SECOND EDITION

Collecting and Interpreting Qualitative Materials

INTERNATIONAL ADVISORY BOARD

SECOND EDITION

Collecting and Interpreting Qualitative Materials

editors

NORMAN K. DENZIN
University of Illinois at Urbana-Champaign

YVONNA S. LINCOLN
Texas A&M University

SAGE Publications
International Educational and Professional Publisher
Thousand Oaks ■ London ■ New Delhi

For information:

Sage Publications, Inc.
2455 Teller Road
Thousand Oaks, California 91320
E-mail: order@sagepub.com

Sage Publications Ltd.
6 Bonhill Street
London EC2A 4PU
United Kingdom

Sage Publications India Pvt. Ltd.
B-42 Panchsheel Enclave
Post Box 4109
New Delhi 110-017 India

Printed in the United States of America

Library of Congress Cataloging-in-Publication Data

Collecting and interpreting qualitative materials / Norman K. Denzin, Yvonna S. Lincoln, editors.— 2nd ed.
  p. cm.
Includes bibliographical references and index.
ISBN 0-7619-2687-9 (Paper)
  1. Social sciences-Research-Methodology. 2. Qualitative reasoning.
I. Denzin, Norman K. II. Lincoln, Yvonna S.
H62 .C566 2003
300'.7'23—dc21   2002156613

Printed on acid-free paper

03 04 05 06 07 08 09 10 9 8 7 6 5 4 3 2 1

Acquiring Editor:	Margaret H. Seawell
Production Editor:	Claudia A. Hoffman
Typesetter:	Christina Hill
Indexer:	Molly Hall
Cover Designer:	Michelle Lee and Ravi Balasuriya
Cover Photograph:	C. A. Hoffman

Contents

Preface

♦   For over than three decades, a quiet methodological revolution has been taking place in the social sciences. A blurring of disciplinary boundaries has occurred. The social sciences and humanities have drawn closer together in a mutual focus on an interpretive, qualitative approach to research and theory. Although these trends are not new, the extent to which the "qualitative revolution" has overtaken the social sciences and related professional fields has been nothing short of amazing.

Reflecting this revolution, a host of textbooks, journals, research monographs, and readers have been published in recent years. In 1994 we published the first edition of the *Handbook of Qualitative Research* in an attempt to represent the field in its entirety, to take stock of how far it had come and how far it might yet go. The immediate success of the first edition suggested the need to offer the *Handbook* in terms of three separate volumes. So in 1998 we published a three-volume set, *The Landscape of Qualitative Research: Theories and Issues*; *Strategies of Inquiry*; and *Collecting and Interpreting Qualitative Materials*. In 2003 we offer a new three-volume set, based on the second edition of the handbook.

In 2000 we published the second edition of the *Handbook*. Although it became abundantly clear that the "field" of qualitative research is still defined primarily by tensions, contradictions, and hesitations—and that they exist in a less-than-unified arena—we believed that the handbook could and would be valuable for solidifying, interpreting, and organizing the field in spite of the essential differences that characterize it.

The first edition attempted to define the field of qualtiative research. The second edition went one step further. Building on themes in the first edition, we asked how the practices of qualitative inquiry could be used to address issues of equity and of social justice.

We have been enormously gratified and heartened by the response to the *Handbook* since its publication. Especially gratifying has been that it has been used and adapted by such a wide variety of scholars and graduate students in precisely the way we had hoped: as a starting point, a springboard for new thought and new work.

◆ The Paperback Project

The second edition of the *Landscape Series* of the *Handbook of Qualitative Research* is virtually all new. Over half of the authors from the first edition have been replaced by new contributors. Indeed, there are 33 new chapter authors or co-authors. There are six totally new chapter topics, including contributions on queer theory, performance ethnography, *testimonio*, focus groups in feminist research, applied ethnography, and anthropological poetics. All returning authors have substantially revised their original contributions, in many cases producing totally new chapters.

The second edition of the *Handbook of Qualitative Research* continues where the first edition ended. With Thomas Schwandt (Chapter 7, Volume 1), we may observe that qualitative inquiry, among other things, is the name for a "reformist movement that began in the early 1970s in the academy." The interpretive and critical paradigms, in their multiple forms, are central to this movement. Indeed, Schwandt argues that this movement encompasses multiple paradigmatic formulations. It also includes complex epistemological and ethical criticisms of traditional social science research. The movement now has its own journals, scientific associations, conferences, and faculty positions.

The transformations in the field of qualitative research that were taking place in the early 1990s continued to gain momentum as we entered the new century. Today, few in the interpretive community look back with skepticism on the narrative turn. The turn has been taken, and that is all there is to say about it. Many have now told their tales from the field. Further, today we know that men and women write culture differently, and that writing itself is not an innocent practice.

Experimental ways of writing first-person ethnographic texts are now commonplace. Sociologists and anthropologists continue to explore new ways of composing ethnography, and many write fiction, drama, performance texts, and ethnographic poetry. Social science journals hold fiction contests. Civic journalism shapes calls for a civic, or public, ethnography. There is a pressing need to show how the practices of qualitative research can help change the world in positive ways. So, at the beginning of the twenty-first century, it is necessary to re-engage the promise of qualitative research as a generative form of inquiry (Peshkin, 1993) and as a form of radical democratic practice. This is the agenda of the second edition of the *Landscape Series*, as it is for the second edition of the *Handbook*; namely to show how the discourses of qualitative research can be used to help imagine and create a free, democratic society. Each of the chapters in the three-volume set takes up this project, in one way or another.

A handbook, we were told by our publisher, should ideally represent the distillation of knowledge of a field, a benchmark volume that synthesizes an existing literature, helping to define and shape the present and future of that discipline. This mandate organized the second edition. In metaphoric terms, if you were to take one book on qualitative research with you to a desert island (or for a comprehensive graduate examination), a handbook would be the book.

We decided that the part structure of the *Handbook* could serve as a useful point of departure for the organization of the paperbacks. Thus Volume 1, titled *The Landscape of Qualitative Research: Theories and Issues*, takes a look at the field from a broadly theoretical perspective and is composed of the *Handbook*'s Parts I ("Locating the Field"), II ("Paradigms and Perspectives in Transition"), and VI ("The Future of Qualitative Research"). Volume 2, titled *Strategies of Qualitative Inquiry*, focuses on just that and consists of Part III of the *Handbook*. Volume 3, titled *Collecting and Interpreting Qualitative Materials*, considers the tasks of collecting, analyzing, and interpreting empirical materials and comprises the *Handbook*'s Parts IV ("Methods of Collecting and Analyzing Empirical Materials") and V ("The Art and Practices of Interpretation, Evaluation, and Representation").

As with the first edition of the *Landscape* series, we decided that nothing should be cut from the original *Handbook*. Nearly everyone we spoke to who used the *Handbook* had his or her own way of using it, leaning heavily on certain chapters and skipping others altogether. But there was consensus that this reorganization made a great deal of sense both pedagogically and economically. We and Sage are committed to making this iteration of the *Handbook* accessible for classroom use. This commitment is reflected in the size, organization, and price of the paperbacks, as well as in the addition of end-of-book bibliographies.

It also became clear in our conversations with colleagues who used the *Handbook* that the single-volume, hard-cover version has a distinct place and value, and Sage will keep the original version available until a revised edition is published.

◆ Organization of This Volume

Collecting and Interpreting Qualitative Materials introduces the researcher to basic methods of gathering, analyzing, and interpreting qualitative empirical materials. Part I moves from interviewing to observing; to the use of artifacts, documents, and records from the past; to visual and auto-ethnographic methods. It then takes up analysis methods, including computer-assisted methodologies, as well as strategies for analyzing talk and text. Esther Madriz reads focus groups through critical feminist inquiry, and Erve Chambers discusses applied ethnography.

◆ Acknowledgments

Of course, this book would not exist without its authors or the editorial board members for the *Handbook* on which it is based. These individuals were able to offer both long-term sustained commitments to the project and short-term emergency assistance.

In addition, we would like to thank the following individuals and institutions for their assistance, support, insights, and patience: our respective universities and departments, as well as Jack Bratich, Ben Scott, Ruoyun Bai, and Francyne Huckaby, our respective graduate students. Without them, we could never have kept this project on course. There are also several people to thank at Sage Publications. We thank Margaret Seawell, our new editor; this three-volume version of the *Handbook* would not have been possible without Margaret's wisdom, support, humor, and grasp of the field in all its current diversity.

As always, we appreciate the efforts of Greg Daurelle, the director of books marketing at Sage, along with his staff, for their indefatigable efforts in getting the word out about the *Handbook* to teachers, researchers, and methodologists around the world. Claudia Hoffman was essential in moving the series through production; we are also grateful to the copy editor, Judy Selhorst, and to those whose proofreading and indexing skills were so central to the publication of the *Handbook* on which these volumes are based. Finally, as ever, we thank our spouses, Katherine Ryan and Egon Guba, for their forbearance and constant support.

The idea for this three-volume paperback version of the *Handbook* did not arise in a vacuum, and we are grateful for the feedback we received from countless teachers and students.

—Norman K. Denzin
University of Illinois at Urbana-Champaign

—Yvonna S. Lincoln
Texas A&M University

1

Introduction

The Discipline and
Practice of Qualitative Research

Norman K. Denzin and Yvonna S. Lincoln

◆ Qualitative research has a long, distinguished, and sometimes an-
guished history in the human disciplines. In sociology, the work of
the "Chicago school" in the 1920s and 1930s established the importance of qualitative inquiry for the study of human group life. In anthropology, during the same time period, the discipline-defining studies of
Boas, Mead, Benedict, Bateson, Evans-Pritchard, Radcliffe-Brown, and
Malinowski charted the outlines of the fieldwork method (see Gupta &
Ferguson, 1997; Stocking, 1986, 1989). The agenda was clear-cut: The
observer went to a foreign setting to study the customs and habits of
another society and culture (see in Volume 1, Vidich & Lyman, Chapter 2;
Tedlock, Volume 2, Chapter 6; see also Rosaldo, 1989, pp. 25-45, for criticisms of this tradition). Soon, qualitative research would be employed in
other social and behavioral science disciplines, including education (especially the work of Dewey), history, political science, business, medicine,
nursing, social work, and communications.

In the opening chapter in Part I of Volume 1, Vidich and Lyman chart
many key features of this history. In this now classic analysis, they note,

1

with some irony, that qualitative research in sociology and anthropology was "born out of concern to understand the 'other.' " Furthermore, this other was the exotic other, a primitive, nonwhite person from a foreign culture judged to be less civilized than that of the researcher. Of course, there were colonialists long before there were anthropologists. Nonetheless, there would be no colonial, and now no postcolonial, history were it not for this investigative mentality that turned the dark-skinned other into the object of the ethnographer's gaze.

Thus does bell hooks (1990, pp. 126-128) read the famous photo that appears on the cover of *Writing Culture* (Clifford & Marcus, 1986) as an instance of this mentality (see also Behar, 1995, p. 8; Gordon, 1988). The photo depicts Stephen Tyler doing fieldwork in India. Tyler is seated some distance from three dark-skinned persons. A child is poking his or her head out of a basket. A woman is hidden in the shadows of a hut. A man, a checkered white-and-black shawl across his shoulder, elbow propped on his knee, hand resting along the side of his face, is staring at Tyler. Tyler is writing in a field journal. A piece of white cloth is attached to his glasses, perhaps shielding him from the sun. This patch of whiteness marks Tyler as the white male writer studying these passive brown and black persons. Indeed, the brown male's gaze signals some desire, or some attachment to Tyler. In contrast, the female's gaze is completely hidden by the shadows and by the words of the book's title, which cross her face (hooks, 1990, p. 127). And so this cover photo of perhaps the most influential book on ethnography in the last half of the 20th century reproduces "two ideas that are quite fresh in the racist imagination: the notion of the white male as writer/authority . . . and the idea of the passive brown/black man [and woman and child] who is doing nothing, merely looking on" (hooks, 1990, p. 127).

In this introductory chapter, we will define the field of qualitative research and then navigate, chart, and review the history of qualitative research in the human disciplines. This will allow us to locate this volume and its contents within their historical moments. (These historical moments are somewhat artificial; they are socially constructed, quasi-historical, and overlapping conventions. Nevertheless, they permit a "performance" of developing ideas. They also facilitate an increasing sensitivity to and sophistication about the pitfalls and promises of ethnography and qualitative research.) We will present a conceptual framework for reading the qualitative research act as a multicultural, gendered process, and then provide a brief introduction to the chapters that follow.

Returning to the observations of Vidich and Lyman as well as those of hooks, we will conclude with a brief discussion of qualitative research and critical race theory (see also in Volume 1, Ladson-Billings, Chapter 9; and in this volume, Denzin, Chapter 13). As we indicate in our preface, we use the metaphor of the bridge to structure what follows. We see this volume as a bridge connecting historical moments, research methods, paradigms, and communities of interpretive scholars.

◆ Definitional Issues

Qualitative research is a field of inquiry in its own right. It crosscuts disciplines, fields, and subject matters.[1] A complex, interconnected family of terms, concepts, and assumptions surround the term *qualitative research*. These include the traditions associated with foundationalism, positivism, postfoundationalism, postpositivism, poststructuralism, and the many qualitative research perspectives, and/or methods, connected to cultural and interpretive studies (the chapters in Part II of Volume 1 take up these paradigms).[2] There are separate and detailed literatures on the many methods and approaches that fall under the category of qualitative research, such as case study, politics and ethics, participatory inquiry, interviewing, participant observation, visual methods, and interpretive analysis.

In North America, qualitative research operates in a complex historical field that crosscuts seven historical moments (we discuss these moments in detail below). These seven moments overlap and simultaneously operate in the present.[3] We define them as the traditional (1900–1950); the modernist or golden age (1950–1970); blurred genres (1970–1986); the crisis of representation (1986–1990); the postmodern, a period of experimental and new ethnographies (1990–1995); postexperimental inquiry (1995–2000); and the future, which is now (2000–). The future, the seventh moment, is concerned with moral discourse, with the development of sacred textualities. The seventh moment asks that the social sciences and the humanities become sites for critical conversations about democracy, race, gender, class, nation-states, globalization, freedom, and community.

The postmodern moment was defined in part by a concern for literary and rhetorical tropes and the narrative turn, a concern for storytelling, for composing ethnographies in new ways (Ellis & Bochner, 1996). Laurel Richardson (1997) observes that this moment was shaped by a new sensibility, by doubt, by a refusal to privilege any method or theory (p. 173).

3

But now, at the beginning of the 21st century, the narrative turn has been taken. Many have learned how to write differently, including how to locate themselves in their texts. We now struggle to connect qualitative research to the hopes, needs, goals, and promises of a free democratic society.

Successive waves of epistemological theorizing move across these seven moments. The traditional period is associated with the positivist, foundational paradigm. The modernist or golden age and blurred genres moments are connected to the appearance of postpositivist arguments. At the same time, a variety of new interpretive, qualitative perspectives were taken up, including hermeneutics, structuralism, semiotics, phenomenology, cultural studies, and feminism.[4] In the blurred genres phase, the humanities became central resources for critical, interpretive theory, and for the qualitative research project broadly conceived. The researcher became a *bricoleur* (see below), learning how to borrow from many different disciplines.

The blurred genres phase produced the next stage, the crisis of representation. Here researchers struggled with how to locate themselves and their subjects in reflexive texts. A kind of methodological diaspora took place, a two-way exodus. Humanists migrated to the social sciences, searching for new social theory, new ways to study popular culture and its local, ethnographic contexts. Social scientists turned to the humanities, hoping to learn how to do complex structural and poststructural readings of social texts. From the humanities, social scientists also learned how to produce texts that refused to be read in simplistic, linear, incontrovertible terms. The line between text and context blurred. In the postmodern experimental moment researchers continued to move away from foundational and quasi-foundational criteria (see in this volume, Smith & Deemer, Chapter 12, and Richardson, Chapter 14; and in Volume 1, Gergen & Gergen, Chapter 13). Alternative evaluative criteria were sought, criteria that might prove evocative, moral, critical, and rooted in local understandings.

Any definition of qualitative research must work within this complex historical field. *Qualitative research* means different things in each of these moments. Nonetheless, an initial, generic definition can be offered: Qualitative research is a situated activity that locates the observer in the world. It consists of a set of interpretive, material practices that make the world visible. These practices transform the world. They turn the world into a series of representations, including field notes, interviews, conversations, photographs, recordings, and memos to the self. At this level, qualitative research involves an interpretive, naturalistic approach to the world. This means that qualitative researchers study things in their natural settings, attempting to make sense of, or to interpret, phenomena in terms of the meanings people bring to them.[5]

Qualitative research involves the studied use and collection of a variety of empirical materials—case study; personal experience; introspection; life story; interview; artifacts; cultural texts and productions; observational, historical, interactional, and visual texts—that describe routine and problematic moments and meanings in individuals' lives. Accordingly, qualitative researchers deploy a wide range of interconnected interpretive practices, hoping always to get a better understanding of the subject matter at hand. It is understood, however, that each practice makes the world visible in a different way. Hence there is frequently a commitment to using more than one interpretive practice in any study.

The Qualitative Researcher as Bricoleur and Quilt Maker

The qualitative researcher may take on multiple and gendered images: scientist, naturalist, field-worker, journalist, social critic, artist, performer, jazz musician, filmmaker, quilt maker, essayist. The many methodological practices of qualitative research may be viewed as soft science, journalism, ethnography, bricolage, quilt making, or montage. The researcher, in turn, may be seen as a *bricoleur*, as a maker of quilts, or, as in filmmaking, a person who assembles images into montages. (On montage, see the discussion below as well as Cook, 1981, pp. 171-177; Monaco, 1981, pp. 322-328. On quilting, see hooks, 1990, pp. 115-122; Wolcott, 1995, pp. 31-33.)

Nelson, Treichler, and Grossberg (1992), Lévi-Strauss (1966), and Weinstein and Weinstein (1991) clarify the meanings of *bricolage* and *bricoleur*.[6] A *bricoleur* is a "Jack of all trades or a kind of professional do-it-yourself person" (Lévi-Strauss, 1966, p. 17). There are many kinds of *bricoleurs*—interpretive, narrative, theoretical, political (see below). The interpretive bricoleur produces a *bricolage*—that is, a pieced-together set of representations that are fitted to the specifics of a complex situation. "The solution [bricolage] which is the result of the *bricoleur's* method is an [emergent] construction" (Weinstein & Weinstein, 1991, p. 161) that changes and takes new forms as different tools, methods, and techniques

5

of representation and interpretation are added to the puzzle. Nelson et al. (1992) describe the methodology of cultural studies "as a bricolage. Its choice of practice, that is, is pragmatic, strategic and self-reflexive" (p. 2). This understanding can be applied, with qualifications, to qualitative research.

The qualitative researcher as *bricoleur* or maker of quilts uses the aesthetic and material tools of his or her craft, deploying whatever strategies, methods, or empirical materials are at hand (Becker, 1998, p. 2). If new tools or techniques have to be invented, or pieced together, then the researcher will do this. The choices as to which interpretive practices to employ are not necessarily set in advance. The "choice of research practices depends upon the questions that are asked, and the questions depend on their context" (Nelson et al., 1992, p. 2), what is available in the context, and what the researcher can do in that setting.

These interpretive practices involve aesthetic issues, an aesthetics of representation that goes beyond the pragmatic, or the practical. Here the concept of *montage* is useful (see Cook, 1981, p. 323; Monaco, 1981, pp. 171-172). Montage is a method of editing cinematic images. In the history of cinematography, montage is associated with the work of Sergei Eisenstein, especially his film *The Battleship Potemkin* (1925). In montage, several different images are superimposed onto one another to create a picture. In a sense, montage is like pentimento, in which something that has been painted out of a picture (an image the painter "repented," or denied) becomes visible again, creating something new. What is new is what had been obscured by a previous image.

Montage and pentimento, like jazz, which is improvisation, create the sense that images, sounds, and understandings are blending together, overlapping, forming a composite, a new creation. The images seem to shape and define one another, and an emotional, gestalt effect is produced. Often these images are combined in a swiftly run filmic sequence that produces a dizzily revolving collection of several images around a central or focused picture or sequence; such effects are often used to signify the passage of time.

Perhaps the most famous instance of montage is the Odessa Steps sequence in *The Battleship Potemkin*.[7] In the climax of the film, the citizens of Odessa are being massacred by czarist troops on the stone steps leading down to the harbor. Eisenstein cuts to a young mother as she pushes her baby in a carriage across the landing in front of the firing troops. Citizens rush past her, jolting the carriage, which she is afraid to push down to the next flight of stairs. The troops are above her firing at the citizens. She is trapped between the troops and the steps. She screams. A line of rifles pointing to the sky erupt in smoke. The mother's head sways back. The wheels of the carriage teeter on the edge of the steps. The mother's hand clutches the silver buckle of her belt. Below her people are being beaten by soldiers. Blood drips over the mother's white gloves. The baby's hand reaches out of the carriage. The mother sways back and forth. The troops advance. The mother falls back against the carriage. A woman watches in horror as the rear wheels of the carriage roll off the edge of the landing. With accelerating speed the carriage bounces down the steps, past the dead citizens. The baby is jostled from side to side inside the carriage. The soldiers fire their rifles into a group of wounded citizens. A student screams as the carriage leaps across the steps, tilts, and overturns (Cook, 1981, p. 167).[8]

Montage uses brief images to create a clearly defined sense of urgency and complexity. Montage invites viewers to construct interpretations that build on one another as the scene unfolds. These interpretations are built on associations based on the contrasting images that blend into one another. The underlying assumption of montage is that viewers perceive and interpret the shots in a "montage sequence not *sequentially*, or one at a time, but rather *simultaneously*" (Cook, 1981, p. 172). The viewer puts the sequences together into a meaningful emotional whole, as if in a glance, all at once.

The qualitative researcher who uses montage is like a quilt maker or a jazz improviser. The quilter stitches, edits, and puts slices of reality together. This process creates and brings psychological and emotional unity to an interpretive experience. There are many examples of montage in current qualitative research (see Diversi, 1998; Jones, 1999; Lather & Smithies, 1997; Ronai, 1998). Using multiple voices, different textual formats, and various typefaces, Lather and Smithies (1997) weave a complex text about women who are HIV positive and women with AIDS. Jones (1999) creates a performance text using lyrics from the blues songs sung by Billie Holiday.

In texts based on the metaphors of montage, quilt making, and jazz improvisation, many different things are going on at the same time— different voices, different perspectives, points of views, angles of vision. Like performance texts, works that use montage simultaneously create and enact moral meaning. They move from the personal to the political, the local to the historical and the cultural. These are dialogical texts. They presume an active audience. They create spaces for give-and-take between reader and writer. They do more than turn the other into the object of the social science gaze (see McCall, Chapter 4, Volume2).

Qualitative research is inherently multimethod in focus (Flick, 1998, p. 229). However, the use of multiple methods, or triangulation, reflects an attempt to secure an in-depth understanding of the phenomenon in question. Objective reality can never be captured. We can know a thing only through its representations. Triangulation is not a tool or a strategy of validation, but an alternative to validation (Flick, 1998, p. 230). The combination of multiple methodological practices, empirical materials, perspectives, and observers in a single study is best understood, then, as a strategy that adds rigor, breadth, complexity, richness, and depth to any inquiry (see Flick, 1998, p. 231).

In Chapter 14 of this volume, Richardson disputes the concept of triangulation, asserting that the central image for qualitative inquiry is the crystal, not the triangle. Mixed-genre texts in the postexperimental moment have more than three sides. Like crystals, Eisenstein's montage, the jazz solo, or the pieces that make up a quilt, the mixed-genre text, as Richardson notes, "combines symmetry and substance with an infinite variety of shapes, substances, transmutations. . . . Crystals grow, change, alter. . . . Crystals are prisms that reflect externalities *and* refract within themselves, creating different colors, patterns, and arrays, casting off in different directions."

In the crystallization process, the writer tells the same tale from different points of view. For example, in *A Thrice-Told Tale* (1992), Margery Wolf uses fiction, field notes, and a scientific article to give an accounting of the same set of experiences in a native village. Similarly, in her play *Fires in the Mirror* (1993), Anna Deavere Smith presents a series of performance pieces based on interviews with people involved in a racial conflict in Crown Heights, Brooklyn, on August, 19, 1991 (see Denzin, Chapter 13, this volume). The play has multiple speaking parts, including conversations with gang members, police officers, and anonymous young girls and boys. There is no "correct" telling of this event. Each telling, like light hitting a crystal, reflects a different perspective on this incident.

Viewed as a crystalline form, as a montage, or as a creative performance around a central theme, triangulation as a form of, or alternative to, validity thus can be extended. Triangulation is the display of multiple, refracted realities simultaneously. Each of the metaphors "works" to create simultaneity rather than the sequential or linear. Readers and audiences are then invited to explore competing visions of the context, to become immersed in and merge with new realities to comprehend.

The methodological *bricoleur* is adept at performing a large number of diverse tasks, ranging from interviewing to intensive self-reflection and introspection. The theoretical *bricoleur* reads widely and is knowledgeable about the many interpretive paradigms (feminism, Marxism, cultural studies, constructivism, queer theory) that can be brought to any particular problem. He or she may not, however, feel that paradigms can be mingled or synthesized. That is, one cannot easily move between paradigms as overarching philosophical systems denoting particular ontologies, epistemologies, and methodologies. They represent belief systems that attach users to particular worldviews. Perspectives, in contrast, are less well developed systems, and one can more easily move between them. The researcher-as-*bricoleur*-theorist works between and within competing and overlapping perspectives and paradigms.

The interpretive *bricoleur* understands that research is an interactive process shaped by his or her personal history, biography, gender, social class, race, and ethnicity, and by those of the people in the setting. The political *bricoleur* knows that science is power, for all research findings have political implications. There is no value-free science. A civic social science based on a politics of hope is sought (Lincoln, 1999). The gendered, narrative *bricoleur* also knows that researchers all tell stories about the worlds they have studied. Thus the narratives, or stories, scientists tell are accounts couched and framed within specific storytelling traditions, often defined as paradigms (e.g., positivism, postpositivism, constructivism).

The product of the interpretive *bricoleur*'s labor is a complex, quiltlike bricolage, a reflexive collage or montage—a set of fluid, interconnected images and representations. This interpretive structure is like a quilt, a performance text, a sequence of representations connecting the parts to the whole.

Qualitative Research as a Site of Multiple Interpretive Practices

Qualitative research, as a set of interpretive activities, privileges no single methodological practice over another. As a site of discussion, or discourse, qualitative research is difficult to define clearly. It has no theory or paradigm that is distinctly its own. As the contributions to Part II of

Volume 1 reveal, multiple theoretical paradigms claim use of qualitative research methods and strategies, from constructivist to cultural studies, feminism, Marxism, and ethnic models of study. Qualitative research is used in many separate disciplines, as we will discuss below. It does not belong to a single discipline.

Nor does qualitative research have a distinct set of methods or practices that are entirely its own. Qualitative researchers use semiotics, narrative, content, discourse, archival and phonemic analysis, even statistics, tables, graphs, and numbers. They also draw upon and utilize the approaches, methods, and techniques of ethnomethodology, phenomenology, hermeneutics, feminism, rhizomatics, deconstructionism, ethnography, interviews, psychoanalysis, cultural studies, survey research, and participant observation, among others.[9] All of these research practices "can provide important insights and knowledge" (Nelson et al., 1992, p. 2). No specific method or practice can be privileged over any other.

Many of these methods, or research practices, are used in other contexts in the human disciplines. Each bears the traces of its own disciplinary history. Thus there is an extensive history of the uses and meanings of ethnography and ethnology in education (see Fine, Weis, Weseen, & Wong, Volume 1, Chapter 4); of participant observation and ethnography in anthropology (see Tedlock, Volume 2, Chapter 6; Ryan & Bernard, this volume, Chapter 7; Brady, this volume, Chapter 15), sociology (see Gubrium & Holstein, Volume 2, Chapter 7; and in this volume, Harper, Chapter 5; Fontana & Frey, Chapter 2; Silverman, Chapter 9), communication (see Ellis & Bochner, this volume, Chapter 6), and cultural studies (see Frow & Morris, Volume 1, Chapter 11); of textual, hermeneutic, feminist, psychoanalytic, semiotic, and narrative analysis in cinema and literary studies (see Olesen, Volume 1, Chapter 8; Brady, this volume, Chapter 15); of archival, material culture, historical, and document analysis in history, biography, and archaeology (see Hodder, this volume, Chapter 4; Tierney, Volume 2, Chapter 9); and of discourse and conversational analysis in medicine, communications, and education (see Miller & Crabtree, Volume 2, Chapter 12; Silverman, this volume, Chapter 9).

The many histories that surround each method or research strategy reveal how multiple uses and meanings are brought to each practice. Textual analyses in literary studies, for example, often treat texts as self-contained systems. On the other hand, a researcher taking a cultural studies or feminist perspective will read a text in terms of its location within a historical moment marked by a particular gender, race, or class ideology. A cultural studies use of ethnography would bring a set of understandings from feminism, postmodernism, and poststructuralism to the project. These understandings would not be shared by mainstream postpositivist sociologists. Similarly, postpositivist and poststructuralist historians bring different understandings and uses to the methods and findings of historical research (see Tierney, Volume 2, Chapter 9). These tensions and contradictions are all evident in the chapters in this volume.

These separate and multiple uses and meanings of the methods of qualitative research make it difficult for researchers to agree on any essential definition of the field, for it is never just one thing.[10] Still, we must establish a definition for our purposes here. We borrow from, and paraphrase, Nelson et al.'s (1992, p. 4) attempt to define cultural studies:

> Qualitative research is an interdisciplinary, transdisciplinary, and sometimes counterdisciplinary field. It crosscuts the humanities and the social and physical sciences. Qualitative research is many things at the same time. It is multiparadigmatic in focus. Its practitioners are sensitive to the value of the multimethod approach. They are committed to the naturalistic perspective and to the interpretive understanding of human experience. At the same time, the field is inherently political and shaped by multiple ethical and political positions.
>
> Qualitative research embraces two tensions at the same time. On the one hand, it is drawn to a broad, interpretive, postexperimental, postmodern, feminist, and critical sensibility. On the other hand, it is drawn to more narrowly defined positivist, postpositivist, humanistic, and naturalistic conceptions of human experience and its analysis. Further, these tensions can be combined in the same project, bringing both postmodern and naturalistic or both critical and humanistic perspectives to bear.

This rather complex statement means that qualitative research, as a set of practices, embraces within its own multiple disciplinary histories constant tensions and contradictions over the project itself, including its methods and the forms its findings and interpretations take. The field sprawls between and crosscuts all of the human disciplines, even including, in some cases, the physical sciences. Its practitioners are variously committed to modern, postmodern, and postexperimental sensibilities and the approaches to social research that these sensibilities imply.

Resistances to Qualitative Studies

The academic and disciplinary resistances to qualitative research illustrate the politics embedded in this field of discourse. The challenges to qualitative research are many. Qualitative researchers are called journalists, or soft scientists. Their work is termed unscientific, or only exploratory, or subjective. It is called criticism and not theory, or it is interpreted politically, as a disguised version of Marxism or secular humanism (see Huber, 1995; see also Denzin, 1997, pp. 258-261).

These resistances reflect an uneasy awareness that the traditions of qualitative research commit the researcher to a critique of the positivist or postpositivist project. But the positivist resistance to qualitative research goes beyond the "ever-present desire to maintain a distinction between hard science and soft scholarship" (Carey, 1989, p. 99; see also in Volume 1, Schwandt, Chapter 7; in this volume, Smith & Deemer, Chapter 12). The experimental (positivist) sciences (physics, chemistry, economics, and psychology, for example) are often seen as the crowning achievements of Western civilization, and in their practices it is assumed that "truth" can transcend opinion and personal bias (Carey, 1989, p. 99; Schwandt, 1997b, p. 309). Qualitative research is seen as an assault on this tradition, whose adherents often retreat into a "value-free objectivist science" (Carey, 1989, p. 104) model to defend their position. They seldom attempt to make explicit, or to critique, the "moral and political commitments in their own contingent work" (Carey, 1989, p. 104; see also Lincoln & Guba, Chapter 6, Volume 1).

Positivists further allege that the so-called new experimental qualitative researchers write fiction, not science, and that these researchers have no way of verifying their truth statements. Ethnographic poetry and fiction signal the death of empirical science, and there is little to be gained by attempting to engage in moral criticism. These critics presume a stable, unchanging reality that can be studied using the empirical methods of objective social science (see Huber, 1995). The province of qualitative research, accordingly, is the world of lived experience, for this is where individual belief and action intersect with culture. Under this model there is no preoccupation with discourse and method as material interpretive practices that constitute representation and description. Thus is the textual, narrative turn rejected by the positivists.

The opposition to positive science by the postpositivists (see below) and the poststructuralists is seen, then, as an attack on reason and truth. At the same time, the positivist science attack on qualitative research is regarded as an attempt to legislate one version of truth over another.

This complex political terrain defines the many traditions and strands of qualitative research: the British tradition and its presence in other national contexts; the American pragmatic, naturalistic, and interpretive traditions in sociology, anthropology, communication, and education; the German and French phenomenological, hermeneutic, semiotic, Marxist, structural, and poststructural perspectives; feminist studies, African American studies, Latino studies, queer studies, studies of indigenous and aboriginal cultures. The politics of qualitative research create a tension that informs each of the above traditions. This tension itself is constantly being reexamined and interrogated, as qualitative research confronts a changing historical world, new intellectual positions, and its own institutional and academic conditions.

To summarize: Qualitative research is many things to many people. Its essence is twofold: a commitment to some version of the naturalistic, interpretive approach to its subject matter and an ongoing critique of the politics and methods of postpositivism. We turn now to a brief discussion of the major differences between qualitative and quantitative approaches to research. We then discuss ongoing differences and tensions within qualitative inquiry.

Qualitative Versus Quantitative Research

The word *qualitative* implies an emphasis on the qualities of entities and on processes and meanings that are not experimentally examined or measured (if measured at all) in terms of quantity, amount, intensity, or frequency. Qualitative researchers stress the socially constructed nature of reality, the intimate relationship between the researcher and what is studied, and the situational constraints that shape inquiry. Such researchers emphasize the value-laden nature of inquiry. They seek answers to questions that stress *how* social experience is created and given meaning. In contrast, quantitative studies emphasize the measurement and analysis of causal relationships between variables, not processes. Proponents of such studies claim that their work is done from within a value-free framework.

13

Research Styles: Doing the Same Things Differently?

Of course, both qualitative and quantitative researchers "think they know something about society worth telling to others, and they use a variety of forms, media and means to communicate their ideas and findings" (Becker, 1986, p. 122). Qualitative research differs from quantitative research in five significant ways (Becker, 1996). These points of difference turn on different ways of addressing the same set of issues. They return always to the politics of research, and to who has the power to legislate correct solutions to these problems.

Uses of positivism and postpositivism. First, both perspectives are shaped by the positivist and postpositivist traditions in the physical and social sciences (see the discussion below). These two positivist science traditions hold to naïve and critical realist positions concerning reality and its perception. In the positivist version it is contended that there is a reality out there to be studied, captured, and understood, whereas the postpositivists argue that reality can never be fully apprehended, only approximated (Guba, 1990, p. 22). Postpositivism relies on multiple methods as a way of capturing as much of reality as possible. At the same time, emphasis is placed on the discovery and verification of theories. Traditional evaluation criteria, such as internal and external validity, are stressed, as is the use of qualitative procedures that lend themselves to structured (sometimes statistical) analysis. Computer-assisted methods of analysis that permit frequency counts, tabulations, and low-level statistical analyses may also be employed.

The positivist and postpositivist traditions linger like long shadows over the qualitative research project. Historically, qualitative research was defined within the positivist paradigm, where qualitative researchers attempted to do good positivist research with less rigorous methods and procedures. Some mid-20th-century qualitative researchers (e.g., Becker, Geer, Hughes, & Strauss, 1961) reported participant observation findings in terms of quasi-statistics. As recently as 1998, Strauss and Corbin, two leaders of the grounded theory approach to qualitative research, attempted to modify the usual canons of good (positivist) science to fit their own postpositivist conception of rigorous research (but see Charmaz, Chapter 8, Volume 2; see also Glaser, 1992). Some applied researchers, while claiming to be atheoretical, often fit within the positivist or postpositivist framework by default.

Flick (1998, pp. 2-3) usefully summarizes the differences between these two approaches to inquiry. He observes that the quantitative approach has been used for purposes of isolating "causes and effects . . . operationalizing theoretical relations . . . [and] measuring and . . . quantifying phenomena . . . allowing the generalization of findings" (p. 3). But today doubt is cast on such projects, because "Rapid social change and the resulting diversification of life worlds are increasingly confronting social researchers with new social contexts and perspectives. . . . traditional deductive methodologies . . . are failing. . . . thus research is increasingly forced to make use of inductive strategies instead of starting from theories and testing them. . . . knowledge and practice are studied as local knowledge and practice" (p. 2).

Spindler and Spindler (1992) summarize their qualitative approach to quantitative materials: "Instrumentation and quantification are simply procedures employed to extend and reinforce certain kinds of data, interpretations and test hypotheses across samples. Both must be kept in their place. One must avoid their premature or overly extensive use as a security mechanism" (p. 69).

Although many qualitative researchers in the postpositivist tradition will use statistical measures, methods, and documents as a way of locating groups of subjects within larger populations, they will seldom report their findings in terms of the kinds of complex statistical measures or methods to which quantitative researchers are drawn (i.e., path, regression, or log-linear analyses).

Acceptance of postmodern sensibilities. The use of quantitative, positivist methods and assumptions has been rejected by a new generation of qualitative researchers who are attached to poststructural and/or postmodern sensibilities (see below; see also in Volume 1, Vidich & Lyman, Chapter 2; and in this volume, Richardson, Chapter 14). These researchers argue that positivist methods are but one way of telling stories about society or the social world. These methods may be no better or no worse than any other methods; they just tell different kinds of stories.

This tolerant view is not shared by everyone (Huber, 1995). Many members of the critical theory, constructivist, poststructural, and postmodern schools of thought reject positivist and postpositivist criteria when evaluating their own work. They see these criteria as irrelevant to their work and contend that such criteria reproduce only a certain kind of science, a science that silences too many voices. These researchers seek alternative methods for evaluating their work, including verisimilitude, emotionality, personal responsibility, an ethic of caring, political praxis, multivoiced texts, and dialogues with subjects. In response, positivists and postpositivists argue that what they do is good science, free of individual bias and subjectivity. As noted above, they see postmodernism and post-structuralism as attacks on reason and truth.

Capturing the individual's point of view. Both qualitative and quantitative researchers are concerned with the individual's point of view. However, qualitative investigators think they can get closer to the actor's perspective through detailed interviewing and observation. They argue that quantitative researchers are seldom able to capture their subjects' perspectives because they have to rely on more remote, inferential empirical methods and materials. The empirical materials produced by interpretive methods are regarded by many quantitative researchers as unreliable, impressionistic, and not objective.

Examining the constraints of everyday life. Qualitative researchers are more likely to confront and come up against the constraints of the everyday social world. They see this world in action and embed their findings in it. Quantitative researchers abstract from this world and seldom study it directly. They seek a nomothetic or etic science based on probabilities derived from the study of large numbers of randomly selected cases. These kinds of statements stand above and outside the constraints of everyday life. Qualitative researchers, on the other hand, are committed to an emic, idiographic, case-based position, which directs their attention to the specifics of particular cases.

Securing rich descriptions. Qualitative researchers believe that rich descriptions of the social world are valuable, whereas quantitative researchers, with their etic, nomothetic commitments, are less concerned with such detail. Quantitative researchers are deliberately unconcerned with rich descriptions because such detail interrupts the process of developing generalizations.

The five points of difference described above (uses of positivism and postpositivism, postmodernism, capturing the individual's point of view, examining the constraints of everyday life, securing thick descriptions) reflect commitments to different styles of research, different epistemologies, and different forms of representation. Each work tradition is governed by its own set of genres; each has its own classics, its own pre-ferred forms of representation, interpretation, trustworthiness, and textual evaluation (see Becker, 1986, pp. 134-135). Qualitative research-ers use ethnographic prose, historical narratives, first-person accounts, still photographs, life histories, fictionalized "facts," and biographical and autobiographical materials, among others. Quantitative researchers use mathematical models, statistical tables, and graphs, and usually write about their research in impersonal, third-person prose.

Tensions Within Qualitative Research

It is erroneous to presume that all qualitative researchers share the same assumptions about the five points of difference described above. As the discussion below will reveal, positivist, postpositivist, and poststructural differences define and shape the discourses of qualitative research. Real-ists and postpositivists within the interpretive qualitative research tradi-tion criticize poststructuralists for taking the textual, narrative turn. These critics contend that such work is navel gazing. It produces conditions "for a dialogue of the deaf between itself and the community" (Silverman, 1997, p. 240). Those who attempt to capture the point of view of the interacting subject in the world are accused of naive humanism, of repro-ducing "a Romantic impulse which elevates the experiential to the level of the authentic" (Silverman, 1997, p. 248).

Still others argue that lived experience is ignored by those who take the textual, performance turn. Snow and Morrill (1995) argue that "this per-formance turn, like the preoccupation with discourse and storytelling, will take us further from the field of social action and the real dramas of every-day life and thus signal the death knell of ethnography as an empirically grounded enterprise" (p. 361). Of course, we disagree.

With these differences within and between the two traditions now in hand, we must now briefly discuss the history of qualitative research. We break this history into seven historical moments, mindful that any history is always somewhat arbitrary and always at least partially a social construction.

◆ The History of Qualitative Research

The history of qualitative research reveals, as Vidich and Lyman remind us in Chapter 2 of Volume 1, that the modern social science disciplines have taken as their mission "the analysis and understanding of the patterned conduct and social processes of society." The notion that this task could be carried out presupposed that social scientists had the ability to observe this world objectively. Qualitative methods were a major tool of such observations.[11]

Throughout the history of qualitative research, investigators have always defined their work in terms of hopes and values, "religious faiths, occupational and professional ideologies" (Vidich & Lyman, Chapter 2, Volume 1). Qualitative research (like all research) has always been judged on the "standard of whether the work communicates or 'says' something to us" (Vidich & Lyman, Chapter 2, Volume 1), based on how we conceptualize our reality and our images of the world. *Epistemology* is the word that has historically defined these standards of evaluation. In the contemporary period, as we have argued above, many received discourses on epistemology are now being reevaluated.

Vidich and Lyman's history covers the following (somewhat) overlapping stages: early ethnography (to the 17th century); colonial ethnography (17th-, 18th-, and 19th-century explorers); the ethnography of the American Indian as "other" (late-19th- and early-20th-century anthropology); the ethnography of the "civic other," or community studies, and ethnographies of American immigrants (early 20th century through the 1960s); studies of ethnicity and assimilation (midcentury through the 1980s); and the present, which we call the *seventh moment*.

In each of these eras, researchers were and have been influenced by their political hopes and ideologies, discovering findings in their research that confirmed prior theories or beliefs. Early ethnographers confirmed the racial and cultural diversity of peoples throughout the globe and attempted to fit this diversity into a theory about the origins of history, the races, and civilizations. Colonial ethnographers, before the professionalization of ethnography in the 20th century, fostered a colonial pluralism that left natives on their own as long as their leaders could be co-opted by the colonial administration.

European ethnographers studied Africans, Asians, and other Third World peoples of color. Early American ethnographers studied the American Indian from the perspective of the conqueror, who saw the life world of the primitive as a window to the prehistoric past. The Calvinist mission to save the Indian was soon transferred to the mission of saving the "hordes" of immigrants who entered the United States with the beginnings of industrialization. Qualitative community studies of the ethnic other proliferated from the early 1900s to the 1960s and included the work of E. Franklin Frazier, Robert Park, and Robert Redfield and their students, as well as William Foote Whyte, the Lynds, August Hollingshead, Herbert Gans, Stanford Lyman, Arthur Vidich, and Joseph Bensman. The post-1960 ethnicity studies challenged the "melting pot" hypothesis of Park and his followers and corresponded to the emergence of ethnic studies programs that saw Native Americans, Latinos, Asian Americans, and African Americans attempting to take control over the study of their own peoples.

The postmodern and poststructural challenge emerged in the mid-1980s. It questioned the assumptions that had organized this earlier history in each of its colonializing moments. Qualitative research that crosses the "postmodern divide" requires one, Vidich and Lyman argue in Volume 1, Chapter 2, to "abandon all established and preconceived values, theories, perspectives . . . and prejudices as resources for ethnographic study." In this new era, the qualitative researcher does more than observe history; he or she plays a part in it. New tales from the field will now be written, and they will reflect the researcher's direct and personal engagement with this historical period.

Vidich and Lyman's analysis covers the full sweep of ethnographic history. Ours is confined to the 20th century and complements many of their divisions. We begin with the early foundational work of the British and French as well the Chicago, Columbia, Harvard, Berkeley, and British schools of sociology and anthropology. This early foundational period established the norms of classical qualitative and ethnographic research (see Gupta & Ferguson, 1997; Rosaldo, 1989; Stocking, 1989).

◆ The Seven Moments of Qualitative Research

As suggested above, our history of qualitative research in North America in this century divides into seven phases, each of which we describe in turn below.

The Traditional Period

We call the first moment the traditional period (this covers Vidich and Lyman's second and third phases). It begins in the early 1900s and continues until World War II. In this period, qualitative researchers wrote "objective," colonializing accounts of field experiences that were reflective of the positivist scientist paradigm. They were concerned with offering valid, reliable, and objective interpretations in their writings. The "other" who was studied was alien, foreign, and strange.

Here is Malinowski (1967) discussing his field experiences in New Guinea and the Trobriand Islands in the years 1914–1915 and 1917–1918. He is bartering his way into field data:

> Nothing whatever draws me to ethnographic studies. . . . On the whole the village struck me rather unfavorably. There is a certain disorganization . . . the rowdiness and persistence of the people who laugh and stare and lie discouraged me somewhat. . . . Went to the village hoping to photograph a few stages of the bara dance. I handed out half-sticks of tobacco, then watched a few dances; then took pictures—but results were poor. . . . they would not pose long enough for time exposures. At moments I was furious at them, particularly because after I gave them their portions of tobacco they all went away. (quoted in Geertz, 1988, pp. 73-74)

In another work, this lonely, frustrated, isolated field-worker describes his methods in the following words:

> In the field one has to face a chaos of facts. . . . in this crude form they are not scientific facts at all; they are absolutely elusive, and can only be fixed by interpretation. . . . *Only laws and generalizations are scientific facts,* and field work consists only and exclusively in the interpretation of the chaotic social reality, in subordinating it to general rules. (Malinowski, 1916/1948, p. 328; quoted in Geertz, 1988, p. 81)

Malinowski's remarks are provocative. On the one hand they disparage fieldwork, but on the other they speak of it within the glorified language of science, with laws and generalizations fashioned out of this selfsame experience.

The field-worker during this period was lionized, made into a larger-than-life figure who went into and then returned from the field with stories about strange people. Rosaldo (1989, p. 30) describes this as the period of the Lone Ethnographer, the story of the man-scientist who went off in search of his native in a distant land. There this figure "encountered the object of his quest . . . [and] underwent his rite of passage by enduring the ultimate ordeal of 'fieldwork' " (p. 30). Returning home with his data, the Lone Ethnographer wrote up an objective account of the culture studied.

These accounts were structured by the norms of classical ethnography. This sacred bundle of terms (Rosaldo, 1989, p. 31) organized ethnographic texts in terms of four beliefs and commitments: a commitment to objectivism, a complicity with imperialism, a belief in monumentalism (the ethnography would create a museumlike picture of the culture studied), and a belief in timelessness (what was studied would never change). The other was an "object" to be archived. This model of the researcher, who could also write complex, dense theories about what was studied, holds to the present day.

The myth of the Lone Ethnographer depicts the birth of classic ethnography. The texts of Malinowski, Radcliffe-Brown, Margaret Mead, and Gregory Bateson are still carefully studied for what they can tell the novice about conducting fieldwork, taking field notes, and writing theory. Today this image has been shattered. The works of the classic ethnographers are seen by many as relics from the colonial past (Rosaldo, 1989, p. 44). Although many feel nostalgia for this past, others celebrate its passing. Rosaldo (1989) quotes Cora Du Bois, a retired Harvard anthropology professor, who lamented this passing at a conference in 1980, reflecting on the crisis in anthropology: "[I feel a distance] from the complexity and disarray of what I once found a justifiable and challenging discipline. . . . It has been like moving from a distinguished art museum into a garage sale" (p. 44).

Du Bois regards the classic ethnographies as pieces of timeless artwork contained in a museum. She feels uncomfortable in the chaos of the garage sale. In contrast, Rosaldo (1989) is drawn to this metaphor: "[The garage sale] provides a precise image of the postcolonial situation where cultural artifacts flow between unlikely places, and nothing is sacred, permanent, or sealed off. The image of anthropology as a garage sale depicts our present global situation" (p. 44). Indeed, many valuable treasures may be found if one is willing to look long and hard, in unexpected places. Old standards no longer hold. Ethnographies do not produce timeless truths. The commitment to objectivism is now in doubt. The complicity with imperialism is openly challenged today, and the belief in monumentalism is a thing of the past.

The legacies of this first period begin at the end of the 19th century, when the novel and the social sciences had become distinguished as separate systems of discourse (Clough, 1992, pp. 21-22; see also Clough, 1998). However, the Chicago school, with its emphasis on the life story and the "slice-of-life" approach to ethnographic materials, sought to develop an interpretive methodology that maintained the centrality of the narrated life history approach. This led to the production of texts that gave the researcher-as-author the power to represent the subject's story. Written under the mantle of straightforward, sentiment-free social realism, these texts used the language of ordinary people. They articulated a social science version of literary naturalism, which often produced the sympathetic illusion that a solution to a social problem had been found. Like the Depression-era juvenile delinquent and other "social problems" films (Roffman & Purdy, 1981), these accounts romanticized the subject. They turned the deviant into a sociological version of a screen hero. These sociological stories, like their film counterparts, usually had happy endings, as they followed individuals through the three stages of the classic morality tale: being in a state of grace, being seduced by evil and falling, and finally achieving redemption through suffering.

Modernist Phase

The modernist phase, or second moment, builds on the canonical works from the traditional period. Social realism, naturalism, and slice-of-life ethnographies are still valued. This phase extended through the postwar years to the 1970s and is still present in the work of many (for reviews, see Wolcott, 1990, 1992, 1995; see also Tedlock, Chapter 6, Volume 2). In this period many texts sought to formalize qualitative methods (see, for example, Bogdan & Taylor, 1975; Cicourel, 1964; Filstead, 1970; Glaser & Strauss, 1967; Lofland, 1971, 1995; Lofland & Lofland, 1984, 1995; Taylor & Bogdan, 1998).[12] The modernist ethnographer and sociological participant observer attempted rigorous qualitative studies of important social processes, including deviance and social control in the classroom and society. This was a moment of creative ferment.

A new generation of graduate students across the human disciplines encountered new interpretive theories (ethnomethodology, phenomenology, critical theory, feminism). They were drawn to qualitative research practices that would let them give a voice to society's underclass. Postpositivism functioned as a powerful epistemological paradigm. Researchers attempted to fit Campbell and Stanley's (1963) model of internal and external validity to constructionist and interactionist conceptions of the research act. They returned to the texts of the Chicago school as sources of inspiration (see Denzin, 1970, 1978).

A canonical text from this moment remains *Boys in White* (Becker et al., 1961; see also Becker, 1998). Firmly entrenched in mid-20th-century methodological discourse, this work attempted to make qualitative research as rigorous as its quantitative counterpart. Causal narratives were central to this project. This multimethod work combined open-ended and quasi-structured interviewing with participant observation and the careful analysis of such materials in standardized, statistical form. In a classic article, "Problems of Inference and Proof in Participant Observation," Howard S. Becker (1958/1970) describes the use of quasi-statistics:

> Participant observations have occasionally been gathered in standardized form capable of being transformed into legitimate statistical data. But the exigencies of the field usually prevent the collection of data in such a form to meet the assumptions of statistical tests, so that the observer deals in what have been called "quasi-statistics." His conclusions, while implicitly numerical, do not require precise quantification. (p. 31)

In the analysis of data, Becker notes, the qualitative researcher takes a cue from statistical colleagues. The researcher looks for probabilities or support for arguments concerning the likelihood that, or frequency with which, a conclusion in fact applies in a specific situation (see also Becker, 1998, pp. 166-170). Thus did work in the modernist period clothe itself in the language and rhetoric of positivist and postpositivist discourse.

This was the golden age of rigorous qualitative analysis, bracketed in sociology by *Boys in White* (Becker et al., 1961) at one end and *The Discovery of Grounded Theory* (Glaser & Strauss, 1967) at the other. In education, qualitative research in this period was defined by George and Louise Spindler, Jules Henry, Harry Wolcott, and John Singleton. This form of qualitative research is still present in the work of such persons as Strauss and Corbin (1998) and Ryan and Bernard (see Chapter 7, this volume).

The "golden age" reinforced the picture of qualitative researchers as cultural romantics. Imbued with Promethean human powers, they valorized villains and outsiders as heroes to mainstream society. They embodied a belief in the contingency of self and society, and held to emancipatory ideals for "which one lives and dies." They put in place a tragic and often ironic view of society and self, and joined a long line of leftist cultural romantics that included Emerson, Marx, James, Dewey, Gramsci, and Martin Luther King, Jr. (West, 1989, chap. 6).

As this moment came to an end, the Vietnam War was everywhere present in American society. In 1969, alongside these political currents, Herbert Blumer and Everett Hughes met with a group of young sociologists called the "Chicago Irregulars" at the American Sociological Association meetings held in San Francisco and shared their memories of the "Chicago years." Lyn Lofland (1980) describes the 1969 meetings as a

> moment of creative ferment—scholarly and political. The San Francisco meetings witnessed not simply the Blumer-Hughes event but a "counterrevolution." . . . a group first came to . . . talk about the problems of being a sociologist and a female. . . . the discipline seemed literally to be bursting with new . . . ideas: labelling theory, ethnomethodology, conflict theory, phenomenology, dramaturgical analysis. (p. 253)

Thus did the modernist phase come to an end.

Blurred Genres

By the beginning of the third stage (1970–1986), which we call the moment of blurred genres, qualitative researchers had a full complement of paradigms, methods, and strategies to employ in their research. Theories ranged from symbolic interactionism to constructivism, naturalistic inquiry, positivism and postpositivism, phenomenology, ethnomethodology, critical theory, neo-Marxist theory, semiotics, structuralism, feminism, and various racial/ethnic paradigms. Applied qualitative research was gaining in stature, and the politics and ethics of qualitative research—implicated as they were in various applications of this work—were topics of considerable concern. Research strategies and formats for reporting research ranged from grounded theory to the case study, to methods of historical, biographical, ethnographic, action, and clinical research. Diverse ways of collecting and analyzing empirical materials were also available, including qualitative interviewing (open-ended and quasi-structured) and observational, visual, personal experience, and documentary methods. Computers were entering the situation, to be fully developed as aids in the analysis of qualitative data in the next decade, along with narrative, content, and semiotic methods of reading interviews and cultural texts.

Two books by Geertz, *The Interpretation of Culture* (1973) and *Local Knowledge* (1983), defined the beginning and end of this moment. In these two works, Geertz argued that the old functional, positivist, behavioral, totalizing approaches to the human disciplines were giving way to a more pluralistic, interpretive, open-ended perspective. This new perspective took cultural representations and their meanings as its point of departure. Calling for "thick descriptions" of particular events, rituals, and customs, Geertz suggested that all anthropological writings are interpretations of interpretations.[13] The observer has no privileged voice in the interpretations that are written. The central task of theory is to make sense out of a local situation.

Geertz went on to propose that the boundaries between the social sciences and the humanities had become blurred. Social scientists were now turning to the humanities for models, theories, and methods of analysis (semiotics, hermeneutics). A form of genre diaspora was occurring: documentaries that read like fiction (Mailer), parables posing as ethnographies (Castañeda), theoretical treatises that look like travelogues (Lévi-Strauss). At the same time, other new approaches were emerging: poststructuralism Barthes), neopositivism (Philips), neo-Marxism (Althusser), micro-macro descriptivism (Geertz), ritual theories of drama and culture (V. Turner), deconstructionism (Derrida), ethnomethodology (Garfinkel). The golden age of the social sciences was over, and a new age of blurred, interpretive genres was upon us. The essay as an art form was replacing the scientific article. At issue now is the author's presence in the interpretive text (Geertz, 1988). How can the researcher speak with authority in an age when there are no longer any firm rules concerning the text, including the author's place in it, its standards of evaluation, and its subject matter?

The naturalistic, postpositivist, and constructionist paradigms gained power in this period, especially in education, in the works of Harry Wolcott, Frederick Erickson, Egon Guba, Yvonna Lincoln, Robert Stake, and Elliot Eisner. By the end of the 1970s, several qualitative journals were in place, including *Urban Life and Culture* (now *Journal of Contemporary Ethnography*), *Cultural Anthropology, Anthropology and Education Quarterly, Qualitative Sociology*, and *Symbolic Interaction*, as well as the book series *Studies in Symbolic Interaction*.

Crisis of Representation

A profound rupture occurred in the mid-1980s. What we call the fourth moment, or the crisis of representation, appeared with *Anthropology as Cultural Critique* (Marcus & Fischer, 1986), *The Anthropology of*

Experience (Turner & Bruner, 1986), *Writing Culture* (Clifford & Marcus, 1986), *Works and Lives* (Geertz, 1988), and *The Predicament of Culture* (Clifford, 1988). These works made research and writing more reflexive and called into question the issues of gender, class, and race. They articulated the consequences of Geertz's "blurred genres" interpretation of the field in the early 1980s.[14]

New models of truth, method, and representation were sought (Rosaldo, 1989). The erosion of classic norms in anthropology (objectivism, complicity with colonialism, social life structured by fixed rituals and customs, ethnographies as monuments to a culture) was complete (Rosaldo, 1989, pp. 44-45; see also Jackson, 1998, pp. 7-8). Critical, feminist, and epistemologies of color now competed for attention in this arena. Issues such as validity, reliability, and objectivity, previously believed settled, were once more problematic. Pattern and interpretive theories, as opposed to causal, linear theories, were now more common, as writers continued to challenge older models of truth and meaning (Rosaldo, 1989).

Stoller and Olkes (1987, pp. 227-229) describe how the crisis of representation was felt in their fieldwork among the Songhay of Niger. Stoller observes: "When I began to write anthropological texts, I followed the conventions of my training. I 'gathered data,' and once the 'data' were arranged in neat piles, I 'wrote them up.' In one case I reduced Songhay insults to a series of neat logical formulas" (p. 227). Stoller became dissatisfied with this form of writing, in part because he learned that "everyone had lied to me and . . . the data I had so painstakingly collected were worthless. I learned a lesson: Informants routinely lie to their anthropologists" (Stoller & Olkes, 1987, p. 9). This discovery led to a second—that he had, in following the conventions of ethnographic realism, edited himself out of his text. This led Stoller to produce a different type of text, a memoir, in which he became a central character in the story he told. This story, an account of his experiences in the Songhay world, became an analysis of the clash between his world and the world of Songhay sorcery. Thus Stoller's journey represents an attempt to confront the crisis of representation in the fourth moment.

Clough (1992) elaborates this crisis and criticizes those who would argue that new forms of writing represent a way out of the crisis. She argues:

> While many sociologists now commenting on the criticism of ethnography view writing as "downright central to the ethnographic enterprise"

[Van Maanen, 1988, p. xi], the problems of writing are still viewed as differ-ent from the problems of method or fieldwork itself. Thus the solution usu-ally offered is experiments in writing, that is a self-consciousness about writing. (p. 136)

It is this insistence on the difference between writing and fieldwork that must be analyzed. (Richardson is quite articulate about this issue in Chap-ter 14 of this volume.)

In writing, the field-worker makes a claim to moral and scientific authority. This claim allows the realist and experimental ethnographic texts to function as sources of validation for an empirical science. They show that the world of real lived experience can still be captured, if only in the writer's memoirs, or fictional experimentations, or dramatic read-ings. But these works have the danger of directing attention away from the ways in which the text constructs sexually situated individuals in a field of social difference. They also perpetuate "empirical science's hegemony" (Clough, 1992, p. 8), for these new writing technologies of the subject become the site "for the production of knowledge/power . . . [aligned] with . . . the capital/state axis" (Aronowitz, 1988, p. 300; quoted in Clough, 1992, p. 8). Such experiments come up against, and then back away from, the difference between empirical science and social criticism. Too often they fail to engage fully a new politics of textuality that would "refuse the identity of empirical science" (Clough, 1992, p. 135). This new social criticism "would intervene in the relationship of information economics, nation-state politics, and technologies of mass communica-tion, especially in terms of the empirical sciences" (Clough, 1992, p. 16). This, of course, is the terrain occupied by cultural studies.

In this series, Richardson (this volume, Chapter 14), Tedlock (Volume 2, Chapter 6), Brady (this volume, Chapter 15), and Ellis and Bochner (this volume, Chapter 6) develop the above arguments, viewing writing as a method of inquiry that moves through successive stages of self-reflection. As a series of written representations, the field-worker's texts flow from the field experience, through intermediate works, to later work, and finally to the research text, which is the public presentation of the ethnographic and narrative experience. Thus fieldwork and writing blur into one another. There is, in the final analysis, no difference between writing and fieldwork. These two perspectives inform one another throughout every chapter in these volumes. In these ways the crisis of rep-resentation moves qualitative research in new and critical directions.

A Triple Crisis

The ethnographer's authority remains under assault today (Behar, 1995, p. 3; Gupta & Ferguson, 1997, p. 16; Jackson, 1998; Ortner, 1997, p. 2). A triple crisis of representation, legitimation, and praxis confronts qualitative researchers in the human disciplines. Embedded in the discourses of poststructuralism and postmodernism (see Vidich & Lyman, Volume 1, Chapter 2; and Richardson, Chapter 14, this volume), these three crises are coded in multiple terms, variously called and associated with *the critical, interpretive, linguistic, feminist*, and *rhetorical* turns in social theory. These new turns make problematic two key assumptions of qualitative research. The first is that qualitative researchers can no longer directly capture lived experience. Such experience, it is argued, is created in the social text written by the researcher. This is the representational crisis. It confronts the inescapable problem of representation, but does so within a framework that makes the direct link between experience and text problematic.

The second assumption makes problematic the traditional criteria for evaluating and interpreting qualitative research. This is the legitimation crisis. It involves a serious rethinking of such terms as *validity, generalizability*, and *reliability*, terms already retheorized in postpositivist (Hammersley, 1992), constructionist-naturalistic (Guba & Lincoln, 1989, pp. 163-183), feminist (Olesen, Chapter 8, Volume 1), interpretive (Denzin, 1997), poststructural (Lather, 1993; Lather & Smithies, 1997), and critical (Kincheloe & McLaren, Chapter 10, Volume 1) discourses. This crisis asks, How are qualitative studies to be evaluated in the contemporary, poststructural moment? The first two crises shape the third, which asks, Is it possible to effect change in the world if society is only and always a text? Clearly these crises intersect and blur, as do the answers to the questions they generate (see in Volume 1, Schwandt, Chapter 7; Ladson-Billings, Chapter 9; and in this volume, Smith & Deemer, Chapter 12).

The fifth moment, the postmodern period of experimental ethnographic writing, struggled to make sense of these crises. New ways of composing ethnography were explored (Ellis & Bochner, 1996). Theories were read as tales from the field. Writers struggled with different ways to represent the "other," although they were now joined by new representational concerns (see Fine et al., Chapter 4, Volume 1). Epistemologies from previously silenced groups emerged to offer solutions to these problems. The concept of the aloof observer has been abandoned. More action, participatory, and activist-oriented research is on the horizon. The search for grand narratives is being replaced by more local, small-scale theories fitted to specific problems and particular situations.

The sixth (postexperimental) and seventh (the future) moments are upon us. Fictional ethnographies, ethnographic poetry, and multimedia texts are today taken for granted. Postexperimental writers seek to connect their writings to the needs of a free democratic society. The demands of a moral and sacred qualitative social science are actively being explored by a host of new writers from many different disciplines (see Jackson, 1998; Lincoln & Denzin, Chapter 6, Volume 1).

Reading History

We draw four conclusions from this brief history, noting that it is, like all histories, somewhat arbitrary. First, each of the earlier historical moments is still operating in the present, either as legacy or as a set of practices that researchers continue to follow or argue against. The multiple and fractured histories of qualitative research now make it possible for any given researcher to attach a project to a canonical text from any of the above-described historical moments. Multiple criteria of evaluation compete for attention in this field (Lincoln, in press). Second, an embarrassment of choices now characterizes the field of qualitative research. There have never been so many paradigms, strategies of inquiry, or methods of analysis for researchers to draw upon and utilize. Third, we are in a moment of discovery and rediscovery, as new ways of looking, interpreting, arguing, and writing are debated and discussed. Fourth, the qualitative research act can no longer be viewed from within a neutral or objective positivist perspective. Class, race, gender, and ethnicity shape the process of inquiry, making research a multicultural process. It is to this topic that we now turn.

◆ Qualitative Research as Process

Three interconnected, generic activities define the qualitative research process. They go by a variety of different labels, including *theory, method, analysis, ontology, epistemology,* and *methodology.* Behind these terms stands the personal biography of the researcher, who speaks from a particular class, gender, racial, cultural, and ethnic community perspective. The gendered, multiculturally situated researcher approaches the world with a set of ideas, a framework (theory, ontology) that specifies a set of questions (epistemology) that he or she then examines in specific ways (methodology, analysis). That is, the researcher collects empirical materials bearing on the question and then analyzes and writes about them. Every researcher speaks from within a distinct interpretive community that configures, in its special way, the multicultural, gendered components of the research act.

In this volume we treat these generic activities under five headings, or phases: the researcher and the researched as multicultural subjects, major paradigms and interpretive perspectives, research strategies, methods of collecting and analyzing empirical materials, and the art, practices, and politics of interpretation. Behind and within each of these phases stands the biographically situated researcher. This individual enters the research process from inside an interpretive community. This community has its own historical research traditions, which constitute a distinct point of view. This perspective leads the researcher to adopt particular views of the "other" who is studied. At the same time, the politics and the ethics of research must also be considered, for these concerns permeate every phase of the research process.

◆ The Other as Research Subject

Since its early-20th-century birth in modern, interpretive form, qualitative research has been haunted by a double-faced ghost. On the one hand, qualitative researchers have assumed that qualified, competent observers can, with objectivity, clarity, and precision, report on their own observations of the social world, including the experiences of others. Second, researchers have held to the belief in a real subject, or real individual, who is present in the world and able, in some form, to report on his or her experiences. So armed, researchers could blend their own observations with the self-reports provided by subjects through interviews and life story, personal experience, case study, and other documents.

These two beliefs have led qualitative researchers across disciplines to seek a method that would allow them to record accurately their own observations while also uncovering the meanings their subjects bring to their life experiences. This method would rely upon the subjective verbal and written expressions of meaning given by the individuals studied as windows into the inner lives of these persons. Since Dilthey (1900/1976), this search for a method has led to a perennial focus in the human disciplines on qualitative, interpretive methods.

Recently, as noted above, this position and its beliefs have come under assault. Poststructuralists and postmodernists have contributed to the understanding that there is no clear window into the inner life of an individual. Any gaze is always filtered through the lenses of language, gender, social class, race, and ethnicity. There are no objective observations, only observations socially situated in the worlds of—and between—the observer and the observed. Subjects, or individuals, are seldom able to give full explanations of their actions or intentions; all they can offer are accounts, or stories, about what they did and why. No single method can grasp all of the subtle variations in ongoing human experience. Consequently, qualitative researchers deploy a wide range of interconnected interpretive methods, always seeking better ways to make more understandable the worlds of experience they have studied.

Table 1.1 depicts the relationships we see among the five phases that define the research process. Behind all but one of these phases stands the biographically situated researcher. These five levels of activity, or practice, work their way through the biography of the researcher. We take them up briefly in order here; we discuss these phases more fully in the introductions to the individual parts of this volume.

Phase 1: The Researcher

Our remarks above indicate the depth and complexity of the traditional and applied qualitative research perspectives into which a socially situated researcher enters. These traditions locate the researcher in history, simultaneously guiding and constraining work that will be done in any specific study. This field has been characterized constantly by diversity and conflict, and these are its most enduring traditions (see Greenwood & Levin, Chapter 3, Volume 1). As a carrier of this complex and contradictory history, the researcher must also confront the ethics and politics of research (see Christians, Chapter 5, Volume 1). The age of value-free inquiry for the human disciplines is over (see in Volume 1, Vidich & Lyman, Chapter 2; and Fine et al., Chapter 4). Today researchers struggle to develop situational and transsituational ethics that apply to all forms of the research act and its human-to-human relationships.

TABLE 1.1   The Research Process

Phase 1: The Researcher as a Multicultural Subject
 history and research traditions
 conceptions of self and the other
 ethics and politics of research

Phase 2: Theoretical Paradigms and Perspectives
 positivism, postpositivism
 interpretivism, constructivism, hermeneutics
 feminism(s)
 racialized discourses
 critical theory and Marxist models
 cultural studies models
 queer theory

Phase 3: Research Strategies
 study design
 case study
 ethnography, participant observation, performance ethnography
 phenomenology, ethnomethodology
 grounded theory
 life history, *testimonio*
 historical method
 action and applied research
 clinical research

Phase 4: Methods of Collection and Analysis
 interviewing
 observing
 artifacts, documents, and records
 visual methods
 autoethnography
 data management methods
 computer-assisted analysis
 textual analysis
 focus groups
 applied ethnography

Phase 5: The Art, Practices, and Politics of Interpretation and Presentation
 criteria for judging adequacy
 practices and politics of interpretation
 writing as interpretation
 policy analysis
 evaluation traditions
 applied research

Phase 2: Interpretive Paradigms

All qualitative researchers are philosophers in that "universal sense in which all human beings . . . are guided by highly abstract principles" (Bateson, 1972, p. 320). These principles combine beliefs about ontology (What kind of being is the human being? What is the nature of reality?), epistemology (What is the relationship between the inquirer and the known?), and methodology (How do we know the world, or gain knowledge of it?) (see Guba, 1990, p. 18; Lincoln & Guba, 1985, pp. 14-15; see also Lincoln & Guba, Chapter 6, Volume 1). These beliefs shape how the qualitative researcher sees the world and acts in it. The researcher is "bound within a net of epistemological and ontological premises which—regardless of ultimate truth or falsity—become partially self-validating" (Bateson, 1972, p. 314).

The net that contains the researcher's epistemological, ontological, and methodological premises may be termed a *paradigm*, or an interpretive framework, a "basic set of beliefs that guides action" (Guba, 1990, p. 17). All research is interpretive; it is guided by a set of beliefs and feelings about the world and how it should be understood and studied. Some beliefs may be taken for granted, invisible, only assumed, whereas others are highly problematic and controversial. Each interpretive paradigm makes particular demands on the researcher, including the questions he or she asks and the interpretations the researcher brings to them.

At the most general level, four major interpretive paradigms structure qualitative research: positivist and postpositivist, constructivist-interpretive, critical (Marxist, emancipatory), and feminist-poststructural. These four abstract paradigms become more complicated at the level of concrete specific interpretive communities. At this level it is possible to identify not only the constructivist, but also multiple versions of feminism (Afrocentric and poststructural)[15] as well as specific ethnic, Marxist, and cultural studies paradigms. These perspectives, or paradigms, are examined in Part II of Volume 1.

The paradigms examined in Part II of Volume 1 work against and alongside (and some within) the positivist and postpositivist models. They all work within relativist ontologies (multiple constructed realities), interpretive epistemologies (the knower and known interact and shape one another), and interpretive, naturalistic methods.

Table 1.2 presents these paradigms and their assumptions, including their criteria for evaluating research, and the typical form that an

TABLE 1.2   Interpretive Paradigms

Paradigm/ Theory	Criteria	Form of Theory	Type of Narration
Positivist/ postpositivist	internal, external validity	logical-deductive, grounded	scientific report
Constructivist	trustworthiness, credibility, transferability, confirmability	substantive-formal	interpretive case studies, ethnographic fiction
Feminist	Afrocentric, lived experience, dialogue, caring, accountability, race, class, gender, reflexivity, praxis, emotion, concrete grounding	critical, standpoint	essays, stories, experimental writing
Ethnic	Afrocentric, lived experience, dialogue, caring, accountability, race, class, gender	standpoint, critical, historical	essays, fables, dramas
Marxist	emancipatory theory, falsifiable, dialogical, race, class, gender	critical, historical, economic	historical, economic, sociocultural analyses
Cultural studies	cultural practices, praxis, social texts, subjectivities	social criticism	cultural theory as criticism
Queer theory	reflexivity, deconstruction	social criticism, historical analysis	theory as criticism, autobiography

interpretive or theoretical statement assumes in each paradigm.[16] These paradigms are explored in considerable detail in Volume 1, Part II by Lincoln and Guba (Chapter 6), Schwandt (Chapter 7), Olesen (Chapter 8), Ladson-Billings (Chapter 9), Kincheloe and McLaren (Chapter 10),

Frow and Morris (Chapter 11), and Gamson (Chapter 12). We have discussed the positivist and postpositivist paradigms above. They work from within a realist and critical realist ontology and objective epistemologies, and rely upon experimental, quasi-experimental, survey, and rigorously defined qualitative methodologies. Ryan and Bernard (Chapter 7, this volume) develop elements of this paradigm.

The constructivist paradigm assumes a relativist ontology (there are multiple realities), a subjectivist epistemology (knower and respondent cocreate understandings), and a naturalistic (in the natural world) set of methodological procedures. Findings are usually presented in terms of the criteria of grounded theory or pattern theories (see in Volume 1, Lincoln & Guba, Chapter 6; in Volume 2, Charmaz, Chapter 8; and in this volume, Ryan & Bernard, Chapter 7). Terms such as *credibility, transferability, dependability*, and *confirmability* replace the usual positivist criteria of internal and external validity, reliability, and objectivity.

Feminist, ethnic, Marxist, and cultural studies and queer theory models privilege a materialist-realist ontology; that is, the real world makes a material difference in terms of race, class, and gender. Subjectivist epistemologies and naturalistic methodologies (usually ethnographies) are also employed. Empirical materials and theoretical arguments are evaluated in terms of their emancipatory implications. Criteria from gender and racial communities (e.g., African American) may be applied (emotionality and feeling, caring, personal accountability, dialogue).

Poststructural feminist theories emphasize problems with the social text, its logic, and its inability ever to represent the world of lived experience fully. Positivist and postpositivist criteria of evaluation are replaced by other terms, including the reflexive, multivoiced text that is grounded in the experiences of oppressed people.

The cultural studies and queer theory paradigms are multifocused, with many different strands drawing from Marxism, feminism, and the postmodern sensibility (see in Volume 1, Frow & Morris, Chapter 11; Gamson, Chapter 12; and in this volume, Richardson, Chapter 14). There is a tension between a humanistic cultural studies, which stresses lived experiences (meaning), and a more structural cultural studies project, which stresses the structural and material determinants (race, class, gender) and effects of experience. Of course, there are two sides to every coin, and both sides are needed and are indeed critical. The cultural studies and queer theory paradigms use methods strategically—that is, as resources for understanding and for producing resistances to local structures of domination. Scholars may do close textual readings and discourse analyses of cultural texts (see in Volume 1, Olesen, Chapter 8; Frow & Morris, Chapter 11; and Silverman, this volume, Chapter 9) as well as conducting local ethnographies, open-ended interviewing, and participant observation. The focus is on how race, class, and gender are produced and enacted in historically specific situations.

Paradigm and personal history in hand, focused on a concrete empirical problem to examine, the researcher now moves to the next stage of the research process—namely, working with a specific strategy of inquiry.

Phase 3: Strategies of Inquiry and Interpretive Paradigms

Table 1.1 presents some of the major strategies of inquiry a researcher may use. Phase 3 begins with research design, which, broadly conceived, involves a clear focus on the research question, the purposes of the study, "what information most appropriately will answer specific research questions, and which strategies are most effective for obtaining it" (LeCompte & Preissle, 1993, p. 30; see also in Volume 2, Janesick, Chapter 2; Cheek, Chapter 3). A research design describes a flexible set of guidelines that connect theoretical paradigms first to strategies of inquiry and second to methods for collecting empirical material. A research design situates researchers in the empirical world and connects them to specific sites, persons, groups, institutions, and bodies of relevant interpretive material, including documents and archives. A research design also specifies how the investigator will address the two critical issues of representation and legitimation.

A strategy of inquiry comprises a bundle of skills, assumptions, and practices that the researcher employs as he or she moves from paradigm to the empirical world. Strategies of inquiry put paradigms of interpretation into motion. At the same time, strategies of inquiry also connect the researcher to specific methods of collecting and analyzing empirical materials. For example, the case study relies on interviewing, observing, and document analysis. Research strategies implement and anchor paradigms in specific empirical sites, or in specific methodological practices, such as making a case an object of study. These strategies include the case study, phenomenological and ethnomethodological techniques, and the use of grounded theory, as well as biographical, autoethnographic, historical, action, and clinical methods. Each of these strategies is connected to a complex literature, and each has a separate history, exemplary works, and preferred ways for putting the strategy into motion.

Phase 4: Methods of Collecting and Analyzing Empirical Materials

The researcher has several methods for collecting empirical materials.[17] These methods are taken up in Part I of this volume. They range from the interview to direct observation, the analysis of artifacts, documents, and cultural records, and the use of visual materials or personal experience. The researcher may also use a variety of different methods of reading and analyzing interviews or cultural texts, including content, narrative, and semiotic strategies. Faced with large amounts of qualitative materials, the investigator seeks ways of managing and interpreting these documents, and here data management methods and computer-assisted models of analysis may be of use. Ryan and Bernard (this volume, Chapter 7) and Weitzman (this volume, Chapter 8) discuss these techniques.

Phase 5: The Art and Politics of Interpretation and Evaluation

Qualitative research is endlessly creative and interpretive. The researcher does not just leave the field with mountains of empirical materials and then easily write up his or her findings. Qualitative interpretations are constructed. The researcher first creates a field text consisting of field notes and documents from the field, what Roger Sanjek (1990, p. 386) calls "indexing" and David Plath (1990, p. 374) calls "filework." The writer-as-interpreter moves from this text to a research text: notes and interpretations based on the field text. This text is then re-created as a working interpretive document that contains the writer's initial attempts to make sense of what he or she has learned. Finally the writer produces the public text that comes to the reader. This final tale from the field may assume several forms: confessional, realist, impressionistic, critical, formal, literary, analytic, grounded theory, and so on (see Van Maanen, 1988).

The interpretive practice of making sense of one's findings is both artistic and political. Multiple criteria for evaluating qualitative research now exist, and those that we emphasize stress the situated, relational, and textual structures of the ethnographic experience. There is no single interpretive truth. As we argued earlier, there are multiple interpretive communities, each with its own criteria for evaluating an interpretation.

Program evaluation is a major site of qualitative research, and qualitative researchers can influence social policy in important ways. The contributions by Greenwood and Levin (Volume 1, Chapter 3), Kemmis and McTaggart (Volume 2, Chapter 11), Miller and Crabtree (Volume 2, Chapter 12), Chambers (this volume, Chapter 11), Greene (this volume, Chapter 16), and Rist (this volume, Chapter 17) trace and discuss the rich history of applied qualitative research in the social sciences. This is the critical site where theory, method, praxis, action, and policy all come together. Qualitative researchers can isolate target populations, show the immediate effects of certain programs on such groups, and isolate the constraints that operate against policy changes in such settings. Action-oriented and clinically oriented qualitative researchers can also create spaces for those who are studied (the other) to speak. The evaluator becomes the conduit through which such voices can be heard. Chambers, Greene, and Rist explicitly develop these topics in their chapters.

◆ Bridging the Historical Moments: What Comes Next?

Ellis and Bochner (this volume, Chapter 6), Gergen and Gergen (Volume 1, Chapter 13), and Richardson (this volume, Chapter 14) argue that we are already in the post "post" period—post-poststructuralist, post-postmodernist, post-postexperimental. What this means for interpretive ethnographic practices is still not clear, but it is certain that things will never again be the same. We are in a new age where messy, uncertain, multivoiced texts, cultural criticism, and new experimental works will become more common, as will more reflexive forms of fieldwork, analysis, and intertextual representation. We take as the subject of our final essay in this volume these fifth, sixth, and seventh moments. It is true that, as the poet said, the center no longer holds. We can reflect on what should be at the new center.

Thus we come full circle. Returning to our bridge metaphor, the chapters that follow take the researcher back and forth through every phase of the research act. Like a good bridge, the chapters provide for two-way traffic, coming and going between moments, formations, and interpretive communities. Each chapter examines the relevant histories, controversies, and current practices that are associated with each paradigm, strategy, and method. Each chapter also offers projections for the future, where a specific paradigm, strategy, or method will be 10 years from now, deep into the formative years of the 21st century.

In reading the chapters that follow, it is important to remember that the field of qualitative research is defined by a series of tensions, contradictions, and hesitations. This tension works back and forth between the broad, doubting postmodern sensibility and the more certain, more traditional positivist, postpositivist, and naturalistic conceptions of this project. All of the chapters that follow are caught in and articulate this tension.

◆ Notes

1. Qualitative research has separate and distinguished histories in education, social work, communications, psychology, history, organizational studies, medical science, anthropology, and sociology.

2. Some definitions are in order here. *Positivism* asserts that objective accounts of the real world can be given. *Postpositivism* holds that only partially objective accounts of the world can be produced, because all methods for examining them are flawed. According to *foundationalism*, we can have an ultimate grounding for our knowledge claims about the world, and this involves the use of empiricist and positivist epistemologies (Schwandt, 1997a, p. 103). *Nonfoundationalism* holds that we can make statements about the world without "recourse to ultimate proof or foundations for that knowing" (p. 102). *Quasi-foundationalism* holds that certain knowledge claims can be made about the world based on neorealist criteria, including the correspondence concept of truth; there is an independent reality that can be mapped (see Smith & Deemer, Chapter 12, this volume).

3. Jameson (1991, pp. 3-4) reminds us that any periodization hypothesis is always suspect, even one that rejects linear, stagelike models. It is never clear to what reality a stage refers, and what divides one stage from another is always debatable. Our seven moments are meant to mark discernible shifts in style, genre, epistemology, ethics, politics, and aesthetics.

4. Some further definitions are in order. *Structuralism* holds that any system is made up of a set of oppositional categories embedded in language. *Semiotics* is the science of signs or sign systems—a structuralist project. According to *poststructuralism*, language is an unstable system of referents, thus it is impossible ever to capture completely the meaning of an action, text, or intention. *Postmodernism* is a contemporary sensibility, developing since World War II, that privileges no single authority, method, or paradigm. *Hermeneutics* is an approach to the analysis of texts that stresses how prior understandings and prejudices shape the interpretive process. *Phenomenology* is a complex system of ideas associated with the works of Husserl, Heidegger, Sartre, Merleau-Ponty, and Alfred Schutz. *Cultural studies* is a complex, interdisciplinary field that merges critical theory, feminism, and poststructuralism.

5. Of course, all settings are natural—that is, places where everyday experiences take place. Qualitative researchers study people doing things together in the places where these

things are done (Becker, 1986). There is no field site or natural place where one goes to do this kind of work (see also Gupta & Ferguson, 1997, p. 8). The site is constituted through the researcher's interpretive practices. Historically, analysts have distinguished between experimental (laboratory) and field (natural) research settings, hence the argument that qualitative research is naturalistic. Activity theory erases this distinction (Keller & Keller, 1996, p. 20; Vygotsky, 1978).

6. According to Weinstein and Weinstein (1991), "The meaning of *bricoleur* in French popular speech is 'someone who works with his (or her) hands and uses devious means compared to those of the craftsman.' . . . the *bricoleur* is practical and gets the job done" (p. 161). These authors provide a history of the term, connecting it to the works of the German sociologist and social theorist Georg Simmel and, by implication, Baudelaire. Hammersley (in press) disputes our use of this term. Following Lévi-Strauss, he reads the *bricoleur* as a mythmaker. He suggests the term be replaced with the notion of the boatbuilder. Hammersley also quarrels with our "moments" model of qualitative research, contending that it implies some sense of progress.

7. Brian De Palma reproduced this baby carriage scene in his 1987 film *The Untouchables*.

8. In the harbor, the muzzles of the *Potemkin*'s two huge guns swing slowly toward the camera. Words onscreen inform us, "The brutal military power answered by guns of the battleship." A final famous three-shot montage sequence shows first a sculptured sleeping lion, then a lion rising from his sleep, and finally the lion roaring, symbolizing the rage of the Russian people (Cook, 1981, p. 167). In this sequence Eisenstein uses montage to expand time, creating a psychological duration for this horrible event. By drawing out this sequence, by showing the baby in the carriage, the soldiers firing on the citizens, the blood on the mother's glove, the descending carriage on the steps, he suggests a level of destruction of great magnitude.

9. Here it is relevant to make a distinction between techniques that are used across disciplines and methods that are used within disciplines. Ethnomethodologists, for example, employ their approach as a method, whereas others selectively borrow that method as a technique for their own applications. Harry Wolcott (personal communication, 1993) suggests this distinction. It is also relevant to make distinctions among topic, method, and resource. Methods can be studied as topics of inquiry; that is how a case study gets done. In this ironic, ethnomethodological sense, method is both a resource and a topic of inquiry.

10. Indeed, any attempt to give an essential definition of qualitative research requires a qualitative analysis of the circumstances that produce such a definition.

11. In this sense all research is qualitative, because "the observer is at the center of the research process" (Vidich & Lyman, Chapter 2, Volume 1).

12. See Lincoln and Guba (1985) for an extension and elaboration of this tradition in the mid-1980s, and for more recent extensions see Taylor and Bogdan (1998) and Creswell (1997).

13. Greenblatt (1997, pp. 15-18) offers a useful deconstructive reading of the many meanings and practices Geertz brings to the term *thick description*.

14. These works marginalized and minimized the contributions of standpoint feminist theory and research to this discourse (see Behar, 1995, p. 3; Gordon, 1995, p. 432).

15. Olesen (Chapter 8, Volume 1) identifies three strands of feminist research: mainstream empirical, standpoint and cultural studies, and poststructural, postmodern. She

places Afrocentric and other models of color under the cultural studies and postmodern categories.

16. These, of course, are our interpretations of these paradigms and interpretive styles.

17. *Empirical materials* is the preferred term for what are traditionally described as data.

◆ References

Aronowitz, S. (1988). *Science as power: Discourse and ideology in modern society.* Minneapolis: University of Minnesota Press.

Bateson, G. (1972). *Steps to an ecology of mind.* New York: Ballantine.

Becker, H. S. (1970). Problems of inference and proof in participant observation. In H. S. Becker, *Sociological work: Method and substance.* Chicago: Aldine. (Reprinted from *American Sociological Review, 1958, 23,* 652-660)

Becker, H. S. (1986). *Doing things together.* Evanston: Northwestern University Press.

Becker, H. S. (1996). The epistemology of qualitative research. In R. Jessor, A. Colby, & R. A. Shweder (Eds.), *Ethnography and human development: Context and meaning in social inquiry* (pp. 53-71). Chicago: University of Chicago Press.

Becker, H. S. (1998). *Tricks of the trade: How to think about your research while you're doing it.* Chicago: University of Chicago Press.

Becker, H. S., Geer, B., Hughes, E. C., & Strauss, A. L. (1961). *Boys in white: Student culture in medical school.* Chicago: University of Chicago Press.

Behar, R. (1995). Introduction: Out of exile. In R. Behar & D. A. Gordon (Eds.), *Women writing culture* (pp. 1-29). Berkeley: University of California Press.

Bogdan, R. C., & Taylor, S. J. (1975). *Introduction to qualitative research methods: A phenomenological approach to the social sciences.* New York: John Wiley.

Campbell, D. T., & Stanley, J. C. (1963). *Experimental and quasi-experimental designs for research.* Chicago: Rand McNally.

Carey, J. W. (1989). *Communication as culture: Essays on media and society.* Boston: Unwin Hyman.

Cicourel, A. V. (1964). *Method and measurement in sociology.* New York: Free Press.

Clifford, J. (1988). *The predicament of culture: Twentieth-century ethnography, literature, and art.* Cambridge, MA: Harvard University Press.

Clifford, J., & Marcus, G. E. (Eds.). (1986). *Writing culture: The poetics and politics of ethnography.* Berkeley: University of California Press.

Clough, P. T. (1992). *The end(s) of ethnography: From realism to social criticism.* Newbury Park, CA: Sage.

Clough, P. T. (1998). *The end(s) of ethnography: From realism to social criticism* (2nd ed.). New York: Peter Lang.

Cook, D. A. (1981). *A history of narrative film.* New York: W. W. Norton.

Creswell, J. W. (1997). *Qualitative inquiry and research design: Choosing among five traditions.* Thousand Oaks, CA: Sage.

Denzin, N. K. (1970). *The research act.* Chicago: Aldine.

Denzin, N. K. (1978). *The research act* (2nd ed.). New York: McGraw-Hill.

Denzin, N. K. (1997). *Interpretive ethnography.* Thousand Oaks, CA: Sage.

Dilthey, W. L. (1976). *Selected writings.* Cambridge: Cambridge University Press. (Original work published 1900)

Diversi, M. (1998). Glimpses of street life: Representing lived experience through short stories. *Qualitative Inquiry, 4,* 131-137.

Ellis, C., & Bochner, A. P. (Eds.). (1996). *Composing ethnography: Alternative forms of qualitative writing.* Walnut Creek, CA: AltaMira.

Filstead, W. J. (Ed.). (1970). *Qualitative methodology.* Chicago: Markham.

Flick, U. (1998). *An introduction to qualitative research: Theory, method and applications.* London: Sage.

Geertz, C. (1973). *The interpretation of cultures: Selected essays.* New York: Basic Books.

Geertz, C. (1983). *Local knowledge: Further essays in interpretive anthropology.* New York: Basic Books.

Geertz, C. (1988). *Works and lives: The anthropologist as author.* Stanford, CA: Stanford University Press.

Glaser, B. G. (1992). *Emergence vs. forcing: Basics of grounded theory.* Mill Valley, CA: Sociology Press.

Glaser, B. G., & Strauss, A. L. (1967). *The discovery of grounded theory: Strategies for qualitative research.* Chicago: Aldine.

Gordon, D. A. (1995). Culture writing women: Inscribing feminist anthropology. In R. Behar & D. A. Gordon (Eds.), *Women writing culture* (pp. 429-441). Berkeley: University of California Press.

Gordon, D. A. (1988). Writing culture, writing feminism: The poetics and politics of experimental ethnography. *Inscriptions, 3/4*(8), 21-31.

Greenblatt, S. (1997). The touch of the real. In S. B. Ortner (Ed.), The fate of "culture": Geertz and beyond [Special issue]. *Representations, 59,* 14-29.

Guba, E. G. (1990). The alternative paradigm dialog. In E. G. Guba (Ed.), *The paradigm dialog* (pp. 17-30). Newbury Park, CA: Sage.

Guba, E. G., & Lincoln, Y. S. (1989). *Fourth generation evaluation.* Newbury Park, CA: Sage.

Gupta, A., & Ferguson, J. (1997). Discipline and practice: "The field" as site, method, and location in anthropology. In A. Gupta & J. Ferguson (Eds.), *Anthropological locations: Boundaries and grounds of a field science* (pp. 1-46). Berkeley: University of California Press.

Hammersley, M. (1992). *What's wrong with ethnography? Methodological explorations*. London: Routledge.

Hammersley, M. (in press). Not bricolage but boatbuilding. *Journal of Contemporary Ethnography*.

hooks, b. (1990). *Yearning: Race, gender, and cultural politics*. Boston: South End.

Huber, J. (1995). Centennial essay: Institutional perspectives on sociology. *American Journal of Sociology, 101*, 194-216.

Jackson, M. (1998). *Minima ethnographica: Intersubjectivity and the anthropological project*. Chicago: University of Chicago Press.

Jameson, F. (1991). *Postmodernism; or, The cultural logic of late capitalism*. Durham, NC: Duke University Press.

Jones, S. H. (1999). Torch. *Qualitative Inquiry, 5*, 235-250.

Keller, C. M., & Keller, J. D. (1996). *Cognition and tool use: The blacksmith at work*. New York: Cambridge University Press.

Lather, P. (1993). Fertile obsession: Validity after poststructuralism. *Sociological Quarterly, 35*, 673-694.

Lather, P., & Smithies, C. (1997). *Troubling the angels: Women living with HIV/ AIDS*. Boulder, CO: Westview.

LeCompte, M. D., & Preissle, J. (with Tesch, R.). (1993). *Ethnography and qualitative design in educational research* (2nd ed.). New York: Academic Press.

Lévi-Strauss, C. (1966). *The savage mind* (2nd ed.). Chicago: University of Chicago Press.

Lincoln, Y. S. (1999, June). Courage, vulnerability and truth. Keynote address delivered at the conference "Reclaiming Voice II: Ethnographic Inquiry and Qualitative Research in a Postmodern Age," University of California, Irvine.

Lincoln, Y. S. (in press). Varieties of validity: Quality in qualitative research. In J. S. Smart & C. Ethington (Eds.), *Higher education: Handbook of theory and research*. New York: Agathon Press.

Lincoln, Y. S., & Guba, E. G. (1985). *Naturalistic inquiry*. Beverly Hills, CA: Sage.

Lofland, J. (1971). *Analyzing social settings*. Belmont, CA: Wadsworth.

Lofland, J. (1995). Analytic ethnography: Features, failings, and futures. *Journal of Contemporary Ethnography, 24*, 30-67.

Lofland, J., & Lofland, L. H. (1984). *Analyzing social settings: A guide to qualitative observation and analysis* (2nd ed.). Belmont, CA: Wadsworth.

Lofland, J., & Lofland, L. H. (1995). *Analyzing social settings: A guide to qualitative observation and analysis* (3rd ed.). Belmont, CA: Wadsworth.

Lofland, L. (1980). The 1969 Blumer-Hughes Talk. *Urban Life and Culture, 8*, 248-260.

Malinowski, B. (1948). *Magic, science and religion, and other essays*. New York: Natural History Press. (Original work published 1916)

Malinowski, B. (1967). *A diary in the strict sense of the term* (N. Guterman, Trans.). New York: Harcourt, Brace & World.

Marcus, G. E., & Fischer, M. M. J. (1986). *Anthropology as cultural critique: An experimental moment in the human sciences.* Chicago: University of Chicago Press.

Monaco, J. (1981). *How to read a film: The art, technology, language, history and theory of film* (Rev. ed.). New York: Oxford University Press.

Nelson, C., Treichler, P. A., & Grossberg, L. (1992). Cultural studies: An introduction. In L. Grossberg, C. Nelson, & P. A. Treichler (Eds.), *Cultural studies* (pp. 1-16). New York: Routledge.

Ortner, S. B. (1997). Introduction. In S. B. Ortner (Ed.), The fate of "culture": Geertz and beyond [Special issue]. *Representations, 59,* 1-13.

Plath, D. W. (1990). Fieldnotes, filed notes, and the conferring of note. In R. Sanjek (Ed.), *Fieldnotes: The makings of anthropology* (pp. 371-384). Ithaca, NY: Cornell University Press.

Richardson, L. (1997). *Fields of play: Constructing an academic life.* New Brunswick, NJ: Rutgers University Press.

Roffman, P., & Purdy, J. (1981). *The Hollywood social problem film.* Bloomington: Indiana University Press.

Ronai, C. R. (1998). Sketching with Derrida: An ethnography of a researcher/erotic dancer. *Qualitative Inquiry, 4,* 405-420.

Rosaldo, R. (1989). *Culture and truth: The remaking of social analysis.* Boston: Beacon.

Sanjek, R. (Ed.). (1990). *Fieldnotes: The makings of anthropology.* Ithaca, NY: Cornell University Press.

Schwandt, T. A. (1997a). *Qualitative inquiry: A dictionary of terms.* Thousand Oaks, CA: Sage.

Schwandt, T. A. (1997b). Textual gymnastics, ethics and angst. In W. G. Tierney & Y. S. Lincoln (Eds.), *Representation and the text: Re-framing the narrative voice* (pp. 305-311). Albany: State University of New York Press.

Silverman, D. (1997). Towards an aesthetics of research. In D. Silverman (Ed.), *Qualitative research: Theory, method and practice* (pp. 239-253). London: Sage.

Smith, A. D. (1993). *Fires in the mirror: Crown Heights, Brooklyn, and other identities.* Garden City, NY: Anchor.

Snow, D., & Morrill, C. (1995). Ironies, puzzles, and contradictions in Denzin and Lincoln's vision of qualitative research. *Journal of Contemporary Ethnography, 22,* 358-362.

Spindler, G., & Spindler, L. (1992). Cultural process and ethnography: An anthropological perspective. In M. D. LeCompte, W. L. Millroy, & J. Preissle (Eds.), *The handbook of qualitative research in education* (pp. 53-92). New York: Academic Press.

Stocking, G. W., Jr. (1986). Anthropology and the science of the irrational: Malinowski's encounter with Freudian psychoanalysis. In G. W. Stocking, Jr.

(Ed.), Malinowski, Rivers, Benedict and others: *Essays on culture and personality* (pp. 13-49). Madison: University of Wisconsin Press.

Stocking, G. W., Jr. (1989). The ethnographic sensibility of the 1920s and the dualism of the anthropological tradition. In G. W. Stocking, Jr. (Ed.), *Romantic motives: Essays on anthropological sensibility* (pp. 208-276). Madison: University of Wisconsin Press.

Stoller, P., & Olkes, C. (1987). *In sorcery's shadow: A memoir of apprenticeship among the Songhay of Niger.* Chicago: University of Chicago Press.

Strauss, A. L., & Corbin, J. (1998). *Basics of qualitative research: Techniques and procedures for developing grounded theory* (2nd ed.). Thousand Oaks, CA: Sage.

Taylor, S. J., & Bogdan, R. (1998). *Introduction to qualitative research methods: A guidebook and resource* (3rd ed.). New York: John Wiley.

Turner, V., & Bruner, E. (Eds.). (1986). *The anthropology of experience.* Urbana: University of Illinois Press.

Van Maanen, J. (1988). *Tales of the field: On writing ethnography.* Chicago: University of Chicago Press.

Vygotsky, L. S. (1978). *Mind in society: The development of higher psychological processes* (M. Cole, V. John-Steiner, S. Scribner, & E. Souberman, Eds.). Cambridge, MA: Harvard University Press.

Weinstein, D., & Weinstein, M. A. (1991). Georg Simmel: Sociological flaneur bricoleur. *Theory, Culture & Society, 8,* 151-168.

West, C. (1989). *The American evasion of philosophy: A genealogy of pragmatism.* Madison: University of Wisconsin Press.

Wolcott, H. F. (1990). *Writing up qualitative research.* Newbury Park, CA: Sage.

Wolcott, H. F. (1992). Posturing in qualitative inquiry. In M. D. LeCompte, W. L. Millroy, & J. Preissle (Eds.), *The handbook of qualitative research in education* (pp. 3-52). New York: Academic Press.

Wolcott, H. F. (1995). *The art of fieldwork.* Walnut Creek, CA: AltaMira.

Wolf, M. A. (1992). *A thrice-told tale: Feminism, postmodernism, and ethnographic responsibility.* Stanford, CA: Stanford University Press.

PART I

Methods of Collecting and Analyzing Empirical Materials

The socially situated researcher creates through interaction the realities that constitute the places where empirical materials are collected and analyzed. In such sites, the interpretive practices of qualitative research are implemented. These methodological practices represent different ways of generating empirical materials grounded in the everyday world. The contributions to Part I of this volume examine the multiple practices and methods of analysis that qualitative researchers-as-methodological-bricoleurs now employ.

◆ The Interview

We live in an interview society, in a society whose members seem to believe that interviews generate useful information about lived experience and its meanings. The interview has become a taken-for-granted feature of our mediated, mass culture. But the interview is a negotiated text, a site where power, gender, race, and class intersect. In Chapter 2, Andrea Fontana and James Frey review the history of the interview in the social sciences, noting its three major forms—structured, unstructured, and open-ended—and showing how the tool is modified and changed during use. They also discuss group (or focused) interviews (see also Madriz, Chapter 10), oral history interviews, creative interviewing, and gendered, feminist, and postmodern, or multivoiced, interviewing.

The interview is a conversation, the art of asking questions and listening. It is not a neutral tool, for at least two people create the reality of the interview situation. In this situation answers are given. Thus the interview produces situated understandings grounded in specific interactional episodes. This method is influenced by the personal characteristics of the interviewer, including race, class, ethnicity, and gender.

Fontana and Frey review the important work of feminist scholars on the interview, especially the arguments of Behar, Reinharz, Hertz, Richardson, Clough, Collins, Smith, and Oakley. British sociologist Oakley (1981) and other feminist scholars have identified a major contradiction between scientific, positivistic research, which requires objectivity and detachment, and feminist-based interviewing, which requires openness, emotional engagement, and the development of a potentially long-term, trusting relationship between the interviewer and the subject.

A feminist interviewing ethic, as Fontana and Frey suggest, redefines the interview situation. This ethic transforms interviewer and respondent into coequals who are carrying on a conversation about mutually relevant, often biographically critical, issues. This narrative, storytelling framework challenges the informed consent and deception models of inquiry discussed by Christians in Volume 1, Chapter 5. This ethic changes the interview into an important tool for both applied action research (see Kemmis & McTaggart, Volume 2, Chapter 11) and clinical research (see Miller & Crabtree, Volume 2, Chapter 12).

◆ Observational Methods

Going into a social situation and looking is another important way of gathering materials about the social world. In Chapter 3, Michael Angrosino and Kimberly Mays de Pérez fundamentally rewrite the methods and practices of naturalistic observation. All observation involves the observer's participation in the world being studied. There is no pure, objective, detached observation; the effects of the observer's presence can never be erased. Further, the colonial concept of the subject (the object of the observer's gaze) is no longer appropriate. Observers now function as collaborative participants in action inquiry settings. Angrosino and Pérez argue that observational interaction is a tentative, situational process. It is shaped by shifts in gendered identity as well as by existing structures of power. As relationships unfold, participants validate the cues generated by others in the setting. Finally, during the observational process people assume situational identities that may not be socially or culturally normative.

Like Christians in Volume 1, Chapter 5, Angrosino and Pérez offer compelling criticisms of institutional review boards (IRBs), noting that positivistic, experimental social scientists seldom recognize the needs of observational ethnographers. In many universities, the IRBs are tied to the experimental, hypothesis-testing, so-called scientific paradigm. This paradigm creates problems for postmodern observers, for scholars who become part of the worlds they study. In order to get approval for their research, scholars may have to engage in deception (in this instance of the IRB). This leads some ethnographers to claim that their research will not be intrusive and hence will not cause harm. Yet interactive observers are by definition intrusive. When collaborative inquiry is undertaken, subjects become stakeholders, persons who shape the inquiry itself. What this means for consent forms—and forms of participatory inquiry more broadly—is not clear. Alternative forms of ethnographic writing, including the use of fictionalized stories, represent one avenue for addressing this ethical quandary.

Angrosino and Pérez offer an ethic of "proportionate reason." This utilitarian ethic attempts to balance the benefits, costs, and consequences of actions in the field, asking if the means to an end are justified by the importance and value of the goals attained. These authors demystify the observation method. Observation is no longer the key to some grand analysis of culture or society. Instead, observational research is a method that focuses on differences, on the lives of particular people in concrete, but constantly changing, human relationships. The relevance and need for a feminist ethics of care and commitment become even more apparent.

◆ Reading Material Culture and Its Records

Mute evidence—that is, written texts and cultural artifacts—endures physically and leaves its traces on the material past. It is impossible to talk to and with these materials. Researchers must interpret them, for in them are found important meanings about the human shape of lived cultures. Archaeologists study material culture. In an essay that moves with ease across and within the postpositivist and postmodern sensibilities, Ian Hodder (Chapter 4) shows how this is done. Central to his position is the constructionist (and constructivist) argument that researchers create, through a set of interpretive practices, the materials and evidence they then theoretically analyze. Today it is understood that material culture, in all its forms, is a gendered, social, and political construction. Previous theories of culture, evolution, and the material past are being rewritten. How the past is reconstructed and interpreted very much determines how it will be constituted in the present and remembered in the future.

◆ Reimagining Visual Methods

Today, visual sociologists and anthropologists use photography, motion pictures, the World Wide Web, interactive CDs, CD-ROMs, and virtual reality as ways of forging connections between human existence and visual perception. These forms of visual representation constitute different ways of recording and documenting what passes as social life. Often called the mirror with a memory, photography takes the researcher into the everyday world, where the issues of observer identity, the subject's point of view, and what to photograph become problematic. In Chapter 5, Douglas Harper presents a history of this method and brings it up against postmodern developments in virtual and real ethnography.

Historically, visual sociology began within the postpositivist tradition; researchers provided visual information to support the realist tales of traditional ethnography. Photographs were a part of the unproblematic "facts" that constituted the "truth" of these tales. Now, visual sociology, like ethnography, is in a period of deep questioning and great change. Visual sociology, Harper contends, must find a place in this new ethnography. He engages this new turn through a close, storied reading of a series of photographs he made on the streets of Bologna. This bicycling sequence is a visual narrative. It tells many different stories at the same time as it mixes and combines multiple images, cultural meanings, points of view, geographic spaces, interactional sequences, and shifting, gendered forms of the gaze. Harper also analyzes the ideological aspects of representation, the social construction of images, the authority of visual knowledge, the mechanical capabilities of the camera, framing (point of view), printing techniques, editing, and image sequencing.

As Harper's bicycle shots indicate, sequences of photos can be connected through visual narratives, stories that connect images to first-person accounts, and cultural stories that unfold through time and space. Of course, every image tells a story, but visual narratives attempt to tell the stories of a culture, of individuals, and of institutions, and their interrelationships. Photo elicitation is one method used to elaborate these meanings.

We need to learn how to experiment with visual (and nonvisual) ways of thinking. We need to develop a critical, visual sensibility, a sensibility that will allow us to bring the gendered material world into play in critically different ways. We need to interrogate critically the hyperlogics of cyberspace and its virtual realities. We also need to understand more fully the rules and methods for establishing truth that hold these worlds together.

◆ Autoethnography and the Researcher as Subject

Personal experience reflects the flow of thoughts and meanings that persons have in their immediate situations. These experiences can be routine or problematic. They occur within the life of a person. When they are talked about, they assume the shape of a story, or a narrative. We cannot study lived experience directly, because language, speech, and systems of discourse mediate and define the very experience we attempt to describe. We study the representations of experience, not experience itself. We examine the stories people tell one another about the experiences they have had. These stories may be personal experience narratives or self-stories, interpretations made up as the person goes along.

Many now argue that we can study only our own experiences. The researcher becomes the research subject. This is the topic of autoethnography. In Chapter 6, Carolyn Ellis and Arthur Bochner reflexively present the arguments for writing reflexive, personal narratives. Indeed, their dialogic text is an example of such writing; it performs its own narrative reflexivity. Ellis and Bochner masterfully review the arguments for studying personal experience narratives, anchoring their text in the discourses of poststructuralism and postmodernism, especially the works of Rorty and Richardson.

They review the history of this writing form, starting with David Hayano's introduction of the term autoethnography in 1979. A variety of terms and methodological strategies are associated with the meanings and uses of autoethnographies, including personal narratives, narratives of the self, writing stories, self-stories, auto-observation, personal ethnography, literary tales, critical autobiography, radical empiricism, evocative narratives, reflexive ethnography, biographical method, co-constructed narrative, indigenous anthropology, anthropological poetics, and performance ethnography. Ellis and Bochner use the case of Sylvia Smith, Ph.D. candidate in psychology, to illustrate the value of this form of writing.

They then turn to their own intellectual biographies, showing how they came to their current understandings concerning the need to write about the researcher as subject. They show that the commitment to this style of writing does not come easily. It involves learning how to write differently, including how to use personal experience and the first-person voice as vehicles for authorizing claims to truth and knowledge. And there are many critics, including those who wonder about narrative truth, emotional recall, and layered texts, who question the point of a storied life and worry as well about such traditional issues as reliability and validity.

Of course, this autoethnography can be read as a variation on the testimonio and the first-person life history. Thus Ellis and Bochner's chapter complements Tierney's (Volume 2, Chapter 9) and Beverley's (Volume 2, Chapter 10) treatments of these narrative forms.

◆ Data Management and Analytic Techniques

The management, analysis, and interpretation of qualitative empirical materials is a complex process involving highly technical languages and systems of discourse. It also entails the mastery of a special set of interpretive practices and narrative techniques. In Chapter 7, Gery Ryan and H. Russell Bernard advance perhaps the most sophisticated and comprehensive model of this process and its discourses.

The management and analysis of empirical materials involves arguments concerning the differences between empiricism (there is a real world out there) and constructivism (the world is constructed). It also involves disputes between empiricists and nonempiricists—between those who would translate their observations into words and those who would translate their observations into numbers. Like others, Ryan and Bernard also distinguish two approaches to texts, the narrative or the linguistic and the sociological. The narrative approach to texts treats them as objects of narrative, conversation, performance, or formal analysis. The sociological approach treats texts as windows into experience and includes both texts generated by the analyst and free-flowing texts, or narratives.

Ryan and Bernard focus on methods used in the sociological tradition, that is, methods for collecting such materials (free lists, pile sorts, frame elicitations, and triad tests) and techniques for their analysis (taxonomies, mental maps, componential analysis). They also discuss methods for analyzing free-flowing texts, starting with texts that use raw text input (keywords-in-context, word counts, semantic network analysis, cognitive maps). They then take up methods that reduce texts to codes: grounded theory, schema analysis, classic content analysis, content dictionaries, analytic induction, and ethnographic decision models.

This is a far-reaching, encyclopedic, elegant, and systematic postpositivist approach to the issues surrounding the rigorous analysis of empirical materials. Ryan and Bernard's treatment of grounded theory, conversation analysis, and computer-assisted models of analysis should be read in conjunction with the treatment of these topics by, respectively, Charmaz (Volume 2, Chapter 8), Silverman (Chapter 9), and Weitzman (Chapter 8).

◆ Computer-Assisted Qualitative Analysis

It is now becoming relatively commonplace for researchers to use computer software programs to assist them in their analysis of qualitative empirical materials. Lee and Fielding (1998, p. 1) call such programs "computer-assisted qualitative data analysis software," or CAQDAS. In Chapter 8, Eben Weitzman presents a comprehensive and user-friendly survey of a wide array of CAQDAS currently available to support qualitative analysis. He reviews computer-based tools that can help researchers to record, store, index, cross-index, code, sort, and interconnect text-based materials. Of course, these tools are not ideologically neutral (Schwandt, 1997, p. 18). They structure the work of interpretation and presume a particular gendered stance toward the material world. They frequently impose a rational, hierarchical, linear or quasi-linear, and sequential framework on the world and its empirical materials. This can create the impression that meaningful patterns actually exist in the data, when in fact they are created by the software and analytic frameworks being used (in the case of analysis that is not assisted by computer, of course, it is the researcher who creates the seeming "order"). These tools can also distance researchers from their fieldwork and their empirical materials. These methods presume an objectivist, realist, foundational epistemology, and their use too often takes for granted the interpretive procedures and assumptions that transform field notes into text-based materials.

Weitzman divides the most frequently used programs into five main software families: textbase managers, code programs, retrieve programs, code-based theory builders, and conceptual network builders. These programs have multiple text management uses, such as helping researchers to locate and retrieve key materials based on phrases and words, build conceptual models, sort categories, attach key words and codes to text segments, isolate negative or deviant cases, and create indices. Multimedia software programs are just now appearing that allow researchers to use audio and video as well as text-based data. CD-ROMs are also functioning as sites where field notes and other versions of ethnographies are stored and made accessible for hypertextual analysis (see Coffey & Atkinson, 1996, p. 186).

Such powerful tools of graphic, visual, and audio representation allow researchers to consolidate and establish patterns of consistency in their materials. However, they can also create negative effects, including the false hope that such programs can actually write a theory (or a case) for researchers. They may even encourage quick-and-dirty, or "blitzkrieg," research. Coding and retrieval schemes can lead to an overemphasis on the discovery of categories and indicators, with a corresponding underemphasis on the multiple meanings of experience in concrete situations (see Fielding & Lee, 1998, pp. 120-121). The search for grounded theory can shift attention away from the theories of interpretation that operate in the social world.

Software programs for the qualitative researcher need to be interactive, allowing for many different interpretive spaces to emerge, spaces that connect patterns with meanings and experience. Nonetheless, it is important that the researcher avoid letting the computer (and the software) determine the form and content of interpretive activity. An emphasis on codes and categories can produce endless variable analyses that fail to take account of important situational and contextual factors.[1] There is frequently a tendency among researchers doing computer-assisted analysis to reduce field materials to only those data that are codable. There is also the danger that researchers will turn over the transcription of their field notes to persons who lack intimate familiarity with the field setting and the processes being studied (Lee & Fielding, 1991, p. 12).

Seidel (1991) speaks of a form of analytic madness that can accompany the use of these methods. This madness can lead researchers to an infatuation with the large volumes of data the computer allows them to deal with. In addition, researchers may develop understandings based on misunderstandings; that is, patterns identified in the data may be "artefacts of a relationship [they] have with the data" (Seidel, 1991, p. 114). Finally, researchers may focus only on those aspects of their research that can be helped by computer methods (Agar, 1991, p. 193). They then select and ready particular software for use in analyzing the materials they gather. Thus the problem arises: Frequently, researchers conduct research that fits the available software and then report that the software constituted their methodology. This is the methodological tail wagging the ethnographic dog.

Finally, ethical problems may arise from the use of such programs. Akeroyd (1991) isolates the crux of the matter: the potential loss of personal privacy that can occur when a personal, confidential database is developed on an individual or group. When such materials are entered into a computer, the problem of security is immediately created. In multiuser systems, privacy cannot be guaranteed (Akeroyd, 1991, p. 100). Nothing is any longer completely private or completely secure.

Fielding and Lee (1998, pp. 186-189) have speculated on the future of CAQDAS, and they suggest that the field is entering a period of "winnowing out," with some software packages becoming more sophisticated and others remaining undeveloped since their initial release. Some developers have left the field. The Windows operating system seems to have "caused a major shake-out of those willing to keep up with its programming and development requirements" (Fielding & Lee, 1998, p. 186). Software that permits the direct transcription of speech stored on CD-ROM continues to be developed. In some programs the speech is actually heard as it is being transcribed. This raises issues about the differences involved in interpreting heard versus written words (Fielding & Lee, 1998, p. 188).

The Internet has also produced changes in CAQDAS. Large-scale projects can now be located on Web sites. Such use of the Internet is not without problems, including the commodification of information, the control of encryption devices, electronic privacy, and the development of ethical protocols to produce subjects (Fielding & Lee, 1998, p. 188). Clearly, computer technology as a whole continues to transform and complicate qualitative research.

◆ Analyzing Talk and Text

Qualitative researchers study spoken and written records of human experience, including transcribed talk, films, novels, and photographs. Historically, there have been three major social science and literary approaches to textual-discourse analysis. Each is associated with a long theoretical and research tradition: content analysis with the quantitative approach to media studies; semiotics with the structural tradition in literary criticism; and narrative, discourse analysis with the recent poststructural development in interpretive theory (see Lieblich, Tuval-Mashiach, & Zilber, 1998, p. 18).

David Silverman contends that the world's business gets done in talk and in conversation. Hence field data are always linguistic, and in Chapter 9 he analyzes three kinds of linguistically mediated data: interviews, texts, and transcripts. With Fontana and Frey (Chapter 2), and Gubrium and Holstein (Volume 2, Chapter 7), Silverman treats interview materials as narrative accounts rather than as true pictures of reality. He poses five questions for interview researchers, including how they use their narrative data to make theoretical claims about the world.

Texts are based on transcriptions of interviews and other forms of talk. These texts are social facts; they are produced, shared, and used in socially organized ways. Silverman objects to those forms of text-based analyses that use the methods of content analysis. Content analyses reify the taken-for-granted understandings persons bring to words, terms, or experiences. Content analyses, he contends, obscure the interpretive processes that turn talk into text.

It is important that researchers not use text-based documentary materials as stand-ins for other kinds of evidence. These documents are social productions. They are not transparent representations of organizational routines, or of decision-making processes. They are situated constructions, particular kinds of representations shaped by certain conventions and understandings (Atkinson & Coffey, 1997, p. 47). Such documents are properly studied through the methods of semiotics, narrative, and discourse analysis. Membership categorization analysis (MCA) is a less familiar form of narrative analysis. Drawing on the work of Harvey Sacks, Silverman illustrates the logic of MCA (on Sacks, see Silverman, 1998). With this method, the researcher asks how persons use everyday terms and categories in their interactions with others. Silverman turns next to transcripts of talk. There are two main social science traditions that inform the analysis of transcripts; conversation analysis (CA) and discourse analysis (DA). Silverman reviews and offers examples of both traditions. He concludes his chapter with four arguments, contending that qualitative research (a) is not based on a set of freestanding techniques, (b) has special strengths for revealing how social interactions are routinely enacted, (c) shows us how people do things, and (d) has uses that extend far beyond exploratory purposes.

To summarize: Text-based documents of experience are complex. But if talk constitutes much of what we have, then the forms of analysis that Silverman outlines represent significant ways of making the world and its words more visible.

◆ Focus Groups in Feminist Research

In Chapter 2, Fontana and Frey note that the group, or focus group, interview relies upon the systematic questioning of several individuals simultaneously in a formal or informal setting. In Chapter 10, Esther Madriz significantly advances the discourse on this method by showing how focus groups are used in feminist research with women of color.[2] Using a feminist/postmodern approach, she offers a model of focus group interviewing that emphasizes a feminist ethic of empowerment, moral community, emotional engagement, and the development of long-term, trusting relationships. This method gives a voice to women of color who have long been silenced. Focus groups facilitate women writing culture together. As a Latina feminist, Madriz places focus groups within the context of collective testimonies and group resistance narratives (see Beverley, Volume 2, Chapter 10; Tierney, Volume 2, Chapter 9). Focus groups reduce the distance between the researcher and the researched. The multivocality of the participants limits the control of the researcher over the research process. The unstructured nature of focus group conversations also reduces the researcher's control over the interview process. Madriz illustrates these points with examples drawn from her study of lower-class women of color.

Drawing on recent developments in critical race theory and feminist theory (see, respectively, Ladson-Billings, Volume 1, Chapter 9; Olesen, Volume 1, Chapter 8), Madriz reminds us that women of color experience a triple subjugation based on class, race, and gender oppression. Focus groups create the conditions for the emergence of a critical race consciousness, a consciousness focused on social change. It seems that with focus groups, critical race theory has found its methodology.

◆ Applied Ethnography

The applied, action themes of Part I are continued in Erve Chambers's comprehensive analysis of the history, forms, and uses of applied ethnography in Chapter 11. Applied research is inquiry intentionally developed within a context of decision making and directed toward the interests of one or more clients. So framed, applied (or action) ethnography is about research that advocates social change and increased cultural understandings between different social groups.

Chambers discusses three distinct traditions within applied ethnography: cognitive, semiotic, and semantic approaches; micro/macro analyses; and action and clinical models. Cognitive approaches attempt to map the native point of view in particular situations, to isolate the language, categories, and terms used in specific locales. Micro/macro analyses examine local contexts with an eye to generalizing to larger, more macro structures—for example, moving from the economy of a local community to the national economy. Action and clinical approaches follow an advocacy model. Researchers build collaborative relations with a variety of different types of persons in the local community, from indigenous experts to informed insiders, leaders in churches, schools, and local government, and representatives of state and federal bureaucracies.

Chambers notes that applied research places great ethical responsibility on the shoulders of the researcher (see also Trotter & Schensul, 1998, p. 692). It carries human, social, and ecological consequences that are immediate and sometimes critical to the life of a community. Its results are change oriented and can be very disruptive.

Chambers also takes up the issue of professional ethics. He indicates that the principle of informed consent has proven to be particularly difficult for applied ethnographers. Maintaining the confidentiality of research subjects can also be problematic. At the same time, applied ethnographers confront moral issues, such as questions of for whom they should advocate and whether or not their services should be available without discrimination.

◆ Conclusion

The researcher-as-methodological-bricoleur should have a working familiarity with all of the methods of collecting and analyzing empirical materials presented in this section of the Handbook. This familiarity should include an understanding of the history of each method and technique as well as hands-on experience with each. Only in this way can a researcher fully appreciate the limitations and strengths of the various methods and, at the same time, see clearly how each, as a set of practices, creates its own subject matter.

In addition, the researcher must understand that each paradigm and perspective, as presented in Part II, has a distinct history with each of these methods of research. Although methods-as-tools are somewhat universal in application, they are not uniformly used by researchers from all paradigms. And when they are used, they are fitted and adapted to the particularities of the paradigm in question.

Of the six specific methods and techniques addressed in Part I of this volume (interviews, observation, cultural artifacts, visual methods, auto-ethnography, focus groups), positivists and postpositivists are most likely to make use of structured interviews and those cultural artifacts that lend themselves to formal analysis. Constructionists and critical theorists also have histories of using each of the methods, as do feminists, queer theorists, ethnic researchers, and cultural studies investigators. Similarly, researchers from all paradigms and perspectives can profitably make use of the data management and analysis methods, as well as the computer-assisted models discussed.

◆ Notes

1. The continued shift toward variable analysis has moved computer-assisted methods firmly in the direction of postpositivist models of interpretation.

2. Also recall Fine, Weis, Weseen, and Wong's discussion of focus groups in Volume 1, Chapter 4.

◆ References

Agar, M. (1991). The right brain strikes back. In N. G. Fielding & R. M. Lee (Eds.), Using computers in qualitative research (pp. 181-194). London: Sage.

Akeroyd, A. V. (1991). Personal information and qualitative research data: Some practical and ethical problems arising from data protection legislation. In N. G. Fielding & R. M. Lee (Eds.), Using computers in qualitative research (pp. 89-106). London: Sage.

Atkinson, P., & Coffey, A. (1997). Analysing documentary realities. In D. Silverman (Ed.), Qualitative research: Theory, method and practice (pp. 45-62). London: Sage.

Coffey, A., & Atkinson, P. (1996). Making sense of qualitative data: Complementary research strategies. Thousand Oaks, CA: Sage.

Fielding, N. G., & Lee, R. M. (1998). Computer analysis and qualitative research. London: Sage.

Hayano, D. M. (1979). Auto-ethnography: Paradigms, problems, and prospects. Human Organization, 38, 113-120.

Lee, R. M., & Fielding, N. G. (1991). Computing for qualitative research: Options, problems and potential. In N. G. Fielding & R. M. Lee (Eds.), Using computers in qualitative research (pp. 1-13). London: Sage.

Lieblich, A., Tuval-Mashiach, R., & Zilber, T. (1998). Narrative research. Thousand Oaks, CA: Sage.

Oakley, A. (1981). Interviewing women: A contradiction in terms. In H. Roberts (Ed.), Doing feminist research (pp. 30-61). London: Routledge & Kegan Paul.

Schwandt, T. A. (1997). Qualitative inquiry: A dictionary of terms. Thousand Oaks, CA: Sage.

Seidel, J. (1991). Method and madness in the application of computer technology to qualitative data analysis. In N. G. Fielding & R. M. Lee (Eds.), Using computers in qualitative research (pp. 107-116). London: Sage.

Silverman, D. (1998). Harvey Sacks: Social science and conversation analysis. Cambridge: Polity.

Trotter, R. T., & Schensul, J. J. (1998). Methods in applied anthropology. In H. R. Bernard (Ed.), Handbook of cultural methods in cultural anthropology (pp. 691-736). Walnut Creek, CA: AltaMira.

2

The Interview

From Structured

Questions to Negotiated Text

Andrea Fontana and James H. Frey

Hamlet: Do you see yonder cloud that's almost in shape of a camel?
Polonius: By the mass, and 'tis like a camel, indeed.
Hamlet: Methink it is like a weasel.
Polonius: It is backed like a weasel.
Hamlet: Or like a whale?
Polonius: Very like a whale.

—William Shakespeare, Hamlet, act 3, scene 2

*Hamlet's interview . . . approximates the threefold ideal of being interpreted, vali-
dated and communicated. . . .*

The interview appears as a display of the power relations at a royal court. . . .

*Hamlet's interview may . . . be seen as an illustration of a pervasive doubt about
the appearance of the world. [Or, we would like to add, the interview can emerge as
an example of a negotiated text.]*

—Kvale, InterViews, 1996

◆   Asking questions and getting answers is a much harder task than it
may seem at first. The spoken or written word has always a residue
of ambiguity, no matter how carefully we word the questions and how
carefully we report or code the answers. Yet interviewing is one of the

most common and powerful ways in which we try to understand our fellow human beings. Interviewing includes a wide variety of forms and a multiplicity of uses. The most common form of interviewing involves individual, face-to-face verbal interchange, but interviewing can also take the form of face-to-face group interchange, mailed or self-administered questionnaires, and telephone surveys. It can be structured, semistructured, or unstructured. Interviewing can be used for marketing research, political opinion polling, therapeutic reasons, or academic analysis. It can be used for the purpose of measurement or its scope can be the understanding of an individual or a group perspective. An interview can be a one-time, brief event—say, 5 minutes over the telephone—or it can take place over multiple, lengthy sessions, at times spanning days, as in life history interviewing.

The use of interviewing to acquire information is so extensive today that it has been said that we live in an "interview society" (Atkinson & Silverman, 1997; Silverman, 1993). Increasingly, qualitative researchers are realizing that interviews are not neutral tools of data gathering but active interactions between two (or more) people leading to negotiated, contextually based results. Thus the focus of interviews is moving to encompass the *hows* of people's lives (the constructive work involved in producing order in everyday life) as well as the traditional *whats* (the activities of everyday life) (Cicourel, 1964; Dingwall, 1997; Gubrium & Holstein, 1997, 1998; Holstein & Gubrium, 1995; Kvale, 1996; Sarup, 1996; Seidman, 1991; Silverman, 1993, 1997a).

In this chapter, after discussing the interview society, we examine interviews by beginning with structured methods of interviewing and gradually moving to more qualitative types, ending with interviews as negotiated texts. We begin by briefly outlining the history of interviewing, then we turn to a discussion of the academic uses of interviewing. Although the focus of this volume is qualitative research, in order to demonstrate the full import of interviewing, we need to discuss the major types of interviewing (structured, group, and unstructured) as well as other ways to conduct interviews. A caveat: In discussing the various interview methods, we use the language and rationales employed by practitioners of these methods; we note our differences with these practitioners and our criticisms later in the chapter, in our discussion of gendered and other new types of qualitative interviewing. Following our examination of structured interviewing, we address in detail the various elements of qualitative interviewing. We then discuss the problems related to gendered interviewing as well as issues of interpretation and reporting, and we broach some considerations related to ethical issues. Finally, we note some of the new trends in qualitative interviewing.

◆ The Interview Society

Before embarking on our journey through interviewing per se, we want to comment briefly on the tremendous reliance on interviewing in U.S. society today, which has reached such a level that a number of scholars have referred to the United States as "the interview society" (Atkinson & Silverman, 1997; Silverman, 1993). Both qualitative and quantitative researchers tend to rely on the interview as the basic method of data gathering, whether the purpose is to obtain a rich, in-depth experiential account of an event or episode in the life of the respondent or to garner a simple point on a scale of 2 to 10 dimensions. There is inherent faith that the results are trustworthy and accurate and that the relation of the interviewer to respondent that evolves in the interview process has not unduly biased the account (Atkinson & Silverman, 1997; Silverman, 1993). The commitment to and reliance on the interview to produce narrative experience reflects and reinforces the view of the United States as an interview society.

It seems that everyone, not just social researchers, relies on the interview as a source of information, with the assumption that interviewing results in true and accurate pictures of respondents' selves and lives. One cannot escape being interviewed; interviews are everywhere, in the forms of political polls, questionnaires about doctor's visits, housing applications, forms regarding social service eligibility, college applications, talk shows, news programs—the list goes on and on. The interview as a means of data gathering is no longer limited to use by social science researchers or police detectives; it is a "universal mode of systematic inquiry" (Holstein & Gubrium, 1995, p. 1). It seems that almost any type of question—personal, sensitive, probing, upsetting, accusatory—is fair game and permissible in the interview setting. Almost all interviews, no matter their purposes (and these can be varied—to describe, to interrogate, to assist, to test, to evaluate), seek various forms of biographical description. As Gubrium and Holstein (1998) have noted, the interview has become a means of contemporary storytelling, where persons divulge life accounts in response to interview inquiries. The media have been especially adept at using this technique.

As a society we rely on the interview and by and large take it for granted. The interview and the norms surrounding the enactment of the respondent and researcher roles have evolved to the point where they are institutionalized and no longer require extensive training; rules and roles are known and shared. However, there is a growing group of individuals who increasingly question the traditional assumptions of the interview— we address their concerns in our later discussion of gendered interviewing and new trends in interview. Many practitioners continue to use and take for granted traditional interviewing techniques. It is as if interviewing is now part of the mass culture, so that it has actually become the most feasible mechanism for obtaining information about individuals, groups, and organizations in a society characterized by individuation, diversity, and specialized role relations. Thus, many feel that it is not necessary to re-invent the wheel for each interview situation, as "interviewing has become a routine technical practice and a pervasive, taken-for-granted activity in our culture" (Mishler, 1986, p. 23).

This is not to say, however, that the interview is so technical and the procedures so standardized that interviewers can ignore contextual, societal, and interpersonal elements. Each interview context is one of interaction and relation; the result is as much a product of this social dynamic as it is a product of accurate accounts and replies. The interview has become a routine, almost unnoticed, part of everyday life. Yet response rates continue to decline, indicating that fewer people are willing to disclose their "selves" or that they are so overburdened by requests for interviews that they are becoming more selective regarding which interviews to grant. Social scientists are more likely to recognize, however, that interviews are interactional encounters and that the nature of the social dynamic of the interview can shape the nature of the knowledge generated. Interviewers with less training and experience than social scientists may not recognize that interview participants are "actively" constructing knowledge around questions and responses (Holstein & Gubrium, 1995).

We turn now to a brief history of interviewing to frame its roots and development.

◆ The History of Interviewing

One form of interviewing or another has been with us for a very long time. Even ancient Egyptians conducted population censuses (Babbie, 1992). In more recent times, the tradition of interviewing evolved from two trends. First, interviewing found great popularity and widespread use in clinical diagnosis and counseling, where the concern was with the quality of responses. Second, during World War I interviewing came to be widely employed in psychological testing; here the emphasis was on measurement (Maccoby & Maccoby, 1954).

The individual generally credited with being the first to develop a social survey relying on interviewing was Charles Booth (Converse, 1987). In 1886, Booth embarked on a comprehensive survey of the economic and social conditions of the people of London, published as *Life and Labour of the People in London* (1902-1903). In his early study, Booth embodied what were to become separate interviewing methods, because he not only implemented survey research but triangulated his work by relying on unstructured interviews and ethnographic observations:

> The data were checked and supplemented by visits to many neighborhoods, streets and homes, and by conferences with various welfare and community leaders. From time to time Booth lived as a lodger in districts where he was not known, so that he could become more intimately acquainted with the lives and habits of the poorer classes (Parten, 1950, pp. 6-7)

Many other surveys of London and other English cities followed, patterned after Booth's example. In the United States a similar pattern ensued. Among others, an 1895 study attempted to do in Chicago what Booth had done in London (see Converse, 1987), and in 1896, self-admittedly following Booth's lead, the American sociologist W. E. B. Du Bois studied the black population of Philadelphia (see Du Bois, 1899). Surveys of cities and small towns followed, most notable among them R. S. Lynd and H. M. Lynd's *Middletown* (1929) and *Middletown in Transition* (1937).

Opinion polling was another early form of interviewing. Some polling took place well before the start of the 20th century, but it really came into its own in 1935 with the formation of the American Institute of Public Opinion by George Gallup. Preceding Gallup, in both psychology and sociology in the 1920s there was a movement toward the study (and usually measurement) of attitudes. W. I. Thomas and Florian Znaniecki used the documentary method to introduce the study of attitudes in social psychology. Thomas's influence, along with that of Robert Park, a former reporter who believed sociology was to be found out in the field, sparked a number of community studies at the University of Chicago that came to be known collectively as the works of the Chicago school. Many other researchers were also greatly influential, such as Albion Small, George H. Mead, E. W. Burgess, Everett C. Hughes, Louis Wirth, W. Lloyd Warner, and Anselm Strauss (for a recent discussion of the relations and influence of various Chicagoans, see Becker, 1999).

Although the members of the Chicago school are reputed to have used the ethnographic method in their inquiries, some disagree, and have noted that many of the Chicago school studies lacked the analytic component of modern-day ethnography, and so were, at best, "firsthand descriptive studies" (Harvey, 1987, p. 50). Regardless of the correct label for the Chicagoans' fieldwork, they clearly relied on a combination of observation, personal documents, and informal interviews in their studies. Interviews were especially in evidence in the work of Thrasher (1927/1963), who in his study of gang members relied primarily on about 130 qualitative interviews, and in that of Nels Anderson (1923), whose classic study of hoboes relied on informal, in-depth conversations.

It was left to Herbert Blumer and his former student Howard Becker to formalize and give impetus to sociological ethnography in the 1950s and 1960s, and interviewing began to lose both the eclectic flavor given to it by Charles Booth and the qualitative accent of the Chicagoans. Understanding gang members or hoboes through interviews lost importance; what became relevant was the use of interviewing in survey research as a tool to quantify data. This was not new, as opinion polls and market research had been doing it for years. But during World War II there was a tremendous increase in survey research as the U.S. armed forces hired great numbers of sociologists as survey researchers. More than half a million American soldiers were interviewed in one manner or another (Young, 1966), and their mental and emotional lives were reported in a four-volume survey titled *Studies in Social Psychology in World War II,* the first two volumes of which were directed by Samuel Stouffer and titled *The American Soldier.* This work had tremendous impact and led the way to widespread use of systematic survey research.

What was new, however, was that quantitative survey research moved into academia and came to dominate sociology as the method of choice for the next three decades. An Austrian immigrant, Paul Lazarsfeld, spearheaded this move. He welcomed *The American Soldier* with great enthusiasm. In fact, Robert Merton and Lazarsfeld (1950) edited a book of reflections on *The American Soldier.* Lazarsfeld moved to Columbia in 1940, taking with him his market research and other applied grants, and became instrumental in the directing of the Bureau of Applied Social Research. Two other "survey organizations" were also formed: one in 1941, by Harry Field, the National Opinion Research Center, first at Denver and then at Chicago; and one in 1946, by Likert and his group, the Survey Research Center at Michigan.

Academia at the time was dominated by theoretical concerns, and there was some resistance toward this applied, numbers-based kind of sociology. Sociologists and other humanists were critical of Lazarsfeld and the other survey researchers. Herbert Blumer, C. Wright Mills, Arthur Schlesinger, Jr., and Pitirin Sorokin, among others, voiced their displeasure. According to Converse (1987), Sorokin felt that "the new emphasis on quantitative work was obsessive, and he called the new practitioners 'quantophrenics'—with special reference to Stouffer and Lazarsfeld" (p. 253). And Converse quotes Mills: "Those in the grip of the methodological inhibition often refuse to say anything about modern society unless it has been through the fine little mill of the Statistical Ritual" (p. 252). Schlesinger, Converse notes, called the survey researchers "social relations hucksters" (p. 253).

But the survey researchers had powerful allies also, such as Merton, who joined the Survey Center at Columbia in 1943, and government moneys were becoming increasing available for survey research. The 1950s saw a growth of survey research in the universities and a proliferation of survey research texts. Gradually, survey research increased its domain over sociology, culminating in 1960 with the election of Lazarsfeld to the presidency of the American Sociological Association. The methodological dominance of survey research continued unabated through the 1970s, 1980s, and 1990s, although other methods began to erode the prominence of survey methods.

Qualitative interviewing continued to be practiced, hand in hand with participant observation methods, but it too assumed some of the quantifiable scientific rigor that so preoccupied survey research. This was especially visible in grounded theory (Glaser & Strauss, 1967), with its painstaking emphasis on coding data, and in ethnomethodology, with its quest for invariant properties of social action (Cicourel, 1970). Other qualitative researchers suggested variations. John Lofland (1971) criticized grounded theory for paying little attention to data gathering techniques, Jack Douglas (1985) suggested lengthy, existential one-on-one interviews lasting one or more days, and James Spradley (1980) tried to clarify the difference between ethnographic observation and ethnographic interviewing.

Recently, postmodernist ethnographers have concerned themselves with some of the assumptions present in interviewing and with the controlling role of the interviewer. These concerns have led to new directions in qualitative interviewing focusing on increased attention to the voices of the respondents (Marcus & Fischer, 1986), the interviewer-respondent relationship (Crapanzano, 1980), the importance of the researcher's gender in interviewing (Gluck & Patai, 1991), and the roles of other elements, such as race, social status, and age (Seidman, 1991).

◆ Structured Interviewing

In structured interviewing, the interviewer asks all respondents the same series of preestablished questions with a limited set of response categories. There is generally little room for variation in responses except where open-ended questions (which are infrequent) may be used. The interviewer records the responses according to a coding scheme that has already been established by the project director or research supervisor. The interviewer controls the pace of the interview by treating the questionnaire as if it were a theatrical script to be followed in a standardized and straightforward manner. Thus all respondents receive the same set of questions asked in the same order or sequence by an interviewer who has been trained to treat all interview situations in a like manner. There is very little flexibility in the way questions are asked or answered in the structured interview setting. Instructions to interviewers often include some of the following guidelines:

- ◆ Never get involved in long explanations of the study; use the standard explanation provided by the supervisor.
- ◆ Never deviate from the study introduction, sequence of questions, or question wording.
- ◆ Never let another person interrupt the interview; do not let another person answer for the respondent or offer his or her opinions on the question.
- ◆ Never suggest an answer or agree or disagree with an answer. Do not give the respondent any idea of your personal views on the topic of the question or the survey.

- ♦ Never interpret the meaning of a question; just repeat the question and give instructions or clarifications that are provided in training or by the supervisors.
- ♦ Never improvise, such as by adding answer categories or making wording changes.

Interviews by telephone, face-to-face interviews in respondents' households, intercept interviews in malls and parks, and interviews generally associated with survey research are most likely to be included in the structured interview category.

This interview context calls for the interviewer to play a neutral role, never interjecting his or her opinion of a respondent's answer. The interviewer must establish what has been called "balanced rapport"; he or she must be casual and friendly on the one hand, but directive and impersonal on the other. The interviewer must perfect a style of "interested listening" that rewards the respondent's participation but does not evaluate the responses (Converse & Schuman, 1974).

In a structured interview, hopefully, nothing is left to chance. However, response effects, or nonsampling errors, that can be attributed to the questionnaire administration process commonly evolve from three sources. The first of these is respondent behavior. The respondent may deliberately try to please the interviewer or to prevent the interviewer from learning something about the respondent. In order to do this, the respondent may embellish a response, give what is described as a "socially desirable" response, or omit certain relevant information (Bradburn, 1983, p. 291). The respondent may also err due to faulty memory. The second source of error is found in the nature of the task: the method of questionnaire administration (face-to-face or telephone) or the sequence or wording of the questions. The third source of error is the interviewer, whose characteristics or questioning techniques can impede proper communication of the questions (Bradburn, 1983). It is the degree of error assigned to the interviewer that is of greatest concern.

Most structured interviews leave little room for the interviewer to improvise or exercise independent judgment, but even in the most structured interview situation not every contingency can be anticipated, and not every interviewer behaves according to the script (Bradburn, 1983; Frey, 1989). In fact, one study of interviewer effects found that interviewers changed the wording to as many as one-third of the questions (Bradburn, Sudman, & Associates, 1979).

In general, research on interviewer effects has shown interviewer characteristics such as age, gender, and interviewing experience to have relatively small impact on responses (Singer & Presser, 1989). However, there is some evidence that student interviewers produce larger response effects than do nonstudents, higher-status interviewers produce larger response effects than do lower-status interviewers, and the race of an interviewer makes a difference only on questions specifically related to race (Bradburn, 1983; Hyman, 1954; Singer, Frankel, & Glassman, 1983).

The relatively minor impact of the interviewer on response quality in structured interview settings is directly attributable to the inflexible, standardized, and predetermined nature of this type of interviewing. There is simply little room for error. However, those who are advocates of structured interviewing are not unaware that the interview takes place in a social interaction context and that it is influenced by that context. Good interviewers recognize this fact and are sensitive to how interaction can influence responses. Converse and Schuman (1974) observe, "There is no single interview style that fits every occasion or all respondents" (p. 53). This means that interviewers must be aware of respondent differences and must be able to make the proper adjustments called for by unanticipated developments. As Raymond Gorden (1992) states, "Interviewing skills are not simple motor skills like riding a bicycle: rather, they involve a high-order combination of observation, empathic sensitivity, and intellectual judgment" (p. 7).

It is not enough to understand the mechanics of interviewing, it is also important to understand the respondent's world and forces that might stimulate or retard response (Kahn & Cannel, 1957). Still, the structured interview proceeds under a stimulus-response format, assuming that the respondent will truthfully answer questions previously determined to reveal adequate indicators of the variable in question, as long as those questions are properly phrased. This kind of interview often elicits rational responses, but it overlooks or inadequately assesses the emotional dimension.

◆ Group Interviews

The group interview is essentially a qualitative data gathering technique (see Madriz, Chapter 10, this volume) that relies upon the systematic questioning of several individuals simultaneously in a formal or informal setting. Thus this technique straddles the line between formal and informal interviewing.

The use of the group interview has ordinarily been associated with marketing research under the label of *focus group,* where the purpose is to gather consumer opinion on product characteristics, advertising themes, or service delivery. This format has also been used to a considerable extent by political parties and candidates who are interested in voter reaction to issues and policies. The group interview has also been used in sociological research. Bogardus used it to test his social distance scale in 1926, Zuckerman (1972) interviewed Nobel laureates, Thompson and Demerath (1952) looked at management problems in the military, Morgan and Spanish (1984) studied health issues, we investigated older-worker labor force reentry (Fontana & Frey, 1990), and Merton and his associates studied the impact of propaganda using group interviews (see Frey & Fontana, 1991). In fact, Merton, Fiske, and Kendall (1956) coined the term *focus group* to apply to a situation in which the researcher/ interviewer asks very specific questions about a topic after having already completed considerable research. There is also some evidence that established anthropologists such as Malinowski used this technique, although they did not report it (Frey & Fontana, 1991). Today, all group interviews are often generically designated *focus group* interviews, even though there are considerable variations in the natures and types of group interviews.

In a group interview, the interviewer/moderator directs the inquiry and the interaction among respondents in a very structured fashion or in a very unstructured manner, depending on the interview's purpose. The purpose may be exploratory; for example, the researcher may bring several persons together to test a methodological technique, to try out a definition of a research problem, or to identify key informants. An extension of this exploratory intent is the use of the group interview for the purpose of pretesting questionnaire wording, measurement scales, or other elements of a survey design. This is now quite common in survey research (Desvousges & Frey, 1989). Group interviews can also be used successfully to aid respondents' recall of specific events or to stimulate embellished descriptions of events (e.g., a disaster or a celebration) or experiences shared by members of a group. Group interviews can also be used for triangulation purposes or can be used in conjunction with other data gathering techniques. For example, group interviews could be helpful in the process of "indefinite triangulation," by putting individual responses into a context (Cicourel,

1974). Finally, phenomenological purposes may be served whether group interviews are the sole basis for gathering data or they are used in association with other techniques.

Group interviews can take different forms depending on their purposes. They can be brainstorming sessions with little or no structure or direction from the interviewer, or they can be very structured, as in nominal, Delphi, and marketing focus groups. In the latter cases the role of the interviewer is very prominent and directive. Fieldwork settings provide both formal and informal occasions for group interviews. The field researcher can bring respondents into a formal setting in the field context and ask very directed questions, or a natural field setting, such as a street corner or a neighborhood tavern, can be a conducive setting for casual but purposive inquiries.

Group interviews can be compared on several dimensions. First, the interviewer can be very formal, taking a very directive and controlling posture, guiding discussion strictly, and not permitting digression or variation from topic or agenda. This is the mode of focus and nominal/Delphi groups. In the latter case participants are physically isolated but share views through a coordinator/interviewer. The nondirective approach is more likely to be implemented in naturally established field settings, such as a street corner, or in controlled settings (e.g., research labs) where the research purpose is phenomenological, to establish the widest range of meaning and interpretation for the topic. Groups can also be differentiated by question format and purpose, which in the case of group interviews usually means exploration, pretest, or phenomenological. Exploratory interviews are designed to establish familiarity with a topic or setting; the interviewer can be very directive (or the opposite), but the questions are usually unstructured or open-ended. The same format is used in interviews with phenomenological purposes, where the intent is to tap intersubjective meaning with depth and diversity. Pretest interviews are generally structured in question format and the interviewer is directive in style. Table 2.1 compares the types of group interviews on various dimensions.

The skills that are required to conduct the group interview are not significantly different from those needed for individual interviews. The interviewer must be flexible, objective, empathic, persuasive, a good listener, and so on. But the group format does present some problems not found in the individual interview. Merton et al. (1956) note three specific

TABLE 2.1   Types of Group Interviews and Dimensions

Type	Setting	Role of Interviewer	Question Format	Purpose
Focus group	formal-preset	directive	structured	exploratory pretest
Brainstorming	formal or informal	nondirective	very structured	exploratory
Nominal/ delphi	formal	directive	structured	pretest exploratory
Field, natural	informal spontaneous	moderately nondirective	very structured	exploratory phenomenological
Field, formal	preset, but in field	somewhat directive	semi-structured	phenomenological

problems: First, the interviewer must keep one person or small coalition of persons from dominating the group; second, the interviewer must encourage recalcitrant respondents to participate; and third, the interviewer must obtain responses from the entire group to ensure the fullest coverage of the topic. In addition, the interviewer must balance the directive, interviewer role with the role of moderator, which calls for the management of the dynamics of the group being interviewed; the group interviewer must simultaneously worry about the script of questions and be sensitive to the evolving patterns of group interaction.

Group interviews have some advantages over individual interviews: They are relatively inexpensive to conduct and often produce rich data that are cumulative and elaborative; they can be stimulating for respondents, aiding recall; and the format is flexible. Group interviews are not, however, without problems: The results cannot be generalized; the emerging group culture may interfere with individual expression, and the group may be dominated by one person; and "groupthink" is a possible outcome. The requirements for interviewer skills are greater than those for individual interviewing because of the group dynamics that are present. In addition, it is difficult to research sensitive topics using this technique. Nevertheless, the group interview is a viable option for both qualitative and quantitative research.

◆ Unstructured Interviewing

Unstructured interviewing can provide a greater breadth of data than the other types, given its qualitative nature. In this section we discuss the traditional type of unstructured interview: the open-ended, ethnographic (in-depth) interview. Many qualitative researchers differentiate between in-depth (or ethnographic) interviewing and participant observation. Yet, as Lofland (1971) points out, the two go hand in hand, and many of the data gathered in participant observation come from informal interviewing in the field. Consider the following report, from Malinowski's (1967/1989) diary:

> Saturday 8 [December 1917]. Got up late, felt rotten, took enema. At about 1 I went out; I heard cries; [people from] Kapwapu were bringing *uri* to Teyava. I sat with the natives, talked, took pictures. Went back. Billy corrected and supplemented my notes about *wasi*. At Teyava, an old man talked a great deal about fishes, but I did not understand him too well. Then we moved to his *bwayama*. Talked about *lili'u*. They kept questioning me about the war—In the evening I talked to the policeman about *bwaga'u*, *lili'u* and *yoyova*. I was irritated by their laughing. Billy again told me a number of interesting things. Took quinine and calomel. (p. 145)

Malinowski's "day in the field" shows how very important unstructured interviewing is in the conduct of fieldwork and clearly illustrates the difference between structured and unstructured interviewing. Malinowski has some general topics he wishes to know about, but he does not use closed-ended questions or a formal approach to interviewing. What's more, he commits (as most field-workers do) what structured interviewers would see as two "capital offenses": (a) He answers questions asked by the respondents, and (b) he lets his personal feelings influence him (as all field-workers do), thus he deviates from the "ideal" of a cool, distant, and rational interviewer.

Malinowski's example captures the differences between structured and unstructured interviewing: The former aims at capturing precise data of a codable nature in order to explain behavior within preestablished categories, whereas the latter attempts to understand the complex behavior of members of society without imposing any a priori categorization that may limit the field of inquiry.

In a way, Malinowski's interviewing is still structured to some degree—that is, there is a setting, there are identified informants, and the respondents are clearly discernible. In other types of interviewing there may be no setting; for instance, Rosanna Hertz (1995, 1997b, 1997c) focused on locating women in a historic moment rather than in a place. Additionally, in their study of single mothers, Hertz and Ferguson (1997) interviewed women who did not know each other, who were not part of a single group or village. At times, informants are not readily accessible or identifiable, but anyone the researcher meets may become a valuable source of information. Hertz and Ferguson relied on tradespeople and friends to identify single mothers for their study. Fontana and Smith (1989) found that respondents are not always readily identifiable. In studying Alzheimer's disease patients, they discovered it was often possible to confuse caregivers and patients in the early stages of the disease. Also, in Fontana's (1977) research on poor elderly, he had no fixed setting at all; he simply wandered from bench to bench in the park where the old folks were sitting, talking to any disheveled old person who would talk back.

Spradley (1979) aptly differentiates among various types of interviewing. He describes the following interviewer-respondent interaction, which would be unthinkable in traditional sociological circles yet is the very essence of unstructured interviewing—the establishment of a human-to-human relation with the respondent and the desire to *understand* rather than to *explain*:

> Presently she smiled, pressed her hand to her chest, and said: "Tsetchwe." It was her name. "Elizabeth," I said, pointing to myself. "Nisabe," she answered. . . . Then, having surely suspected that I was a woman, she put her hand on my breast gravely, and, finding out that I was, she touched her own breast. Many Bushmen do this; to them all Europeans look alike. "Tasu si" (women), she said. Then after a moment's pause Tsetchwe began to teach me. (pp. 3-4)

Spradley goes on to discuss all the things an interviewer learns from the natives about them, their culture, their language, their ways of life. Although each and every study is different, these are some of the basic elements of unstructured interviewing. These elements have been discussed in details already, and we need not elaborate upon them too much (for detailed accounts of unstructured interviewing, see, among others, Adams & Preiss, 1960; Denzin, 1989b; Lofland, 1971; Spradley, 1979). Here we provide brief synopses. Please remember that these are presented only as heuristic devices; every study uses slightly different elements and often in different combinations.

Later in this chapter, in discussing new trends, we will deconstruct these notions as we frame the interview as an active, emergent process. We contend that our interview society gives people instructions on how to comply with these heuristics (see Silverman, 1993, 1997a, 1997b). Similarly, James Scheurich (1997) is openly critical of both positivistic and interpretive interviewing, as they are both based on modernist assumptions. Rather than being a process "by the numbers," for Scheurich, interviewing (and its language) are "persistently slippery, unstable, and ambiguous from person to person, from situation to situation, from time to time" (p. 62).

Accessing the setting. How do we "get in"? That, of course, varies according to the group one is attempting to study. One may have to disrobe and casually stroll in the nude if doing a study of nude beaches (Douglas & Rasmussen, 1977), or one may have to buy a huge motorbike and frequent seedy bars in certain locations if attempting to befriend and study the Hell's Angels (Thompson, 1985). The different ways and attempts to "get in" vary tremendously, but they all share the common goal of gaining access to the setting. Sometimes there is no setting per se, as when Fontana (1977) attempted to study poor elderly on the streets and had to gain access anew with each and every interviewee.

Understanding the language and culture of the respondents. Rosalie Wax (1960) gives perhaps the most poignant description of learning the language and culture of the respondents in her study of "disloyal" Japanese in concentration camps in the United States between 1943 and 1945. Wax had to overcome a number of language and cultural problems in her study. Although respondents may be fluent in the language of the interviewer, there are different ways of saying things and, indeed, certain things that should not be said at all, linking language and cultural manifestations. Wax makes this point:

I remarked that I would like to see the letter. The silence that fell on the chatting group was almost palpable, and the embarrassment of the hosts was painful to see. The *faux pas* was not asking to see a letter, for letters were passed about rather freely. It rested on the fact that one did not give a Caucasian a letter in which the "disloyal" statement of a friend might be expressed. (p. 172)

Some researchers, especially in anthropological interviews, tend to rely on interpreters, and thus become vulnerable to added layers of meanings, biases, and interpretations, which may lead to disastrous misunderstandings (Freeman, 1983). At times, specific jargon, such as the medical metalanguage of physicians, may be a code that is hard for nonmembers to understand.

Deciding on how to present oneself. Do we present ourselves as representatives from academia studying medical students (Becker, 1956)? Do we approach the interview as a woman-to-woman discussion (Spradley, 1979)? Do we "dress down" to look like the respondents (Fontana, 1977; Thompson, 1985)? Do we represent the colonial culture (Malinowsky, 1922), or do we humbly present ourselves as "learners" (Wax, 1960)? This decision is very important, because once the interviewer's presentational self is "cast," it leaves a profound impression on the respondents and has great influence over the success (or lack of it) of the study. Sometimes, inadvertently, the researcher's presentational self may be misrepresented, as John Johnson (1976) discovered in studying a welfare office, when some of the employees assumed he was a "spy" for management despite his best efforts to the contrary.

Locating an informant. The researcher must find an insider, a member of the group studied, who is willing to be an informant and act as a guide and a translator of cultural mores and, at times, jargon or language. Although the researcher can conduct interviews without an informant, he or she can save much time and avoid mistakes if a good informant becomes available. The "classic" sociological informant is Doc in William Foote Whyte's *Street Corner Society* (1943). Without Doc's help and guidance, it is doubtful that Whyte would have been able to access his subjects at the level he did. Very instructive is Paul Rabinow's (1977) discussion of his relationship with his main informant, Abd al-Malik ben Lahcen. Malik acted as a translator but also provided Rabinow with access to the cultural ways of the subjects, and by his actions provided Rabinow with insights into the vast differences between a University of Chicago researcher and a native Moroccan.

Gaining trust. Survey researchers asking respondents whether they would or would not favor the establishment of a nuclear dump in their state (Frey, 1993) do not have too much work to do in the way of gaining trust; respondents have opinions about nuclear dumps and are very willing to express them, sometimes forcefully. But it is clearly a different story if one wants to ask about a person's frequency of sexual intercourse or preferred method of birth control. The interviewer needs to establish some trust with the respondents (Cicourel, 1974). Paul Rasmussen (1989) had to spend months as a "wallflower" in the waiting room of a massage parlor before any of the masseuses gained enough trust in him to divulge to him, in unstructured interviews, the nature of their "massage" relations with clients. Gaining trust is essential to the success of the interviews and, once gained, trust can still be very fragile. Any faux pas by the researcher may destroy days, weeks, or months of painfully gained trust.

Establishing rapport. Because the goal of unstructured interviewing is *understanding,* it is paramount that the researcher establish rapport with respondents; that is, the researcher must be able to take the role of the respondents and attempt to see the situation from their viewpoint, rather than superimpose his or her world of academia and preconceptions upon them. Although a close rapport with the respondents opens the doors to more informed research, it may create problems as the researcher may become a spokesperson for the group studied, losing his or her distance and objectivity, or may "go native" and become a member of the group and forgo his or her academic role. At times, what the researcher may feel is good rapport turns out not to be, as Thompson (1985) found out in a nightmarish way when he was subjected to a brutal beating by the Hell's Angels just as his study of them was coming to a close. At the other end of the spectrum, some researchers may never feel they have established rapport with their subjects. Malinowski (1967/1989), for example, always mistrusted the motives of the natives and at times was troubled by their brutish sensuality or angered by their outright lying or deceptions: "After lunch I [carried] yellow calico and spoke about the *baloma.* I made a small *sagali,* Navavile. I was *fed up* with the *niggers*" (p. 154).

Collecting empirical materials. Being out in the field does not afford researchers the luxury of video cameras, soundproof rooms, and high-quality recording equipment. Lofland (1971) provides detailed information on doing and writing up interviews and on the types of field notes researchers ought to take and how to organize them. Yet field-workers often must make do; their "tales" of their methods range from holding a miniature tape recorder as inconspicuously as possible to taking mental notes and then rushing to the privacy of a bathroom to jot notes down, on toilet papers at times. We agree with Lofland that regardless of the circumstances, researchers ought to (a) take notes regularly and promptly: (b) write everything down, no matter how unimportant it may seem at the time; (c) try to be as inconspicuous as possible in note taking; and (d) analyze their notes frequently.

◆ Other Types of Unstructured Interviewing

We consider the issues of interpreting and reporting empirical material later in this chapter. In this section, we briefly outline some different types of unstructured interviews.

Oral History

The oral history differs from other unstructured interviews in purpose, but not methodologically. The oral collection of historical materials goes back to ancient times, but its modern-day formal organization can be traced to 1948, when Allan Nevins began the Oral History Project at Columbia University (Starr, 1984, p. 4). Oral history captures a variety of forms of life, from common folks talking about their jobs in Studs Terkel's *Working* (1975) to the historical recollections of president Harry Truman in Merle Miller's *Plain Speaking* (1974; see Starr, 1984). Often, oral history transcripts are not published, but many may be found in libraries, silent memoirs waiting for someone to rummage through them and bring their testimony to life. Recently, oral history has found great popularity among feminists (Gluck & Patai, 1991), who see it as a way to understand and bring forth the history of women in a culture that has traditionally relied on masculine interpretation: "Refusing to be rendered historically voiceless any longer, women are creating a new history—using our own voices and experiences" (Gluck, 1984, p. 222).

Relevant to the study of oral history (and, in fact, to all interviewing) is the study of memory and its relation to recall. For instance, Barry Schwartz (1999) has examined the ages at which we recall critical episodes in our lives; he concludes that "biographical memory . . . is better understood as a social process" and that "as we look back, we find ourselves remembering our lives in terms of our experience with others" (p. 15; see also Schwartz, 1996). Carolyn Ellis (1991) has resorted to the use of "sociological introspection" to reconstruct biographical episodes of her past life. Notable among Ellis's works in this genre is her reconstruction of her 9-year relationship with her partner, Gene Weinstein, in which she describes the emotional negotiations the two of them went through as they coped with his downward-spiraling health, until the final negotiation with death (Ellis, 1995).

Creative Interviewing

Close to oral history, but used more conventionally as a sociological tool, is Jack Douglas's (1985) "creative interviewing." Douglas argues against "how-to" guides to conducting interviews because unstructured interviews take place in the largely situational everyday worlds of members of society. Thus interviewing and interviewers must necessarily be creative, forget how-to rules, and adapt themselves to the ever-changing situations they face. Similar to oral historians, Douglas sees interviewing as collecting oral reports from the members of society. In creative interviewing, these reports go well beyond the length of conventional unstructured interviews and may become "life histories," with interviewing taking place in multiple sessions over many days with the subject(s).

Postmodern Interviewing

Douglas's concern with the important role played by the interviewer qua human being, which is also shared by feminist oral historians, became a paramount element in the interviewing approaches of postmodern anthropologists and sociologists in the mid-1980s. Marcus and Fischer (1986) address ethnography at large, but their discussion is germane to unstructured interviewing because, as we have seen, such interviewing constitutes the major way of collecting data in fieldwork. Marcus and Fischer voice reflexive concerns about the ways in which the researcher influences the study, both in the methods of data collection and in the techniques of reporting findings; this concern leads to new ways to conduct interviews, in the hope of minimizing, if not eliminating, interviewer influence. One such way is *polyphonic* interviewing, in which the voices of the subjects are recorded with minimal influence from the researcher and are not collapsed together and reported as one, through the interpretation of the researcher. Instead, the multiple perspectives of the various subjects are reported and differences and problems encountered are discussed, rather than glossed over (see Krieger, 1983). *Interpretive* interactionism follows in the footsteps of creative and polyphonic interviewing, but, borrowing from James Joyce, adds a new element, that of epiphanies, which Denzin (1989a) describes as "those interactional moments that leave marks on people's lives [and] have the potential for creating transformational experiences for the person" (p. 15). Thus the topic of inquiry becomes dramatized by the focus on existential moments in people's lives, hopefully producing richer and more meaningful data. Finally, as postmodernists seek new ways of understanding and reporting data, we wish to note the concept of *oralysis,* which refers "to the ways in which oral forms, derived from everyday life, are, with the recording powers of video, applied to the analytical tasks associated with literate forms" (Ulmer, 1989, p. xi). In oralysis, the traditional product of interviewing, talk, is coupled with the visual, providing, according to Ulmer (1989), a product consonant with a society that is dominated by the medium of television.

◆ Gendered Interviews

> The housewife goes into a well-stocked store to look for a frying pan. Her thinking probably does not proceed exactly this way, but it is helpful to think of the many possible two-way choices she might make: Cast iron or aluminum? Thick or thin? Metal or wooden handle? Covered or not? Deep or shallow? Large or small? This brand or that? Reasonable or too high in price? To buy or not? Cash or charge? Have it delivered or carry it. . . . The two-way question is simplicity itself when it comes to recording answers and tabulating them. (Payne, 1951, pp. 55-56)

The above quote represents the prevalent paternalistic attitude toward women in interviewing (see Oakley, 1981, p. 39) as well as the paradigmatic concern with coding answers and therefore with presenting limited, dichotomous choices. Apart from a tendency to be condescending to women, the traditional interview paradigm does not account for gendered differences. In fact, Babbie's classic text *The Practice of Social Research* (1992) briefly references gender only three times and says nothing about the influence of gender on interviews. As Ann Oakley (1981) cogently points out, both the interviewers and the respondents are considered faceless and invisible, and they must be if the paradigmatic assumption of gathering value-free data is to be maintained. Yet, as Denzin (1989a, p. 116) tells us, "gender filters knowledge"; that is, the sex of the interviewer and that of the respondent do make a difference, as the interview takes place within the cultural boundaries of a paternalistic social system in which masculine identities are differentiated from feminine ones.

In the typical interview there exists a hierarchical relation, with the respondent being in the subordinate position. The interviewer is instructed to be courteous, friendly, and pleasant:

> The interviewer's manner should be friendly, courteous, conversational and unbiased. He should be neither too grim nor too effusive; neither too talkative nor too timid. The idea should be to put the respondent at ease, *so that he will talk freely and fully.* (Selltiz, Jahoda, Deutsch, & Cook, 1965, p. 576; emphasis added)

Yet, as the last above-quoted line shows, this demeanor is a ruse to gain the trust and confidence of the respondent without reciprocating those feelings in any way. Interviewers are not to give their own opinions and are to evade direct questions. What seems to be a conversation is really a one-way pseudoconversation, raising the ethical dilemma (Fine, 1983-1984) inherent in the study of people for opportunistic reasons. When the respondent is female, the interview presents added problems, because the preestablished format directed at information relevant for the study tends both to ignore the respondent's own concerns and to curtail any attempts to digress and elaborate. This format also stymies any revelation of personal feelings and emotions.

Warren (1988) discusses problems of gender in both anthropological and sociological fieldwork, and many of these are found as well in the ethnographic interview. Some of these problems are the traditional ones of entrée and trust, which may be heightened by the sex of the interviewer, especially in highly sex-segregated societies: "I never witnessed any ceremonies that were barred to women. Whenever I visited compounds I sat with the women while the men gathered in the parlors or in front of the compound. . . . I never entered any of the places where men sat around to drink beer or palm wine and to chat" (Sudarkasa, 1986; quoted in Warren, 1988, p. 16).

Solutions to the problem have been to view the female anthropologist as androgyne or to grant her honorary male status for the duration of her research. Warren (1988) also points to some advantages of a researcher's being female and therefore seen as harmless or invisible. Other problems are associated with the researcher's status and race and with the context of the interview; again, these problems are magnified for female researchers in a paternalistic world. Female interviewers at times face the added burden of sexual overtures or covert sexual hassle (Warren, 1988, p. 33).

Feminist researchers have suggested ways to circumvent the traditional interviewing paradigm. Oakley (1981) notes that interviewing is a masculine paradigm, embedded in a masculine culture and stressing masculine traits while at the same time excluding traits such as sensitivity, emotionality, and others that are culturally viewed as feminine traits. There is, however, a growing reluctance, especially among female researchers (Oakley, 1981; Reinharz, 1992; Smith, 1987), to continue interviewing women as "objects," with little or no regard for them as individuals. Although this reluctance stems from moral and ethical reasons, it is also relevant methodologically. As Oakley (1981) points out, in interviewing there is "no intimacy without reciprocity" (p. 49). Thus the emphasis is shifting to allow the development of a closer relation between interviewer and respondent; researchers are attempting to minimize status differences and are doing away with the traditional hierarchical situation in interviewing. Interviewers can show their human side and answer questions and express feelings. Methodologically, this new approach provides a greater spectrum of responses and greater insight into the lives of respondents—or "participants," to avoid the hierarchical pitfall (Reinharz, 1992, p.22)—because it encourages them to control the sequencing and the language of the interview and also allows them the freedom of open-ended responses (Oakley, 1981; Reinharz, 1992; Smith, 1987). To wit: "Women were always . . . encouraged to 'digress' into details of their personal histories and to recount anecdotes of their working lives. Much important information was gathered in this way" (Yeandle, 1984; quoted in Reinharz, 1992, p. 25).

Rosanna Hertz (1997a) makes the self of the researcher visible and suggests that it is only one of many selves the researcher takes to the field. She asserts that interviewers need to be reflexive; that is, they need "to have an ongoing conversation about experience while simultaneously living in the moment" (p. viii). By doing so, they will heighten the understanding of differences of ideologies, cultures, and politics between interviewers and interviewees.

Hertz also underscores the importance of "voices"—how we, as authors, express and write our stories, which data we include and which we exclude, whose voices we choose to represent and which we do not. The concern with voices is also found, very powerfully, in a volume edited by Kim Marie Vaz titled *Oral Narrative Research With Black Women* (1997). One of the contributors, Christine Obbo (1997), states:

> This chapter is a modest exercise in giving expression to women's voices and in rescuing their perceptions and experiences from being mere murmurs or backdrop to political, social and cultural happenings. Women's voices have been devalued by male chronicles of cultural history even when the men acknowledge female informants; they are overshadowed by the voice of male authority and ascendance in society. (pp. 42-43)

This commitment to maintaining the integrity of the phenomena and preserving the viewpoint of the subjects, as expressed in their everyday language, is akin to the stand taken by phenomenological and existential sociologies (Douglas & Johnson, 1977; Kotarba & Fontana, 1984) and also reflects the concerns of postmodern ethnographers (Marcus & Fischer, 1986). The differences are (a) the heightened moral concern for subjects/participants, (b) the attempt to redress the male/female hierarchy and existing paternalistic power structure, and (c) the paramount importance placed upon membership, because the effectiveness of male researchers in interviewing female subjects has been largely discredited.

Ruth Behar (1996) addresses the ambiguous nature of the enterprise of interviewing by asking: Where do we locate the researcher in the field? How much do we reveal about ourselves? How do we reconcile our different roles and positions? Behar makes us see that interviewer, writer, respondent, and interview are not clearly distinct entities; rather, they are intertwined in a deeply problematic way.

Some feminist sociologists have gone beyond concerns with interviewing or fieldwork in itself. Laurel Richardson (1992a) is striving for new forms of expression to report her findings and has presented some of her fieldwork in the form of poetry. Patricia Clough (1998) questions the whole enterprise of fieldwork under the current paradigm and calls for a reassessment of the whole sociological enterprise and for a rereading of existing sociological texts in a light that is not marred by a paternalistic bias. Their voices echo the concern of Dorothy Smith (1987), who eloquently states:

> The problem [of a research project] and its particular solution are analogous to those by which fresco painters solved the problems of representing the different temporal moments of a story in the singular space of the wall. The problem is to produce in a two-dimensional space framed as a wall a world of action and movement in time. (p. 281)

A growing number of researchers feel that we cannot isolate gender from other important elements that also "filter knowledge." Among others, Patricia Hill Collins (1990) has written eloquently about the filtering of knowledge through memberships—of being black and female in American culture, in her case. Kath Weston (1998) makes just as powerful a case for sexuality, which, she contends, should not be treated as a compartmentalized subspecialty, because it underlies and is integral to the whole of the social sciences. Clearly, gender, sexuality, and race cannot be considered in isolation; race, class, hierarchy, status, and age (Seidman, 1991) are all part of the complex, yet often ignored, elements that shape interviewing.

◆ Framing and Interpreting Interviews

Aside from the problem of framing real-life events in a two-dimensional space, we face the added problems of how the framing is being done and who is doing the framing. In sociological terms, this means that the type of interviewing selected, the techniques used, and the ways of recording information all come to bear on the results of the study. Additionally, data must be interpreted, and the researcher has a great deal of influence on what part of the data will be reported and how it will be reported.

Framing Interviews

Numerous volumes have been published on the techniques of structured interviewing (see, among others, Babbie, 1992; Bradburn et al., 1979; Gorden, 1980; Kahn & Cannel, 1957). There is also a voluminous literature on group interviewing, especially in marketing and survey research (for a comprehensive review of literature in this area, see Stewart & Shamdasani, 1990). The uses of group interviewing have also been linked to qualitative sociology (Morgan, 1988). Unstructured interviewing techniques have been covered thoroughly (Denzin, 1989b; Lofland, 1971; Lofland & Lofland, 1984; Spradley, 1979).

As we have noted, unstructured interviews vary widely, given their informal nature and depending on the nature of the setting, and some eschew the use of any preestablished set of techniques (Douglas, 1985). Yet there are techniques involved in interviewing whether the interviewer is just being "a nice person" or is following a format. Techniques can be varied to meet various situations, and varying one's techniques is known as using tactics. Traditionally, the researcher is involved in an informal conversation with the respondent, thus he or she must maintain a tone of "friendly" chat while trying to remain close to the guidelines of the topic of inquiry he or she has in mind. The researcher begins by "breaking the ice" with general questions and gradually moves on to more specific ones, while also—as inconspicuously as possible—asking questions intended to check the veracity of the respondent's statements. The researcher should avoid getting involved in a "real" conversation in which he or she answers questions asked by the respondent or provides personal opinions on the matters discussed. A researcher can avoid "getting trapped" by shrugging off the relevance of his or her opinions ("It doesn't matter how I feel, it's your opinion that's important") or by feigning ignorance ("I really don't know enough about this to say anything; you're the expert"). Of course, as we have seen in the case of gendered interviewing, the researcher may reject these techniques and "come down" to the level of the respondent to engage in a "real" conversation, with give-and-take and shared empathic understanding.

The use of language, particularly the use of specific terms, is important in the creation of a "sharedness of meanings" in which both interviewer and respondent understand the contextual nature of specific referents. For instance, in studying nude beaches, Douglas and Rasmussen (1977) discovered that the term *nude beach virgin* had nothing to do with chastity; rather, it referred to the fact that a person's buttocks were white, thus indicating to others that he or she was a newcomer to the nude beach. Language is also important in delineating the type of question (broad, narrow, leading, instructive, and so on).

Nonverbal techniques are also important in interviewing. There are four basic modes of nonverbal communication:

> *Proxemic* communication is the use of interpersonal space to communicate attitudes, *chronemics* communication is the use of pacing of speech and length of silence in conversation, *kinesic* communication includes any body movements or postures, and *paralinguistic* communication includes all the variations in volume, pitch and quality of voice. (Gorden, 1980, p. 335)

All four of these modes represent important techniques for the researcher; in addition, the researcher should carefully note and record respondents' uses of these modes, for interview data are more than verbal records and should include, as much as possible, nonverbal features of the interaction. Finally, techniques vary with the groups being interviewed; for instance, interviewing a group of children requires a different approach from the one an interviewer might use when interviewing a group of elderly widows (Lopata, 1980).

Interpreting Interviews

Many studies using unstructured interviews are not reflexive enough about the interpreting process; common platitudes proclaim that the data speak for themselves, that the researcher is neutral, unbiased, and "invisible." The data reported tend to flow nicely, there are no contradictory data and no mention of what data were excluded and/or why. Improprieties never happen and the main concern seems to be the proper, if unreflexive, filing, analyzing, and reporting of events. But anyone who has engaged in fieldwork knows better; no matter how organized the researcher may be, he or she slowly becomes buried under an increasing mountain of field notes, transcripts, newspaper clippings, and audiotapes. Traditionally, readers were presented with the researcher's interpretation of the data, cleaned and streamlined and collapsed in rational, non-contradictory accounts. More recently, sociologists have come to grips with the reflexive, problematic, and, at times, contradictory nature of data and with the tremendous, if unspoken, influence of the researcher as author. What Van Maanen (1988) calls "confessional style" began in earnest in the 1970s (see Johnson, 1976) and continues unabated to our day, in a soul cleansing by researchers of problematic feelings and sticky situations in the field. Although perhaps somewhat overdone at times, these "confessions" are very valuable, as they make the readers aware of the complex and cumbersome nature of interviewing people in their natural settings and lend a tone of realism and veracity to studies. For example: "Yesterday I slept very late. Got up around 10. The day before I had engaged Omaga, Koupa, and a few others. They didn't come. Again I fell into a rage" (Malinowski, 1967/1989, p. 67).

Showing the human side of the researcher and the problematics of unstructured interviewing has taken new forms in deconstructionism (Derrida, 1976). Here the influence of the author is brought under scrutiny. Thus the text created by the researcher's rendition of events is "deconstructed"; the author's biases and taken-for-granted notions are exposed, and, at times, alternative ways to look at the data are introduced (Clough, 1998).

Postmodern social researchers, as we have seen, attempt to expose and minimize the role of the researcher qua field-worker and qua author. Thus, for instance, Crapanzano (1980) reports Tuhami's accounts, whether they be sociohistorical renditions, dreams, or outright lies, because they all constitute a part of this Morrocan Arab subject's sense of self and personal history. In interviewing Tuhami, Crapanzano learns not only about his subject but about himself:

> As Tuhami's interlocutor, I became an active participant in his life history, even though I rarely appear directly in his recitations. Not only did my presence, and my questions, prepare him for the text he was to produce, but they produced what I read as a change of consciousness in him. They produced a change of consciousness in me too. We were both jostled from our assumptions about the nature of the everyday world and ourselves and groped for common reference points within this limbo of interchange. (p. 11)

No longer pretending to be faceless subject and invisible researcher, Tuhami and Crapanzano are portrayed as individual human beings with their own personal histories and idiosyncrasies, and we, the readers, learn about two people and two cultures.

◆ Ethical Considerations

Because the objects of inquiry in interviewing are human beings, researchers must take extreme care to avoid any harm to them. Traditionally, ethical concerns have revolved around the topics of *informed consent* (receiving consent by the subject after having carefully and truthfully informed him or her about the research), *right to privacy* (protecting the identity of the subject), and *protection from harm* (physical, emotional, or any other kind).

No sociologist or other social scientist would dismiss these three ethical concerns. Yet, there are other concerns that are less unanimously upheld. The controversy concerning overt/covert fieldwork is more germane to participant observation, but could include the surreptitious use of tape-recording devices. Warwick (1973) and Douglas (1985) argue for the use of covert methods, because they mirror the deceitfulness of everyday-life reality, whereas others, including Kai Erikson (1967), are vehemently opposed to the study of uninformed subjects.

Another problematic issue stems from the researcher's degree of involvement with the group under study. Whyte (1943) was asked to vote more than once during the same local elections (i.e., to vote illegally) by members of the group he had gained access to, and befriended, gaining their trust. He used "situational ethics," judging the legal infraction to be minor in comparison to the loss of his fieldwork if he refused to vote. Thompson (1985) was faced with a more serious possible legal breach. He was terrified of having to witness one of the alleged rapes for which the Hell's Angels had become notorious, but, as he reports, none took place during his research. The most famous, and widely discussed, case of questionable ethics in qualitative sociology took place during Laud Humphreys's research for *Tearoom Trade* (1970). Humphreys studied homosexual encounters in public restrooms in parks ("tearooms") by acting as a lookout ("watchqueen"). Although this fact in itself may be seen as ethically incorrect, it is the following one that has raised many academic eyebrows. Humphreys, unable to interview the men in the "tearoom," recorded their cars' license-plate numbers, which led him to find their residences with the help of police files. He then interviewed many of the men in their homes without being recognized as having been their "watchqueen."

Another ethical problem is raised by the veracity of the reports made by researchers. For example, Whyte's (1943) famous study of Italian street corner men in Boston has come under severe scrutiny (Boelen, 1992), as some have alleged that Whyte portrayed the men in demeaning ways that did not reflect their visions of themselves. Whyte's case is still unresolved, but it does illustrate the delicate issue of ethical decisions in the field and in reporting field notes, even more than 50 years later (Richardson, 1992b).

A growing number of scholars, as we have seen (Oakley, 1981), feel that most of traditional in-depth interviewing is unethical, whether wittingly or unwittingly. The techniques and tactics of interviewing, they say, are really ways of manipulating the respondents while treating them as objects or numbers rather than individual human beings. Should the quest for objectivity supersede the human side of those we study? Consider the following:

> One day while doing research at the convalescent center, I was talking to one of the aides while she was beginning to change the bedding of one of the patients who had urinated and soaked the bed. He was the old, blind, ex-wrestler confined in the emergency room. Suddenly, the wrestler decided he was not going to cooperate with the aide and began striking violently at the air about him, fortunately missing the aide. Since nobody else was around, I had no choice but to hold the patient pinned down to the bed while the aide proceeded to change the bedding. It was not pleasant: The patient was squirming and yelling horrible threats at the top of his voice; the acid smell of urine was nauseating; I was slowly loosing my grip on the much stronger patient, while all along feeling horribly like Chief Bromden when he suffo-cates the lobotomized Mac Murphy in Ken Kesey's novel. *But there was no choice, one just could not sit back and take notes while the patient tore apart the aide.* (Fontana, 1977, p. 187; emphasis added)

Clearly, as we move forward with sociology, we cannot, to paraphrase what Herbert Blumer said so many years ago, let the methods dictate our images of human beings. As Punch (1986) suggests, as field-workers we need to exercise common sense and responsibility, and, we would like to add, to our subjects first, to the study next, and to ourselves last.

◆ New Trends in Interviewing

The latest trends in interviewing have come some distance from structured questions; we have reached the point of interview as negotiated text. Eth-nographers have realized for quite some time that researchers are not invis-ible, neutral entities; rather, they are part of the interactions they seek to study and influence those interactions. At last, interviewing is being brought in line with ethnography. There is a growing realization that inter-viewers are not the mythical, neutral tools envisioned by survey research. Interviewers are increasingly seen as active participants in interactions with respondents, and interviews are seen as negotiated accomplishments of both interviewers and respondents that are shaped by the contexts and situations in which they take place. As Schwandt (1997) notes, "It has become increasingly common in qualitative studies to view the interview as a form of discourse between two or more speakers or as a linguistic event in which the meanings of questions and responses are contextually grounded and jointly constructed by interviewer and respondent" (p. 79). We are beginning to realize that we cannot lift the results of interviews out of the contexts in which they were gathered and claim them as objective data with no strings attached.

Interview as Negotiated Accomplishment

Let us briefly recap the two traditional approaches to the interview, following Holstein and Gubrium (1995, 1997). These authors use Jean Converse and Howard Schuman's *Conversations at Random* (1974) as an exemplar of the interview as used in survey research. In this context the interviewer is carefully instructed to remain as passive as possible, so as to reduce his or her influence—the scope of the interviewer's function is to access respondents' answers. This is a *rational* type of interviewing; it assumes that there is an objective knowledge out there and that if one is skilled enough one can access it, just as a skilled surgeon can remove a kidney from a donor and use it in a different context (e.g., for a patient awaiting transplant).

Holstein and Gubrium (1995, 1997) regard Jack Douglas's (1985) creative interviewing as a romanticist type of interviewing. Creative interviewing is based on *feelings*; it assumes that researchers, qua interviewers, need to "get to know" respondents beneath their rational facades, and that researchers can reach respondents' deep wells of emotion by engaging them, by sharing feelings and thoughts with them. Douglas's interviewer is certainly more active and far less neutral than Converse and Schuman's, but the assumptions are still the same: that it is the *skills* of interviewers that will provide access to knowledge and that there is a *core knowledge* that researchers can access.

Holstein and Gubrium finally consider the new type of interviewing—well, "new" isn't exactly accurate, given that their reference for this is the work of Ithiel de Sola Pool, published in 1957. To wit: "Every interview . . . is an interpersonal drama with a developing plot" (Pool, 1957, p. 193; quoted in Holstein & Gubrium, 1995, p. 14). Holstein and

Gubrium (1995) go on to note that thus far we have focused on the *whats* of the interview, the substantive findings, and it is time that we pay attention to the *hows* of the interview—the contexts, particular situations, nuances, manners, people involved, and so on in which interview interactions take place. This concept harks back to ethnomethodology, according to Holstein and Gubrium (1995): "To say that the interview is an interpersonal drama with a developing plot is part of a broader claim that reality is an ongoing, interpretive accomplishment" (p. 16). Garfinkel, Sacks, and others clearly stated in the late 1960s that reality is an ever-changing, ongoing accomplishment based on the practical reasoning of the members of society. It is time to consider the interview as a practical production, the meaning of which is accomplished at the intersection of the interaction of interviewer and respondent.

In a later essay, Gubrium and Holstein (1998) continue their argument by looking at interviews as storytelling, which they see as a practical production used by members of society to accomplish coherence in their accounts. Once more they encourage us to examine the *hows* as well as the *whats* of storytelling. Similarly, Madan Sarup (1996) tells us:

> Each narrative has two parts; a story (*histoire*) and a discourse (*discourse*). The story is the content, or chain of events. The story is the "what" in a narrative, the discourse is the "how." The discourse is rather like a plot, how the reader becomes aware of what happened, the order of appearance of the events. (p. 17)

Gubrium and Holstein are not alone in advocating this reflexive approach to interviews. Both David Silverman (1993) and Robert Dingwall (1997) credit Cicourel's classic work *Method and Measurement in Sociology* (1964) with pointing to the interview as a social encounter. Dingwall (1997) notes:

> If the interview is a social encounter, then, logically, it must be analyzed in the same way as any other social encounter. The products of an interview are the outcome of a socially situated activity where the responses are passed through the role-playing and impression management of both the interviewer and the respondent. (p. 56)

I. E. Seidman (1991) discusses interviewing as a relationship by relying upon a principal intellectual antecedent of the ethnomethodologist Alfred

Schutz (1967). Seidman analyzes the interviewer-respondent relation in terms of Schutz's "I-thou" relation, in which the two share a reciprocity of perspective and, by both being "thou" oriented, create a "we" relationship. Thus the respondent is no longer "an object or a type" (Seidman, 1991, p. 73) but becomes an equal participant in the interaction.

The Problematics of New Approaches

Some of the proponents of the ethnomethodologically informed interview are critical of interactionist as well as positivist interview methods. Dingwall (1997), as well as others, speaks of the romantic movement in ethnography (and interviewing)—the idea that the nearer we come to the respondent, the closer we are to apprehending the "real self." This assumption neglects the fact that the self is a process, ever negotiated and accomplished in the interaction. Dingwall also faults the "postmodern" turn; that is, if there is no real self, there is no real world and I can create one of my own. Finally, he is troubled by the "crusading" nature of the romantics and asks, "What is the value of a scholarly enterprise that is more concerned with being 'right on' than with being right?" (p. 64).

In a similar vein, Atkinson and Silverman (1997) reject the postmodern notion of "polyphonic voices," correctly noting that interviewer and respondent collaborate together to create an essentially monologic view of reality. This same rejection could be made using Schutz's (1967) argument—that is, "I" and "thou" create a unified "we," not two separate versions of it.

Ethnomethodologically informed interviewing is not, however, immune from criticism itself. Schutz assumes a reciprocity of perspective that may not exist. Granted, in our interview society we all know the common-sense routines and ground rules of interviewing, but in other societies this may not be the case. Isabel Bowler (1997) attempted to interview Pakistani women about their experience with maternity services and found a total lack of understanding of the value of social research and interviewing: "I had told them that I was writing a book on my findings. Yams, who spoke the better English, translated this with a look of disbelief on her face, and then they both dissolved into laughter. The hospitals were very good. There weren't any problems. All was well" (p. 72). Bowler was forced to conclude that interviewing may not work where there is no "shared notion of the process of research" (p. 66).

Silverman (1993) envisions a different problem. He seems to feel that some ethnomethodologists have suspended their interest in substantive concerns of everyday life, claiming that they cannot address them until they know more about the ways (methods) in which these realities are accomplished. He notes, "Put simply, according to one reading of Cicourel, we would focus on the conversational skills of the participants rather than on the content of what they are saying and its relation to the world outside the interview" (p. 98).

Cicourel (1970) states that sociologists need to outline a workable model of the actor before engaging in the study of self and society. Garfinkel held similar beliefs. For instance, in his famous study of a transsexual, Agnes, Garfinkel (1967) was examining the routines by which societal members pass as males or females; he had little or no interest in issues of transsexuality per se. Thus it would follow that, according to Silverman's reading of ethnomethodology, we should learn the conversational methods before attempting to learn substantive matters in interviewing.

Future Directions

To borrow from Gubrium and Holstein (1997): "Where do we go from here?" (p. 97). We share with these two authors a concern with appreciating the new horizons of postmodernism while simultaneously remaining conservatively committed to the empirical description of everyday life. Gubrium and Holstein (1998) introduce a technique they call "analytic bracketing" to deal with the multiple levels of interviewing (and ethnography):

> We may focus, for example, on *how* a story is being told, while temporarily deferring our concern for the various *whats* that are involved—for example, the substance, structure, or plot of the story, the context within which it is told, or the audience to which it is accountable. We can later return to these issues. (p. 165)

The use of this analytic bracketing allows the authors to analyze interviewing in its coherence and diversity as an event collaboratively achieved, in which product and process are mutually constituted.

A pressing problem in interviewing concerns the kinds of standards we should apply to these new and different types of interviews. To assume absolute relativism is not the solution, for it would lead, in Silverman's (1997b) words, to the "sociology of navel-gazing" (p. 240). Silverman proposes an aesthetics for research; he rejects attempts to use literary forms in sociology: "If I want to read a good poem, why on earth should I turn to a social science journal?" (p. 240). Silverman's critique of inter-actionist sociology and proposal for aesthetic values seems to focus on the following three points: (a) He attacks the grandiose, political theorizing of British sociology and invokes a return to more modest, more minute goals; (b) he rejects the romanticist notion of equating experience (from the members' viewpoint) with authenticity; and (c) he notes that in sociology we mimic the mass media of the interview society, thus succumbing to the trivial, the kitschy, the gossipy, and the melodramatic and ignoring sim-plicity and profundity.

Silverman's notion that we should pay attention to minute details in sociological studies, rather than embarking on grandiose, abstract proj-ects, in a way is not dissimilar to Lyotard's appeal for a return to local ele-ments and away from metatheorizing. For Silverman, the "minute" are the small details that go on in front of our eyes in our everyday lives—very similar to Garfinkel's mundane routines, which allow us to sustain the world and interact with each other.

We are in agreement with Silverman that we need to stop deluding our-selves that in our particular method (whichever it may be) we have the key to the understanding of the self. We also agree that it is imperative that we look for new standards, as we are quickly digressing into a new form of the theater of the absurd (without the literary flair, we fear). But we cannot wait to find a model of the methods used by participants in interviews or in everyday life before we proceed; Cicourel's (1970) invariant properties of interaction turned out to be so general as to be of little use to sociological inquiry.

We need to proceed by looking at the substantive concerns of the mem-bers of society while simultaneously examining the constructive activities used to produce order in everyday life, and, all along, remaining reflexive about how interviews are accomplished (see Gubrium & Holstein, 1997, 1998). For instance, as Carolyn Baker (1997) points out, a researcher's telling a respondent "I am a mother of three" versus telling her "I am a university professor" accesses different categories and elicits different accounts. We need to move on with sociological inquiry, even though we realize conditions are less than perfect. To paraphrase Robert Solow, as cited by Geertz (1973): Just because complete asepsis is impossible it doesn't mean we may just as well perform surgery in a sewer.

A different kind of future direction for interviewing stems largely from the new feminist interviewing practices. Traditional interview has painstakingly attempted to maintain neutrality and achieve objectivity, and has kept the role of the interviewer as invisible as possible. Feminists, instead, are rebelling at the practice of *exploiting* respondents and wish to use interviewing for ameliorative purposes. To wit: "As researchers with a commitment to change, we must decenter ourselves from the 'ivory tower' and construct more participatory, democratic practices. *We must keep people and politics at the center of our research*" (Benmayor, 1991, pp. 172-173; emphasis added). Denzin (1989a) refers to this approach as the "feminist, communitarian ethical model" (see also Lincoln, 1995) and tells us:

> The feminist, communitarian researcher does not invade the privacy of others, use informed consent forms, select subjects randomly, or measure research designs in term of their validity. This framework presumes a researcher who builds collaborative, reciprocal, trusting, and friendly relations with those studied. . . . It is also understood that those studied have claims of ownership over any material that are produced in the research process, including field notes.

Combining the roles of the scholar and the feminist may be problematic and, at times, may lead to conflict if the researcher has a different political orientation than that of the people studied (Wasserfall, 1993), but this approach may also be very rewarding in allowing the researcher to see positive results stemming from the research (see Gluck, 1991).

Electronic Interviewing

Another direction currently being taken in interviewing is related to the changing technologies available. The reliance on the interview as a means of information gathering has most recently expanded to electronic outlets, with questionnaires being administered via fax, electronic mail, and Web site. Estimates suggest that nearly 50% of all households have computers, and nearly half of these utilize the Internet. Software is now available that allows researchers to schedule and archive interview data gathered via chat-room interviews. The limited population of potential respondents with access to computers makes general-population surveys infeasible, but electronic interviewing can reach 100% of some specialized populations (Schaefer & Dillman, 1998).

It is now possible to engage in "virtual interviewing," in which Internet connections are used synchronously or asynchronously to obtain information. The advantages include low cost, as the result of no telephone or interviewer charges, and speed of return. Of course, face-to-face interaction is eliminated, as is the possibility, for both interviewer and respondent, of reading nonverbal behavior or of cuing from gender, race, age, class, and other personal characteristics. Thus, establishing an interviewer-interviewee "relationship" and "living the moment" while gathering information (Hertz, 1997a) is difficult, if not impossible. Internet surveys make it easy for respondents to manufacture fictional social realities without anyone knowing the difference (Markham, 1998). Of course, interviewers can also deceive respondents by claiming experiences or characteristics they do not have in hopes of establishing better rapport. They can feign responses for the same purpose by claiming "false nonverbals," such as telling respondents that they "laughed" or "were pained" by particular comments. Markham (1998), in her autoethnography of Internet interviewing, reports that electronic interviews take longer than their traditional counterparts and that responses are more cryptic and less in depth, but the interviewer has more time to phrase follow-up questions or probes properly.

It is also virtually impossible to preserve anonymity in Internet e-mail surveys, but chat rooms and similar sites do permit the use of pseudonyms. Although electronic interviews are currently used primarily for quantitative research and usually employ structured questionnaires, it is only a matter of time before researchers adapt these techniques to qualitative work, just as they have adapted electronic techniques of data analysis. For example, Markham immersed herself in the process of engaging with various electronic or Internet formats (i.e., chat rooms, listservs) to interview other participants and to document her journey in the virtual world, learning the experience of cyberspace and the meaning participants attached to their on-line lifestyles. She asks an intriguing question: "Can I have a self where my body does not exist?" (p. 8).

The future may see considerable ethnography by means of computer-mediated communication, where virtual space rather than a living room or a workplace is the setting of the interview. It remains to be seen whether electronic interviewing will allow researchers to obtain "thick descriptions" or accounts of subjective experiences, and whether such interviewing will provide the "process context" so important to qualitative interviews. In addition, researchers conducting such interviewing can never be sure they are receiving answers from desired or eligible respondents. Interviewing via the Internet is so prominent today that researchers are studying its effects on response quality. Schaefer and Dillman (1998), for example, found that e-mail surveys achieved similar response rates to mail surveys but yielded better-quality data in terms of item completion and more detailed responses to open-ended questions.

There are clearly many unanswered questions and problems related to the use of electronic interviewing. This mode of interviewing will obviously increase in the forthcoming millennium, as people rely increasingly on electronic modes of communication. But just how much Internet communication will displace face-to-face interviewing is a matter that only time will tell.

◆ Conclusion

In this chapter we have examined the interview, from structured types to interview as negotiated text. We have outlined the history of interviewing, with its qualitative and quantitative origins. We have looked at structured, group, and various types of unstructured interviewing. We have examined the importance of gender in interviewing and the ways in which framing and interpreting affect interviews. We have examined the importance of ethics in interviewing, and, finally we have discussed the latest trends in interviewing.

We have included discussion of the whole gamut of interviews, despite the fact that this book is concerned with qualitative research, because we believe that researchers must be cognizant of all the various types of interviews if they are to gain a clear understanding of interviewing. Clearly, certain types of interviewing are better suited to particular kinds of situations, and researchers *must be aware of the implications, pitfalls, and problems of the types of interviews they choose.* If we wish to find out how many people oppose the establishment of a nuclear repository in their area, a structured type of interview, such as that used in survey research, is the best tool; we can quantify and code the responses and use mathematical models to explain our findings. If we are interested in opinions about a given product, a focus group interview will provide us with the most efficient results, whereas if we wish to know about the lives of Palestinian women in the resistance (Gluck, 1991), we need to interview them at length and in depth in an unstructured way. In the first example used above, and perhaps in the second, we can speak in the formal language of scientific rigor and verifiability of findings; in the third example we can speak of understanding a negotiated way of life.

More scholars are realizing that to pit one type of interviewing against another is futile, a leftover from the paradigmatic quantitative/qualitative hostility of past generations. Thus an increasing number of researchers are using multimethod approaches to achieve broader and often better results. This multimethod approach, referred to as *triangulation* (Denzin, 1989b; Flick, 1998), allows researchers to use different methods in different combinations. For instance, group interviewing has long been used to complement survey research and is now being used to complement participant observation (Morgan, 1988). Human beings are complex, and their lives are ever changing; the more methods we use to study them, the better our chances to gain some understanding of how they construct their lives and the stories they tell us about them.

The brief journey we have taken through the world of interviewing should allow us to be better informed and perhaps more sensitized to the problematics of asking questions for sociological reasons. We must remember that each individual has his or her own social history and an individual perspective on the world. Thus we cannot take our task for granted. As Oakley (1981) notes, "Interviewing is rather like a marriage: everybody knows what it is, an awful lot of people do it, and yet behind each closed front door there is a world of secrets" (p. 41). She is quite correct— we all think we know how to ask questions and talk to people, from common, everyday folks to highly qualified quantophrenic experts. Yet to learn about people we must treat them as people, and they will work with us to help us create accounts of their lives. As long as many researchers continue to treat respondents as unimportant, faceless individuals whose only contribution is to fill one more boxed response, the answers we, as researchers, get will be commensurable with the questions we ask and the ways we ask them. We are no different from Gertrude Stein, who, on her deathbed, asked her lifelong companion, Alice B. Toklas, "What is the answer?" And when Alice could not bring herself to speak, Gertrude asked, "In that case, what is the question?"

◆ References

Adams, R. N., & Preiss, J. J. (Eds.). (1960). *Human organizational research: Field relations and techniques.* Homewood, IL: Dorsey.

Anderson, N. (1923). *The hobo: The sociology of the homeless man.* Chicago: University of Chicago Press.

Atkinson, P., & Silverman, D. (1997). Kundera's *Immortality*: The interview society and the invention of self. *Qualitative Inquiry, 3,* 304-325.

Babbie, E. (1992). *The practice of social research* (6th ed.). Belmont, CA: Wadsworth.

Baker, C. (1997). Membership categorization and interview accounts. In D. Silverman (Ed.), *Qualitative research: Theory, method and practice* (pp. 130-143). London: Sage.

Becker, H. S. (1956). Interviewing medical students. *American Journal of Sociology, 62,* 199-201.

Becker, H. S. (1999). The Chicago school, so-called. *Qualitative Sociology, 22,* 3-12.

Behar, R. (1996). *The vulnerable observer: Anthropology that breaks your heart.* Boston: Beacon.

Benmayor, R. (1991). Testimony, action research, and empowerment: Puerto Rican women and popular education. In S. B. Gluck & D. Patai (Eds.), *Women's words: The feminist practice of oral history* (pp. 159-174). New York: Routledge.

Boelen, W. A. M. (1992). *Street corner society*: Cornerville revisited. *Journal of Contemporary Ethnography, 21,* 11-51.

Bogardus, E. S. (1926). The group interview. *Journal of Applied Sociology, 10,* 372-382.

Booth, C. (1902-1903). *Life and labour of the people in London.* London: Macmillan.

Bowler, I. (1997). Problems with interviewing: Experiences with service providers and clients. In G. Miller & R. Dingwall (Eds.), *Context and method in qualitative research* (pp. 66-76). Thousand Oaks, CA: Sage.

Bradburn, N. M. (1983). Response effects. In P. H. Rossi, J. D. Wright, & A. B. Anderson (Eds.), *Handbook of survey research* (pp. 289-328). New York: Academic Press.

Bradburn, N. M., Sudman, S., & Associates. (1979). *Improving interview method and questionnaire design.* San Francisco: Jossey-Bass.

Cicourel, A. (1964). *Method and measurement in sociology.* New York: Free Press.

Cicourel, A. (1970). The acquisition of social structure: Toward a developmental sociology of language and meaning. In J. D. Douglas (Ed.), *Understanding everyday life: Toward a reconstruction of social knowledge* (pp. 136-168). Chicago: Aldine.

Cicourel, A. (1974). *Theory and method in a study of Argentine fertility.* New York: John Wiley.

Clough, P. T. (1998). *The end(s) of ethnography: From realism to social criticism* (2nd ed.). New York: Peter Lang.

Collins, P. H. (1990). *Black feminist thought: Knowledge, consciousness, and the politics of empowerment.* New York: Routledge, Chapman & Hall.

Converse, J. M. (1987). *Survey research in the United States: Roots and emergence 1890-1960.* Berkeley: University of California Press.

Converse, J. M., & Schuman, H. (1974). *Conversations at random: Survey research as interviewers see it.* New York: John Wiley.

Crapanzano, V. (1980). *Tuhami: Portrait of a Moroccan.* Chicago: University of Chicago Press.

Denzin, N. K. (1989a). *Interpretive interactionism.* Newbury Park, CA: Sage.

Denzin, N. K. (1989b). *The research act: A theoretical introduction to sociological methods* (3rd ed.). Englewood Cliffs, NJ: Prentice Hall.

Derrida, J. (1976). *Of grammatology* (G. C. Spivak, Trans.). Baltimore: Johns Hopkins University Press.

Desvousges, W. H., & Frey, J. H. (1989). Integrating focus groups and surveys: Examples from environmental risk surveys. *Journal of Official Statistics, 5,* 349-363.

Dingwall, R. (1997). Accounts, interviews, and observations. In G. Miller & R. Dingwall (Eds.), *Context and method in qualitative research* (pp. 51-65). Thousand Oaks, CA: Sage.

Douglas, J. D. (1985). *Creative interviewing.* Beverly Hills, CA: Sage.

Douglas, J. D., & Johnson, J. M. (1977). *Existential sociology.* Cambridge: Cambridge University Press.

Douglas, J. D., & Rasmussen, P. (with Flanagan, C. A.). (1977). *The nude beach.* Beverly Hills, CA: Sage.

Du Bois, W. E. B. (1899). *The Philadelphia Negro: A social study.* Philadelphia: Ginn.

Ellis, C. (1991). Sociological introspection and emotional experience. *Symbolic Interaction, 14,* 23-50.

Ellis, C. (1995). *Final negotiations: A story of love, loss, and chronic illness.* Philadelphia: Temple University Press.

Erikson, K. T. (1967). A comment on disguised observation in sociology. *Social Problems, 14,* 366-373.

Fine, M. (1983-1984). Coping with rape: Critical perspectives on consciousness. *Imagination, Cognition and Personality, 3,* 249-267.

Flick, U. (1998). *An introduction to qualitative research: Theory, method and applications.* London: Sage.

Fontana, A. (1977). *The last frontier: The social meaning of growing old.* Beverly Hills, CA: Sage.

Fontana, A., & Frey, J. H. (1990). Postretirement workers in the labor force. *Work and Occupations, 17,* 355-361.

Fontana, A., & Smith, R. (1989). Alzheimer's disease victims: The "unbecoming" of self and the normalization of competence. *Sociological Perspectives, 32,* 35-46.

Freeman, D. (1983). *Margaret Mead and Samoa: The making and unmaking of an anthropological myth.* Cambridge, MA: Harvard University Press.

Frey, J. H. (1989). *Survey research by telephone* (2nd ed.). Newbury Park, CA: Sage.

Frey, J. H. (1993). Risk perception associated with a high-level nuclear waste repository. *Sociological Spectrum, 13,* 139-151.

Frey, J. H., & Fontana, A. (1991). The group interview in social research. *Social Science Journal, 28,* 175-187.

Garfinkel, H. (1967). *Studies in ethnomethodology.* Englewood Cliffs, NJ: Prentice Hall.

Geertz, C. (1973). Thick description: Toward an interpretive theory of culture. In C. Geertz, *The interpretation of cultures: Selected essays* (pp. 3-30). New York: Basic Books.

Glaser, B. G., & Strauss, A. L. (1967). *The discovery of grounded theory: Strategies for qualitative research.* Chicago: Aldine.

Gluck, S. B. (1984). What's so special about women: Women's oral history. In D. Dunaway & W. K. Baum (Eds.), *Oral history: An interdisciplinary anthology* (pp. 221-237). Nashville, TN: American Association for State and Local History.

Gluck, S. B. (1991). Advocacy oral history: Palestinian women in resistance. In S. B. Gluck & D. Patai (Eds.), *Women's words: The feminist practice of oral history* (pp. 205-220). New York: Routledge.

Gluck, S. B., & Patai, D. (Eds.). (1991). *Women's words: The feminist practice of oral history.* New York: Routledge.

Gorden, R. L. (1980). *Interviewing: Strategy, techniques, and tactics.* Homewood, IL: Dorsey.

Gorden, R. L. (1992). *Basic interviewing skills.* Itasca, IL: F. E. Peacock.

Gubrium, J. F., & Holstein, J. A. (1997). *The new language of qualitative method.* New York: Oxford University Press.

Gubrium, J. F., & Holstein, J. A. (1998). Narrative practice and the coherence of personal stories. *Sociological Quarterly, 39,* 163-187.

Harvey, L. (1987). *Myths of the Chicago school of sociology.* Aldershot, England: Avebury.

Hertz, R. (1995). Separate but simultaneous interviewing of husbands and wives: Making sense of their stories. *Qualitative Inquiry, 1,* 429-451.

Hertz, R. (1997a). Introduction: Reflexivity and voice. In R. Hertz (Ed.), *Reflexivity and voice.* Thousand Oaks, CA: Sage.

Hertz, R. (Ed.). (1997b). *Reflexivity and voice.* Thousand Oaks, CA: Sage.

Hertz, R. (1997c). A typology of approaches to child care: The centerpiece of organizing family life for dual-earner couples. *Journal of Family Issues, 18,* 355-385.

Hertz, R., & Ferguson, F. (1997). Kinship strategies and self-sufficiency among single mothers by choice: Postmodern family ties. *Qualitative Sociology, 20*(2), 13-37.

Holstein, J. A., & Gubrium, J. F. (1995). *The active interview.* Thousand Oaks, CA: Sage.

Holstein, J. A., & Gubrium, J. F. (1997). Active interviewing. In D. Silverman (Ed.), *Qualitative research: Theory, method and practice* (pp. 113-129). London: Sage.

Humphreys, L. (1970). *Tearoom trade: Impersonal sex in public places.* Chicago: Aldine.

Hyman, H. H. (1954). *Interviewing in social research.* Chicago: University of Chicago Press.

Johnson, J. (1976). *Doing field research.* New York: Free Press.

Kahn, R., & Cannell, C. F. (1957). *The dynamics of interviewing.* New York: John Wiley.

Kotarba, J. A., & Fontana, A. (Eds.). (1984). *The existential self in society.* Chicago: University of Chicago Press.

Krieger, S. (1983). *The mirror dance: Identity in a women's community.* Philadelphia: Temple University Press.

Kvale, S. (1996). *InterViews: An introduction to qualitative research interviewing.* Thousand Oaks, CA: Sage.

Lincoln, Y. S. (1995). The sixth moment: Emerging problems in qualitative research. In N. K. Denzin (Ed.), *Studies in symbolic interaction: A research annual* (Vol. 19, pp. 37-55). Greenwich, CT: JAI.

Lofland, J. (1971). *Analyzing social settings.* Belmont, CA: Wadsworth.

Lofland, J., & Lofland, L. H. (1984). *Analyzing social settings: A guide to qualitative observation and analysis* (2nd ed.). Belmont, CA: Wadsworth.

Lopata, H. Z. (1980). Interviewing American widows. In W. Shaffir, R. Stebbins, & A. Turowetz (Eds.), *Fieldwork experience: Qualitative approaches to social research* (pp. 68-81). New York: St. Martin's.

Lynd, R. S., & Lynd, H. M. (1929). *Middletown: A study in American culture.* New York: Harcourt, Brace.

Lynd, R. S., & Lynd, H. M. (1937). *Middletown in transition: A study in cultural conflicts.* New York: Harcourt, Brace.

Maccoby, E. E., & Maccoby, N. (1954). The interview: A tool of social science. In G. Lindzey (Ed.), *Handbook of social psychology: Vol. 1. Theory and method* (pp. 449-487). Reading, MA: Addison-Wesley.

Malinowski, B. (1922). *Argonauts of the western Pacific.* New York: E. P. Dutton.

Malinowski, B. (1989). *A diary in the strict sense of the term.* Stanford, CA: Stanford University Press. (Original work published 1967)

Marcus, G. E., & Fischer, M. M. J. (1986). *Anthropology as cultural critique: An experimental moment in the human sciences.* Chicago: University of Chicago Press.

Markham, A. N. (1998). *Life online: Researching real experience in virtual space.* Walnut Creek, CA: AltaMira.

Merton, R. K., Fiske, M., & Kendall, P. L. (1956). *The focused interview.* Glencoe, IL: Free Press.

Merton, R. K., & Lazarsfeld, P. F. (Eds.). (1950). *Continuities in social research: Studies in the scope and method of "The American soldier."* Glencoe, IL: Free Press.

Miller, M. (1974). *Plain speaking: An oral biography of Harry S Truman.* New York: Putnam.

Mishler, E. G. (1986). *Research interviewing: Context and narrative.* Cambridge, MA: Harvard University Press.

Morgan, D. (1988). *Focus groups as qualitative research.* Newbury Park, CA: Sage.

Morgan, D., & Spanish, M. T. (1984). Focus groups: A new tool for qualitative research. *Qualitative Sociology, 7,* 253-270.

Oakley, A. (1981). Interviewing women: A contradiction in terms. In H. Roberts (Ed.), *Doing feminist research* (pp. 30-61). London: Routledge & Kegan Paul.

Obbo, C. (1997). What do women know? . . . As I was saying! In K. M. Vaz (Ed.), *Oral narrative research with black women* (pp. 41-63). Thousand Oaks, CA: Sage.

Parten, M. (1950). *Surveys, polls, and samples.* New York: Harper.

Payne, S. L. (1951). *The art of asking questions.* Princeton, NJ: Princeton University Press.

Pool, I. de S. (1957). A critique of the twentieth anniversary issue. *Public Opinion Quarterly, 21,* 190-198.

Punch, M. (1986). *The politics and ethics of fieldwork.* Newbury Park, CA: Sage.

Rabinow, P. (1977). *Reflections on fieldwork in Morocco.* Berkeley: University of California Press.

Rasmussen, P. (1989). *Massage parlor prostitution.* New York: Irvington.

Reinharz, S. (1992). *Feminist methods in social research.* New York: Oxford University Press.

Richardson, L. (1992a). The poetic representation of lives: Writing a postmodern sociology. In N. K. Denzin (Ed.), *Studies in symbolic interaction: A research annual* (Vol. 13, pp. 19-28). Greenwich, CT: JAI.

Richardson, L. (1992b). Trash on the corner: Ethics and technography. *Journal of Contemporary Ethnography, 21,* 103-119.

Sarup, M. (1996). *Identity, culture and the postmodern world.* Athens: University of Georgia Press.

Schaefer, D. R., & Dillman, D. A. (1998). Development of a standard e-mail methodology. *Public Opinion Quarterly, 62,* 378-397.

Scheurich, J. J. (1997). *Research method in the postmodern.* London: Falmer.

Schutz, A. (1967). *The phenomenology of the social world.* Evanston, IL: Northwestern University Press.

Schwandt, T. A. (1997). *Qualitative inquiry: A dictionary of terms.* Thousand Oaks, CA: Sage.

Schwartz, B. (Ed.). (1996). Collective memory [Special issue]. *Qualitative Sociology, 19*(3).

Schwartz, B. (1999). Memory and the practice of commitment. In B. Glassner & R. Hertz (Eds.), *Qualitative sociology as everyday life.* Thousand Oaks, CA: Sage.

Seidman, I. E. (1991). *Interviewing as qualitative research.* New York: Teachers College Press.

Selltiz, C., Jahoda, M., Deutsch, M., & Cook, S. W. (1965). *Research methods in social relations.* London: Methuen.

Silverman, D. (1993). *Interpreting qualitative data: Strategies for analysing talk, text and interaction.* London: Sage.

Silverman, D. (Ed.). (1997a). *Qualitative research: Theory, method and practice.* London: Sage.

Silverman, D. (1997b). Towards an aesthetics of research. In D. Silverman (Ed.), *Qualitative research: Theory, method and practice* (pp. 239-253). London: Sage.

Singer, E., Frankel, M., & Glassman, M. B. (1983). The effect of interviewer characteristics and expectations on response. *Public Opinion Quarterly, 47,* 68-83.

Singer, E., & Presser, S. (1989). *Survey research methods.* Chicago: University of Chicago Press.

Smith, D. E. (1987). *The everyday world as problematic: A feminist sociology.* Boston: Northeastern University Press.

Spradley, J. P. (1979). *The ethnographic interview.* New York: Holt, Rinehart & Winston.

Spradley, J. P. (1980). *Participant observation.* New York: Holt, Rinehart & Winston.

Starr, L. (1984). Oral history. In D. Dunaway & W. K. Baum (Eds.), *Oral history: An interdisciplinary anthology* (pp. 3-26). Nashville, TN: American Association for State and Local History.

Stewart, D., & Shamdasani, P. (1990). *Focus groups: Theory and practice.* Newbury Park, CA: Sage.

Sudarkasa, N. (1986). In a world of women: Field work in a Yoruba community. In P. Golde (Ed.), *Women in the field: Anthropological experiences* (pp. 167-191). Berkeley: University of California Press.

Terkel, S. (1975). *Working*. New York: Avon.

Thompson, H. (1985). *Hell's Angels*. New York: Ballantine.

Thompson, J., & Demerath, M. J. (1952). Some experiences with the group interview. *Social Forces, 31,* 148-154.

Thrasher, F. M. (1963). *The gang: A study of 1,313 gangs in Chicago*. Chicago: University of Chicago Press. (Original work published 1927)

Ulmer, G. (1989). *Teletheory: Grammatology in an age of video*. New York: Routledge.

Van Maanen, J. (1988). *Tales of the field: On writing ethnography*. Chicago: University of Chicago Press.

Vaz, K. M. (Ed.). (1997). *Oral narrative research with black women*. Thousand Oaks, CA: Sage.

Warren, C. A. B. (1988). *Gender issues in field research*. Newbury Park, CA: Sage.

Warwick, D. P. (1973). Tearoom trade: Means and ends in social research. *Hastings Center Studies, 1,* 27-38.

Wasserfall, R. (1993). Reflexivity, feminism and difference. *Qualitative Sociology, 16,* 23-41.

Wax, R. (1960). Twelve years later: An analysis of field experiences. In R. N. Adams & J. J. Preiss (Eds.), *Human organizational research: Field relations and techniques* (pp. 166-178). Homewood, IL: Dorsey.

Weston, K. (1998). *Long slow burn: Sexuality and social science*. New York: Routledge.

Whyte, W. F. (1943). *Street corner society: The social structure of an Italian slum*. Chicago: University of Chicago Press.

Yeandle, S. (1984). *Women's working lives: Patterns and strategies*. New York: Tavistock.

Young, P. (1966). *Scientific social surveys and research* (4th ed.). Englewood Cliffs, NJ: Prentice Hall.

Zuckerman, H. (1972). Interviewing an ultra-elite. *Public Opinion, 36,* 159-175.

3

Rethinking Observation

From Method to Context

Michael V. Angrosino and

Kimberly A. Mays de Pérez

◆ Observation: Basic Assumptions

Observation has been characterized as "the fundamental base of all research methods" in the social and behavioral sciences (Adler & Adler, 1994, p. 389) and as "the mainstay of the ethnographic enterprise" (Werner & Schoepfle, 1987, p. 257). Even studies based on direct interviews employ observational techniques to note body language and other gestural cues that lend meaning to the words of the persons being interviewed. Social scientists are observers both of human activities and of the physical settings in which such activities take place. Some such observation may take place in a lab or clinic, in which case the activity may be the result of a controlled experiment. On the other hand, it is also possible to conduct observations in settings that are the "natural" loci of those activities. Some scholars have criticized the very concept of the "natural" setting,

AUTHORS' NOTE: We thank Alvin W. Wolfe and Kathryn Borman for sharing their insights and experiences with us during the preparation of this chapter. We also gratefully acknowledge the advice and constructive criticism of Arthur Bochner, Norman Denzin, Yvonna Lincoln, and Barbara Tedlock.

particularly when fieldwork is conducted in Third World locations (or in domestic inner-city sites) that are the products of inherently "unnatural" colonial relationships (Gupta & Ferguson, 1996c, p. 6), but the designation is still prevalent throughout the literature. In that case, it is proper to speak of "naturalistic observation," or fieldwork, which is the focus of this chapter.

Observations in natural settings can be rendered as descriptions either through open-ended narrative or through the use of published checklists or field guides (Rossman & Rallis, 1998, p. 137; see Stocking, 1983a, for a historical overview of this dichotomy). In either case, it has generally been assumed that naturalistic observation does not interfere with the people or activities under observation. Most social scientists have long recognized the possibility of the observer's affecting what he or she observes, but careful researchers are nonetheless supposed to adhere to rigorous standards of objective reporting designed to overcome that potential bias. Even cultural anthropologists, who have usually thought of themselves as "participant observers" and who have deliberately set out to achieve a degree of subjective immersion in the cultures they study (Cole, 1983, p. 50; Wolcott, 1995, p. 66), still claim to be able to maintain their scientific objectivity. Failure to do so would mean that they had "gone native," with their work consequently rendered suspect as scientific data (Pelto & Pelto, 1978, p. 69). The achievement of the delicate balance between participation and observation remains the ideal of anthropologists (Stocking, 1983b, p. 8), even though it is no longer "fetishized" (Gupta & Ferguson, 1996c, p. 37). Objectivity remains central to the self-images of most practitioners of the social and behavioral *sciences*. Objective rigor has most often been associated with quantitative research methods, and so important has been the harmonization of empathy and detachment that even those dedicated to qualitative methods have devoted considerable effort to organizing their observational data in the most nearly objective form (i.e., the form that looks most quantitative) for analysis (see, e.g., Altheide & Johnson, 1994; Bernard, 1988; Miles & Huberman, 1994; Silverman, 1993).

Adler and Adler (1994) have, in fact, suggested that in the future, observational research will be found as "part of a methodological spectrum," but that in that spectrum, it will serve as "the most powerful source of validation" (p. 389). Observation, they claim, rests on "something researchers can find constant," by which they mean "their own direct knowledge and their own judgment" (p. 389). In social science research, as in legal cases,

eyewitness testimony from trustworthy observers has been seen as a particularly convincing form of verification (Pelto & Pelto, 1978, p. 69). In
actuality, the production of a convincing narrative report of the research
has most often served as de facto validation, even if the only thing it validates is the ethnographer's writing skill and not his or her observational
capacities (Kuklick, 1996, p. 60).

Whatever else may be said about the postmodernist turn in contemporary studies of society and culture, its critique of assumptions about the
objectivity of science and its presumed authoritative voice has raised issues
that all qualitative researchers need to address.[1] Earlier criticism might
have been directed at particular researchers, with the question being
whether they had lived up to the expected standards of objective scholarship. In the postmodernist milieu, by contrast, the criticism is directed at
the standards themselves. In effect, it is now possible to question whether
observational objectivity is either desirable or feasible as a goal. James
Clifford (1983a), who has written extensively and critically about the
study of culture and society, has called into question even the work of the
revered Bronislaw Malinowski, the archetype of the scientific participant
observer, who, according to Stocking (1983a), is the scholar most directly
responsible for the "shift in the conception of the ethnographer's role,
from that of inquirer to that of participant 'in a way' in village life" (p. 93).
Perhaps more surprisingly, Clifford has also questioned the research of the
very influential contemporary interpretivist Clifford Geertz; he takes
Geertz to task for suggesting that through empathy, the ethnographer can
describe a culture in terms of the meanings specific to members of that culture. In other words, the ethnographer, as a distinct person, disappears—
just as he or she was supposed to do in Malinowski's more openly
positivistic world. This assessment is echoed by Sewell (1997), who points
out that Geertz did not expect field-workers to "achieve some miracle of
empathy with the people whose lives they briefly and incompletely share;
they acquire no preternatural capacity to think, feel, and perceive like a
native" (p. 40). The problem is not that Geertz failed to achieve some sort
of idealized empathic state; rather, the question is whether such a state is
even relevant to ethnographic research, and whether it is desirable to
describe and/or interpret cultures as if those depictions could exist without the ethnographer's being part of the action.

The postmodernist critique, which emphasizes the importance of understanding the ethnographer's "situation" (e.g., his or her gender, class,
ethnicity) as part of interpreting the ethnographic product, is particularly

salient because the remote, traditional folk societies that were the anthropologists' stock-in-trade have virtually disappeared; most cultural anthropology is now carried out in literate societies that are part of global
communication and transportation networks. Like sociologists, anthropologists now "study up" (i.e., conduct research among elites) almost as
often as they study the poor and the marginalized. Doing so overcomes
some of the problems associated with the lingering colonialist bias of traditional ethnography (D. L. Wolf, 1996, p. 37), but it raises new issues
regarding the position and status of the observational researcher. For one
thing, ethnographers can no longer claim to be the sole arbiters of knowledge about the societies and cultures they study, because they are in a position to have their analyses read and contested by those for whom they presume to speak (Bell & Jankowiak, 1992; Larcom, 1983, p. 191). In effect,
objective truth about a society or a culture cannot be established, because
there are inevitably going to be conflicting versions of what happened.
Sociologists and other social scientists were working in such settings long
before the anthropologists came on the scene, and were already beginning
to be aware of the problems inherent in claiming the privilege of objective,
authoritative knowledge when there are all too many "natives" ready and
able to challenge them. As Margery Wolf (1992) wryly comments: "We
can no longer assume that an isolated village will not within an amazingly
short period of time move into the circuit of rapid social and economic
change. A barefoot village kid who used to trail along after you *will* one
day show up on your doorstep with an Oxford degree and your book in
hand" (p. 137). The validity of the traditional assumption, that the truth
can be established through careful cross-checking of ethnographers' and
insiders' reports, is no longer universally granted, as contemporary social
and behavioral scientists are increasingly inclined to expect differences in
testimony grounded in gender, class, ethnicity, and other factors that are
not easy to mix into a consensus. Ethnographic truth has come to be seen
as a thing of many parts, and no one perspective can claim exclusive privilege in the representation thereof. Indeed, the result of ethnographic research "is never reducible to a form of knowledge that can be packaged in
the monologic voice of the ethnographer alone" (Marcus, 1997, p. 92).

Some ethnographers (of various disciplines) have responded to this
new situation by revising the ways in which they conduct observation-
based research and present their analyses. No longer can it be taken for
granted that ethnographers operate at a distance from their subjects.
Indeed, the very term *subject,* with its implicit colonialist connotations, is

no longer appropriate. Rather, there is said to be a *dialogue* between researchers and those whose cultures/societies are to be described.[2] Discussions of ethnographers' own interactions, relationships, and emotional states while in the field have as a result been moved from their traditional discreet place in acknowledgments or forewords to the centers of the ethnographies themselves. Although this practice has certainly opened up new horizons in ethnographic reportage, it raises further issues of its own. For example, because it is likely to be the ethnographers who write up (or at least collate or edit) the results of the field studies, do they not continue to claim the implicit status of arbiters/mediators of social/cultural knowledge (Wolf, 1992, p. 120)? Ethnographers may assert that they represent the many voices involved in the research, but we still have only their assurance that such is the case.

Nonetheless, we now function in a context of "collaborative" research. *Collaboration* no longer refers only to the conduct of multidisciplinary teams of professional researchers; it often means the presumably equal participation of professional researchers and their erstwhile "subjects" (Kuhlmann, 1992; D. L. Wolf, 1996, p. 26). Matsumoto (1996), for example, sent a prepared list of questions to the people she was interested in interviewing for an oral history project. She assured them all that any questions to which they objected would be eliminated. The potential respondents reacted favorably to this invitation to participate in the formulation of the research design. As such situations become more common, it is important that we rethink our received notions about "observation"— what it is, how it is done, what role it plays in the generation of ethnographic knowledge. To that end, it might be useful to shift from a concentration on observation as a "method" per se to a perspective that emphasizes observation as a context for interaction among those involved in the research collaboration.

◆ Observation: The Classic Tradition

As a prelude to an exploration of observation-as-context, we will briefly review the traditions of observation-as-method that form the basis of our exercise in "rethinking." Conscientious ethnographers have, in fact, long been aware that in naturalistic settings, the interaction of researcher and subjects of study can change behaviors in ways that would not have occurred in the absence of such interaction. They have believed, however, that it is both possible and desirable to develop standardized procedures that can "maximize observational efficacy, minimize investigator bias, and allow for replication and/or verification to check out the degree to which these procedures have enabled the investigator to produce valid, reliable data that, when incorporated into his or her published report, will be regarded by peers as objective findings" (Gold, 1997, p. 397). True objectivity has been held to be the result of agreement between participants and observers as to what is really going on in a given situation. Such agreement has been thought to be attained through the elicitation of feedback from those whose behaviors were being reported. Ethnography's "self-correcting investigative process" has typically included adequate and appropriate sampling procedures, systematic techniques for gathering and analyzing data, validation of data, avoidance of observer bias, and documentation of findings (Clifford, 1983b, p. 129; Gold, 1997, p. 399). The main difference between sociological and anthropological practitioners of ethnography seems to have been that the former have generally felt the need to validate their eyewitness accounts through other forms of documentation, whereas the latter have tended to use participant observation, "relatively unsystematized" though it may be, as the ultimate reality check on "all the other, more refined, research techniques" (Pelto & Pelto, 1978, p. 69).

The possibility of "observer bias" looms large in the thinking of both sociologists and anthropologists in the ethnographic tradition (Werner & Schoepfle, 1987, p. 259). Even setting aside the expected distortion of ethnocentrism (which can presumably be controlled for as long as the ethnographer is conscious of it), the plain fact is that each person who conducts observational research brings his or her distinctive talents and limitations to the enterprise; therefore, the quality of what is *recorded* becomes the measure of usable observational data (because it can be monitored and replicated) rather than the quality of the observation itself (which is, by definition, idiosyncratic and not subject to replication). Although theoretical or conceptual frames of analysis inevitably direct observers' observations, it was traditionally assumed that researchers could keep these in the background when recording basic observational data. For this reason, the emphasis was placed on observational *methods,* the basic theme of which was, as one important manual of field procedures puts it, "Primary reporting of concrete events and things in field work should proceed at as low a level of abstraction as possible" (Pelto & Pelto,

1978, p. 70). Theoretical analysis was therefore an epiphenomenon to the process of observation.

According to Gold (1958), the sociological ethnographers of the first half of the 20th century often made implicit reference to a typology of roles that might characterize naturalistic research: the complete partici-pant (a highly subjective stance whose scientific validity was suspect), the participant-as-observer (only slightly less problematic), the observer-as-participant, and the complete observer. The complete observer was one who was to all intents and purposes removed from the setting, and who functioned without interacting in any way with those being observed. Because of the difficulty of maintaining the purity of such a stance (Werner & Schoepfle, 1987, p. 259), and because such research was sometimes conducted without the informed consent of the observed (an ethical lapse that is no longer tolerated by responsible social researchers), the observer-as-participant role was considered an acceptable compromise, allowing the researcher to interact "casually and nondirectively" with subjects; the researcher remained a researcher, however, and did not cross over the line into friendship (Adler & Adler, 1994, p. 380). Perhaps the most important contemporary use of this role is in classroom observational studies con-ducted by educational researchers (Rossman & Rallis, 1998, p. 137).

Ethnographers trained in sociology are nowadays more inclined than were their predecessors to accept participation as a legitimate base from which to conduct observation. Adler and Adler (1987) have therefore pro-posed a modification of Gold's familiar typology in recognition of the increasing emphasis in contemporary ethnographic research on "member-ship roles" as opposed to roles grounded in pure observation. In other words, the older assumption that "participation" (which bothered sociol-ogists more than it did anthropologists) seriously compromises the valid-ity of observational data has given way to the realities of contemporary re-search, which is often conducted with a greater degree of researcher immersion (deliberate or otherwise) in the culture under study than was once considered desirable. Adler and Adler describe, for example, "peripheral-member researchers" as those who believe that they can develop a desirable insider's perspective without participating in those activities constituting the core of group membership. By contrast, "active-member researchers" are those who become involved with the central activities of the group, sometimes even assuming responsibilities that advance the group; they do not, however, necessarily fully commit them-selves to members' values and goals. A third category, that of "complete-member researchers," is composed of those who study settings in which they are already members or with which they become fully affiliated in the course of research. Even though practitioners in this category celebrate the "subjectively lived experience," they still strive to use their membership "so as not to alter the flow of interaction unnaturally" (Adler & Adler, 1994, p. 380).

Traditional anthropological ethnographers did not question the utility of participation or membership as a base for observation, but they often worried about the unsystematic nature of their observational methods. Werner and Schoepfle (1987, pp. 262-264) have addressed this concern by suggesting a typology of observation undertaken in naturalistic settings that focuses on process rather than on role. In this system, there are three types of observational process, representing increasingly deep understanding of the social group under study. First, there is "descriptive observation," which is, to all intents and purposes, the observation of everything. The ethnographer assumes a childlike attitude, assuming that he or she knows nothing about what is going on and taking nothing for granted. Such an approach quickly leads to a morass of "irrelevant minutiae," although it is only with increased exposure to the culture that the ethnographer begins to understand what is and is not irrelevant. At that point, he or she moves into "focused observation," in which certain things, defined as irrelevant, can be ignored. Focused observation necessarily entails interviewing, because the insights gleaned from the experience of "natives" guide the ethnographer in his or her decisions about what is more or less important in that culture. Focused observations usually concentrate on well-defined types of group activity (e.g., religious rituals, classroom instruction, political elections). Finally, and most systematically, there is "selective observation," in which the ethnographer concentrates on the attributes of different types of activities (e.g., apart from the obvious difference in content, what makes instructing a class in language arts different from instructing a class in social studies?)

◆ Rethinking Observation as Context of Interaction

Contemporary social research may be characterized by (a) the increasing willingness of ethnographers to affirm or develop a "membership" role in the communities they study, (b) the recognition of the possibility that it may be neither feasible nor possible to harmonize observer and "insider" perspectives so as to achieve a consensus about "ethnographic truth," and (c) the transformation of the erstwhile "subjects" of research into ethnographers' collaborative partners. The traditional concern with process and method has therefore been supplemented with (but by no means supplanted by) an interest in the ways in which ethnographic observers interact with or enter into a dialogic relationship with members of the group being studied. In this section, we discuss several selected works by contemporary ethnographers in order to illustrate these supplemental factors in the contemporary interactive context of observational research. We use five very general principles of social interaction to organize the following review of this otherwise quite disparate body of theoretical, methodological, and substantive literature.

The Conscious Adoption of a Situational Identity

The first principle is as follows: *The basis of social interaction is the decision (which may be spontaneous or part of a careful plan) to take part in a social setting rather than react passively to a position assigned by others.* In some of the older sociological literature, this process is referred to as "role making," as opposed to "role taking." In the context of this discussion, this principle animates those ethnographers who actively seek out situational identities based on "membership" rather than on "observation" as traditionally understood.

For example, Angrosino has conducted a long-term study of adults with mental retardation and/or chronic mental illness who are served by community-based agencies in the United States. The question at the heart of this research project concerned how these adults, who had been socialized as youths in large-scale institutions, adapted to life in the community in the wake of the move to deinstitutionalize all but the most seriously disturbed individuals. Answering such a question required an immersion into the lives of these people, because they would not likely respond adequately to questionnaires or clinical survey instruments. Angrosino also expressed a desire to understand what it might feel like to be mentally "disabled" in a society that places high value on technical competence. To investigate this issues, it would not be reasonable to "observe" people served by the selected agencies in the older, neutralist, objective manner discussed above, because the ethnographer could not presume to be able to "read" the attitudes and responses of people whose behavioral cues were, by definition, not "normal." On the other hand, engaging in intensive interviewing in and of itself would not work very well, because the clients would not likely trust someone with whom they were not already familiar outside the interview setting.

Angrosino therefore actively sought out a membership role in the world in which the clients lived and worked. He did not want to adopt one of the recognized professional roles that would have been familiar to the clients (e.g., therapist, social worker, teacher, parole officer) because the very familiarity would have resulted in stereotypical responses. On the other hand, he could not just "hang out." Unlike other kinds of communities, where strangers do often show up and stay to become friends, no one just "shows up" in a sheltered workshop or at a group home. So Angrosino opted for a role as a "volunteer." He assisted the teacher as a tutor in the classroom, he occasionally drove clients to and from appointments, he clerked at the thrift shop run by one of the agencies as a fund-raising effort and that was staffed by the clients, and he helped out at special events (e.g., he helped to organize a charity softball game). By assuming these duties, he made it clear that he fit no preconceived model of what someone did in this community, and yet he was able to demonstrate that he did indeed have a meaningful function (other than simply "researcher," which would not have explained anything as far as the clients were concerned). He was thus able to spend a considerable amount of time making detailed observations of the settings in which the clients lived and worked, because his presence after a while ceased to be novel enough to be disruptive, and he was able to conduct interviews with the clients, who had already learned that he was someone who could be trusted. (For further details about this project, see Angrosino, 1992, 1994, 1995a, 1997b, 1998; Angrosino & Zagnoli, 1992.)

Behar's (1993) study of Esperanza illustrates the ways in which an ethnographer was led, by the force of her collaborator's personality, to adopt more of a membership role than she had originally expected. Indeed, that study could fairly be described as an account by a feminist ethnographer who realized only in the course of writing the book that she was a feminist. In relating the story of a poor Mexican Indian woman who has defined herself through her life's struggles, Behar comes to understand more about herself as a Cuban immigrant to the United States who had always felt outside the social and academic systems in which she sought membership. Behar first encountered Esperanza when the latter was selling flowers on a street corner. Behar asked the woman permission to photograph her, expecting some sort of deferential acquiescence. Instead, Esperanza asked her (in a "haughty" manner) why she needed the picture. Behar (1993) admits, "I jumped on her as an alluring image of Mexican womanhood, ready to create my own exotic portrait of her, but the image turned around and spoke back to me, questioning my project and daring me to carry it out" (p. 4). Behar responded to Esperanza's challenge by questioning her own assumptions about the power relationship in ethnographic research (see also D. L. Wolf, 1996, p. 2; M. A. Wolf, 1992, p. 5); in this case, Behar felt herself to be directed by the more assertive woman she wished to study. Esperanza could in no sense be described as a "subject" of research. If she wished to understand Esperanza and the world in which she lived, Behar would ultimately have to become part of Esperanza's family network; she did so, becoming *comadre* to Esperanza's daughter in the process.

The decision to insert oneself in a social setting other than one's own has emotional consequences, which Behar (1996) discusses at some length. She translates the old anthropological problem of establishing rapport without "going native" (a question of methodology, with strong *ethical* overtones) into a problem of allowing oneself to be vulnerable without being "too" vulnerable (a question of personal psychology, with strong *moral* overtones). She is wary of using the language of theory and analysis; it is her only tool for "making sense" of new experiences, but it is also a way of distancing herself from an emotionally affecting (and perhaps painful) encounter.

An even more emotionally affecting (and definitely more painful) encounter is reported by Eva Moreno (a pseudonym), who writes about being raped while conducting fieldwork in Ethiopia. Moreno (1995, p. 246) admits that it is neither feasible nor desirable to "maintain a fiction of a genderless self" while in the field, which means that when an ethnographer chooses how to express her own sexuality, she must always be aware of the degree to which she thereby makes herself the object of attention of others who may see her as a target of (unwanted) sexual advances. Moreno suspects that the sexual violence she suffered was directed as much against her "professional" identity as against her "private" self—there was, at the time of her research, a generalized hostility aimed at foreigners, particularly those who presented themselves as "experts" and who were blamed for the civil disorder that had overtaken the country. She had heard, for example, that at least one other foreign woman had been raped by the very police to whom she had gone to report an assault perpetrated by local men. Moreno (1995) concludes that "women must always, everywhere, deal with the spectre of sexual violence" (p. 248). It is difficult to believe that males are not also victimized in this way—although it is much less likely that they would discuss it openly—but Moreno is undoubtedly correct in her assumption that as a generalized pattern, sexual violence is most often, in most situations, directed against women. It would therefore be a painfully naïve female ethnographer who was not prepared to factor this possibility into her plan for her observations, as "reasonable precautions" should almost certainly affect what, where, how, and with whom one conducts research.

In sum, "making a role" may mean assuming a quasi-professional stance, becoming part of a family network, or becoming hyperconscious of one's sexuality—or some combination of them all. In no case is it advantageous for the ethnographer to be passive in the face of the assumptions of the community he or she is studying.

The Perception of Power

The second principle is as follows: *In most social interactions, people assess behavior not in terms of its conformity to social or cultural norms in the abstract, but in regard to its consistency, which is a perceived pattern that somehow makes sense to others in a given social situation.* This principle is related to the traditional anthropological distinction between "ideal" and "real" culture. An ethnographer who took the observer-as-participant role was largely concerned with the ideal culture and took steps not to transgress general norms of propriety. But an ethnographer who actively makes a membership role must be more familiar with behavior as it is lived. Members of a social group typically work their way through given situations in ways that do not necessarily conform to the principles enshrined in ideal tradition.

We often function in terms of an ideology that leads us to expect (and, therefore, possibly also to see) power working downward from white, Western institutions (and their representatives, such as ethnographers) to various subordinated or marginalized peoples. Yet the literature is increasingly filled with examples of "how people in subordinate positions managed to oppose and evade the predations of higher powers" (Maddox, 1996, p. 277). We also have a lingering bias in favor of conceptualizing both culture and society as unified, cohesive wholes. Yet ethnographers increasingly find themselves studying "communities" that are defined as much by their conflicts, factions, and divisions as they are by their commonalities (Hubbard, 1997; McCall, Ngeva, & Mbebe, 1997).

For example, Angrosino (1991) compiled an oral history of a Benedictine monastery in Florida on the occasion of the centennial of its founding. He spent a month living at the monastery while conducting the interviews, during which time he adhered to the round of daily prayer, work, and reflective leisure that is prescribed by the Rule of St. Benedict. The research was approved by the abbot (to whom all the monks in the community have vowed obedience), and although Angrosino was not a vowed member of the community, the abbot made it clear that he expected the same deference from the ethnographer that he received from the monks. The abbot was always very cordial, but he demarcated his position very clearly in ways both subtle (sitting behind a desk when it came time for his interview) and blatant (reserving the final say as to which members of the community Angrosino could approach for interviews). The other members of the community claimed to be very supportive of the research, but Angrosino found that a fair number of them gave very truncated interviews, explaining that it is not seemly for a monk to speak too much about his own experiences—doing so smacks of vanity. In the course of living in and observing the community, Angrosino came to realize that this humble reticence, although sincere to a point, covered other motives. For one thing, it expressed a quiet rebellion against the authority of the abbot, who had mandated their cooperation. In the ordinary course of things, they would not have dared to be seen as less than eager to carry out the abbot's wishes, but because the ethnographer was, for all his temporary immersion in the life of the monastery, an outsider, he could be disobliged in a way that would have spelled trouble had it been directed against any insider, much less the abbot himself. Moreover, this tactic allowed some of the monks to make an oblique criticism of those who had been more fully cooperative; their own humility was a kind of symbolic indictment of their brothers, who could be seen as either toadying to the abbot or preening in their own vanity by "telling all" to the researcher. In any event, it was clear that the ideal arrangements of monastic life—with its formal, even codified system of hierarchy and deference—were not what happened in real life. Even in such a highly circumscribed culture, people could experiment with styles of interaction and involve the visitor in subtle, yet very revealingly subversive, power games, games that inevitably shaped both *what* the ethnographer observed and *how* he interpreted what he saw.

Behar (1993) discusses her inclination to fit Esperanza's story into the prevailing model of feminist studies of Latin American women. She realized, however, that Esperanza could not fit the part of the "exemplary feminist heroine." The reality of Esperanza was no less admirable and heroic, for her life was a kind of epic of female struggle, rage, and defiance of the patriarchal institutions of her culture; but she was a flesh-and-blood woman capable of "misbehavior," and not a stereotypical Third World feminist plaster saint. Behar concludes that an ethnographer's desire to produce stories that empower the people she studies must be grounded in an allowance for the way women in other cultures "misbehave." There must be respect for their "different ways of making sense," even if their sense does not conform to the European or North American expectations of the feminist ideal (p. 270). In a similar vein, Hirsh and Olson (1995, p. 23) cite Sandra Harding to the effect that feminist scholarship in general has sought to surmount the established categories of social knowledge, which have been developed from a male point of view (even when applied in the past by female scholars). Margery Wolf (1992), however, asks "whether by studying our subjects we are also exploiting them and whether by attempting to improve women's living situations we are imposing another (powerful) society's values" (p. 2). Moreover, it may be misleading to conceptualize the "power relationship" as that obtaining between researcher and "subject." In fact, Hsiung (1996) claims that this standard binary view overlooks the patriarchal context in which both the (female) ethnographer and her female informants are situated. It may be more useful to think in terms of a "multidimensional power relationship, of which the patriarchal/capitalist system, individual agents of the system, female informants, and female feminist researcher are the key constituents" (p. 123).

The injunction to pay attention to what makes sense in a given setting takes on particular importance when, as is now so often the case, ethnography is conducted "without the ethnos" (Gupta & Ferguson, 1996b, p. 2). In other words, few ethnographers function within the circumscribed communities that lent coherence to the cultures or societies that figured so prominently in the conceptual frameworks of earlier generations of observational researchers. It is no longer possible to assume that "the cultural object of study is fully accessible within a particular site" (Marcus, 1997, p. 96). Much of the contemporary ethnographic field consists of studies of those who inhabit the "borders between culture areas," of localities that demonstrate a diversity of behavioral and attitudinal patterns, of "postcolonial hybrid cultures," and of the social changes and cultural transformations that typically are found "within interconnected spaces" (Gupta & Ferguson, 1996a, p. 35). People, after all, "live in different overlapping but not always overdetermining spaces and times: domestic spaces; national spaces; broadcasting and narrowcasting spaces; biographical times; daily times; scheduled, spontaneous, but also sociogeological times" (Abu-Lughod, 1997, p. 112). Malkki (1996b), for example, describes working in "accidental communities of memory," which include "people who have experienced war together . . . ; people who were bombed in Hiroshima or Nagasaki; people who all fled a particular revolution; people who are stricken by a particular illness; or people who worked together on a particular humanitarian or development project" (p. 92). In all of these cases, "it is the communities that are accidental, not the happenings" (p. 92). The ethnographer therefore no longer enjoys the luxury of assuming that the local scene he or she is observing is somehow typical or representative of "a" culture of "a" society. It is a nexus of interactions defined by "interstitiality and hybridity" (Gupta & Ferguson, 1996a, p. 48), factors of "the globalizing discourses and images of the media" (Peters, 1996, p. 81), that the ethnographer, the classic neither-here-nor-there person, helps to define. In some cases, the ethnographer may even be said to *create* a community simply by virtue of studying certain people and by implying that the links he or she has perceived among them constitute a society. The "street corner society" studied by Whyte (1955), or Liebow (1967), or Hannerz (1969) became a "society" only because an ethnographer chose to treat that "nexus of interaction" as a site. Oral historians are often in the position of creating virtual communities by linking several personal experiences around a central theme of their own choosing (Hareven, 1996).

The principle is confounded when gender—that "enormous, extreme" question, in the words of Jean-François Lyotard (quoted in Olson, 1995a, p. 186)—and sexual orientation enter the picture, because "differing sexualized perspectives of 'the field' influence the kind of relationship that the ethnographer has with the field and this, in turn, affects interpretation" (Willson, 1995, p. 253). Gender and sexual orientation are extremely meaningful elements in defining an ethnographer's personal identity; they can also become filters through which the observation of communities is mediated. The problem is that the meanings shift from one community to another. The observer cannot assume a universal, let alone an ideal, symbolism of gender and/or sexual orientation. The cues of personal identity must always be interpreted in the context of the reality of a given social setting.

Dubisch (1995, p. 34), for example, notes that female anthropologists, simply by virtue of being female, have not been granted the indulgence to engage in casual sex, whether their sexual encounters occur at home or in the field. Male anthropologists, by contrast, have long been assumed to have had casual flings while in the field (Newton, 1993, p. 5). There was a tacit assumption that such male behavior did not matter because it was expected and approved by all parties, whereas analogous behavior by women was always disruptive because it was neither expected nor approved. This assumption must now be called into question, because the decision of *any* ethnographer to insert him- or herself into the social setting in a sexual manner must be seen to have repercussions with respect to what he or she is able to observe. Whether or not such behavior is approved is less important than the recognition that it will make a difference to the entire set of relationships initiated by the ethnographer, and hence to the type and quality of observations he or she is able to conduct. In recognition of this reality, Killick (1995) seems to counsel abstinence, noting that "while in the field, the fear of upsetting the delicate balance of relationships with informants is likely to be a significant curb on the libido" (p. 81). On the other hand, Killick advises those whose libidos are unrestrained by such methodological niceties to "keep quiet about it if their behavior is likely to be seen as either uninteresting (a possibility we should not discount) or reprehensible" (p. 81). Altork (1995), however, argues against both repression and concealment. She believes that "instead of blocking out [the] wealth of sensory (and sensual) input, or relegating it to private field journals, we might consider making room for our sensual responses in our work" (p. 116). In her view, whether or not one "did it" in the field is less important than whether or not one is able to be honest in acknowledging what did or did not happen and why, because such admissions leave the ethnographer "open to the fertile possibilities for dialogue about the ways in which 'it' changed, enhanced, or detracted from what we felt, witnessed, and interpreted in the field" (p. 121). In an ironic twist on this old (but only recently public) dilemma, Altork suggests that "perhaps by acknowledging our own feelings and desires, we might actually look at other people and places *more objectively,* by being able to ferret out our own biases and distortions as we do our work" (p. 132; emphasis added).

The process of open acknowledgment may be hindered in the case of lesbian or gay ethnographers, who may be habituated to a degree of concealment in both their personal and professional lives. Goodman (1996, p. 50) notes that lesbian and gay male ethnographers *expect* to engage in subterfuge while in the field, but Burkhart (1996) believes that his initial efforts at concealment (rationalized as an effort to achieve the "ideal of observer neutrality") led only to "spells of inertia and depression" (p. 34). Williams (1996, p. 74) suggests a compromise: being completely honest with people in the community although less so with granting agencies. He claims to have had positive experiences with people to whom he divulged his sexual orientation in the communities in which he conducted research, but he has found it prudent to apply for funding by stressing other research topics, and then studying homosexual behavior once in the field. Even AIDS research, now a reasonably well-funded area for social scientists, was initially not something funding agencies wanted to hear about, because it was assumed that AIDS was a purely homosexual concern (Bolton, 1996, p. 157).

Lesbians and gay men are used to "constant, and conscious, identity management" and have typically carried this mind-set from their personal lives into their research settings (Lewin & Leap, 1996, p. 13). A fair number of homosexual ethnographers have chosen to study homosexual behavior in the field (apparently on the assumption that they have a ready point of reference), but it is easy to be disappointed if one assumes that the understanding of and manifestation of homosexuality is the same in all communities, just as it is easy to be misled into assuming that female ethnographers are in an advantaged position when it comes to understanding women in all cultures (Lewin & Leap, 1996, p. 17). The point is that one's gender, as well as one's sexual orientation, are matters that must be taken into conscious account when one endeavors to conduct observational ethnography; but neither factor can be considered a source of privileged knowledge in and of itself. As Lang (1996) notes, "Quite obviously, there is no 'universal gay community'" (p. 103). At the very least, homosexuality does not "override the social hierarchies of the contemporary world" (Kennedy & Davis, 1996, p. 193); it is still necessary to investigate the impact of "the hierarchies of class and race" even within a presumed "gay community."

In any case, it is clear that "no longer is it generally acceptable for [ethnographic researchers] to conceal or deny the significance of their gender identity, age, class, or ethnicity. (Sexual identity represents a sort of final frontier in this regard.) Instead, contemporary ethnographic writing tends to acknowledge these attributes as factors that shape an [ethnographer's] interpretations of what she or he observed in the field" (Weston, 1996, p. 276). For example, Edelman (1996) discusses the varying impacts his Jewish ethnicity had in three different field sites. Other factors, less well established as demographic categories, may also play a part in how an ethnographer relates to what is studied—for example, the ethnographer's personal struggle with bulimia (Tillman-Healy, 1996) or breast cancer (Kolker, 1996), or the ethnographer's having survived a nonmainstream childhood (Fox, 1996; Ronai, 1996) or having undergone detoxification therapy (Mienczakowski, 1996). In all of the cases just cited, the ethnographers' personal experiences were the main focus of both observation and interpretation. But it is clear that if these ethnographers should go on to study other people with those same characteristics, they would have to shift from a perspective that implicitly elevates the personal to the normative in order to observe what is going on in a natural setting.

Negotiating a Situational Identity

The third principle is as follows: *Interaction is always a tentative process that involves the continuous testing by all participants of the conceptions they have of the roles of others.* In other words, ethnographers and their collaborators do not step into fixed and fully defined positions; rather, their behaviors and expectations of each other are part of a dynamic process that continues to grow (one hopes in healthy ways, although the outcome is sometimes problematic) throughout the course of single research projects or as they move from one project to another (Wolcott, 1995, p. 77). Giroux (1995) speaks of the need for "intellectuals" in general (and ethnographers in particular) to "reinvent themselves in diverse sites" (p. 197). Denzin (1997a) discusses the "mobile consciousness" of an ethnographer who is aware of his or her "relationship to an ever-changing external world" (p. 46).

For example, Angrosino (1997a) conducted an oral history of the Southern Anthropological Society on the occasion of the 30th anniversary of its founding. He had been a member of the SAS almost since its establishment and had served over the years in both elective and appointive offices. As a professional anthropologist affiliated with a department at a university in the South, and whose research often dealt with aspects of life in the contemporary South, he was in terms of status a fully integrated member of the institutional culture of the organization. Moreover, he had long-term personal and professional ties with all of the people who were scheduled to be interviewed. The bulk of the interviews were conducted during the special anniversary meetings of the society, and Angrosino brought along three graduate students to work as his assistants—and, more important, to serve as "reality checks" to make sure that he did not act like too much of an "insider" and thereby miss important cues or take for granted too many items that outsiders would find in need of clarification. The interviews, however, began awkwardly, as many of the participants seemed annoyed at being questioned by someone they assumed already knew the answers. "Oh, you remember what happened in New Orleans in '70 . . ." someone would say. "Well, why don't you tell about it in your own words?" Angrosino would respond. They usually sighed in frustration at that suggestion. It was very difficult for professional anthropologists to act as informants, particularly when the interviewer was already assumed to be in the know. Some others decided to short-circuit an uncomfortable situation and, in effect, to hijack the interview, carrying on in lecture/monologue fashion without paying attention to the interviewer's questions. Still others demanded to be interviewed by one of the graduate assistants; "I can't talk to you with a straight face," one of them told Angrosino.

After a while, the awkwardness wore off, presumably as members began to share with one another their reactions to having been interviewed. They reaffirmed all the reasons they had thought of collecting an oral history in the first place, primarily because doing so would be a good idea "for posterity." The later interviews went much more smoothly, as participants had clearly made a tacit decision to treat the overly familiar Angrosino as simply a naïve outsider to whom *everything* needed to be explained. The ethnographer came to think of himself as if he were one of his students, so that he would remember to ask all the questions that someone who had not been in on the action would want ask. Although most ethnographers seek to move from outsider status to a status of participant/member, Angrosino in this case (abetted by his collaborators) reinvented himself from complete insider to interested-but-ignorant bystander. Within the interactive context of observational research, roles mutate in response to changing circumstances and are never defined with finality.

Behar describes this process in terms of her own evolution from "feminist anthropologist" to "feminist ethnographer," by which she means a researcher who is attentive to the "reflexiveness about the politics of practicing feminism and experimental cultural writing." The focus of such reflexiveness must be "women's relationships to other women" (Behar, 1993, p. 301) rather than a scientific observer's relationship to a "subject" of research. For Behar (1996, p. 5), the very term *participant observation* is an "oxymoron." The ethnographer must, Behar suggests, be defined by the creative tension in the role of member/observer, not by some finite quantity of information gathered by one who plays that role. According to Ferguson (1996, p. 153), the exploration of how shifting connections frame experiences of place, community, and society among "the partially and provisionally dislocated" may well represent the most fertile ground for future ethnographic research.

Blackwood (1995, p. 53) therefore speaks of the *identities* assumed by the ethnographer in the field in terms of the many different ways he or she is perceived by "others." As a woman, she has "continually tacked back and forth between various assigned and constructed identities: researcher, friend, daughter, professional, American" (p. 58), and she concludes that "identities [in the field] are never stable, never simply defined" (p. 70). At this point in the psychosocial history of Western culture, it is probably clear that our "identities" in the existential sense are always in a process of evolution and never achieve a fixed, final point. The naïve assumption that ethnographers' identities in the field should be clearly defined and finite is, perhaps, the last vestige of the old belief that "wholeness" means personal autonomy and fixity of identity. Nevertheless, there is a very strong sense in which ethnographers continue to believe, as they have since the days of the ascendancy of the Freudian perspective in social analysis, that doing fieldwork is a way in which they can come to terms with themselves. "Sharing a different lifestyle," according to Barnett (1983), "has a mirror effect, providing glimpses of an observer's foibles as well as his dignity" (p. 169).

Walters (1996) expresses this view with an interesting figure of speech: In the matter of establishing one's identity, one must "constantly . . . pivot the center" (p. 63). She was led to this perspective when it became necessary for her to deal with the problem of bringing her partner to the field—the Yemen Arab Republic. She assumed that a conservative Islamic society would not be a friendly place for two openly homosexual women, and she considered various strategies of concealment (e.g., claiming to be relatives, going through a process of adoption); she finally decided to refer to the other woman as her "companion," which, while perfectly true, seemed vague enough to avoid the suspicion of the authorities. (It even had a whiff of Victorian propriety about it—a young woman traveling in the company of an older female companion has long been a well-known image in many parts of the world.)

Despite such occasionally successful strategies, it remains true that women researchers often feel pressured to conform to the gender behavior norms of the cultures they study, even if those norms are not the ones they would freely choose for themselves, and even if they have to resort to a certain amount of deception so as to appear to conform. According to Diane Wolf (1996), "Feminist fieldworkers have lied about their marital status, . . . about their national identity or ethnic/religious background . . . , about divorce and former marriages . . . , and about their class background" (p. 11). Even in those cases where the deception did no real harm to the people the researcher was observing, the ethnographers often felt guilty, in part because the very act of deception "directly contradicts attempts at a more feminist approach to fieldwork, which includes attempts to equalize a relationship and create more of a friendship" (Berik, 1996, p. 56; see also D. L. Wolf, 1996, p. 12). On the other hand, the refusal to deceive—in effect, to defy the norms of the community being studied in order to make a principled stand for what one actually believes—can sometimes have unintended negative consequences. Berik (1996, p. 65), for example, admits that her openly feminist stance while conducting research in a Turkish village unwittingly led to one of her female informants' being beaten by an outraged husband, who assumed she was being led astray by the insufficiently submissive ethnographer.

Lang (1996) conducted a research project focusing on Native American lesbians. Although she is openly gay herself, she found it unacceptable to locate potential informants in bars or other obvious meeting places. She was concerned lest the other women assume, because she was hanging out in a bar, that she was therefore interested in finding sexual, rather than research, partners. She decided that it would be unethical to pose as a potential sexual partner in order to elicit information (Lang, 1996, p. 94), and so she had to seek her "community" in less symbolically charged environments. In this case, Lang decided that her status as "ethnographer" would take precedence over her sexual orientation as a way of defining herself to the people she intended to study, despite the fact that sexual orientation was the thematic focus of her study. Her decision was a matter of strategy dictated by her reading of the nature of the particular community.

Much of the recent literature bearing on the creation, maintenance, and creative evolution of observers' identities (and on the pros and cons of deception and disclosure) has dealt with issues particular to women and lesbians/gay men, as shown above. It is worth mentioning, however, that there are other issues of identity that are of concern to researchers who study situations of political unrest and who come to be identified with politically proscribed groups (Hammond, 1996; Mahmood, 1996; Sluka, 1990), or who work with groups that are defined by their need for deceptive concealment, such as illegal migrants (Chavez, Flores, & Lopez-Garza, 1990; Stepick & Stepick, 1990) or those involved in criminal activities (Agar & Feldman, 1980; Brewer, 1992; Dembo, Hughes, Jackson, & Mieczkowski, 1993; Koester, 1994; van Gelder & Kaplan, 1992).

Criteria for Validation

The fourth principle is as follows: *Participants validate the cues generated by others in the setting by internal and/or external criteria.* Internal criteria are those by which members of a community check their behavior against the prevailing norms of their own group. External criteria are those by which members of a community check their behavior in terms of presumably universal standards. In other words, participants in the interaction ask, "Does it work?" or, perhaps less nobly, "Can I get away with it?" (that is, "Does my interpretation help me and my potential collaborator work out a viable relationship?") rather than, "Is it correct?" (That is, "Does 'the culture' somehow 'require' people to act in a certain manner?")

For example, Angrosino (1995b) led a team of graduate students in a study of local responses to the AIDS epidemic. The research centered on a particular agency that provided limited direct service (mostly testing) but was far more important as an information and referral network. The agency had been founded by partners and relatives of people who had contracted AIDS; these people believed that their personal involvement in—indeed, their emotional commitment to—the cause was a primary reason for the success of their project. They were somewhat put out by the apparent transformation of the agency into a more professional outfit, with leadership positions being increasingly taken by human service managers and development specialists with no special concern for the particular characteristics of the AIDS crisis except for the recognition that it was a major public health concern. The professional managers were helpful to the researchers, but in a rather distant fashion; by contrast, the "old-line" founders were eager to draw the team members into a kind of social circle, the better for them to learn "what it's really all about."

This situation was one in which internal and external criteria seemed to work at cross-purposes. On the one hand, the two factions within the agency were reacting to very different criteria for validation. One side validated its activities and sense of mission with reference to the *quality* of interpersonal interactions (an internal criterion) and to general humanitarian concerns (an external criterion). The other group sought validation in the *efficiency* of interpersonal interactions (an internal criterion) and in "objective" standards of professional conduct (an external criterion). There was clearly no "correct" corporate culture in such an agency or in the client community it served; the question was, "What worked?" and the answer was, "It depends on what you want to accomplish." The founders vigorously sought to convince the ethnographers that the key to success in the crisis was to "work from the heart, not from the head." People with AIDS and their caretakers needed emotional support more than sound fiscal management from an agency like theirs. They did not deny that the clients appreciated good management, but believed that a coolly competent accountant was not the "face" potential clients wanted to see when they contacted the agency for help. They sought empathy, having already gotten quite enough unfeeling "competence" in clinical settings. The ethnographers, for their part, tended to agree, although they certainly appreciated the way in which the "competent" managers facilitated the research process for them.

It may be useful to characterize this aspect of the interactive context in terms of the ways in which personal experience serves as an organizing principle in the process of mediating internal and external criteria in social settings. For Denzin (1997a), "the starting point is experience" (p. 55), which leads to a discourse between the ethnographer and other members of the community, a discourse that "often begins from the painful autobiographical experiences of the writer" (p. 57). Indeed, there is increasing tolerance for a discourse that ends with those same experiences as well (Quinney, 1996). "Life in the field," Hinsley (1983) points out, "is an individual experience" (p. 55), and "ethnography" (despite the traditional connotation of the term as the study of "a people") is seen in certain quarters as a species of autobiography, the "personal ethnography" (Quinney, 1996). Olson (1995b) cites Donna Haraway to the effect that ethnographic observation must be translated into written representations that place "the writer's own situatedness in history" in the foreground (p. 46). Denzin's (1997a)—and, more obliquely, Olson's—remarks are directed mainly to the production of "standpoint texts" that flow from the

particular experiences of those who have been excluded from "the dominant discourses in the human disciplines" (p. 55). Stocking (1983b) refers
to the same trend in somewhat less favorable terms as the proliferation of
"adjectival anthropologies" (p. 4).

It is nevertheless certainly possible to apply the same perspective to
anyone engaging in ethnographic research. Even those who come from
traditionally "dominant" social groups must engage in a process of consciousness-raising about the nature and effects of their interaction with
others. For them, as for those previously marginalized, the starting point
of observational research *is* experience, for their own existential immersion in the "cultural displacement" of people, things, and cultural products is a defining quality of the state of the world today (Malkki, 1996a,
p. 53). According to Mary Belenky: "We all need to understand how writing the same material for different audiences changes the voice. This is
very empowering knowledge to have" (quoted in Ashton-Jones &
Thomas, 1995, p. 86). On the other hand, one cannot be "preoccupied"
with one's audience, because such a focus can lead to "self-censorship,"
according to bell hooks (quoted in Olson & Hirsh, 1995, p. 110). In
effect, the ethnographer who is a member/observer is an artifact of the
very situation of cultural displacement that he or she intends to study. It
may not, in fact, be possible to resolve the tension between what the ethnographer "is" and what he or she must "become" in the field; rather than
fret about that tension, it may now be time to "find some practical use" for
it in our analysis (M. A. Wolf, 1996, p. 217).

Bolton (1995) points out that when the topic of an ethnographic study
is sexuality, the ethnographer is limited by his or her inability to "observe"
the behavior in the strict, traditional sense of the term. Much of the social
scientific discourse on sexual behavior has been recorded via hearsay
rather than eyewitness testimony, although it has often been conducted
within the compass of supposedly observational research designs. The best
way for the ethnographer to overcome this limitation, Bolton suggests, is
through participation, *if* the ethnographer feels comfortable doing so. He
admits that "I learned more through participation than by simple observation or direct interviewing" (p. 148). This solution raises some additional
issues of an interactional nature: Is the ethnographer who "participates"
in this manner really learning about the norms of sexual practice in the
community he or she is studying, or is the ethnographer importing attitudes and emotions from his or her own culture into the field setting? Is
the ethnographer, in effect, confusing internal and external criteria? More

provocatively, is he or she participating in the creation of a new set of norms or standards that are specific to this particular interaction, and not of either the host community or the home community? If the latter, is the ethnographer still doing social research, or has a new field for observation been introduced, requiring at minimum the much-discussed "blurring of genres" in reporting and at maximum a blurring of traditional academic/ disciplinary boundaries in order to conceive of a new topic of discourse? As Murray (1996) notes: "Having sex with the natives is not a royal road to insight about alien sexuality. . . . In answering questions or inscribing life histories at a researcher's behest, as in having sex with them, the person whose sexuality is being studied is likely to be guessing what the researcher wants to hear rather than representing his or her most fundamental desires and identities" (p. 250).

A female variant of Bolton's point of view is provided by Gearing (1995), who fell in love with and married her "best informant" while conducting field research. Ethnographic research, she contends, is always a "joint endeavor" between the would-be observer and those he or she would observe; it is therefore dependent on the "quality of our personal relationships" (p. 207). Gearing advocates abandoning the "model of the dispassionate participant observer" and adopting instead the persona of "an emotionally aware inter-actor engaged with other actors" (p. 211).

The validation of the individual experience of the ethnographer has traditionally been bound up in the ethnography (usually written) produced as the result of observational research. The only audience that really matters has been the academic, although there have been recent attempts to write for an audience composed (at least in part) of the "subjects" of research. Nevertheless, there are now many formats in which a report can be generated (Polkinghorne, 1997), reflecting the variety of constituencies to which the ethnographer is now responsible. Thus the ethnographic observer must be concerned with the different "voices" in which he or she presents material. Traditional ethnographic reportage favored the supposedly objective third-person voice, emanating from the "omniscient narrator," as Tierney (1997, p. 27) notes. The move toward greater participation allowed the ethnographer to acknowledge his or her own presence, although this was often done via circumlocution, with the ethnographer referring to him- or herself, for example, as "the interviewer" (Tierney, 1997, p. 26). The once-banned "I" is now much more common as subjective experience comes to the fore (Tierney, 1997, p. 25; see also Ellis, 1997; Lather, 1997; Tanaka, 1997). Wolcott (1995) declares his preference for "an approach that keeps humans always visibly present, re-searcher as well as the researched" (p. 15). Margery Wolf (1992, p. 52) suggests that it was women and others previously marginalized by the academic world who first dared challenge orthodoxy by writing in the first person, a trend that she believes has now entered the mainstream—now that male academics are also doing so. These shifts in reference are not irrelevant matters of style; they reflect evolving self-images of the ethnographic observer, changing relations between the observer and the observed, and new perceptions about the diverse (and possibly even contradictory) audiences to whom ethnographic research must now be addressed. Certain kinds of ethnographic texts can have professional, participatory, lay, and aesthetic audiences (Denzin, 1997b, p. 188). It is clear that validating what "I" say is a very different matter—philosophically as well as scientifically—from validating what "the interviewer" says.

Perhaps the most widely cited case study of the subtle interplay of internal and external criteria is the "thrice-told tale" of Margery Wolf (1992). In her book, Wolf embarks on a personal, reflexive journey by revisiting a fictional short story she had written some 30 years earlier, when she was the wife/assistant of an anthropologist conducting his first field research in Taiwan. Since that time, she had become an anthropologist in her own right, as well as a feminist. The original story (which was based on real events) is reprinted first, followed by the field notes and journal entries referring to the same events. The third part of the book is a formal ethnographic article that was originally published in *American Ethnologist,* a mainstream academic journal. Each section of the book is followed by commentary in which Wolf explains what she remembers about the events as represented in each of the three written accounts and what she now thinks about those same events from the perspective of three decades. In the process she sees changes in herself as both a woman and an ethnographer. For example, she notes, "Where once I was satisfied to describe what I thought I saw and heard as accurately as possible, to the point of trying to resolve differences of opinion among my informants, I have come to realize the importance of retaining these 'contested meanings' " (p. 4).

Wolf's point is that no ethnographic research, including supposedly objective naturalistic observation, can be considered complete and valid until it has undergone what Polkinghorne (1997) describes as the transformation of a "list or sequence of disconnected research events into a unified story with a thematic point" (p. 14). A good observer can develop the skill of catching cultural meanings as members of the community themselves understand them, but equally important is the skill of writing up the report in such a way as "to convey that meaning to an interested reader from another culture" (Wolf, 1992, p. 5).

Contextualizing Meaning

The fifth principle is as follows: *People come into interactions by assuming situational identities that enhance their own self-conceptions or serve their own needs, which may be context specific rather than socially or culturally normative.* Members of the community are reacting to *this particular ethnographer* and the cues he or she generates, not to "an outsider" in a generic sense. Some of those cues are matters over which the ethnographer can exercise some control if he or she is made aware of them (e.g., improving language facility, dressing in an "appropriate" way), although many others are simply part of the package (e.g., gender, race/ethnicity, relative age). In the latter case, the ethnographer may need to realize that what *he or she* observes is conditioned by who *he or she* is, and that different ethnographers—equally well trained and well versed in theory and method but of different gender, race, or age—might well stimulate a very different set of interactions, and hence a different set of observations leading to a different set of conclusions.

Angrosino, for example, has been involved with a long-term project documenting the patterns and impacts of inter-island labor migration in the Netherlands Antilles. One of his informants was an elderly woman now living on Saba, the smallest of the islands, and he published her life history in an anthology devoted to the Saba part of the project. Shortly thereafter, the same woman was interviewed by a Saba-born folklorist (and political leader) who was publishing a collection dedicated to "the island's treasures" (i.e., the accumulated wisdom of its senior citizens). The general outlines of the woman's life story were the same in both accounts, but there were clear differences as well. As might be expected, the story she told Angrosino had many more explanatory details than the one she told her fellow islander. Angrosino had obviously asked her many questions to clarify matters about which a nonnative would have no knowledge. But there were more subtle, yet telling differences. The woman had lived a life of great hardship, and yet she had survived to raise (virtually single-handedly) a large family; all of her children had gone on to become pillars of the community, and she herself was recognized as a person of the utmost integrity. When she told her story to the ethnographer, she allowed herself a bit of pride in recounting how she had surmounted all her travails; she comes across in that account as a humble, yet definitely heroic figure. In the story she told her fellow Sabian, she is considerably more self-deprecating; the island culture is not very cordial to those who "try to get above themselves." On the other hand, she included anecdotes in her discourse with the Sabian about her defiance of the white establishment, incidents she suppressed when talking with the (white) ethnographer. The point is that Angrosino, who is white, from another country, and of the same generation as this woman's grandsons, evoked a qualitatively different story from the one she told the black Sabian of her own generation. There is little evidence of conscious dissimulation; she merely responded to cues both obvious and covert in her two "audiences," and, like any good performer, she engaged her interlocutors in terms that resonated most clearly with them and their personal circumstances. (For a more detailed comparison of the two life stories, see Angrosino, 1989.) As Behar (1996) notes, citing George Devereux, the observer "*never* observes the behavioral event which 'would have taken place' in his absence, nor hears an account identical with that which the same narrator would give to another person" (p. 6).

Denzin (1997a) points out that it is now important to be aware of class, race, gender, and ethnicity, and of how these factors "shape the process of inquiry, thereby making research a multicultural process" (p. 19). This insight is not in and of itself new; what is new and important for the purposes of this discussion is the implication that the ethnographer must become aware of these factors not to minimize them or "hold them constant," as classic observers were taught to do, but to integrate them creatively into both the process of observation and the production of a written representation of the fruits of that observation. Diane Wolf (1996) echoes this position in a feminist context; she advises ethnographers to analyze their field research in terms that use, rather than deny, their "intuition, feelings, and viewpoint" (p. 5).

Morton (1995), for example, conducted research in Tonga, a "seductive," "exotic" culture. On her first visit, she "nearly" succumbed to the seduction; 10 years later, she was pregnant while conducting research, and she was able to wear her pregnancy as a "chastity belt" to avoid sexual pursuit (p. 168). The reader assumes that Morton had other motives for her pregnancy, but it certainly helped her out of an undesirable situation (that of being sexually active in the field); it probably also meant that she was able to hear a significantly different side of the story of Tongan culture from the one to which she was privy as a single, childless woman.

◆ The Ethical Dimension of Observational Research

Observation was once thought of as a data collection technique employed primarily by ethnographers who thought of themselves as objective researchers extrinsic to the social settings they studied. It has become a context in which researchers who define themselves as members of those social settings interact in dialogic fashion with other members of those settings. This transition has also effected a shift in the parameters of our ongoing reflections on the ethics of social research.

Institutional Structures

For good or ill, virtually all social research in our time is governed by the structure of institutional review boards (IRBs), which grew out of federal regulations beginning in the 1960s that mandated informed consent for all those participating in federally funded research. The perceived threat was from "intrusive" research (usually biomedical), participation in which was to be under the control of the "subjects," who had a right to know what was going to happen to them and to agree formally to all provisions of the research. The right of informed consent, and the review boards that were eventually created to enforce it at each institution receiving federal moneys (assuming a function originally carried out by the federal Office of Management and Budget), radically altered the power relationship between researcher and "subject," allowing both parties to have a say in the conduct and character of research. (For more detailed reviews of this history, see Fluehr-Lobban, 1994; Wax & Cassell, 1979.)

Ethnographic researchers, however, have always been uncomfortable with this situation—not, of course, because they wanted to conduct covert, harmful research, but because they did not believe that their research was "intrusive." Such a claim was of a piece with the assumptions typical of the "observer-as-participant" role, although it is certainly possible to interpret it as a relic of the "paternalism" that traditional researchers often adopted with regard to their "subjects" (Fluehr-Lobban, 1994, p. 8). Ethnographers were also concerned that the proposals sent to IRBs had to be fairly complete, so that all possibilities for doing harm might be adequately assessed. Their research, they argued, often grew and changed as it went along and could not always be set out with the kind of predetermined specificity that the legal experts seemed to expect. They further pointed out that the statements of professional ethics promulgated by the relevant disciplinary associations already provided for informed consent, such that IRBs were merely being redundant in their oversight.

In the 1980s, social scientists won from the federal Department of Health and Human Services an exemption from review for all social research except that dealing with children, people with disabilities, and others defined as members of "vulnerable" populations. Nevertheless, legal advisers at many universities (including the University of South Florida, where we are both based) have opted for caution and have been very reluctant to allow this near-blanket exemption to be applied. Indeed, at USF it is possible for a research proposal to undergo "expedited" (or "partial") review if it seems to meet the federal criteria for exemption, and even those that are judged worthy of full exemption must still be on file. USF now has two IRBs—one for biomedical research and one for "behavioral research." Because the latter is dominated by psychologists (by far the largest department in the social sciences division of the College of Arts and Sciences), this separate status rarely works to the satisfaction of ethnographic researchers. The psychologists, used to dealing with hypothesis-testing, experimental, or clinical or lab-based research, have been reluctant to recognize a subcategory of "observational" research design. As a result, the form currently required by the behavioral research IRB is couched in terms of the individual subject rather than in terms of populations or communities, and it mandates the statement of a hypothesis to be tested and a "protocol for the experiment." Concerned ethnographers at USF have discovered that some other institutions have developed forms more congenial to their particular needs, but as of this writing they have had no success in convincing the USF authorities to adopt any of them as an alternative to the current "behavioral research" form for review.

It is interesting to note that the only kind of "observational" research that is explicitly mentioned and routinely placed in the "exempt" category at USF is that defined as "public"—for example, studying patterns of where people sit in airport waiting rooms, one of the rare remaining classic "pure observer" types of ethnography. The exemption, however, disappears if the researcher intends to publish photos or otherwise identify the people who make up "the public."

Issues for Contemporary Observational Researchers

Ethical ethnographers who adopt more clearly "membership"-oriented identities—certainly a very strong trend, as this review has demonstrated—are therefore caught between two equally untenable models of research. On the one hand is the official IRB, which is tied to the experimental, hypothesis-testing, clinical model. On the other hand are those ethnographers who, in their zeal to win exemption from irrelevant and time-consuming strictures, appear to be claiming that their research is not, should not be, "intrusive" at all. Yet the interactive, membership-oriented researchers *are*, by definition, intrusive—not in the negative sense of the word, to be sure, but they are still deeply involved in the lives and activities of the communities they study, a stance fraught with all sorts of possibilities for "harm." There are ethnographers with an "applied" orientation (i.e., those who seek to use their research to effect social or institutional change), those interested in using their research as part of a project for social criticism, and those who advocate for "universalistic" values (e.g., women's rights, ecological justice) even when the local communities they happen to be studying act in ways inimical to those values. All of these researchers may do "harm" in the strict sense of the term, but it has not been satisfactorily determined whether such "harm" is necessarily and inevitably to be avoided by the ethical researcher. It is difficult to prepare an informed consent form when one cannot even begin to anticipate the possibilities that might flow from personalized interaction. In principle, at least, it might be possible to say that because research collaborators are no longer subjects, by definition they have as much power as do researchers in shaping the research agenda; they do not need to be warned or protected. But in reality, the researcher is still in a privileged position, at least insofar as actually *doing* the research and disseminating its results are concerned. The researcher probably does not want to retreat to the objective cold of the classic observer role, but neither does he or she want to shirk the responsibility for doing everything possible to avoid hurting or embarrassing people who have been trusting partners in the research endeavor. As Fluehr-Lobban (1994) concludes:

> Openness and disclosure; reference in social studies to participants instead of informants; models of collaborative research that incorporate informed consent; all are components of [ethnographic] research, whether academic or applied, federally or privately funded, that is fully current with develop-

ments taking place in the world we study and the professions that study it. Informed consent may only be a convenient summary term for what has taken place in biomedical and social science research, but when its spirit is implemented it results in better researchers and better research. (p. 8)

An Interim Solution

This ethical dilemma would seem to be the pivot on which further developments in observational research will turn, although there have been only provisional efforts to resolve it. One example of such an attempt is Angrosino's *Opportunity House* (1998), his summative report on the study, discussed above, of nearly two decades' duration of community-based agencies serving adult clients with mental disabilities. Informed consent was secured from those clients who were classified as "legally competent" and from the legal guardians of those who were not. Nevertheless, Angrosino never felt confident that the people with whom he worked fully understood the ramifications of their consent, particularly given that much of the ethnographic research was conducted in the form of extended life history interviews that often went off in directions that could not have been predicted at the time the original study was proposed and approved. Various interim publications about the project were written in the standard authoritative voice of the objective scientist, with aggregated observations and limited excerpts from interview data (attributed to pseudonymous informants) as illustrations. When it came time to write an overall analysis of the entire project, Angrosino found that such a strategy seemed inadequate. It was necessary to draw the reader into both the experiences of people with mental disabilities (people who are so much like us, and yet with a critical difference somewhat beyond our capacities to imagine) and the experiences of a researcher trying to figure out the patterns of the communities in which those people interact. But doing so by means of an implicitly distancing language of expository scientific writing and a blurring of individual differences was not an attractive option.

Angrosino therefore decided to try a form of "alternative ethnographic writing" and to present his material in the form of fictionalized stories that preserved the truth of individual experience without making explicit identifications of particular people with specific situations. There are many valid reasons for experimenting with nonexpository presentations of ethnographic material, but it may also be useful to think of such alterna-

tive genres as one response to the ethical quandary of observational research in transition.

Steps Toward an Ethic of
Proportionate Reason in Observational Research

Because observational research, as it has evolved in recent times, is
essentially a matter of interpersonal interaction and not a matter of objective hypothesis testing, it would seem that a standard for the making of
ethical judgments appropriate to the analysis of "the morality of human
action" (Gula, 1989, p. 272) is in order. Human action must always be
interpreted in situational context, and not in terms of objective "codes."
As Gula (1989) has pointed out, "No one enjoys an ahistorical vantage
point which will give absolute certitude on moral matters" (p. 275). The
notion of "proportionate reason" is the key to such an interpretation
(Cahill, 1981; Curran, 1979; Hoose, 1987; Walter, 1984). *Proportionalism* can sometimes refer to a strictly utilitarian cost-benefit analysis,
but it is more properly thought of in this context as that which gives an
action its moral meaning. In that sense, " 'proportionate' refers to the relation between the specific value at stake and the . . . limitations, the harm,
or the inconvenience which will inevitably come about in trying to achieve
that value" (Gula, 1989, p. 273). In other words, it is certainly important
to "weigh the consequences" of an action, but consequences are only one
part of the total meaning of the action. From this perspective, proportionate reason defines what a person is doing in an action (as an ethnographer
engaged in an observational context) and not something merely added to
the action already defined (i.e., the old notion of the ethnographic observer as extrinsic to the "action" he or she was recording).

There are three criteria that help us decide whether a proper relationship exists between the specific value and the other elements of the act
(McCormick, 1973; McCormick & Ramsey, 1978). First, *the means used
will not cause more harm than necessary to achieve the value.* In traditional
moral terms, the ends cannot be said to justify the mans. If we take "the
value" to refer to the production of some form of ethnography, then we
must be careful to assure that "the means used" (e.g., inserting oneself into
a social network, using photographs or other personal records) do not
cause disproportionate harm. We might all agree that serving as *comadre*
to an "informant's" child is sufficiently proportionate; we might well
argue about whether becoming the lover of an "informant" (particularly

if that sexual liaison is not intended to last beyond the time of the research) does more harm than an ethnographic book, paper, or presentation might be worth. Volunteering as a classroom tutor in a program serving adults with mental retardation whom one is interested in observing and interviewing is probably sufficiently proportionate; becoming a bill-paying benefactor to induce cooperation would, by contrast, be morally questionable.

The second criterion is that *no less harmful way exists at present to protect the value*. Some might argue that observational research always and inevitably compromises personal privacy, such that no form of research can ethically protect that cherished value. But most researchers (and others) would probably reject such an extreme view and take the position that there is real value in disseminating the fruits of ethnographic research so as to increase our knowledge and understanding of cultural diversity, or the nature of coping strategies, or any number of currently salient social justice issues. Granted that *all* methods have the potential to harm, we must be sure to choose those that do the *least* amount of harm, but that still enable us to come up with the sort of product that will be effective in communicating the valuable message. The strategy of writing ethnographic fiction, for example, is certainly not foolproof, as anyone with a knowledge of the population with which the ethnographer worked would be able to identify the "characters." But there is far less chance that an outside reader would be able to do so than would be the case with a report based on "objective" materials that are on the public record.

The third criterion is that *the means used to achieve the value will not undermine it*. If one sets out, for example, to use research in order to promote the dignity of people defined as mentally disabled, one must make sure that the research techniques do not subject such people to ridicule. Videotaping a group of people with mental retardation as they play a game of softball might conceivably result in viewers' concluding that such people are gallantly trying their best, but more likely it will result in confirming the popular stereotypes of such people as clumsy and inept, objects of pity (at best) or of scorn (at worst) rather than dignified individuals. Videotaping as an ethnographic method is ethically neutral; its appropriateness must be evaluated in this proportionate context.

McCormick (1973) suggests three modes of knowing whether there is a proportionate reason to carry out a suggested action. First, we know that a proper relation exists between a specific value and all other elements of an act through *experience*, which sometimes amounts to plain common sense.

For example, although we may think that it is important to encourage individual expression, we know from experience that doing so in the context of a community (such as a monastery) in which the individual is, by tradition, subordinate to the group will do real violence to the precepts by which the people we are intent on studying have historically formed themselves into a community. Experience might suggest that we rethink a decision to collect personal life histories of people in such groups in favor of focusing on the collective reconstruction of remembered common activities or events.

Second, we may know that a proper relationship exists through our own *intuition* that some actions are inherently disproportionate, even if we do not have personal experience of their being so. Janssens (1979, p. 63) asserts that we can discover disproportion through "feelings of disunity" within the self. For example, we should intuitively know that publishing personal material collected from people living in an oppressive, totalitarian society might ultimately result in that material being used against them, even in the absence of a direct or explicit threat. Our righteous goal of exposing the tyrannical regime might well backfire on the very people we are trying to help. Our intuition might warn us that an otherwise praiseworthy research proposal (e.g., to collect life histories or genealogies, or to observe the daily activities at the local market) could have harmful consequences if the product of the research were to fall into the wrong hands. A perception of what *could* happen (the result of intuition) is, of course, different from a perception of what *will* happen (the result of experience), and we are clearly not well served by dreaming up every conceivable disaster. It serves no purpose to allow ourselves to be paralyzed beforehand by overactive guilty consciences. But there is certainly a commonsensical hierarchy of plausibility that obtains in such cases—some things that *could* happen are more likely to come about than others.

Third, we know through *trial and error*. This is a mode of knowing that would be completely impossible under current institutional ethical guidelines. But the fact is that we do not and cannot know all possible elements in any given human social interaction, and the idea that we can predict—and thereby forestall—all harm is naïve in the extreme. An ethical research design would omit (or seek to modify) that which experience and intuition tell us is most likely to do harm; we can then proceed, but only on the understanding that the plan will be modified in the midst of the action when it becomes clear what is feasible and desirable in the real-life situation. For those uncomfortable with the indeterminacy of the term *trial and error,* Walter (1984) suggests "rational analysis and argument" (p. 38). By gathering evidence and formulating logical arguments, we try to give reasons to support our choices for certain actions over others. But the plain fact is that this way of knowing does, indeed, involve the possibility of committing an "error," perhaps one that may have unexpected harmful consequences. It is nonetheless disingenuous to hold that all possibility of harm can be anticipated and that any human action (including a research project based on interpersonal interaction) can be made risk-free. The moral advantage of the proportionate reasoning strategy is that it encourages the researcher to admit to an error once it has occurred, to correct it as far as possible, and to move on; the "objective" mode of research ethics, by contrast, encourages researchers to believe that they have eliminated all such problems, so that they are disinclined to own up to those problems that (perhaps inevitably) crop up and hence are less capable of repairing the damage. Those who work with people with developmental disabilities are familiar with the expression "the dignity of risk"; it is used to describe the "habilitation" of clients for full participation in the community. To deny the clients the possibility of making mistakes (by assuming that all risk can be eliminated beforehand and by failing to provide training in reasonable problem-solving techniques) is to deny them one of the fundamental characteristics of responsible adult living. One either lives in a shelter, protected from risk by objectified "codes," or one lives real life. The ethical paradigm suggested here does nothing more than allow the observational researcher the dignity of risk.

The logic of proportionate reason as a foundation for an ethical practice of social research might seem, at first glance, to slide into subjective relativism. Indeed, the conscience of the individual researcher plays a very large part in determining the morality of a given interaction. But proper proportionalism cannot be reduced to a proposition that an action can mean anything an individual wants it to mean, or that ethics is simply a matter of personal soul-searching. The strategy, rather, is based on a sense of community—the individual making the ethical decision must ultimately be guided by a kind of "communal discernment" (Gula, 1989, p. 278). When we speak of "experience," for example, we refer not just to personal experience, but to the "wisdom of the past" as it is embodied in the community's traditions. As such, it "demands broad consultation to seek the experience and reflection of others in order to prevent the influence of self interest from biasing perception and judgment. Using proportionalism requires more moral consultation with the community than would ever be required if the morality of actions were based on only one aspect . . . apart from its relation to all the . . . features of the action" (Gula, 1989, p. 278). That being the case, the ideal IRB would not be content with a utilitarian checklist of presumed consequences; it would constitute a circle of "wise" peers with whom the researcher could discuss and work out the sometimes conflicting demands of experience, intuition, and the potential for rational analysis and argument. The essential problem with current ethical codes, from the standpoint of qualitative observational researchers, is that they set up an arbitrary—and quite unnecessary—adversarial relationship between researchers and the rest of the scholarly community. The framework of proportionate reason implies that ethical research is the product of shared discourse, not of a species of prosecutorial inquisition.

◆ Prospects for Observational Research

As Adler and Adler (1994) remark in their chapter appearing in the first edition of this *Handbook,* "Forecasting the wax and wane of social science research methods is always uncertain" (p. 389), although they were able to do so by extrapolating from existing trends. In that same cautious spirit, we suggest that the future of observational research will most likely be in the direction of what Barrett (1996) refers to as "qualitative investigation with a difference" (p. 237). Barrett refers to the "demystification" of methodology; whereas once ethnographers spoke in a vague way about "rapport" or "empathy," they now publish and lecture extensively in the soul-baring manner suggested by the preceding literature review. One important result of that demystification is that observation can no longer be said to be a key to those grand, but somewhat opaque, units of analysis, "culture" and "society." Abu-Lughod (1991) has, indeed, urged qualitative researchers to use their techniques to undermine those concepts, which, she feels, have become the contemporary equivalents of "race"—categories that separate people, arrange them into hierarchies, and freeze the system so that institutionalized inequality prevails. To speak in such terms reifies the treatment of difference and hierarchy as somehow "natural." Observational research, by contrast, has the potential to turn our attention to what Abu-Lughod (1991) calls "the ethnography of the particular" (p. 154). Rather than attempting to describe the composite culture of a group or analyze the full range of institutions that supposedly constitute the society, the observational ethnographer will be able to provide a rounded account of the lives of particular people, the focus being on individuals and their ever-changing relationships rather than on the supposedly homogeneous, coherent, patterned, and (particularly in the case of traditional anthropologists) timeless nature of the supposed "group."

Abu-Lughod's position was foreshadowed by Geertz (1973) more than two decades ago (an indication of how slowly it takes some predictions to come to pass). Geertz advocated setting aside the traditional social science concern for "complexes of concrete behavior patterns" in favor of a "concern with the particular" based on the interpretation of "significant symbols" (p. 44). The above literature review clearly indicates that this shift is already taking place, in the interest of feminists and postmodernists of all persuasions in life history and "meaning." At present, the type of social science represented by this approach to the observation of the particular coexists uneasily with more quantitative and positivistic schools of sociology, anthropology, and social psychology. There is, however, considerable doubt as to how long that link can survive, given the very different aims and approaches of the diverging branches of the once epistemologically unified social sciences. It seems not unlikely that observational techniques will find a home in a redefined genre of cultural studies (composed of the qualitative elements of the older disciplines), leaving their positivist colleagues to carry on in a redefined social science discipline.

Humanists though they may be, observational researchers are as dependent on the evolution of technology as their quantitative colleagues. *Observation* once implied a notebook and pencil, and perhaps a sketch pad; first still and then motion pictures were later added to the ethnographer's resources. Tape recorders have been supplemented (and, in some cases, even supplanted) by video recorders. Note taking has been enhanced by the advent of the laptop computer, and computer programs for the analysis of narrative data are being developed at a brisk pace. Observation-based ethnographers are, as a consequence, being pulled in two directions. On the one hand, they speak the theoretical language of "situatedness," indeterminacy, and relativism; but on the other hand, they rely more and more on technology that suggests the capturing of "reality" in ways that could be said to transcend the individual researcher's relatively limited capacity to interpret. The technology makes it possible for the ethnographer to record and analyze people and events with a degree of particularity that would have been impossible just a decade ago, but it also has the potential to privilege what is captured on the record at the expense of the lived experience as the ethnographer has personally known it. It would be foolish to suggest that for the sake of consistency, observation-based ethnographers should eschew further traffic with sophisticated recording and analyzing technology. But it would be equally foolish to assume that the current very strong trend in the direction of individualized particularization can continue without significant modification in the face of technology that has the perceived power to objectify and turn into "data" everything it encounters. Perhaps it will become necessary for us to turn our observational powers on the very process of observation, to understand ourselves not only as psychosocial creatures (which is the current tendency) but as users of technology. As Postman (1993) has pointed out, technological change is never merely additive or subtractive, never simply an aid to doing what has always been done. It is, rather, "ecological" in the sense that a change in one aspect of behavior has ramifications throughout the entire system of which that behavior is a part. "Surrounding every technology are institutions whose organization . . . reflects the world-view promoted by that technology" (p. 18). Under those circumstances, perhaps the most effective use we can make of observational techniques in the near future will be to discern the ethos of the technology that we can no longer afford to think of as a neutral adjunct to our business-as-usual. It is a technology that itself has the capacity to define our business. We need to turn our observational powers to what happens not just when "we" encounter "them," but when "we" do so with a particular kind of totalizing technology.

Nevertheless, it seems quite clear that the once-unquestioned hegemony of positivistic epistemology that encompassed even so fundamentally humanistic a research technique as observation has now been shaken to its roots. One telling indication of the power of that transition—and a challenging indication of things to come—is a recent comment by Stephen Jay Gould (1998), the renowned paleontologist and historian of science, who has ruefully admitted:

> No faith can be more misleading than an unquestioned personal conviction that the apparent testimony of one's eyes must provide a purely objective account, scarcely requiring any validation beyond the claim itself. Utterly unbiased observation must rank as a primary myth and shibboleth of science, for we can only see what fits into our mental space, and all description includes interpretation as well as sensory reporting. (p. 72)

145

◆ Notes

1. The critique of objectivity was certainly not invented by the postmodernists. Indeed, a good case can be made that the prescient, discipline-spanning scholar Gregory Bateson (1972) was contributing rigorous and systematic analyses of the place of observers in the field long before it was considered possible to question the rationale of striving to eliminate "observer bias." His "cybernetic" theory suggested that the observer is inevitably tied to what is observed. Nevertheless, the debate that currently commands the attention of ethnographic researchers was jump-started by critics of the cultural studies persuasion, and the debate is most deeply informed by their vocabulary as well as by their specific epistemological concerns.

2. *Dialogue* need not be taken literally to mean a conversation between two parties; in practice, it often consists of multiple—even contradictory—voices.

◆ References

Abu-Lughod, L. (1991). Writing against culture. In R. G. Fox (Ed.), *Recapturing anthropology: Working in the present* (pp. 137-162). Santa Fe, NM: School of American Research Press.

Abu-Lughod, L. (1997). The interpretation of culture(s) after television. *Reflections, 59*, 109-134.

Adler, P. A., & Adler, P. (1987). *Membership roles in field research*. Newbury Park, CA: Sage.

Adler, P. A., & Adler, P. (1994). Observational techniques. In N. K. Denzin & Y. S. Lincoln (Eds.), *Handbook of qualitative research* (pp. 377-392). Thousand Oaks, CA: Sage.

Agar, M., & Feldman, H. (1980). A four-city study of PCP users: Methodology and findings. In C. Akins & G. Beschner (Eds.), *Ethnography: A research tool for policymakers in the drug and alcohol fields* (pp. 80-146). Rockville, MD: National Institute on Drug Abuse.

Altheide, D. L., & Johnson, J. M. (1994). Criteria for assessing interpretive validity in qualitative research. In N. K. Denzin & Y. S. Lincoln (Eds.), *Handbook of qualitative research* (pp. 485-499). Thousand Oaks, CA: Sage.

Altork, K. (1995). Walking the fire line: The erotic dimension of the fieldwork experience. In D. Kulick & M. Willson (Eds.), *Taboo: Sex, identity and erotic subjectivity in anthropological fieldwork* (pp. 107-139). London: Routledge.

Angrosino, M. V. (1989). The two lives of Rebecca Levenstone: Symbolic interaction in the generation of the life history. *Journal of Anthropological Research, 45*, 315-326.

Angrosino, M. V. (1991). Conversations in a monastery. *Oral History Review, 19*, 55-73.

Angrosino, M. V. (1992). Metaphors of stigma: How deinstitutionalized mentally retarded adults see themselves. *Journal of Contemporary Ethnography, 21,* 171-199.

Angrosino, M. V. (1994). On the bus with Vonnie Lee: Explorations in life history and metaphor. *Journal of Contemporary Ethnography, 23,* 14-28.

Angrosino, M. V. (1995a). Eutaw Jack: The man born blind. In B. Grindal & F. Salamone (Eds.), *Bridges to humanity: Narratives on anthropology and friendship* (pp. 7-22). Prospect Heights, IL: Waveland.

Angrosino, M. V. (1995b). *The Tampa AIDS Network: An oral history.* Tampa: University of South Florida, Center for Applied Anthropology.

Angrosino, M. V. (1997a). Among the savage Anthros: Reflections on the SAS oral history project. *Southern Anthropologist, 24,* 25-32.

Angrosino, M. V. (1997b). The ethnography of mental retardation: An applied perspective. *Journal of Contemporary Ethnography, 26,* 98-109.

Angrosino, M. V. (1998). *Opportunity House: Ethnographic stories of mental retardation.* Walnut Creek, CA: AltaMira.

Angrosino, M. V., & Zagnoli, L. J. (1992). Gender constructs and social identity: Implications for community-based care of retarded adults. In T. Whitehead & B. Reid (Eds.), *Gender constructs and social issues* (pp. 40-69). Urbana: University of Illinois Press.

Ashton-Jones, E., & Thomas, D. K. (1995). Composition, collaboration, and women's ways of knowing: A conversation with Mary Belenky. In G. A. Olson & E. Hirsh (Eds.), *Women writing culture* (pp. 81-104). Albany: State University of New York Press.

Barnett, H. G. (1983). Learning about culture: Reconstruction, participation, administration, 1934-1954. In G. W. Stocking, Jr. (Ed.), *Observers observed: Essays on ethnographic fieldwork* (pp. 157-174). Madison: University of Wisconsin Press.

Barrett, S. R. (1996). *Anthropology: A student's guide to theory and method.* Toronto: University of Toronto Press.

Bateson, G. (1972). *Steps to an ecology of mind: Collected essays in anthropology, psychiatry, evolution, and epistemology.* San Francisco: Chandler.

Behar, R. (1993). *Translated woman: Crossing the border with Esperanza's story.* Boston: Beacon.

Behar, R. (1996). *The vulnerable observer: Anthropology that breaks your heart.* Boston: Beacon.

Bell, J., & Jankowiak, W. R. (1992). The ethnographer vs. the folk expert: Pitfalls of contract ethnography. *Human Organization, 51,* 412-417.

Berik, G. (1996). Understanding the gender system in rural Turkey: Fieldwork dilemmas of conformity and intervention. In D. L. Wolf (Ed.), *Feminist dilemmas in fieldwork* (pp. 56-71). Boulder, CO: Westview.

Bernard, H. R. (1988). *Research methods in cultural anthropology*. Newbury Park, CA: Sage.

Blackwood, E. (1995). Falling in love with an-Other lesbian: Reflections on identity in fieldwork. In D. Kulick & M. Willson (Eds.), *Taboo: Sex, identity and erotic subjectivity in anthropological fieldwork* (pp. 51-75). London: Routledge.

Bolton, R. (1995). Tricks, friends, and lovers: Erotic encounters in the field. In D. Kulick & M. Willson (Eds.), *Taboo: Sex, identity and erotic subjectivity in anthropological fieldwork* (pp. 140-167). London: Routledge.

Bolton, R. (1996). Coming home: The journey of a gay ethnographer in the years of the plague. In E. Lewin & W. L. Leap (Eds.), *Out in the field: Reflections of lesbian and gay anthropologists* (pp. 147-170). Urbana: University of Illinois Press.

Brewer, D. D. (1992). Hip hop graffiti writers' evaluations of strategies to control illegal graffiti. *Human Organization, 51,* 188-196.

Burkhart, G. (1996). Not given to personal disclosure. In E. Lewin & W. L. Leap (Eds.), *Out in the field: Reflections of lesbian and gay anthropologists* (pp. 31-48). Urbana: University of Illinois Press.

Cahill, L. S. (1981). Teleology, utilitarianism, and Christian ethics. *Theological Studies, 42,* 601-629.

Chavez, L. R., Flores, E. T., & Lopez-Garza, M. (1990). Here today, gone tomorrow? Undocumented settlers and immigration reform. *Human Organization, 49,* 193-205.

Clifford, J. (1983a). On ethnographic authority. *Representations, 1,* 118-146.

Clifford, J. (1983b). Power and dialogue in ethnography: Marcel Griaule's initiation. In G. W. Stocking, Jr. (Ed.), *Observers observed: Essays on ethnographic fieldwork* (pp. 121-156). Madison: University of Wisconsin Press.

Cole, D. (1983). "The value of a person lies in his *Herzenbildung*": Franz Boas' Baffin Island letter-diary, 1883-1884. In G. W. Stocking, Jr. (Ed.), *Observers observed: Essays* on ethnographic fieldwork (pp. 13-52). Madison: University of Wisconsin Press.

Curran, C. E. (1979). Utilitarianism and contemporary moral theology: Situating the debates. In C. E. Curran & R. A. McCormick (Eds.), *Readings in moral theology* (pp. 341-362). Ramsey, NJ: Paulist Press.

Dembo, R., Hughes, P., Jackson, L., & Mieczkowski, T. (1993). Crack cocaine dealing by adolescents in two public housing projects: A pilot study. *Human Organization, 52,* 89-96.

Denzin, N. K. (1997a). *Interpretive ethnography: Ethnographic practices for the 21st century*. Thousand Oaks, CA: Sage.

Denzin, N. K. (1997b). Performance texts. In W. G. Tierney & Y. S. Lincoln (Eds.), *Representation and the text: Re-framing the narrative voice* (pp. 179-218). Albany: State University of New York Press.

Dubisch, J. (1995). Lovers in the field: Sex, dominance, and the female anthropologist. In D. Kulick & M. Willson (Eds.), *Taboo: Sex, identity and erotic subjectivity in anthropological fieldwork* (pp. 29-50). London: Routledge.

Edelman, M. (1996). Devil, not-quite-white, rootless cosmopolitan: *Tsuris* in Latin America, the Bronx, and the USSR. In C. Ellis & A. P. Bochner (Eds.), *Composing ethnography: Alternative forms of qualitative writing* (pp. 267-300). Walnut Creek, CA: AltaMira.

Ellis, C. (1997). Evocative autoethnography: Writing emotionally about our lives. In W. G. Tierney & Y. S. Lincoln (Eds.), *Representation and the text: Reframing the narrative voice* (pp. 115-142). Albany: State University of New York Press.

Ferguson, J. (1996). The country and the city on the copperbelt. In A. Gupta & J. Ferguson (Eds.), *Culture, power, place: Explorations in critical anthropology* (pp. 137-154). Durham, NC: Duke University Press.

Fluehr-Lobban, C. (1994). Informed consent in anthropological research: We are not exempt. *Human Organization, 53,* 1-10.

Fox, K. V. (1996). Silent voices: A subversive reading of child sexual abuse. In C. Ellis & A. P. Bochner (Eds.), *Composing ethnography: Alternative forms of qualitative writing* (pp. 330-356). Walnut Creek, CA: AltaMira.

Gearing, J. (1995). Fear and loving in the West Indies: Research from the heart (as well as the head). In D. Kulick & M. Willson (Eds.), *Taboo: Sex, identity and erotic subjectivity in anthropological fieldwork* (pp. 186-218). London: Routledge.

Geertz, C. (1973). *The interpretation of cultures: Selected essays.* New York: Basic Books.

Giroux, H. A. (1995). Writing the space of the public intellectual. In G. A. Olson & E. Hirsh (Eds.), *Women writing culture* (pp. 195-198). Albany: State University of New York Press.

Gold, R. L. (1958). Roles in sociological field observation. *Social Forces, 36,* 217-223.

Gold, R. L. (1997). The ethnographic method in sociology. *Qualitative Inquiry, 3,* 388-402.

Goodman, L. (1996). Rites of passing. In E. Lewin & W. L. Leap (Eds.), *Out in the field: Reflections of lesbian and gay anthropologists* (pp. 49-57). Urbana: University of Illinois Press.

Gould, S. J. (1998). The sharp-eyed lynx, outfoxed by nature (part two). *Natural History, 107,* 23-27, 69-73.

Gula, R. M. (1989). *Reason informed by faith.* New York: Paulist Press.

Gupta, A., & Ferguson, J. (1996a). Beyond "culture": Space, identity, and the politics of difference. In A. Gupta & J. Ferguson (Eds.), *Culture, power, place: Explorations in critical anthropology* (pp. 33-52). Durham, NC: Duke University Press.

Gupta, A., & Ferguson, J. (1996b). Culture, power, place: Ethnography at the end of an era. In A. Gupta & J. Ferguson (Eds.), *Culture, power, place: Explorations in critical anthropology* (pp. 1-32). Durham, NC: Duke University Press.

Gupta, A., & Ferguson, J. (1996c). Discipline and practice: "The field" as site, method, and location in anthropology. In A. Gupta & J. Ferguson (Eds.), *Anthropological locations: Boundaries and grounds of a field science* (pp. 1-46). Berkeley: University of California Press.

Hammond, J. L. (1996). Popular education in the Salvadoran guerrilla army. *Human Organization, 55,* 436-445.

Hannerz, U. (1969). *Soulside.* New York: Columbia University Press.

Hareven, T. (1996). The search for generational memory. In D. K. Dunaway & W. K. Baum (Eds.), *Oral history: An interdisciplinary anthology* (2nd ed., pp. 241-256). Walnut Creek, CA: AltaMira.

Hinsley, C. (1983). Ethnographic charisma and scientific routine: Cushing and Fewkes in the American Southwest, 1879-1893. In G. W. Stocking, Jr. (Ed.), *Observers observed: Essays on ethnographic fieldwork* (pp. 53-69). Madison: University of Wisconsin Press.

Hirsh, E., & Olson, G. A. (1995). Starting from marginalized lives: A conversation with Sandra Harding. In G. A. Olson & E. Hirsh (Eds.), *Women writing culture* (pp. 3-44). Albany: State University of New York Press.

Hoose, B. (1987). *Proportionalism.* Washington: Georgetown University Press.

Hsiung, P.-C. (1996). Between bosses and workers: The dilemma of a keen observer and a vocal feminist. In D. L. Wolf (Ed.), *Feminist dilemmas in fieldwork* (pp. 122-137). Boulder, CO: Westview.

Hubbard, A. S. (1997). Face-to-face at arm's length: Conflict norms and extra-group relations in grassroots dialogue groups. *Human Organization, 56,* 265-274.

Janssens, L. (1979). Ontic evil and moral evil. In C. E. Curran & R. A. McCormick (Eds.), *Readings in moral theology* (pp. 49-72). Ramsey, NJ: Paulist Press.

Kennedy, E. L., & Davis, M. (1996). Constructing an ethnohistory of the Buffalo lesbian community: Reflexivity, dialogue, and politics. In E. Lewin & W. L. Leap (Eds.), *Out in the field: Reflections of gay and lesbian anthropologists* (pp. 171-199). Urbana: University of Illinois Press.

Killick, A. P. (1995). The penetrating intellect: On being white, straight, and male in Korea. In D. Kulick & M. Willson (Eds.), *Taboo: Sex, identity and erotic subjectivity in anthropological fieldwork* (pp. 76-106). London: Routledge.

Koester, S. K. (1994). Copping, running, and paraphernalia laws: Contextual variables and needle risk behavior among injection drug users in Denver. *Human Organization, 53,* 287-295.

Kolker, A. (1996). Thrown overboard: The human costs of health care rationing. In C. Ellis & A. P. Bochner (Eds.), *Composing ethnography: Alternative forms of qualitative writing* (pp. 132-159). Walnut Creek, CA: AltaMira.

Kuhlmann, A. (1992). Collaborative research among the Kickapoo tribe of Oklahoma. *Human Organization, 51,* 274-283.

Kuklick, H. (1996). After Ishmael: The fieldwork tradition and its future. In A. Gupta & J. Ferguson (Eds.), *Anthropological locations: Boundaries and grounds of a field science* (pp. 47-65). Berkeley: University of California Press.

Lang, S. (1996). Traveling woman: Conducting a fieldwork project on gender variance and homosexuality among North American Indians. In E. Lewin & W. L. Leap (Eds.), *Out in the field: Reflections of lesbian and gay anthropologists* (pp. 86-110). Urbana: University of Illinois Press.

Larcom, J. (1983). Following Deacon: The problem of ethnographic reanalysis, 1926-1981. In G. W. Stocking, Jr. (Ed.), *Observers observed: Essays on ethnographic fieldwork* (pp. 175-195). Madison: University of Wisconsin Press.

Lather, P. (1997). Creating a multilayered text: Women, AIDS, and angels. In W. G. Tierney & Y. S. Lincoln (Eds.), *Representation and the text: Re-framing the narrative voice* (pp. 233-258). Albany: State University of New York Press.

Lewin, E., & Leap, W. L. (1996). Introduction. In E. Lewin & W. L. Leap (Eds.), *Out in the field: Reflections of lesbian and gay anthropologists* (pp. 1-30). Urbana: University of Illinois Press.

Liebow, E. (1967). *Tally's corner: A study of Negro street corner men.* Boston: Little, Brown.

Maddox, R. (1996). Bombs, bikinis, and the popes of rock 'n' roll: Reflections on resistance, the play of subordinations, and liberalism in Andalusia and academia, 1983-1995. In A. Gupta & J. Ferguson (Eds.), *Culture, power, place: Explorations in critical anthropology* (pp. 277-290). Durham, NC: Duke University Press.

Mahmood, C. K. (1996). Why Sikhs fight. In A. Wolfe & H. Yang (Eds.), *Anthropological contributions to conflict resolution* (pp. 7-30). Athens: University of Georgia Press.

Malkki, L. H. (1996a). National geographic: The rooting of peoples and the territorialization of national identity among scholars and refugees. In A. Gupta & J. Ferguson (Eds.), *Culture, power, place: Explorations in critical anthropology* (pp. 53-74). Durham, NC: Duke University Press.

Malkki, L. H. (1996b). News and culture: Transitory phenomena and the fieldwork tradition. In A. Gupta & J. Ferguson (Eds.), *Anthropological locations: Boundaries and grounds of a field science* (pp. 86-101). Berkeley: University of California Press.

Marcus, G. E. (1997). The uses of complicity in the changing mise-en-scène of anthropological fieldwork. *Reflections, 59,* 85-108.

Matsumoto, V. (1996). Reflections on oral history: Research in a Japanese American community. In D. L. Wolf (Ed.), *Feminist dilemmas in fieldwork* (pp. 160-169). Boulder, CO: Westview.

McCall, G. J., Ngeva, J., & Mbebe, M. (1997). Mapping conflict cultures: Interpersonal disputing in a South African black township. *Human Organization, 56,* 71-78.

McCormick, R. A. (1973). *Ambiguity and moral choice.* Milwaukee, WI: Marquette University Press.

McCormick, R. A., & Ramsey, P. (1978). *Doing evil to achieve good.* Chicago: Loyola University Press.

Mienczakowski, J. (1996). An ethnographic act: The construction of consensual theater. In C. Ellis & A. P. Bochner (Eds.), *Composing ethnography: Alternative forms of qualitative writing* (pp. 244-266). Walnut Creek, CA: AltaMira.

Miles, M. B., & Huberman, A. M. (1994). *Qualitative data analysis: An expanded sourcebook* (2nd ed.). Thousand Oaks, CA: Sage.

Moreno, E. (1995). Rape in the field: Reflections from a survivor. In D. Kulick & M. Willson (Eds.), *Taboo: Sex, identity and erotic subjectivity in anthropological fieldwork* (pp. 219-250). London: Routledge.

Morton, H. (1995). My "chastity belt": Avoiding seduction in Tonga. In D. Kulick & M. Willson (Eds.), *Taboo: Sex, identity and erotic subjectivity in anthropological fieldwork* (pp. 168-185). London: Routledge.

Murray, S. P. (1996). Male homosexuality in Guatemala: Possible insights and certain confusions from sleeping with the natives. In E. Lewin & W. L. Leap (Eds.), *Out in the field: Reflections of lesbian and gay anthropologists* (pp. 236-260). Urbana: University of Illinois Press.

Newton, E. (1993). My best informant's dress: The erotic equation in fieldwork. *Cultural Anthropology, 8,* 3-23.

Olson, G. A. (1995a). Resisting a discourse of mastery: A conversation with Jean-François Lyotard. In G. A. Olson & E. Hirsh (Eds.), *Women writing culture* (pp. 169-194). Albany: State University of New York Press.

Olson, G. A. (1995b). Writing, literacy and technology: Toward a cyborg writing. In G. A. Olson & E. Hirsh (Eds.), *Women writing culture* (pp. 45-80). Albany: State University of New York Press.

Olson, G. A., & Hirsh, E. (1995). Feminist praxis and the politics of literacy: A conversation with bell hooks. In G. A. Olson & E. Hirsh (Eds.), *Women writing culture* (pp. 105-140). Albany: State University of New York Press.

Pelto, P. J., & Pelto, G. H. (1978). *Anthropological research: The structure of inquiry* (2nd ed.). New York: Cambridge University Press.

Peters, J. D. (1996). Seeing bifocally: Media, place, culture. In A. Gupta & J. Ferguson (Eds.), *Culture, power, place: Explorations in critical anthropology* (pp. 75-92). Durham, NC: Duke University Press.

Polkinghorne, D. E. (1997). Reporting qualitative research as practice. In W. G. Tierney & Y. S. Lincoln (Eds.), *Representation and the text: Re-framing the narrative voice* (pp. 3-22). Albany: State University of New York Press.

Postman, N. (1993). *Technopoly: The surrender of culture to technology.* New York: Vintage.

Quinney, R. (1996). Once my father traveled west to California. In C. Ellis & A. P. Bochner (Eds.), *Composing ethnography: Alternative forms of qualitative writing* (pp. 357-382). Walnut Creek, CA: AltaMira.

Ronai, C. R. (1996). My mother is mentally retarded. In C. Ellis & A. P. Bochner (Eds.), *Composing ethnography: Alternative forms of qualitative writing* (pp. 109-131). Walnut Creek, CA: AltaMira.

Rossman, G. B., & Rallis, S. F. (1998). *Learning in the field: An introduction to qualitative research.* Thousand Oaks, CA: Sage.

Sewell, W. H. (1997). Geertz and history: From synchrony to transformation. *Reflections, 59,* 35-55.

Silverman, D. (1993). *Interpreting qualitative data: Strategies for analysing talk, text and interaction.* London: Sage.

Sluka, J. A. (1990). Participant observation in violent social contexts. *Human Organization, 49,* 114-126.

Stepick, A., & Stepick, C. D. (1990). People in the shadows: Survey research among Haitians in Miami. *Human Organization, 49,* 64-77.

Stocking, G. W., Jr. (1983a). The ethnographer's magic: Fieldwork in British anthropology from Tylor to Malinowski. In G. W. Stocking, Jr. (Ed.), *Observers observed: Essays on ethnographic fieldwork* (pp. 70-120). Madison: University of Wisconsin Press.

Stocking, G. W., Jr. (1983b). History of anthropology: Whence/whither. In G. W. Stocking, Jr. (Ed.), *Observers observed: Essays on ethnographic fieldwork* (pp. 3-12). Madison: University of Wisconsin Press.

Tanaka, G. (1997). Pico College. In W. G. Tierney & Y. S. Lincoln (Eds.), *Representation and the text: Re-framing the narrative voice* (pp. 259-304). Albany: State University of New York Press.

Tierney, W. G. (1997). Lost in translation: Time and voice in qualitative research. In W. G. Tierney & Y. S. Lincoln (Eds.), *Representation and the text: Re-framing the narrative voice* (pp. 23-36). Albany: State University of New York Press.

Tillman-Healy, L. M. (1996). A secret life in a culture of thinness: Reflections on body, food, and bulimia. In C. Ellis & A. P. Bochner (Eds.), *Composing ethnography: Alternative forms of qualitative writing* (pp. 76-108). Walnut Creek, CA: AltaMira.

van Gelder, P. J., & Kaplan, C. D. (1992). The finishing moment: Temporal and spatial features of sexual interactions between streetwalkers and car clients. *Human Organization, 51,* 253-263.

Walter, J. (1984). Proportionate reason and its three levels of inquiry: Structuring the ongoing debate. *Louvain Studies, 10,* 30-40.

Walters, D. M. (1996). Cast among outcastes: Interpreting sexual orientation, racial, and gender identity in the Yemen Arab Republic. In E. Lewin & W. L. Leap (Eds.), *Out in the field: Reflections of lesbian and gay anthropologists* (pp. 58-69). Urbana: University of Illinois Press.

Wax, M. L., & Cassell, J. (1979). *Federal regulations: Ethical issues and social research.* Boulder, CO: Westview.

Werner, O., & Schoepfle, G. M. (1987). *Systematic fieldwork: Vol. 1. Foundations of ethnography and interviewing.* Newbury Park, CA: Sage.

Weston, K. (1996). Requiem for a street fighter. In E. Lewin & W. L. Leap (Eds.), *Out in the field: Reflections of lesbian and gay anthropologists* (pp. 274-286). Urbana: University of Illinois Press.

Whyte, W. F. (1955). *Street corner society: The social structure of an Italian slum* (2nd ed.). Chicago: University of Chicago Press.

Williams, W. L. (1996). Being gay and doing fieldwork. In E. Lewin & W. L. Leap (Eds.), *Out in the field: Reflections of lesbian and gay anthropologists* (pp. 70-85). Urbana: University of Illinois Press.

Willson, M. (1995). Perspective and difference: Sexualization, the field, and the ethnographer. In D. Kulick & M. Willson (Eds.), *Taboo: Sex, identity and erotic subjectivity in anthropological fieldwork* (pp. 251-275). London: Routledge.

Wolcott, H. F. (1995). *The art of fieldwork.* Walnut Creek, CA: AltaMira.

Wolf, D. L. (1996). Situating feminist dilemmas in fieldwork. In D. L. Wolf (Ed.), *Feminist dilemmas in fieldwork* (pp. 1-55). Boulder, CO: Westview.

Wolf, M. A. (1992). *A thrice-told tale: Feminism, postmodernism, and ethnographic responsibility.* Stanford, CA: Stanford University Press.

Wolf, M. A. (1996). Afterword: Musings from an old gray wolf. In D. L. Wolf (Ed.), *Feminist dilemmas in fieldwork* (pp. 215-222). Boulder, CO: Westview.

4

The Interpretation of Documents and Material Culture

Ian Hodder

◆ This chapter is concerned with the interpretation of mute
evidence—that is, with written texts and artifacts. Such evidence,
unlike the spoken word, endures physically and thus can be separated
across space and time from its author, producer, or user. Material traces
thus often have to be interpreted without the benefit of indigenous commentary. There is often no possibility of interaction with spoken emic
"insider" as opposed to etic "outsider" perspectives. Even when such
interaction is possible, actors often seem curiously inarticulate about the
reasons they dress in particular ways, choose particular pottery designs, or
discard dung in particular locations. Material traces and residues thus
pose special problems for qualitative research. The main disciplines that
have tried to develop appropriate theory and method are history, art history, archaeology, anthropology, sociology, cognitive psychology, technology, and modern material culture studies, and it is from this range of
disciplines that my account is drawn.

◆ Written Documents and Records

Lincoln and Guba (1985, p. 277) distinguish documents and records on the basis of whether the text was prepared to attest to some formal transaction. Thus records include marriage certificates, driving licenses, building contracts, and banking statements. Documents, on the other hand, are prepared for personal rather than official reasons and include diaries, memos, letters, field notes, and so on. In fact, the two terms are often used interchangeably, although the distinction is an important one and has some parallels with the distinction between writing and speech, to be discussed below. Documents, closer to speech, require more contextualized interpretation. Records, on the other hand, may have local uses that become very distant from officially sanctioned meanings. Documents involve a personal technology, and records a full state technology of power. The distinction is also relevant for qualitative research, in that researchers may often be able to get access to documents, whereas access to records may be restricted by laws regarding privacy, confidentiality, and anonymity.

Despite the utility of the distinction between documents and records, my concern here is more the problems of interpretation of written texts of all kinds. Such texts are of importance for qualitative research because, in general terms, access can be easy and low cost, because the information provided may differ from and may not be available in spoken form, and because texts endure and thus give historical insight.

It has often been assumed, for example, in the archaeology of historical periods, that written texts provide a "truer" indication of original meanings than do other types of evidence (to be considered below). Indeed, Western social science has long privileged the spoken over the written and the written over the nonverbal (Derrida, 1978). Somehow it is assumed that words get us closer to minds. But as Derrida has shown, meaning does not reside in a text but in the writing and reading of it. As the text is reread in different contexts it is given new meanings, often contradictory and always socially embedded. Thus there is no "original" or "true" meaning of a text outside specific historical contexts. Historical archaeologists have come to accept that historical documents and records give not a better but simply a different picture from that provided by artifacts and architecture. Texts can be used alongside other forms of evidence so that the particular biases of each can be understood and compared.

Equally, different types of texts have to be understood in the contexts of their conditions of production and reading. For example, the analyst will be concerned with whether a text was written as a result of firsthand experience or from secondary sources, whether it was solicited or unsolicited, edited or unedited, anonymous or signed, and so on (Webb, Campbell, Schwartz, & Sechrest, 1966). As Ricoeur (1971) demonstrates, concrete texts differ from the abstract structures of language in that they are written to do something. They can be understood only as what they are—a form of artifact produced under certain material conditions (not everyone can write, or write in a certain way, or have access to relevant technologies of reproduction) embedded within social and ideological systems.

Words are, of course, spoken to do things as well as to say things—they have practical and social impact as well as communication function. Once words are transformed into a written text, the gap between the "author" and the "reader" widens and the possibility of multiple reinterpretations increases. The text can "say" many different things in different contexts. But also the written text is an artifact, capable of transmission, manipulation, and alteration, of being used and discarded, reused and recycled— "doing" different things contextually through time. The writing down of words often allows language and meanings to be controlled more effectively, and to be linked to strategies of centralization and codification. The word, concretized or "made flesh" in the artifact, can transcend context and gather through time extended symbolic connotations. The word made enduring in artifacts has an important role to play in both secular and religious processes of the legitimation of power. Yet there is often a tension between the concrete nature of the written word, its enduring nature, and the continuous potential for rereading meanings in new contexts, undermining the authority of the word. Text and context are in a continual state of tension, each defining and redefining the other, saying and doing things differently through time.

In a related way, the written texts of anthropologists and archaeologists are increasingly coming under scrutiny as employing rhetorical strategies in order to establish positions of authority (e.g., Tilley, 1989). Archaeologists are used to the idea that their scientific activities leave traces and transform the worlds they study. Excavations cannot be repeated, and the residues of trenches, spoil tips, and old beer cans remain as specific expressions of a particular way of looking at the world. The past has been transformed into a present product, including the field notes and site reports. Ethnographic field notes (Sanjek, 1990) also transform the object of study into a historically situated product, "capturing" the "other" within a familiar routine. The field text has to be contextualized within specific historical moments.

I shall in this chapter treat written texts as special cases of artifacts, subject to similar interpretive procedures. In both texts and artifacts the problem is one of situating material culture within varying contexts while at the same time entering into a dialectic relationship between those contexts and the context of the analyst. This hermeneutical exercise, in which the lived experience surrounding the material culture is translated into a different context of interpretation, is common for both texts and other forms of material culture. I will note various differences between language and material culture in what follows, but the interpretive parallels have been widely discussed in the consideration of material culture as text (e.g., Hodder, 1991; Moore, 1986; Tilley, 1990).

◆ Artifact Analysis and Its Importance for the Interpretation of Social Experience

Ancient and modern buildings and artifacts, the intended and unintended residues of human activity, give alternative insights into the ways in which people perceived and fashioned their lives. Shortcuts across lawns indicate preferred traffic patterns, foreign-language signs indicate the degree of integration of a neighborhood, the number of cigarettes in an ashtray betrays a nervous tension, and the amount of paperwork in an "in" tray is a measure of workload or of work efficiency and priority (Lincoln & Guba, 1985, p. 280). Despite the inferential problems surrounding such evidence, I wish to establish at the outset that material traces of behavior give an important and different insight from that provided by any number of questionnaires.

"What people say" is often very different from "what people do." This point has perhaps been most successfully established over recent years by research stemming from the work of Bill Rathje (Rathje & Murphy, 1992; Rathje & Thompson, 1981). In studies in Tucson, Arizona, and elsewhere, Rathje and his colleagues collected domestic garbage bags and itemized the contents. It became clear that, for example, people's estimates about the amounts of garbage they produced were wildly incorrect, that discarded beer cans indicated a higher level of alcohol consumption than was admitted to, and that in times of meat shortage people threw away more meat than usual as a result of overhoarding. Thus a full sociological analysis cannot be restricted to interview data. It must also consider the material traces.

In another series of studies, the decoration of rooms as well as pots and other containers has been interpreted as a form of silent discourse conducted by women, whose voice has been silenced by dominant male interests. Decoration may be used to mark out, silently, and to draw attention to, tacitly, areas of female control, such as female areas of houses and the preparation and provision of food in containers. The decoration may at one level provide protection from female pollution, but at another level it expresses female power (Braithwaite, 1982; Donley, 1982; Hodder, 1991).

The study of material culture is thus of importance for qualitative researchers who wish to explore multiple and conflicting voices, differing and interacting interpretations. Many areas of experience are hidden from language, particularly subordinate experience. Ferguson (1991) has shown how study of the material traces of food and pots can provide insight into how slaves on plantations in the American South made sense of and reacted to their domination. The members of this normally silenced group expressed their own perspective in the mundane activities of everyday life.

Analysis of such traces is not a trivial pursuit, as the mundane and the everyday, because unimportant to dominant interests, may be of great importance for the expression of alternative perspectives. The material expression of power (parades, regalia, tombs, and art) can be set against the expression of resistance. The importance of such analysis is increased by the realization that material culture is not simply a passive by-product of other areas of life. Rather, material culture is active (Hodder, 1982). By this I mean that artifacts are produced so as to transform, materially, socially, and ideologically. It is the exchange of artifacts themselves that constructs social relationships; it is the style of spear that creates a feeling of common identity; it is the badge of authority that itself confers authority. Material culture is thus *necessary for* most social constructs. An adequate study of social interaction thus depends on the incorporation of mute material evidence.

◆ Toward a Theory of Material Culture

Having established that the study of material culture can be an important tool for sociological and anthropological analysis, we must attempt to build a theory on which the interpretation of material culture can be based. A difficulty here has been the diversity of the category "material culture," ranging from written texts to material symbols surrounding death, drama, and ritual to shopping behavior and to the construction of roads and airplanes. As a result, theoretical directions have often taken rather different paths, as one can see by comparing attempts to build a comprehensive theory for technological behavior (Lemonnier, 1986) and attempts to consider material culture as text (Tilley, 1990).

Ultimately, material culture always has to be interpreted in relation to a situated context of production, use, discard, and reuse. In working toward that contextual interpretation, it may be helpful to distinguish some general characteristics and analogies for the different types of material culture. In this attempt to build a general theory, recent research in a range of disciplines has begun to separate two areas of material meaning.

Some material culture is designed specifically to be communicative and representational. The clearest example is a written text, but this category extends, for example, to the badge and uniform of certain professions, to red and green stop and go traffic lights, to smoke signals, to the images of Christ on the cross. Because this category includes written texts, it is to be expected that meaning in this category might be organized in ways similar to language. Thus, as with words in a language, the material symbols are, outside a historical context, often arbitrary. For example, any design on a flag could be used as long as it differs from the designs on other flags and is recognizable with its own identity. Thus the system of meanings in the case of flags is constructed through similarities and differences in a semiotic code. Miller (1982) has shown how dress is organized both syntagmatically and paradigmatically. The choice of hat, tie, shirt, trousers, shoes, and so on for a particular occasion is informed by a syntax that allows a particular set of clothes to be put together. On the other hand, the distinctions among different types of hats (bowler, straw, cloth, baseball) or jackets constitute paradigmatic choices.

The three broad areas of theory that have been applied to this first type of material meaning derive from information technology, Marxism, and structuralism. In the first, the aim has been to account for the ways in which material symboling can provide adaptive advantage to social groups. Thus the development of complex symboling systems allows more information to be processed more efficiently (e.g., Wobst, 1977). This type of approach is of limited value to qualitative research because it is not concerned with the interpretation and experience of meaningful symbols.

In the second, the ideological component of symbols is identified within relations of power and domination (Leone, 1984; Miller & Tilley, 1984) and increasingly power and systems of value and prestige are seen as multiple and dialectical (Miller, Rowlands, & Tilley, 1989; Shanks & Tilley, 1987). The aim of structuralist analysis has been to examine design (e.g., Washburn, 1983) or spatial relationships (e.g., Glassie, 1975; McGhee, 1977) in terms of underlying codes, although here too the tendency has been to emphasize multiple meanings contested within active social contexts as the various directions of poststructuralist thought have been debated (Tilley, 1990).

In much of this work the metaphor of language has been applied to material culture relatively unproblematically. The pot appears to "mean" in the same way as the word *pot*. Recent work has begun to draw attention to the limitations of this analogy between material culture and language, as will become clear in my consideration of the second type of material culture meaning. One can begin to explore the limitations of the analogy by considering that many examples of material culture are not produced to "mean" at all. In other words, they are not produced with symbolic functions as primary. Thus the madeleine cookie discussed in Proust's *A la recherche du temps perdu* (*Swann's Way*) was produced as an enticing food made in a shape representing a fluted scallop. But Proust describes its meaning as quite different from this symbolic representation. Rather, the meaning was the evocation of a whole series of childhood memories, sounds, tastes, smells surrounding Proust's having tea with his mother in winter.

Many if not most material symbols do not work through rules of representation, using a language-like syntax. Rather, they work through the evocation of sets of practices within individual experience. It would be relatively difficult to construct a grammar or dictionary of material symbols except in the case of deliberately representational or symbolic items, such as flags and road signs. This is because most material symbols do not mean in the same way as language. Rather, they come to have abstract meaning through association and practice. Insofar as members of society experience common practices, material symbols can come to have common evocations and common meanings. Thus, for example, the ways in which certain types of food, drink, music, and sport are experienced are embedded within social convention and thus come to have common meaning. A garlic crusher may not be used overtly in Britain to represent or symbolize class, but through a complex set of practices surrounding food and its preparation, the crusher has come to mean class through evocation.

Because objects endure, have their own traces, their own grain, individual objects with unique evocations can be recognized. The specific memory traces associated with any particular object (a particular garlic crusher) will vary from individual to individual. The particularity of material experience and meaning derives not only from the diversity of human life but also from the identifiability of material objects. The identifiable particularity of material experience always has the potential to work against and transform societywide conventions through practice. Because of this dialectic between structure and practice, and because of the multiple local meanings that can be given to things, it would be difficult to construct dictionaries and grammars for most material culture meanings.

Another reason for the inability to produce dictionaries of material culture returns us to the difficulty with which people give discursive accounts of material symbolism. The meanings often remain tacit and implicit. A smell or taste of a madeleine cookie may awake strong feelings, but it is notoriously difficult to describe a taste or a feel or to pin down the emotions evoked. We may know that in practice this or that item of clothing "looks good," "works well," or "is stylish," but we would be at a loss to say what it "means" because the item does not mean—rather, it is embedded in a set of practices that include class, status, goals, aesthetics. We may not know much about art, but we know what we like. On the basis of a set of practical associations, we build up an implicit knowledge about the associations and evocations of particular artifacts or styles. This type of embedded, practical experience seems to be different from the manipulation of rules of representation and from conscious analytic thought. Material symbolic meanings may get us close to lived experience, but they cannot easily be articulated.

The importance of practice for the social and symbolic meanings of artifacts has been emphasized in recent work on technology (Schlanger, 1990). Each technical operation is linked to others in operational chains (Leroi-Gourhan, 1964) involving materials, energy, and gestures. For example, some clays are better for throwing than others, so the type of clay constrains whether a manufacturer can make thrown pots or hand-built statuettes. Quality of clay is related to types of temper that should be used. All such operational chains are nondeterministic, and some degree of social choice is involved (Lemonnier, 1986; Miller, 1985). All operational chains involve aspects of production, exchange, and consumption, and so

162

are part of a network of relations incorporating the material, the economic, the social, and the conceptual.

The practical operational chains often have implications that extend into not only social but also moral realms. For example, Latour (1988) discusses hydraulic door closers, devices that automatically close a door after someone has opened it. The material door closer thus takes the place of, or delegates, the role of a porter, someone who stands there and makes sure that the door stays shut after people have gone through. But use of this particular delegate has various implications, one of which is that very young or infirm people have difficulty getting through the door. A social distinction is unwittingly implied by this technology. In another example, Latour discusses a key used by some inhabitants of Berlin. This double-ended key forces the user to lock the door in order to get the key out. The key delegates for staff or signs that might order a person to "relock the door behind you." Staff or signs would be unreliable—they could be outwitted or ignored. The key enforces a morality. In the same way, "sleeping policemen" (speed bumps) force the driver of a car to be moral and to slow down in front of a school, but this morality is not socially encoded. That would be too unreliable. The morality is embedded within the practical consequences of breaking up one's car by driving too fast over the bumps. The social and moral meanings of the door closer, the Berlin key, or the speed bump are thoroughly embedded in the implications of material practices.

I have suggested that in developing a theory of material culture, the first task is to distinguish at least two different ways in which material culture has abstract meaning beyond primary utilitarian concerns. The first is through rules of representation. The second is through practice and evocation—through the networking, interconnection, and mutual implication of material and nonmaterial. Whereas it may be the case that written language is the prime example of the first category and tools the prime example of the second, language also has to be worked out in practices from which it derives much of its meaning. Equally, we have seen that material items can be placed within language-like codes. But there is some support from cognitive psychology for a general difference between the two types of knowledge. For example, Bechtel (1990, p. 264) argues that rule-based models of cognition are naturally good at quite different types of activity from connectionist models. Where the first is appropriate for problem solving, the second is best at tasks such as pattern recognition and motor control. It seems likely, then, that the skills involved in material practice and the social, symbolic, and moral meanings that are implicated in such practices might involve different cognitive systems from those involved in rules and representations.

Bloch (1991) argues that practical knowledge is fundamentally different from linguistic knowledge in the way it is organized in the mind. Practical knowledge is "chunked" into highly contextualized information about how to "get on" in specific domains of action. Much cultural knowledge is nonlinear and purpose dedicated, formed through the practice of closely related activities. I have argued here that even the practical world involves social and symbolic meanings that are not organized representational codes but that are chunked or contextually organized realms of activity in which emotions, desires, morals, and social relations are involved at the level of implicit taken-for-granted skill or know-how.

It should perhaps be emphasized that the two types of material symbolism—the representational and the evocative or implicative—often work in close relation to each other. Thus a set of practices may associate men and women with different parts of houses or times of day, but in certain social contexts these associations might be built upon to construct symbolic rules of separation and exclusion and to build an abstract representational scheme in which mythology and cosmology play a part (e.g., Yates, 1989). Such schemes also have ideological components that feed back to constrain the practices. Thus practice, evocation, and representation interpenetrate and feed off each other in many if not all areas of life. Structure and practice are recursively related in the "structuration" of material life (Giddens, 1979; see also Bourdieu, 1977).

◆ Material Meanings in Time

It appears that people both experience and "read" material culture meanings. There is much more that could be said about how material culture works in the social context. For instance, some examples work by direct and explicit metaphor, where similarities in form refer to historical antecedents, whereas others work by being ambiguous and abstract, by using spectacle or dramatic effect, by controlling the approach of the onlooker, by controlling perspective. Although there is not space here to explore the full range of material strategies, it is important to establish the temporal dimension of lived experience.

As already noted, material culture is durable and can be given new meanings as it is separated from its primary producer. This temporal variation in meaning is often related to changes in meaning across space and culture. Archaeological or ethnographic artifacts are continually being taken out of their contexts and reinterpreted within museums within different social and cultural contexts. The Elgin Marbles housed in the British Museum take on new meanings that are in turn reinterpreted antagonistically in some circles in Greece. American Indian human and artifact remains may have a scientific meaning for archaeologists and biological anthropologists, but they have important emotive and identity meanings for indigenous peoples.

Material items are continually being reinterpreted in new contexts. Also, material culture can be added to or removed from, leaving the traces of reuses and reinterpretations. In some cases, the sequence of use can give insight into the thought processes of an individual, as when flint flakes that have been struck off a core in early prehistory are refitted by archaeologists today (e.g., Pelegrin, 1990) in order to rebuild the flint core and to follow the decisions made by the original flint knapper in producing flakes and tools. In other cases, longer frames of time are involved, as when a monument such as Stonehenge is adapted, rebuilt, and reused for divergent purposes over millennia up to the present day (Chippindale, 1983). In such an example, the narrative held within traces on the artifact has an overall form that has been produced by multiple individuals and groups, often unaware of earlier intentions and meanings. Few people today, although knowledgeable about Christmas practices, are aware of the historical reasons behind the choice of Christmas tree, Santa Claus, red coats, and flying reindeer.

There are many trajectories that material items can take through shifting meanings. For example, many are made initially to refer to or evoke metaphorically, whereas through time the original meaning becomes lost or the item becomes a cliché, having lost its novelty. An artifact may start as a focus but become simply a frame, part of an appropriate background. In the skeuomorphic process a functional component becomes decorative, as when a gas fire depicts burning wood or coal. In other cases the load of meaning invested in an artifact increases through time, as in the case of a talisman or holy relic. Material items are often central in the backward-looking invention of tradition, as when the Italian fascist movement elevated the Roman symbol of authority—a bundle of rods—to provide authority for a new form of centralized power.

This brief discussion of the temporal dimension emphasizes the contextuality of material culture meaning. As is clear from some of the examples given, changing meanings through time are often involved in antagonistic relations between groups. Past and present meanings are continually being contested and reinterpreted as part of social and political strategies. Such conflict over material meanings is of particular interest to qualitative research in that it expresses and focuses alternative views and interests. The reburial of American Indian and Australian Aboriginal remains is an issue that has expressed, but perhaps also helped to construct, a new sense of indigenous rights in North America and Australia. As "ethnic cleansing" reappears in Europe, so too do attempts to reinterpret documents, monuments, and artifacts in ethnic terms. But past artifacts can also be used to help local communities in productive and practical ways. One example of the active use of the past in the present is provided by the work of Erickson (1988) in the area around Lake Titicaca in Peru. Information from the archaeological study of raised fields was used to reconstruct agricultural systems on the ancient model, with the participation and to the benefit of local farmers.

◆ Method

The interpretation of mute material evidence puts the interactionist view under pressure. How can an approach that gives considerable importance to interaction with speaking subjects (e.g., Denzin, 1989) deal with material traces for which informants are long dead or about which informants are not articulate?

I have already noted the importance of material evidence in providing insight into other components of lived experience. The methodological issues that are raised are not, however, unique. In all types of interactive research the analyst has to decide whether or not to take commentary at face value and how to evaluate spoken or unspoken responses. How does what is said fit into more general understanding? Analysts of material culture may not have much spoken commentary to work with, but they do have patterned evidence that has to be evaluated in relation to the full range of available information. They too have to fit different aspects of the evidence into a hermeneutical whole (Hodder, 1992; Shanks & Tilley, 1987). They ask, How does what is done fit into more general understanding?

In general terms, the interpreter of material culture works between past and present or between different examples of material culture, making analogies between them. The material evidence always has the potential to be patterned in unexpected ways. Thus it provides an "other" against which the analyst's own experience of the world has to be evaluated and can be enlarged. Although the evidence cannot "speak back," it can confront the interpreter in ways that enforce self-reappraisal. At least when a researcher is dealing with prehistoric remains, there are no "member checks" because the artifacts are themselves mute. On the other hand, material culture is the product of and is embedded in "internal" experience. Indeed, it could be argued that some material culture, precisely because it is not overt, self-conscious speech, may give deeper insights into the internal meanings according to which people lived their lives. I noted above some examples of material culture being used to express covert meanings. Thus the lack of spoken member checks is counteracted by the checks provided by unspoken material patterning that remain able to confront and undermine interpretation.

An important initial assumption made by those interpreting material culture is that belief, idea, and intention are important to action and practice (see above). It follows that the conceptual has some impact on the patterning of material remains. The ideational component of material patterning is not opposed to but is integrated with its material functioning. It is possible therefore to infer both utilitarian and conceptual meaning from the patterning of material evidence.

The interpreter is faced with material data that are patterned along a number of different dimensions simultaneously. Minimally, archaeologists distinguish technology, function, and style, and they use such attributes to form typologies and to seek spatial and temporal patterning. In practice, however, as the discussion above has shown, it has become increasingly difficult to separate technology from style or to separate types from their spatial and temporal contexts. In other words, the analytic or pattern-recognition stage has itself been identified as interpretive.

Thus at all stages, from the identification of classes and attributes to the understanding of high-level social processes, the interpreter has to deal simultaneously with three areas of evaluation. First, the interpreter has to identify the contexts within which things had similar meaning. The boundaries of the context are never "given"; they have to be interpreted. Of course, physical traces and separations might assist the definition of contextual boundaries, such as the boundaries around a village or the separation in time between sets of events. Ritual contexts might be more formalized than or may invert mundane contexts. But despite such clues there is an infinity of possible contexts that might have been constructed by indigenous actors. The notion of context is always relevant when different sets of data are being compared and where a primary question is whether the different examples are comparable, whether the apparent similarities are real.

Second, in conjunction with and inseparable from the identification of context is the recognition of similarities and differences. The interpreter argues for a context by showing that things are done similarly, that people respond similarly to similar situations, within its boundaries. The assumption is made that within the context similar events or things had similar meaning. But this is true only if the boundaries of the context have been correctly identified. Many artifacts initially identified as ritual or cultic have later been shown to come from entirely utilitarian contexts. Equally, claimed cross-cultural similarities always have to be evaluated to see if their contexts are comparable. Thus the interpretations of context and of meaningful similarities and differences are mutually dependent.

The identification of contexts, similarities, and differences within patterned materials depends on the application of appropriate social and material culture theories. The third evaluation that has to be made by the interpreter is of the relevance of general or specific historical theories to the data at hand. Observation and interpretation are theory laden, although theories can be changed in confrontation with material evidence in a dialectical fashion. Some of the appropriate types of general theory for material culture have been identified above. The more specific theories include the intentions and social goals of participants, or the nature of ritual or cultic as opposed to secular or utilitarian behavior.

In terms of the two types of material meaning identified earlier, rules of representation are built up from patterns of association and exclusion. For example, if a pin type is exclusively associated with women in a wide variety of contexts, then it might be interpreted as representing women in all situations. The aspect of womanhood that is represented by this association with pins is derived from other associations of the pins—perhaps with foreign, nonlocal artifacts (Sorensen, 1987). The more richly networked the associations that can be followed by the interpreter, and the thicker the description (Denzin, 1989) that can be produced, the subtler the interpretations that can be made.

For the other type of material meaning, grounded in practice, the initial task of the interpreter is to understand all the social and material implications of particular practices. This is greatly enhanced by studies of modern material culture, including ethnoarchaeology (Orme, 1981). Experimental archaeologists (Coles, 1979) are now well experienced in reconstructing past practices, from storage of cereals in pits to flaking flint tools. Such reconstructions, always unavoidably artificial to some degree, allow some direct insight into another lived experience. On the basis of such knowledge the implications of material practices, extending into the social and the moral, can be theorized. But again it is detailed thick description of associations and contexts that allows the material practices to be set within specific historical situations and the particular evocations to be understood.

An example of the application of these methods is provided by Merriman's (1987) interpretation of the intentions behind the building of a wall around the elite settlement of Heuneberg, Germany, in the sixth century B.C. (an example similar to that provided by Collingwood, 1956). In cultural terms, the Hallstatt context in central Europe, including Germany, can be separated from other cultural areas such as the Aegean at this time. And yet the walls are made of mud brick and they have bastions, both of which have parallels only in the Aegean. In practice, mud brick would not have been an effective long-term form of defense in the German climate. Thus some purpose other than defense is supposed. The walls are different from other contemporary walls in Germany and yet they are similar to walls found in the Aegean context. Other similarities and differences that seem relevant are the examples of prestige exchange—valuable objects such as wine flagons traded from the Aegean to Germany. This trade seems relevant because of a theory that elites in central Europe based their power on the control of prestige exchange with the Mediterranean. It seems likely, in the context of such prestige exchange, that the walls built in a Mediterranean form were also designed to confer prestige on the elites who organized their construction. In this example the intention of the wall building is interpreted as being for prestige rather than for defense. The interpretation is based on the simultaneous evaluation of similarities and differences, context and theory. Both representational symbolism (conferring prestige) and practical meanings (the building of walls by elites in a non-Mediterranean climate) are considered. For other examples of the method applied to modern material culture, see Hodder (1991) and Moore (1986).

◆ Confirmation

How is it possible to confirm such hypotheses about the meanings of mute material and written culture? Why are some interpretations more plausible than others? The answers to such questions are unlikely to differ radically from the procedures followed in other areas of interpretation, and so I will discuss them relatively briefly here (see Denzin, 1989; Lincoln & Guba, 1985). However, there are some differences in confirming hypotheses regarding material objects. Perhaps the major difficulty is that material culture, by its very nature, straddles the divide between a universal, natural science approach to materials and a historical, interpretive approach to culture. There is thus a particularly marked lack of agreement in the scientific community about the appropriate basis for confirmation procedures. In my view, an interpretive position can and should accommodate scientific information about, for example, natural processes of transformation and decay of artifacts. It is thus an interpretive position that I describe here.

The twin struts of confirmation are coherence and correspondence. Coherence is produced if the parts of the argument do not contradict each other and if the conclusions follow from the premises. There is a partial autonomy of different types of theory, from the observational to the global, and a coherent interpretation is one in which these different levels do not produce contradictory results. The partial autonomy of different types of theory is especially clear in relation to material culture. Because material evidence endures, it can continually be reobserved, reanalyzed, and reinterpreted. The observations made in earlier excavations are continually being reconsidered within new interpretive frameworks. It is clear from these reconsiderations of earlier work that earlier observations can be used to allow different interpretations—the different levels of theory are partially autonomous. The internal coherence between different levels of theory is continually being renegotiated.

As well as internal coherence there is external coherence—the degree to which the interpretation fits theories accepted in and outside the discipline. Of course, the evaluation of a coherent argument itself depends on the application of theoretical criteria, and I have already noted the lack of agreement in studies of material culture about foundational issues such as the importance of a natural science or humanistic approach. But whatever their views on such issues, most of those working with material culture seem to accept implicitly the importance of simplicity and elegance. An argument in which too much special pleading is required in order to claim coherence is less likely to be adopted than is a simple or elegant theory. The notion of coherence could also be extended to social and political issues within and beyond disciplines, but I shall here treat these questions separately.

The notion of correspondence between theory and data does not imply absolute objectivity and independence, but rather embeds the fit of data and theory within coherence. The data are made to cohere by being linked within theoretical arguments. Similarly, the coherence of the arguments is supported by the fit to data. On the other hand, data can confront theory, as already noted. Correspondence with the data is thus an essential part of arguments of coherence. There are many aspects of correspondence arguments that might be used. One is the exactness of fit, perhaps measured in statistical terms, between theoretical expectation and data, and this is a particularly important aspect of arguments exploiting the mute aspects of material culture. Other arguments of correspondence include the number of cases that are accounted for, their range in space and time, and the variety of different classes of data that are explained. However, such numerical indications of correspondence always have to be evaluated against contextual relevance and thick description to determine whether the different examples of fit are relevant to each other. In ethnographic and historical contexts correspondence with indigenous accounts can be part of the argument that supports contextual relevance.

Other criteria that affect the success of theories about material culture meaning include fruitfulness—how many new directions, new lines of inquiry, new perspectives are opened up. Reproducibility concerns whether other people, perhaps with different perspectives, come to similar results. Perhaps different arguments, based on different starting points, produce similar results. I have already noted that one of the advantages of material evidence is that it can continually be returned to, unexcavated parts of sites excavated and old trenches dug out and reexamined. Intersubjective agreement is of considerable importance although of particular difficulty in an area that so completely bridges the science-humanity divide. The success of interpretations depends on peer review (either informal or formally in journals) and on the number of people who believe, cite, and build on them.

But much depends too on the trustworthiness, professional credentials, and status of the author and supporters of an interpretation. Issues here include how long the interpreter spent in the field and how well she or he knows the data: their biases, problems, and unusual examples. Has the author obtained appropriate degrees and been admitted into professional societies? Is the individual an established and consistent writer, or has he or she yet to prove her- or himself? Does the author keep changing her or his mind?

In fact, the audience does not respond directly to an interpretation but to an interpretation written or staged as an article or presentation. The audience thus responds to and reinterprets a material artifact or event. The persuasiveness of the argument is closely tied to the rhetoric within which it is couched (Gero, 1991; Hodder, 1989; Spector, 1991; Tilley, 1989). The rhetoric determines how the different components of the discipline talk about and define problems and their solutions.

◆ Conclusion

Material culture, including written texts, poses a challenge for interpretive approaches that often stress the importance of dialogue with and spoken critical comment from participants. Material culture evidence, on the other hand, may have no living participants who can respond to its interpretation. Even if such participants do exist, they may often be unable to be articulate about material culture meanings. In any case, material culture endures, and so the original makers and users may be able to give only a partial picture of the full history of meanings given to an object as it is used and reinterpreted through time.

The challenge posed by material culture is important for anthropological and sociological analysis because material culture is often a medium in which alternative and often muted voices can be expressed. But the "reader" of material culture must recognize that only some aspects of material culture meaning are language-like. The meaning of much material culture comes about through use, and material culture knowledge is often highly chunked and contextualized. Technical operations implicate a wide network of material, social, and symbolic resources and the abstract meanings that result are closely tied in with the material.

The methods of interpretation of material culture center on the simultaneous hermeneutical procedures of context definition, the construction of patterned similarities and differences, and the use of relevant social and material culture theory. The material culture may not be able directly to "speak back," but if appropriate procedures are followed, there is room for the data and for different levels of theory to confront interpretations.

The interpreter learns from the experience of material remains—the data and the interpreter bring each other into existence in dialectical fashion. The interpretations can be confirmed or made more or less plausible than others using a fairly standard range of internal and external (social) criteria.

◆ References

Bechtel, W. (1990). Connectionism and the philosophy of mind: An overview. In W. G. Lycan (Ed.), *Mind and cognition: A reader.* Oxford: Basil Blackwell.

Bloch, M. (1991). Language, anthropology and cognitive science. *Man, 26,* 183-198.

Bourdieu, P. (1977). *Outline of a theory of practice.* Cambridge: Cambridge University Press.

Braithwaite, M. (1982). Decoration as ritual symbol. In I. Hodder (Ed.), *Symbolic and structural archaeology* (pp. 80-88). Cambridge: Cambridge University Press.

Chippindale, C. (1983). *Stonehenge complete.* London: Thames & Hudson.

Coles, J. M. (1979). *Experimental archaeology.* London: Academic Press.

Collingwood, R. (1956). *The idea of history.* Oxford: Oxford University Press.

Denzin, N. K. (1989). *Interpretive interactionism.* Newbury Park, CA: Sage.

Derrida, J. (1978). *Writing and difference.* London: Routledge & Kegan Paul.

Donley, L. (1982). House power: Swahili space and symbolic markers. In I. Hodder (Ed.), *Symbolic and structural archaeology* (pp. 63-73). Cambridge: Cambridge University Press.

Erickson, C. L. (1988). Raised field agriculture in the Lake Titicaca Basin: Putting ancient agriculture back to work. *Expedition, 30*(3), 8-16.

Ferguson, L. (1991). Struggling with pots in colonial South Carolina. In R. McGuire & R. Paynter (Eds.), *The archaeology of inequality* (pp. 28-39). Oxford: Basil Blackwell.

Gero, J. (1991). Who experienced what in prehistory? A narrative explanation from Queyash, Peru. In R. Preucel (Ed.), *Processual and postprocessual archaeologies* (pp. 126-189). Carbondale: Southern Illinois University.

Giddens, A. (1979). *Central problems in social theory.* London: Macmillan.

Glassie, H. (1975). *Folk housing in middle Virginia.* Knoxville: University of Tennessee Press.

Hodder, I. (1982). *Symbols in action.* Cambridge: Cambridge University Press.

Hodder, I. (1989). Writing archaeology: Site reports in context. *Antiquity, 63,* 268-274.

Hodder, I. (1991). *Reading the past.* Cambridge: Cambridge University Press.

Hodder, I. (1992). *Theory and practice in archaeology*. London: Routledge.

Latour, B. (1988). Mixing humans and nonhumans together: The sociology of a door closer. *Social Problems, 35,* 298-310.

Lemonnier, P. (1986). The study of material culture today: Towards an anthropology of technical systems. *Journal of Anthropological Archaeology, 5,* 147-186.

Leone, M. (1984). Interpreting ideology in historical archaeology. In D. Miller & C. Tilley (Eds.), *Ideology, power and prehistory* (pp. 25-36). Cambridge: Cambridge University Press.

Leroi-Gourhan, A. (1964). *Le geste et la parole*. Paris: Michel.

Lincoln, Y. S., & Guba, E. G. (1985). *Naturalistic inquiry*. Beverly Hills, CA: Sage.

McGhee, R. (1977). Ivory for the sea woman. *Canadian Journal of Archaeology, 1,* 141-159.

Merriman, N. (1987). Value and motivation in prehistory: The evidence for "Celtic spirit." In I. Hodder (Ed.), *The archaeology of contextual meanings* (pp. 111-116). London: Unwin Hyman.

Miller, D. (1982). Artifacts as products of human categorisation processes. In I. Hodder (Ed.), *Symbolic and structural archaeology* (pp. 89-98). Cambridge: Cambridge University Press.

Miller, D. (1985). *Artifacts as categories*. Cambridge: Cambridge University Press.

Miller, D., Rowlands, M., & Tilley, C. (1989). *Domination and resistance*. London: Unwin Hyman.

Miller, D., & Tilley, C. (1984). *Ideology, power and prehistory*. Cambridge: Cambridge University Press.

Moore, H. (1986). *Space, text and gender*. Cambridge: Cambridge University Press.

Orme, B. (1981). *Anthropology for archaeologists*. London: Duckworth.

Pelegrin, J. (1990). Prehistoric lithic technology. *Archaeological Review From Cambridge, 9,* 116-125.

Rathje, W., & Murphy, C. (1992). *Rubbish! The archaeology of garbage*. New York: HarperCollins.

Rathje, W., & Thompson, B. (1981). *The Milwaukee Garbage Project*. Washington, DC: American Paper Institute, Solid Waste Council of the Paper Industry.

Ricoeur, P. (1971). The model of the text: Meaningful action considered as text. *Social Research, 38,* 529-562.

Sanjek, R. (Ed.). (1990). *Fieldnotes: The makings of anthropology*. Albany: State University of New York Press.

Schlanger, N. (1990). Techniques as human action: Two perspectives. *Archaeological Review From Cambridge, 9,* 18-26.

Shanks, M., & Tilley, C. (1987). *Reconstructing archaeology*. Cambridge: Cambridge University Press.

Sorensen, M.-L. (1987). Material order and cultural classification. In I. Hodder (Ed.), *The archaeology of contextual meanings* (pp. 90-101). Cambridge: Cambridge University Press.

Spector, J. (1991). What this awl means: Toward a feminist archaeology. In J. M. Gero & M. W. Conkey (Eds.), *Engendering archaeology* (pp. 388-406). Oxford: Basil Blackwell.

Tilley, C. (1989). Discourse and power: The genre of the Cambridge inaugural. In D. Miller, M. Rowlands, & C. Tilley (Eds.), *Domination and resistance* (pp. 41-62). London: Unwin Hyman.

Tilley, C. (Ed.). (1990). *Reading material culture*. Oxford: Basil Blackwell.

Washburn, D. (1983). *Structure and cognition in art*. Cambridge: Cambridge University Press.

Webb, E. J., Campbell, D. T., Schwartz, R. C., & Sechrest, L. (1966). *Unobtrusive measures: Nonreactive research in the social sciences*. Chicago: University of Chicago Press.

Wobst, M. (1977). Stylistic behavior and information exchange. *University of Michigan Museum of Anthropology, Anthropological Paper, 61*, 317-342.

Yates, T. (1989). Habitus and social space. In I. Hodder (Ed.), *The meanings of things* (pp. 248-262). London: Unwin Hyman.

◆ Suggested Further Readings

Hodder, I. (1999). *The archaeological process*. Oxford: Basil Blackwell.

Hodder, I., & Shanks, M. (1995). *Interpreting archaeology*. London: Routledge.

Miller, D. (Ed.). (1997). *Material cultures*. London: University College Press.

Tilley, C. (1994). *The phenomenology of landscape*. London: Berg.

Tilley, C. (1999). *Metaphor and material culture*. Oxford: Basil Blackwell.

5

Reimagining
Visual Methods

Galileo to Neuromancer

Douglas Harper

◆   This chapter is based on my sense that the chapter I prepared for the first edition of this *Handbook* might help a researcher understand the relationship between visual and other methods, but it would not be very useful to a student or researcher trying to use visual methods, or to a researcher looking for a framework in which to understand visual methods.[1] In this chapter I take a different approach. First, I suggest a context in which to see photography and social research, this being the history of recorded perception. Next, I present visual sociology as fieldwork photography guided by several research traditions. Third, I describe the social influences around which "picture making" has taken place, noting how the social power involved in making images redefines institutions, groups, and individuals. Finally, I suggest that visual sociology is, above all, a process of seeing guided by theory. Because visual sociology is a grab bag of research approaches and perspectives on understanding images in society, I aim to make several attenuated arguments and to weave them into a whole.

◆ Visual Methods and the History of Recorded Perception

Logical positivism assumed its modern form in the 16th century, when Roger Bacon suggested that observable data are the basis of knowledge. Bacon also argued that knowledge ought to be practically applied to solving social problems, anticipating Comte's mandate for sociology in the early 19th century. I note that Bacon's insights traced to the rationalist philosophers of 6th-century B.C. Greece to remind us that the roots of this perspective are nearly as old as recorded thought.

Bacon and logical positivism were contemporary to the invention of the telescope and the microscope, tools that showed that the world observed with human eyes was not complete or even correct. In the 16th century this was such a challenging idea that philosophers at the University of Padua, where Galileo was a professor, refused to look through the telescope. Galileo, censured and threatened with death, recanted the discoveries his telescope had revealed. But, of course, the scientific revolution was not stopped by the violence of the Church, and the revolution inspired by Galileo and Bacon flourished in the 17th century and became the basis of the modern scientific world.

In the 19th century, the camera became part of the revolution in seeing and understanding that was the scientific revolution, and several subsequent instruments and tools, which I will describe below, further redefined the relationship between seeing and knowing.

There are two important implications to the changes brought by Galileo's telescope. The first is that the new, instrument-based perception was treated as more real than was the world based on faith and belief. It became understood that to see through an instrument (such as the telescope or microscope, and, eventually, the camera) was to see a more profound reality than could be observed by the eye. The second implication of these changes is that the legitimacy of science came to be based in large part on its claim to describe a world in visual terms. In this way the eye became the privileged sense of science, and of modernism.

The hegemony of science and the image did not last, due a succession of tools and instruments that redefined both image making and the social role of images. The first and perhaps most important of these is the camera itself. The cameras used today are essentially similar to cameras designed 150 years ago, although they have the ability to see farther, closer, faster, and in lower light. In surprising ways, the public use of cameras has remained constant. The middle-class public enthusiastically adopted photography in the 19th century and continues to do so. Different social classes and groups, of course, use photography differently (Bourdieu, 1990), but the 19th-century family snapshooter would have no trouble interpreting the modern-day family album.

In the meantime, motion pictures, video, the World Wide Web, and virtual reality have offered new connections between human existence and visual perception. These new instruments influence the meanings of images, their relationship to spoken words and sounds, and the emergence and development of visual sociology.

By the end of the 19th century, it became possible to link individual frames of film together, giving a succession of images a verisimilitude the still image could never achieve. Suddenly it seemed that the process of life itself could be recorded. But at first this record was limited to images alone (synchronized sound could not be recorded with the images), and because cameras were bulky and heavy, filming the flow of natural life was nearly impossible. The earliest documentary films, such as *Nanook of the North* (filmed during the 1920s), were thus extraordinary technical achievements. Because there was no sound track (except for a piano score for a live musician), the film contained frames of typed words between sequences of images. These had to be brief statements, quickly readable by an audience impatient to rejoin the visual narrative of the film. These texts were what we now call "captions," and they performed the same function, which was to summarize the visual text.

By the 1930s it became possible to add sound to film, but it was nearly impossible to do so outside of a studio. Documentaries such as Pare Lorentz's *The River* and *The Plow That Broke the Plains* (see Snyder, 1968) introduced voice-over commentary. This commentary functioned as did the captions of the silent film, in that it defined and provided closure for the images. In this sense it can be thought of as the confident voice of (modernist) science.

The era of television brought documentaries in this form to the living rooms of America in the weekly *Omnibus* series shown during the 1950s. Again, the voice-over-image narrator supplied the logic that tied the film statements together. As a result, these films are linear and narrative in organization, and unambiguous in structure and message.

Portable cameras that could simultaneously record sound were developed in the early 1960s. These capabilities potentially eliminated the hegemony of image and scientific authority. Film could now explain itself; it leaped closer to reality, and the results resembled the messy flow of life.

Interestingly enough, the movement was called cinema verité, or truth-cinema. Jean Rouch and Edgar Morin's (a French sociologist) *Chronique d'un Eté* (*Chronicle of a Summer*; 1960), one of the first cinema verité films, took cameras to the streets of Paris to measure the public reaction to the Algerian war and to comment on several cultural themes. In a departure from previous film structure, in *Chronique d'un Eté* the subjects of the film are shown watching their earlier filmed interviews, adding a layer of interpretation to the already ambiguous film statement.

In the United States, the early cinema verité movement (see Mamber, 1974) coincided with the emergence of experimental ethnography, although only a handful of sociological filmmakers and sociologists and anthropologists made the connection. Several films of this era offered bridges between ethnography and experimental filmmaking. These included the Maysles brothers' documentary *The Salesman* (1969), which follows the day-to-day routines of a Bible salesman; Robert Drew's *Primary* (1960), which shows the mundane events of a political primary; and Richard Leacock's *Happy Mother's Day* (1963), which explores how a small town experienced and marketed the birth of quintuplets. Frederick Wiseman's *Titicut Follies* (1967), which depicts the day-to-day routines of a prison for the criminally insane, was the first in a series of more than 20 cinema verité studies of mostly American institutions that offered an extraordinary resource for experimental sociology and anthropology. Cinema verité showed sociological dimensions to everyday life, and the movement embraced a technology that redefined what, in fact, could be filmed. Sadly for the social sciences, the potential of this technology has been little used or even recognized.

Although cinema verité redefined the relationship between film and reality, its adoption, for example, as a common research technique was limited by its expense. By the early 1980s a typical budget for a documentary film, not including salaries, was more than $1,000 per minute. The cameras could record only a few minutes of simultaneous sound and images, and generally there needed to be a sound recorder working in tandem with the filmmaker, which added to the intrusion of the recorders of reality on reality itself.

Advances in video technology, dating to the early 1980s, made it possible for videographers to record hours of synchronized visual and audio information at a fraction of the cost of film. Video cameras have become smaller and yet produce higher-quality images and sound (most recently in the Hi 8 format), and they have also become simpler to operate and cheap enough to be a routine home expense. Video wrested image making from the monopoly of well-heeled experts. It is reasonable to say that with this change, visual representations of the world lost their close connection with the authority of science. Yet the implications of this change are ambiguous. For the most part, the video revolution has not worked hand in hand with experimental ethnography to redefine the social science. Indeed, the social effects have been trivialized into "funniest home videos" television programs (now worldwide), in which the extraordinary power of the camera is used to present the lowest common denominator of public life.

Contemporary electronic technologies continue to redefine the image and its social meaning. Now that images can be created and/or changed digitally, the connection between image and "truth" has been forever severed. What was once disturbing (such as the addition of Hitler-like visual cues to a portrait of Saddam Hussein on the cover of a national newsmagazine) is now commonplace. Electronically altered images have become part of our entertainment (in *Zelig*, Woody Allen appears alongside Lenin; in *Forrest Gump*, Tom Hanks is shown in conversation with John Kennedy); advertising juxtaposes the images of people who have nothing to do with each other, who in fact do not even live in the same era, presenting them as enthusiastic product spokespersons.

But the electronic revolution is a great deal more than the ability to alter photographic or video images. Because of what is now called *hyperlogic,* there is an alternative to linear or narrative form of visual presentation. Hyperlogic, which began in the Hypercard program (packaged with early Macintosh computers) is the basis of the World Wide Web. As is common knowledge today, the Web is organized so that viewers can create their own paths through text, images, and even film or video clips. The most successful current example is Peter Biella, Napoleon Chagnon, and Gary Seaman's (1997) interactive CD-ROM of the anthropological film *The Ax Fight,* by Timothy Asch, and additional hyperlinked materials. The interactive CD allows a viewer to view the actual film in any of several possible ways (in real time, backward as well as forward, frame by frame, in slow motion, or keyed to significant moments as identified by the anthropologists). The viewer can also link to scene-by-scene descriptions of the film, or can link to any individual shown in the film to get information on that person's age, sex, spouses, children, birthplace, lineage, residence, year of death, place in the kin systems (presented in kin charts), and other anthropological details. The CD contains complete footage and edited versions of the film, hundreds of photographs, and several full-length essays. The viewer can access any part of the film and digress to any of several analyses.

The CD is a curious step in the evolution I have described. On one hand, it represents the scientific expert whose claims are reinforced visually; on the other, it deconstructs the authority of the scientist and makes the viewer the author of the viewing and learning experience.

The last step in the process that began with Galileo's telescope is the jumbling up of our senses through electronic manipulation, called *virtual reality*. Giovanni Artieri (1996) suggests that the "technological image is the real marker of the postmodern, able to trace out subjects' experience as border lines between natural and artificial" (p. 56). By wearing machines that transform nerve stimuli into visual and tactile sensations, users alter the boundaries separating the body and society, and experience itself loses its link to authenticity. Now it is no longer what we see (or hear and feel) that is real, as in the case of a science based on unchallenged claims to represent the world. Rather, we choose to immerse ourselves in a fictional perceptional reality—that is, a perceptual world that is the result of our imagination and a machine. In the next step, still fictional (best represented in cyberpunk novels such as William Gibson's *Neuromancer*, 1985), computer chips implanted into the brain allow a person to jack directly into the Web, to experience viscerally what is a fictional, yet operative, space.

Because visual sociology comprises images and science, it is appropriate that we study the relationship between these elements. The images that visual sociologists make are also part of these issues; we should study our work as part of the study of visual society. As new technologies alter what and how we see (even changing the nature of sight, reality, and imagination), the issues will become both more complex and more important.

◆ A Visual Social Science Through Research Photography

The above comments offer a broad view. I now shift to the mundane operation of visual sociology, showing the operation of several paradigms of visual methodology in photos of a bike ride in Italy.[2]

I made the photographs that accompany this text while I was teaching visual sociology at the University of Bologna, experiencing a culture I was pretty much new to. My students and I explored the idea of seeing (and photographing) forms and levels of social control. In all cultures, the relationship between formal and informal social control is complex, and in Italy it seems extremely so. It would be only fair, I reasoned, for me to explore this assignment myself. Participating in traffic from the vantage point of a bicycle seemed sufficiently complex and visual to be a suitable photographic project. Thus, armed with my intrepid Leica, I photographed the same route, a main street that bisects the circle of the inner city of Bologna, on several occasions.

From a personal standpoint, I certainly found it intimidating to mount my beaten-up (pink) bike and take on Italian traffic, with or without a camera. I was a guest of my colleague Patrizia Faccioli, who told me to simply follow her through the moving maze of dangerous vehicles and vulnerable, darting pedestrians. Of course, this is the point: Things taken for granted by a cultural insider (which rules are followed, which norms guide behavior that is not regulated by rules, and what areas of social life lie primarily outside the perusal or rules) are not obvious to cultural outsiders. In the case of negotiating the street, not knowing is dangerous.

I had already photographed a different European city from a bicycle, and I'd become rather adept at the process. My camera is not automatic, so I steered with my left hand, holding the camera in my right. I focused and set apertures and shutter speeds before starting off. I framed the images as I biked, advancing the film with the thumb of my right hand. The resulting photos can be used to illustrate complementary paradigms of visual research, which is to say that their sociological meanings can be organized within the logics of at least four research strategies.

The first of these strategies can be referred to (cautiously!) as *empirical*. This orientation toward photography recognizes that a photographic image is created when light leaves its trace on an element that has a memory. For the image to exist, there had to be light reflected off a subject; thus the photograph is a record of the subject at a particular moment.

From this perspective, the photographs document several levels of social life. The simplest is a bicycle commute through Italian traffic. The photographs record such mundane information as how many vehicles of what types share the Italian streets at a certain time of day. The photographs suggest some of the jockeying that regulates a complex mix of human interaction mediated by machines. If they are read carefully, with the help of a cultural insider, they begin to offer evidence of normative behavior. This is simple information, but it is precisely the daily occurrences of life that are often the basis of sociological analysis. Above all, the visual cataloging of life is efficient; it would take a lot of words to convey the information in the photographs.

Although these images produce what I consider to be empirical data, I do not claim that these images represent "objective truth." The very act of observing is interpretive, for to observe is to choose a point of view. To elaborate: As a photographer, I choose a point of view by aiming the camera and by choosing the focal length of the lens. Camera lenses do not see precisely what the human eye sees—some magnify a small visual area, like a telescope; some see wider than the normal vision but move the foreground of the subject farther away; others act as microscopes. For the bike photographs, I used a 35 mm focal-length lens because it sees nearly what the eye sees (but cuts off the edges of normal vision); thus when I hold the camera in front of my face I need not look through the range finder to imagine the image I'll make. The person looking at the photograph sees the frame as familiar because it is rather close to how the eye records information. Thus the decisions of the image maker have profound effects on the kinds of sociological statements that result from their images.[3]

In this project I used 400 ASA (black-and-white) film, which is properly exposed with a small amount of light. Thus I could use a fast shutter speed (freezing the motion in the frame), and I could also use a small aperture, which created a deep depth of field (in lay terms, the images are in focus from the front nearly to the back). These are decisions that rendered the photographs a certain way. Different film, shutter speeds, apertures, and lenses would have created different visual statements. These statements would not be "better" or "worse," but they would be decidedly different. For example, Photo 5 freezes the action of about 10 individuals on different kinds of two-wheeled vehicles in an extremely dangerous confluence. The image, crisp and frozen, suggests order. Likewise, the elderly man in Photo 8 is not a passive spectator, as he appears, but a pedestrian about to make a decision as to whether or not to venture into my path. If I had used different shutter speeds and even different angles of the frame (point of view), the photographs would have communicated more of the chaos and uncertainties in the negotiation of the public space.

It is easy to see that empirical evidence is both constructed and real. Becoming a visual ethnographer means becoming conscious of the potential to make visual statements by knowing how the camera interprets social reality. This means learning how cameras work, making the technical decisions that, in fact, create the photograph self-consciously, and relegating the automatic camera to the wastebasket.

1

2

3

4

6

5

7

8

9

10

11

12

13

14

15

All photographs © by Douglas Harper

185

◆ Visual Narratives

To expand the idea of empirical data in single images to a sequence of photos is to introduce the concept of visual narrative. Sociologists use verbal narratives to tell sociological stories, both as first-person accounts and as cultural stories that unfold through time and space. On the level of microanalysis, the narrative view is consistent with symbolic interaction, which makes us sensitive to how we process interaction based on interpretations. Interaction, by definition, is narrative; it embodies the flow of human experience.

Visual materials are often narrative in form. The most common visual narrative is film or video, as described above: single images taken sequentially (often many per second) that, when viewed in rapid succession, seem to re-create the movement the eye sees. But still photographs can also create sociological narratives (Harper, 1982, 1987). For example, a succession of photographs of a tramp worker coming down from a drunk, boarding a freight train for a 1,500-mile trip, reassembling his identity as a worker, and taking on another job tells the story of a culture, a story that is repeated with subtle variations. The most respected photojournalists have used this narrative form to great advantage. Eugene Smith and Ailene Smith's (1975) visual narrative of a social movement surrounding the lethal poisoning of a fishing village by a corporation describes the scenarios of several social groups. Kent Klich's visual narrative *The Book of Beth* (1989) traces events in the life of a Swedish heroin addict who is also a prostitute; here the sad narrative moves from the individual to several institutional connections.

My narrative study of the cultural phenomenon of bicycling down the same street at the same time of day over several days is constructed in several ways. It mixes images made at different times on the same route, which is indicated by the varying patterns of light and shadows that appear in different images. Even assembled in this way, the sequence is a sociological narrative, although the relationship of these images to the narrative flow of time is arbitrary.

The bicycle narrative is framed at either end by images that suggest the cultural definition of the bicycle and that locate the narrative in a larger geographic context. The advertising image that opens the sequence suggests that the bicycle represents both utility and fashion. The final image was taken from a tower (the same tower that appears in Photos 9-13), looking down at the street along which the bicyclist travels. The increasingly larger tower in the photos is a way to note the progress of the sequence. Seeing the context of the photographs from the bird's-eye view of the tower, one realizes that the path of the bicycle trip is through one of the main drags of the inner city of Bologna. The overview is a visual summary of the images that precede it.

The second image in the series frames the series from the perspective of a spectator rather than a participant. We gain the sense that cars, motor scooters, and bicycles are waiting for the signal to begin a race. In fact, that is exactly what the moment is like, as recorded in Photo 3. At the intersection where we wait, a small street suddenly becomes a much larger street, and oncoming traffic crosses immediately to the right. Photo 4 shows the moment just out of the "starting gate," with several different kinds of bikes and scooters roughly following the white lines marking a place for two-wheelers. Noteworthy is the presence of a "sportsman" on a touring bike, seemingly out of place in the urban stop-and-go traffic. The two buses pictured are going opposite directions, one leading traffic to the right and the other bearing toward the dispersing traffic. The remaining images show different points on the route, as recorded on different days (note the presence of shadows on some images, and disappearing buses and cars). Photo 5 shows the close reckoning between the scooters that are turning left immediately after the scooters moving ahead (a crash seems imminent, as is often the case). Photo 11 records a moment in a game of "chicken" where I did not faint at the onrush of a cab (and a woman on a scooter), causing the cabbie to slam on his brakes halfway through his turn into my path. Several images show how pedestrians and motorized traffic interact. The elderly man in Photo 8 appears alone halfway across the street; several groups in Photo 12 are crossing the street using different strategies. Finally, in Photo 7 I am observed photographing and the onlookers seem surprised, perhaps perturbed. This is such usual behavior it is by itself a norm violation. In any case, it is a record of the impact of the researcher on the reality he studies. By choosing images from several bike trips along the same path, I was able to include several events that occurred at different times.

Every visual narrative involves a decision concerning how much information to include per time unit. A film or video shows so much information it appears to reproduce reality. Thus it is not surprising that video and film are used in the analysis of face-to-face interaction. The example here stretches a small number of images over several minutes of social life. It may be in the sequence that questions of social norms can be approached, but it is clear that one would need more visual information to explore this subject in satisfying depth. Probably video, with simultaneous sound, would yield more meaningful data.

The visual narrative, like the individual frames from which it is made, is a result of choices and decisions. If the researcher is conscious of these choices, the visual narrative may become a useful way to study certain kinds of social patterns. The methods used will, of course, influence the questions asked.

◆ Eliciting Cultural Explanation

Photo elicitation has become a familiar, if underutilized, qualitative method.[4] Simply described, in using this technique, rather than asking a subject, for example, "What is the role of the bicycle in Italian culture?" a researcher might present a set of images such as those in this chapter to an Italian or a group of Italians to elicit their explanations. Of course, responses to the images could well vary according to whether the respondents participate in the pictured reality as bicyclists, scooter or car drivers, or pedestrians. As such, the images function as a kind of "cultural Rorschach" test.

To demonstrate how photo elicitation works, I presented these images to my Italian colleague Patrizia Faccioli (PF), who appears in Photos 9 and 13 as lead driver in our convoy. Because she is a visual sociologist, the photo-elicitation interview provided a natural way for her to share her responses to the photographs. Her responses to these few images filled several pages; the edited excerpts presented below show the range of topics and the depth of the information produced but do not reflect the full range of her responses. As a demonstration, this is the tip of a larger cultural study iceberg.

The photos led PF to comment generally on the overall meanings of the bike in Italian culture:

> The bicycle stands for: rapidity, convenience, physical exercise, danger, risk, challenge, reduction of stress, increase of stress, cancer in the lungs, cold in the winter, hot in the summer . . . flexibility of the [traffic] rules, aggressiveness, attention, negotiation, social conscience, no pollution, autonomy.

> The bike increases your stress; you must have 1,000 eyes open (behind you, in front of you, at right, at left, above, under . . .) because every 10

seconds you risk your life. Nobody in the street cares about cyclists; they seem not to exist: pedestrians who suddenly cross the road, ignoring that you are coming; motorbikes which pass you on right and left and almost touch you; cars which don't give you the way even if you have the right of way. And the buses . . . It seems that among the bus drivers in Bologna, there is a sort of bet on who can pass the most closely to a bike without touching it.

So, using the bike means paying much attention, but also being aggressive and brutal. You have to stare at the car or motor scooter driver (the bus is too high) telling him, through the eyes, that you are going to pass first and that you will not stop.

In reference to Photos 5 and 6, PF comments:

The light has turned green and the scooters and the bikes went quickly in front of the cars, because the light is green also for those coming from the other side who want to turn left. The challenge is to pass first, before the others cross. You can see this in Photo 5; those going toward the two towers have the right of way, but if those arriving from the direction of the two towers can arrive first to turn left, they will turn and the others will have to stop. That is especially the case if you are on a bike (recall what I said about the use of the eyes to communicate you are going to pass anyway). This is one of the most dangerous moments in my everyday experience of going to work.

Understanding the experience of the bicyclist, PF tells us, leads us to understand what Italians call "minor deviance":

Using the bike means . . . not being obligated to follow rules. You are half machine and half pedestrian, and you are not very dangerous for the others, you can glance around and, if possible, pass when the light is red. When there is a traffic jam you can enter the portico [the covered sidewalks of Bologna, which weave 42 kilometers through the city, visible in Photos 8 and 11] and move among pedestrians. You can go the opposite direction in one-way streets, paying attention to the cars, of course. As an American you might say: "The rule is the rule, always and anyway!" But you are wrong! . . . Certain types of rules have to be evaluated in order to decide if it is right to follow them or not. This attitude is very diffused in Italy, especially regarding the rules of the road. Of course it's not the same for the penal code . . . but regarding certain types of rules we Italians think that we have the right to judge the rule and behave accordingly. For example, Italian people decided (with their behavior) that the safety belts are important and useful on the freeways, but not in the town. The police have tried for a long time to have the rule followed, but nothing could bring this about. So now the police have accepted that behavior, as if there were an unwritten rule that tolerates the absence of belts when people drive in towns. . . . We can't accept any sort of rule just because someone decided that the rule is right. People who make rules can also make mistakes; people who live every day in the road can understand which is the best behavior.

A bicycle in a window display with female models is a difficult cultural symbol for an outsider to understand. Referring to Photo 1, PF explains the cultural meaning of several forms of transportation:

This perfume shop shows a bike that is the prize drawn by lot among those who buy a certain product, the perfume. The statement translates "The autographed bike could be yours." That's an indicator of how much the bike has become part of Italian culture and everyday life. Women who wear a famous perfume use bikes in everyday life: the woman in the poster is wearing elegant dresses, not sport ones. In the '60s those who used bikes were people belonging to the working class, who did not have money to buy (or to use every day) a car. A lot of people used the car only on Sunday, with their family. Nowadays, because of the increased standard of living . . . all people have one or more cars and the towns, mainly the old centers, are crowded. So the bike has become an alternative to the car, not linked to social class or money. It has become one of the most rapid ways to move across town. This is a similar consideration for the scooters: students, young people, but also employees, lawyers, doctors (teachers like me), etc., have scooters more and more fine and expensive, costing as much as $3,000. So the scooter means both rapidity and a status symbol. The motorcycles are different; used mainly for vacation or races on the road. In a town you can see scooters (for the rich people) or mopeds (for poor people) or bikes (for both the very poor people and the urban "ecologist"). These are ideal types, of course. The reality is more complex and mixed.

These interview excerpts show how images elicit cultural information that ranges from the micro (normative negotiation of social action) to cultural definition. The photo-elicitation interview is really a completion of the empirical and narrative efforts, the critical point being that the meaning supplied is from a cultural insider. This is in recognition that what constitutes a "fact" is culturally defined.

◆ Experience and Image

I next address a fourth way to look at these images, which I call the *phenomenological mode*. The vantage point from this view is the self, in this instance a self who happens to be driving a bicycle through crowded streets of an alien culture. From the phenomenological perspective, photographs express the artistic, emotional, or experiential intent of the photographer. Here sociology borrows from art; the phenomenological mode draws from early photographic art movements, as photographers sought to define themselves as more than technicians and to assert that photographic expression is equivalent to artistic expression in other media.[5]

Treating photographs phenomenologically is not common in sociology. Perhaps the best examples are found in the work of Richard Quinney (e.g., 1991, 1995), who uses images to interpret and render his own experiences, reflections, and memories. In the case of the Italian bicycle photography, my intent was to photograph what was new to me, but routine to natives.

There was a mix of euphoria and fear in the experience of biking to work. To photograph the experience was to look as I was doing—a harder thing than one might imagine. If you look at the photographs with this in mind, you see the photographer choosing points of view that illuminate different aspects of the unfolding social reality. The sentiments behind the image making must be understood through another mode of expression: a diary, a poem, or other expressive form. The photographs by themselves seem curiously detached, even quiet and subdued, yet they emerged from an adrenaline-saturated experience. Here I question whether the same photographs serve both the empirical and the phenomenological mode equally well. The clinical distance in the crisp images of the empirical rendering does not communicate the experience of the moment.

Photography can produce data that enlarge our understanding of sociological processes, from the formation of one's own definition of the situation to the negotiation of actors with different machines. Photographs record details that may engage viewers to reflect upon larger cultural realities. Using photos as sequences allows us to see how social actions take place.

The example above shows how the most mundane of events, biking through a city street, may be thought about in several sociological ways. These four approaches do not begin to exhaust the possibilities for using photography in the research process.

◆ The Social Construction of Photography and Visual Sociology

It is not enough to describe visual research in the terms offered above. Like all research, visual research depends upon and redistributes social power. In the case of visual research, these issues are compounded by the power associated with photography. Thus we speak of the "social construction of the photograph" as part of the discussion of the politics of visual sociology itself.

The photograph is socially constructed in the sense that the social positions of the photographer and the subject come into play when a photograph is made. It takes social power to make photographs (Tagg, 1988), partly because making photographs defines identities (Spence, 1988), institutional relationships (Jackson, 1977), and histories (Copeland, 1969; Rieger, 1996). A father may photograph his children in ridiculous poses, but the children do not generally have the social power to photograph their parents arguing (or making love) and to present those images as the "official" family story (Chalfen, 1987). Sociologists and anthropologists have assumed that it is their right to photograph the people they study, and thus to present them as academic subjects (and in ways in which the ideological bases of their relationships are disguised). Edwards's (1992) collection of essays on early British anthropological photography demonstrates exactly this point: The images are not objective renderings of objects of scientific studies, as interpreted by early-20th-century anthropologists; rather, they are markers of colonial relationships. Anthropology was a science of the colonizer, and the images made in the service of anthropology defined the native in ways that reified the relationships of superiority and inferiority endemic to colonialism. There are no photographic records made by natives of colonialism (or colonials), but in recent decades prior "natives" have assumed the right to make their own images and tell their own visual stories. This has, of course, called the relationships of traditional anthropology into question.

The social construction of photography is also a matter of gender. For example, in my current research I am using about 110 documentary photographs made just after World War II in a study of the evolution of dairy farming in the northeastern United States. The photographs are part of a collection of nearly 70,000 images produced under the sponsorship of Standard Oil of New Jersey and directed by Roy Stryker. My farming collection includes about 40 images made by a female photographer, Charlotte Brooks, and about 70 by several male photographers. When I compared the photographs on the basis of the gender of the photographers, I was startled by what I found. For the men, the farm women's work was largely invisible. They did not photograph women as productive parts of the farm, nor did they photograph the work of maintaining and provisioning the house (and taking care of children). Brooks's photographs, however, cover many of these excluded topics. The difference is significant because it shows clearly that if we regard these photographs as a document of farm life during the World War II era, we accept an incomplete portrait as a full record. Indeed, the photos, in this case, are a result of the social construction of "maleness" and "femaleness" typical of 1940s America. The role of gender in creating photographic meaning is yet another largely unexplored subject.[6]

Social scientists should be aware of the social construction of the image for several reasons. We need to acknowledge that photography embodies the unequal relationships that are part of most research activities. I can enter into the worlds of the poor by living temporarily on the street, and I can photograph the worlds I encounter there, but a homeless person cannot infiltrate and photograph the life of my university president. This realization has led many social scientists to abandon the use of photography. For others it is a cautioning awareness that should help us to overcome the inevitable power differentials of subject and researcher. Some sociologists have confronted the issue by giving up their own photography and instead teaching their subjects to use photography and writing to investigate their own cultures and, perhaps, to empower themselves. Wendy Ewald is a leader in this field, for she takes on the asymmetry of adult/child as well as First World/Third World power differences. Her first published project on Appalachian children is a good introduction to this approach. The photographs and writings of her students contradict the stereotypes long associated with the internal colony of Appalachia (Ewald, 1985). In this method, photographs (often accompanied by text that expands upon the images) represent inspired reflection—they are not social science in and of themselves, but data that sociologists and others should put to use.

◆ The Essence of Visual Sociology; and, Where Are We Going?

Assuming we are talking about research methods (given that this is a handbook of qualitative methods), and assuming we are speaking about the photographic end of the movement, the simplest way to do visual sociology is to photograph with sociological consciousness. Howard Becker (1974) was the first to make this argument and the point has not been made more elegantly since then.

Becker suggests that we think theoretically when we do photography. What does this mean, exactly? For Becker, all photography is done from a theoretical perspective, but little of the theory is sociological. Our normal views of the world (which Becker calls "lay" theory) tell us where to point the camera and how to use the camera (speaking technically) to make images. Thus, when we photograph, we re-create our unexamined, taken-for-granted perceptions. We are interpreting sociological topics in our unexamined theorizing, and our photographs are our conclusions. If we are photojournalists (see Hagaman, 1996), we learn to present the theories of our newspaper editors and the recent conventions of photojournalism. We do this not only by choosing topics and specific images of those topics, but by using particular lenses (frames), apertures, and shutter speeds. If we are sociologists, we presumably have theoretical knowledge of our subject, the way Bateson and Mead (1942) knew the Balinese before they began photographing their still unequaled study of Bali culture. This prior knowledge will tell the researcher: "There is the enactment of a ritual my subjects have described. . . . It lasts 20 minutes and has four stages. . . . I will photograph it to highlight the transitions and interactions among actors." From this perspective, the work of visual sociology is straightforward: We bring it into the research process to extend our knowledge of the subject.

But not all field-workers have the kind of preexisting knowledge that Bateson and Mead had. There are at least two alternatives for visual sociologists. The first is to use the camera as an information-gathering instrument, to discover what Glaser and Strauss (1967) call "grounded theory." Photographs made during the research experience concretize the observations that field-workers use continually to redefine their theories. In this way photographs help build theory. In fact, the need to make photographs in the field requires that the field-worker look at something, and these beginning observations can be the starting point for making theory.

The second alternative is to use photographs to confirm and develop existing theory through photo elicitation, as described above. Researchers may use photos of events people experienced in the past to draw out memories of their history. Margolis (1998) studied the political consciousness of coal miners, using decades-old photos of mine work to interview elderly miners about events and their interpretations. In this case, one senses that the intervening years between when the photographs were taken and their interpretation led to deeper reflection than would normally be associated with the photo-elicitation process.

Other researchers have engaged subjects in the photography as well as the interviews in photo-elicitation research. Van der Dos, Gooskens, Liefting, and van Mierlo (1992) photographed a multiethnic Dutch neighborhood under the direction of five subjects. The researchers then interviewed their subjects using the images made on their earlier "photo tour." Finally, the researchers interviewed other informants using photos made by their neighbors, who were of a different age, gender, and ethnic background. The result is that as researchers we understand that a neighborhood is made up of people who share a material space but define it differently; but in this case, the five subjects also came to understand and appreciate the perspectives of their neighbors.

In all examples of photo-elicitation research, the photograph loses its claim to objectivity. Indeed, the power of the photo lies in its ability to unlock the subjectivity of those who see the image differently from the researcher.

A final thought: One can say that visual sociologists seek to find a way to integrate seeing into the research process. A sensitive field-worker is already nearly equipped to do visual sociology. It helps a great deal to understand how the camera records information, and it is important to understand the impact of photography on the research process. Finally, it is important to understand how various constructions (technical and social) influence how the photograph is made and interpreted.

We are living in a time of electronic revolution, which, as I have pointed out, has affected how images are made, distributed, experienced, and understood. Surely these changes should have an impact on visual sociology. Yet we are in a curious place. Sociology remains essentially uninterested in visual culture (Denzin, 1995, being an exception) or visual methods. Our textbooks contribute to the problem rather than solve it. The books most professors use for first courses in sociology are filled with colorful, uncomplicated images (chosen by art directors primarily to spiff up pages of text). The photographs restate the most obvious themes of the already watered-down text. Given that these images are the entirety of what most sociologists experience as "visual sociology," it is perhaps not surprising that the visual sociology movement remains tangential rather than in the mainstream of the discipline. In anthropology, with its long tradition of anthropological filmmaking and examples like Bateson and

Mead's still-admired visual ethnography, the case is a bit better. Still, most articles published in the two journals of visual anthropology are primarily words-about-images rather than reports of experiments and demonstrations of visual thinking.

What is the future? One possibility has visual sensibility leading an energized social science that is experimentally ethnographic and theoretically interdisciplinary. The new technologies promise myriad ways to bring changing visual experience into the production of social science and the understanding of visual dimensions of society. Another possible future has social science largely unconnected with a rapidly changing technological world, only mildly interested in studying society as an observed phenomenon. In this scenario, those of us in the small movement of visually inspired thinkers continue to wave our banners from the sidelines. I suppose the actual future will be some mix of the two.

◆ Notes

1. In my chapter for the first edition of this book, I suggest that the area in visual sociology most relevant to qualitative methods is photographic fieldwork, or visual ethnography; I note that visual ethnography, however, is the focal point of several criticisms (Harper, 1994). These include a postmodern critique of scientific ethnography, a postmodern critique of documentary photography, and a criticism that the portrayal of subjects inevitable in much visual ethnography violates ethical principles of fieldwork. These critiques raise substantial and serious issues, but I argue that it is better to reform visual methods than to discard visual ethnography in a sweeping rejection of modernism, science, ethnography, and documentary photography. Because that paper was subsequently updated (Harper, 1998), I have sought new ground for this chapter.

2. I first suggested these "types" of visual sociology in a paper that was inspired by Nichols's (1981) discussion of film theory (Harper, 1988). For a broader view of visual sociology, see also John Grady's (1996) argument for an enlarged scope for visual sociology and Charles Suchar's (1997) plea for an "interrogatory principle" for visual sociology. A collection edited by Chris Jenks (1995b) explores several dimensions of the sociology of visual perception on this general theme. Jenks (1995a) notes that " 'idea' derives from the Greek verb meaning 'to see.' This lexical etymology reminds us that the way that we think about the way that we think in Western culture is guided by a visual paradigm" (p. 1). Jenks later anticipates some ideas I have offered in this chapter with the statement: "The modern world is very much a 'seen' phenomenon. Sociology, however, itself in many senses the emergent discourse of modernity, has been rather neglectful of addressing cultural ocular conventions and has subsequently become somewhat inarticulate in relation to the visual dimensions of social relations" (p. 2).

3. Steiger's (1995) analysis of the relationship between photographers' choices and sociological statements is the best place to become acquainted with this topic.

4. Collier (1967; Collier & Collier, 1986) first described photo elicitation, a process used in the 1950s in Cornell University research on rural assimilation to urban centers in Canada. The researchers came to the realization that without photographs to indicate common understandings, their interviews did not make a great deal of sense. Photographs made in the research became a bridge between the subjects and the researchers.

5. A good place to start on this topic is with Dorothy Norman's (1960) study of Alfred Stieglitz, for whom photography was integral to the emergence of modern art.

6. After a thorough search (and on-line discussion), I found no references to the influence of gender in documentary expression. There have been many studies of the impact of gender on artistic photography. Thus although my example is limited because of the difficulty of comparing the work of a single female to the work of several men, it is an interesting first study.

◆ References

Artieri, G. (1996). The virtual image: Technology, media, and construction of the visual reality. *Visual Sociology, 11*(2), 56-61.

Bateson, G., & Mead, M. (1942). *Balinese character: A photographic analysis.* New York: New York Academy of Sciences.

Becker, H. S. (1974). Photography and sociology. *Studies in the Anthropology of Visual Communication, 1*(1), 1-19.

Biella, P., Chagnon, N., & Seaman, G. (1997). *Yanomamo interactive: The ax fight* [CD-ROM and text]. New York: Harcourt Brace Jovanovich.

Bourdieu, P. (1990). *Photography: A middle-brow art.* Stanford, CA: Stanford University Press.

Chalfen, R. (1987). Snapshot versions of life. Bowling Green, OH: Bowling Green Popular Press.

Collier, J., Jr. (1967). *Visual anthropology: Photography as a research method.* New York: Holt, Rinehart & Winston.

Collier, J., Jr., & Collier, M. (1986). *Visual anthropology: Photography as a research method* (Rev. ed.). Albuquerque: University of New Mexico Press.

Copeland, A. (Ed.). (1969). *People's Park.* New York: Ballantine.

Denzin, N. K. (1995). *The cinematic society: The voyeur's gaze.* Thousand Oaks, CA: Sage.

Edwards, E. (Ed.). (1992). *Anthropology and photography 1860-1920.* New Haven, CT: Yale University Press.

Ewald, W. (1985). *Portraits and dreams: Photographs and stories by children of the Appalachians.* New York: Writers & Readers.

Gibson, W. (1985). *Neuromancer.* New York: Ace.

Glaser, B. G., & Strauss, A. L. (1967). *The discovery of grounded theory: Strategies for qualitative research.* Chicago: Aldine.

Grady, J. (1996). The scope of visual sociology. *Visual Sociology, 11*(2), 10-24.

Hagaman, D. (1996). *How I learned not to be a photojournalist*. Lexington: University Press of Kentucky.

Harper, D. (1982). *Good company*. Chicago: University of Chicago Press.

Harper, D. (1987). The visual ethnographic narrative. *Visual Anthropology, 1*(1), 1-19.

Harper, D. (1988). Visual sociology: Expanding sociological vision. *American Sociologist, 19*(1), 54-70.

Harper, D. (1994). On the authority of the image: Visual methods at the crossroads. In N. K. Denzin & Y. S. Yvonna Lincoln (Eds.), *Handbook of qualitative research* (pp. 403-412). Thousand Oaks, CA: Sage.

Harper, D. (1998). An argument for visual sociology. In J. Prosser (Ed.), *Image-based research: A sourcebook for qualitative researchers* (pp. 24-41). London: Falmer.

Jackson, B. (1977). *Killing time*. Ithaca, NY: Cornell University Press.

Jenks, C. (1995a). The centrality of the eye in Western culture: An introduction. In C. Jenks (Ed.), *Visual culture* (pp. 1-25). London: Routledge.

Jenks, C. (Ed.). (1995b). *Visual culture*. London: Routledge.

Klich, K. (1989). *The book of Beth*. Millertown, NY: Aperture.

Mamber, S. (1974). *Cinema vérité in America: Studies in uncontrolled documentary*. Cambridge: MIT Press.

Margolis, E. (1998). Picturing labor: A visual ethnography of the coal mine labor process. *Visual Sociology, 13*(2), 5-37.

Nichols, B. (1981). *Ideology and the image*. Bloomington: Indiana University Press.

Norman, D. (1960). *Alfred Stieglitz: An American seer*. New York: Random House.

Quinney, R. (1991). *Journey to a far place*. Philadelphia: Temple University Press.

Quinney, R. (1995). A sense sublime: Visual sociology as a fine art. *Visual Sociology, 10*(1-2), 61-84.

Rieger, J. (1996). Photographing social change. *Visual Sociology, 11*(1), 5-49.

Smith, W. E., & Smith, A. (1975). *Minamata*. New York: Holt, Rinehart & Winston.

Snyder, R. L. (1968). *Pare Lorentz and the documentary film*. Norman: Oklahoma University Press.

Spence, J. (1988). *Putting myself in the picture: A political, personal and photographic autobiography*. Seattle: Real Comet.

Steiger, R. (1995). First children and family dynamics. *Visual Sociology, 10*(1-2), 28-49.

Suchar, C. (1997). Grounding visual sociology research in shooting scripts. *Qualitative Sociology, 20*, 33-55.

Tagg, J. (1988). *The burden of representation: Essays on photographies and histories*. Basingstoke, Hampshire, England: Macmillan.

van der Dos, S. E., Gooskens, I., Liefting, M., & van Mierlo, M. (1992). Reading images: A study of a Dutch neighborhood. *Visual Sociology, 7*(1), 4-68.

6

Autoethnography, Personal Narrative, Reflexivity

Researcher as Subject

Carolyn Ellis and Arthur P. Bochner

◆ Overview: Extending the Handbook Genre

"Hi, glad it's you," I say, relieved to hear Art's voice on the other end of the line.

"You sound upset. What's the matter?" Art asks.

"Oh, it's been a zoo in the office today—long distance calls, forms to fill out, a barrage of e-mail, one student after another. I'm feeling that end-of-the-semester panic. I'd hoped to finish reading class papers and turn in

AUTHORS' NOTE: Thanks to our graduate students at University of South Florida and to Mitch Allen, Norman Denzin, Rosanna Hertz, Yvonna Lincoln, Laurel Richardson, and William Tierney for commenting on the chapter manuscript. Carolyn Ellis gave a short portion of this article as a keynote address at The International Advances in Qualitative Methods Conference held in Edmonton, Alberta, Canada, February 1999, and published it in *Qualitative Health Research* (Vol. 9, no. 5, September 1999, pp. 653-667) as "Heartful Autoethnography."

semester grades, but I haven't gotten to them yet. How's everything at home? Are the dogs okay?"

"They're fine," Art replies quickly, "but I'm not. I started working on our chapter for the *Handbook of Qualitative Research*. The more I think about it, the more frustrated I become."

"I thought you really wanted to do this."

"Well, the first edition of the *Handbook* didn't sufficiently highlight autoethnography and personal narrative. So I initially thought it would be a good opportunity to show how important it is to make the researcher's own experience a topic of investigation in its own right."

"Well, the timing is right now to do that," I respond. "When the first edition was published a lot of academics were trying to figure out how to write their way out of the crisis of representation, but there weren't many examples of authors who made themselves and their personal experience a central focus of their research. Over the past 5 years, however, that's changed significantly, what with the beginning of the Ethnographic Alternatives series, Denzin's emphasis on personal writing in *Interpretive Ethnography*, Behar's *The Vulnerable Observer...*"

"Granted, there's been a wave of interest in more personal, intimate, and embodied writing," Art assents.

"So what's the problem?"

"I think we've underestimated the constraints imposed by the genre of the handbook chapter as a form of writing," Art continues, apparently deep in thought.

"But you've written many handbook chapters before," I point out. "Why is this different?"

"Because those chapters conformed to the conventions of the handbook genre. They were essays, not stories. But in this piece we want to *show*, not just tell *about* autoethnography. Look at any handbook on your shelf and what you'll find is that most chapters are written in third-person, passive voice. It's as if they're written from nowhere by nobody. The conventions militate against personal and passionate writing. These books are filled with dry, distant, abstract, propositional essays."

"That's called academic writing, darling." When Art doesn't laugh, I continue in a more serious tone, "But some of the authors in the first edition of the *Handbook of Qualitative Research* wrote in first person."

"Yes, but the 'I' usually disappeared after the introduction and then reappeared abruptly in the conclusion," Art replies.

"And the 'I' usually was a 'we,' and an ambiguous 'we' at best, which sometimes referred to the authors as writers of the chapters and sometimes included all of us, whoever we might be," I add.

"And the authors almost never became characters in the stories they wrote . . ."

"They couldn't," I interrupt, now immersed in the conversation, "because their chapters weren't really stories. They included little in the way of dialogue, dramatic tension, or plotline, for that matter."

"But, look, handbooks do provide a service," I continue, fearing that Art will decide not to collaborate on the chapter. "They provide citations and sources, a sense of history, and arguments others can use as justifications for their own work."

"I don't question that they serve an important purpose. Hundreds of students have been inspired to do qualitative research by the first edition of the *Handbook of Qualitative Research,* for example."

"That's true, and we can't criticize handbook writers for failing to do what they're not asked to do."

"But we can ask why authors aren't encouraged to write academic articles in the first person, " Art retorts. "Why should we take it for granted that an author's personal feelings and thoughts should be omitted in a handbook chapter? After all, who is the person collecting the evidence, drawing the inferences, and reaching the conclusions? By not insisting on some sort of personal accountability, our academic publications reinforce the third-person, passive voice as the standard, which gives more weight to abstract and categorical knowledge than to the direct testimony of personal narrative and the first-person voice. It doesn't even occur to most authors that writing in the first person is an option. They've been shaped by the prevailing norms of scholarly discourse within which they operate. Once the anonymous essay became the norm, then the personal, autobiographical story became a delinquent form of expression."

Just as I'm beginning to doubt that we can do this project, Art says, "This morning I wrote out some of my concerns in conventional social science prose. Maybe this will give us a place to start. If you have a minute, I'd like to read it to you."

Relieved, I say, "Sure, go ahead." I glance toward the large stack of term papers. They'll have to wait.

Art reads:

Like most social scientists educated in the 1960s and 1970s, I was socialized into the legacy of empiricism. I developed an appetite for

201

generalizable abstractions and unified knowledge. The first social science handbooks were published when I was in graduate school, and they fed this hunger for received knowledge. My professors pressed the point that scientific knowledge is cumulative and linear, so every once in a while scholars have to step back and assess the state of the field. Ironically, these assessments sometimes were referred to as "state-of-the-art" essays (an art that was supposedly science). That's what a handbook did—it gave an objective, neutral read on the evidence. The authors were the experts, but they wrote as if they were anonymous. Because it wasn't important who gathered the evidence or who judged and weighed it, handbook writers followed the conventions of using a passive voice that erases subjectivity and personal accountability.

After I earned my Ph.D., I became increasingly circumspect about the possibilities and limitations of the human sciences. In the mid-1970s, one of my colleagues, who was teaching a graduate seminar on "the rhetoric of science," suggested that I study the growing literature on "the crisis of confidence" in social science. I began by reading Kuhn (1962), who showed that the building-block model of science lacked foundations; then Rorty (1982), Toulmin (1969), and other philosophers who illustrated how the "facts" scientists see are inextricably connected to the vocabulary they use to express or represent them; Lyotard (1984) debunked the belief in a unified totality of knowledge, questioning whether master narratives were either possible or desirable; poststructuralist and deconstructionist writers, such as Barthes (1977), Derrida (1978, 1981), and Foucault (1970), effectively obliterated the modernist conception of the author, altering how we understand the connections among author, text, and readers; under the influence of Bakhtin (1981), the interpretive space available to the reader was broadened, encouraging multiple perspectives, unsettled meanings, plural voices, and local and illegitimate knowledges that transgress against the claims of a unitary body of theory; feminist critical theorists such as Clough (1994), Harding (1991), Hartsock (1983), and Smith (1990, 1992) promoted the unique and marginalized standpoints and particularities of women; and standpoint boundary-crossing textualists such as Trinh (1989, 1992), Anzaldúa (1987), and Behar (1993, 1996) opened our eyes and ears to the necessity of exposing how the complex contingencies of race, class, sexuality, disability, and ethnicity are woven into the fabric of concrete, personal lived experiences, championing the cause of reflexive, experimental, autobiographical, and vulnerable texts.

In the wake of these developments, I doubt whether a handbook chapter can help guide the work of those who have turned toward autoethnography and personal narrative if it holds to the voice and authority of a form of writing that this work seeks to transgress. How helpful would it be to list references, define terms, abstract from and critique exemplars, formulate criteria for evaluation, or theorize the perspective of the "I," so readers can make our knowledge theirs? No, we need a form that will allow readers to feel the moral dilemmas, think with our story instead of about it, join actively in the decision points that define an autoethnographic project, and consider how their own lives can be made a story worth telling.

When Art stops reading, I say, "Well, that's clever. Although you started with the 'I,' you quickly fell into using the handbook genre to argue against writing in the handbook genre." I can't stop laughing. "Reminds me of how so many of our texts argue in postmodern abstract jargon for greater accessibility and experimental forms."

"See how powerful the conventions are?" Art agrees, now chuckling as well. Then he adds more seriously, "Let's just write to Norman and Yvonna and bow out. Think of the time we could spend on the beach instead. Get some immediate gratification for a change."

"It's tempting, especially given how we've been feeling lately that our life is too dominated by our work—but no way. Not after I've already agonized over writing the section on 'what is autoethnography?' You know how I resist doing this kind of writing. At the same time, I know it's important," I reply, as I hear a knock at my door.

"I don't think I'll be satisfied, nor will you, unless we find a way to transgress the conventions. What if we were to create a story that would work within the handbook genre but also outside it, showing what we do as we tell about it? That could be fun," Art suggests playfully.

"How delightfully paradoxical," I add in a mischievous tone. "But we'd have to be careful not to give the impression that we're being oppositional and advocating that everyone should write the way we do," I warn, expressing something we hear often and try hard to dispel. Then I get back into the irony of Art's idea. "Won't our critics love it—you know, the ones who already accuse us of being irreverent, self-absorbed, sentimental, and romantic?"

Before Art can answer, I tell him I have to go. "Someone's at the door. Bye—Come in," I say in one breath, in response to the third knock.

◆ Introduction to Autoethnography

A woman in her mid-40s opens the door and hesitates in the entryway. A large-brimmed, floppy straw hat covered with purple bangles hides her face. A matching scarf hangs loosely around her neck. "Professor Ellis?" I nod. "My name is Sylvia Smith. I'm a Ph.D. student in the Psychology Department. I'm planning to do my dissertation on breast cancer, and your name was given to me as a social scientist interested in research on illness. I'd like you to be on my dissertation committee. Three members of my committee are from the Psychology Department and the fourth is a research oncologist."

"Hold it," I say, my hands extended in front of me to slow down her monologue. "Back up. Have a seat and let's talk about your project."

Sylvia removes her scarf and hat with a sweeping crisscross motion of both hands and continues speaking as rapidly as before. "I want to interview breast cancer survivors to understand how they're adjusting after cancer. I hope to combine qualitative and quantitative approaches. Send out a survey and then interview . . . oh, maybe 30 women and include African Americans and lesbians, older and young women, professional and working-class women. That way I can generalize . . ."

"How'd you get interested in this topic?" I interrupt.

"Well, uh," she says, now slowing down and looking at me quizzically, "I've had breast cancer." Then, going back to her rapid-fire, assertive style, "But I won't let that bias my research. You can count on that."

"Of course you will," I say, and she immediately assumes a downcast, defeated posture, before I add, "as you should."

"What do you mean?" she asks, looking straight at me with penetrating eyes. "I thought I had to keep my personal experience out of my research. If I want my study to be valid, I can't mention to my participants that I've had cancer, can I?"

"Hold that question," I say again, and move my chair closer to hers. "Would you be willing to tell me a little about your breast cancer first? It'll help me understand more about your academic interest in the topic. Are you okay talking about your own experience?"

"Of course," she responds, "but I didn't think anybody at the university would be interested in my personal experience." She breathes deeply and slowly begins her story about the lump she discovered 7 years before, her mastectomy, and follow-up chemotherapy. Then, "And it's had a big impact on my family, especially my relationship with my daughter, and how I see myself . . . ," she says, her voice trailing off.

"How has it impacted your relationship with your daughter?" I ask quietly.

"She has to worry about getting cancer as well now. You know, the genetic link, and we seem to have trouble talking openly about the risks and about our feelings."

Sylvia continues to talk about her daughter, and after a while, I ask, "And your self-image?"

"I could write a book about that," she says, shaking her head back and forth. "You know, I'm a therapist. I thought I could deal with it all. But it's hard to feel like a whole person. I don't mean because I lost a breast. Good riddance, I say to that. They were always too big anyway. I had breast reduction on the other one when I had reconstruction. It's just . . . well . . . my life has changed so drastically, except the day-to-day, well actually that's not all that different . . ."

She becomes animated as she tells her story. Sensing that she is comfortable and desires to keep going, I continue asking questions. Her story inspires thoughts about myself. How would I feel if I had a breast removed? As she talks, I glance at her small breasts, then casually glide my hands across my own large ones. I can't imagine their not being there. Wouldn't I feel incomplete, desexualized? Did she really feel "good riddance" or is that a cover?

". . . And the hair," I hear her say through my thoughts. "Just look at my fuzz. It never really grew back like before. Shaving it was the most difficult yet exhilarating thing I've ever done." The thin, inch-long brown and gray strands don't move as she casually tosses her head from side to side. My fingers reach for my fine-textured, shoulder-length brown hair—I'd feel naked without it. I even resist pulling my hair back from my face. I wonder why she cuts hers so short now, as if she's drawing attention to having had cancer. But what about the hat and scarf? Does she use them in case she wants to "pass"? I wonder.

Sylvia and I are about the same age. This could happen to me. No, it couldn't. I get an annual mammogram.

". . . I'd had a mammogram just a few months before I found the lump," her voice intrudes into my thoughts.

But I do self-examinations every month, I argue back from inside my head.

"I found it during my monthly self-exam," she continues, shaking the false predictability of my world. I listen intently, understanding that Sylvia has a lot to teach me.

"Anyway, I'm interested in other women's experience," she says, adding hesitantly, "you know, how it compares to mine. That's not something I've admitted before, the personal part, I mean."

I nod. What do I do now? I don't want to wean another student off the science model and deal with a science-oriented committee. And I'm wary of getting involved in another study that simplifies, categorizes, slices and dices the illness process. But Sylvia is a therapist and forthcoming about her feelings and what happened to her. Maybe her study could explore the feelings associated with breast cancer and be useful for other women. The pain on Sylvia's face, in spite of the casualness of her words, also makes me think that this study might be a useful exploration for her. And I know it could be a valuable experience for me as well. But what am I getting into?

"Do you have any idea what I do?" I ask.

"Just that you study illness and do qualitative work. Nobody does qualitative research in my department. But I've taken a qualitative course in education and I think I could get my committee to accept grounded theory for my dissertation research."

"I don't use grounded theory much anymore," I say. "Most of what I do is autoethnography."

"What's that?" she asks, writing the word *autoethnography* on her notepad as she looks at me.

"I start with my personal life. I pay attention to my physical feelings, thoughts, and emotions. I use what I call systematic sociological introspection and emotional recall to try to understand an experience I've lived through. Then I write my experience as a story. By exploring a particular life, I hope to understand a way of life, as Reed-Danahay says."

"Who?" she asks, pen poised in the air.

"Reed-Danahay, an anthropologist who wrote a book on autoethnography."

"How do I get a copy?"

"Don't worry about that yet. There's plenty of time to read *about* autoethnography. I want you to *experience* autoethnography first."

I ignore Sylvia's confused look, as I dig through my file cabinet. "So if I understand you correctly, the goal is to use your life experience to generalize to a larger group or culture," Sylvia speaks to my back.

"Yes, but that's not all. The goal is also to enter and document the moment-to-moment, concrete details of a life. That's an important way of knowing as well."

"So, you just write about your life? That doesn't sound too difficult," Sylvia says casually.

I turn around, stare at her for a moment, as though I'll get a sign as to whether I should promote autoethnography to Sylvia. When no sign is forthcoming, I say, "Oh, it's amazingly difficult. It's certainly not something that most people can do well. Most social scientists don't write well enough to carry it off. Or they're not sufficiently introspective about their feelings or motives, or the contradictions they experience. Ironically, many aren't observant enough of the world around them. The self-questioning autoethnography demands is extremely difficult. So is confronting things about yourself that are less than flattering. Believe me, honest autoethnographic exploration generates a lot of fears and doubts—and emotional pain. Just when you think you can't stand the pain anymore, well, that's when the real work has only begun. Then there's the vulnerability of revealing yourself, not being able to take back what you've written or having any control over how readers interpret it. It's hard not to feel your life is being critiqued as well as your work. It can be humiliating. And the ethical issues," I warn, "just wait until you're writing about family members and loved ones who are part of your story."

Sylvia holds on to her chair, her eyes wide. I smile and let out the breath I've been holding. "I'm sorry. I get really passionate about all this," I say more gently. "Of course, there are rewards too—for example, you come to understand yourself in deeper ways. And with understanding yourself comes understanding others. Autoethnography provides an avenue for doing something meaningful for yourself and the world . . ."

"Ah, here they are," I interrupt myself as I pull two stapled papers from my autoethnography file. "The one on top is 'Survivors,' a paper I wrote about my brother's death. The other one's a chapter from Butler and Rosenblum's book *Cancer in Two Voices,* a co-constructed narrative about a woman with breast cancer and her lesbian lover who takes care of her."

"Co-constructed?"

"We'll talk about that later. For now, just see how you respond to these stories. I think that after you've read them, what I've been saying will be clearer. If you're still interested then, leave me a note and I'll mail you some other materials."

"One more thing," I add, pointing to the syllabi on my desk. "I'll want to meet often and you'll have to read the assignments from my classes on 'illness narratives' and 'communicating emotion.' Also, I want you to meet with Art Bochner, my coauthor, who teaches courses on narrative and, by the way, also happens to be my husband." Her down-turned mouth changes to a smile for a brief moment, until I add, "These are minimum requirements if I'm going to be on your committee."

"Oh, my. I don't know if I'll have time, given my program," she says. "I still have to take 'Tests and Measurement' and 'Advanced Experimental Research Design.' I hope to finish my course work during this coming fall, and then take my prelims in early spring and finish my proposal by the beginning of next summer."

I shrug my shoulders as I stand and open the door. My exuberance, the warnings, all the requirements—any of these could scare her off. Oh, well, better if it happens now than later. Suspecting this will be the last I see of her, I'm glad I've given her an easy way out. Sylvia winds her scarf around her neck, throws her hat along with the papers I've given her into her large open bag, says good-bye, and quickly scurries from view.

Two days later, I arrive at school and find a faxed message from Sylvia.

Dear Professor Ellis:

> *This is some of the most powerful writing I've ever read. I identified with your grief over losing your brother so suddenly. You reminded me of how I felt when I found out I had cancer. So did Butler and Rosenblum. I recall experiencing that kind of turmoil, confusion, and meaninglessness. This work violates everything I've been taught about social science research, but I'm fascinated and want to know more. Will you mail some materials to help clarify the origins and practices of autoethnography? Maybe some kind of a literature review would suffice. While you're at it, do you mind including a few more autoethnographies?*

I smile and pull out articles from my autoethnography file. Jago, Kiesinger, Kolker, Ronai, Tillmann-Healy—that ought to do it—and a section on defining autoethnography I have just written as part of a chapter for Denzin and Lincoln's second edition of the *Handbook of Qualitative Research*. I pause to read the draft, which is titled "What Is Autoethnography?"

◆ What Is Autoethnography?

Autoethnography is an autobiographical genre of writing and research that displays multiple layers of consciousness, connecting the personal to the cultural. Back and forth autoethnographers gaze, first through an ethnographic wide-angle lens, focusing outward on social and cultural aspects of their personal experience; then, they look inward, exposing a vulnerable self that is moved by and may move through, refract, and resist cultural interpretations (see Deck, 1990; Neumann, 1996; Reed-Danahay, 1997). As they zoom backward and forward, inward and outward, distinctions between the personal and cultural become blurred, sometimes beyond distinct recognition. Usually written in first-person voice, autoethnographic texts appear in a variety of forms—short stories, poetry, fiction, novels, photographic essays, personal essays, journals, fragmented and layered writing, and social science prose. In these texts, concrete action, dialogue, emotion, embodiment, spirituality, and self-consciousness are featured, appearing as relational and institutional stories affected by history, social structure, and culture, which themselves are dialectically revealed through action, feeling, thought, and language.

The term **autoethnography** *has been in circulation for at least two decades. Although anthropologist Karl Heider referred in 1975 to the Dani's own account of what people do as autoethnography, David Hayano (1979) usually is credited as the originator of the term. Hayano limited the term to cultural-level studies by anthropologists of their "own people," in which the researcher is a full insider by virtue of being "native," acquiring an intimate familiarity with the group, or achieving full membership in the group being studied (p. 100).*

Like many terms used by social scientists, the meanings and applications of autoethnography have evolved in a manner that makes precise definition and application difficult. It seems appropriate now to include under the broad rubric of autoethnography those studies that have been referred to by other similarly situated terms, such as personal narratives (Personal Narratives Group, 1989), narratives of the self (Richardson, 1994b), personal experience narratives (Denzin, 1989), self-stories (Denzin, 1989), first-person accounts (Ellis, 1998a), personal essays (Krieger, 1991), ethnographic short stories (Ellis, 1995d), writing-stories (Richardson, 1997); complete-member research (Adler & Adler, 1987), auto-observation (Adler & Adler, 1994), opportunistic research (Riemer, 1977), personal ethnography (Crawford, 1996), literary tales (Van Maanen, 1988), lived experience (Van Maanen, 1990), critical autobiography (Church, 1995), self-ethnography (Van Maanen, 1995), radical empiricism (Jackson, 1989), socioautobiography (Zola, 1982), autopathography (Hawkins, 1993), evocative narratives (Bochner, Ellis, & Tillmann-Healy, 1997), personal writing (DeVault, 1997), reflexive ethnography (Ellis & Bochner, 1996a), confessional tales (Van Maanen, 1988), ethnographic memoir (Tedlock, 1991), ethnobiography (Lejeune, 1989), autobiology (Payne, 1996), collaborative autobiography (Goldman, 1993), ethnographic autobiography (Brandes, 1982), emotionalism (Gubrium & Holstein, 1997), experiential texts (Denzin, 1997), narrative ethnography (Abu-Lughod, 1993), autobiographical ethnography (Reed-Danahay, 1997), ethnographic poetics (Marcus & Fischer, 1986), native ethnography (Ohnuki-Tierney, 1984), indigenous ethnography (Gonzalez & Krizek, 1994), and ethnic autobiography (Reed-Danahay, 1997). Nevertheless, social scientists often discuss autoethnography as a subtype of some other forms, such as impressionistic accounts (Van Maanen, 1988), narrative ethnography (Tedlock, 1991), interpretive biography (Denzin, 1989), new or experimental ethnography (Ellis & Bochner, 1996b), sociopoetics (Ellis & Bochner, 1996a), or postmodern ethnography (Tyler, 1986).

Various methodological strategies have been developed in connection with autoethnographic projects, although they may be applied to other forms of qualitative research as well. These include systematic sociological introspection (Ellis, 1991b), biographical method (Denzin, 1989), personal experience methods (Clandinin & Connelly, 1994), feminist methods (Reinharz, 1992), experiential analysis (Reinharz, 1979), narrative inquiry (Bochner, 1994), consciousness-raising methods (Hollway, 1989), co-constructed narrative (Bochner & Ellis, 1992), and interactive interviewing (Ellis, Kiesinger, & Tillmann-Healy, 1997). In some disciplines, terms endemic to a particular field have evolved, such as in sociology, personal sociology (Higgins & Johnson, 1988), autobiographical sociology (Friedman, 1990), sociological autobiography (Merton, 1972/1988), private sociology (Shostak, 1996), and emotional sociology (Ellis, 1991a); in anthropology, anthropological autobiography (Brandes, 1982), native anthropology (Narayan, 1993), indigenous anthropology (Tedlock, 1991), autoanthropology (Strathern, 1987), self-conscious anthropology (Cohen, 1992), anthropology of the self (Kondo, 1990), anthropology at home (Jackson, 1987), anthropological poetics (Brady, 1991), and autoethnology (Lejeune, 1989); and in communication, rhetorical autoethnography

(French, 1998), performance autobiography (Miller & Taylor, 1997), and autoethnographic performance (Park-Fuller, 1998). Increasingly, however, autoethnography has become the term of choice in describing studies and procedures that connect the personal to the cultural, frequently appearing in titles of books, theses, sections of books, articles, special issues of journals, and book series (for example, Clough, 1997; Deck, 1990; Ellis, 1997, 1998a; Ellis & Bochner, 1996a; Gravel, 1997; Herndon, 1993; Lionnet, 1989; Pratt, 1994; Reed-Danahay, 1997; Trotter, 1992).

Autoethnographers vary in their emphasis on the research process (graphy), on culture (ethnos), and on self (auto) (see Reed-Danahay, 1997, p. 2). Different exemplars of autoethnography fall at different places along the continuum of each of these three axes. Researchers disagree on the boundaries of each category and on the precise definitions of the types of autoethnography. Indeed, many writers move back and forth among terms and meanings even in the same articles. Recognizing this limitation, I will mention, for heuristic purposes, a few widely used expressions that provide a sense of the range of approaches associated with autoethnography.

*Although **reflexive ethnographies** primarily focus on a culture or subculture, authors use their own experiences in the culture reflexively to bend back on self and look more deeply at self-other interactions. In native ethnographies, researchers who are natives of cultures that have been marginalized or exoticized by others write about and interpret their own cultures for others. In texts by **"complete-member researchers,"** researchers explore groups of which they already are members or in which, during the research process, they have become full members with complete identification and acceptance. In **personal narratives**, social scientists take on the dual identities of academic and personal selves to tell autobiographical stories about some aspect of their experience in daily life. In **literary autoethnographies**, an author's primary identification is as an autobiographical writer rather than a social scientist, and the text focuses as much on examining a self autobiographically as on interpreting a culture for a nonnative audience (see Deck, 1990).*

*In **reflexive ethnographies**, the researcher's personal experience becomes important primarily in how it illuminates the culture under study. Reflexive ethnographies range along a continuum from starting research from one's own experience to ethnographies where the researcher's experience is actually studied along with other participants, to confessional tales where the researcher's experiences of doing the study become the focus of investigation.*

Feminism has contributed significantly to legitimating the autobio-graphical voice associated with reflexive ethnography (for example, Behar, 1996; Behar & Gordon, 1995; Krieger, 1991, 1996; Personal Narratives Group, 1989; Richardson, 1997). Many feminist writers have advocated starting research from one's own experience (e.g., Smith, 1979). Thus, to a greater or lesser extent, researchers incorporate their personal experiences and standpoints in their research by starting with a story about them-selves, explaining their personal connection to the project, or by using per-sonal knowledge to help them in the research process (for examples, see Jones, 1998; Linden, 1992; for a summary of reflexive studies, see Reinharz, 1992, pp. 258-263).

*Jackson (1989) uses the term **radical empiricism** to refer to a process that includes the ethnographer's experiences and interaction with other participants as vital parts of what is being studied. Reflexive ethnographers ideally use all their senses, their bodies, movement, feeling, and their whole being—they use the "self" to learn about the other (Cohen, 1992; Jack-son, 1989; Okely, 1992; Turner & Bruner, 1986). Particularly controver-sial is the notion of the role of sexuality in learning about the other (Kulick & Willson, 1995; Lewin & Leap, 1996).*

In summarizing reflexive ethnography and tracing its history thor-oughly, Tedlock (1991) distinguishes between ethnographic memoir (also called confessional tales by Van Maanen, 1988), in which the ethnographer, who is the focus of the story, tells a personal tale of what went on in the backstage of doing research, and narrative ethnography, where the ethnog-rapher's experiences are incorporated into the ethnographic description and analysis of others and the emphasis is on the "ethnographic dialogue or encounter" between the narrator and members of the group being studied (p. 78). The ethnographic memoir is rooted historically in the personal dia-ries and journals kept by Malinowski (1967). Standing on his shoulders, many ethnographers who followed wrote confessional tales about their re-search in volumes separate from their research documents (e.g., Dumont, 1976, 1978; Rabinow, 1975, 1977); some wrote under pen names in order to avoid losing academic credibility (e.g., Bowen, 1954). The development of this kind of reflexive writing is connected, according to Tedlock (1991), to a shift in the 1970s from an emphasis on participant observation to the "observation of participation" and to an emphasis on the process of writ-ing. This shift was inspired by the epistemological doubt associated with the crisis of representation and the changing composition of those who become ethnographers, with more women, lower-class, ethnic and racial groups, and Third and Fourth World scholars now represented (Bochner & Ellis, 1999).

This changing composition also is associated with concerns about power and praxis and with more ethnographers writing about their own people. *Native ethnography*, for example, is written by researchers from the Third and Fourth Worlds who share a history of colonialism or economic subordination, including subjugation by ethnographers who have made them subjects of their work. Now as bicultural insiders/outsiders, native ethnographers construct their own cultural stories (often focusing on their own autobiographies; for example, see Kinkaid, 1988; Rodriguez, 1983), raise serious questions about the interpretations of others who write about them, and use their dual positionality to problematize the distinction between observer and observed, insider and outsider (see, for example, Motzafi-Haller, 1997; Trinh, 1989; for more detailed discussions, see Neumann, 1996; Reed-Danahay, 1997; Tedlock, 1991).

Complete-member researchers is a term coined by Adler and Adler (1987) to refer to researchers who are fully committed to and immersed in the groups they study. During the research process, the "convert" researcher identifies with the group and "becomes the phenomenon" (Mehan & Wood, 1975) being studied. For example, Jules-Rosette (1975) became a baptized true believer in the African Apostolic church she studied. The "opportunistic" researcher (Riemer, 1977; sometimes called an indigenous researcher in anthropology—see Tedlock, 1991) studies settings of which he or she is already a member (such as Hayano's 1982 study of poker or Krieger's 1983 study of a lesbian community).

In contrast to complete-member research, where the emphasis is on the research process and the group being studied, social scientists recently have begun to view themselves as the phenomenon and to write **evocative personal narratives** specifically focused on their academic as well as their personal lives. Their primary purpose is to understand a self or some aspect of a life lived in a cultural context. In personal narrative texts, authors become "I," readers become "you," subjects become "us." Participants are encouraged to participate in a personal relationship with the author/researcher, to be treated as coresearchers, to share authority, and to author their own lives in their own voices. Readers, too, take a more active role as they are invited into the author's world, evoked to a feeling level about the events being described, and stimulated to use what they learn there to reflect on, understand, and cope with their own lives. The goal is to write meaningfully and evocatively about topics that matter and may make a difference, to include

213

sensory and emotional experience (Shelton, 1995), and to write from an ethic of care and concern (Denzin, 1997; Noddings, 1984; Richardson, 1997).

Literary and cultural critics *often join social scientists in employing the term* **autoethnography** *in reference to autobiographies that self-consciously explore the interplay of the introspective, personally engaged self with cultural descriptions mediated through language, history, and ethnographic explanation (see Deck, 1990; Lionnet, 1989; Pratt, 1994). For example, Lionnet (1989) and Deck (1990) both label and explore Hurston's (1942/1991) memoirs as autoethnography, in which the traditional historical frame and specific dates and events associated with autobiography are minimized and the attempt to demonstrate the lived experience and humanity of authors and their peoples to outside audiences is maximized. As Hurston (1942/1991) explains about the folk songs she gathered in her own research, "The words do not count.... The tune is the unity of the thing" (p. 144). Deck compares literary autoethnographies to self-reflexive fieldwork accounts, such as Shostak's* Nisa: The Life and Words of a !Kung Woman *(1981) and Crapanzano's* Tuhami: Portrait of a Moroccan *(1980), in which the authors ground themselves in their field experiences, reference other social scientists who serve to validate the characters in their stories, keep the autobiographical components mainly in the introductions and epilogues, and focus personal revelations directly on the fieldwork at hand rather than on their own personal development.*

Social scientists also write literary and poetic ethnography. Dan Rose (1991), for example, distinguishes between his own personal poetry, which is not connected to his anthropology, and the poetry of other anthropologists such as Stanley Diamond (1982), which focuses on the ethnographic experience of anthropologists as observers. Many anthropologists, such as Edward Sapir and Ruth Benedict, have published realist ethnography in mainstream anthropology journals and personal poetry in literary outlets (Bruner, 1993). Now Anthropology and Humanism *publishes fiction and poetry by anthropologists. In sociology, Laurel Richardson, for example, has published essays in literary (1995) and social science journals (1996) and poetry as ethnography (1994a).*

Autoethnography, native ethnography, self-ethnography, memoir, autobiography, even fiction, have become blurred genres. In many cases, whether a social science work is called an autoethnography or an ethnography depends on the claims made by those who write and those who write about the work. Whether a work is called fiction or fact, autoethnography

214

*or memoir, is connected to writing practices—social science autoethnographies usually contain citations to other academics and use an academic, disciplinary vocabulary; publishing practices—who publishes the book, how it is promoted (for example, the field identified on the outside cover) and labeled (ISBN number), and who the targeted audience is; and reviewing practices—who endorses it, who reviews it, and who writes about it. Literary critics treat some autobiographies as autoethnographies and not others; Hurston, who sees herself as essayist, anthropologist, and fiction writer (Lionnet, 1989), provides a good example of the messiness and overlap. Mainstream social science tends to classify autoethnographies (for example, Ellis, 1995b) and life histories about academic careers (for example, Berger, 1990; Goetting & Fenstermaker, 1995; Riley, 1988) into the genre of memoir or autobiography (see Zussman, 1996). Perhaps the loose application of the term **autoethnography** only signifies a greater tolerance now for the diverse goals of ethnography and a better understanding of the fallibility and indeterminacy of language and concepts.*

Smiling at the social science prose, I place the copy of the *Handbook* draft in the package with the stories I'm sending Sylvia. I try to imagine how she will take it in.

A week later, Sylvia again appears at my door. "Okay, I read everything you sent me. Wow, those personal narratives just blew me away. Your autoethnography piece was interesting, but hard to get through. It'll be more helpful later, I'm sure," she reassures, then continues quickly, "but now I'm very confused."

"Listen, I only have 5 minutes," I say. "I'm going to a department colloquium."

"Oh, I'm sorry. I'll come back another time," Sylvia responds, retreating through the doorway.

"No, wait. What confuses you?" I ask.

"Well, in my methods classes I was taught that I had to protect against my own biases interfering with my observations and that my research should produce general knowledge and theory. But the articles you gave me emphasize concrete expressions over abstractions. So, I'm confused about what my objectives would be if I do an autoethnography. Why would others be interested? How could I prove that what I have to say about my experience is true? Autoethnography isn't really social science, is it?"

215

"Your timing is perfect. Come with me," I say, grabbing my keys and walking down the hall. "I want you to hear somebody."

We enter a crowded room where a talk is about to begin. "That's Art, my partner, the good-looking guy sitting at the table," I whisper to Sylvia, as we take seats in the back.

"Welcome to another session of our Interdisciplinary Colloquium Series on Interpretive Research in the Social Sciences," says Jim Spiro, a departmental colleague who organizes the talks. "Today's speaker is Art Bochner, who teaches a Ph.D. seminar on 'narrative inquiry.' "

"We have these talks every week," I whisper to Sylvia. "They're pretty informal."

"Art will present his remarks for about 15 minutes and then turn to questions from the audience," Jim announces. "I've asked him to talk about what some writers have called 'the narrative turn in the human sciences' and to focus specifically on personal narratives. His talk is entitled 'Why Personal Narrative Matters.' Please welcome Art Bochner."

Art stands with his right foot hooked behind his left leg, runs his fingers through his hair, and begins.

◆ Why Personal Narrative Matters

It's my pleasure to be here today and to have this opportunity to speak on a topic about which I feel so passionately. As many of you know, I was educated as a traditional empiricist and spent most of the first decade of my academic life plying the trade I had learned as a graduate student. In the late 1970s I began to feel uneasy about the political, philosophical, ethical, and ideological foundations of social science research (Bochner, 1981). In my chosen field, communication research, empiricism rested largely on the premise that communication between humans could be described as an object. But human communication is not an object, or a discipline studying objects. Communication is a process consisting of sequences of interactions and the dynamic human activity of studying them. Moreover, as communicating humans studying humans communicating, we are inside what we are studying. The reflexive qualities of human communication should not be bracketed "in the name of science." They should be accommodated and integrated into research and its products.

Like many other social scientists who took these matters seriously, my confidence in orthodox, social science methodology was shaken by the

216

critiques of poststructuralist, postmodernist, and feminist writers. I turned to narrative as a mode of inquiry because I was persuaded that social science texts needed to construct a different relationship between researchers and subjects and between authors and readers. I wanted a more personal, collaborative, and interactive relationship, one that centered on the question of how human experience is endowed with meaning and on the moral and ethical choices we face as human beings who live in an uncertain and changing world. I also wanted to understand the conventions that constrain which stories we can tell and how we can tell them, and to show how people can and do resist the forms of social control that marginalize or silence counternarratives, stories that deviate from or transgress the canonical ones. The texts produced under the rubric of what I call **narrative inquiry** *would be stories that create the effect of reality, showing characters embedded in the complexities of lived moments of struggle, resisting the intrusions of chaos, disconnection, fragmentation, marginalization, and incoherence, trying to preserve or restore the continuity and coherence of life's unity in the face of unexpected blows of fate that call one's meanings and values into question.*

I refer to these personal stories as evocative narratives (Bochner, Ellis, & Tillmann-Healy, 1997, 1998). The word evocative contrasts the expressive and dialogic goals of this work with the more traditional orientations of mainstream, representational social science. Usually the author of an evocative narrative writes in the first person, making herself the object of research and thus breaching the conventional separation of researcher and subjects (Jackson, 1989); the story often focuses on a single case and thus breaches the traditional concerns of research from generalization across cases to generalization within a case (Geertz, 1973); the mode of storytelling is akin to the novel or biography and thus fractures the boundaries that normally separate social science from literature; the accessibility and readability of the text repositions the reader as a coparticipant in dialogue and thus rejects the orthodox view of the reader as a passive receiver of knowledge; the disclosure of hidden details of private life highlights emotional experience and thus challenges the rational actor model of social performance; the narrative text refuses the impulse to abstract and explain, stressing the journey over the destination, and thus eclipses the scientific illusion of control and mastery; and the episodic portrayal of the ebb and flow of relationship experience dramatizes the motion of connected lives across the curve of time, and thus resists the standard practice of portraying social life and relationships as a snapshot. Evocative stories activate

217

subjectivity and compel emotional response. They long to be used rather than analyzed; to be told and retold rather than theorized and settled; to offer lessons for further conversation rather than undebatable conclusions; and to substitute the companionship of intimate detail for the loneliness of abstracted facts.

Personal writing akin to evocative narrative has recently proliferated in the mainstream press, in new journalism, in creative nonfiction, and in the genres of literary memoir, autobiography, and autopathography (Buford, 1996; Harrington, 1997; Hawkins, 1993; Parini, 1998; "True Confessions," 1996). All of the life writing genres (Tierney, 1998; see also Chapter 9, Volume 2) seem to have turned toward more intimate, personal, and self-conscious writing. I think the move in the social sciences toward less anonymous, more personal writing parallels the same trend in literature and journalism (Denzin, 1997; Neumann, 1996). Whatever the reasons, I see ample evidence of a burgeoning interest among diverse fields of social science in the genres of personal narrative and autoethnography. The examples I have in mind include the recent special issues of such journals as Journal of Contemporary Ethnography (Ellis & Bochner, 1996b) and Qualitative Sociology (Glassner, 1997; Hertz, 1996); the book series Ethnographic Alternatives, published by AltaMira Press; the edited collections by anthropologists (Benson, 1993; Brady, 1991; Okely & Callaway, 1992), sociologists (Ellis & Flaherty, 1992; Hertz, 1997), and educators (Tierney & Lincoln, 1997); the many articles and monographs published in academic journals such as American Anthropologist, Anthropology and Humanism Quarterly, Feminist Studies, Journal of Personal and Interpersonal Loss, Qualitative Inquiry, Sociological Quarterly, Symbolic Interaction, Text and Performance Quarterly, Western Journal of Communication, and Women's Studies International Forum.

By way of example, let me briefly mention three published evocative narratives. Each highlights the communicative practices through which the author's identity evolves, is displayed, and put to use (Bruner, 1990). In particular, these writers illustrate how certain metaphors and meanings are narrativized into their lives. Mukaia (1989) shows the lived experience of "anorexia from within," expressing the ways in which food and starvation are emplotted into her identity; Ronai (1992) presents a layered story in which she performs her situated, multiple selves, expressing her tortured ambivalence in assuming the dual identities of social science researcher and erotic dancer; and Ellis (1993) navigates the emotional maze of shock and grief as she copes with conflicting academic and family personas in the aftermath of her brother's sudden death in an airplane crash. Each is a first-person account, written as a story, that expresses vivid details about the author's own experience. The "research text" is the story, complete (but open) in itself, largely free of academic jargon and abstracted theory. The authors privilege stories over analysis, allowing and encouraging alternative readings and multiple interpretations. They ask their readers to feel the truth of their stories and to become coparticipants, engaging the story line morally, emotionally, aesthetically, and intellectually (Richardson, 1994b).

The question that I'm usually asked is, "To what kind of truth do these stories aspire?" Often this question is asked in a tone that expresses skepticism, doubt, and even hostility. Some critics (e.g., Mink, 1969-1970; Shotter, 1987) argue that stories give life a structure it does not have and, thus, stories fictionalize life. Since the experiences on which narratives are based may be vague and uncertain, the stories they arouse can never be determinate or complete (e.g. Shotter, 1987). Given the distortions of memory and the mediation of language, narrative is always a story about the past and not the past itself.

A second criticism is that personal narrative reflects or advances a "romantic construction of the self" (Atkinson, 1997) unworthy of being classified as part of social science. If you are "a storyteller rather than a story analyst," argues Atkinson (1997, p. 335), then your goal becomes therapeutic rather than analytic. Atkinson believes that a text that acts as an agent of self-discovery or self-creation—precisely the narrative challenge one faces when an expected life story is interrupted by illness, violence, or accident—cannot be an academic text. Presumably, if you don't subject narrative to sociological, cultural, or some other form of analysis, treating stories as "social facts," then you are not doing social science. While passionately protesting the ways in which some writers want "to privilege certain kinds and occasions of narrative performance," Atkinson (1997) aims to redeem (and privilege) the standard version of representational social science by trivializing or dismissing any work that does not, in his words, "use narrative to achieve serious social analysis" (pp. 338-339).

Let me briefly address the reservations expressed by these critics. First, there is the question of narrative truth. What is the point of a storied life? Narrative truth seeks to keep the past alive in the present. Stories show us that the meanings and significance of the past are incomplete, tentative, and revisable according to contingencies of our present life circumstances, the present from which we narrate. Doesn't this mean that the stories we tell always run the risk of distorting the past? Of course, it does. After all, stories rearrange, redescribe, invent, omit, and revise. They can be wrong in numerous ways—tone, detail, substance, etc. Does this attribute of story-telling threaten the project of personal narrative? Not at all, because a story is not a neutral attempt to mirror the facts of one's life; it does not seek to recover already constituted meanings. Only within the memoro-politics surrounding the accuracy of recovered memories, which emerged within the context of positivist psychology, would such a criticism be threatening (Hacking, 1995).

The truth of narrative is not akin to correspondence with prior meanings assumed to be located in some sort of prenarrative experience. One narra-tive interpretation of events can be judged against another, but there is no standard by which to measure any narrative against the meaning of events themselves, because the meaning of prenarrative experience is constituted in its narrative expression. Life and narrative are inextricably connected. Life both anticipates telling and draws meaning from it. Narrative is both about living and part of it.

I titled this little talk "Why Personal Narrative Matters" to emphasize that we live within the tensions constituted by our memories of the past and anticipations of the future. Personal narrative, the project of telling a life, is a response to the human problem of authorship, the desire to make sense and preserve coherence over the course of our lives. Our personal identities seem largely contingent on how well we bridge the remembered past with the anticipated future to provide what Stephen Crites (1971) calls "a conti-nuity of experience over time." The narrative challenge that we face as nar-rators is the desire for continuity, to make sense of our lives as a whole. "The present of things past and the present of things future," says Crites (1971), "are the tension of every moment of experience, both united in that present and qualitatively differentiated by it" (p. 302). The work of self-narration is to produce this sense of continuity: to make a life that sometimes seems to be falling apart come together again, by retelling and restorying the events of one's life. Thus, narrative matters to us because, as David Carr (1986) observes, "coherence seems to be a need imposed upon us whether we seek it or not" (p. 97). At stake in our narrative attempts to achieve a coherent sense of ourselves are the very integrity and intelligibility of our selfhood, which rest so tenderly and fallibly on the story we use to link birth to life to death (MacIntyre, 1981). In the final analysis, the self is indistin-guishable from the life story it constructs for itself out of what is inherited, what is experienced, and what is desired (Freeman, 1993, 1998; Kerby, 1991).

So the question is not, "Does my story reflect my past accurately?" as if I were holding a mirror to my past. Rather I must ask, "What are the consequences my story produces? What kind of a person does it shape me into? What new possibilities does it introduce for living my life?" The crucial issues are what narratives do, what consequences they have, to what uses they can be put. These consequences often precede rather than follow the story because they are enmeshed in the act of telling. "The story of our lives becomes our lives," writes Adrienne Rich (1978, p. 34). Thus personal narrative is part of the human, existential struggle to move life forward. Through the narrative activity of self-creation we seek to become identical to the story we tell. Anaïs Nin underscores this desire for self-created, narrative meaning when she announces, "I could not live in any of the worlds offered to me. . . . I believe one writes because one has to create a world in which to live" (quoted in Oakley, 1984).

I get impatient with writers who belittle or diminish the therapeutic consequences of stories. They tend to draw a hard-and-fast distinction between therapy and social research, implying that narratives are useful only insofar as they advance sociological, anthropological, or psychological theory. For these critics, narrative threatens the whole project of science. They reply angrily, shouting the canonically given, professional response: "If you can't pitch a theory, then you can't play in the big leagues." The most important thing is to be smart, clever, analytical; that's what it means to be academic. What they oppose is what they equate with the therapeutic: the sentimental, the mushy, the popular. Thus they engage surreptitiously in what feminist critic Jane Tompkins (1989) calls "the trashing of emotion," a war waged ceaselessly by academic intellectuals "against feeling, against women, against what is personal" (p. 138).

A text that functions as an agent of self-discovery or self-creation, for the author as well as for those who read and engage the text, is only threatening under a narrow definition of social inquiry, one that eschews a social science with a moral center and a heart. Why should caring and empathy be secondary to controlling and knowing? Why must academics be conditioned to believe that a text is important only to the extent it moves beyond the merely personal? We need to question our assumptions, the metarules that govern the institutional workings of social science—arguments over feelings, theories over stories, abstractions over concrete events, sophisticated jargon over accessible prose. Why should we be ashamed if our work has therapeutic or personal value? Besides, haven't our personal stories always been embedded in our research monographs? The question is whether we should express our vulnerability and subjectivity openly in the text or hide them behind "social analysis."

Sometimes I think: Art, if only you could do a better job communicating the important differences between a representational and an evocative social science. Why is it so hard to grasp that personal narrative is moral work and ethical practice? When the narrator is the investigator, to a certain extent she is always asking what it is right to do and good to be. At its most extreme, those who want "to put narrative in its place" (Atkinson, 1997, p. 343) seem to think there is only one right place to put it. They seek to preserve what already has been lost (Gergen, 1994; Schwandt, 1996). They think that if these personal voices can be silenced, then perhaps they can return to business as usual in the social sciences, protected against the contingencies of human experience, restored in their traditional belief in a transcendent position from which to speak (and interpret) with authority, freed of moral choices and emotional dilemmas, and inspired to champion control over fate, facts over meanings, and rigor over peace of mind.

"Well, I guess this is a good place to stop and throw this session open for comments or questions," Art invites. People in the audience shuffle in their seats anxiously, then several hands go up. "Yes, Billy," Art says, pointing toward a philosophy professor I recognize.

"Art, you mentioned that your turn toward narrative was provoked by postmodernism. Could you elaborate on that?"

"I had read Thomas Kuhn's *The Structure of Scientific Revolutions* and was impressed by his argument that there was no way to distinguish unequivocally what's in our minds from what's out there in the world. About the same time, I was introduced to the writings of Wittgenstein (1953), Heidegger (1971), Gadamer (1989), and Derrida (1978), and to speech act theory. In quite diverse ways, all of this work stood in opposition to the view—that now seems incredibly naïve—that language could be a neutral or transparent medium of communication. Whether we apply language to ourselves or to the world there always is slippage, inexactness, indeterminacy. Then along came Richard Rorty's *Philosophy and the Mirror of Nature* (1979), which provided a powerful synthesis of the challenges to our most venerable notions about truth and knowledge. It was hard to read Rorty without feeling totally shaken. I came away convinced that the foundations of traditional epistemology were fallible. No strong case could be made that human knowledge was independent of the human mind. All truths were contingent on the describing activities of human beings. No sharp distinctions could be made between facts and values. If you couldn't eliminate the influence of the observer on the observed, then no theories or findings could ever be completely free of human values. The investigator would always be implicated in the product. So why not observe the observer, focus on turning our observations back on ourselves? And why not write more directly, from the source of your own experience? Narratively. Poetically. Evocatively. No longer was there any deep reason to believe that social science is closer to physics than to literature or poetry. Besides, I became a social scientist because I thought it was a way to address deep and troubling questions about how to live a meaningful, useful, and ethical life. Somewhere along the way these questions took a backseat to methodological rigor. Now I felt liberated to grapple with these questions again, more dialogically, through personal narrative."

A woman I don't recognize stands and shouts from the back of the room, "I've always found the postmodernists depressing and cynical. They seem to be saying you can't know anything. It all seems so destructive." Laughter circulates through the audience and I notice a number of people nodding in agreement.

Art responds, "Well there's an affirming strain of postmodernism too. At least I read it that way. In the writings of certain postmodernists and particularly within feminist and queer theory you see a renewed appreciation for emotion, intuition, personal experience, embodiment, and spirituality. They've helped us cross some of the boundaries separating the arts and the sciences and to focus attention on diversity and difference instead of unity and similarity. I don't regard these moves as negative or depressing. Perhaps, like you, I find them unsettling, even painful at times. But that's where the learning is. We lose our innocence and our lost innocence validates some good values. We gain tolerance and humility. Sometimes we're ashamed of how much we've excluded from our experience, tried not to see, hidden from. And we should be. We don't need to run from the fear or anxiety we feel. We need to learn from it. Racism, sexism, poverty, homophobia, disability—these issues touch all of us. We can't hide from them. We're all complicit in some way. No one's immune, invulnerable. So it's important to get exposed to local stories that bring us into worlds of experience that are unknown to us, show us the concrete daily details of people whose lives have been underrepresented or not represented at all, help us reduce their marginalization, show us how partial and situated our understanding of the world is. Maybe that's depressing to some of you, but I think it's enlightening and possibly transforming."

"I think you misunderstood her," a man in the front row interjects. I recognize the voice of a colleague wedded to mainstream social science methods. "The resistance and political dimensions are clear enough, but some of us still want to know how we can tell when we're right, when our representations are accurate and we can generalize."

Art sighs in frustration and continues, "We may have to agree to disagree. I take the crisis of representation more seriously than you do. For me, it necessitates a radical transformation in the goals of our work—from description to communication. That's the inspiration for the narrative turn. As I see it, the practices of human communication—the negotiation and performance of acts of meaning—should become our model for how we tell about the empirical world (Bochner & Waugh, 1995). Then, we would feel compelled to produce narrative, evocative, dialogic texts that show human beings, including ourselves, in the process of creating, negotiating, and performing meaning in a world of others, making our way through a world that poses obstacles, interruptions, contingencies, turning points, epiphanies, and moral choices."

"So what are the goals? I don't quite follow," the same man continues. "Could you be more precise?"

"The goal is to encourage compassion and promote dialogue. Actually, I would be pleased if we understood our whole endeavor as a search for better conversation in the face of all the barriers and boundaries that make conversation difficult. The stories we write put us into conversation with ourselves as well as with our readers. In conversation with ourselves, we expose our vulnerabilities, conflicts, choices, and values. We take measure of our uncertainties, our mixed emotions, and the multiple layers of our experience. Our accounts seek to express the complexities and difficulties of coping and feeling resolved, showing how we changed over time as we struggled to make sense of our experience. Often our accounts of ourselves are unflattering and imperfect, but human and believable. The text is used, then, as an agent of self-understanding and ethical discussion.

"In conversation with our readers, we use storytelling as a method for inviting them to put themselves in our place. Our dialogue centers on moral choices, questions having more to do, as Michael Jackson (1995) observes, with how to live than with how to know. The usefulness of these stories is their capacity to inspire conversation from the point of view of the readers, who enter from the perspective of their own lives. The narrative rises or falls on its capacity to provoke readers to broaden their horizons, reflect critically on their own experience, enter empathically into worlds of experience different from their own, and actively engage in dialogue regarding the social and moral implications of the different perspectives and standpoints encountered. Invited to take the story in and use it for themselves, readers become coperformers, examining themselves through the evocative power of the narrative text."

Art pauses to take a sip of water. Jim, the colloquium organizer, turns toward him and says, "I liked your attempt to enter into dialogue with the critics of narrative inquiry, but you left out one of my main reservations. How do you react to critics who say that personal narratives simulate reality TV? Aren't these narratives reflective of the culture of confession and victimization and don't they end up as spectacles that sentimentalize, humiliate, and take pleasure in revealing anguish and pain? Personal narratives remind me of victim art. They play on your sympathies and manipulate your emotions."

"I've heard that one before, Jim. My first response is to consider the source. That's a particular reading, by a particular person. So it's always the case, in my view, that the criticism speaks the critic's life too. The text's meanings are never transparent. There is always a connection being made between the reader's consciousness and what is being read. So I want to know something about the reader—her interests, desires, values, premises, and what she resists and why.

"So, Jim, where are you in this picture?" Art teases. He pauses and smiles gently as the audience chuckles and Jim looks around quizzically, shrugging his shoulders.

"Seriously, Jim," Art continues. "I didn't mean to put you on the spot. Well, maybe I did. But, as a critic, I don't think it's your job to condemn something categorically. I think you have to look at the merits of each case. It's hard for me to respond in terms of some general principle. If you take a genre of stories that might be called 'illness narratives,' for example, the sorts of stories that Arthur Frank (1995) has analyzed, well, I think the goal is to reduce the stigma and marginalization of illness and disability. Most of these stories are written by people who don't want to surrender to the victimization and marginal identities promoted by the canonical narrative of medicine. Many of them try to write themselves as survivors, displaying their embodiment as a source of knowledge. It's hard to understand how anyone could read Anatole Broyard (1992) or Nancy Mairs (1986, 1990, 1998) or Audre Lorde (1980)—and I could name dozens more—as victim confessionals. They aren't seeking pity and they don't portray themselves as pathetic, helpless, downtrodden characters. If anything, they use narrative as a source of empowerment and a form of resistance to counter the domination and authority of canonical discourses. I think that Couser (1997) thoroughly discredits the 'victim art' argument by showing that the vast majority of narratives focused on the 'recovering body' 'are much more likely to *de*victimize their subjects and others like them' (p. 291). Their main function is to confirm and humanize the experience of illness by bearing witness to what it means to live with bodily dysfunction and to gain agency through testimony. So, what are the choices, Jim? Erasure? Silence? Surrender? I think you have to understand some of the identity politics that are involved here too. Whose stories get told? By whom? And for what purpose? I know you're interested in cultural and political implications of narrative. Don't you think these stories help us understand how culture and politics are written on the body?"

"I see your point," Jim says, "but I still worry about voyeurism and the way these personal stories indulge our culture's perverse curiosity about the private, peeking in on damaged selves. How do we judge the merits of these stories? When do we know they're reliable and telling?"

"I think it's the same judgment we make about any author or any character. Is the work honest or dishonest? Does the author take the measure of herself, her limitations, her confusion, ambivalence, mixed feelings? Do you gain a sense of emotional reliability? Do you sense a passage through emotional epiphany to some communicated truth, not resolution per se, but some transformation from an old self to a new one (Rhett, 1997)? Does the story enable you to understand and feel the experience it seeks to convey? There is complexity, multiplicity, uncertainty, desire. Phillip Lopate (1994) refers to the personal essay as something akin to basic research on the self that ends up as 'a mode of being' (p. xliv). It's not science; it's not philosophy. The same can be said for the evocative, personal story. It's an existential struggle for honesty and expansion in an uncertain world."

I tap Sylvia's shoulder and whisper, "Notice how Art dodges questions that try to get him to stipulate categorical criteria. He always wants to balance rigor and imagination. He thinks if you're too bound up with rules, you probably won't do anything interesting. Anyway, I've got to meet another student in my office for a makeup exam. I'll meet you back here after the talk."

When I return, Sylvia is standing alone watching the students gathered around Art talking passionately about their writing projects. "The woman facing us is Lisa Tillmann-Healy," I tell Sylvia. "She's published a story about her own eating disorder, and she's recently finished her dissertation on straight couples' relationships with gay men, telling the story of her own friendships. The woman to her left is Deborah Austin, who writes lyrical poems and did her dissertation on African American marriages in the aftermath of the Million Man March. For her dissertation defense, she performed a script she wrote based on focus groups she studied. Christine Kiesinger, the woman talking to Art, has published several stories from her dissertation on women with eating disorders. You might be interested in looking at her dissertation to see how she weaves her story with the story of one of her participants. Over there, that's Laura Ellingson," I say, nodding just to the left of the group. "She published an article recently in *Qualitative Inquiry* on how her own illness affected her understanding of other cancer patients and the organizational environment at the cancer hospital she is studying, and how, in turn, this experience helped her reinterpret her own illness. I'll give you a reprint. Laura is talking with Leigh Berger, who published a story about her relationship with her hearing-impaired sister and another about her father who was institutionalized for mental illness. She's studying Messianic Judaism now, observing her own transformation as she participates in a religious group. Come, I'll introduce you to them."

"I read the articles by Lisa and Christine," Sylvia reminds me. "Interesting that they are all women," she says thoughtfully, and then exclaims, "Wow! This is exciting!" I smile, but before I can say anything, Sylvia blurts out, "I want to write my story. But I haven't been keeping notes or anything. How would I do it? Where would I start?"

◆ Doing Autoethnography: Considerations

"Answering your questions will take a while. Let's go get a cup of coffee. You can meet the other students later," I decide, waving to them over my shoulder. "There are a number of ways to go about writing autoethnography," I say as we walk. "It really depends on where along the continuum of art and science you want to locate yourself. What claims do you want to make? If you want to claim you're following traditional rules of ethnographic method, then it would be best if you had kept notes on the experience as it happened. The notes would serve as field notes and you'd write from those."

"If you didn't have notes, how would you remember what actually happened?" Sylvia asks.

"Do you think the notes would tell you what actually happened? Aren't they partial interpretations as well?"

"Well, yes, but then how would I make sure that what I said was truthful?"

"The truth is that we can never capture experience. As Art said, 'Narrative is always a story about the past,' and that's really all field notes are— one selective story about what happened written from a particular point of view for a particular purpose. But if representation is your goal, it's best to have as many sources and levels of story recorded at different times as possible. Even so, realize that every story is partial and situated."

I take four quarters from my pocket and insert them into the coffee machine. "I'm buying," I say. "Cream and sugar?"

"Oh, no. Let me pay," she insists, opening her purse.

"Next time. Okay?"

"Okay. Just black for me." We take our coffees outside and sit under a tree to enjoy the perfect Florida spring day. "Is there a way other than representation to think about personal narrative?" Sylvia asks.

"Well, yes, if you viewed your project as closer to art than science, then your goal would not be so much to portray the *facts* of what happened to you accurately, but instead to convey the *meanings* you attached to the experience. You'd want to tell a story that readers could enter and feel a part of. You'd write in a way to evoke readers to feel and think about your life, and their lives in relation to yours. You'd want them to experience the experience you're writing about—in your case, breast cancer."

"If these were your goals," I continue, "writing notes at the time the experience occurred would have been helpful, but not absolutely necessary. If you're writing about an epiphany, which you usually are in this kind of research, you may be too caught up in living it to write about it."

"But then how do you remember all the dialogue and details later?"

"When I wrote *Final Negotiations,* about the chronic illness and death of my first husband, I didn't actually remember everything I wrote about, certainly not the exact words we spoke, anyway. I had notes for much of what I described, but I still had to construct scenes and dialogue from the partial descriptions in my notes. And I hadn't kept immediate notes for everything I wrote about, though I constructed them later. But it's amazing what you can recall, and for how long, if the event was emotionally evocative. Another story I wrote, about race relations in a small town, was constructed without notes more than 25 years after the event occurred."

"But how can that be valid?"

"It depends on your definition of validity. I start from the position that language is not transparent and there's no single standard of truth. To me validity means that our work seeks verisimilitude; it evokes in readers a feeling that the experience described is lifelike, believable, and possible. You might also judge validity by whether it helps readers communicate with others different from themselves, or offers a way to improve the lives of participants and readers or even your own. Take a look at Lather's discussion of validity and counterpractices of authority in the *Sociological Quarterly*, 1993, I believe it is."

Sylvia looks up from her note taking and grimaces, "What about reliability?"

"Since we always create our personal narrative from a situated location, trying to make our present, imagined future, and remembered past cohere, there's no such thing as orthodox reliability in autoethnographic research. However, we can do reliability checks. When other people are involved, you might take your work back to them and give them a chance to comment, add materials, change their minds, and offer their interpretations."

"Generalizability? Is that a concern?"

"Of course, though again not in the usual sense. Our lives are particular, but they also are typical and generalizable, since we all participate in a limited number of cultures and institutions. We want to convey both in our stories. A story's generalizability is constantly being tested by readers as they determine if it speaks to them about their experience or about the lives of others they know. Likewise, does it tell them about unfamiliar people or lives? Does a work have what Stake calls 'naturalistic generalization,' meaning that it brings 'felt' news from one world to another and provides opportunities for the reader to have vicarious experience of the things told?"

"That's sure different from what I've learned, but I think I understand. Still I don't know where to start my own project."

"Why don't you start by writing a draft of your story. Think of it as making retrospective field notes on your life. Include all the details you can recall. I find it helpful to organize my writing chronologically first, using the main events to structure the tale. I try to write daily, rereading what I wrote the day before, then filling in new memories. Remember, you are creating this story; it is not there waiting to be found. Your final story will be crafted from these notes."

"But how will I know when I'm writing from my perspective then and when my current perspective is clouding my memory of what happened?"

"Well, you won't really. Memory doesn't work in a linear way, nor does life, for that matter. As Denzin and also Ronai say in *Investigating Subjectivity*, the book I edited with Michael Flaherty, thoughts and feelings circle around us, flash back, then forward, the topical is interwoven with the chronological, thoughts and feelings merge, drop from our grasp, then reappear in another context. In real life, we don't always know when we know something. Remember Art's talk—events in the past are always interpreted from our current position. Yet that doesn't mean there's no value in trying to disentangle now from then, as long as you realize it's not a project you'll ever complete or get completely right; instead, you strive to get it 'differently contoured and nuanced' in a meaningful way, as Richardson says in her *Handbook* chapter."

"What do you mean? How do you do that?"

"I use a process of emotional recall in which I imagine being back in the scene emotionally and physically. If you can revisit the scene emotionally, then you remember other details. The advantage of writing close to the time of the event is that it doesn't take much effort to access lived emotions—they're often there whether you want them to be or not. The disadvantage is that being so involved in the scene emotionally means that it's difficult to get outside of it to analyze from a cultural perspective. Yet both of these processes, moving in and moving out, are necessary to produce an effective autoethnography. That's why it's good to write about an event while your feelings are still intense, and then to go back to it when you're emotionally distant. I've had students who were great at getting *inside* emotional experience, but they had tunnel vision. They couldn't move around in the experience. They were unable to see it as it might appear to others. They had trouble analyzing their thoughts and feelings as socially constructed processes. I'll give you my article on systematic sociological introspection, which talks more about introspection as a social process."

"I'd like that. But I'm not sure I'd want to feel all those emotions again. And some of the feelings I've had and still have about my cancer I wouldn't want to share. I'd feel so vulnerable."

"Well, that's your call. But if you're not willing to become a vulnerable observer, then maybe you ought to reconsider doing autoethnography. If

230

you let yourself be vulnerable, then your readers are more likely to respond vulnerably, and that's what you want, vulnerable readers. I agree with Ruth Behar, who wrote in *The Vulnerable Observer* that social science 'that doesn't break your heart just isn't worth doing.' My goal is the same as Dorothy Allison's—'to take the reader by the throat, break her heart, and heal it again.' Vulnerability can be scary, but it also can be the source of growth and understanding."

"I've always assumed my task as a social scientist was to deliver knowledge and stay invulnerable," Sylvia responds. "I didn't know I had a choice.

"So, suppose I am willing to be vulnerable," she continues slowly. "How do I get from field notes to writing in a way that opens up myself and readers to being vulnerable?"

"Do you ever read fiction?" When she nods, I continue, "Well, think about how a good novel makes you feel. It does make you feel, right?" She nods again, waiting for what I will say next. "What provokes these feelings?"

"Sometimes I identify with the characters. I feel for them. Or I think about being in the situations they're in, doing what they're doing, or imagine what I'd do in the same situation. And sometimes I stop reading to think about how my life is different or similar."

"Exactly. Good fiction writers make you feel the feelings of the characters, smell the smells, see the sights, hear the sounds, as though you were there. They do this with devices of fictional writing such as internal monologue, dialogue among the characters, dramatic recall, strong imagery, things like scene setting, character development, flashbacks, suspense, and action. You enter the reality of the novel through a dramatic plotline, which is developed through the specific actions of specific characters with specific bodies doing specific things."

"Then how is what you do different from fiction writing?"

"A number of social scientists have addressed your question. Take a look at Denzin's discussion of the relationship of social science writers to the new journalists in *Interpretive Ethnography*. Susan Krieger's early piece on fiction and social science and Richardson and Lockridge's new work on fiction and ethnography also might be helpful."

"The two genres are more similar than different," I continue. "As Walt Harrington says about intimate journalism, in autoethnography you try to write from inside the heads of participants and evoke the tone of their felt lives."

"Of course, writing and publishing conventions are different," I add, now switching gears. "You're a social scientist, so that probably will affect what you look at and how you see. And, among social scientists, auto-ethnography often has more of an overt analytic purpose and an analytic frame. Remember how Carol Ronai in the piece I gave you layers analysis through her personal narrative? But in *Final Negotiations,* I emphasized that analysis can come through story and dialogue too. Arthur Frank says in *The Wounded Storyteller* that it is important to think *with* a story, not just about a story. Thinking with a story means allowing yourself to reso-nate with the story, reflect on it, become a part of it.

"I'd suggest you read some exemplars of this work and note the differ-ent ways authors intersect story and analytic frame. Look at some of the books in the AltaMira Ethnographic Alternatives series edited by Art and me. For example, Jones's *Kaleidoscope Notes* uses conversation, songs, poetry, stories, performance, and autoethnography to examine women's music, a folk music club, and ethnography; Angrosino's *Opportunity House* is made up of fictional stories of adults with mental illness that are based on his decade of participant observation work; and Markham's *Life Online* uses her own experiences to study life on the Internet. Our *Com-posing Ethnography* and *Fiction and Social Research* by Banks and Banks both showcase a multitude of creative forms of narrative writing."

"Aren't decisions social scientists make different from fiction writers?"

"Well, generally, autoethnographers limit themselves, unlike fiction writers, to what they remember actually happened. Or at least they don't tell something they know to be false. Well, even that's not so clear-cut. It depends . . ."

"On what?"

"Well, say you want to protect the privacy of a character in your story. Then you might use composites or change some identifying information. Or you might collapse events to write a more engaging story, which might be more truthful in a narrative sense though not in a historical one."

When Sylvia looks at me questioningly, I say, "You know—the story evokes in readers the feeling that the tale is true. The story is coherent. It connects readers to writers and provides continuity in their lives." When I see a look of recognition on Sylvia's face, I continue, "Even realist ethnographers, who claim to follow the rules for doing science, use de-vices such as composites or collapsing events to tell better stories and pro-tect their participants. Yet they worship 'accuracy' in description. A friend of mine, Sherryl Kleinman, says, If it didn't happen, don't tell it. That's another version of 'Don't put words in participants' mouths if they didn't say them.' But, of course, ethnographers do put words in participants' mouths all the time."

"Really? How can they get away with that?"

"By relying on memory, editing, and selecting verbatim prose out of context and then surrounding it with their own constructed analytic contexts. When it comes to analysis, most traditional ethnographers have no problems reaching beyond description for all kinds of interpretation."

"Give me an example."

"Oh, from limited time and access in the field, they create the 'typical' person or day, the 'common' event. They use ambiguous and qualifying descriptors like *most, some, frequent,* and *few.* And, of course, they reify concepts such as social structure and organizational climate. I did this too in my first study of two fishing villages. Let me tell you, when community members read what I wrote—well, what I saw as typical was certainly not what they saw as typical. What I wrote told you more about how I organize my world than how they organized theirs."

"Don't believe the propaganda," Art says, suddenly walking toward us with a stack of books piled in his arms.

I laugh and ask, "Hi, where have you been?"

"In the library, retrieving some sources for our *Handbook* paper."

"They look pretty heavy to me," I say, smiling as I eye the titles on the spines of the books. "Art, this is my student Sylvia, the one who is studying breast cancer."

"Oh, yes, hi. I noticed you sitting next to Carolyn at my talk today."

"Yes, I found it very interesting," Sylvia replies.

"We were just talking about how autoethnography differs from fiction," I explain.

"Oh, was Carolyn giving you her rap on how you have to be systematic and stick to the facts?" Art asks, turning to Sylvia. "Just the facts, ma'am," he mimics.

"Ah . . . ," Sylvia stalls.

"Art, stop it," I say playfully. Then turning to Sylvia, I explain, "Art and I have this running commentary on writing autoethnography. I argue that you try to construct the story as close to the experience as you can remember it, especially in the initial version. That doing so helps you work through the meaning and purpose of the story. He likes to argue that what's important is the usefulness of the story. Of course, I agree that our stories should have therapeutic value . . ."

"Therapeutic value?" Sylvia stammers.

"Yes, I think of it as action research for the individual. Though therapy might not be the major objective in our research, it often is a useful result of good writing," I respond.

"That reminds me, Art . . . uh, may I call you Art?" Sylvia inquires. When Art nods, she continues, "What you said in your talk about the focus of stories, well, I thought therapy and research were separate entities. I mean, I'm a therapist, but I assumed I had to keep that role separate from my interviewer identity, because if I acted as a therapist it might bias the data. And wouldn't it be unethical?"

Art and I look at each other and try not to smile. Her questions and concerns help us realize how close together our positions are. I quickly interject, "But you told me you hoped your research would provide understanding of what happened to you and help others who face similar circumstances cope. So what will you do if an interviewee breaks down or if you see a place where you could be of help?"

She looks at me, waiting for the answer, then murmurs, "I'm not sure."

"What would you want someone in a similar situation to do for you if you were a research participant?"

"Well, I'd want them to care about me and try to understand where I was coming from, " she responds softly. "Otherwise I wouldn't want to share my life stories with them."

"And wouldn't it be unethical for a researcher not to help or empathize with you if you were in need?"

"I've never thought of it that way before, but I would want my subjects to feel that I care about them. What good would my research be if it doesn't help others who are going through this experience, especially my subjects?"

"Participants," I say quietly.

"Participants," she repeats, her face turning red. "But isn't it true that not everybody can do good therapy? I mean most academics aren't trained therapists."

"Being able to do therapy and being a trained therapist are not synonymous," I respond, and Sylvia nods in agreement. "In fact, ethnographic training might be just as important for a therapist as therapeutic training."

"And therapeutic training probably should be a prerequisite to being an ethnographer," Art adds, laughing.

I smile and continue, "But you're right, not everybody is comfortable or capable of dealing with emotionality. Those who aren't probably shouldn't be doing this kind of research in the first place, or directing students who are."

"Perhaps you should give her citations to articles on some of these issues, like the ethic of caring and personal accountability, maybe Collins," Art suggests, as several of his books fall to the ground.

"I will," I say, helping to retrieve the books. "Other feminist writers would be helpful too. Let's see, Lieblich, Miller, Cook and Fonow, and Oakley. They'd be a good start," I say, marking them off as I return each book to Art's stack.

"And there are good summaries in Reinharz and also in Denzin's *Interpretive Ethnography*," Art adds. He then turns to Sylvia, "But enough literature, I want to know more about how you'd respond if you were an interviewee. What would make you comfortable enough to tell your story?"

"To know the other person was listening, really listening. I'd want someone I could cry in front of, actually who might cry with me. A person who might tell me some of her story if she had been through a similar experience."

"So are you going to share your story with your participants?" I ask.

"Ah . . . I think . . ."

"Go on."

"Well, I was going to say that my story would contaminate theirs, but I'm not so sure anymore."

Art and I smile. "This is probably enough for now," I say. "We've come a long way. Why don't you think about how this conversation provides clues for how you might want to do your own interviews and let's pick up this topic next time we meet."

We say our good-byes, and Art and I make our way to our car. "Are you sure this is the right move?" Art asks. "Is she ready to write her story?"

"Oh, I think she's ready. I sense she wants to tell her story."

"What if it opens up things for her that are just too painful?"

"I'll keep in close contact with her, just in case. But in my experience with personal narrative, people pretty quickly find their own comfort zone. They know when the time's right. But I'll make sure to provide opportunities for her to pull back or change gears in the project, if she needs to. She can always do that survey," I add, playfully tugging at his arm and then skipping ahead.

"I admire how much you're willing to risk with your students," Art says lovingly when I return to help him pick up the books that once again have toppled to the ground. "And how much you care about them."

"Same with you," I say.

"It's not easy being vulnerable, especially in the academy, where you're expected to be in control and keep your private life removed from your professional life. That's what I tried to say in 'It's About Time.' "

"It's scary, when you think about the professor at Colby who asked students to write personal narratives and ended up being charged with sexual harassment. Of course, we don't know what really happened there; we have only Ruth Shalit's report," I add. "Maybe his private and professional lives did become too entwined."

"That's certainly a possibility. But what about the article in the *Chronicle of Higher Education* that described how some of Jane Tompkins's colleagues attacked her for suggesting that the emotional and spiritual lives of university students are just as important as their intellects?"

"Maybe we should just write fiction," I offer.

"Now wait a minute," Art reprimands. "You know everything we write is fiction . . ."

◆ Doing Autoethnography: Method and Form

Two weeks later, Sylvia appears in my office. "Hi, I've written most of my story about my past now, and I waited until I was almost finished before I began reading other personal narratives of breast cancer. It's been very therapeutic," she says, "to write and to read. But I'm not sure I'm getting anywhere on my dissertation. I have so many questions."

"Like what?" I ask.

"Why would anybody want to read my story? How does my story differ from what's already published? And how will my story fit with the interviews I want to do of other women?"

"Slow down. Are you learning anything?"

"Oh, yes, at every turn."

"Tell me what you're learning."

"Well, that I have a lot in common with other women's breast cancer stories. For example, most women tell of their discovery of the lump— that's always a traumatic event—then the diagnosis and assessment of treatment options, then they describe waking up from the surgery, going through the follow-up treatment, and finally there's recovery and some kind of resolution at the end."

"Interesting, that's almost exactly how Couser summarized breast cancer narratives in his book on illness narratives," I respond, pleased with how much reading Sylvia has done.

"Most survivors describe making decisions about reconstructive surgery, shopping for a prosthesis—if they decide to wear one—their hair falling out, and seeking alternative treatment," she continues without skipping a beat. "I wrote about these things as well, and . . ."

"And have you learned anything new from writing *your* story? Sorry, I didn't mean to cut you off, but I'm curious."

"Yes, that cancer is more than a medical story, it's a feeling story. I learned how scared I am even though I've been a survivor now for 7 years. And that's the interesting thing—there's little about long-term survivors in stories or in social science research. Most survivors tell their stories soon after recovery from treatment and they're usually pretty optimistic about recovery and often claim to be better off at the end than the beginning.

"I felt that too, the optimism I mean, immediately after my treatment was over, that is," Sylvia continues passionately. "But I don't feel that way now. I try so hard to pretend that I'm an upbeat, optimistic person with no worries, a warrior who has learned from her experiences. But what I had to face as I wrote my story is that I'm scared all the time that the cancer will come back. I've had carpal tunnel syndrome and it's probably from the chemo. And now I have sweats at night, and I don't know if it's early menopause—another gift of chemo—or signs of the cancer returning. I'm sorry, but cancer has not improved my life and I can't make it into a gift. Holding in these feelings, all these years, has been difficult and I think it's had negative effects on my psychological and physical well-being and on my family."

Sylvia begins to cry. I touch her shoulder and hand her a Kleenex. We sit silently for a while, sadness connecting us. Needing to stay in the role of adviser, I hold back my tears. "Do you still want to continue this project?" I ask gently. "Or is it too painful?"

"Oh, no, I *have* to continue it," she responds forcefully, although her voice shakes. "What I'm experiencing is important to me. It was hard pretending; sometimes I thought I was going crazy. Now I realize I don't have to pretend. There are other stories to live and write. Maybe through writing and talking with other women about their experiences, I can figure out another story to live, one that might help me cope better and not take so much out of me. Maybe I can write myself as a survivor in a deeper, more meaningful way, like Art was talking about. You know, I can't help wondering how other women feel years after their treatment. That's what I want to know—how it feels to them, how they cope . . . or don't," she adds, the tears starting up again. "Does the experience continue to be as fresh and scary to them as it still is to me? Maybe I can both contribute to knowledge and help others—and myself—write a story we can live with. How I'm living now, denying my feelings—well, this is no way to live."

"Okay, we're getting somewhere now," I say softly. "I think you have your topic. I imagine that other women share your sense of vulnerability and loss of control over their lives. I think I would," I add, involuntarily shivering as I imagine how difficult it would be to have cancer hanging over me in such an intrusive way. "Now how do we find out how other long-term survivors experience cancer?"

"I'd like to do intensive interviews with survivors of more than 5 years," Sylvia responds energetically, "and include an African American woman—there's so little on their experience of breast cancer—and maybe even a lesbian woman, because I think their experiences might be different. How many participants would I need? Twenty-five?"

"Oh no," I laugh. "If you're going to do intensive interviews, you'd need only a few, maybe five or six including yourself. You'll want to interview each woman a number of times to build trust in the relationship, and also so they can read and respond to each transcript before you follow up with the next interview."

"How much will I participate?"

"Given that you share aspects of their experience, the interviews should be an interactive conversation, I would think. But you have to play that by ear. Rather than overlay method onto experience, you want to relate your approach to each woman's life and think about what would help her to tell her story. In some cases, participants will feel comfortable having a conversation, if you set it up that way. But as a society, we're so accustomed to the authoritative interview situation that some women still will expect you to be the authority and ask all the questions. Some might inquire about your story; others will be too glad for an opportunity to tell their own to pay attention to yours. They'll want you to be the researcher and therapist. Perhaps a few of the women will want to write their stories. Remind me next time to give you an article on interactive interviewing that I wrote with Christine Kiesinger and Lisa Tillmann-Healy, where we had conversations over dinner about eating disorders. It'll get you thinking about form and the problems of doing interactive interviews—the time involved and the emotional commitment and ethical issues of dealing in such a personal realm. I'll also give you a piece I wrote with Art on co-constructed narrative, which describes a two-part process of individually writing stories that are then shared and co-constructed by several participants."

"I guess there's no interview schedule then?" Sylvia asks, but since she's smiling, I don't respond. "How will the chapters look and where will my story be?" she asks, this time seriously.

"The form will evolve during the research process. You might start the dissertation with a short personal story, to position yourself for the reader, or tell your longer story as a chapter. Or you might integrate parts of your experience into each participant's story, each of which could form separate chapters. Or write your story in comparison to one of the participants who is similar to you, as Christine Kiesinger did in her study of eating disorders.

"Perhaps you will write each chapter in a unique form to reflect the different experiences you had in each interview," I continue, "or to reflect something about the character of each woman's story. For example, if a participant tells her story without much input or questioning from you, you might write in the thoughts you had as you listened to her and reflected on your life. If another interview is interactive, you might write dialogue to show the process of communication and interpretation that occurred between you. If you're successful, you should not only 'unmask' them and yourself for others, but, as Harold Rosen says, you should also discover the face under the mask.

"Or," I continue hesitantly, "you could write the dissertation, as Elliot Eisner suggests, in the form of a novel. The plot would consist of your research journey. You'd let readers experience with you your search for understanding, the questions you ask, how the women respond, what their answers open up for you, new questions that arise, and how you interpret their stories. In that case, you might end by showing how your stories compare and finally how your story changed as you took in and interacted with the other women's stories. You'd have to be careful, though, that your story didn't overshadow theirs."

"Yes, and it would probably be hard to get my committee to buy a novel."

I nod in agreement, and then remind her, "No matter how you tell the story, the writing has to be engaging and evocative. That's not how social scientists have been taught to write. You'll essentially have to learn how to write by reading novels, and by writing and rewriting and getting feedback. Of course, I'll provide response, but you might want to consider joining a writing group as well."

"That's a good idea," Sylvia responds, jotting down notes as she talks. "Won't I also have to do traditional writing? What about analysis, for example? Will I do grounded theory?"

"Well, your committee will demand an analytic chapter, you can bet on that. I also think you need one. The article I wrote on stigma convinced me of the benefits of moving between narrative and categorical knowledge, though I don't think that is necessary in every study."

I continue hesitantly, "You could do a straight grounded theory analysis. Then you'd divide chapters by concepts that emerge, or types, or some kind of category. Or each chapter might represent a stage in the illness process, like David Karp did in his study of depression. If you choose grounded theory, you'd need to pay a lot of attention to coding your materials and comparing and analyzing your data along the way, and you'd write in an authoritative voice about the patterns you saw. If you choose this strategy, I'd recommend you follow the procedures that Kathy Charmaz describes in the new *Handbook of Qualitative Research*."

"What would happen then to the women's stories? And my story?"

"Well, you'd use snippets from all the stories where they applied in each chapter."

Sylvia pauses for a moment, jots down some notes, and then says thoughtfully, "I don't think so. It seems to me that would take away from the evocative nature of the stories as a whole, which is the value of my study. Besides, the women deserve to tell their own stories, though I know I'll influence how they get told . . ."

"I agree," I interrupt, relieved, "given the nature of your project and your goals. But just because we decide to do analysis doesn't mean we have to do it traditionally." Sylvia's eyes open wide. "What about inviting all your participants to read each other's stories and then meet together and tape-record the discussion? This could serve as the basis for your analysis—you'd 'ground' the analysis in your participants' understandings, as well as your own. You might provide your own interpretations for them to respond to."

"Okay," Sylvia says, leaning forward, speaking passionately. "I really like this idea. I'll invite my participants over for dinner one night. It'll be my way of doing something for them. Before they come, I'll send them the stories I wrote about each of the women. Then . . ."

"As long as you get permission," I caution.

"Oh, yes, I know that's important. Maybe I'll only send them their own stories." She pauses, then suddenly blurts, "What if somebody wants me to leave out something?"

"Then you might omit it, or ask your participant to help you rewrite it. Or you could fictionalize a detail in a way that camouflages the actual event but still conveys the meaning you want to get across. Or use pseudonyms or composite characters, if that helps."

"I'd also want them to listen and respond to my interpretations. But what if they disagree with my analysis?" she asks suddenly, frowning.

"That can happen, so you have to have some understanding up front about how you'll handle that. Perhaps you'll put alternative interpretations, yours and theirs, into the text. Or you could listen to their interpretations without giving them yours."

To provide an example, I say, "Susan Chase, a sociologist, chose not to give her analysis to participants to read before publication, though she asked for permission to use their words and gave them an opportunity to amend their narratives. She makes a distinction between what she wanted to communicate in her analysis—how culture shapes narrative process—and what her participants wanted to communicate in their narrations—their life experiences.

"In any case," I continue, "you'll need to explain in your dissertation the kinds of decisions you made and on what grounds you made them. You owe that to readers.

"It's a hard balance," I continue, suddenly reminded of readers, "giving readers the information they expect without betraying the trust of participants, I mean. As Ruth Josselson says, when we get to the writing stage, we tend to take ourselves out of relationship with our participants to form a relationship with readers. How can we help then but have feelings of betraying our participants?

"Oh, and it gets even more complicated," I say to Sylvia, whose hand covers her open mouth as she shakes her head in disbelief. "We haven't even talked about your family members yet. They may become central characters in your very personal story. Say your husband or daughter doesn't want you to reveal things about them or your relationship to them. What do you do then?"

"Oh, my, I hadn't thought of that," she says quietly. "But I'd *have* to talk about my family in order to penetrate the depths of my experience. How could I ask my participants to do this, if I couldn't?"

"This is one of the most important ethical problems in this kind of research. Because now we're not just talking about faceless, nameless, unidentifiable subjects—if we ever were. Your intimates are identifiable individuals with names. Don't they deserve the same consideration as your participants who have given you permission to write about them?"

"Well, of course . . ."

"Are there any situations in which the 'greater good' outweighs individuals' rights to privacy, in which you have a right to tell your story even if other characters in it object?"

When I see the look of defeat on Sylvia's face, I realize that I am transferring too many of my own concerns to her too quickly. "Hey, these issues don't all have to be resolved today. I just wanted you to know that they will come up. We'll discuss each one as it arises and try to make good, ethical decisions."

Then, before Sylvia has a chance to be too relieved, I add, "But by the next time we talk, we do have to consider how to get your proposal past the IRB committee. You'll want to read Michael Angrosino and Kimberly Mays de Pérez's discussion of IRBs in the new *Handbook*. You'll have to be strategic in writing your proposal, because the first thing the committee will ask is about your independent and dependent variables. Then they'll want to see a copy of your interview schedule. All the talk of risk and ceding of responsibility by the university that they'll want you to put into your consent form, well, that will likely scare away some participants. But we have to go through the process to protect the university and ourselves, especially since you're dealing with an at-risk population. The board will be concerned with how you're protecting your participants—their identities and their well-being. At the least, you'll have to provide the name of a therapist your participants can see. I don't know how the board would respond to your telling them that you'll be the therapist," I laugh. Then I add more seriously, "But really protecting the participants and your family members—well, in the end that's left up to you and me." I pick up the book I was reading when Sylvia arrived to indicate our time is up.

"I think I'm ready for those syllabi now. You know, from the courses you've taught." I smile and hand Sylvia the syllabi waiting on my desk. In turn, she hands me a folded piece of paper. "It's a poem I wrote about losing my breast. I know it isn't research, but . . ."

"Of course it's research. Think about including it as part of your story. Have you read any of Laurel Richardson's ethnographic poetry?"

I'm about to get started again, when Sylvia says with a twinkle in her eye, "So will you be on my committee?"

"Only if you're still planning to do that survey," I say, both of us chuckling as we wave good-bye.

◆ Defending and Expanding Autoethnography (One Year Later)

"Hi, Art, I just had to call."

"Why? What's the matter?"

"I just got out of Sylvia's proposal defense. Actually it wasn't as bad as I expected. I think she held her ground. Hey, would you quiet the dogs? I can hardly hear you."

"Oh, yeah. I guess that antibark contraption you bought for Christmas isn't working any better than all the other ones we've purchased. Likker, Traf, Ande, Sunya—quiet, your mom's on the phone," Art yells, and I'm amazed when they actually stop barking. "So what happened?"

"Well, I started the questioning and at first it went very well. Committee members seemed to understand what we were proposing. But then when it was their turn to ask questions, suddenly we moved from talking about the experience of breast cancer to talking about bias, validity, eligibility criteria, operationalization, control variables, confounding factors, building models, replicability, and objectivity. In response, I found myself giving long speeches peppered with words like *literature, literary license, evocative, vulnerable, narrative truth, verisimilitude, interactive,* and *therapeutic.*"

"Nothing like these forays out into the other world to make you realize how fortunate we are to have created what we have in the Communication Department, where we take the significance of this work for granted," Art responds.

"That's for sure. The experience gave me a lot of empathy for what students and young faculty members in other universities may have to go through to do this kind of work.

"But," I continue, "something very interesting happened near the end of the defense. I was listening to the oncologist talk about prediction and control when I began thinking about how important these goals must seem in his daily work life. So instead of giving yet another speech, I asked the oncologist what it is like to have to tell women the bad news, to deal with illness and death all the time. Before I knew it, we were having a

243

conversation about feelings, how emotionally difficult his job is, and how he'd like to do it better. He told the story of how upset he was yesterday, when he had to tell a 34-year-old women, a mother of two young children, that she probably has less than 6 months to live and how bad he felt when she apologized for taking up too much of his time. He had tears in his eyes when he was telling the story. I mentioned Robert Cole's work and he told me he had read *The Call of Stories* and admired the writings of William Carlos Williams. I tried to show him how the goals of Sylvia's work relate to what Coles was saying about how we use stories to try to figure out how to live our lives meaningfully. I felt I had reached him where he lived, at the site of his subjectivity and deep feelings. Unlike the first part of the meeting, it seemed both of us had let down our guards and were communicating with each other as human beings."

"Wow, that must have been some moment."

"It was. You know, I think this is the future of what we do. To figure out how to introduce personal ethnography into the practical contexts of everyday life, to people whose work would be enhanced by it, like doctors, nurses, social workers, administrators, and teachers."

"I've been giving that issue a great deal of thought lately," Art responds. "I think there's a lot to gain from extending all of ethnography beyond the academy so that we stop thinking of it as exclusively an academic practice. Couldn't the work of many people in the service and helping professions be thought of as ethnography? To do their work effectively, service workers have to gain intersubjective understanding in contexts that cross the boundaries of age, ability, race, class, and ethnicity. I mean any time the success of your work depends on developing some degree of intercultural understanding, then you have to use the social skills we associate with ethnographic empathy. Wouldn't you say that psychotherapists do this? Aren't they ethnographers of the self?"

"Of course. And good teaching involves ethnography too," I add. "Over time you try to work your way through the barriers of unfamiliarity, distance, and difference toward a spirit of collaboration, understanding, and openness to experience and participation. When we learn how to open ourselves to ourselves and to each other, we find it easier to drop some of our resistance to different ideas. I like to think of this as working toward an ethnographic consciousness in the classroom that is personal, intimate, and empathic."

244

"That's very close to how I see the private geriatric care managers I've been studying for the past 2 years," Art responds. "As they work between long-distanced families and their elderly relatives, they become ethnographers of aging. They aren't academics. They don't do academic research and they don't write articles. Yet in every other respect they think and act as ethnographers. In each case they manage, they function as a channel through which pass the emotional, economic, medical, and social crises that must be negotiated by families coping with the contingencies of aging. They occupy a unique, dynamic, holistic, and engaged perspective. They are participants and observers and their private lives are deeply affected by their public and professional services. As storytellers and autoethnographers, they have as much, if not more, to teach us about the concrete, everyday details associated with aging as do scholars of aging."

"We like to think we have a lot to teach people in the public sector, but they have a lot to teach us as well, if we just listen," I add. "Yet I know, as Elliot Eisner discusses, that it will be difficult to wean scholars and the American public from a view that measuring, comparison, and outcomes are all that matter."

"But I think we're slowly knocking down some of the walls," Arts says encouragingly. "We've opened a space to write between traditional social science prose and literature and to stimulate more discussion of working the spaces between subjectivity and objectivity, passion and intellect, and autobiography and culture. Look at all the book manuscripts we've received to review for our series. I take that as strong evidence that more and more academics think it's possible to write from the heart, to bring the first-person voice into their work, and to merge art and science. I don't think there's any danger of going back to the way it used to be, not in our lifetimes anyway."

"Yes, we've encouraged writers to make ethnography readable, evocative, engaging, and personally meaningful. And it's working. Autoethnography is being read widely by graduate and undergraduate students. Now it's time to show its usefulness in the public realm. It's interesting that this is the same argument being made in some of the mainstream sociology journals. Have you seen the symposium in *Contemporary Sociology* on 'engaging publics in social dialogue'?" I ask.

"Yes, I read it yesterday. Perhaps our purposes are coming together for a change. After all, that's what we are trying to do in the Ethnographic

Alternatives series, to publish books that say something meaningful and attract a wide audience."

"Like Mike Angrosino's stories of adult mental illness. Now we just need to get the book into the hands of those who work with and make policies about mental illness."

"I don't know if this *Handbook* piece will help with that," Art says. "But it may encourage more people to do autoethnography and help legitimate this approach for those students and young faculty members you're worried about. Those are important goals we've tried to achieve in our chapter. I'm glad we've written it."

"Me, too," I say, smiling as I think of Art's initial resistance to writing for the *Handbook*.

"So, then, we're finished with this piece?" Art asks.

"Looks like it," I reply. "Let's reward ourselves and go to the beach for the weekend. We need to get out of our offices and engage in some other life experiences, or else the only thing we're going to be able to write about is writing."

"But what about the chapter for the *Handbook of Loss and Trauma* and the one for the *Handbook of Interpersonal Communication* we just committed to do? We really should get started," Art says.

"Art!" I yell, as I hear simultaneously his laughter and a knock on my office door.

◆ References

Abu-Lughod, L. (1993). *Writing women's worlds: Bedouin stories.* Berkeley: University of California Press.

Adler, P. A., & Adler, P. (1987). *Membership roles in field research.* Newbury Park, CA: Sage.

Adler, P. A., & Adler, P. (1994). Observational techniques. In N. K. Denzin & Y. S. Lincoln (Eds.), *Handbook of qualitative research* (pp. 377-392). Thousand Oaks, CA: Sage.

Allison, D. (1994). *Skin: Talking about sex, class, and literature.* Ithaca, NY: Firebrand.

Angrosino, M. (1998). *Opportunity House: Ethnographic stories of mental retardation.* Walnut Creek, CA: AltaMira.

Anzaldúa, G. (1987). *Borderlands/la frontera: The new mestiza.* San Francisco: Aunt Lute.

Atkinson, P. (1997). Narrative turn in a blind alley? *Qualitative Health Research, 7,* 325-344.

Austin, D. (1996). Kaleidoscope: The same and different. In C. Ellis & A. P. Bochner (Eds.), *Composing ethnography: Alternative forms of qualitative writing* (pp. 206-230). Walnut Creek, CA: AltaMira.

Austin, D. (1998). *Understanding close relationships among African Americans in the context of the Million Man March.* Unpublished doctoral dissertation, University of South Florida.

Bakhtin, M. M. (1981). *The dialogic imagination: Four essays* (M. Holquist, Ed.; M. Holquist & C. Emerson, Trans.). Austin: University of Texas Press.

Banks, A., & Banks, S. P. (Eds.). (1998). *Fiction and social research: By ice or fire.* Walnut Creek, CA: AltaMira.

Barthes, R. (1977). *Image, music, text* (S. Heath, Trans.). New York: Hill & Wang.

Behar, R. (1993). *Translated woman: Crossing the border with Esperanza's story.* Boston: Beacon.

Behar, R. (1996). *The vulnerable observer: Anthropology that breaks your heart.* Boston: Beacon.

Behar, R., & Gordon, D. A. (Eds.). (1995). *Women writing culture.* Berkeley: University of California Press.

Benson, P. (Ed.). (1993). *Anthropology and literature.* Urbana: University of Illinois Press.

Berger, B. (Ed.). (1990). *Authors of their own lives: Intellectual autobiographies by twenty American sociologists.* Berkeley: University of California Press.

Berger, L. (1997). Between the candy store and the mall: The spiritual loss of a father. *Journal of Personal and Interpersonal Loss, 2,* 397-409.

Berger, L. (1998). Silent movies: Scenes from a life. In A. Banks & S. P. Banks (Eds.), *Fiction and social research: By ice or fire* (pp. 137-146). Walnut Creek, CA: AltaMira.

Bochner, A. P. (1981). Forming warm ideas. In C. Wilder-Mott & J. H. Weakland (Eds.), *Rigor and imagination: Essays from the legacy of Gregory Bateson* (pp. 65-81). New York: Praeger.

Bochner, A. P. (1994). Perspectives on inquiry II: Theories and stories. In M. L. Knapp & G. R. Miller (Eds.), *Handbook of interpersonal communication* (2nd ed., pp. 21-41). Thousand Oaks, CA: Sage.

Bochner, A. P. (1997). It's about time: Narrative and the divided self. *Qualitative Inquiry, 3,* 418-438.

Bochner, A. P., & Ellis, C. (1992). Personal narrative as a social approach to interpersonal communication. *Communication Theory, 2,* 165-172.

Bochner, A. P., & Ellis, C. (1999). Which way to turn? *Journal of Contemporary Ethnography, 28,* 500-509.

Bochner, A. P., Ellis, C., & Tillmann-Healy, L. (1997). Relationships as stories. In S. Duck (Ed.), *Handbook of personal relationships: Theory, research and interventions* (2nd ed., pp. 307-324). New York: John Wiley.

Bochner, A. P., Ellis, C., & Tillmann-Healy, L. (1998). Mucking around looking for truth. In B. M. Montgomery & L. A. Baxter (Eds.). *Dialectical approaches to studying personal relationships* (pp. 41-62). Mahwah, NJ: Lawrence Erlbaum.

Bochner, A. P., & Waugh, J. B. (1995). Talking-with as a model for writing-about: Implications of Rortyean pragmatism. In L. Langsdorf & A. R. Smith (Eds.), *Recovering pragmatism's voice: The classical tradition, Rorty, and the philosophy of communication* (pp. 211-233). Albany: State University of New York Press.

Bowen, E. S. (1954). *Return to laughter: An anthropological novel.* New York: Harper & Row.

Brady, I. (Ed.). (1991). *Anthropological poetics.* Savage, MD: Rowman & Littlefield.

Brandes, S. (1982). Ethnographic autobiographies in American anthropology. In E. A. Hoebel, R. Currier, & S. Kaiser (Eds.), *Crisis in anthropology: View from Spring Hill, 1980* (pp. 187-202). New York: Garland.

Broyard, A. (1992). *Intoxicated by my illness and other writings on life and death.* New York: Fawcett-Columbine.

Bruner, J. (1990). *Acts of meaning.* Cambridge, MA: Harvard University Press.

Bruner, J. (1993). Introduction: The ethnographic self and the personal self. In P. Benson (Ed.), *Anthropology and literature* (pp. 2-26). Urbana: University of Illinois Press.

Buford, B. (1996, June 24). The seductions of storytelling. *New Yorker,* pp. 11-12.

Butler, S., & Rosenblum, B. (1991). *Cancer in two voices.* San Francisco: Spinster.

Carr, D. (1986). *Time, narrative, and history.* Bloomington: Indiana University Press.

Charmaz, K. (1991). *Good days, bad days: The self in chronic illness and time.* New Brunswick, NJ: Rutgers University Press.

Chase, S. (1996). Personal vulnerability and interpretive authority in narrative research. In R. Josselson (Ed.), *Ethics and process in the narrative study of lives* (pp. 45-59). Thousand Oaks, CA: Sage.

Church, K. (1995). *Forbidden narratives: Critical autobiography as social science.* Newark, NJ: Gordon & Breach.

Clandinin, D. J., & Connelly, F. M. (1994). Personal experience methods. In N. K. Denzin & Y. S. Lincoln (Eds.), *Handbook of qualitative research* (pp. 413-427). Thousand Oaks, CA: Sage.

Clough, P. T. (1994). *Feminist thought: Desire, power and academic discourse.* Cambridge, MA: Blackwell.

Clough, P. (1997). Autotelecommunication and autoethnography: A reading of Carolyn Ellis's *Final negotiations. Sociological Quarterly, 38,* 95-110.

Cohen, A. (1992). Self-conscious anthropology. In J. Okely & H. Callaway (Eds.), *Anthropology and autobiography* (pp. 221-241). London: Routledge.

Coles, R. (1989). *The call of stories: Teaching and the moral imagination.* Boston: Houghton Mifflin.

Collins, P. H. (1986). Learning from the outsider within: The sociological significance of black feminist thought. *Social Problems, 33,* 14-32.

Cook, J. A., & Fonow, M. M. (1986). Knowledge and women's interests: Issues of epistemology and methodology in feminist sociological research. *Sociological Inquiry, 56,* 2-27.

Couser, G. T. (1997). *Recovering bodies: Illness, disability, and life writing.* Madison: University of Wisconsin Press.

Crapanzano, V. (1980). *Tuhami: Portrait of a Moroccan.* Chicago: University of Chicago Press.

Crawford, L. (1996). Personal ethnography. *Communication Monographs, 63,* 158-170.

Crites, S. (1971). The narrative quality of experience. *Journal of the American Academy of Religion, 39,* 291-311.

Deck, A. (1990). Autoethnography: Zora Neale Hurston, Noni Jabavu, and cross-disciplinary discourse. *Black American Literature Forum, 24,* 237-256.

Denzin, N. K. (1989). *Interpretive biography.* Newbury Park, CA: Sage.

Denzin, N. K. (1997). *Interpretive ethnography: Ethnographic practices for the 21st century.* Thousand Oaks, CA: Sage.

Denzin, N. K., & Lincoln, Y. S. (Eds.). (1994). *Handbook of qualitative research.* Thousand Oaks, CA: Sage.

Derrida, J. (1978). *Writing and difference* (A. Bass, Trans.). Chicago: University of Chicago Press.

Derrida, J. (1981). *Positions* (A. Bass, Trans.). Chicago: University of Chicago Press.

DeVault, M. (1997). Personal writing in social science: Issues of production and interpretation. In R. Hertz (Ed.). *Reflexivity and voice* (pp. 216-228). Thousand Oaks, CA: Sage.

Diamond, S. (1982). *Totems.* Barrytown, NY: Open Book/Station Hill.

Dumont, J.-P. (1976). *Under the rainbow: Nature and supernature among the Panare Indians.* Austin: University of Texas Press.

Dumont, J.-P. (1978). *The headman and I: Ambiguity and ambivalence in the fieldworking experience.* Austin: University of Texas Press.

Eisner, E. (1996). Should a novel count as a dissertation in education? *Research in the Teaching of English, 30,* 403-427.

Eisner, E. (1997). The new frontier in qualitative research methodology. *Qualitative Inquiry, 3,* 259-273.

Ellingson, L. (1998). "Then you know how I feel": Empathy, identification, and reflexivity in fieldwork. *Qualitative Inquiry, 4,* 492-514.

Ellis, C. (1986). *Fisher folk: Two communities on Chesapeake Bay.* Lexington: University Press of Kentucky.

Ellis, C. (1991a). Emotional sociology. In N. K. Denzin (Ed.), *Studies in symbolic interaction: A research annual* (Vol. 12, pp. 123-145). Greenwich, CT: JAI.

Ellis, C. (1991b). Sociological introspection and emotional experience. *Symbolic Interaction, 14,* 23-50.

Ellis, C. (1993). "There are survivors": Telling a story of sudden death. *Sociological Quarterly, 34,* 711-730.

Ellis, C. (1995a). Emotional and ethical quagmires in returning to the field. *Journal of Contemporary Ethnography, 24,* 711-713.

Ellis, C. (1995b). *Final negotiations: A story of love, loss, and chronic illness.* Philadelphia: Temple University Press.

Ellis, C. (1995c). The other side of the fence: Seeing black and white in a small, southern town. *Qualitative Inquiry, 1,* 147-167.

Ellis, C. (1995d). Speaking of dying: An ethnographic short story. *Symbolic Interaction, 18,* 73-81.

Ellis, C. (1997). Evocative autoethnography: Writing emotionally about our lives. In W. G. Tierney & Y. S. Lincoln (Eds.), *Representation and the text: Reframing the narrative voice* (pp. 115-142). Albany: State University of New York Press.

Ellis, C. (1998a). Exploring loss through autoethnographic inquiry: Autoethnographic stories, co-constructed narratives, and interactive interviews. In J. H. Harvey (Ed.), *Perspectives on loss: A sourcebook* (pp. 49-62). Philadelphia: Taylor & Francis.

Ellis, C. (1998b). "I hate my voice": Coming to terms with minor bodily stigmas. *Sociological Quarterly, 39,* 517-537.

Ellis, C., & Bochner, A. P. (1992). Telling and performing personal stories: The constraints of choice in abortion. In C. Ellis & M. G. Flaherty (Eds.), *Investigating subjectivity: Research on lived experience* (pp. 79-101). Newbury Park, CA: Sage.

Ellis, C., & Bochner, A. P. (Eds.). (1996a). *Composing ethnography: Alternative forms of qualitative writing.* Walnut Creek, CA: AltaMira.

Ellis, C., & Bochner, A. P. (Eds.). (1996b). Taking ethnography into the twenty-first century [Special issue]. *Journal of Contemporary Ethnography, 25*(1).

Ellis, C., & Flaherty, M. G. (Eds.). (1992). *Investigating subjectivity: Research on lived experience.* Newbury Park, CA: Sage.

Ellis, C., Kiesinger, C., & Tillmann-Healy, L. (1997). Interactive interviewing: Talking about emotional experience. In R. Hertz (Ed.), *Reflexivity and voice* (pp. 119-149). Thousand Oaks, CA: Sage.

Engaging publics in sociological dialogue [Symposium]. (1998). *Contemporary Sociology, 27,* 435-462.

Foucault, M. (1970). *The order of things: An archaeology of the human sciences.* New York: Random House.

Frank, A. (1991). *At the will of the body: Reflections on illness.* Boston: Houghton Mifflin.

Frank, A. (1994). Reclaiming an orphan genre: The first-person narrative of illness. *Literature and Medicine, 13,* 1-21.

Frank, A. (1995). *The wounded storyteller: Body, illness, and ethics.* Chicago: University of Chicago Press.

Freeman, M. (1993). *Rewriting the self: History, memory, narrative.* London: Routledge.

Freeman, M. (1998). Mythical time, historical time, and the narrative fabric of self. *Narrative Inquiry, 8,* 27-50.

French, D. (1998). *Through the eyes of the comic mask: An ethnographic exploration of the identity of a stand-up comedian.* Unpublished doctoral dissertation, University of South Florida.

Friedman, N. (1990, Spring). Autobiographical sociology. *American Sociologist, 21,* 60-66.

Gadamer, H.-G. (1989). *Truth and method* (2nd rev. ed.; J. Weinsheimer & D. G. Marshall, Eds. & Trans.). New York: Crossroad.

Geertz, C. (1973). *The interpretation of cultures: Selected essays.* New York: Basic Books.

Gergen, K. J. (1994). *Realities and relationships: Soundings in social construction.* Cambridge, MA: Harvard University Press.

Glassner, B. (Ed.). (1997). Qualitative sociology as everyday life [Special issue]. *Qualitative Sociology, 20*(4).

Goetting, A., & Fenstermaker, S. (1995). *Individual voices, collective visions: Fifty years of women in sociology.* Philadelphia: Temple University Press.

Goldman, A. (1993, Fall). Is that what she said? The politics of collaborative autobiography. *Cultural Critique,* pp. 177-204.

Gonzalez, M. C., & Krizek, R. L (1994). *Indigenous ethnography.* Paper presented at the annual meeting of the Western States Communication Association, San Jose, CA.

Gravel, A. (1997). *The ideological functions of autoethnography.* Unpublished manuscript, University of Wisconsin–Whitewater.

Gubrium, J. F., & Holstein, J. A. (1997). *The new language of qualitative method.* New York: Oxford University Press.

Hacking, I. (1995). *Rewriting the soul: Multiple personality and the sciences of memory.* Princeton, NJ: Princeton University Press.

Harding, S. (1991). *Whose science? Whose knowledge? Thinking from women's lives.* Ithaca, NY: Cornell University Press.

Harrington, W. (1997). *Intimate journalism: The art and craft of reporting everyday life.* Thousand Oaks, CA: Sage.

Hartsock, N. C. M. (1983). The feminist standpoint: Developing the ground for a specifically feminist historical materialism. In S. Harding & M. B. Hintikka (Eds.), *Discovering reality* (pp. 283-310). Amsterdam: D. Reidel.

Harvey, J. (Ed.). (in press). *Handbook of loss and trauma.* London: Taylor & Francis.

Hawkins, A. H. (1993). *Reconstructing illness: Studies in pathography.* West Lafayette, IN: Purdue University Press.

Hayano, D. M. (1979). Auto-ethnography: Paradigms, problems, and prospects. *Human Organization, 38,* 113-120.

Hayano, D. M. (1982). *Poker faces.* Berkeley: University of California Press.

Heidegger, M. (1971). *On the way to language* (P. D. Hertz & J. Stambaugh, Trans.). New York: Harper & Row.

Herndon, C. (1993). *Gendered fictions of self and community: Autobiography and autoethnography in Caribbean women's writing.* Unpublished doctoral dissertation, University of Texas at Austin.

Hertz, R. (Ed.). (1996). Ethics, reflexivity and voice [Special issue]. *Qualitative Sociology, 19*(1).

Hertz, R. (Ed.). (1997). *Reflexivity and voice.* Thousand Oaks, CA: Sage.

Higgins, P., & Johnson, J. (Eds.). (1988). *Personal sociology.* New York: Praeger.

Hollway, W. (1989). *Subjectivity and method in psychology: Gender, meaning and science.* London: Sage.

Hurston, Z. N. (1991). *Dust tracks on a road.* New York: HarperCollins. (Original work published 1942)

Jackson, A. (Ed.). (1987). *Anthropology at home.* London: Tavistock.

Jackson, M. (1989). *Paths toward a clearing: Radical empiricism and ethnographic inquiry.* Bloomington: Indiana University Press.

Jackson, M. (1995). *At home in the world.* Durham, NC: Duke University Press.

Jago, B. (1996). Postcards, ghosts, and fathers: Revising family stories. *Qualitative Inquiry, 2,* 495-516.

Jones, S. H. (1998). *Kaleidoscope notes: Writing women's music and organizational culture.* Walnut Creek, CA: AltaMira.

Josselson, R. (1996). On writing other people's lives: Self-analytic reflections of a narrative researcher. In R. Josselson (Ed.), *Ethics and process in the narrative study of lives* (pp. 60-71). Thousand Oaks, CA: Sage.

Jules-Rosette, B. (1975). *African apostles.* Ithaca, NY: Cornell University Press.

Karp, D. (1996). *Speaking of sadness.* New York: Oxford University Press.

Kerby, A. (1991). *Narrative and the self.* Bloomington: Indiana University Press.

Kiesinger, C. (1995). *Anorexic and bulimic lives: Making sense of food and eating.* Unpublished doctoral dissertation, University of South Florida.

Kiesinger, C. (1998a). From interviewing to story: Writing Abbie's life. *Qualitative Inquiry, 4,* 71-95.

Kiesinger, C. (1998b). Portrait of an anorexic life. In A. Banks & S. P. Banks (Eds.), *Fiction and social research: By ice or fire* (pp. 115-136). Walnut Creek, CA: AltaMira.

Kinkaid, J. (1988). *A small place.* New York: Penguin.

Kleinman, S. (1997). Essaying the personal: Making sociological stories stick. *Qualitative Sociology, 20,* 553-564.

Kolker, A. (1996). Thrown overboard: The human costs of health care rationing. In C. Ellis & A. P. Bochner (Eds.), *Composing ethnography: Alternative forms of qualitative writing* (pp. 132-159). Walnut Creek, CA: AltaMira.

Kondo, D. (1990). *Crafting selves: Power, gender, and discourses of identity in a Japanese workplace.* Chicago: University of Chicago Press.

Krieger, S. (1983). *The mirror dance: Identity in a women's community.* Philadelphia: Temple University Press.

Krieger, S. (1984). Fiction and social science. In N. K. Denzin (Ed.), *Studies in symbolic interaction: A research annual* (Vol. 5, pp. 269-286). Greenwich, CT: JAI.

Krieger, S. (1991). *Social science and the self: Personal essays on an art form.* New Brunswick, NJ: Rutgers University Press.

Krieger, S. (1996). *The family silver: Essays on relationships among women.* Berkeley: University of California Press.

Kuhn, T. (1962). *The structure of scientific revolutions.* Chicago: University of Chicago Press.

Kulick, D., & Willson, M. (Eds.). (1995). *Taboo: Sex, identity and erotic subjectivity in anthropological fieldwork.* London: Routledge.

Lather, P. (1986). Research as praxis. *Harvard Educational Review, 56,* 257-277.

Lather, P. (1993). Fertile obsession: Validity after poststructuralism. *Sociological Quarterly, 34,* 673-693.

Lejeune, P. (1989). *On autobiography* (K. Leary, Trans.). Minneapolis: University of Minnesota Press.

Lewin, E., & Leap, W. L. (Eds.). (1996). *Out in the field: Reflections of lesbian and gay anthropologists.* Urbana: University of Illinois Press.

Lieblich, A. (1996). Some unforeseen outcomes of conducting narrative research with people of one's own culture. In R. Josselson (Ed.). *Ethics and process in the narrative study of lives* (pp. 151-184). Thousand Oaks, CA: Sage.

Linden, R. R. (1992). *Making stories, making selves: Feminist reflections on the Holocaust.* Columbus: Ohio State University Press.

Lionnet, F. (1989). Autoethnography: The an-archic style of *Dust tracks on a road.* In F. Lionnet, *Autobiographical voices: Race, gender, self-portraiture* (pp. 97-129). Ithaca, NY: Cornell University Press.

Lopate, P. (1994). Introduction. In P. Lopate (Ed.), *The art of the personal essay: An anthology from the classical era to the present.* Garden City, NY: Anchor.

Lorde, A. (1980). *The cancer journals.* Argyle, NY: Spinsters.

Lyotard, J.-F. (1984). *The postmodern condition: A report on knowledge* (G. Bennington & B. Massumi, Trans.). Minneapolis: University of Minnesota Press.

MacIntyre, A. (1981). *After virtue: A study in moral theory.* Notre Dame, IN: University of Notre Dame Press.

Mairs, N. (1986). *Plain text.* Tucson: University of Arizona Press.

Mairs, N. (1990). *Carnal acts: Essays.* New York: Harper.

Mairs, N. (1998). *Waist-high in the world: A life among the nondisabled.* Boston: Beacon.

Malinowski, B. (1967). *A diary in the strict sense of the term.* (N. Guterman, Trans.). New York: Harcourt, Brace & World.

Marcus, G. E., & Fischer, M. M. J. (1986). *Anthropology as cultural critique: An experimental moment in the human sciences.* Chicago: University of Chicago Press.

Markham, A. (1998). *Life online: Researching real experience in virtual space.* Walnut Creek, CA: AltaMira.

Mehan, H., & Wood, H. (1975). *The reality of ethnomethodology.* New York: John Wiley.

Merton, R. (1988). Some thoughts on the concept of sociological autobiography. In M. Riley (Ed.), *Sociological lives* (pp. 17-21). Newbury Park, CA: Sage. (Original work published 1972)

Miller, L., & Taylor, J. (1997). Performing autobiography: Editors' introduction. *Text and Performance Quarterly, 4,* v-vi.

Miller, M. (1996). Ethics and understanding through interrelationship: I and thou in dialogue. In R. Josselson (Ed.), *Ethics and process in the narrative study of lives* (pp. 129-147). Thousand Oaks, CA: Sage.

Mink, L. (1969-1970). History and fiction as modes of comprehension. *New Literary History, 1,* 541-558.

Motzafi-Haller, P. (1997). Writing birthright: On native anthropologists and the politics of representation. In D. Reed-Danahay, *Auto/ethnography: Rewriting the self and the social* (pp. 195-222). Oxford: Berg.

Mukaia, T. (1989). A call for our language: Anorexia from within. *Women's Studies International Forum, 12,* 613-638.

Narayan, K. (1993). How native is a "native" anthropologist? *American Anthropologist, 95,* 671-686.

Neumann, M. (1996). Collecting ourselves at the end of the century. In C. Ellis & A. P. Bochner (Eds.), *Composing ethnography: Alternative forms of qualitative writing* (pp. 172-198). Walnut Creek, CA: AltaMira.

Noddings, N. (1984). *Caring: A feminine approach to ethics and moral education.* Berkeley: University of California Press.

Oakley, A. (1981). Interviewing women: A contradiction in terms. In H. Roberts (Ed.), *Doing feminist research* (pp. 30-61). London: Routledge & Kegan Paul.

Oakley, A. (1984). *Taking it like a woman.* New York: Random House.

Ohnuki-Tierney, E. (1984). Native anthropologists. *American Ethnologist, 2,* 584-586.

Okely, J. (1992). Participatory experience and embodied knowledge. In J. Okely & H. Callaway (Eds.), *Anthropology and autobiography* (pp. 1-28). London: Routledge.

Okely, J., & Callaway, H. (Eds.). (1992). *Anthropology and autobiography.* London: Routledge.

Parini, J. (1998, July 10). The memoir versus the novel in a time of transition. *Chronicle of Higher Education,* p. A40.

Park-Fuller, L. (1998). *Introduction to session on arguing the shifting shapes and speaking tongues of autoethnographic performance.* Paper presented at the annual meeting of the National Communication Association, New York.

Payne, D. (1996). Autobiology. In C. Ellis & A. P. Bochner (Eds.), *Composing ethnography: Alternative forms of qualitative writing* (pp. 49-75). Walnut Creek, CA: AltaMira.

Personal Narratives Group. (1989). *Interpreting women's lives: Feminist theory and personal narratives.* Bloomington: Indiana University Press.

Pratt, M. L. (1994). Transculturation and autoethnography: Peru 1615/1980. In F. Barker, P. Holme, & M. Iverson (Eds.), *Colonial discourse/postcolonial theory* (pp. 24-46). Manchester: Manchester University Press.

Quinney, R. (1991). *Journey to a far place: Autobiographical reflections.* Philadelphia: Temple University Press.

Rabinow, P. (1975). *Symbolic domination: Cultural form and historical change in Morocco.* Chicago: University of Chicago Press

Rabinow, P. (1977). *Reflections on fieldwork in Morocco.* Berkeley: University of California Press.

Reed-Danahay, D. (1997). *Auto/ethnography: Rewriting the self and the social.* Oxford: Berg.

Reinharz, S. (1979). *On becoming a social scientist: From survey research and participation to experiential analysis.* San Francisco: Jossey-Bass.

Reinharz, S. (1992). *Feminist methods in social research.* New York: Oxford University Press.

Rhett, K. (Ed.). (1997). *Survival stories: Memoirs of crisis.* Garden City, NY: Doubleday.

Rich, A. (1978). *On lies, secrets and silence: Selected prose 1966-1978.* New York: W. W. Norton.

Richardson, L. (1990a). Narrative and sociology. *Journal of Contemporary Ethnography, 19,* 116-135.

255

Richardson, L. (1990b). *Writing strategies: Reaching diverse audiences.* Newbury Park, CA: Sage.

Richardson, L. (1994a). Nine poems: Marriage and the family. *Journal of Contemporary Ethnography, 23,* 3-14.

Richardson, L. (1994b). Writing: A method of inquiry. In N. K. Denzin & Y. S. Lincoln (Eds.), *Handbook of qualitative research* (pp. 516-529). Thousand Oaks, CA: Sage.

Richardson, L. (1995). Vespers. *Chicago Review, 41,* 129-146.

Richardson, L. (1996). Speech lessons. In C. Ellis & A. P. Bochner (Eds.), *Composing ethnography: Alternative forms of qualitative writing* (pp. 231-239). Walnut Creek, CA: AltaMira.

Richardson, L. (1997). *Fields of play: Constructing an academic life.* New Brunswick, NJ: Rutgers University Press.

Richardson, L., & Lockridge, E. (1998). Fiction and ethnography: A conversation. *Qualitative Inquiry, 4,* 328-336.

Riemer, J. W. (1977). Varieties of opportunistic research. *Urban Life, 5,* 467-477.

Riley, M. W. (1988). *Sociological lives.* Newbury Park, CA: Sage.

Rodriguez, R. (1983). *Hunger of memory: The education of Richard Rodriguez.* New York: Bantam.

Ronai, C. R. (1992). The reflexive self through narrative: A night in the life of an erotic dancer/researcher. In C. Ellis & M. G. Flaherty (Eds.), *Investigating subjectivity: Research on lived experience* (pp. 102-124). Newbury Park, CA: Sage.

Ronai, C. R. (1995). Multiple reflections of child sex abuse: An argument for a layered account. *Journal of Contemporary Ethnography, 23,* 395-426.

Rorty, R. (1979). *Philosophy and the mirror of nature.* Princeton, NJ: Princeton University Press.

Rorty, R. (1982). *Consequences of pragmatism (essays 1972-1980).* Minneapolis: University of Minnesota Press.

Rose, D. (1991). In search of experience: The anthropological poetics of Stanley Diamond. In I. Brady (Ed.), *Anthropological poetics* (pp. 219-233). Savage, MD: Rowman & Littlefield.

Rosen, H. (1988). The autobiographical impulse. In D. Tannen (Ed.), *Linguistics in context: Connecting observation and understanding* (pp. 69-88). Norwood, NJ: Ablex.

Schneider, A. (1998, July 10). Jane Tompkins's message to academe: Nurture the individual, not just the intellect. *Chronicle of Higher Education,* pp. A8-A10.

Schwandt, T. A. (1996). Farewell to criteriology. *Qualitative Inquiry, 2,* 58-72.

Shalit, R. (1998, February). The man who knew too much. *Lingua Franca,* pp. 32-40.

Shelton, A. (1995). Foucault's Madonna: The secret life of Carolyn Ellis. *Symbolic Interaction, 18,* 83-87.

Shostak, A. (Ed.). (1996). *Private sociology: Unsparing reflections, uncommon gains.* Dix Hills, NY: General Hall.

Shostak, M. (1981). *Nisa: The life and words of a !Kung woman.* Cambridge, MA: Harvard University Press.

Shotter, J. (1987). The social construction of an "us": Problems of accountability and narratology. In R. Burnett, P. McGee, & D. Clarke (Eds.), *Accounting for relationships: Explanation, representation, and knowledge* (pp. 225-247). London: Methuen.

Smith, D. (1979). A sociology for women. In J. Sherman & E. Beck (Eds.), *The prism of sex: Essays in the sociology of knowledge.* Madison: University of Wisconsin Press.

Smith, D. (1990). *The conceptual practices of power: A feminist sociology of knowledge.* Boston: Northeastern University Press.

Smith, D. (1992). Sociology from women's perspective: A reaffirmation. *Sociological Theory, 10,* 88-97.

Sontag, S. (1978). *Illness as a metaphor.* New York: Farrar, Straus & Giroux.

Stake, R. E. (1994). Case studies. In N. K. Denzin & Y. S. Lincoln (Eds.). *The handbook of qualitative research* (pp. 236-247). Thousand Oaks, CA: Sage.

Strathern, M. (1987). The limits of auto-anthropology. In A. Jackson (Ed.), *Anthropology at home* (pp. 59-67). London: Tavistock.

Tedlock, B. (1991). From participant observation to the observation of participation: The emergence of narrative ethnography. *Journal of Anthropological Research, 41,* 69-94.

Tierney, W. (1998). Life history's history: Subjects foretold. *Qualitative Inquiry, 4,* 49-70.

Tierney, W. G., & Lincoln, Y. S. (Eds.). (1997). *Representation and the text: Reframing the narrative voice.* Albany: State University of New York Press.

Tillmann-Healy, L. (1996). A secret life in a culture of thinness: Reflections on body, food, and bulimia. In C. Ellis & A. P. Bochner (Eds.), *Composing ethnography: Alternative forms of qualitative writing* (pp. 76-108). Walnut Creek, CA: AltaMira.

Tillmann-Healy, L. (1999). *Life projects: A narrative ethnography of gay-straight friendship.* Unpublished doctoral dissertation, University of South Florida.

Tompkins, J. (1989). Me and my shadow. In L. Kauffman (Ed.), *Gender and theory: Dialogues on feminist criticism* (pp. 121-139). Cambridge, MA: Blackwell.

Toulmin, S. (1969). Concepts and the explanation of human behavior. In T. Mischel (Ed.), *Human action* (pp. 71-104). New York: Academic Press.

Trinh T. M. (1989). *Woman, native, other: Writing postcoloniality and feminism.* Bloomington: Indiana University Press.

Trinh T. M. (1992). *Framer framed.* New York: Routledge.

Trotter, M. (1992). *Life writing: Exploring the practice of autoethnography in anthropology.* Unpublished master's thesis, University of Illinois, Urbana-Champaign.

True confessions: The age of the literary memoir [Special issue]. (1996, May 12). *New York Times Magazine.*

Turner, V., & Bruner, E. (Eds.). (1986). *The anthropology of experience.* Urbana: University of Illinois Press.

Tyler, S. (1986). Post-modern ethnography: From document of the occult to occult document. In J. Clifford and G. E. Marcus (Eds.), *Writing culture: The poetics and politics of ethnography* (pp. 122-140). Berkeley: University of California Press.

Van Maanen, J. (1988). *Tales of the field: On writing ethnography.* Chicago: University of Chicago Press.

Van Maanen, J. (1995). An end to innocence: The ethnography of ethnography. In J. Van Maanen (Ed.), *Representation in ethnography* (pp. 1-35). Thousand Oaks, CA: Sage.

Van Maanen, M. (1990). *Researching lived experience: Human science for an action sensitive pedagogy.* Albany: State University of New York Press.

Wittgenstein, L. (1953). *Philosophical investigations* (G. Anscombe, Trans.). New York: Macmillan.

Zola, I. K. (1982). *Missing pieces: A chronicle of living with a disability.* Philadelphia: Temple University Press.

Zussman, R. (1996). Autobiographical occasions. *Contemporary Sociology, 25,* 143-148.

7

Data Management and Analysis Methods

Gery W. Ryan and H. Russell Bernard

◆ Texts Are Us

This chapter is about methods for managing and analyzing qualitative data. By *qualitative data* we mean text: newspapers, movies, sitcoms, e-mail traffic, folktales, life histories. We also mean narratives—narratives about getting divorced, about being sick, about surviving hand-to-hand combat, about selling sex, about trying to quit smoking. In fact, most of the archaeologically recoverable information about human thought and human behavior is text, the "good stuff" of social science.

Scholars in content analysis began using computers in the 1950s to do statistical analysis of texts (Pool, 1959), but recent advances in technology are changing the economics of the social sciences. Optical scanning today makes light work of converting written texts to machine-readable form. Within a few years, voice-recognition software will make light work of transcribing open-ended interviews. These technologies are blind to epistemological differences. Interpretivists and positivists alike are using these technologies for the analysis of texts, and will do so more and more.

Like Tesch (1990), we distinguish between the *linguistic tradition,* which treats text as an object of analysis itself, and the *sociological tradition,* which treats text as a window into human experience (see Figure 7.1). The linguistic tradition includes narrative analysis, conversation (or

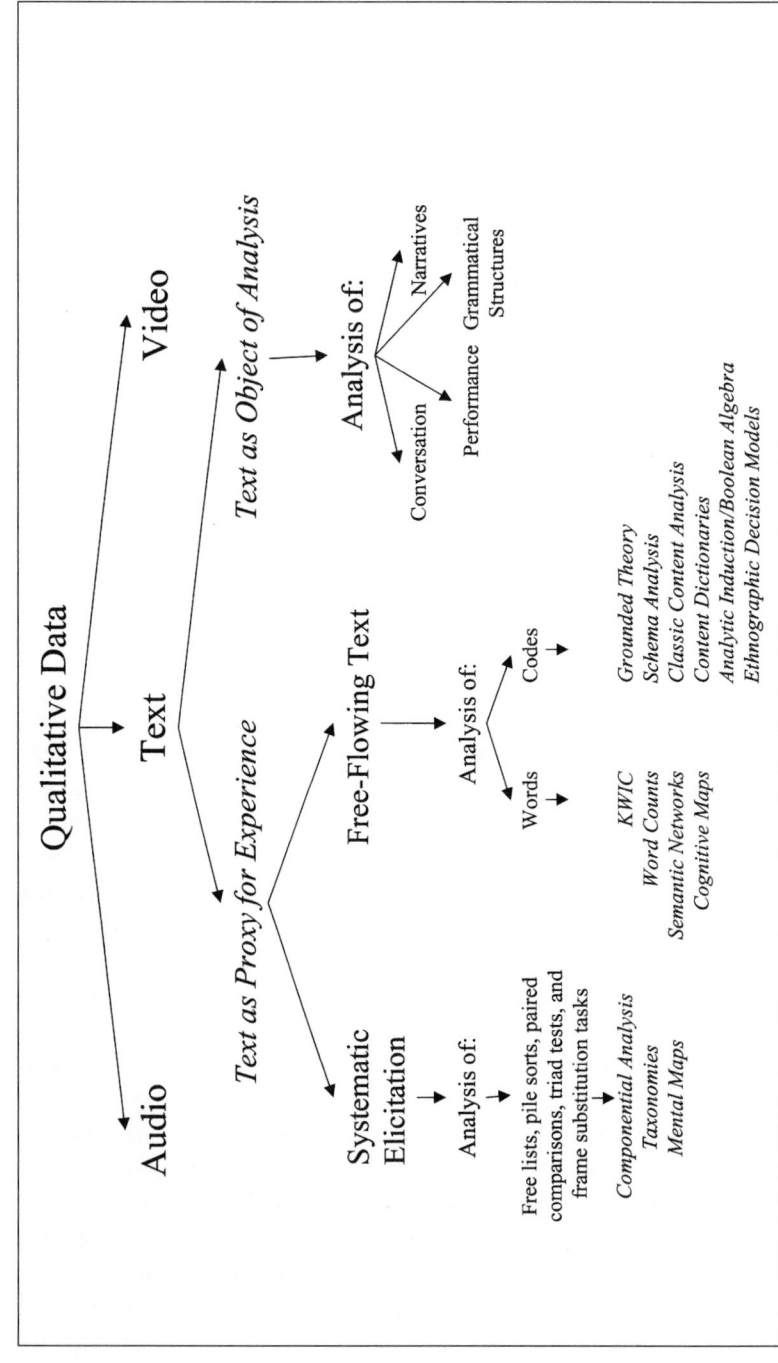

Figure 7.1. Typology of Qualitative Analysis Techniques

discourse) analysis, performance analysis, and formal linguistic analysis. Methods for analyses in this tradition are covered elsewhere in this *Handbook*. We focus here on methods used in the sociological tradition, which we take to include work across the social sciences.

There are two kinds of written texts in the sociological tradition: (a) words or phrases generated by techniques for systematic elicitation and (b) free-flowing texts, such as narratives, discourse, and responses to open-ended interview questions. In the next section, we describe some methods for collecting and analyzing words or phrases. Techniques for data collection include free lists, pile sorts, frame elicitations, and triad tests. Techniques for the analysis of these kinds of data include componential analysis, taxonomies, and mental maps.

We then turn to the analysis of free-flowing texts. We look first at methods that use raw text as their input—methods such as key-words-in-context, word counts, semantic network analysis, and cognitive maps. We then describe methods that require the reduction of text to codes. These include grounded theory, schema analysis, classical content analysis, content dictionaries, analytic induction, and ethnographic decision models. Each of these methods of analysis has advantages and disadvantages. Some are appropriate for exploring data, others for making comparisons, and others for building and testing models. Nothing does it all.

◆ Collecting and Analyzing Words or Phrases

Techniques for Systematic Elicitation

Researchers use techniques for systematic elicitation to identify lists of items that belong in a cultural domain and to assess the relationships among these items (for detailed reviews of these methods, see Bernard, 1994; Borgatti, 1998; Weller, 1998; Weller & Romney, 1988). Cultural domains comprise lists of words in a language that somehow "belong together." Some domains (such as animals, illnesses, things to eat) are very large and inclusive, whereas others (animals you can keep at home, illnesses that children get, brands of beer) are relatively small. Some lists (such as the list of terms for members of a family or the names of all the Major League Baseball teams) are agreed on by all native speakers of a language; others (such as the list of carpenters' tools) represent highly specialized knowledge, and still others (like the list of great left-handed baseball pitchers of the 20th century) are matters of heated debate. Below we review some of the most common systematic elicitation techniques and discuss how researchers analyze the data they generate.

Free Lists

Free lists are particularly useful for identifying the items in a cultural domain. To elicit domains, researchers might ask, "What kinds of illnesses do you know?" Some short, open-ended questions on surveys can be considered free lists, as can some responses generated from in-depth ethnographic interviews and focus groups. Investigators interpret the frequency of mention and the order in which items are mentioned in the lists as indicators of items' salience (for measures of salience, see Robbins & Nolan, 1997; Smith, 1993; Smith & Borgatti, 1998). The co-occurrence of items across lists and the proximity with which items appear in lists may be used as measures of similarity among items (Borgatti, 1998; Henley, 1969; for a clear example, see Fleisher & Harrington, 1998).

Paired Comparisons, Pile Sorts, Triad Tests

Researchers use paired comparisons, pile sorts, and triads tests to explore the *relationships* among items. Here are two questions we might ask someone in a paired comparison test about a list of fruits: (a) "On a scale of 1 to 5, how similar are lemons and watermelons with regard to sweetness?" (b) "Which is sweeter, watermelons or lemons?" The first question produces a set of fruit-by-fruit matrices, one for each respondent, the entries of which are scale values on the similarity of sweetness among all pairs of fruits. The second question produces, for each respondent, a perfect rank ordering of the set of fruits.

In a pile sort, the researcher asks each respondent to sort a set of cards or objects into piles. Item similarity is the number of times each pair of items is placed in the same pile (for examples, see Boster, 1994; Roos, 1998). In a triad test, the researcher presents sets of three items and asks each respondent either to "choose the two most similar items" or to "pick the item that is the most different." The similarity among pairs of items is the number of times people choose to keep pairs of items together (for some good examples, see Albert, 1991; Harman, 1998).

Frame Substitution

In the frame substitution task (D'Andrade, 1995; D'Andrade, Quinn, Nerlove, & Romney, 1972; Frake, 1964; Metzger & Williams, 1966), the researcher asks the respondent to link each item in a list of items with a list of attributes. D'Andrade et al. (1972) gave people a list of 30 illness terms and asked them to fill in the blanks in frames such as "You can catch _____ from other people," "You can have _____ and never know it," and "Most people get _____ at one time or other" (p. 12; for other examples of frame substitution, see Furbee & Benfer, 1983; Young, 1978).

Techniques for Analyzing Data About Cultural Domains

Researchers use these kinds of data to build several kinds of models about how people think. *Componential analysis* produces formal models of the elements in a cultural domain, and *taxonomies* display hierarchical associations among the elements in a domain. *Mental maps* are best for displaying fuzzy constructs and dimensions. We treat these in turn.

Componential Analysis

As we have outlined elsewhere, componential analysis (or feature analysis) is a formal, qualitative technique for studying the content of meaning (Bernard, 1994; Bernard & Ryan, 1998). Developed by linguists to identify the features and rules that distinguish one sound from another (Jakobson & Halle, 1956), the technique was elaborated by anthropologists in the 1950s and 1960s (Conklin, 1955; D'Andrade, 1995; Frake, 1962; Goodenough, 1956; Rushforth, 1982; Wallace, 1962). (For a particularly good description of how to apply the method, see Spradley, 1979, pp. 173-184.)

Componential analysis is based on the principle of distinctive features. Any two items (sounds, kinship terms, names of plants, names of animals, and so on) can be distinguished by some minimal set ($2n$) of binary features—that is, features that either occur or do not occur. It takes two features to distinguish four items ($2^2 = 4$, in other words), three features to distinguish eight items ($2^3 = 8$), and so on. The trick is to identify the smallest set of features that best describes the domain of interest. Table 7.1 shows that just three features are needed to describe kinds of horses.

TABLE 7.1 A Componential Analysis of Six Kinds of Horses

Name	Female	Neuter	Adult
Mare	+	–	+
Stallion	–	–	+
Gelding	–	+	+
Foal	–	+	–
Filly	+	–	–
Colt	–	–	–

SOURCE: Adapted from D'Andrade (1995).

Componential analysis produces models based on logical relationships among features. The models do not account for variations in the meanings of terms across individuals. For example, when we tried to do a componential analysis on the terms for cattle (*bull, cow, heifer, calf, steer,* and *ox*), we found that native speakers of English in the United States (even farmers) disagreed about the differences between *cow* and *heifer,* and between *steer* and *ox.* When the relationships among items are less well defined, taxonomies or mental models may be useful. Nor is there any intimation that componential analyses reflect how "people really think."

Taxonomies

Folk taxonomies are meant to capture the hierarchical structure in sets of terms and are commonly displayed as branching tree diagrams. Figure 7.1 presents a taxonomy of our own understanding of qualitative analysis techniques. Figure 7.2 depicts a taxonomy we have adapted from Pamela Erickson's (1997) study of the perceptions among clinicians and adolescents of methods of contraception. Researchers can elicit folk taxonomies directly by using successive pile sorts (Boster, 1994; Perchonock & Werner, 1969). This involves asking people to continually subdivide the piles of a free pile sort until each item is in its own individual pile. Taxonomic models can also be created with cluster analysis on the similarity data from paired comparisons, pile sorts, and triad tests. *Hierarchical cluster analysis* (Johnson, 1967) builds a taxonomic tree where each item appears in only one group.

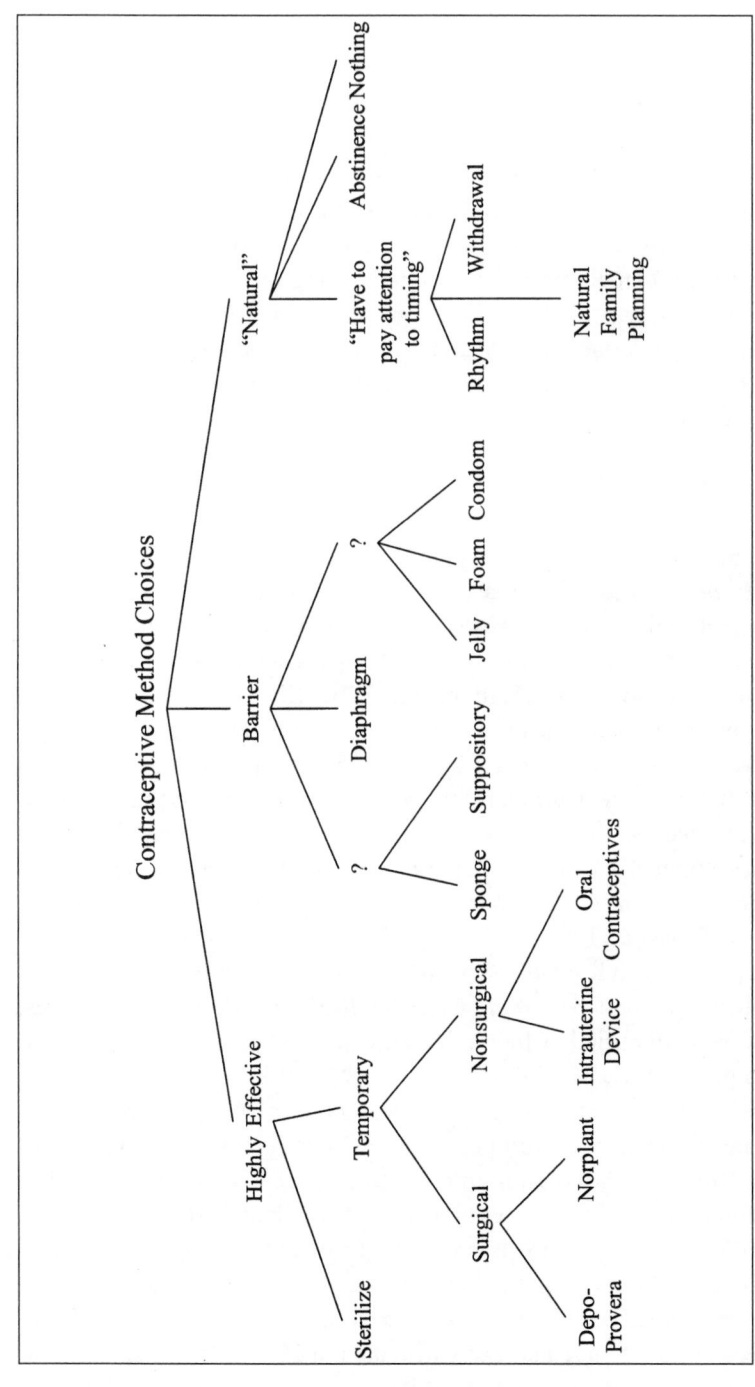

Figure 7.2. Clinicians' Taxonomy of Contraceptive Methods
SOURCE: Based on Erickson (1997).

Interinformant variation is common in folk taxonomies. That is, different people may use different words to refer to the same category of things. Some of Erickson's (1997) clinician informants referred to the "highly effective" group of methods as "safe," "more reliable," and "sure bets." Category labels need not be simple words, but may be complex phrases; for example, see the category in Figure 7.2 comprising contraceptive methods in which you "have to pay attention to timing." Sometimes, people have no labels at all for particular categories—at least none that they can dredge up easily—and categories, even when named, may be fuzzy and may overlap with other categories. *Overlapping cluster analysis* (Hartigan, 1975) identifies groups of items where a single item may appear in multiple groups.

Mental Maps

Mental maps are visual displays of the similarities among items, whether or not those items are organized hierarchically. One popular method for making these maps is by collecting data about the cognitive similarity or dissimilarity among a set of objects and then applying multidimensional scaling, or MDS, to the similarities (Kruskal & Wish, 1978).

Cognitive maps are meant to be directly analogous to physical maps. Consider a table of distances between all pairs of cities on a map. Objects (cities) that are very dissimilar have high mileage between them and are placed far apart on the map; objects that are less dissimilar have low mileage between them and are placed closer together. Pile sorts, triad tests, and paired comparison tests are measures of cognitive distance. For example, Ryan (1995) asked 11 literate Kom speakers in Cameroon to perform successive pile sorts on Kom illness terms. Figure 7.3 presents an MDS plot of the collective mental map of these terms. The five major illness categories, circled, were identified by hierarchical cluster analysis of the same matrix used to produce the MDS plot.[1]

Data from frame substitution tasks can be displayed with correspondence analysis (Weller & Romney, 1990).[2] Correspondence analysis scales both the rows and the columns into the same space. For example, Kirchler (1992) analyzed 562 obituaries of managers who had died in 1974, 1980, and 1986. He identified 31 descriptive categories from adjectives used in the obituaries and then used correspondence analysis to display how these categories were associated with men and women managers over time. Figure 7.4 shows that male managers who died in 1974 and 1980 were seen

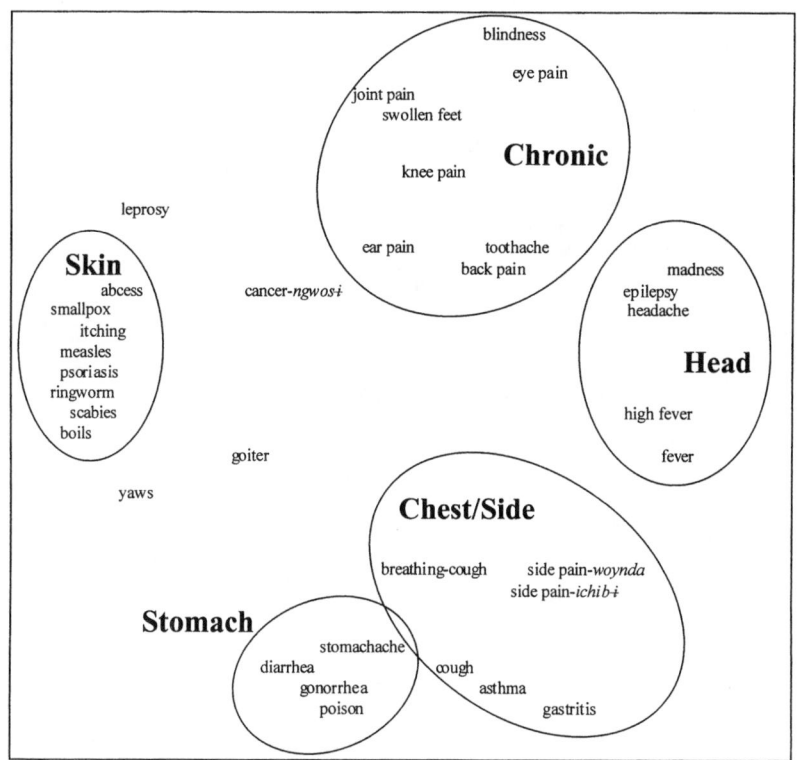

Figure 7.3. Mental Map of Kom Illness Terms

by their surviving friends and family as *active, intelligent, outstanding, conscientious,* and *experienced experts.* Although the managers who died in 1986 were still respected, they were more likely to be described as *entrepreneurs, opinion leaders,* and *decision makers.* Perceptions of female managers also changed, but they did not become more like their male counterparts. In 1974 and 1980, female managers were remembered for being nice people. They were described as *kind, likable,* and *adorable.* By 1986, women were remembered for their *courage* and *commitment.* Kirchler interpreted these data to mean that gender stereotypes changed in the early 1980s. By 1986, both male and female managers were perceived as working for success, but men impressed their colleagues through their knowledge and expertise, whereas women impressed their colleagues with motivation and engagement.

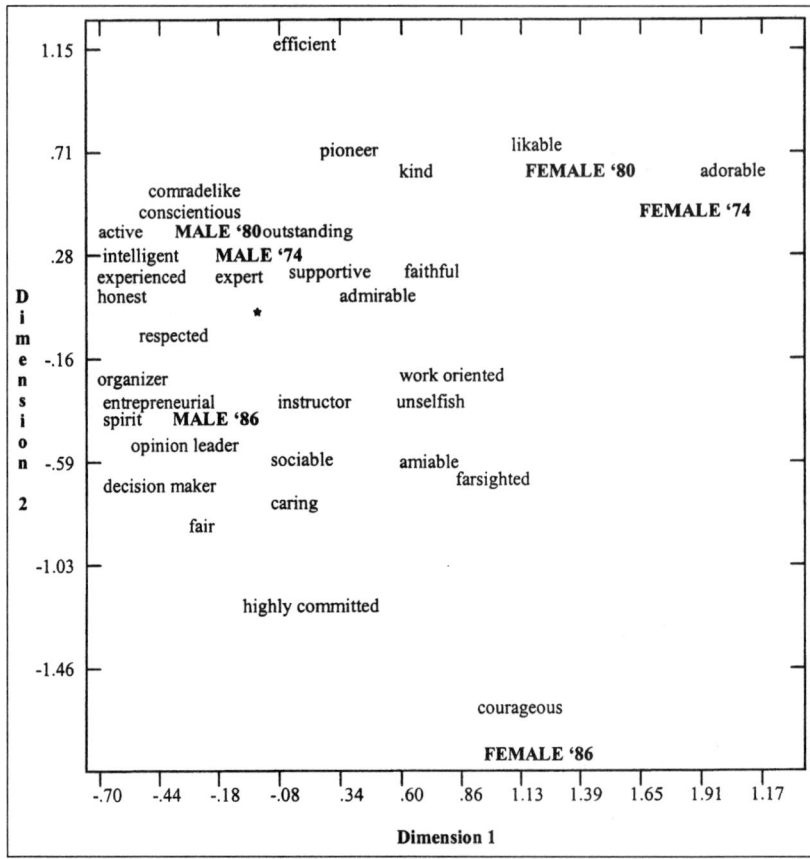

Figure 7.4. Correspondence Analysis of the Frequencies of 31 Disruptive Obituary Categories by Gender and Year of Publication

SOURCE: Erich Kirchler, "Adorable Woman, Expert Man: Changing Gender Images of Women and Men in Management," *European Journal of Social Psychology, 22* (1992), p. 371. Copyright 1992 by John Wiley & Sons Limited. Reproduced by permission of John Wiley & Sons Limited.

◆ Methods for Analyzing Free-Flowing Text

Although taxonomies, MDS maps, and the like are useful for analyzing short phrases or words, most qualitative data come in the form of free-flowing texts. There are two major types of analysis. In one, the text is segmented into its most basic meaningful components: words. In the other, meanings are found in large blocks of text.

Analyzing Words

Techniques for word analysis include key-words-in-context, word counts, structural analysis, and cognitive maps. We review each below.

Key-Words-in-Context

Researchers create key-words-in-context (KWIC) lists by finding all the places in a text where a particular word or phrase appears and printing it out in the context of some number of words (say, 30) before and after it. This produces a *concordance*. Well-known concordances have been done on sacred texts, such as the Old and New Testaments (Darton, 1976; Hatch & Redpath, 1954) and the Koran (Kassis, 1983), and on famous works of literature from Euripides (Allen & Italie, 1954) to Homer (Prendergast, 1971), to Beowulf (Bessinger, 1969), to Dylan Thomas (Farringdon & Farringdon, 1980). (On the use of concordances in modern literary studies, see Burton, 1981a, 1981b, 1982; McKinnon, 1993.)

Word Counts

Word counts are useful for discovering patterns of ideas in any body of text, from field notes to responses to open-ended questions. Students of mass media have used use word counts to trace the ebb and flow of support for political figures over time (Danielson & Lasorsa, 1997; Pool, 1952). Differences in the use of words common to the writings of James Madison and Alexander Hamilton led Mosteller and Wallace (1964) to conclude that Madison and not Hamilton had written 12 of the *Federalist Papers*. (For other examples of authorship studies, see Martindale & McKenzie, 1995; Yule 1944/1968.)

Word analysis (like constant comparison, memoing, and other techniques) can help researchers to discover themes in texts. Ryan and Weisner (1996) instructed fathers and mothers of adolescents in Los Angeles: "Describe your children. In your own words, just tell us about them." Ryan and Weisner identified all the unique words in the answers they got to that grand-tour question and noted the number of times each word was used by mothers and by fathers. Mothers, for example, were more likely to use words like *friends, creative, time,* and *honest;* fathers were more likely to use words like *school, good, lack, student, enjoys, independent,* and *extremely.* This suggests that mothers, on first mention, express concern

269

over interpersonal issues, whereas fathers appear to prioritize achieve-ment-oriented and individualistic issues. This kind of analysis considers neither the contexts in which the words occur nor whether the words are used negatively or positively, but distillations like these can help research-ers to identify important constructs and can provide data for systematic comparisons across groups.

Structural Analysis and Semantic Networks

Network, or structural, analysis examines the properties that emerge from relations among things. As early as 1959, Charles Osgood created word co-occurrence matrices and applied factor analysis and dimensional plotting to describe the relations among words. Today, semantic network analysis is a growing field (Barnett & Danowski, 1992; Danowski, 1982, 1993). For example, Nolan and Ryan (1999) asked 59 undergraduates (30 women and 29 men) to describe their "most memorable horror film." The researchers identified the 45 most common adjectives, verbs, and nouns used across the descriptions of the films. They produced a 45(word)-by-59(person) matrix, the cells of which indicated whether each student had used each key word in his or her description. Finally, Nolan and Ryan cre-ated a 59(person)-by-59(person) similarity matrix of *people* based on the co-occurrence of the words in their descriptions.

Figure 7.5 shows the MDS of Nolan and Ryan's data. Although there is some overlap, it is pretty clear that the men and women in their study used different sets of words to describe horror films. Men were more likely to use words such as *teenager, disturbing, violence, rural, dark, country,* and *hillbilly,* whereas women were more likely to use words such as *boy, little, devil, young, horror, father,* and *evil.* Nolan and Ryan interpreted these results to mean that the men had a fear of rural people and places, whereas the women were more afraid of betrayed intimacy and spiritual posses-sion. (For other examples of the use of word-by-word matrices, see Jang & Barnett, 1994; Schnegg & Bernard, 1996.) This example makes abun-dantly clear the value of turning qualitative data into quantitative data: Doing so can produce information that engenders deeper interpretations of the meanings in the original corpus of qualitative data. Just as in any mass of numbers, it is hard to see patterns in words unless one first does some kind of data reduction. More about this below.

As in word analysis, one appeal of semantic network analysis is that the data processing is done by computer. The only investigator bias intro-

Figure 7.5. Multidimensional Scaling of Informants Based on Words Used in Descriptions of Horror Films

duced in the process is the decision to include words that occur at least 10 times or 5 times or whatever. (For discussion of computer programs that produce word-by-text and word-by-word co-occurrence matrices, see Borgatti, 1992; Doerfel & Barnett, 1996.) There is, however, no guarantee that the output of any word co-occurrence matrix will be meaningful, and it is notoriously easy to read patterns (and thus meanings) into any set of items.

Cognitive Maps

Cognitive map analysis combines the intuition of human coders with the quantitative methods of network analysis. Carley's work with this technique is instructive. Carley argues that if cognitive models or schemata exist, they are expressed in the texts of people's speech and can be represented as networks of concepts (see Carley & Palmquist, 1992,

271

p. 602), an approach also suggested by D'Andrade (1991). To the extent that cognitive models are widely shared, Carley asserts, even a very small set of texts will contain the information required for describing the models, especially for narrowly defined arenas of life.

In one study, Carley (1993) asked students some questions about the work of scientists. Here are two examples she collected:

> Student A: I found that scientists engage in research in order to make discoveries and generate new ideas. Such research by scientists is hard work and often involves collaboration with other scientists which leads to discoveries which make the scientists famous. Such collaboration may be informal, such as when they share new ideas over lunch, or formal, such as when they are coauthors of a paper.

> Student B: It was hard work to research famous scientists engaged in collaboration and I made many informal discoveries. My research showed that scientists engaged in collaboration with other scientists are coauthors of at least one paper containing their new ideas. Some scientists make formal discoveries and have new ideas. (p. 89)

Carley compared the students' texts by analyzing 11 concepts: *I, scientists, research, hard work, collaboration, discoveries, new ideas, formal, informal, coauthors, paper.* She coded the concepts for their strength, sign (positive or negative), and direction (whether one concept is logically prior to others), not just for their existence. She found that although students used the same concepts in their texts, the concepts clearly had different meanings. To display the differences in understandings, Carley advocates the use of maps that show the relations between and among concepts. Figure 7.6 shows Carley's maps of two of the texts.

Carley's approach is promising because it combines the automation of word counts with the sensitivity of human intuition and interpretation. As Carley recognizes, however, a lot depends on who does the coding. Different coders will produce different maps by making different coding choices. In the end, native-language competence is one of the fundamental methodological requirements for analysis (see also Carley, 1997; Carley & Kaufer, 1993; Carley & Palmquist, 1992; Palmquist, Carley, & Dale, 1997).

Key-words-in-context, word counts, structural analysis, and cognitive maps all reduce text to the fundamental meanings of specific words. These reductions make it easy for researchers to identify general patterns and

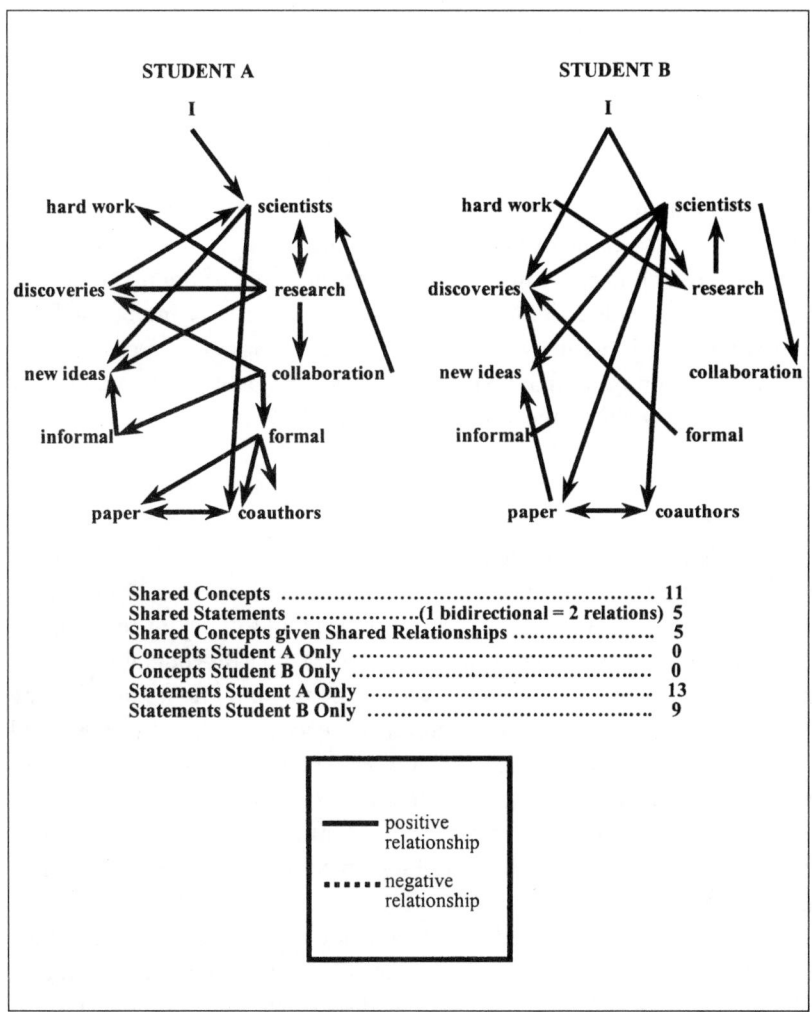

Figure 7.6. Coded Maps of Two Students' Texts
SOURCE: Kathleen Carley, "Coding Choices for Textual Analysis: A Comparison of Content Analysis and Map Analysis," in P. Marsden (Ed.), *Sociological Methodology* (Oxford: Blackwell, 1993), p. 104. Copyright 1993 by the American Sociological Association. Reproduced by permission of the American Sociological Association.

make comparisons across texts. With the exception of KWIC, however, these techniques remove words from the contexts in which they occur. Subtle nuances are likely to be lost—which brings us to the analysis of whole texts.

Analyzing Chunks of Text: Coding

Coding is the heart and soul of *whole-text analysis.* Coding forces the researcher to make judgments about the meanings of contiguous blocks of text. The fundamental tasks associated with coding are sampling, identifying themes, building codebooks, marking texts, constructing models (relationships among codes), and testing these models against empirical data. We outline each task below. We then describe some of the major coding traditions: grounded theory, schema analysis, classic content analysis, content dictionaries, analytic induction, and ethnographic decision trees. We want to emphasize that no particular tradition, whether humanistic or positivistic, has a monopoly on text analysis.

Sampling

Investigators must first identify a *corpus of texts,* and then select the *units of analysis within the texts.* Selection can be either random or purposive, but the choice is not a matter of cleaving to one epistemological tradition or another. Waitzkin and Britt (1993) did a thoroughgoing interpretive analysis of encounters between patients and doctors by selecting 50 texts at random from 336 audiotaped encounters. Trost (1986) used classical content analysis to test how the relationships between teenagers and their families might be affected by five different dichotomous variables. He intentionally selected five cases from each of the 32 possible combinations of the five variables and conducted $32 \times 5 = 160$ interviews.

Samples may also be based on extreme or deviant cases, cases that illustrate maximum variety on variables, cases that are somehow typical of a phenomenon, or cases that confirm or disconfirm a hypothesis. (For reviews of nonrandom sampling strategies, see Patton, 1990, pp. 169-186; Sandelowski, 1995b.) A single case may be sufficient to display something of substantive importance, but Morse (1994) suggests using at least six participants in studies where one is trying to understand the essence of experience. Morse also suggests 30-50 interviews for ethnographies and grounded theory studies. Finding themes and building theory may require fewer cases than comparing across groups and testing hypotheses or models.

Once the researcher has established a sample of texts, the next step is to identify the basic units of analysis. The units may be entire texts (books, interviews, responses to an open-ended question on a survey), grammatical segments (words, word senses, sentences, themes, paragraphs), formatting units (rows, columns, or pages), or simply chunks of text that reflect a single theme—what Krippendorf (1980, p. 62) calls *thematic units*. In general, where the objective is to compare across texts (as in the case of classical content analysis), the units of analysis need to be nonoverlapping. (For discussion of additional kinds of units of analysis, see Krippendorf, 1980, pp. 57-64; Tesch, 1990.)

Finding Themes

Themes are abstract (and often fuzzy) constructs that investigators identify before, during, and after data collection. Literature reviews are rich sources for themes, as are investigators' own experiences with subject matter. More often than not, however, researchers induce themes from the text itself.

There is more than one way to induce themes. Grounded theorists suggest a careful, line-by-line reading of the text while looking for processes, actions, assumptions, and consequences. Schema analysts suggest looking for metaphors, for repetitions of words, and for shifts in content (Agar & Hobbs, 1985). Content analysts have used KWIC to identify different meanings. Spradley (1979, pp. 199-201) suggests looking for evidence of social conflict, cultural contradictions, informal methods of social control, things that people do in managing impersonal social relationships, methods by which people acquire and maintain achieved and ascribed status, and information about how people solve problems. Each of these arenas is likely to yield major themes in cultures. Barkin, Ryan, and Gelberg (1999) had multiple coders independently sort informants' statements into thematic piles. They then used multidimensional scaling and cluster analysis on the pile-sort data to identify subthemes shared across coders. (For another example, see Patterson, Bettini, & Nussbaum, 1993.)

Willms et al. (1990) and Miles and Huberman (1994) suggest that researchers start with some general themes derived from reading the literature and add more themes and subthemes as they go. Shelley (1992) followed this advice in her study of how social networks affect people with end-stage kidney disease. She used the *Outline of Cultural Materials* (Murdock, 1971) as the basis of her coding scheme and then added additional themes based on a close reading of the text. Bulmer (1979) lists 10 different sources of themes, including literature reviews, professional definitions, local commonsense constructs, and researchers' values and prior experiences. He also notes that investigators' general theoretical orientations, the richness of the existing literature, and the characteristics of the phenomena being studied influence the themes researchers are likely to find.

No matter how the researcher actually *does* inductive coding, by the time he or she has identified the themes and refined them to the point where they can be applied to an entire corpus of texts, a lot of interpretive analysis has already been done. Miles and Huberman (1994) say simply, "Coding is analysis" (p. 56).

Building Codebooks

Codebooks are simply organized lists of codes (often in hierarchies). How a researcher can develop a codebook is covered in detail by Dey (1993, pp. 95-151), Crabtree and Miller (1992), and Miles and Huberman (1994, pp. 55-72). MacQueen, McLellan, Kay, and Milstein (1998) suggest that a good codebook should include a detailed description of each code, inclusion and exclusion criteria, and exemplars of real text for each theme. If a theme is particularly abstract, we suggest that the researcher also provide examples of the theme's boundaries and even some cases that are closely related but *not* included within the theme. Coding is supposed to be data *reduction,* not proliferation (Miles, 1979, pp. 593-594). The codes themselves are mnemonic devices used to identify or mark the specific themes in a text. They can be either words or numbers—whatever the researcher finds easiest to remember and to apply.

Qualitative researchers working as a team need to agree up front on what to include in their codebook. Morse (1994) suggests beginning the process with a group meeting. MacQueen et al. (1998) suggest that a single team member should be designated "Keeper of the Codebook"—we strongly agree.

Good codebooks are developed and refined as the research goes along. Kurasaki (1997) interviewed 20 *sansei*—third-generation Japanese Americans—and used a grounded theory approach to do her analysis of ethnic identity. She started with seven major themes. As the analysis progressed, she split the major themes into subthemes. Eventually, she combined two of the major themes and wound up with six major themes and a total of 18 subthemes. (Richards & Richards, 1991, discuss the theoretical principles related to hierarchical coding structures that emerge out of the data.

Araujo, 1995, uses an example from his own research on the traditional British manufacturing industry to describe the process of designing and refining hierarchical codes.)

The development and refinement of coding categories have long been central tasks in classical content analysis (see Berelson, 1952, pp. 147-168; Holsti, 1969, pp. 95-126) and are particularly important in the construction of concept dictionaries (Deese, 1969; Stone, Dunphy, Smith, & Ogilvie, 1966, pp. 134-168). Krippendorf (1980, pp. 71-84) and Carey, Morgan, and Oxtoby (1996) note that much of codebook refinement comes during the training of coders to mark the text and in the act of checking for intercoder agreement. Disagreement among multiple coders shows when the codebook is ambiguous and confusing. The first run also allows the researcher to identify good examples to include in the codebook.

Marking Texts

The act of coding involves the assigning of codes to contiguous units of text. Coding serves two distinct purposes in qualitative analysis. First, codes act as *tags* to mark off text in a corpus for later retrieval or indexing. Tags are not associated with any fixed units of text; they can mark simple phrases or extend across multiple pages. Second, codes act as *values* assigned to fixed units (see Bernard, 1991, 1994; Seidel & Kelle, 1995). Here, codes are nominal, ordinal, or ratio scale values that are applied to fixed, nonoverlapping units of analysis. The nonoverlapping units can be texts (such as paragraphs, pages, documents), episodes, cases, or persons. *Codes as tags* are associated with grounded theory and schema analysis (reviewed below). *Codes as values* are associated with classic content analysis and content dictionaries. The two types of codes are not mutually exclusive, but the use of one gloss—*code*—for both concepts can be misleading.

Analyzing Chunks of Texts: Building Conceptual Models

Once the researcher identifies a set of things (themes, concepts, beliefs, behaviors), the next step is to identify how these things are linked to each other in a theoretical model (Miles & Huberman, 1994, pp. 134-137). Models are sets of abstract constructs and the relationships among them

(Bulmer, 1979). Grounded theory, schema analysis, ethnographic decision modeling, and analytic induction all include model-building phases.

Once a model starts to take shape, the researcher looks for negative cases—cases that don't fit the model. Negative cases either disconfirm parts of a model or suggest new connections that need to be made. In either instance, negative cases need to be accommodated. Negative case analysis is discussed in detail by Becker, Geer, Hughes, and Strauss (1961, pp. 37-45), Strauss and Corbin (1990, pp. 108-109), Lincoln and Guba (1985, pp. 309-313), Dey (1993, pp. 226-233), Miles and Huberman (1994, p. 271), and Becker (1998), and is used by schema analysts (Quinn, 1997), ethnographic decision modelers (Gladwin, 1989), and scholars who use analytic induction (Bloor, 1976; Cressey, 1953/1971; Lindesmith, 1947/1968).

In ethnographic decision modeling and in classical content analysis, models are built on one set of data and tested on another. In their original formulation, Glaser and Strauss (1967) emphasized that building grounded theory models is a step in the research process and that models need to be validated. Grounded theorists and schema analysts today are more likely to validate their models by seeking confirmation from expert informants than by analyzing a second set of data. For example, Kearney, Murphy, and Rosenbaum (1994) checked the validity of their model of crack mothers' experiences by presenting it to knowledgeable respondents who were familiar with the research.

Regardless of the kind of reliability and validity checks, models are simplifications of reality. They can be made more or less complicated and may capture all or only a portion of the variance in a given set of data. It is up to the investigator and his or her peers to decide how much a particular model is supposed to describe.

Below we review some of the most common methods researchers use to analyze blocks of texts. These include grounded theory, schema analysis, classical content analysis, content dictionaries, analytic induction, and ethnographic decision tree analysis.

Grounded Theory

Grounded theorists want to understand people's experiences in as rigorous and detailed a manner as possible. They want to identify categories and concepts that emerge from text and link these concepts into substantive and formal theories. The original formulation of the method (Glaser & Strauss, 1967) is still useful, but later works are easier to read and more practical (Charmaz, 1990; Lincoln & Guba, 1985; Lonkila, 1995; Strauss, 1987). Strauss and Corbin (1990), Dey (1993), and Becker (1998) provide especially useful guidance. (For some recent examples of grounded theory research, see Hunt & Ropo, 1995; Irurita, 1996; Kearney et al., 1994; Kearney, Murphy, Irwin, & Rosenbaum, 1995; Sohier, 1993; Strauss & Corbin, 1997; Wilson & Hutchinson, 1996; Wright, 1997.)

Grounded theory is an iterative process by which the analyst becomes more and more "grounded" in the data and develops increasingly richer concepts and models of how the phenomenon being studied really works. To do this, the grounded theorist collects verbatim transcripts of interviews and reads through a small sample of text (usually line by line). Sandelowski (1995a) observes that analysis of texts begins with proof-reading the material and simply underlining key phrases "because they make some as yet inchoate sense" (p. 373). In a process called "open coding," the investigator identifies potential themes by pulling together real examples from the text (Agar, 1996; Bernard, 1994; Bogdan & Biklen, 1992; Lincoln & Guba, 1985; Lofland & Lofland, 1995; Strauss & Corbin, 1990; Taylor & Bogdan, 1984). Identifying the categories and terms used by informants themselves is called "*in vivo* coding" (Strauss & Corbin, 1990). As grounded theorists develop their concepts and categories, they often decide they need to gather more data from informants.

As coding categories emerge, the investigator links them together in theoretical models. One technique is to compare and contrast themes and concepts. When, why, and under what conditions do these themes occur in the text? Glazer and Strauss (1967, pp. 101-116) refer to this as the "constant comparison method," and it is similar to the contrast questions Spradley (1979, pp. 160-172) suggests researchers ask informants. (For other good descriptions of the comparison method, see Glaser, 1978, pp. 56-72; Strauss & Corbin, 1990, pp. 84-95.)

Another useful tool for building theoretical models is the conditional matrix described by Strauss and Corbin (1990, pp. 158-175). The conditional matrix is a set of concentric circles, each level corresponding to a different unit of influence. At the center are actions and interactions; the outer rings represent international and national concerns, and the inner rings represent individual and small group influences on action. The matrix is designed to help investigators to be more sensitive to conditions, actions/interactions, and consequences of a phenomenon and to order these conditions and consequences into theories.

Memoing is one of the principal techniques for recording relationships among themes. Strauss and Corbin (1990, pp. 18, 73-74, 109-129, 197-219) discuss three kinds of memos: code notes, theory notes, and operational notes. Code notes describe the concepts that are being discovered in "the discovery of grounded theory." In theory notes, the researcher tries to summarize his or her ideas about what is going on in the text. Operational notes are about practical matters.

Once a model starts to take shape, the researcher uses negative case analysis to identify problems and make appropriate revisions. The end results of grounded theory are often displayed through the presentation of segments of text—verbatim quotes from informants—as exemplars of concepts and theories. These illustrations may be prototypical examples of central tendencies or they may represent exceptions to the norm. Grounded theory researchers also display their theoretical results in maps of the major categories and the relationships among them (Kearney et al., 1995; Miles & Huberman, 1994, pp. 134-137). These "concept maps" are similar to the personal semantic networks described by Leinhardt (1987, 1989), Strauss (1992), and D'Andrade (1991) (see below).

Schema Analysis

Schema analysis combines elements of the linguistic and sociological traditions. It is based on the idea that people must use cognitive simplifications to help make sense of the complex information to which they are constantly exposed (Casson, 1983, p. 430). Schank and Abelson (1977) postulate that schemata—or scripts, as they call them—enable culturally skilled people to fill in details of a story or event. It is, says Wodak (1992, p. 525), our schemata that lead us to interpret Mona Lisa's smile as evidence of her perplexity or her desperation.

From a methodological view, schema analysis is similar to grounded theory. Both begin with a careful reading of verbatim texts and seek to discover and link themes into theoretical models. In a series of articles, Quinn (1982, 1987, 1992, 1996, 1997) has analyzed hundreds of hours of interviews to discover concepts underlying American marriage and to show how these concepts are tied together. Quinn's (1997) method is to "exploit clues in ordinary discourse for what they tell us about shared cognition—to glean what people must have in mind in order to say the things they do" (p. 140). She begins by looking at patterns of speech and the repetition of key words and phrases, paying particular attention to informants' use of metaphors and the commonalities in their reasoning about marriage. Quinn found that the hundreds of metaphors in her corpus of texts fit into just eight linked classes, which she calls lastingness, sharedness, compatibility, mutual benefit, difficulty, effort, success (or failure), and risk of failure.

Metaphors and proverbs are not the only linguistic features used to infer meaning from text. D'Andrade (1991) notes that "perhaps the simplest and most direct indication of schematic organization in naturalistic discourse is the repetition of associative linkages" (p. 294). He observes that "indeed, anyone who has listened to long stretches of talk—whether generated by a friend, spouse, workmate, informant, or patient—knows how frequently people circle through the same network of ideas" (p. 287).

In a study of blue-collar workers in Rhode Island, Claudia Strauss (1992) refers to these ideas as "personal semantic networks." She describes such a network from one of her informants. On rereading her intensive interviews with one of the workers, Strauss found that her informant repeatedly referred to ideas associated with greed, money, businessmen, siblings, and "being different." She displays the relationships among these ideas by writing the concepts on a page of paper and connecting them with lines and explanations.

Price (1987) observes that when people tell stories, they assume that their listeners share with them many assumptions about how the world works, and so they leave out information that "everyone knows." Thus she looks for what is *not* said in order to identify underlying cultural assumptions (p. 314).

For more examples of the search for cultural schemata in texts, see Holland's (1985) study of the reasoning that Americans apply to interpersonal problems, Kempton's (1987) study of ordinary Americans' theories of home heat control, Claudia Strauss's (1997) study of what chemical plant workers and their neighbors think about the free enterprise system, and Agar and Hobbs's (1985) analysis of how an informant became a burglar. We next turn to the two other methods used across the social sciences for analyzing text: classical content analysis and content dictionaries.

Displaying Concepts and Models

Visual displays are an important part of qualitative analysis. Selecting key quotes as exemplars, building matrices or forms, and laying theories out in the form of flowcharts or maps are all potent ways to communicate ideas visually to others. Models are typically displayed using boxes and arrows, with the boxes containing themes and the arrows representing the relationships among them. Lines can be unidirectional or bidirectional. For example, taxonomies are models in which the lines represent the super- and subordinate relationships among items. Relationships can include causality, association, choices, and time, to name a few.

A widely used method for describing themes is the presentation of direct quotes from respondents—quotes that lead the reader to understand quickly what it may have taken the researcher months or years to figure out. The researcher chooses segments of text—verbatim quotes from respondents—as exemplars of concepts, of theories, and of negative cases. Ryan (1999) has used multiple coders to identify typical quotes. He asks 10 coders to mark the same corpus of text for three themes. Ryan argues that the text marked by all the coders represents the central tendency or typical examples of the abstract constructs, whereas text marked by only some of the coders represents less typical examples and is more typical of the "edges" of the construct.

Tables can be used to organize and display raw text or can be used to summarize qualitative data along multiple dimensions (rows and columns). The cells can be filled with verbatim quotes (Bernard & Ashton-Voyoucalos, 1976; Leinhardt & Smith, 1985, p. 254; Miles & Huberman, 1994, p. 130), summary statements (Yoder, 1995), or symbols (Fjellman & Gladwin, 1985; Van Maanen, Miller, & Johnson, 1982). (For a range of presentation formats, see Bernard, 1994; Miles & Huberman, 1994; Werner & Schoepfle, 1987.)

Classical Content Analysis

Whereas grounded theory is concerned with the discovery of data-induced hypotheses, classical content analysis comprises techniques for reducing texts to a unit-by-variable matrix and analyzing that matrix quantitatively to test hypotheses. The researcher can produce a matrix by applying a set of codes to a set of qualitative data (including written texts as well as audio and video media). Unlike grounded theory or schema analysis, content analysis assumes that the codes of interest have already been discovered and described.

Once the researcher has selected a sample of texts, the next step in classical content analysis is to code each unit for each of the themes or variables in the codebook. This produces a unit-by-variable matrix that can be analyzed using a variety of statistical techniques. For example, Cowan and O'Brien (1990) tested whether males or females are more likely to be survivors in slasher films. Conventional wisdom about such films suggests that victims are mostly women and slashers are mostly men. Cowan and O'Brien selected a corpus of 56 slasher films and identified 474 victims. They coded each victim for gender and survival. They found that slashers are mostly men, but it turned out that victims are equally likely to be male or female. Women who survive are less likely to be shown engaging in sexual behavior and are less likely to be physically attractive than their nonsurviving counterparts. Male victims are cynical, egotistical, and dictatorial. Cowan and O'Brien conclude that, in slasher films, sexually pure women survive and "unmitigated masculinity" leads to death (p. 195).

The coding of texts is usually assigned to multiple coders so that the researcher can see whether the constructs being investigated are shared and whether multiple coders can reliably apply the same codes. Typically, investigators first calculate the percentage of agreement among coders for each variable or theme. They then apply a correction formula to take account of the fact that some fraction of agreement will always occur by chance. The amount of that fraction depends on the number of coders and the precision of measurement for each code. If two people code a theme present or absent, they could agree, ceteris paribus, on any answer 25% of the time by chance. If a theme, such as wealth, is measured ordinally (low, medium, high), then the likelihood of chance agreement changes accordingly. Cohen's (1960) kappa, or K, is a popular measure for taking these chances into account. When K is zero, agreement is what might be expected by chance. When K is negative, the observed level of agreement is less than one would expect by chance. How much intercoder agreement is enough? The standards are still ad hoc, but Krippendorf (1980, pp. 147-148) advocates agreement of at least .70 and notes that some scholars (e.g., Brouwer, Clark, Gerbner, & Krippendorf, 1969) use a cutoff of .80. Fleiss (1971) and Light (1971) expand kappa to handle multiple coders. For other measures of intercoder agreement, see Krippendorf (1980, pp. 147-154) and Craig (1981).

Reliability "concerns the extent to which an experiment, test, or any measuring procedure yields the same results on repeated trials" (Carmines & Zeller, 1979, p. 11). A high level of intercoder agreement is evidence that a theme has some external validity and is not just a figment of the investigator's imagination (Mitchell, 1979). Not surprisingly, investigators have suggested many ways to assess validity (for reviews of key issues, see Campbell, 1957; Campbell & Stanley, 1963; Cook & Campbell, 1979; Denzin, 1997; Fielding & Fielding, 1986; Guba, 1981; Guba & Lincoln, 1982; Hammersley, 1992; Kirk & Miller, 1986; Lincoln & Guba, 1985). Bernard (1994) argues that, ultimately, the validity of a concept depends on the utility of the device that measures it and the collective judgment of the scientific community that a construct and its measure are valid. "In the end," he says, "we are left to deal with the effects of our judgments, which is just as it should be. Valid measurement makes valid data, but validity itself depends on the collective opinion of researchers" (p. 43). *Generalizability* refers to the degree to which the findings are applicable to other populations or samples. It draws on the degree to which the original data were representative of a larger population.

For reviews of work in content analysis, see Pool (1959); Gerbner, Holsti, Krippendorf, Paisley, and Stone (1969); Holsti (1969); Krippendorf (1980); Weber (1990); and Roberts (1997). Examples of classical content analysis can be found in media studies (Hirschman, 1987; Kolbe & Albanese, 1996; Spiggle, 1986), political rhetoric (Kaid, Tedesco, & McKinnon, 1996), folklore (Johnson & Price-Williams, 1997), business relations (Spears, Mowen, & Chakraborty, 1996), health care delivery (Potts, Runyan, Zerger, & Marchetti, 1996; Sleath, Svarstad, & Roter, 1997), and law (Imrich, Mullin, & Linz, 1995). Classical content analysis is also the fundamental means by which anthropologists test cross-cultural hypotheses (Bradley, Moore, Burton, & White, 1990; Ember & Ember, 1992; White & Burton, 1988). For early, but fundamental, criticisms of the approach, see Kracauer (1953) and George (1959).

Content Dictionaries

Computer-based, general-purpose content analysis dictionaries allow investigators to automate the coding of texts. To build such dictionaries, researchers assign words, by hand, to one or more categories (there are typically 50-60 categories in computerized content analysis dictionaries) according to a set of rules. The rules are part of a computer program that parses new texts, assigning words to categories.

Work on content dictionaries began in the 1960s with the General Inquirer and continues to this day (Kelly & Stone, 1975; Stone et al., 1966; Zuell, Weber, & Mohler, 1989). The General Inquirer is a computer program that uses a dictionary (the *Harvard Psychosocial Dictionary*) to parse and assign text to coded categories. Over time, the dictionary has been updated. The latest version (*Harvard IV*) contains more than 10,000 words and can distinguish among multiple meanings of words (Rosenberg, Schnurr, & Oxman, 1990, p. 303). Because such dictionaries do not contain all the words in the English language, investigators can assign unrecognized words to categories as they see fit, a process of further modifying the "codebook."

How effective are computer-based dictionaries? An early version of the General Inquirer was tested on 66 suicide notes—33 written by men who had actually taken their own lives and 33 written by men who were asked to produce simulated suicide notes. The program parsed the texts and picked the actual suicide notes 91% of the time (Ogilvie, Stone, & Schneidman, 1966). Content dictionaries do not need to be very big to be useful. Colby (1966) created a simple dictionary to distinguish between Navaho and Zuni responses to thematic apperception tests. For additional examples of special-purpose dictionaries in content analysis, see Fan and Shaffer (1990), Furbee (1996), Holsti (1966), Jehn and Werner (1993), Laffal (1990, 1995), McTavish and Pirro (1990), and Schnurr, Rosenberg, Oxman, and Tucker (1986).

Content dictionaries are attractive because they are entirely reliable and automated, but, as Shapiro (1997) argues, this may be offset by a decrease in validity. For the time being, only humans can parse certain subtleties of meaning reflected in context (Viney, 1983), but computer-based dictionaries are getting better all the time. For example, texts are now scored by computer for the Gottschalk-Gleser psychological scales (measuring various forms of anxiety and hostility) with greater than .80 reliability (Gottschalk & Bechtel, 1993).

Analytic Induction and Boolean Tests

Analytic induction is a formal, nonquantitative method for building up causal explanations of phenomena from a close examination of cases. It was proposed as an alternative to statistical analysis by Znaniecki (1934, pp. 249-331), modified by Lindesmith (1947/1968) and Cressey (1953/ 1971), and is discussed by Denzin (1978), Bulmer (1979), Manning (1982), and Becker (1998), among others. (For critiques of the approach, see Robinson, 1951.) The method is a formal kind of negative case analysis.

The technique can be described in a series of steps: First, define a phenomenon that requires explanation and propose an explanation. Next, examine a case to see if the explanation fits. If it does, then examine another case. An explanation is accepted until a new case falsifies it. When a case is found that doesn't fit, then, under the rules of analytic induction, the alternatives are to change the explanation (so that you can include the new case) or redefine the phenomenon (so that you exclude the nuisance case). Ideally, the process continues until a universal explanation for all known cases of a phenomenon is attained. Explaining cases by declaring them all unique is a tempting but illegitimate option. Classic examples of analytic induction include Lindesmith's (1947/1968) study of drug addicts, Cressey's (1953/1971) study of embezzlers, and McCleary's (1978) study of how parole officers decide when one of their charges is in violation of parole. For a particularly clear example of the technique, see Bloor's (1976, 1978) analysis of how doctors decide whether or not to remove children's tonsils.

Ragin (1987, 1994) formalized the logic of analytic induction, using a Boolean approach, and Romme (1995) applies the approach to textual data. Boolean algebra involves just two states (true and false, present and absent), but even with such simple inputs, things can get very complicated, very quickly. With just three dichotomous causal conditions (A and not A, B and not B, and C and not C) and one outcome variable (D and not D), there are 16 possible cases: A, B, C, D; A, not B, C, D; A, B, not C, D; and so on. Boolean analysis involves setting up what is known as a truth table, or a matrix of the actual versus the possible outcomes. (For more on truth tables and how they are related to negative case analysis, see Becker, 1998, pp. 146-214.)

Schweizer (1991, 1996) applied this method in his analysis of conflict and social status among residents of Chen Village, China. (For a discussion of Schweizer's data collection and analysis methods, see Bernard & Ryan, 1998.) All the data about the actors in this political drama were extracted from a historical narrative about Chen Village. Like classic content analysis and cognitive mapping, analytic induction requires that human coders read and code text and then produce an event-by-variable matrix. The object of the analysis, however, is not to show the relationships among all codes, but to find the minimal set of logical relationships among the concepts that accounts for a single dependent variable. With more than three variables, the analysis becomes much more difficult. Computer programs such as QCA (Drass, 1980) and ANTHROPAC (Borgatti, 1992) test all possible multivariate hypotheses and find the optimal solution. (QCA is reviewed in Weitzman & Miles, 1995.)

Ethnographic Decision Models

Ethnographic decision models (EDMs) are qualitative, causal analyses that predict behavioral choices under specific circumstances. An EDM, often referred to as a decision tree or flowchart, comprises a series of nested *if-then* statements that link criteria (and combinations of criteria) to the behavior of interest (Figure 7.7). EDMs have been used to explain how fishermen decide where to fish (Gatewood, 1983), what prices people decide to place on their products (Gladwin, 1971; Quinn, 1978), and which treatments people choose for an illness (Mathews & Hill, 1990; Ryan & Martínez, 1996; Young, 1980).

EDMs combine many of the techniques employed in grounded theory and classic content analysis. Gladwin (1989) lays out the fundamental steps for building an ethnographic decision tree model. (For other clear descriptions of the steps, see Hill, 1998; Ryan & Martínez, 1996.)

EDMs require exploratory data collection, preliminary model building, and model testing. First, researchers identify the decisions they want to explore and the alternatives that are available. Typically, EDMs are done on simple yes/no types of behaviors. They can be used, however, to predict multiple behaviors (Mathews & Hill, 1990; Young, 1980) as well as the order of multiple behaviors (Ryan & Martínez, 1996).

Next, the researchers conduct open-ended interviews to discover the criteria people use to select among alternatives. The researchers first ask people to recall the most recent example of an actual—not a hypothetical—behavior and to recall *why* they did or did not do the behavior. Here is an example from a study we've done recently: "Think about the last time you had a can of something to drink in your hand—soda, juice, water, beer, whatever. Did you recycle the can? Why [Why not]?" This kind of question generates a list of *decision criteria*. To

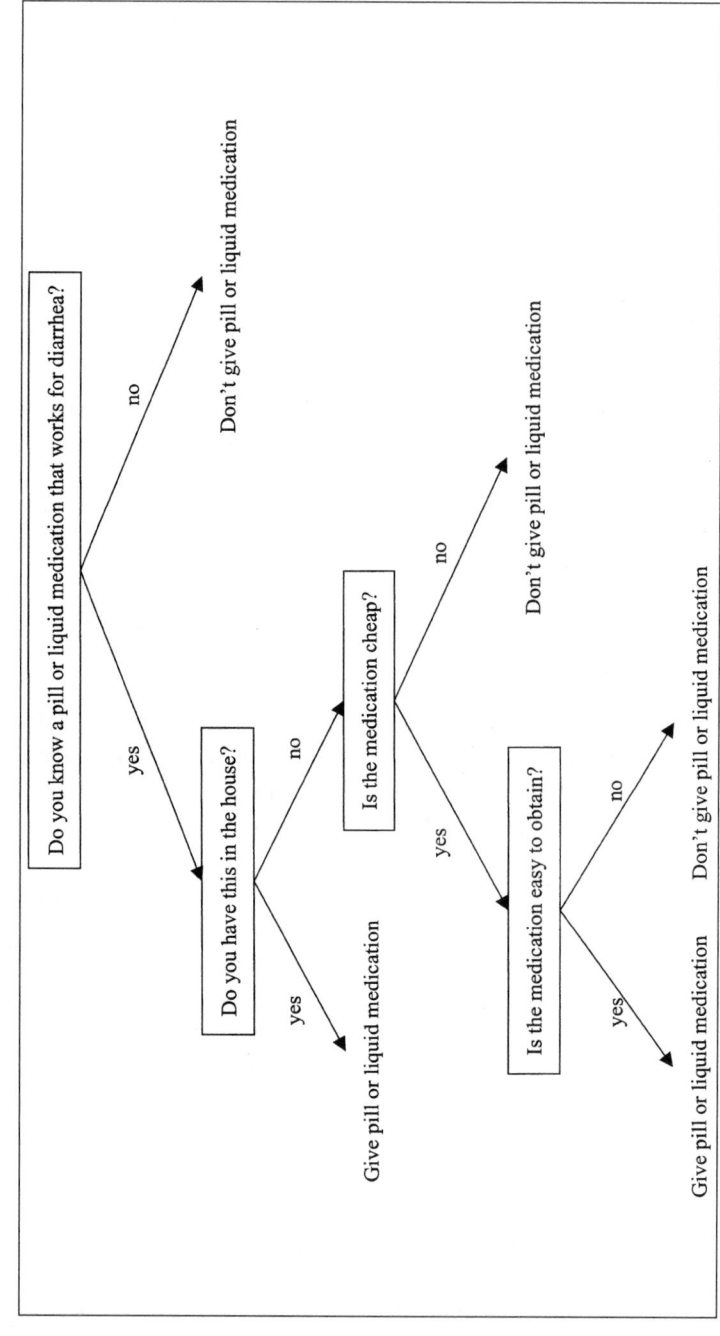

Figure 7.7. Decision Model of Constraints on the Use of Pills or Liquid Medications for Mothers Treating Children with Diarrhea in Rural Mexico

SOURCE: Based on data in Ryan and Martínez (1996).

understand how these criteria might be linked, EDM researchers ask people to compare the latest decision with other similar decisions made in the past. Some researchers have used vignettes to elicit the relationships among criteria (e.g., Weller, Ruebush, & Klein, 1997; Young, 1980).

With a list of decision criteria in hand, the researchers' next step is to systematically collect data, preferably from a new group of people, about how each criterion applies or does not apply to a recent example of the behavior. "Was a recycling bin handy?" and "Do you normally recycle cans at home?" are 2 of the 30 questions we've asked people in our study of recycling behavior. The data from this stage are used to build a preliminary model of the decision process for the behavior under scrutiny. Cases that do not fit the model are examined closely and the model is modified. Researchers tweak, or tune, the model until they achieve a satisfactory level of postdictive accuracy—understood to be at least 80% among EDM researchers. Parsimonious models are favored over more complicated ones. (For automated ways of building and pruning decision trees, see Mingers, 1989a, 1989b.)

The process doesn't end there—the same data are used in building a preliminary model and in testing its postdictive accuracy. When EDM researchers feel confident in their model, they test it on an independent sample to see if it predicts as well as it postdicts. Typically, EDMs predict more than 80% of whatever behavior is being modeled, far above what we expect by chance. (For more detailed arguments on how to calculate accuracy in EDMs, see Ryan & Martínez, 1996; Weller et al., 1997.)

Because of the intensive labor involved, EDMs have been necessarily restricted to relatively simple decisions in relatively small and homogeneous populations. Recently, however, we found we could effectively test, on a nationally representative sample, our ethnographically derived decision models for whether or not to recycle cans and whether or not to ask for paper or plastic bags at the grocery store (Bernard, Ryan, & Borgatti, 1999).

EDMs can be displayed as decision trees (e.g., Gladwin, 1989), as decision tables (Mathews & Hill, 1990; Young, 1980), or as sets of rules in the form of *if-then* statements (Ryan & Martínez, 1996). Like componential analysis, folk taxonomies, and schema analysis, EDMs represent an aggregate decision process and do not necessarily represent what is going on inside people's heads (Garro, 1998).

◆ Breaking Down the Boundaries

Text analysis as a research strategy permeates the social sciences, and the range of methods for conducting text analysis is inspiring. Investigators examine words, sentences, paragraphs, pages, documents, ideas, meanings, paralinguistic features, and even what is missing from the text. They interpret, mark, retrieve, and count. By turns, they apply interpretive analysis and numerical analysis. They use text analysis for exploratory and confirmatory purposes. Researchers identify themes, describe them, and compare them across cases and groups. Finally, they combine themes into conceptual models and theories to explain and predict social phenomena.

Figure 7.1 depicts a broad range of analysis techniques found across the social sciences. To conform our presentation with the literature on qualitative methods, we have organized these techniques according to the goals of the investigators and the kinds of texts to which the techniques are typically applied.

In this chapter, we focus on the sociological tradition that uses text as a "window into experience" rather than the linguistic tradition that describes how texts are developed and structured. Texts such as conversations, performances, and narratives are analyzed by investigators from both the sociological and linguistic traditions. Although the agendas of the investigators may differ, we see no reason why many of the sociological techniques we describe could not be useful in the linguistic tradition and vice versa.

We also distinguish between those analyses associated with systematically elicited data and those associated with free-flowing texts. We argue, however, that these data-analytic pairings are ones of convention rather than necessity. Investigators want to (a) identify the range and salience of key items and concepts, (b) discover the relationships among these items and concepts, and (c) build and test models linking these concepts together. They use free-listing tasks, KWIC, word counts, and the exploratory phases of grounded theory, schema analysis, and EDM to discover potentially useful themes and concepts.

Researchers use pile sorts, paired comparisons, triads tests, frame substitution tasks, semantic networks, cognitive maps, content analysis and content dictionaries, and the modeling phases of grounded theory, schema analysis, and EDM to discover how abstract concepts are related to each other. They display the relationships as models or frameworks. These frameworks include formal models that rely on Boolean logic (componential analysis and analytic induction), hierarchical models (taxonomies and ethnographic decision models), probabilistic models (classic content analysis and content dictionaries), and more abstract models such as those produced by grounded theory and schema analysis. Below we describe two important examples of studies in which researchers combined methods to understand their data more fully.

Jehn and Doucet (1996, 1997) used word counts, classical content analysis, and mental mapping to examine conflicts among Chinese and U.S. business associates. They asked 76 U.S. managers who had worked in Sino-American joint ventures to describe recent interpersonal conflicts with business partners. Each person described a situation with a same-culture manager and a different-cultural manager. The researchers made sure that each manager interviewed included information about his or her relationship to the other person, who was involved, what the conflict was about, what caused the conflict, and how the conflict was resolved.

After collecting the narratives, Jehn and Doucet asked their informants to help identify the emic themes in the narratives. First, they generated separate lists of words from the intercultural and intracultural conflict narratives. They asked three expatriate managers to act as judges and to identify all the words that were related to conflict. They settled on a list of 542 conflict words from the intercultural list and 242 conflict words from the intracultural list. Jehn and Doucet then asked the three judges to sort the words into piles or categories. The experts identified 15 subcategories for the intercultural data (things like *conflict, expectations, rules, power,* and *volatile*) and 15 categories for the intracultural data (things like *conflict, needs, standards, power, contentious,* and *lose*). Taking into consideration the total number of words in each corpus, conflict words were used more in intracultural interviews and resolution terms were more likely to be used in intercultural interviews.

Jehn and Doucet also used traditional content analysis on their data. The had two coders read the 152 conflict scenarios (76 intracultural and 76 intercultural) and evaluate (on a 5-point scale) each on 27 different themes they had identified from the literature. This produced two 76×27 scenario-by-theme profile matrices—one for the intracultural conflicts and one for the intercultural conflicts. The first three factors from the intercultural matrix reflect (a) interpersonal animosity and hostility, (b) aggravation, and (c) the volatile nature of the conflict. The first two factors from the intracultural matrix reflect (a) hatred and animosity with a volatile nature and (b) conflicts conducted calmly with little verbal intensity.

Finally, Jehn and Doucet identified the 30 intracultural and the 30 intercultural scenarios that they felt were the clearest and pithiest. They recruited 50 *more* expatriate managers to assess the similarities (on a 5-point scale) of 60-120 randomly selected pairs of scenarios. When combined across informants, the managers' judgments produced two aggregate, scenario-by-scenario, similarity matrices—one for the intracultural conflicts and one for the intercultural conflicts. Multidimensional scaling of the intercultural similarity data identified four dimensions: (a) open versus resistant to change, (b) situational causes versus individual traits, (c) high- versus low-resolution potential based on trust, and (d) high- versus low-resolution potential based on patience. Scaling of the intracultural similarity data identified four different dimensions: (a) high versus low cooperation, (b) high versus low confrontation, (c) problem solving versus accepting, and (d) resolved versus ongoing.

The work of Jehn and Doucet is impressive because the analysis of the data from these tasks produced different sets of themes. All three emically induced theme sets have some intuitive appeal, and all three yield analytic results that are useful. The researchers could have also used the techniques of grounded theory or schema analysis to discover even more themes.

Jehn and Doucet are not the only researchers ever to combine different analytic techniques. In a series of articles on young adult "occasional" drug users, Agar (1979, 1980, 1983) used grounded theory methods to build models of behavior. He then used classical content analysis to test his hypotheses. Agar conducted and transcribed three interviews with each of his three informants. In his 1979 article, Agar describes his initial, intuitive analysis. He pulled all the statements that pertained to informants' interactions or assessments of other people. He then looked at the statements and sorted them into piles based on their content. He named each pile as a theme and assessed how the themes interacted. He found that he had three piles. The first contained statements in which the informant was expressing negative feelings toward a person in a dominant social position. The second was made up of statements emphasizing the other's knowledge or awareness. The statements in the third small cluster emphasized the importance of change or openness to new experiences.

292

From this intuitive analysis, Agar felt that his informants were telling him that those in authority were only interested in displaying their authority unless they had knowledge or awareness; that knowledge or awareness comes through openness to new experience; and that most in authority are closed to new experience or change.

To test his intuitive understanding of the data, Agar (1983) used all the statements from a single informant and coded the statements for their role type (kin, friend/acquaintance, educational, occupational, or other), power (dominant, symmetrical, subordinate, or undetermined), and affect (positive, negative, ambivalent, or absent). Agar was particularly interested in whether negative sentiments were expressed toward those in dominant social roles. For one informant, Agar found that out of 40 statements coded as dominant, 32 were coded negative and 8 were coded positive. For the 36 statements coded as symmetrical, 20 were coded positive and 16 negative, lending support to his original theory.

Next, Agar looked closely at the deviant cases—the 8 statements where the informant expressed positive affect toward a person in a dominant role. These counterexamples suggested that the positive affect was expressed toward a dominant social other when the social other possessed, or was communicating to the informant, knowledge that the informant valued.

Finally, Agar (1980) developed a more systematic questionnaire to test his hypothesis further. He selected 12 statements, 4 from each of the control, knowledge, and change themes identified earlier. He matched these statements with eight roles from the informant's transcript (father, mother, employer, teacher, friend, wife, coworker, and teammate). Agar then returned to his informant and asked if the resulting statements were true, false, or irrelevant. (In no case did the informant report "irrelevant.") Agar then compared the informant's responses to his original hypotheses. He found that on balance his hypotheses were correct, but discrepancies between his expectations and his results suggested areas for further research.

These examples show that investigators can apply one technique to different kinds of data and they can apply multiple techniques to the same data set. Text analysis is used by avowed positivists and interpretivists alike. As we have argued elsewhere (Bernard, 1993; Bernard & Ryan, 1998), methods are simply tools that belong to everyone.

◆ What's Next?

We do not want to minimize the profound *intellectual* differences in the epistemological positions of positivists and interpretivists. We think, however, that when researchers can move easily and cheaply between qualitative and quantitative data collection and analysis, the distinctions between the two epistemological positions will become of less *practical* importance. That is, as researchers recognize the full array of tools at their disposal, and as these tools become easier to use, the pragmatics of research will lessen the distinction between qualitative and quantitative data and analysis.

The process is under way—and is moving fast—with the development of increasingly useful software tools for qualitative data analysis. Useful tools create markets, and market needs create increasingly useful tools. Qualitative data analysis packages (ATLAS/ti, NUD•IST, Code-A-Text, the Ethnograph, AnSWR, and others) have improved dramatically over the past few years (Fischer, 1994; Kelle, 1995; Weitzman & Miles, 1995). These products, and others, make it easier and easier for researchers to identify themes, build codebooks, mark text, create memos, and develop theoretical models. Based loosely on a grounded theory type of approach to qualitative analysis, many program suites have recently folded in techniques from classical content analysis. Several programs, for example, allow researchers to export data to matrices that they can then analyze using other programs.

Investigators, however, remain constrained by program-defined units of analysis—usually marked blocks of text or informants. Researchers need the flexibility to create matrices on demand, whether they be word-by-theme or word-by-informant matrices for word analysis and sentence-by-code or paragraph-by-code matrices for content analysis. A series of word analysis functions would greatly enhance the automated coding features found in programs that are geared to the interests of scholars in the grounded theory school. Investigators should be able to code a section of text using grounded theory, then identify the key words associated with each theme. They should be able to use key words to search for additional occurrences of the theme in large corpuses of text.

When programs make it easy to use multiple coders and to identify intercoder agreements and disagreements systematically, researchers will be better able to describe themes and to train assistants. Adding a variety of measures for calculating intercoder agreement, which only some programs do, would also be helpful. Some programs offer researchers the option of recording the marking behavior of multiple coders, yet offer no direct way to measure intercoder agreement.

The evolution of text analysis software is just beginning. Some 15 years ago, spell checkers, thesauruses, and scalable fonts were all sold separately. Today, these functions are integrated into all full-featured word-processing packages. Just 10 years ago, graphics programs were sold separately from programs that do statistical analysis. Today, graphics functions are integrated into all full-featured packages for statistical analysis. As programmers of text analysis software compete for market share, packages will become more inclusive, incorporating methods from both sides of the epistemological divide. It can't happen too soon.

◆ Notes

1. MDS displays are highly evocative. They beg to be interpreted. In fact, they *must* be interpreted. Why are some illnesses at the top of Figure 7.3 and some at the bottom? We think the illnesses at the top are more of the chronic variety, whereas those at the bottom are more acute. We also think that the illnesses on the left are less serious than those on the right. We can test ideas like these by asking key informants to help us understand the arrangement of the illnesses in the MDS plot. (For more examples of mental maps, see Albert, 1991; D'Andrade et al., 1972; Erickson, 1997.) (There is a formal method, called property fitting analysis, or PROFIT, for testing ideas about the distribution of items in an MDS map. This method is based on linear regression. See Kruskal & Wish, 1978.)

2. Alternatively, profile matrices (the usual thing-by-variable attribute matrix ubiquitous in the social sciences) can be converted to similarity matrices (thing-by-thing matrices in which the cells contain measures of similarity among pairs of things) and then analyzed with MDS (for step-by-step instructions, see Borgatti, 1999).

◆ References

Agar, M. (1979). Themes revisited: Some problems in cognitive anthropology. *Discourse Processes, 2,* 11-31.

Agar, M. (1980). Getting better quality stuff: Methodological competition in an interdisciplinary niche. *Urban Life, 9,* 34-50.

Agar, M. (1983). Microcomputers as field tools. *Computers and the Humanities, 17,* 19-26.

Agar, M. (1996). *Speaking of ethnography* (2nd ed.). Thousand Oaks, CA: Sage.

Agar, M., & Hobbs, J. (1985). How to grow schemata out of interviews. In J. W. D. Dougherty (Ed.), *Directions in cognitive anthropology* (pp. 413-431). Urbana: University of Illinois Press.

Albert, S. M. (1991). Cognition of caregiving tasks: Multidimensional scaling of the caregiver task domain. *The Gerontologist, 31,* 726-734.

Allen, J. T., & Italie, G. (1954). *A concordance to Euripides.* Berkeley: University of California Press.

Araujo, L. (1995). Designing and refining hierarchical coding frames. In U. Kelle (Ed.), *Computer-aided qualitative data analysis: Theory, methods and practice* (pp. 96-104). London: Sage.

Barkin, S., Ryan, G. W., & Gelberg, L. (1999). What clinicians can do to further youth violence primary prevention: A qualitative study. *Injury Prevention, 5,* 53-58.

Barnett, G. A., & Danowski, J. A. (1992). The structure of communication: A network analysis of the International Communication Association. *Human Communication Research, 19,* 164-285.

Becker, H. S. (1998). *Tricks of the trade: How to think about your research while you're doing it.* Chicago: University of Chicago Press.

Becker, H. S., Geer, B., Hughes, E. C., & Strauss, A. L. (1961). *Boys in white: Student culture in medical school.* Chicago: University of Chicago Press.

Berelson, B. (1952). *Content analysis in communication research.* Glencoe, IL: Free Press.

Bernard, H. R. (1991). About text management and computers. *CAM Newsletter, 3*(1), 1-4, 7, 12.

Bernard, H. R. (1993). Methods belong to all of us. In R. Borofsky (Ed.), *Assessing cultural anthropology* (pp. 168-178). New York: McGraw-Hill.

Bernard, H. R. (1994). *Research methods in anthropology: Qualitative and quantitative approaches* (2nd ed.). Walnut Creek, CA: AltaMira.

Bernard, H. R., & Ashton-Voyoucalos, S. (1976). Return migration to Greece. *Journal of the Steward Anthropological Society, 8*(1), 31-51.

Bernard, H. R., & Ryan, G. W. (1998). Qualitative and quantitative methods of text analysis. In H. R. Bernard (Ed.), *Handbook of methods in cultural anthropology* (pp. 595-646). Walnut Creek, CA: AltaMira.

Bernard, H. R., Ryan, G. W., & Borgatti, S. (1999). *Green cognition and behaviors.* Report submitted to Ford Research Laboratories, Dearborn, MI.

Bessinger, J. B. (1969). *A concordance to Beowulf.* Ithaca, NY: Cornell University Press.

Bloor, M. (1976). Bishop Berkeley and the adenotonsillectomy dilemma. *Sociology, 10,* 43-61.

Bloor, M. (1978). On the analysis of observational data: A discussion of the worth and uses of inductive techniques and respondent validation. *Sociology, 12,* 545-557.

Bogdan, R. C., & Biklen, S. K. (1992). *Qualitative research for education: An introduction to theory and methods* (2nd ed.). Boston: Allyn & Bacon.

Borgatti, S. P. (1992). *ANTHROPAC 4.0*. Columbia, SC: Analytic Technologies. Available Internet: http://www.analytictech.com

Borgatti, S. P. (1998). The methods. In V. C. De Munck & E. J. Sobo (Eds.), *Using methods in the field: A practical introduction and casebook* (pp. 249-252). Walnut Creek, CA: AltaMira.

Borgatti, S. P. (1999). Elicitation methods for cultural domain analysis. In J. Schensul, M. LeCompte, S. Borgatti, & B. Nastasi (Eds.), *The ethnographer's toolkit: Vol. 3. Enhanced ethnographic methods* (pp. 115-151). Walnut Creek, CA: AltaMira.

Boster, J. (1994). The successive pile sort. *Cultural Anthropology Methods Journal, 6*(2), 11-12.

Bradley, C., Moore, C. C., Burton, M. L., & White, D. R. (1990). A cross-cultural historical analysis of subsistence change. *American Anthropologist, 92,* 447-457.

Brouwer, M., Clark, C. C., Gerbner, G., & Krippendorf, K. (1969). The television world of violence. In R. K. Baker & S. J. Ball (Eds.), *Mass media and violence: A report to the National Commission on the Causes and Prevention of Violence* (pp. 311-339, 519-591). Washington, DC: Government Printing Office.

Bulmer, M. (1979). Concepts in the analysis of qualitative data. *Sociological Review, 27,* 651-677.

Burton, D. M. (1981a). Automated concordances and word indexes: The early sixties and the early centers. *Computers and the Humanities, 15,* 83-100.

Burton, D. M. (1981b). Automated concordances and word indexes: The process, the programs, and the products. *Computers and the Humanities, 15,* 139-154.

Burton, D. M. (1982). Automated concordances and word indexes: Machine decisions and editorial revisions. *Computers and the Humanities, 16,* 195-218.

Campbell, D. T. (1957). Factors relevant to the validity of experiments in social settings. *Psychological Bulletin, 54,* 297-312.

Campbell, D. T., & Stanley, J. C. (1963). *Experimental and quasi-experimental designs for research.* Chicago: Rand McNally.

Carey, J. W., Morgan, M., & Oxtoby, M. J. (1996). Intercoder agreement in analysis of responses to open-ended interview questions: Examples from tuberculosis research. *Cultural Anthropology Methods Journal, 8*(3), 1-5.

Carley, K. (1993). Coding choices for textual analysis: A comparison of content analysis and map analysis. In P. Marsden (Ed.), *Sociological methodology* (pp. 75-126). Oxford: Blackwell.

Carley, K. (1997). Network text analysis: The network position of concepts. In C. W. Roberts (Ed.), *Text analysis for the social sciences: Methods for drawing statistical inferences from texts and transcripts* (pp. 79-100). Mahwah, NJ: Lawrence Erlbaum.

Carley, K., & Kaufer, D. S. (1993). Semantic connectivity: An approach for analyzing semantic networks. *Communication Theory, 3,* 182-213.

Carley, K., & Palmquist, P. (1992). Extracting, representing, and analyzing mental models. *Social Forces, 70,* 601-636.

Carmines, E. G., & Zeller, R. A. (1979). *Reliability and validity assessment.* Beverly Hills, CA: Sage.

Casson, R. (1983). Schemata in cultural anthropology. *Annual Review of Anthropology, 12,* 429-462.

Charmaz, K. (1990). "Discovering" chronic illness: Using grounded theory. *Social Science and Medicine, 30,* 1161-1172.

Cohen, J. (1960). A coefficient of agreement for nominal scales. *Educational and Psychological Measurement, 20,* 37-48.

Colby, B. N. (1966). The analysis of culture content and the patterning of narrative concern in texts. *American Anthropologist, 68,* 374-388.

Conklin, H. (1955). Hanunóo color categories. *Southwest Journal of Anthropology, 11,* 339-344.

Cook, T. D., & Campbell, D. T. (1979). *Quasi-experimentation: Design and analysis issues for field settings.* Chicago: Rand McNally.

Cowan, G., & O'Brien, M. (1990). Gender and survival versus death in slasher films: A content analysis. *Sex Roles, 23*(3-4), 187-196.

Crabtree, B. F., & Miller, W. L. (1992). A template approach to text analysis: Developing and using codebooks. In B. F. Crabtree & W. L. Miller (Eds.), *Doing qualitative research* (pp. 93-109). Newbury Park, CA: Sage.

Craig, R. T. (1981). Generalization of Scott's index of intercoder agreement. *Public Opinion Quarterly, 45,* 260-264.

Cressey, D. R. (1971). *Other people's money: A study in the social psychology of embezzlement.* Montclair, NJ: Patterson Smith. (Original work published 1953)

D'Andrade, R. (1991). The identification of schemas in naturalistic data. In M. J. Horowitz (Ed.), *Person schemas and maladaptive interpersonal patterns* (pp. 279-301). Chicago: University of Chicago Press.

D'Andrade, R. (1995). *The development of cognitive anthropology.* Cambridge: Cambridge University Press.

D'Andrade, R., Quinn, N., Nerlove, S., & Romney, A. K. (1972). Categories of disease in American-English and Mexican-Spanish. In A. K. Romney et al. (Eds.), *Multidimensional scaling: Theory and applications in the behavioral sciences* (Vol. 2, pp. 9-54). New York: Seminar.

Danielson, W. A., & Lasorsa, D. L. (1997). Perceptions of social change: 100 years of front-page content in the *New York Times* and the *Los Angeles Times.* In C. W. Roberts (Ed.), *Text analysis for the social sciences: Methods for drawing statistical inferences from texts and transcripts* (pp. 103-116). Mahwah, NJ: Lawrence Erlbaum.

Danowski, J. A. (1982). A network-based content analysis methodology for computer-mediated communication: An illustration with a computer bulletin board. In M. Burgoon (Ed.), *Communication yearbook 6* (pp. 904-925). Beverly Hills, CA: Sage.

Danowski, J. A. (1993). Network analysis of message content. In W. D. Richards & G. A. Barnett (Eds.), *Progress in communication science* (Vol. 12, pp. 197-221). Norwood, NJ: Ablex.

Darton, M. (1976). *Modern concordance to the New Testament.* Garden City, NY: Doubleday.

Deese, J. (1969). Conceptual categories in the study of content. In G. Gerbner, O. R. Holsti, K. Krippendorf, W. J. Paisley, & P. J. Stone (Eds.), *The analysis of communication content: Developments in scientific theories and computer techniques* (pp. 39-56). New York: John Wiley.

Denzin, N. K. (1978). *The research act: A theoretical introduction to sociological methods* (2nd ed.). New York: McGraw-Hill.

Denzin, N. K. (1997). *Interpretive ethnography: Ethnographic practices for the 21st century.* Thousand Oaks, CA: Sage.

Dey, I. (1993). *Qualitative data analysis: A user-friendly guide for social scientists.* London: Routledge & Kegan Paul.

Doerfel, M. L., & Barnett, G. A. (1996). The use of Catpac for text analysis. *Cultural Anthropology Methods Journal, 8*(2), 4-7.

Drass, K. (1980). The analysis of qualitative data: A computer program. *Urban Life, 9,* 332-353.

Ember, C. R., & Ember, M. (1992). Resource unpredictability, mistrust, and war: A cross-cultural study. *Journal of Conflict Resolution, 36,* 242-262.

Erickson, P. (1997). Contraceptive methods: Do Hispanic adolescents and their family planning care providers think about contraceptive methods the same way? *Medical Anthropology, 17,* 65-82.

Fan, D. P., & Shaffer, C. L. (1990). Use of open-ended essays and computer content analysis to survey college students' knowledge of AIDS. *College Health, 38,* 221-229.

Farringdon, J. M., & Farringdon, M. G. (1980). *A concordance and word-lists to the poems of Dylan Thomas.* Swansea, England: Ariel House.

Fielding, N. G., & Fielding, J. L. (1986). *Linking data.* Beverly Hills, CA: Sage.

Fischer, M. D. (1994). *Applications in computing for social anthropologists.* London: Routledge.

Fjellman, S. M., & Gladwin, H. (1985). Haitian family patterns of migration to South Florida. *Human Organization, 44,* 301-312.

Fleisher, M. S., & Harrington, J. A. (1998). Freelisting: Management at a women's federal prison camp. In V. C. De Munck & E. J. Sobo (Eds.), *Using methods in the field: A practical introduction and casebook* (pp. 69-84). Walnut Creek, CA: AltaMira.

Fleiss, J. L. (1971). Measuring nominal scale agreement among many raters. *Psychological Bulletin, 76,* 378-382.

Frake, C. O. (1962). The ethnographic study of cognitive systems. In T. Gladwin & W. C. Sturtevant (Eds.), *Anthropology and human behavior* (pp. 72-85). Washington, DC: Anthropology Association of Washington.

Frake, C. O. (1964). Notes on queries in ethnography. *American Anthropologist, 66,* 132-145.

Furbee, L. (1996). *The religion of politics in Chiapas: Founding a cult of communicating saints.* Paper presented at the 96th Annual Meeting of the American Anthropological Association, San Francisco.

Furbee, L., & Benfer, R. (1983). Cognitive and geographic maps: Study of individual variation among Tojolabal Mayans. *American Anthropologist, 85,* 305-333.

Garro, L. (1998). On the rationality of decision-making studies: Part 1. Decision models of treatment choice. *Medical Anthropology Quarterly, 12,* 319-340.

Gatewood, J. B. (1983). Deciding where to fish: The skipper's dilemma in Southeast Alaskan salmon seining. *Coastal Zone Management Journal, 10,* 347-367.

George, A. L. (1959). Quantitative and qualitative approaches to content analysis. In I. de S. Pool (Ed.), *Trends in content analysis* (pp. 7-32). Urbana: University of Illinois Press.

Gerbner, G., Holsti, O. R., Krippendorf, K., Paisley, W. J., & Stone, P. J. (Eds.). (1969). *The analysis of communication content: Developments in scientific theories and computer techniques* New York: John Wiley.

Gladwin, C. (1989). *Ethnographic decision tree modeling.* Newbury Park, CA: Sage.

Gladwin, H. (1971). *Decision making in the Cape Coast (Fante) fishing and fish marketing system.* Unpublished doctoral dissertation, Stanford University.

Glaser, B. G. (1978). *Theoretical sensitivity.* Mill Valley, CA: Sociology Press.

Glaser, B. G., & Strauss, A. L. (1967). *The discovery of grounded theory: Strategies for qualitative research.* Chicago: Aldine.

Goodenough, W. H. (1956). Componential analysis and the study of meaning. *Language, 32,* 195-216.

Gottschalk, L. A., & Bechtel, R. J. (1993). *Psychological and neuropsychiatric assessment applying the Gottschalk-Gleser content analysis method to verbal sample analysis using the Gottschalk-Bechtel computer scoring system.* Palo Alto, CA: Mind Garden.

Guba, E. G. (1981). Criteria for assessing the trustworthiness of naturalistic inquiries. *Educational Communications and Technology Journal, 29,* 75-92.

Guba, E. G., & Lincoln, Y. S. (1982). Epistemological and methodological bases for naturalistic inquiry. *Educational Communications and Technology Journal, 30,* 233-252.

Hammersley, M. (1992). *What's wrong with ethnography? Methodological explorations.* London: Routledge.

Harman, R. C. (1998). Triad questionnaires: Old age in Karen and Maya cultures. In V. C. De Munck & E. J. Sobo (Eds.), *Using methods in the field: A practical introduction and casebook* (pp. 121-138). Walnut Creek, CA: AltaMira.

Hartigan, J. A. (1975). *Clustering algorithms.* New York: John Wiley.

Hatch, E., & Redpath, H. (1954). *A concordance to the Septuagint and the other Greek versions of the Old Testament.* Graz, Austria: Akademische Druck-u. Verlagsanstalt.

Henley, N. M. (1969). A psychological study of the semantics of animal terms. *Journal of Verbal Learning and Verbal Behavior, 8,* 176-184.

Hill, C. E. (1998). Decision modeling: Its use in medical anthropology. In V. C. De Munck & E. J. Sobo (Eds.), *Using methods in the field: A practical introduction and casebook* (pp. 139-164). Walnut Creek, CA: AltaMira.

Hirschman, E. C. (1987). People as products: Analysis of a complex marketing exchange. *Journal of Marketing, 51,* 98-108.

Holland, D. (1985). From situation to impression: How Americans get to know themselves and one another. In J. W. D. Dougherty (Ed.), *Directions in cognitive anthropology* (pp. 389-412). Urbana: University of Illinois Press.

Holsti, O. R. (1966). External conflict and internal consensus: The Sino-Soviet case. In P. J. Stone, D. C. Dunphy, M. S. Smith, & D. M. Ogilvie (Eds.), *The General Inquirer: A computer approach to content analysis* (pp. 343-358). Cambridge: MIT Press.

Holsti, O. R. (1969). *Content analysis for the social sciences and humanities.* Reading, MA: Addison-Wesley.

Hunt, J. G., & Ropo, A. (1995). Multi-level leadership: Grounded theory and mainstream theory applied to the case of General Motors. *Leadership Quarterly, 6,* 379-412.

Imrich D. J., Mullin, C., & Linz, D. (1995). Measuring the extent of prejudicial pretrial publicity in major American newspapers: A content analysis. *Journal of Communication, 45*(3), 94-117.

Irurita, V. F. (1996). Hidden dimensions revealed: Progressive grounded theory study of quality care in the hospital. *Qualitative Health Research, 6,* 331-349.

Jakobson, R., & Halle, M. (1956). *Fundamentals of language.* The Hague: Mouton.

Jang, H.-Y., & Barnett, G. A. (1994, September). Cultural differences in organizational communication: A semantic network analysis. *Bulletin de Méthodologie Sociologique, 44,* 31-59.

Jehn, K. A., & Doucet, L. (1996). Developing categories from interview data: Part 1. Text analysis and multidimensional scaling. *Cultural Anthropology Methods Journal, 8*(2), 15-16.

Jehn, K. A., & Doucet, L. (1997). Developing categories for interview data: Part 2. Consequences of different coding and analysis strategies in understanding text. *Cultural Anthropology Methods Journal, 9*(1), 1-7.

Jehn, K. A., & Werner, O. (1993). Hapax Legomenon II: Theory, a thesaurus, and word frequency. *Cultural Anthropology Methods Journal, 5*(1), 8-10.

Johnson, A., & Price-Williams, D. R. (1997). *Oedipus ubiquitous: The family complex in world folk literature.* Stanford, CA: Stanford University Press.

Johnson, S. C. (1967). Hierarchical clustering schemes. *Psychometrika, 32,* 241-253.

Kaid, L. L., Tedesco, J. C., & McKinnon, L. M. (1996). Presidential ads as nightly news: A content analysis of 1988 and 1992 televised Adwatches. *Journal of Broadcasting Electronic Media, 40,* 297-308.

Kassis, H. (1983). *A concordance of the Qur'an.* Berkeley: University of California Press.

Kearney, M. H., Murphy, S., Irwin, K., & Rosenbaum, M. (1995). Salvaging self: A grounded theory of pregnancy on crack cocaine. *Nursing Research, 44,* 208-213.

Kearney, M. H., Murphy, S., & Rosenbaum, M. (1994). Mothering on crack cocaine: A grounded theory analysis. *Social Science and Medicine, 38,* 351-361.

Kelle, U. (1995). An overview of computer-aided methods in qualitative research. In U. Kelle (Ed.), *Computer-aided qualitative data analysis: Theory, methods and practice* (pp. 1-18). London: Sage.

Kelly, E. F., & Stone, P. J. (1975). *Computer recognition of English word senses.* Amsterdam: North-Holland.

Kempton, W. (1987). Two theories of home heat control. In D. Holland & N. Quinn (Eds.), *Cultural models in language and thought* (pp. 222-242). Cambridge: Cambridge University Press.

Kirchler, E. (1992). Adorable woman, expert man: Changing gender images of women and men in management. *European Journal of Social Psychology, 22,* 363-373.

Kirk, J., & Miller, M. L. (1986). *Reliability and validity in qualitative research.* Beverly Hills, CA: Sage.

Kolbe, R. H., & Albanese, J. P. (1996). Man to man: A content analysis of sole-male images in male-audience magazines. *Journal of Advertising, 25*(4), 1-20.

Kracauer, S. (1953. The challenge of qualitative content analysis. *Public Opinion Quarterly, 16,* 631-642.

Krippendorf, K. (1980). *Content analysis: An introduction to its methodology.* Beverly Hills, CA: Sage.

Kruskal, J. B., & Wish, M. (1978). *Multidimensional scaling*. Beverly Hills, CA: Sage.

Kurasaki, K. S. (1997). *Ethnic identity and its development among third-generation Japanese Americans*. Unpublished doctoral dissertation, DePaul University.

Laffal, J. (1990). *A concept dictionary of English, with computer programs for content analysis*. Essex, CT: Gallery.

Laffal, J. (1995). A concept analysis of Jonathan Swift's *A tale of a tub* and *Gulliver's travels*. *Computers and the Humanities, 29*, 339-361.

Leinhardt, G. (1987). Development of an expert explanation: An analysis of a sequence of subtraction lessons. *Cognition and Instruction, 4*, 225-282.

Leinhardt, G. (1989). Math lessons: A contrast of novice and expert competence. *Journal for Research in Mathematics Education, 20*(1), 52-75.

Leinhardt, G., & Smith, D. A. (1985). Expertise in mathematics instruction: Subject matter knowledge. *Journal of Educational Psychology, 77*, 247-271.

Light, R. J. (1971). Measures of response agreement for qualitative data: Some generalizations and alternatives. *Psychological Bulletin, 76*, 365-377.

Lincoln, Y. S., & Guba, E. G. (1985). *Naturalistic inquiry*. Beverly Hills, CA: Sage.

Lindesmith, A. R. (1968). *Addiction and opiates*. Chicago: Aldine. (Original work published 1947)

Lofland, J., & Lofland, L. H. (1995). *Analyzing social settings* (3rd ed.). Belmont, CA: Wadsworth.

Lonkila, M. (1995). Grounded theory as an emerging paradigm for computer-assisted qualitative data analysis. In U. Kelle (Ed.), *Computer-aided qualitative data analysis: Theory, methods and practice* (pp. 41-51). London: Sage.

MacQueen, K. M., McLellan, E., Kay, K., & Milstein, B. (1998). Codebook development for team-based qualitative research. *Cultural Anthropology Methods Journal, 10*(2), 31-36.

Manning, P. K. (1982). Analytic induction. In R. Smith & P. K. Manning (Eds.), *Handbook of social science methods: Vol. 2. Qualitative methods* (pp. 273-302). New York: Harper.

Martindale, C., & McKenzie, D. (1995). On the utility of content analysis in author attribution: The Federalist. *Computers and the Humanities, 29*, 259-270.

Mathews, H. F., & Hill, C. (1990). Applying cognitive decision theory to the study of regional patterns of illness treatment choice. *American Anthropologist, 91*, 155-170.

McCleary, R. (1978). *Dangerous men: The sociology of parole*. Beverly Hills, CA: Sage.

McKinnon, A. (1993). The multi-dimensional concordance: A new tool for literary research. *Computers and the Humanities, 27*, 165-183.

McTavish, D. G., & Pirro, E. B. (1990). Contextual content analysis. *Quality and Quantity, 24*, 44-63.

Metzger, D., & Williams, G. (1966). Some procedures and results in the study of native categories: Tzeltal "firewood." *American Anthropologist, 68,* 389-407.

Miles, M. B. (1979). Qualitative data as an attractive nuisance: The problem of analysis. *Administrative Science Quarterly, 24,* 590-601.

Miles, M. B., & Huberman, A. M. (1994). *Qualitative data analysis: An expanded sourcebook* (2nd ed.). Thousand Oaks, CA: Sage.

Mingers, J. (1989a). An empirical comparison of pruning methods for decision tree induction. *Machine Learning, 4,* 227-243.

Mingers, J. (1989b). An empirical comparison of selection measures for decision-tree induction. *Machine Learning, 3,* 319-342.

Mitchell, S. K. (1979). Interobserver agreement, reliability, and generalizability of data collected in observational studies. *Psychological Bulletin, 86,* 376-390.

Morse, J. M. (1994). Designing funded qualitative research. In N. K. Denzin & Y. S. Lincoln (Eds.), *Handbook of qualitative research* (pp. 220-235). Thousand Oaks, CA: Sage.

Mosteller, F., & Wallace, D. L. (1964). *Inference and disputed authorship: The Federalist Papers.* Reading, MA: Addison-Wesley.

Murdock, G. P. (1971). *Outline of cultural materials* (4th rev. ed.). New Haven, CT: Human Relations Area Files.

Nolan, J., & Ryan, G. W. (in press). *Fear and loathing at the cinemaplex: Differences in gender perceptions and descriptions of slasher films.* Manuscript submitted for publication.

Ogilvie, D. M., Stone, P. J., & Schneidman, E. S. (1966). Some characteristics of genuine versus simulated suicide notes. In P. J. Stone, D. C. Dunphy, M. S. Smith, & D. M. Ogilvie (Eds.), *The General Inquirer: A computer approach to content analysis* (pp. 527-535). Cambridge: MIT Press.

Osgood, C. (1959). The representational model and relevant research methods. In I. de S. Pool (Eds.), *Trends in content analysis* (pp. 33-88). Urbana: University of Illinois Press.

Palmquist, M., Carley, K., & Dale, T. (1997). Applications of computer-aided text analysis: Analyzing literary and nonliterary texts. In C. W. Roberts (Ed.), *Text analysis for the social sciences: Methods for drawing statistical inferences from texts and transcripts* (pp. 171-189). Mahwah, NJ: Lawrence Erlbaum.

Patterson, B. R., Bettini, L., & Nussbaum, J. F. (1993). The meaning of friendship across the life-span: Two studies. *Communication Quarterly, 41,* 145-160.

Patton, M. Q. (1990). *Qualitative evaluation and research methods* (2nd ed.). Newbury Park, CA: Sage.

Perchonock, N., & Werner, O. (1969). Navaho systems of classification. *Ethnology, 8,* 229-242.

Pool, I. de S. (1952). *Symbols of democracy.* Stanford, CA: Stanford University Press.

Pool, I. de S. (Ed.). (1959). *Trends in content analysis.* Urbana: University of Illinois Press.

Potts R., Runyan, D., Zerger, A., & Marchetti, K. (1996). A content analysis of safety behaviors of television characters: Implications for children's safety and injury. *Journal of Pediatric Psychology, 21,* 517-528.

Prendergast, G. L. (1971). *A complete concordance to the Iliad of Homer.* Hildesheim, Germany: G. Olms.

Price, L. (1987). Ecuadorian illness stories. In D. Holland & N. Quinn (Eds.), *Cultural models in language and thought* (pp. 313-342). Cambridge: Cambridge University Press.

Quinn, N. (1978). Do Mfantse fish sellers estimate probabilities in their heads? *American Ethnologist, 5,* 206-226.

Quinn, N. (1982). "Commitment" in American marriage: A cultural analysis. *American Ethnologist, 9,* 755-798.

Quinn, N. (1987). Convergent evidence for a cultural model of American marriage. In D. Holland & N. Quinn (Eds.), *Cultural models in language and thought* (pp. 173-192). Cambridge: Cambridge University Press.

Quinn, N. (1992). The motivational force of self-understanding: Evidence from wives' inner conflicts. In R. D'Andrade & C. Strauss (Eds.), *Human motives and cultural models* (pp. 90-126). New York: Cambridge University Press.

Quinn, N. (1996). Culture and contradiction: The case of Americans reasoning about marriage. *Ethos, 24,* 391-425.

Quinn, N. (1997). Research on shared task solutions. In C. Strauss & N. Quinn (Eds.), *A cognitive theory of cultural meaning* (pp. 137-188). Cambridge: Cambridge University Press.

Ragin, C. C. (1987). *The comparative method: Moving beyond qualitative and quantitative strategies.* Berkeley: University of California Press.

Ragin, C. C. (1994). Introduction to qualitative comparative analysis. In T. Janowski & A. M. Hicks (Eds.), *The comparative political economy of the welfare state* (pp. 299-317). Cambridge: Cambridge University Press.

Richards, T. J., & Richards, L. (1991). The NUD•IST qualitative data analysis system. *Qualitative Sociology, 14,* 307-325.

Robbins, M. C., & Nolan, J. M. (1997). A measure of dichotomous category bias in free listing tasks. *Cultural Anthropology Methods Journal, 9*(3), 8-12.

Roberts, C. W. (1997). A theoretical map for selecting among text analysis methods. In C. W. Roberts (Ed.), *Text analysis for the social sciences: Methods for drawing statistical inferences from texts and transcripts* (pp. 275-283). Mahwah, NJ: Lawrence Erlbaum.

Robinson, W. S. (1951). The logical structure of analytic induction. *American Sociological Review, 16,* 812-818.

Romme, A. G. L. (1995). Boolean comparative analysis of qualitative data: A methodological note. *Quality and Quantity, 29,* 317-329.

Roos, G. (1998). Pile sorting: "Kids like candy." In V. C. De Munck & E. J. Sobo (Eds.), *Using methods in the field: A practical introduction and casebook* (pp. 97-110). Walnut Creek, CA: AltaMira.

Rosenberg, S. D., Schnurr, P. P., & Oxman, T. E. (1990). Content analysis: A comparison of manual and computerized systems. *Journal of Personality Assessment, 54,* 298-310.

Rushforth, S. (1982). A structural semantic analysis of Bear Lake Athapaskan kinship classification. *American Ethnologist, 9,* 559-577.

Ryan, G. W. (1995). *Medical decision making among the Kom of Cameroon: Modeling how characteristics of illnesses, patients, caretakers, and compounds affect treatment choice in a rural community.* Unpublished doctoral dissertation, University of Florida, Gainesville.

Ryan, G. W. (1999). Measuring the typicality of text: Using multiple coders for more than just reliability and validity checks. *Human Organization, 58*(3), 313-322.

Ryan, G. W., & Martínez, H. (1996). Can we predict what mothers do? Modeling childhood diarrhea in rural Mexico. *Human Organization, 55,* 47-57.

Ryan, G. W., & Weisner, T. (1996). Analyzing words in brief descriptions: Fathers and mothers describe their children. *Cultural Anthropology Methods Journal, 8*(3), 13-16.

Sandelowski, M. (1995a). Qualitative analysis: What it is and how to begin. *Research in Nursing and Health, 18,* 371-375.

Sandelowski, M. (1995b). Sample size in qualitative research. *Research in Nursing and Health, 18,* 179-183.

Schank, R. C., & Abelson, R. P. (1977). *Scripts, plans, goals, and understanding: An enquiry into human knowledge structures.* Hillsdale, NJ: Lawrence Erlbaum.

Schnegg, M., & Bernard, H. R. (1996). Words as actors: A method for doing semantic network analysis. *Cultural Anthropology Methods Journal, 8*(2), 7-10.

Schnurr, P. P., Rosenberg, S. D., Oxman, T. E., & Tucker, G. (1986). A methodological note on content analysis: Estimates of reliability. *Journal of Personality Assessment, 50,* 601-609.

Schweizer, T. (1991). The power struggle in a Chinese community, 1950-1980: A social network analysis of the duality of actors and events. *Journal of Quantitative Anthropology, 3,* 19-44.

Schweizer, T. (1996). Actor and event orderings across time: Lattice representation and Boolean analysis of the political disputes in Chen Village, China. *Social Networks, 18,* 247-266.

Seidel, J., & Kelle, U. (1995). Different functions of coding in the analysis of textual data. In U. Kelle (Ed.), *Computer-aided qualitative data analysis: Theory, methods and practice* (pp. 52-61). London: Sage.

Shapiro, G. (1997). The future of coders: Human judgments in a world of sophisticated software. In C. W. Roberts (Ed.), *Text analysis for the social sciences: Methods for drawing statistical inferences from texts and transcripts* (pp. 225-238). Mahwah, NJ: Lawrence Erlbaum.

Shelley, G. A. (1992). *The social networks of people with end-stage renal disease: Comparing hemodialysis and peritoneal dialysis patients.* Unpublished doctoral dissertation, University of Florida.

Sleath, B., Svarstad, B., & Roter, D. (1997). Physician versus patient initiation of psychotropic prescribing in primary care settings: A content analysis of audiotapes. *Social Science and Medicine, 44,* 541-548.

Smith, J. J. (1993). Using ANTHROPAC 3.5 and a spreadsheet to compute a free-list salience index. *Cultural Anthropology Methods Journal, 5*(3), 1-3.

Smith, J. J., & Borgatti, S. P. (1998). Salience counts—and so does accuracy: Correcting and updating a measure for free-list-item salience. *Journal of Linguistic Anthropology, 7,* 208-209.

Sohier, R. (1993). Filial reconstruction: A theory on development through adversity. *Qualitative Health Research, 3,* 465-492.

Spears, N. E, Mowen, J. C., & Chakraborty, G. (1996). Symbolic role of animals in print advertising: Content analysis and conceptual development. *Journal of Business Research, 37*(2), 87-95.

Spiggle, S. (1986). Measuring social values: A content analysis of Sunday comics and underground comix. *Journal of Consumer Research, 13,* 100-113.

Spradley, J. P. (1979). *The ethnographic interview.* New York: Holt, Rinehart & Winston.

Stone, P. J., Dunphy, D. C., Smith, M. S., & Ogilvie, D. M. (Eds.). (1966). *The General Inquirer: A computer approach to content analysis.* Cambridge: MIT Press.

Strauss, A. L. (1987). *Qualitative analysis for social scientists.* New York: Cambridge University Press.

Strauss, A. L., & Corbin, J. (1990). *Basics of qualitative research: Grounded theory procedures and techniques.* Newbury Park, CA: Sage.

Strauss, A. L., & Corbin, J. (Eds.). (1997). *Grounded theory in practice.* Thousand Oaks, CA: Sage.

Strauss, C. (1992). What makes Tony run? Schemas as motive reconsidered. In R. D'Andrade & C. Strauss (Eds.), *Human motives and cultural models* (pp. 191-224). New York: Cambridge University Press.

Strauss, C. (1997). Research on cultural discontinuities. In C. Strauss & N. Quinn (Eds.), *A cognitive theory of cultural meaning* (pp. 210-251). Cambridge: Cambridge University Press.

Taylor, S. J., & Bogdan, R. C. (1984). *Introduction to qualitative research methods: The search for meanings* (2nd ed.). New York: John Wiley.

Tesch, R. (1990). *Qualitative research: Analysis types and software tools.* New York: Falmer.

Trost, J. E. (1986). Statistically nonrepresentative stratified sampling: A sampling technique for qualitative studies. *Qualitative Sociology, 9,* 54-57.

Van Maanen, J., Miller, M., & Johnson, J. (1982). An occupation in transition: Traditional and modern forms of commercial fishing. *Work and Occupations, 9,* 193-216.

Viney, L. L. (1983). The assessment of psychological states through content analysis of verbal communications. *Psychological Bulletin, 94,* 542-563.

Waitzkin, H., & Britt, T. (1993). Processing narratives of self-destructive behavior in routine medical encounters: Health promotion, disease prevention, and the discourse of health care. *Social Science and Medicine, 36,* 1121-1136.

Wallace, A. F. C. (1962). Culture and cognition. *Science, 135,* 352-357.

Weber, R. (1990). *Basic content analysis* (2nd ed.). Newbury Park, CA: Sage.

Weitzman, E. A., & Miles, M. B. (1995). *Computer programs for qualitative data analysis: A software sourcebook.* Thousand Oaks, CA: Sage.

Weller, S. C. (1998). Structured interviewing and questionnaire construction. In H. R. Bernard (Ed.), *Handbook of methods in cultural anthropology* (pp. 365-409). Walnut Creek, CA: AltaMira.

Weller, S. C., & Romney, A. K. (1988). *Systematic data collection.* Newbury Park, CA: Sage.

Weller, S. C., & Romney, A. K. (1990). *Metric scaling: Correspondence analysis.* Newbury Park, CA: Sage.

Weller, S. C., Ruebush, T. K., II, & Klein, R. E. (1997). Predicting treatment-seeking behavior in Guatemala: A comparison of the health services research and decision-theoretic approaches. *Medical Anthropology Quarterly, 11,* 224-245.

Werner, O., & Schoepfle, G. M. (1987). *Systematic fieldwork: Vol. 2. Ethnographic analysis and data management.* Newbury Park, CA: Sage.

White, D. R., & Burton, M. L. (1988). Causes of polygyny: Ecology, economy, kinship, and warfare. *American Anthropologist, 90,* 871-887.

Willms, D. G., Best, J. A., Taylor, D. W., Gilbert, J. R., Wilson, D. M. C., Lindsay, E. A., & Singer, J. (1990). A systematic approach for using qualitative methods in primary prevention research. *Medical Anthropology Quarterly, 4,* 391-409.

Wilson, H. S., & Hutchinson, S. A. (1996). Methodological mistakes in grounded theory. *Nursing Research, 45,* 122-124.

Wodak, R. (1992). Strategies in text production and text comprehension: A new perspective. In D. Stein (Ed.), *Cooperating with written texts* (pp. 493-528). New York: Mouton de Gruyter.

Wright, K. B. (1997). Shared ideology in Alcoholics Anonymous: A grounded theory approach. *Journal of Health Communication, 2*(2), 83-99.

Yoder, S. (1995). Examining ethnomedical diagnoses and treatment choices for diarrheal disorders in Lubumbashi Swahili. *Medical Anthropology, 16*, 211-248.

Young, J. C. (1978). Illness categories and action strategies in a Tarascan town. *American Ethnologist, 5*, 81-97.

Young, J. C. (1980). A model of illness treatment decisions in a Tarascan town. *American Ethnologist, 7*, 106-151.

Yule, G. U. (1968). *The statistical study of literary vocabulary.* Hamden, CT: Archon. (Original work published 1944)

Znaniecki, F. (1934). *The method of sociology.* New York: Farrar & Rinehart.

Zuell, C., Weber, R. P., & Mohler, P. (Eds.). (1989). *Computer-assisted text analysis for the social sciences: The General Inquirer III.* Mannheim, Germany: Center for Surveys, Methods, and Analysis (ZUMA).

8

Software and
Qualitative Research

Eben A. Weitzman

◆ The array of software available to support the work of qualitative researchers is maturing. A wide variety of useful tools are now available to support many different approaches to qualitative research. Most qualitative researchers can now find software that is appropriate to their analysis plans, the structure of their data, and their ease-of-use and cost preferences. However, making that appropriate match still requires systematic analysis of the needs of the project and the researcher(s), and careful comparison of the software options available at the time of purchase with an eye kept fixed firmly on those needs. There is still no one best program.

To help researchers understand what software can and cannot do to support their research efforts, understand both the potential benefits and pitfalls of using computers in qualitative research projects, and find software that is suited to their needs, I provide in this chapter (a) an introduction to and overview of the role of software in qualitative research, (b) a discussion of the critical debates and concerns in the field about the impact and appropriateness of using qualitative data analysis (QDA) software, (c) guidelines for choosing software to match individual needs, and

AUTHOR'S NOTE: My thanks to Norman Denzin, Nigel Fielding, Udo Kelle, Ray Lee, and Morten Levin for their comments on an earlier draft of this chapter.

(d) an indication of future directions for both scholarship on the use of QDA software and development of such software.

◆ A Minihistory of theUse of Computers in Qualitative Research

Traditionally, qualitative researchers have carried out the mechanics of analysis by hand: typing up field notes and interviews, photocopying them, "coding" by marking them up with markers or pencils, cutting and pasting the marked segments onto file cards, sorting and shuffling cards, and typing up their analyses. This picture has been slowly changing since the early to mid-1980s. At that point, some researchers were beginning to use word processors for the typing work, and just a few were beginning to experiment with database programs for storing and accessing their texts. Most qualitative methods textbooks at the time (e.g., Bogdan & Biklen, 1982; Goetz & LeCompte, 1984; Lofland & Lofland, 1984; Miles & Huberman, 1984) made little, if any, reference to the use of computers.

In the early 1980s, a couple of programs designed specifically for the analysis of qualitative data began to appear (Drass, 1980; Seidel & Clark, 1984; Shelly & Sibert, 1985). Early programs like QUALOG and the first versions of The Ethnograph and NUD•IST reflected the state of computing at that time. Researchers typically accomplished the coding of texts (tagging chunks of text with labels—codes—that indicate the conceptual categories the researcher wants to sort them into) by typing in line numbers and code names at a command prompt, and there was little or no facility for memoing or other annotation or markup of text. In comparison to marking up text with colored pencils, this felt awkward to many researchers. And computer support for the analysis of video or audio data was at best a fantasy.

But the landscape has changed dramatically, in terms of both software and the literature devoted to it. By the time the late Matt Miles and I wrote *Computer Programs for Qualitative Data Analysis* (Weitzman & Miles, 1995b), we reviewed no fewer than 24 different programs that were useful for analyzing qualitative data. Half of those programs had been developed specifically for qualitative data analysis, whereas the other half had been developed for more general-purpose applications, such as text search and storage. Since then, the field has continued to grow rapidly. Programs are being revised at a regular rate, new programs appear on the scene at the rate of one or two a year, and programs that don't find users disappear. There has been some convergence as good features in one program are imitated by the developers of others. And there has also been divergence, as developers look for new and different ways to conceptualize support for analysis.

There are now tools available that can help researchers who are using a wide variety of research and analysis methodologies, from grounded theory to textual analysis to narrative analysis to interpretive interactionism. It is important to emphasize that software is not now, if it ever was, something that is relevant only to "positivist" or "quasi-positivist" approaches to qualitative research. If you see language in this chapter that does not match your approach, you may find it helpful to do some speculative translation. For example, if the discussion is about "verification" or "hypothesis testing" and your approach is postmodern, the discussion may seem irrelevant. But it may be that there is a way to understand the concept that makes sense from your perspective, such as "looking to see whether there is more material supporting, or contradicting, a certain assumption or interpretation." The same software tools that someone else might use for classical hypothesis testing might be very useful for *your* purposes.

Many programs now allow the researcher to specify relationships among codes and use these relationships in analysis, and to write memos and link them to text and codes. Some programs allow the researcher to create links between different points in the text (hypertext), and a small but growing handful allow the use of audio and video in place of, or in addition to, text. And there are a variety of approaches to linking categorical and quantitative data (e.g., demographics, test scores, quantitative ratings) to text and for exporting categorical and quantitative data (e.g., word frequencies or coding summaries) to quantitative analysis programs for statistical analysis. Finally, there are now some free programs available, notably two from the U.S. Centers for Disease Control: EZ-Text, which focuses on qualitative surveys, and AnSWR, intended for a more general range of qualitative data. The software continues to vary widely, and it remains very much the case that there is no one best program for all needs.

In parallel with the growth in software, literature reporting studies and commenting on the software has begun to appear regularly. There has been an outpouring of journal articles, a series of international conferences on computers and qualitative methodology, thoughtful books on the topic (Fielding & Lee, 1991, 1998; Kelle, 1995; Tesch, 1990; Weitzman & Miles, 1995b), and special journal issues (Mangabeira, 1996; Tesch, 1991).

Periodically, commentators have raised concerns about whether the range of available software is dominated by a particular approach, methodology, or epistemology (see, e.g., Coffey, Holbrook, & Atkinson, 1996; Lonkila, 1995). Although there is certainly room for further development to support certain specific analytic processes (I offer some suggestions later in this chapter, and the list appearing in the chapter titled "Reflections and Hopes" in Weitzman & Miles, 1995b, has only begun to be addressed), these concerns are clearly missing the mark. In this chapter, I suggest a wide variety of types of programs that are available to support a wide variety of research approaches. Qualitative researchers are not limited only to coding-oriented programs, or even to programs explicitly marketed to qualitative researchers. For example, as Fielding and Lee (1998) point out, there are a variety of options for those wishing to follow the suggestion of Coffey and Atkinson (1996) that text retrievers may be more helpful for discourse analysis than code-and-retrieve programs. Fielding and Lee go on to argue that

> developers of CAQDAS [computer-aided qualitative data analysis software] programs have increasingly included facilities for proximity searching, which might be useful for narrative analysis, and for "autocoding" which could be adapted to some kinds of semiotic analysis. The provision of new features in CAQDAS programs reflects the generally close relationship between users and developers characteristic of the field, and the general willingness of developers to incorporate features desired by users even if these do not always accord with the epistemological preferences of the developer. Since packages increasingly support procedures, routines and features which are new to qualitative analysis or make procedures possible that were not practicable without the power of the computer, it is less and less plausible either to argue that the software is merely an aid to code-and-retrieve or to argue that code-and-retrieve is the *sine qua non* of qualitative analysis. (p. 175)

I address these issues at more length through much of this chapter, particularly in the subsections below headed "False Hopes and Fears," "Real Hopes," and "Real Fears," and in the later section headed "Debates in the Field."

◆ What Software Can and Cannot Do

Simply put, software can provide tools to help you analyze qualitative data, but it cannot do the analysis for you, not in the same sense in which a statistical package like SPSS or SAS can do, say, multiple regression. Many researchers have had the hope—for others it is a fear—that the computer could somehow read the text and decide what it all means. That is, generally speaking, not the case.[1] Thus it is particularly important to emphasize that using software cannot be a substitute for learning data analysis methods: The researcher must know what needs to be done, and do it. The software provides tools to do it with.

The following are some of the things computers *can* be used for to facilitate the analysis process:

1. *Making notes* in the field;
2. *Writing up* or transcribing field notes;
3. *Editing:* correcting, extending, or revising field notes;
4. *Coding:* attaching key words or tags to segments of text, graphics, audio, or video to permit later retrieval;
5. *Storage:* keeping text in an organized database;
6. *Search and retrieval:* locating relevant segments of text and making them available for inspection;
7. *Data "linking":* connecting relevant data segments to each other, forming categories, clusters, or networks of information;
8. *Memoing:* writing reflective commentaries on some aspect of the data, theory, or method as a basis for deeper analysis;
9. *Content analysis:* counting frequencies, sequences, or locations of words and phrases;
10. *Data display:* placing selected or reduced data in a condensed, organized format, such as a matrix or network, for inspection;
11. *Conclusion drawing and verification:* aiding in the interpretation of displayed data and the testing or confirmation of findings;
12. *Theory building:* developing systematic, conceptually coherent explanations of findings; testing hypotheses;
13. *Graphic mapping:* creating diagrams that depict findings or theories;
14. *Report writing:* interim and final (adapted from Miles & Huberman, 1994, p. 44).

Obviously, many of these are things that researchers can do with a word processor. Other software, which is the focus of this chapter, helps with the other tasks. The developments seen in recent years have made it possible for researchers to do these things more and more easily, and more and more powerfully. In the section headed "Types and Functions of Software for QDA," below, you will find more specific details about what software can do. But first, consider some of the hopes and fears, both real and false, that people have concerning QDA software.

False Hopes and Fears

In Weitzman and Miles (1995b), we argue:

> As Pfaffenberger . . . points out, it's equally naïve to believe that a program is (a) a neutral technical tool or (b) an overdetermining monster. The issue is understanding a program's properties and presuppositions, and how they can support or constrain your thinking to produce unanticipated effects. (p. 330)

As already mentioned, many people apparently continue to believe that QDA software intends to *do* the data analysis. Skeptical researchers raise challenges to the notion of "dumping my text into a program and seeing what comes out." Others express this more as a hope that if they buy the right program, they will not have to engage in the often very time-consuming process of analyzing all that text themselves. QDA software provides tools that help you do these things; it does not do them for you.

In an extension of this concern, many researchers have worried about the software going yet a step further and "building theory." But, as Miles and I also argued in 1995, "Software will never 'do' theory building for you . . . , but it can explicitly support your intellectual efforts, making it easier for you to think coherently about the meaning of your data" (Weitzman & Miles, 1995b, p. 330).

This situation may change in the coming years. There are some current efforts to use artificial intelligence (AI) approaches to get computers to interpret text. For example, the SPSS module TextSmart uses information about frequency of occurrence of words and proximity of words to each other to categorize text responses automatically. Microsoft Word97 has an "Auto Summarize" feature that aims to identify the most important "concepts" in a document according to word frequency. Other developers are thinking about using AI techniques to get software to participate in the theory-building process with researchers. These approaches rely on things like frequency to indicate importance and proximity in the text to indicate relatedness. For some qualitative researchers these are acceptable assumptions, but for many others they are not, and for such researchers the results of these approaches do not yield useful interpretations of text.

Real Hopes

What can we really expect to gain from the use of software? QDA software provides tools for searching, marking up, linking, and reorganizing the data, and representing and storing your own reflections, ideas, and theorizing. Some of it gives you tools for further exploration—which in some cases might amount to hypothesis testing or conclusion verification—based on your theorizing and interpretive work.

Consistency. Software can help with consistency. If I can search for *all* the places a given key word appears, or *all* the places where a given code or combination of codes was applied, or always see the relationship between two features of the data that I have recorded, it becomes possible for me to be more consistent in a couple of ways. I can be much more careful about not missing the data that contradict my brilliant, but wrong, new hypothesis. I can easily review all the data I assigned to a given conceptual category or theme and check to see if they (a) all belong together and (b) still seem to support the interpretation I started out with; if not, I can easily reorganize. (Note that the problem of my making bad interpretations has not been removed. But the kinds of facilities mentioned here can be tremendously helpful to competent researchers in checking their own work, as well as in allowing colleagues or research participants to check it and provide feedback.)

Speed. The speed of computers is a critical issue in making QDA software helpful. First, a caution: It can take time to learn to use a program, and once you have, it can take some time to prepare and set up the data for analysis. But once that is done, the speed of the computer quickly pays for that investment. Being able to search and re-search almost instantaneously encourages the researcher to conduct multiple searches to zero in on the data that really apply to a particular question. Being able to quickly re-sort a database, redefine codes, and reassign chunks of text enables and encourages the researcher to revise the analysis and the thinking about it whenever necessary. Being able to quickly pull together all the text for cells in a complex matrix display enables and encourages the researcher to run down provocative leads and new ideas—as well as worries that the current conclusions may be way off track—much more often and with much less cost.

An example from quantitative research may be instructive. In the days of slide rules, and even of handheld calculators, before statistical software was available, doing factor analysis was a months-long enterprise. Now a factor analysis can be run in minutes or seconds on a desktop computer. As a result, researchers can run factor analyses much more often, as part of other analyses rather than only as major undertakings of their own, and on multiple sets of scores in the same project. The speed of the computer alone can change what researchers even contemplate undertaking.

Representation. Software that allows dynamic, real-time representation of a researcher's thinking can be a substantial aid to theorizing. Software that provides a graphic map of relationships among codes, text segments, or cases can help researchers to visualize and extend their thinking about the data or theory at hand. Researchers often use drawings to depict these relationships, but software can keep maps tied to the underlying project, so that changes to the links in the drawing change the links among the objects in the database, and vice versa.

Consolidation. Finally, allowing the researcher to record field notes, interviews, codes, memos, annotations, reflective remarks, diagrams, audio and video recordings, demographic variables, and structural maps of the data and the theory all in one place can be a tremendously powerful support to the analysis process. If the design of the program is such that it allows the researcher to move from one intellectual activity to another with minimal effort, and carry over the results of one sort of thinking to others, it can both free up large amounts of energy for the critical tasks and help the researcher to see and keep track of connections that might otherwise easily fall through the cracks.

Real Fears

What do we really have to be worried about? Many of the advantages touted above have flip sides. The very ease, speed, and power of the software have the potential to encourage the kind of thinking I have referred to as "false hopes and fears" above. Although the software will not figure out what a complex account of a childhood trauma really means in the context of the current study, the ease of searching for key words and "autocoding" them may encourage the researcher to take shortcuts. We may fail to check to see what passages were actually coded in the autocoding process, and to use their own intelligence to analyze whether they fit. There is the real potential that we will get lazy. As Lee and Fielding (1991) have noted, "There is the possibility that the use of computers may tempt qualitative researchers into 'quick and dirty' research with its attendant danger of premature theoretical closure" (p. 8).

It is also possible that the availability of software may tempt researchers to skip over the process of learning properly about research. Again from Lee and Fielding (1991):

> Of course, the ultimate fear here is of Frankenstein's monster. It is susceptible to the same caveats, too. Like the monster, the programs are misunderstood. The programs are innocent of guile. It is their misapplication which poses the threat. It was exposure to human depravity which made a threat of Frankenstein's creation. Equally, the untutored use of analysis programs can certainly produce banal, unedifying and off-target analyses. But the fault would lie with the user. This is why teaching the use of the programs to novice researchers has to be embedded in a pedagogy which has a sense of the exemplars of qualitative analysis, rather than as skills and techniques to be mechanically applied. (p. 8)

The final fear that has some truth to it is that the conceptual assumptions behind the program—for example, that the relationships among codes are always strictly hierarchical—will shape the analysis. This fear both has truth to it and is often overstated. For example, if the program allows you to directly represent hierarchical relationships among codes, but not nonhierarchical relationships, such as circular loops or unstructured networks, it will probably encourage you to think primarily or only in terms of hierarchical relationships among your codes/concepts. If you are aware of the assumptions behind a program, you have a couple of options: You can choose another program or you can find a way to work around the assumptions in the program—for example, by keeping an ever-changing, nonhierarchical code map pinned to the wall. More on this in the section headed "Debates in the Field," below.

◆ Types and Functions of Software for QDA

In this section I offer a rough sorting of available software into types. There is naturally quite a bit of overlap among categories, with individual programs having functions that would seem to belong to more than one type. However, it is possible to focus on the "heart and soul" of a program: what it is mainly intended for. This categorization scheme was first presented in Weitzman and Miles (1995b).

Text Retrievers

Text retrievers specialize in finding all the instances of words and phrases in text, in one or several files. They typically also allow you to search for places where two or more words or phrases coincide within a specified distance (a number of words, sentences, pages, and so on) and allow you to sort the resulting passages into different output files and reports. They may do other things as well, such as content analysis functions like counting, displaying key words in context or creating concordances (organized lists of all words and phrases in their contexts), or they may allow you to attach annotations or even variable values (for things like demographics or source information) to points in the text. Examples of text retrievers are Sonar Professional, the Text Collector, and ZyINDEX; there are also a variety of free (but hard to use) GREP tools available on the World Wide Web.

Textbase Managers

Textbase managers are database programs specialized for storing text in more or less organized fashion. They are good at holding text, together with information about it, and allowing you to quickly organize and sort your data in a variety of ways and retrieve it according to different criteria. Some are better suited to highly structured data that can be organized into "records" (that is, specific cases) and "fields" (variables—information that appears for each case), whereas others easily manage "free-form" text. They may allow you to define fields in the fixed manner of a traditional database such as Microsoft Access® or FileMaker Pro®, or they may allow significantly more flexibility, for example, allowing different records to have different field structures. Their search operations may be as good as, or sometimes even better than, those of some text retrievers. Examples of

319

textbase managers are askSam, Folio Views, Idealist, InfoTree32 XT, and TEXTBASE ALPHA.

Code-and-Retrieve Programs

Code-and-retrieve programs are often developed by qualitative researchers specifically for the purpose of qualitative data analysis. The programs in this category specialize in allowing you to apply category tags (codes) to passages of text and later retrieve and display the text according to your coding. These programs have at least some search capacity, allowing you to search either for codes or words and phrases in the text. They may have a capacity to store memos. Even the weakest of these programs represent a quantum leap forward from the old scissors-and-paper approach: they're more systematic, more thorough, less likely to miss things, more flexible, and much, much faster. Examples of code-and-retrieve programs are HyperQual2, Kwalitan, QUALPRO, Martin, and the Data Collector.

Code-Based Theory Builders

Most of the code-based theory-building programs are also based on a code-and-retrieve model, but they go beyond the functions of code-and-retrieve programs. They do not, nor would you want them to, build theory for you. Rather, they have special features or routines that go beyond those of code-and-retrieve programs in supporting *your* theory-building efforts. For example, they may allow you to represent relations among codes, build higher-order classifications and categories, or formulate and test theoretical propositions about the data. They may have more powerful memoing features (allowing you, for example, to categorize or code your memos) or more sophisticated search-and-retrieval functions than code-and-retrieve programs. They may have extended and sophisticated hyperlinking features, allowing you to link segments of text together or to create links among segments of text, graphics, photos, video, audio, Web sites, and more. They may also offer capabilities for "system closure," allowing you to feed results of your analyses (such as search results or memos) back into the system as data. Examples of code-based theory builders are AFTER, AnSWR, AQUAD, ATLAS/ti, Code-A-Text, Hyper-RESEARCH, NUD•IST, NVivo, QCA, the Ethnograph, and winMAX. Two of these programs, AQUAD and QCA, support cross-case configural analysis (Ragin, 1987), QCA being dedicated wholly to this method and not having any text-coding capabilities.

Conceptual Network Builders

Conceptual network builders are programs that emphasize the creation and analysis of network displays. Some of them are focused on allowing you to create network drawings: graphic representations of the relationships among concepts. Examples of these are Inspiration, MetaDesign, and Visio. Others are focused on the analysis of cognitive or semantic networks, for example, the program MECA. Still others offer some combination of the two approaches, for example, SemNet and Decision Explorer. Finally, ATLAS/ti, a program also mentioned above under code-based theory builders, also has a fine graphical network builder connected to the analytic work you do with your text and codes.

Summary

In concluding this discussion of the five main software family types, I want to emphasize that functions often cross type boundaries. For example, Folio VIEWS can code and retrieve, and has an excellent text search facility. ATLAS/ti, NUD•IST, NVivo, the Ethnograph, and winMAX graphically represent the relationships among codes, although among these, only ATLAS/ti allows you to work with and manipulate the drawing.[2] The Ethnograph and winMAX both have systems for attaching variable values (text, date, numeric, and so on) to text files and/or cases. Sphinx Survey allows you to work with survey data consisting of a mix of qualitative and quantitative data. The implication: Do not decide too early which family you want to choose from. Instead, stay focused on the functions you need.

Multimedia. Multimedia capabilities are just beginning to emerge as a significant issue in software choice. There are now several programs in the code-based theory builder category that allow you to use audio and video, as well as text, as data: AFTER, ATLAS/ti, and Code-A-Text all allow you to code and annotate audio and video files, and search and retrieve from them, in ways quite similar to the ways they let you manipulate text, as does version 2 of HyperRESEARCH, which is under development at the time of this writing. In these programs, you can play a media file (audio or video), mark the beginning and ending points of segments, and then treat those segments much like segments of text. A program now in beta testing called InterClipper is designed primarily for audio files, with the assumption that you only bother to transcribe the segments that you find most important (it is targeted at focus group researchers in commercial environments who need to be able to generate analyses and reports quickly). This program will probably fall in the code-and-retrieve family when it is ready for release. There is also a growing field of software dedicated exclusively to managing video.

◆ How to Make Intelligent, Individualized Software Choices

I have emphasized from the beginning of this chapter that there is no one best software program for analyzing qualitative data. Furthermore, there is no one best program for a particular type of research or analytic method. Researchers will sometimes ask, What's the best program for a school ethnography? or, What's the best program for doing grounded theory? or, What's the best program for analyzing focus groups? None of these questions has a good answer. Instead, analysts need to approach choice based on the structure of the data, the specific things they will want to do as part of the analysis, and their needs around issues such as ease of use, cost, time available, and collaboration.

Researchers can ask themselves four broad questions, as well as consider two cut-across issues, to help guide their choices (Weitzman & Miles, 1995a, 1995b). These guidelines for choice have seen wide use in practice since their original formulation, and have proven to be effective for guiding researchers to appropriate choices. Because this approach to choice emphasizes matching functions, rather than specific programs, to particular needs, these guidelines can continue to be useful long after the programs referenced here as examples have evolved into new versions and new programs have arrived on the scene.[3]

Specifically, there are four key questions you need to ask and answer as you move toward choosing one or more software packages:

1. What kind of computer user am I?

2. Am I choosing for one project or for the next few years?

3. What kind of project(s) and database(s) will I be working on?
4. What kinds of analyses am I planning to do?

In addition to these four key questions, there are two cut-across issues to bear in mind:

♦ How important is it to you to maintain a sense of "closeness" to your data?
♦ What are your financial constraints when buying software and the hardware it needs to run on?

With these basic issues clear, you will be able to look at specific programs in a more active, deliberate way, seeing what does or does not meet your needs. (You may find it helpful to organize your answers to these questions on a worksheet, such as the one proposed in Weitzman & Miles, 1995b, which has rows for each of the questions below and columns for answers, implications/notes, and candidate programs.) Work your way from answering questions, to the implications of those answers for program choice, to candidate programs. For example, if you are working on a complex evaluation study, with a combination of structured interviews, focus groups, and case studies, you will need strong tools for tracking cases through different documents. You might find good support for this in a program's code structures, or through the use of speaker identifiers that track individuals throughout the database (see Question 3, below). Such suggestions are elaborated below.

Question 1:
What Kind of Computer User Are You?

Your present level of computer use is an important factor in choice of a program. If you are new to computers, your best bet is probably to choose a word-processing program with advice from friends and begin using it, learning to use your computer's operating system (e.g., MS-DOS, Windows, or Mac) and getting comfortable with the idea of creating text, moving around in it, and revising it. That would bring you to what we'll call Level 1. Or you may have gotten acquainted with several different programs, use your operating system easily, and feel comfortable with the idea of exploring and learning new programs (Level 2). Or you may be a person with active interest in the ins and outs of how programs work (Level 3) and feel easy with customization, writing macros, and the like.

(I will not deal here with the "hacker," a Level 4 person who lives and breathes computing.)

Being more of a novice does not mean you have to choose a "baby" program, or even that you shouldn't choose a very complex program. It does mean, however, allowing for extra learning time, perhaps placing more emphasis on user-friendliness, and finding sources of support for your learning, such as friends or colleagues, or on-line discussion groups on the Internet. People at different levels seem to have quite different reactions to the same programs. So, for example, a person at Level 2 or 3 might like a program that puts the maximum information on one screen because this allows her to find what she wants quickly, and she might learn the program very quickly. A person at Level 1 might find all that information overwhelming at first, and might take a little longer to learn that program because of it. But, once he has learned the program, our Level 1 person would probably benefit from the layout in the same way as the more advanced computer user.

Question 2:
Are You Choosing for One Project or for the Next Few Years?

A word processor does not care what you are writing about, so most people pick one and stick with it until something better comes along and they feel motivated to learn it. But particular qualitative analysis programs tend to be good for certain types of analyses. Switching will cost you learning time and money. Think about whether you should choose the best program for this project or the program that best covers the kinds of projects you are considering over the next few years. For example, a particular code-and-retrieve program might look adequate for the current project and be cheaper or look easier to learn than some other program. But if you are likely to need a more fully featured code-based theory builder down the road, it might make more sense to get started with one of those now (assuming you choose one that includes good code-and-retrieve capabilities).

Question 3:
What Kind of Database and Project Will You Be Working On?

Here the questions begin to get a bit more specific. As you look at detailed software features, you need to play them against a series of detailed issues. Because of the nature of computers, it becomes essential to give careful attention to the issue of understanding the nature and structure of qualitative data sets. The issues here have to do with the physical and logical form of the data: how structured and how consistent it is, how data about a case are organized, and so on. In terms of the issues presented below, there may be great variation from project to project, even within a given analytic approach (say, grounded theory, ethnography, or narrative analysis). Epistemological issues, such as the interpretive nature of observational notes, coding, or memos, or the social construction of interview data, although very important for research methodology, do not come into play here; the question is whether the program you choose provides the organizational tools for the text, graphics, audio, or video you want to put into it.

Data sources per case: single versus multiple. You may be collecting data on a case from many different sources (say your case is defined as a student, and you talk with several teachers, the student's parents and friends, the principal, and the student herself). Some programs are specifically designed to handle data organized like this, others are not designed this way but can handle multiple sources pretty well, and some really do not have the flexibility you'll need. As mentioned above, you should look for strong tools for tracking cases through different documents. Some programs provide good support for this in code structures (particularly programs with highly structured code systems, like NUD•IST and NVivo, and to lesser degrees in programs with flexible code systems like ATLAS/ti) or through the use of speaker identifiers in programs like AFTER, the Ethnograph, or Code-A-Text. Also, look for programs that are good at making links, such as those with hypertext capability, and that attach "source tags" telling you where information is coming from.

Single versus multiple cases. If you have multiple cases, you usually will want to sort them out according to different patterns or configurations, and/or work with only some of the cases, and/or do cross-case comparisons. Multicase studies can get complicated. For example, your cases might be students (and you might have data from multiple sources for each student). Your students might all be "nested" in (grouped by) classrooms, which might be nested within schools, which in turn might be nested in districts. Look for software that will easily select different portions of the database, and/or do configurational analysis (Ragin, 1987) across your cases; software that can help you create multiple-case matrix displays, usually by gathering together the data that correspond to the different cells of the matrix, is also useful.

Fixed records versus revised. Will you be working with data that are fixed (such as official documents or survey responses) or data that will be revised (with corrections, added codes, annotations, memos, and so on)? Some programs make database revision easy, whereas others are quite rigid, so that revising can use up a lot of time and energy. Some will let you revise annotations and coding easily, but not the underlying text, and some will let you revise both. Although this has been a constraining issue up to now, the trend in new programs and upcoming revisions of existing ones is toward programs that allow you to edit underlying text easily.

Structured versus open. Are your data strictly organized (for example, responses to a standard questionnaire or interview) or free-form (running field notes, participant observation, and so on)? Highly organized data can usually be more easily, quickly, and powerfully managed in programs set up to accommodate them—for example, those with well-defined "records" for each case and "fields" (or variables) with data for each record. Structured surveys may benefit from survey-oriented programs like Sphinx Survey or EZ-Text, which take advantage of predictable structure to provide good data-manipulation tools. Free-form text demands a more flexible program. There are programs that specialize in one or the other type of data, and some that work fairly well with either.

Uniform versus diverse entries. Your data may all come from interviews, or you may have information of many sorts: archival documents, field observations, questionnaires, pictures, audiotapes, videotapes (this issue overlaps with single versus multiple sources, above). Some programs handle diverse data types easily, and others are narrow and stern in their requirements. If you will have diverse entries, look for software designed to handle multiple sources and types of data, with good source tags and good linking features in a hypertext mode. The ability to handle "off-line" data—referring you to material not actually loaded into your program—is a plus. Many programs can be tricked into doing this if you are clever about it. If you want to be able to code, and then retrieve, audio or video, look for programs like AFTER, ATLAS/ti, Code-A-Text, and InterClipper, which let you treat these media much like text.

326

Size of database. A program's database capacity may be expressed in terms of numbers of cases, numbers of data documents (files), size of individual files, and/or total database size, often expressed in kilobytes (K) or megabytes (MB). (Roughly, consider that a *single*-spaced page of printed text is about 2 to 3K.) Estimate your total size in whatever terms the program's limits are expressed, and at least double it. Most programs today are generous in terms of total database size. A few are still stingy when it comes to the size of individual texts. For example, in some programs when a document goes beyond about 10 pages, the program will insist on breaking it into smaller chunks or will open it only in a "read-only mode" browser.[4]

Question 4:
What Kind of Analyses Are You Planning to Do?

As mentioned above, identifying the name of your analysis methodology really won't do the trick here. Your choice of software depends on how you expect to go about analysis. This does not mean a detailed analysis plan, but a general sense of the style and approach you are expecting, which in turn will tell you the kinds of things you will need to be able to do with the data. For an excellent overview of a range of approaches to qualitative data analysis, and a discussion of some of the procedures associated with them, see Fielding and Lee (1998, chap. 2).

If you will be coding your data, you need a program that will let you code the way your methodology requires. If you are doing narrative analysis you may need to track temporal or narrative structures in certain ways. Or you may be focusing on building a web of hypertext links as a way of understanding the phenomena in your data, and your needs may be better served by one or another way of creating and representing that hypertext web. Coding is probably the best-supported approach at the current writing, and many researchers who use other approaches may find that their best option is to use a "coding" system for their own purposes—for example, to mark up the narrative structure of a text. More on this in the section headed "The Future," below.

The subsections below, laying out the parts of Question 4, should help you move beyond just the name of your methodology. They should help you identify the specific analytic moves you will need to make; the specific operations you will need to perform; the kinds of insights, inferences, and interpretations you will need to record; and the manner in which you plan to record them. In other words, they should help you to get specific about the things you would do if working with paper and to translate these into the functions you will need from software.

Exploratory versus confirmatory. Are you mainly planning to poke around in your data to see what they are like, evolving your ideas inductively? Or do you have some specific hypotheses in mind linked to an existing theory to test deductively? If the former, it is especially important that you have features of fast and powerful search and retrieval, easy coding and revision, along with good text and/or graphic display.

If, on the other hand, you have a beginning theory and want to test some specific hypotheses, programs with strong theory-building and -testing features are better bets. Look for programs that test propositions, or those that help you develop and extend conceptual networks.

Coding scheme firm at start versus evolving. Does your study have a fairly well defined a priori scheme for codes (categories, key words), perhaps theoretically derived, that you will apply to your data? Or will such a scheme evolve as you go, in a grounded theory style, using the "constant comparative" method (Glaser, 1965; Glaser & Strauss, 1967; Strauss & Corbin, 1998)? If the latter, it is especially important that you have easy on-screen coding (rather than being required to code on hard copy, or having to deal with cumbersome on-screen coding procedures) and features supporting easy or automated revision of codes. Hypertext linking capabilities are helpful here too. "Automated" coding (in which the program applies a code according to a rule you set up, such as when a certain phrase or a combination of other codes exists) can be helpful in either case.

Multiple versus single coding. Some programs let you assign several different codes to the same segment of text, including higher-order codes, and may let you overlap or nest coded "chunks" (the ranges of text you apply codes to). Others are stern: one chunk, one code. Still other programs will let you apply more than one code to a chunk, but will not "know" that there are multiple codes on the chunk—they'll treat it like two chunks, one for each code.

Iterative versus one pass. Do you want—and do you have the time—to keep walking through your data several times, taking different and revised cuts? Or will you limit yourself to one pass? An iterative intent should point you toward programs that give you a good display of your previous coding, are flexible, invite repeated runs, make coding revision easy, have good search and autocoding features, allow you to track connections between different parts of the text with hypertext, and can make a log of your work as you go. (See also the question of whether your records are fixed or revisable during analysis.)

Fineness of analysis. Will your analysis focus on specific words? Or lines of text? Or sentences? Paragraphs? Pages? Whole files? Look to see what the program permits (or requires, or forbids) you to do. How flexible is it? Can you look at *varying* sizes of chunks in your data? Can you define freeform segments with ease? Some programs make you choose the size of your codable segments when you first import the data, whereas others let you mix and match chunk sizes as you go.

Interest in context of data. When the program pulls out chunks of text in response to your search requests, how much surrounding information do you want to have? Do you need only the word, phrase, or line itself? Do you want the preceding and following lines/sentences/paragraphs? Do you want to see the entire file? Do you need to be able to jump right to that place in the file and do some work on it (e.g., code, edit, annotate)? Do you want the information to be marked with a "source tag" that tells you where it came from (e.g., Interview 3 with Janice Chang, page 22, line 6)? Or do you just want the source information without the text itself? Programs vary widely on this.

Intentions for displays. Analysis goes much better when you can see organized, compressed information in one place rather than in page after page of unreduced text. Some programs produce output in list form (lists of text segments, hits, codes, and so on). Some can help you produce matrix displays. They may list text segments or codes for each cell of a matrix, although you will have to actually arrange them in a matrix for display. Look for programs that let you edit, reduce, or summarize hits before you put them into a text-filled matrix with your word processor. Some programs can give you quantitative data (generally frequencies) in a matrix. Others can give you networks or hierarchical diagrams, the other major form of data display.

Qualitative only or numbers included. If your data, and/or your analyses, include the possibility of number crunching, look to see whether the program will count things and/or whether it can share information with quantitative analysis programs such as SPSS or SAS. Think carefully about what kind of quantitative analysis you'll be doing, and make sure the program you are thinking about can arrange the data appropriately. Consider, too, whether the program can link qualitative and quantitative data in a meaningful way (in terms of the analytic approach you are taking). For example, do you need to be able to select subsets of your qualitative data based on quantitative scores or demographics? Or do you need to use your qualitative coding to generate scaled variables for statistical analysis in SPSS? Or do you want to be able to generate word or code frequency tables for statistical analysis?

Collaboration. If you will be working with a team and more than one of you will be working on data analysis, look to see how the program supports collaboration. Some are fine if you just want to divide up the work with each of you coding different parts of the data and then combining the work. Others will support comparing multiple researchers' interpretations of the same data. Some programs will allow multiple users to access a shared database over a network; others will allow you to merge periodically separate copies of the database that different researchers have been working on. Programs differ in how much control they give you over the merge process. Some allow you to specify what the program will do if it finds, say, codes or memos with the same name in each of the copies being merged, whereas others follow a fixed rule. Some programs are good at letting you tell which copy a code, memo, or other object came from; others lose all identifying information so you have to use tricks like using different names in each copy (e.g., I might start the names of all codes I create with my initials, and you start yours with your initials). Some programs offer specific features for letting you compare the coding of two different researchers, for example, by showing you a table in which you can see the coding done by each.

Cut-Across Issues

The two main cut-across issues are closeness to the data and financial resources. Let's dispense quickly with the latter question first. Software varies dramatically in price. The range of prices for the programs we reviewed in Weitzman and Miles (1995b) was $0 to $1,644 per user. That is

330

still the range. (Look for discounts for educational users and multiple-user "site licenses.") In addition, programs vary a lot in the hardware they require to run efficiently. You obviously cannot use a program if it is too expensive for you, if it requires a machine you cannot afford, or if it runs on the wrong platform—say, PC instead of Mac. Happily, the U.S. Centers for Disease Control now distributes two programs free via the Web: EZ-Text for qualitative surveys and AnSWR for unstructured text. Also happily, reports from the field are that the Macintosh computers being sold today (the G3 is today's top Mac) run even the most powerful new PC programs satisfactorily with PC "emulation" software. This will, presumably, continue to be the case with future generations of Macs.

The remaining issue, closeness to the data, is more complex, and I also address it below in the section headed "Debates in the Field." For choice purposes, remember to think about what *kind* of closeness to the data is important to you. Many researchers fear that working with qualitative data on a computer will have the effect of "distancing" them from their data. This can in fact be the case. You may wind up looking at only small chunks of text at a time, or maybe even just line-number references to where the text is. This is a far cry from the feeling of deep immersion in the data that comes from reading and flipping through piles of paper.

But other programs minimize this effect. They typically keep your data files onscreen in front of you at all times; show you search results by scrolling to the hit, so that you see it in its full context; and allow you to execute most or all actions from the same data-viewing screen. Programs that allow you to build in hypertext links between different points in your data, provide good facilities for keeping track of where you are in the database, display your coding and memoing, and allow you to pull together related data quickly can in some ways help you get even *closer* to the data than you can with paper transcripts. If you choose with this consideration in mind, software can *help*, rather than hinder, your work at staying close to the data. It can, in fact, help keep you from drowning in those piles of paper.

However, having software that enhances the sense of closeness to the data may not be a crucial issue for everyone. Some researchers do not mind relying heavily on printed transcripts to get a feeling of closeness, whereas others think such heavy reliance defeats the purpose of QDA software. Furthermore, some projects simply do not require intense closeness to the data. You may be doing more abstract work, and in fact may *want* to move away from the raw data.

◆ Debates in the Field

A number of debates have taken place over the past two decades in the qualitative research community about whether the use of software is a good idea and, if so, what kinds of software are a good idea. I will address four of the debated issues here: closeness to the data, whether software drives methodology, whether new researchers should start off doing analysis by hand, and whether software really affects rigor, consistency, and thoroughness.[5]

Closeness to the Data

The issue of closeness to the data, which I have just discussed in terms of program choice, has been one of the big concerns raised by qualitative researchers over the years. Experienced researchers have often found that as difficult as it was, the process of spending endless hours sitting on the floor surrounded by piles and piles of paper led them, by necessity, to a very rich and thorough familiarity with their data. But as I have tried to argue above, software need not cut down on this familiarity. Software neither makes it better nor worse, it simply changes it. Although some programs still create the sense that you are staring at just a small window of text with no sense of what lies around it, there are now many programs available that provide rich contextual information (such as source information, graphical maps of hypertext links, navigable outlines, and linked lists of codes, documents, and text segments), and may in fact help you get to know your data better than ever before.

Does Software Drive Methodology?

Another concern has been that researchers might wind up adapting their research to the software they use, rather than the other way around (Coffey et al., 1996; Kelle, 1997; Lonkila, 1995)—that is, that the software will impose a methodological or conceptual approach. In fact, software developers bring assumptions, conceptual frameworks, and sometimes even methodological and theoretical ideologies to the development of their products. These have important implications for the impact that using a particular program will have on your analyses. However, as I have argued elsewhere, you need not, and in fact should not, be trapped by these assumptions and frameworks; there are often ways of bending a program to your own purposes (see Weitzman, in press). For example, a program may allow you to define only hierarchical relations among codes. You might work around this by creating redundant codes in different parts of the hierarchy, or by keeping track of the extra relationships *you* want to define with memos and network diagrams.

The fact that developers bring conceptual assumptions to their work is in fact one of the strengths of the field. Many of the developers, particularly of code-and-retrieve and code-based theory builder programs, are researchers themselves. They have invested enormous intellectual energy in finding the right tools for analyses of different types, and the user can benefit greatly from their investment.

It is also true that the design of the software can have an impact on analysis. For example, different programs work with different "metaphors"—that is, different ways of presenting the relationships among codes, and between codes and text. Kwalitan, NUD•IST, the Ethnograph, and winMAX all allow hierarchical relations among codes. For studies in which you are organizing your conceptual categories hierarchically, these programs offer significant strengths. If you want to represent nonhierarchical relationships, even if you choose to try to work around this metaphor, it may be less comfortable than using a program like ATLAS/ti that explicitly supports more flexible networks. HyperRESEARCH emphasizes the relationship between codes and cases, rather than codes and chunks of text. When you code a chunk of text, you create an entry on what looks like an index card for a particular case. This strongly supports and encourages thinking that stresses casewise and cross-case phenomena, but makes it harder to look for and think about relationships among codes *within* a text (although version 2, under development at the time of this writing, appears to be solving this problem). Finally, Code-A-Text offers a quite different set of coding metaphors: (a) codes arranged into "scales" (you can assign only one code from each scale to a segment of text, useful if you want to code your text chunks by making mutually exclusive judgments on a variety of factors), (b) codes automatically assigned according to words in the text, and (c) open-ended "interpretations" you write about each text chunk. Working with this collection of coding metaphors could be expected to lead you to consider your text in somewhat different ways than with one of the other metaphors described above.

Similar issues exist in the choice of other types of software, such as textbase managers. InfoTree32 XT allows you to arrange texts in a hierarchical tree and lets you drag texts around to rearrange them. Folio Views also allows you to create a hierarchical outline, but gives you the additional capability of creating multiple, nonsequential "groupings" of texts that you can activate any time you wish. Folio Views and askSam let you insert fields whenever and wherever you want in any given record, whereas InfoTree32 XT requires that you use a standard field set (of your own design) throughout the whole database. Idealist not only lets you customize the field set for each record, you can also create a variety of record types, each with its own set of fields, and mix them in the same database. Finally, whereas most of these programs show you just one record at a time, Folio Views shows you a word processor-like view in which records appear one right after the other as paragraphs. Clearly, each of these programs shows you a quite different view of your data, and so each may encourage different ways of thinking about your data. The different programs all have different strengths and weaknesses. It is also true that a clever user will be able to bend each of these flexible packages to a wide variety of different tasks, overcoming many of the differences between them.

Each of these assumptions is both a benefit for some modes of analysis and a constraint. The key, then, is not to get trapped by the assumptions of the program. If you are aware of what they are, you can be clever and work around them. The program should serve *your* analytic needs, goals, and assumptions, not the other way around. Researchers interested in empirical work on the impacts of different programs on research are again encouraged to refer to Fielding and Lee (1998).

Should New Researchers Start Off Doing Analysis by Hand?

There is no clear-cut answer to this question. Certainly, it is important that new researchers begin by learning about how to do good analysis, rather than just how to use a program. Whether that means doing a first project by hand or learning about analysis and software to do it with in the same course is a question best left to teachers. I have taught both ways, and in my experience students benefit from having some experience with manual methods, if only a few coding exercises, so that they can get the feel of what is happening analytically before they start worrying about using the software.

Does Software Really Affect
Rigor? Consistency? Thoroughness?

Some researchers are dedicated to the notion that software makes for more rigorous research. There are even rumors floating around of federal funding agencies requiring the use of software in grant proposals. Yet, as I have argued above, software will not pull good work out of a poor researcher. On the other hand, for all the reasons outlined above in the subsection headed "Real Hopes," software can in fact help competent researchers do more rigorous, consistent, and thorough analysis than they otherwise might. The issue should be conceptualized not as whether the software makes the work more rigorous, but whether the researcher uses the software to do more rigorous work than he or she could without it.

◆ The Future

It is my hope that the future will see a continuation of current trends, both in scholarship and in software development. Some of my specific hopes are outlined below.

Needs for Scholarship on the Topic

Ongoing review work. In addition to books like Weitzman and Miles (1995b) and its upcoming revision (which I am coauthoring with Nigel Fielding and Ray Lee), which offer comprehensive comparative reviews of the range of software available at a particular time, there is a need for regularly appearing reviews of new and revised programs as they appear. The journal *Field Methods* (formerly *Cultural Anthropology Methods*) offers regular software reviews (of quantitative as well as qualitative programs) in the same way that many journals feature regular book reviews. More journals that serve qualitative research audiences should follow this lead.

Debate on methodological questions. The kind of controversial issues addressed in this chapter need to be subjected to continued debate in the literature and among researchers. We need to be both wary of unintended influences of software and actively participating in shaping the future development of software by arguing (constructively) with developers about what we need and what we do not like.

More empirical work. The kind of empirical work on the impact of software on analysis that has been pioneered by Fielding and Lee (1998), Weaver and Atkinson (1995), Horney and Healey (1991), and Walker (1993) needs to be continued. Opinions about the impact of software are nice, but we also need to continue to subject our hypotheses to empirical research.

Needs for Software Development

We can at this point identify some of the needs of researchers that are not yet met. For example, the field is still lagging in its support for case-oriented work. A few programs have features built in for explicitly tracking individual cases through multiple documents, but few programs are set up with a strong case-oriented structure.

Display building, especially of matrices, still needs much development. A product newly released at the time of this writing, NVivo (from the developers of NUD•IST), allows you to build an interactive matrix in which you can click on cells to call up the corresponding text. Matt Miles's dream of a program that would combine this sort of functionality with the ability to actually compose the summary text for the output matrix (rather than switching to a word processor) is still one step away.

Tools for narrative and discourse analysis are still lagging as well. Researchers using these approaches continue to call for features that let them flexibly describe the structure of text and discourse, and longitudinal researchers do not yet have much in the way of tools built explicitly for tracking cases over time, though NVivo has an "attributes" feature that allows you to attach date values to codes or documents.[6] In each of these cases, researchers can either adapt coding systems to their needs or look for yet other kinds of software (such as hypertext authoring programs, project schedulers, and so on) that they can adapt to their needs.

Finally, because no one program will ever do it all best, researchers need developers to create the possibility of importing and exporting marked-up, coded, annotated data from one program to another. At this writing, there is just a little of this beginning to happen. The developers of Code-A-Text, the Ethnograph, and winMAX have agreed to work on a common structure, partially realized at this point. And ATLAS/ti has become the first program to support export of fully developed projects in XML, a new markup language that may succeed HTML, the World Wide Web formatting standard. A common standard like this, if adopted by other developers, would allow researchers to move fully developed projects easily from one program to another, just as we can now move tabular data among multiple spreadsheet and database programs.

◆ Conclusion

Unlike the situation just a decade or so ago, qualitative researchers now have available to them an array of very good software tools to assist in their research, and the use of software—including, but not limited to, word processors—seems more and more to be a regular part of the qualitative research process. There is still no one "best" program, not even for a particular methodology, and that's good. It means that researchers have to think through their methods and choose programs that fit, which should keep them from becoming reliant on the software to lead them. As researchers continue to hunt around for programs that will do the things they want, and do them better, software developers will likely continue to respond by making their programs more and more useful.

What else can we hope will come out of this collaboration between users and developers in the near future? More and better tools for sharing analyses and raw data, perhaps by allowing posting of project databases, with analytic markups, links, and memos, to the World Wide Web, as ATLAS/ti allows, or on CDs; tools for building complex reports that include analyses and data right in the report itself; and more and better tools for supporting collaboration among research teams, and for involving informants in the research process without intensive computer training.

◆ Notes

1. I discuss some exceptions in the subsection below headed "False Hopes and Fears."

2. The first release of NVivo lets you draw diagrams, but any connections you draw are represented only in the diagram, they are not representations of the defined relationships among codes and other objects, as in ATLAS/ti. You see the actual relationships among codes in a hierarchical "explorer" with expandable and collapsible branches, as in NUD•IST, the Ethnograph, and winMAX.

3. This section does not contain much in the way of references to specific software, both because the landscape changes every few years and because a single chapter does not allow for responsible comparisons among programs.

4. For any warning like this, check at the time you are choosing to see if the program under consideration presents this problem. This type of problem is worked at so regularly by developers that it would be unfair and unhelpful for me to name particular programs. Things change.

5. The reader interested in pursuing these questions further is referred to Fielding and Lee (1998) for reports of users' experiences of these and other issues when using different programs.

6. You can, in fact, attach not only date values, but text or numerical values as well.

◆ References

Bogdan, R. C., & Biklen, S. K. (1982). *Qualitative research for education: An introduction to theory and methods.* Boston: Allyn & Bacon.

Coffey, A., & Atkinson, P. (1996). *Making sense of qualitative data: Complementary research strategies.* Thousand Oaks, CA: Sage.

Coffey, A., Holbrook, B., & Atkinson, P. (1996). Qualitative data analysis: Technologies and representations. *Sociological Research Online, 1*(1). Available Internet: http://www. socresonline.org.uk/socresonline/1/1/4.html

Drass, K. A. (1980). The analysis of qualitative data: A computer program. *Urban Life, 9,* 322-353.

Fielding, N. G., & Lee, R. M. (Eds.). (1991). *Using computers in qualitative research.* London: Sage.

Fielding, N. G., & Lee, R. M. (1998). *Computer analysis and qualitative research.* London: Sage.

Glaser, B. G. (1965). The constant comparative method of qualitative analysis. *Social Problems, 12,* 436-445.

Glaser, B. G., & Strauss, A. L. (1967). *The discovery of grounded theory: Strategies for qualitative research.* Chicago: Aldine.

Goetz, J. P., & LeCompte, M. D. (1984). *Ethnography and qualitative design in educational research.* New York: Academic Press.

Horney, M. A., & Healey, D. (1991, April). *Hypertext and database tools for qualitative research.* Paper presented at the annual meeting of the American Educational Research Association, Chicago.

Kelle, U. (Ed.). (1995). *Computer-aided qualitative data analysis: Theory, methods and practice.* London: Sage.

Kelle, U. (1997). Theory building in qualitative research and computer programs for the management of textual data. *Sociological Research Online, 2*(2). Available Internet: http://www.socresonline.org.uk/socresonline/2/2/1.html

Lee, R. M., & Fielding, N. G. (1991). Computing for qualitative research: Options, problems and potential. In N. G. Fielding & R. M. Lee (Eds.), *Using computers in qualitative research* (pp. 1-13). London: Sage.

Lofland, J., & Lofland, L. H. (1984). *Analyzing social settings: A guide to qualitative observation and analysis* (2nd ed.). Belmont, CA: Wadsworth.

Lonkila, M. (1995). Grounded theory as an emerging paradigm for computer-assisted qualitative data analysis. In U. Kelle (Ed.), *Computer-aided qualitative data analysis: Theory, methods and practice* (pp. 41-51). London: Sage.

Mangabeira, W. (Ed.). (1996). Qualitative sociology and computer programs: Advent and diffusion of CAQDAS [Special issue]. *Current Sociology, 44*(1).

Miles, M. B., & Huberman, A. M. (1984). *Qualitative data analysis: A sourcebook of new methods.* Beverly Hills, CA: Sage.

Miles, M. B., & Huberman, A. M. (1994). *Qualitative data analysis: An expanded sourcebook* (2nd ed.). Thousand Oaks, CA: Sage.

Ragin, C. C. (1987). *The comparative method: Moving beyond qualitative and quantitative strategies.* Berkeley: University of California Press.

Seidel, J. V., & Clark, J. A. (1984). The Ethnograph: A computer program for the analysis of qualitative data. *Qualitative Sociology, 7,* 110-125.

Shelly, A., & Sibert, E. (1985). *The QUALOG users' manual.* Syracuse, NY: Syracuse University, School of Computer and Information Science.

Strauss, A. L., & Corbin, J. (1998). *Basics of qualitative research: Techniques and procedures for developing grounded theory* (2nd ed.). Thousand Oaks, CA: Sage.

Tesch, R. (1990). *Qualitative research: Analysis types and software tools.* New York: Falmer.

Tesch, R. (1991). Computers and qualitative data II. *Qualitative Sociology, 14*(3).

Walker, B. L. (1993). Computer analysis of qualitative data: A comparison of three packages. *Qualitative Health Research, 3*(1), 91-111.

Weaver, A., & Atkinson, P. (1995). From coding to hypertext: Strategies for microcomputing and qualitative data analysis. In R. G. Burgess (Ed.), *Studies in qualitative methodology.* Greenwich, CT: JAI.

Weitzman, E. A. (1999). Analyzing qualitative data with computer software. *Health Services Research, 34*(5), 1241-1263.

Weitzman, E. A., & Miles, M. B. (1995a). Choosing software for qualitative data analysis: An overview. *Cultural Anthropology Methods, 7*(1), 1-5.

Weitzman, E. A., & Miles, M. B. (1995b). *Computer programs for qualitative data analysis: A software sourcebook.* Thousand Oaks, CA: Sage.

9

Analyzing

Talk and Text

David Silverman

◆ The linguistic character of field data is most obvious in the case of texts and interviews. Even if our aim is to search for supposedly "external" realities (e.g., class, gender, power), our raw material is inevitably the words written in documents or spoken by interview respondents. Moreover, although observational data should properly include descriptions of contextual aspects of social interaction (what Stimson, 1986, calls "the sociology of space and place"), much of what we observe in formal and informal settings will inevitably consist of conversations.

Of course, if our data are transcripts of audiotapes, then we come face-to-face with how talk organizes the world. Although talk is sometimes seen as trivial ("mere" talk), it has increasingly become recognized as the primary medium through which social interaction takes place. In households and in more "public" settings, families and friends assemble their activities through talk. At work, we converse with one another and have accounts of our activities placed in dossiers and files. As Heritage (1984)

AUTHOR'S NOTE: I am most grateful for the comments of Norman Denzin, Jaber Gubrium, and Yvonna Lincoln on a first draft of this chapter.

argues, "The social world is a pervasively conversational one in which an overwhelming proportion of the world's business is conducted through the medium of spoken interaction" (p. 239). Indeed, what Heritage calls "the world's business" includes such basic features as telling news, deciding if one should commit suicide, and children's learning how to converse with their mothers (see Sacks, 1992a; Silverman, 1998b, chap. 1).

Yet a curiously prelinguistic sensibility pervades much social research. This is most obvious in quantitative researchers' preference for "operational definitions" that arbitrarily define the meaning of (linguistically mediated) phenomena. Less apparently, an inattention to participants' talk-in-interaction is shown by those qualitative researchers who claim to have direct access to the external "realities" mentioned earlier. These "realities" are often simply "read off" interview respondents' answers or transcripts of talk, with little or no reference to whether (and how) they are made reference to by the speakers. So, for instance, our "knowledge" that the speaker is a woman or that the setting is, say, a medical consultation is of no analytic relevance unless we can demonstrate the relevance of these features in the actions of the parties concerned (see Schegloff, 1991).

By contrast, 20th-century thought has resisted such researchers' assumptions that words are simply a transparent medium to "reality." From Saussure (1974), the Swiss linguist, we learn that signs derive meaning from their relation to other signs. From Wittgenstein (1968), the philosopher, we understand that the meaning of a word derives largely from its *use*. Consequently, as Wittgenstein puts it,

> when philosophers use a word—"knowledge," "being," "object" (etc.) . . . —and try to grasp the *essence* of the thing, one must first ask oneself: is the word ever actually used in this way in the language-game which is its original home?
>
> What *we* do is to bring words back from their metaphysical to their everyday use. (para. 116)

Wittgenstein's critique of some philosophers can, of course, be turned upon those quantitative researchers who arbitrarily construct "operational definitions" of phenomena without ever studying the "language-game" in which a phenomenon has its everyday home. However, what Wittgenstein is saying constitutes an equally relevant critique of qualitative research that claims to discover social "realities" unaddressed by participants.

As Garfinkel (1967) implies, both quantitative researchers' scientism and qualitative researchers' claims for "empathic understanding" are deeply commonsensical, because both trade off the capacity of societal members to "see through" appearances to an underlying reality. In this sense, there is a strong similarity between social researchers who claim to be able to access some social structure or emotion "behind" their data and, say, TV sports commentators who tell their audiences what sportspeople are "feeling." Both parties use (as a tacit resource) what Garfinkel calls the "documentary method of interpretation" to produce their "findings" (see Gubrium & Holstein, Chapter 7, Volume 2).

This link between social research and society is hardly surprising. Such activities as observation and interviewing are not unique to social researchers. For instance, as Foucault (1977) has noted, the observation of the prisoner has been at the heart of modern prison reform, and the method of questioning used in the interview reproduces many of the features of the Catholic confessional or the psychoanalytic consultation. Its pervasiveness is reflected by the centrality of the interview study in so much contemporary social research. Think, for instance, of how much interviews are a central (and popular) feature of mass-media products, from "talk shows" to "celebrity interviews." Perhaps we all live in what might be called an "interview society," in which interviews seem central to making sense of our lives (see Atkinson & Silverman, 1997).

This broader societal context may explain qualitative researchers' temptation to gloss their methodology as "empathic understanding" and to use methods such as the interview. Of course, such a link between culture and method should be an opportunity to question ourselves about our methodological preferences. However, such self-questioning (sometimes—mistakenly, I think—referred to as reflexivity) does not itself provide a warrant for the choices we make.[1] As I argue below, such a warrant depends on our preparedness to describe societal members' actual methods for achieving whatever they do achieve.

These large-scale questions need, of course, to be embedded in our data analysis. I now turn to such issues, examining three kinds of linguistically mediated data: interviews, texts, and transcripts. It should be apparent that here, as elsewhere, I am concerned with data *analysis* rather than the mechanics of data gathering.

◆ Interviews

For the qualitative-minded researcher, the open-ended interview apparently offers the opportunity for an authentic gaze into the soul of another, or even for a politically correct dialogue in which researcher and researched offer mutual understanding and support. The rhetoric of interviewing "in depth" repeatedly hints at such a collection of assumptions. Here we see a stubbornly persistent romantic impulse in contemporary sociology: the elevation of the experiential as the authentic—the selfsame gambit that can make the TV talk-show or news interview so appealing.

Such qualitative researchers share survey researchers' assumption that interview responses index some external reality ("facts" or "events" for the latter group and "feelings" or "meanings" for the former). Both groups build into their research designs various devices to ensure the accuracy of their interpretations. So you can try to ensure that you have accurately depicted such realities and experiences by such measures as intercoder agreement and computer-assisted qualitative data programs. And you can check the accuracy of what your respondents tell you through other observations. Let us call this a *realist* approach to interview data.

An alternative approach treats interview data as accessing various stories or narratives through which people describe their worlds (see Holstein & Gubrium, 1995, 1997). This *narrative* approach claims that, by abandoning the attempt to treat respondents' accounts as potentially "true" pictures of "reality," we open up for analysis the culturally rich methods through which interviewers and interviewees, in concert, generate plausible accounts of the world (e.g., Gubrium, 1993; Voysey, 1975).

I am aware that many readers of this volume will favor the former approach. In this light, I want to give an example of how one realist interview study was eventually driven in a narrative direction. Jody Miller and Barry Glassner (1997) describe a study involving in-depth, open-ended interviews with young women (aged 13 to 18) who claim affiliation with youth gangs in their communities (Miller, 1996). These interviews followed the completion of survey interviews administered by Miller. Here is how Miller and Glassner (1997) describe the purposes of each form of data:

> While the survey interview gathers information about a wide range of topics, including the individual, her school, friends, family, neighborhood, delinquent involvement, arrest history, sexual history, and victimization, in

addition to information about the gang, the in-depth interview is concerned exclusively with the roles and activities of young women in youth gangs, and the meanings they describe as emerging from their gang affiliation. (p. 105)

Let us focus on the data that Miller obtained in her in-depth interviews. This is one example:

> Describing why she joined her gang, one young women told Miller, "well, I didn't get any respect at home. I wanted to get some love and respect from somebody somewhere else." (p. 107)

Here is another respondent's explanation of why she joined a gang:

> I didn't have *no* family. . . . I had nothin' else. (p. 107)

Another young woman, when asked to speculate on why young people join gangs, suggested:

> Some of 'em are like me, don't have, don't really have a basic home or steady home to go to, you know, and they don't have as much love and respect in the home so they want to get it elsewhere. And, and, like we get, have family members in gangs or that were in gangs, stuff like that. (p. 107)

Let us assume that you have gathered these data and now want to begin analysis. Put at its starkest, what are you to do with them?

In line with the realist approach, using programs such as the Ethnograph or NUD•IST (see Weitzman, Chapter 8, this volume), you may start by coding respondents' answers into the different sets of reasons they give for participation in gangs. From these data, two reasons seem to predominate: "push" factors (unsupportive families) and "pull" factors (supportive gangs).

Moreover, given the availability of survey data on the same respondents, you are now in a position to correlate each factor with various background characteristics that they have. This seems to set up your research in good shape. Not only can you search for the "subjective" meanings of adolescent gangs, you can relate these meanings to "objective" social structures.

The realist approach thus has a high degree of plausibility to social scientists who theorize the world in terms of the impact of (objective) social structures upon (subjective) dispositions. Moreover, the kind of research outputs that this approach seeks to deliver are precisely those demanded by "users" in the community, who seek immediate practical payoffs from social science research.

Calling their approach a "methodology for listening," Miller and Glassner (1997) are thus centrally concerned with "seeing the world from the perspective of our subjects" (Glassner & Loughlin, 1987, p. 37). In this respect, they share the same assumptions about the "authenticity" of "experience" as other realists and, therefore, fail to detect culturally (and locally) specific elements in several "personal" tales (see Gubrium, 1993; Voysey, 1975).

However, say we are not entirely satisfied by the apparent plausibility of realism. How can the narrative approach kick-start data analysis? Miller and Glassner (1997, pp. 103-104) suggest that one way to begin is to think about how respondents are using culturally available resources in order to construct their stories. They refer to Richardson's (1990) suggestion that "participation in a culture includes participation in the narratives of that culture, a general understanding of the stock of meanings and their relationships to each other" (p. 24).

How, then, can the data above be read in these terms? The idea is to see respondents' answers as *cultural stories*. This means examining the rhetorical force of what interviewees say as "interviewees deploy these narratives to make their actions explainable and understandable to those who otherwise may not understand" (Miller & Glassner, 1997, p. 107).

In the data already presented, Miller and Glassner note that respondents make their actions understandable in two ways. First, they do not attempt to challenge public views of gangs as bad. But, second, they do challenge the notion that the interviewee herself is bad. However, Miller and Glassner (1997) note that not all their respondents glibly recycle conventional cultural stories. As they put it, "Some of the young women go farther and describe their gang involvement in ways that directly challenge prevailing stereotypes about gangs as groups that are inherently bad or antisocial and about females' roles within gangs" (p. 108). Here are some of the respondents' accounts that they have in mind:

It was really, it was just normal life, the only difference was, is, that we had meetings. (p. 109)

[We] play cards, smoke bud, play dominoes, play video games. That's basically all we do is play. You would be surprised. This is a bunch of big kids. It's a bunch of big old kids in my set. (p. 109)

345

In accounts like these, Miller and Glassner argue that there is an explicit challenge to what the interviewees know to be popular beliefs about youth gangs. Instead of accepting the conventional definition of their behavior as "deviant," the girls attempt to convey the normalcy of their activities.

These narratives directly challenge stereotypical cultural stories of the gang. Following Richardson, Miller and Glassner (1997) refer to such accounts as "collective stories" that "resist the cultural narratives about groups of people and tell alternative stories" (Richardson, 1990, p. 25). Miller and Glassner's sensitive address of the narrative forms from which perspectives arise suggests an alternative path for interview analysis (for a more developed version of the narrative approach, see Gubrium & Holstein, 1997).

Summary

In light of the discussion above, I suggest below five questions that interview researchers might ask themselves.

What status do you attach to your data? Many interview studies are used to elicit respondents' perceptions. How far is it appropriate to think that people attach single meanings to their experiences? May there not be multiple meanings of a situation (e.g., living in a community home) or of an activity (e.g., being a male football fan) represented by what people say to the researcher, to each other, to caregivers, and so on (Gubrium, 1975/ 1997)?

This raises the important methodological issue of whether interview responses are to be treated as giving direct access to "experience" or as actively constructed "narratives" involving activities that themselves demand analysis (Holstein & Gubrium, 1995; Silverman, 1993). Both positions are entirely legitimate, but you need to justify and explain the position you take.

Is your analytic position appropriate to your practical concerns? Some ambitious analytic positions (e.g., hermeneutics, discourse analysis) may actually cloud the issue if your aim is simply to respond to a given social problem (e.g., living and coping in a community of elderly people, students' views of evaluation and feedback). If so, it might be simpler to acknowledge that there are more complex ways of addressing your data but to settle on presenting your research as a *descriptive* study based upon a clear social problem.

Do interview data really help in addressing your research topic? If you are interested in, say, what happens in school classrooms, should you be using interviews as your major source of data? Think about exactly why you have settled on an interview study. Certainly, it can be relatively quick to gather interview data, but not as quick as, say, gathering texts and documents. How far are you being influenced by the prominence of interviews in the media (see Atkinson & Silverman, 1997)?

In the case of the classroom, couldn't you observe what people do there instead of asking them what they think about it? Or gather documents that routinely arise in schools, such as pupils' reports, mission statements, and so on? Of course, you may still want to do an interview study. But, whatever your method, you will need to justify it and show you have thought through the practical and analytic issues involved in your choice.

Are you making too-large claims about your research? It always helps to make limited claims about your own research. Grandiose claims about originality, scope, or applicability to social problems are all hostages to fortune. Be careful in how you specify the claims of your approach. Show that you understand that it constitutes one way of "slicing the cake" and that other approaches, using other forms of data, may not be directly competitive.

Does your analysis go beyond a mere list? Identifying the main elements in your data according to some theoretical scheme should be only the first stage of your data analysis. By examining how these elements are linked together, you can bring out the active work of both interviewer and interviewee and, like them, say something lively and original.

◆ Texts

To introduce a separate section on "texts" now begins to look a little artificial. After all, to treat an interview as a narrative can mean looking for the same textual features as researchers working with printed material. Indeed, the mere act of transcription of an interview turns it into a written text. In this section, I use *text* as a heuristic device to identify data consisting of words and images that have become recorded without the intervention of a researcher (e.g., through an interview).

Of course, every way of seeing is also a way of not seeing. As Atkinson (1992, p. 459) points out, one of the disadvantages of the coding schemes used in both interview and text-based analysis is that, because they are based upon given sets of categories, they furnish "a powerful conceptual grid" from which it is difficult to escape. Although this grid is very helpful for organizing the data analysis, it also deflects attention away from uncategorized activities.

In part, Atkinson's critique vitiates the claims of many quantitative researchers in their attempts to produce reliable evidence about large samples of texts. Their favored method is "content analysis," in which the researchers establish a set of categories and then count the number of instances that fall into each category. The crucial requirement is that the categories are sufficiently precise to enable different coders to arrive at the same results when the same body of material (e.g., newspaper headlines) is examined (see Berelson, 1952).

The meat of the problem with content analysis (and its relatives) is not simply Atkinson's point about overlooked categories, but how analysts usually simply trade off their tacit members' knowledge in coining and applying whatever categories they do use. For instance, in a lecture given in the 1960s, Harvey Sacks compared the social psychologist Bales's (1950) tendency to produce immediate categories of "interaction process" with the relatively long time taken by experienced physicians to read the output of electroencephalographs. According to Sacks (1992b), one should not "categorize . . . as it comes out" (p. 28). Indeed, as we shall see shortly, our ability to categorize quickly is properly treated as a research topic rather than a research resource.

By contrast, in some qualitative research, small numbers of texts and documents may be analyzed for a very different purpose. The aim is to understand the participants' categories and to see how these are used in concrete activities such as telling stories (Propp, 1968; Sacks, 1974), assembling files (Cicourel, 1968; Gubrium & Buckholdt, 1982), and describing "family life" (Gubrium, 1992). The theoretical orientation of these qualitative researchers makes them more concerned with the processes through which texts depict "reality" than with whether such texts contain true or false statements. As Atkinson and Coffey (1997) put it:

> In paying due attention to such materials, however, one must be quite clear about what they can and cannot be used for. They are "social facts," in that they are produced, shared and used in socially organised ways. They are not, however, transparent representations of organizational routines, decision-making processes, or professional diagnoses. They construct particular kinds of representations with their own conventions. (p. 47)

The implications of this are clear:

> We should not use documentary sources as surrogates for other kinds of data. We cannot, for instance, learn through records alone how an organization actually operates day-by-day. Equally, we cannot treat records—however "official"—as firm evidence of what they report. . . . That strong reservation does not mean that we should ignore or downgrade documentary data. On the contrary, our recognition of their existence as social facts alerts us to the necessity to treat them very seriously indeed. We have to approach them for what they are and what they are used to accomplish. (p. 47)

What does it mean to approach texts "for what they are"? Potential examples are semiotics, ethnographically oriented narrative analysis, and discourse analysis. In crude terms, semiotics treats texts as systems of signs on the basis that no meaning every resides in a single term (see Silverman, 1993, pp. 71-80), narrative analysis focuses on how accounts artfully use local cultural resources (e.g., Atkinson & Coffey, 1997; Denzin, 1990; Holstein & Gubrium, 1997), and discourse analysis focuses on how different versions of the world are produced through the use of interpretive repertoires, claims to "stakes" in an account (see Potter, 1997), and constructions of knowing subjects (Prior, 1997).

Following my interest in ethnomethodology's focus on members' methods, I will sketch out a less familiar example—Sacks's account of membership categorization analysis (see also Silverman, 1998b; Watson, 1997).

Membership Categorization Analysis

Like some contemporary ethnographers concerned with narratives, Sacks (1992b) believes the issue is not to second-guess societal members, but to try to work out "how it is that people can produce sets of actions that provide that others can see such things . . . [as] persons doing inti-macy . . . persons lying, etc." (p. 119). Given that many categories can be used to describe the same person or act, Sacks's task was "to find out how they [members] go about choosing among the available sets of categories for grasping some event" (p. 41). So Sacks does not mean to imply that "society" determines which category one chooses. Instead, he wants to show the active interpretive work involved in rendering any description and the local implications of choosing any particular category. Whether or not we choose to use Sacks's precise method, he offers an inspiring way to begin to analyze the productivities of any text.

As we have already seen, "coding" is not the preserve of research scientists. All of us "code" what we hear and see in the world around us. This is what Garfinkel (1967) and Sacks (1992a) mean when they say that societal members, like social scientists, make the world observable and report-able. Put at its simplest, this means that researchers must be very careful how they use categories. For instance, Sacks (1992b) quotes from two linguists who appear to have no problem characterizing particular (invented) utterances as "simple," "complex," "casual," or "ceremonial." For Sacks (1992a), such rapid characterizations of data assume "that we can know that [such categories are accurate] without an analysis of what it is [members] are doing" (p. 429).

At this point, the experienced researcher might respond that Sacks has characterized conventional research as overly naïve. In particular, most researchers are aware of the danger of assuming any one-to-one corre-spondence between their categories and the aspects of "reality" that they purport to describe. Instead, following Weber (1949), many researchers claim that they are simply using hypothetical constructs (or "ideal types") that are to be judged only in relation to whether they are *useful,* not whether they are "accurate" or "true." However, Sacks (1992a) was aware of this argument:

> It is a very conventional way to proceed in the social sciences to propose that the machinery you use to analyze some data you have is acceptable if it is not intendedly the analysis of real phenomena. That is, you can have machinery which is a "valid hypothetical construct," and it can analyze something for you. (p. 315)

By contrast, the "machinery" in which Sacks is interested is not a set of "hypothetical constructs." Instead, Sacks's (1992a) ambitious claim throughout is "to be dealing with the real world" (p. 316). The "machinery" he sets out, then, is not to be seen as a set of more or less useful categories, but as the *actual* categories and mechanisms that members use.

Let us take a concrete example. In two of Harvey Sacks's lectures, he refers to a *New York Times* story about an interview with a U.S. Navy pilot about the pilot's missions in the Vietnam War (see Sacks, 1992b, pp. 205-222, 306-311). Sacks is especially interested in the story's report of the pilot's reported answer to a question:

> How did he feel about knowing that even with all the care he took in aiming only at military targets someone was probably being killed by his bombs?
>
> "I certainly don't like the idea that I might be killing anybody," he replied. "But I don't lose any sleep over it. You have to be impersonal in this business. Over North Vietnam I condition myself to think that I'm a military man being shot at by another military man like myself." (Sacks, 1992b, p. 205)

Sacks invites us to see how the pilot's immediate reply ("I certainly don't like the idea") shows his commitment to the evaluational scheme offered by the journalist's question. For instance, if the pilot had instead said, "Why do you ask?" he would have shown that he did not necessarily subscribe to the same moral universe as the reporter (and, by implication, the readers of the article) (Sacks, 1992b, p. 211).

Having accepted this moral schema, the pilot, as Sacks shows, now builds an answer that helps us to see him in a favorable light. The category "military man" works to defend his bombing as a category-bound activity that reminds us this is, after all, what military pilots do. The effect of this is magnified by the pilot's identification of his coparticipant as "another military man like myself." In this way, the pilot creates a pair (military man/military man) with recognizable mutual obligations (bombing/shooting at the other). In terms of this pair, the other party cannot properly complain, or, as Sacks (1992b) puts it, "there are no complaints to be offered on their part about the error of his ways, except if he happens to violate the norms that, given the device used, are operative" (p. 206).

Notice also that the pilot suggests, "You have to be impersonal in this business." Note how the category "this business" sets up the terrain on which the specific pair of military men will shortly be used. So this account could be offered by either pair-part. However, as Sacks (1992b) argues, the implication is that "this business" is one of many where impersonality is required, for "if it were the case that, that you had to be impersonal in this business held only for this business, then it might be that doing this business would be wrong in the first instance" (p. 206).

Moreover, the impersonality involved is of a special sort. Sacks points out that we hear the pilot as saying not that it is unfortunate that he cannot kill "personally," but rather that being involved in this "business" means that one must not consider that one is killing persons (p. 209). However, the pilot is only *proposing* a pair of military man/military man. In that sense, he is inviting the North Vietnamese to "play the game" in the same way a child might say to another, "I'll be third base." However, as Sacks (1992b) notes, in children's baseball, such proposals can be rejected: "If you say 'I'll be third base,' unless someone else says 'and I'll be . . .' another position, and the others say they'll be the other positions, then you're not that thing. You can't play" (p. 307).

Of course, the North Vietnamese indeed did reject the pilot's proposal. Instead, they proposed the identification of the pilot as a "criminal" and defined themselves as "doing police action." As Sacks notes, these competing definitions had implications that went beyond mere propaganda. For instance, if the navy pilot were shot down, then the Geneva Conventions about his subsequent treatment would be properly applied only if he indeed were a "military man" rather than a "criminal" (p. 307).

Unlike more formalistic accounts of action (Mead, 1934; Parsons, 1937), Sacks's analysis shows us the nitty-gritty mechanisms through which we construct moral universes "involving appropriate kinds of action and particular actors with motives, desires, feelings, aspirations and sense of justice" (J. F. Gubrium, personal communication, January 1997). Like Garfinkel (1967), Sacks wants to avoid treating people as "cultural dopes," representing the world in ways that some culture demanded. Instead, Sacks approaches "culture" as an "inference-making machine": a descriptive apparatus, administered and used in specific contexts.

Summary

I will conclude my discussion of texts with a further summary statement. Here I will not use questions, but take the risk of offering three pieces of advice that emerge out of the preceding discussion (for a development of this argument, see Silverman, 2000).

Have a clear analytic approach. Successful textual studies recognize the value of working with a clearly defined approach. Having chosen your approach (e.g., Foucauldian discourse analysis, Saussurian semiotics, Sacks's analysis of membership categorizations), treat it as a "toolbox" providing a set of concepts and methods to select your data and to illuminate your analysis.

Recognize that successful analysis goes beyond a list. I make no apology for repeating a point that I made above in my discussion of interview studies. It seems to me that the distinctive contribution qualitative researchers can make is in utilizing their theoretical resources in the deep analysis of small bodies of publicly shareable data. This means that, unlike many quantitative researchers, we are not satisfied with a simple coding of data. Instead, we have to work to show how the (theoretically defined) elements we have identified are assembled or mutually laminated.

Limit your data. Like many other qualitative approaches, textual analysis depends upon very detailed data analysis. To make such analysis effective, it is imperative that you have a limited body of data with which to work. So, although it may be useful initially to explore different kinds of data (e.g., newspaper reports, scientific textbooks, magazine advice pages), you should usually do this only to establish the data set with which you can most effectively work. Having chosen your data set, you should limit your material further by taking only a few texts or parts of texts (e.g., headlines).

◆ Transcripts

The three types of qualitative data discussed here all end up in the form of some kind of text. In interviews, researchers usually work with written transcripts. Similarly, audiotapes of naturally occurring interaction are usually transcribed prior to (and as part of) the analysis.

The two main social science traditions that inform the analysis of transcripts of tapes are conversation analysis (CA) and discourse analysis (DA). For an introduction to CA, see ten Have (1998); on DA, see Potter and Wetherell (1987) and Potter (1997).[2] In the rest of this chapter, I will deal with two more practical issues: (a) the advantages of working with tapes

and transcripts of naturally occurring talk and (b) the elements of how to
do analysis of such tapes.

Why Work With Tapes?

> The kind of phenomena I deal with are always transcriptions of actual oc-
> currences in their actual sequence. (Sacks, 1984, p. 25)

In contemporary philosophy, Sacks was attracted to speech-act theory,
which, like him, treats talk as an activity. However, Austin (1962) and
Searle (1969) did not study actual talk but worked with invented examples
and their own intuitions about what it makes sense to say. Sacks (1992b),
on the contrary, notes:

> One cannot invent new sequences of conversation and feel happy with
> them. You may be able to take "a question and answer," but if we have to ex-
> tend it very far, then the issue of whether somebody would really say that,
> after, say, the fifth utterance, is one which we could not confidently argue.
> One doesn't have a strong intuition for sequencing in conversation. (p. 5)

The earlier ethnographers had generally relied on recording their
observations through field notes. Why did Sacks prefer to use an audio recorder? Sacks's answer is that we cannot rely on our recollections of conversations. Certainly, depending on our memories, we can usually summarize what different people said. But it is simply impossible to remember (or
even to note at the time) such matters as pauses, overlaps, and inbreaths.

Now, whether you think these kinds of things are important or not will
depend upon what you can show with or without them. Indeed, you may
not even be convinced that conversation itself is a particularly interesting
topic. But, at least by studying tapes of conversations, you are able to focus
on the "actual details" of one aspect of social life. As Sacks (1992b) puts it:

> My research is about conversation only in this incidental way, that we can
> get the actual happenings on tape and transcribe them more or less, and
> therefore have something to begin with. If you can't deal with the actual de-
> tail of actual events then you can't have a science of social life. (p. 26)

Tapes and transcripts also offer more than just "something to begin
with." In the first place, they are a public record, available to the scientific
community, in a way that field notes are not. Second, they can be replayed

and transcriptions can be improved, and analyses can take off on different tacks unlimited by the original transcript. As Sacks (1992b) told his students:

> I started to play around with tape recorded conversations, for the single virtue that I could replay them; that I could type them out somewhat, and study them extendedly, who knew how long it might take. . . . It wasn't from any large interest in language, or from some theoretical formulation of what should be studied, but simply by virtue of that; I could get my hands on it, and I could study it again and again. And also, consequentially, others could look at what I had studied, and make of it what they could, if they wanted to disagree with me. (p. 622)

A third advantage of detailed transcripts is that, if you want to, you can inspect sequences of utterances without being limited to the extracts chosen by the first researcher. For it is within these sequences, rather than in single turns of talk, that we make sense of conversation. As Sacks (1992b) points out:

> Having available for any given utterance other utterances around it, is extremely important for determining what was said. If you have available only the snatch of talk that you're now transcribing, you're in tough shape for determining what it is. (p. 729)

There remains the potential charge that data based mainly on audio recordings is incomplete. We see Sacks's response to this issue when a student asks a question about "leaving out things like facial expressions" from his analysis (1992b, p. 26). Sacks at once concedes that "it would be great to study them [such things]. It's an absence." Nonetheless, he constructs a two-part defense of his data.

First, the idea of "completeness" may itself be an illusion. Surely, there cannot be totally "complete" data any more than there can be a "perfect" transcript? Second, Sacks (1992b, pp. 26-27) recognized some of the undoubted technical problems involved in camera positioning and the like if one were to use videos. These are the very issues that have been addressed, if not resolved, by more recent work based on video-recorded data (e.g., Heath, 1986, 1997; Heath & Luff, 1992). Rather, as always in science, everything will depend on what you are trying to do and where it seems that you may be able to make progress. As Sacks (1992b) puts it, "One gets started where you can maybe get somewhere" (p. 26).

It should not be assumed that the preparation of transcripts is simply a technical detail prior to the main business of the analysis. The convenience of transcripts for presentational purposes is no more than an added bonus. As Atkinson and Heritage (1984) point out, the production and use of transcripts are essentially "research activities." They involve close, repeated listenings to recordings that often reveal previously unnoted recurring features of the organization of talk. Such listenings can most fruitfully be done in group data sessions. As described by Paul ten Have (1998), work in such groups usually begins with the members listening to an extract from a tape with a draft transcript and agreeing upon improvements to the transcript. Then

> the participants are invited to proffer some observations on the data, to select an episode which they find "interesting" for whatever reason, and formulate their understanding or puzzlement, regarding that episode. Then anyone can come in to react to these remarks, offering alternatives, raising doubts, or whatever. (p. 124)

However, as ten Have makes clear, such group data sessions should be rather more than anarchic free-for-alls:

> Participants are, on the one hand, *free* to bring in anything they like, but, on the other hand, *required* to ground their observations in the data at hand, although they may also support them with reference to their own data-based findings or those published in the literature. (p. 124)

Analyzing Tapes

As with any kind of data, the analysis of tapes and transcripts depends upon the generation of some research problem out of a particular theoretical orientation. Like the writing of field notes, the preparation of a transcript from an audio- or videotape is a theoretically saturated activity. Where there is more than one researcher, debate about what you are seeing and hearing is never just about collating data—it is data *analysis*.

But how do you push the analysis beyond an agreed transcript? The temptation is to start at line 1 of your transcript and work your way down the page, making observations as you go. However, the danger of proceeding in this way is that your observations are likely to be ad hoc and commonsensical. Moreover, if you are committed to an approach (like CA

TABLE 9.1   How to Do Conversation Analysis

1. Always try to identify sequences of related talk.
2. Try to examine how speakers take on certain roles or identities through their talk (e.g., questioner/answerer or client-professional).
3. Look for particular outcomes in the talk (e.g., a request for clarification, a repair, laughter) and work backward to trace the trajectory through which a particular outcome was produced.

SOURCE: Silverman (1998a).

or DA) that looks at how the participants coproduce some meaning, then beginning with a single utterance gets you off on the wrong foot.

How else can you proceed? Jennifer Mason (1996) suggests that you can formulate a research topic in terms of different kinds of puzzles. Identifying a puzzle can also be a way to kick-start the analysis of a transcript. Once you have found your puzzle, the best method is often to *work back and forth* through your transcript to see how the puzzle arises and is resolved. This implies a strongly inductive bent to this kind of research. It follows that any research claims need to be identified in precise analyses of detailed transcripts. It is therefore necessary to avoid premature theory construction and the "idealization" of research materials that uses only general, nondetailed characterizations. Heritage (1984) sums up these assumptions as follows:

> Specifically, analysis is strongly "data-driven"—developed from phenomena which are in various ways evidenced in the data of interaction. Correspondingly, there is a strong bias against *a priori* speculation about the orientations and motives of speakers and in favour of detailed examination of conversationalists' actual actions. Thus the empirical conduct of speakers is treated as the central resource out of which analysis may develop. (p. 243)

In practice, Heritage adds, this means that it must be demonstrated that the regularities described can be shown to be produced by the participants and attended to by them as grounds for their own inferences and actions. Further, deviant cases, in which such regularities are absent, must be identified and analyzed.

However, the way in which CA obtains its results is rather different from how we might intuitively try to analyze talk. It may be helpful,

357

TABLE 9.2   Common Errors in Conversation Analysis

1. Explaining a turn at talk by reference to the speaker's intentions (except insofar as such intentions are topicalized in the conversation).
2. Explaining a turn at talk by reference to a speaker's role or status (e.g., as a doctor or as a man or woman).
3. Trying to make sense of a single line of transcript or utterance in isolation from the surrounding talk.

SOURCE: Silverman (1998a).

therefore, if I conclude this section by offering a crude set of prescriptions about how to do CA (Table 9.1) and a list of things to avoid in doing CA (Table 9.2). If we follow these rules, the analysis of conversations does not require exceptional skills. As Schegloff (1992) puts it in his introduction to Sacks's collected lectures, all we need to do is "begin with some observations, then find the problem for which these observations could serve as . . . the solution" (p. xlviii).

This means that doing the kind of systematic data analysis that CA demands is not an impossibly difficult activity. As Harvey Sacks (1992a) once pointed out, in doing CA we are only reminding ourselves about things we already know:

> I take it that lots of the results I offer, people can see for themselves. And they needn't be afraid to. And they needn't figure that the results are wrong because they can see them. . . . [It is] as if we found a new plant. It may have been a plant in your garden, but now you see it's different than something else. And you can look at it to see how it's different, and whether it's different in the way that somebody has said. (p. 488)

Wittgenstein (although mentioned only twice in Sacks's lectures), and his concern for assembling reminders of what we know already, is clearly relevant. Wittgenstein (1968) writes: "The aspects of things that are most important for us are hidden because of their simplicity and familiarity" (para. 129). Now Wittgenstein, of course, is referring to what is hidden from philosophers. But the same issue often arises for social scientists—to whom things can be "hidden because of their simplicity and familiarity."

◆ Conclusion

In a sense, nearly all qualitative research touches upon talk and text. In this chapter, however, I have resisted such inclusiveness in favor of a much more strictly defined version of appropriate ways of responding to the linguistically mediated character of qualitative data.

Although my own approach derives from Garfinkel's and Sacks's concern with members' methods, I have nonetheless tried to avoid adopting a "take it or leave it" approach. In particular, I have highlighted points of contact with a wide range of other approaches, including narrative-based ethnography, discourse analysis, and semiotics.

Above all, I have endeavored to offer practical advice to novice researchers who may be considering setting out in this direction. However, rather than offering a simple cookbook of techniques, this chapter, I hope, derives from a coherent set of principles. At the risk of restating what is already obvious, I conclude with a statement of four of those principles:

- ◆ Qualitative research is best viewed not as a set of freestanding techniques but as based on some analytically defined perspective.
- ◆ From my perspective, the particular strength of qualitative research, for both researchers and practitioners, is its ability to focus on actual practice in situ, looking at how social interactions are routinely *enacted*.
- ◆ The fashionable identification of qualitative method with an analysis of how people "see things" ignores the importance of how people "do things." This means that the apparent identification of nonquantitative social science with the open-ended interview needs to be reexamined. This does *not* mean that we should never interview, but that, as a minimum, we should first think through the alternatives.
- ◆ Qualitative researchers ought to question the conventional wisdom that their kind of research can only be "exploratory" or "anecdotal." Case study methods can be applied to large data sets and standard issues of "reliability" can, in part, be addressed by systematic transcription of data (see Peräkylä, 1997; Silverman, 1993, pp. 144-170).

◆ Notes

1. In Garfinkel's (1967) sense, *reflexivity* refers not to self-questioning but to how context is constituted through interaction (see Gubrium & Holstein, Chapter 7, Volume 2).

2. The difference between DA and CA is a matter for debate. Some DA researchers find CA's refusal to engage directly with cultural and political context disconcerting (see Wetherell, 1998). Equally, CA specialists question the validity of some DA researchers' appeals to their own sense of context (see Schegloff, 1998).

◆ References

Atkinson, J. M., & Heritage, J. C. (Eds.). (1984). *Structures of social action*. Cambridge: Cambridge University Press.

Atkinson, P. A. (1992). The ethnography of a medical setting: Reading, writing and rhetoric. *Qualitative Health Research, 2,* 451-474.

Atkinson, P. A., & Coffey, A. (1997). Analysing documentary realities. In D. Silverman (Ed.), *Qualitative research: Theory, method and practice* (pp. 45-62). London: Sage.

Atkinson, P. A., & Silverman, D. (1997). Kundera's *Immortality*: The interview society and the invention of self. *Qualitative Inquiry, 3,* 304-325.

Austin, J. L. (1962). *How to do things with words*. Oxford: Clarendon.

Bales, R. F. (1950). *Interaction process analysis*. Cambridge, MA: Addison-Wesley.

Berelson, B. (1952). *Content analysis in communicative research*. New York: Free Press.

Cicourel, A. (1968). *The social organization of juvenile justice*. New York: John Wiley.

Denzin, N. K. (1990). Harold and Agnes: A feminist narrative's undoing. *Sociological Theory, 8,* 198-216.

Foucault, M. (1977). *Discipline and punish: The birth of the prison* (A. Sheridan, Trans.). New York: Pantheon.

Garfinkel, H. (1967). *Studies in ethnomethodology*. Englewood Cliffs, NJ: Prentice Hall.

Glassner, B., & Loughlin, J. (1987). *Drugs in adolescent worlds: Burnouts to straights*. New York: St. Martin's.

Gubrium, J. F. (1992). *Out of control: Family therapy and domestic disorder*. Newbury Park, CA: Sage.

Gubrium, J. F. (1993). *Speaking of life: Horizons of meaning for nursing home residents*. New York: Aldine de Gruyter.

Gubrium, J. F. (1997). *Living and dying at Murray Manor*. Charlottesville: University Press of Virginia. (Original work published 1975)

Gubrium, J. F., & Buckholdt, D. (1982). *Describing care: Image and practice in rehabilitation*. Cambridge, MA: Oelschlager, Gunn & Hain.

Gubrium, J. F., & Holstein, J. A. (1997). *The new language of qualitative method*. New York: Oxford University Press.

Heath, C. C. (1986). *Body movement and speech in medical interaction.* Cambridge: Cambridge University Press.

Heath, C. C. (1997). Using video: Analysing activities in face to face interaction. In D. Silverman (Ed.), *Qualitative research: Theory, method and practice* (pp. 183-200). London: Sage.

Heath, C. C., & Luff, P (1992). Collaboration and control: Crisis management and multimedia technology in London underground line control rooms. *Journal of Computer Supported Cooperative Work, 1*(1-2), 69-94.

Heritage, J. C. (1984). *Garfinkel and ethnomethodology.* Cambridge: Polity.

Holstein, J. A., & Gubrium, J. F. (1995). *The active interview.* Thousand Oaks, CA: Sage.

Holstein, J. A., & Gubrium, J. F. (1997). Active interviewing. In D. Silverman (Ed.), *Qualitative research: Theory, method and practice* (pp. 113-129). London: Sage.

Mason, J. (1996). *Qualitative researching.* London: Sage.

Mead, G. H. (1934). *Mind, self, and society: From the standpoint of a social behaviorist* (C. W. Morris, Ed.). Chicago: University of Chicago Press.

Miller, J. (1996). *Female gang involvement in the Midwest: A two-city comparison.* Unpublished doctoral dissertation, University of Southern California.

Miller, J., & Glassner, B. (1997). The "inside" and the "outside": Finding realities in interviews. In D. Silverman (Ed.), *Qualitative research: Theory, method and practice* (pp. 99-112). London: Sage.

Parsons, T. (1937). *The structure of social action.* New York: McGraw-Hill.

Peräkylä, A. (1997). Reliability and validity in research based upon transcripts. In D. Silverman (Ed.), *Qualitative research: Theory, method and practice* (pp. 201-220). London: Sage.

Potter, J. (1997). Discourse analysis as a way of analysing naturally-occurring talk. In D. Silverman (Ed.), *Qualitative research: Theory, method and practice* (pp. 144-160). London: Sage.

Potter, J., & Wetherell, M. (1987). *Discourse and social psychology: Beyond attitudes and behaviour.* London: Sage.

Prior, L. (1997). Following in Foucault's footsteps: Text and context in qualitative research. In D. Silverman (Ed.), *Qualitative research: Theory, method and practice* (pp. 63-79). London: Sage.

Propp, V. I. (1968). *The morphology of the folktale* (L. A. Wagner, Ed.; 2nd rev. ed.). Austin: University of Texas Press.

Richardson, L. (1990). *Writing strategies: Reaching diverse audiences.* Newbury Park, CA: Sage.

Sacks, H. (1974). On the analyzability of stories by children. In R. Turner (Ed.), *Ethnomethodology* (pp. 216-232). Harmondsworth: Penguin.

Sacks, H. (1984). Notes on methodology. In J. M. Atkinson & J. Heritage (Eds.), *Structures of social action: Studies in conversation analysis* (pp. 21-27). Cambridge: Cambridge University Press.

Sacks, H. (1992a). *Lectures on conversation* (G. Jefferson, Ed.; Vol. 1). Oxford: Blackwell.

Sacks, H. (1992b). *Lectures on conversation* (G. Jefferson, Ed.; Vol. 2). Oxford: Blackwell.

Saussure, F. de. (1974). *Course in general linguistics*. London: Fontana.

Schegloff, E. A. (1991). Reflections on talk and social structure. In D. Boden & D. Zimmerman (Eds.), *Talk and social structure: Studies in ethnomethodology and conversation analysis* (pp. 44-70). Cambridge: Polity.

Schegloff, E. A. (1992). Introduction. In H. Sacks, *Lectures on conversation* (G. Jefferson, Ed.; Vol. 1). Oxford: Blackwell.

Schegloff, E. A. (1998). Reply to Wetherell. *Discourse and Society, 9,* 413-416.

Searle, J. R. (1969). *Speech acts*. Cambridge: Cambridge University Press.

Silverman, D. (1993). *Interpreting qualitative data: Strategies for analysing talk, text and interaction*. London: Sage.

Silverman, D. (1998a). Analysing conversation. In C. Seale (Ed.), *Researching society and culture* (pp. 261-274). London: Sage.

Silverman, D. (1998b). *Harvey Sacks: Social science and conversation analysis*. Cambridge: Polity.

Silverman, D. (2000). *Doing qualitative research: A practical handbook*. London: Sage.

Stimson, G. (1986). Place and space in sociological fieldwork. *Sociological Review, 34,* 641-656.

ten Have, P. (1998). *Doing conversation analysis: A practical guide*. Thousand Oaks, CA: Sage.

Voysey, M. (1975). *A constant burden*. London: Routledge.

Watson, R. (1997). Ethnomethodology and textual analysis. In D. Silverman (Ed.), *Qualitative research: Theory, method and practice* (pp. 80-98). London: Sage.

Weber, M. (1949). *The methodology of the social sciences* (E. A. Shils & H. A. Finch, Eds. & Trans.). New York: Free Press.

Wetherell, M. (1998). Positioning and interpretative repertoires: Conversation analysis and post-structuralism in dialogue. *Discourse and Society, 9,* 387-412.

Wittgenstein, L. (1968). *Philosophical investigations*. Oxford: Basil Blackwell.

10

Focus Groups in
Feminist Research

Esther Madriz

Me gusta mas conversar así, con un grupo de mujeres. . . .
Cuando estoy sola con un entrevistador, me siento
intimidada, asustada. Y, si ellos me llaman por el telefono,
yo nunca les contesto sus preguntas. ¿Como puedo saber
quienes son o que quieren?

[I'd rather talk this way, with a group of women. . . .
When I am alone with an interviewer, I feel intimidated,
scared. And if they call me over the telephone, I never
answer their questions. *How can I know what they really*
want or who they are?]

—María Fernández, 25-year-old Dominican woman
(participant in a focus group I led in Washington
Heights, New York City, spring 1995)

◆ The two major techniques used by researchers to collect qualitative
data are participant observation and individual interviews. Focus
groups, or group interviews, possess elements of both techniques while
maintaining their own uniqueness as a distinctive research method
(Morgan, 1988). Fundamentally, they are "a way of listening to people

and learning from them" (Morgan, 1998, p. 9). As María Fernández's words suggest, focus groups allow access to research participants who may find one-on-one, face-to-face interaction "scary" or "intimidating." By creating multiple lines of communication, the group interview offers participants such as María a safe environment where they can share ideas, beliefs, and attitudes in the company of people from the same socioeconomic, ethnic, and gender backgrounds. Some of the studies that have been conducted on focus groups show that group participants find the experience more gratifying and stimulating than individual interviews (Morgan, 1988; Wilkinson, 1998).

This chapter deals specifically with the use of focus groups from a feminist/postmodernist framework. The major concerns of feminist/postmodernist ethnographers are the moral dilemmas present in the process of interviewing and the role of the interviewer in this process. These concerns have given particular significance to the voices and feelings of the participants (Fontana & Frey, 1994). Moreover, by acknowledging the absence and invisibility that have surrounded certain population groups in the social sciences, and more specifically women of color, feminist/postmodernist researchers have made the race and ethnicity of the researchers and the respondents focal points in their studies.

For years, the voices of women of color have been silenced in most research projects. Focus groups may facilitate women of color "writing culture together" by exposing not only the layers of oppression that have suppressed these women's expressions, but the forms of resistance that they use every day to deal with such oppressions. In this regard, I argue that focus groups can be an important element in the advancement of an agenda of social justice for women, because they can serve to expose and validate women's everyday experiences of subjugation and their individual and collective survival and resistance strategies.

The focus group is a collectivistic rather than an individualistic research method that focuses on the multivocality of participants' attitudes, experiences, and beliefs. In the social sciences, however, individualistic research methods have been prevalent for several reasons. First, the dominance of positivistic, quantitative studies, particularly in the United States, has led to a preference for the individual questionnaire as the favored and more accepted data gathering method. Second, even among qualitative researchers, the one-to-one, face-to-face interview is the most widely used research tool. It is only recently that collective testimonies and narratives have gained limited ascendancy among qualitative researchers. Even among feminist scholars, who—paradoxically—emphasize the communal and collectivist nature of women's lives, the most important research method is still the individual interview (Finch, 1984; Oakley, 1981; Wilkinson, 1998). As a Latina feminist, I place focus groups within the context of collective testimonies and group resistance narratives. They can be used by women in general and by women of color in particular to unveil specific and little-researched aspects of women's daily existences, their feelings, attitudes, hopes, and dreams.

The singularity of focus groups is that they allow social scientists to observe the most important sociological process—collective human interaction. Furthermore, they enable researchers to gather large amounts of information about such interactions in limited periods of time. Curiously, although focus groups have been used extensively in market research, it has taken some time for qualitative and ethnographic social researchers to accept them and to get acquainted with the method. Hence the existing information regarding focus groups is not only scarce but unsystematic. As Morgan and Krueger (1993) suggest, "Social science and evaluation research are still at a stage at which most of our knowledge about focus groups comes from personal experience rather than systematic investigation" (p. 3). During the past 5 years, however, group interviews have gained in popularity among a few feminist and postmodernist social researchers.

Compared with participant observation, focus groups have the disadvantage of—sometimes—taking place outside of the settings where social interaction typically occurs. Therefore, the range of behavioral information that can be gathered through group interviews is narrower and is—with some exceptions—limited to verbal communication, body language, and self-report data. In addition, given the necessary presence of a facilitator, it is difficult to discern how "authentic" the social interaction in a focus group really is. This last limitation, however, is also shared with participant observation, for it has been argued that the presence of the researcher may also alter the behavior of those he or she observes.

Compared with individual interviews, the clear advantage of focus groups is that they make it possible for researchers to observe the interactive processes occurring among participants. Often these processes include spontaneous responses from the members of the group that ease their involvement and participation in the discussion. Moreover, the interaction among group participants often decreases the amount of interaction between the facilitator and the individual members of the group.

This gives more weight to the participants' opinions, decreasing the influence the researcher has over the interview process.

◆ History of Focus Groups

Morgan (1998) explains how focus groups developed in three phases: First, during the 1920s, social scientists used the technique for a variety of purposes, one of the most important being the development of survey questionnaires. Second, between World War II and the 1970s, focus groups were used mainly by market researchers to understand people's wants and needs. Finally, from the 1980s to the present, focus group interviews have been used by various professionals to do research on issues dealing with health, sexual behavior, and other social issues. Indeed, in recent years, social scientists have begun to consider the focus group to be an important qualitative research technique.

Although some early field researchers acknowledged using group interviews, few made explicit reference to them as a distinctive methodology. Bronislaw Malinowski, for example, one of the major figures in cultural anthropology, acknowledged in his diaries conversations among groups of native Trobriand Islanders. Nevertheless, he did not explicitly describe the particularities of these group interviews in his reports (Frey & Fontana, 1993). William Foote Whyte, author of *Street Corner Society* (1943), made use of group interviews with gang members in Boston, but he did not explicitly acknowledge the use of group interviews as a unique research technique.

During the early 1940s, Robert Merton and Paul Lazarsfeld introduced the method of group interviewing into the social sciences. In their pioneering work, they used focused group interviews to evaluate the reaction of a group of subjects to wartime radio programs at the Office of Radio Research at Columbia University (Merton, 1987; Stewart & Shamdasani, 1990). Since then, focus group interviews have been used consistently, especially by market researchers, among whom they are one of the favored qualitative research techniques (Morgan, 1988).

For about 40 years after Merton and Lazarsfeld's work, there was little acceptance of group interviews as a method of social science inquiry. Since the late 1980s, however, there has been a renewed interest in promoting the use of group interviews as a recognized social science research method. This interest is not limited to sociologists and anthropologists. Indeed, a diversity of social scientists and other professionals are finding this qualitative technique useful. Political scientists, for example, are using focus groups to assess the public perceptions of political candidates and their views on specific issues. Stewart and Shamdasani (1990) document how focus groups were used in the 1980s during President Ronald Reagan's administration to understand the perception of U.S. and Soviet citizens regarding relations between the two countries. Similarly, they illustrate their own use of this technique to learn about consumer practices in the purchase of new automobiles. In sum, focus groups have become a valuable tool for social researchers and other professionals, regardless of their particular fields of inquiry (Frey & Fontana, 1993; Morgan, 1998).

In the social sciences, group interviews developed as reservations concerning the effectiveness of individual information gathering techniques grew. Such reservations focused on the influence of the interviewer on research participants and on the limitations imposed by closed-ended questions. Traditional interview techniques, which used highly structured questionnaires, had a major disadvantage—the interviewer's framework, viewpoint, and beliefs, consciously or not, influenced the nature of the questions asked and the choices given to research participants (Krueger, 1994). Less directed methods were based on the premise that they were more appropriate to elicit responses that better reflected the social reality of the interviewee.

As Krueger (1994) argues, the acceptance of qualitative techniques, especially focus group interviews, has been slow due to the positivistic legacy of reliance on numbers as the most accepted way to measure social reality and due to the emphasis on quantitative methods, considered more "scientific" than qualitative methods. Although quantitative methods have dominated the social sciences, particularly in the United States, many contemporary social researchers are interested in learning more about research participants' opinions, attitudes, and everyday interactions. Feminist and postmodernist researchers, particularly, believe that traditional methods are alien to population groups who have been traditionally marginalized. These researchers also consider such methods inappropriate to recover the voices of members of marginalized groups because, among other reasons, those methods force upon participants an agenda that it is not their own but the researcher's (Maynard & Purvis, 1994). Even more important, feminist and postmodern researchers believe that traditional research methods do not result in high-quality data (Wilkinson, 1998).

◆ Focus Groups, Postmodernism, and Feminism

Influenced by feminist and postmodernist ethnographic studies, a few social researchers have "rediscovered" focus groups and are now increasingly utilizing them in their specific areas of research. This technique is particularly useful to postmodernist ethnographers, who attempt to remain as close as possible to accounts of everyday life while trying to minimize the distance between themselves and their research participants. It is believed that the group situation may reduce the influence of the interviewer on the research subjects by tilting the balance of power toward the group. Because focus groups emphasize the collective, rather than the individual, they foster free expression of ideas, encouraging the members of the group to speak up (Denzin, 1986; Frey & Fontana, 1993).

Feminist scholars, disenchanted with the disengagement and aloofness of positivistic research and with its inability to explore women's experiences and life situations, have also begun to advocate a more integrative, experiential approach to research. Such an approach regards women's everyday experiences as an important area of study that necessitates alternative methods of scrutiny. Among these methods, ethnography has been regarded as "particularly suited to feminist research" (Stacey, 1991, p. 112). Feminists have advanced many arguments to justify their preference for ethnographic research over traditional survey research methods. First, they have pointed to the potential for one-to-one interviewing to reproduce power relationships between the researcher and the participants (Finch, 1984; Oakley, 1981; Wilkinson, 1998). Their argument is that the researcher usually dominates the whole research process, from the selection of the topic to the choice of the method and the questions asked, to the imposition of her own framework on the research findings. Focus groups minimize the control the researcher has during the data gathering process by decreasing the power of the researcher over research participants. The collective nature of the group interview empowers the participants and validates their voices and experiences.

Second, feminist research attempts to lessen the dichotomy that traditional research imposes between thought and feeling, between the personal and the political, between the observed and the observer, between "dispassionate" or "objective" research and "passionate" or "subjective" knowledge. Giving voice to the subjective experiences of women becomes the focus of inquiry (Stacey, 1991). Rather than seeing research as a linear, one-way process, feminist researchers emphasize the contradictions and complexities encountered in their work.

It should be noted, however, that feminist researchers hold several and conflicting views; they do not take one unified approach. Olesen (1994) characterizes three types of feminist research. First is standpoint research, which emphasizes the need to focus on women's experiences in everyday life as it is familiar to them. Those experiences are constantly shaped, created, and re-created by women. Second is feminist empiricism, which adheres to "the standards of the current norms of qualitative inquiry" (p. 163). This also creates new and strict research practices to make research findings believable. Third is postmodernist feminism, which focuses on stories and narratives and on the construction and reproduction of knowledge. In spite of their differences, however, feminist researchers share the common need of centering and "problematizing" women's diversity of views and life experiences. Group interviews, I believe, offer a viable qualitative research method that satisfies the requirements of all three models of feminist research. Group interviews are particularly suited for uncovering women's daily experience through collective stories and resistance narratives that are filled with cultural symbols, words, signs, and ideological representations that reflect the different dimensions of power and domination that frame women's quotidian experiences.

However, in order to enhance the requirements and standards of qualitative inquiry (Olesen, 1994), as feminist empiricists demand, we must pay greater attention to the following questions: How can a social scientist conduct ethical research that uses subjects not only as providers of information but as human agents with potential to exert social change? What is the potential of group interviews and of qualitative research projects in general for fostering such change? Can the focus group be a data gathering technique as well as part of a consciousness-raising process through which human sharing and interaction take place? Is the focus group a valid research method that minimizes the voice and influence of the researcher?

Black feminists (e.g., Collins, 1986; hooks, 1990), Latina feminists (e.g., Benmayor, 1991; Garcia, 1989; Madriz, 1997), and Asian feminists (e.g., Chow, 1987; Espiritu, 1997) remind us that women of color experience a triple subjugation based on class, race, and gender oppression. Researchers should take such subjugation into account in their selection of methods for studying women's lives. Not all methods are suitable for interviewing women and much less women of color, who, understandably, may feel apprehensive about talking with an interviewer about their lives. As Collins (1998) argues, the contemporary debate about quantitative versus qualitative research reflects the polarization that exists between what is male, White, and scientific on one side and what is considered soft, subjective, female, and possibly Black, Latino, or Asian on the other.

Some researchers have documented the reluctance of some Latinas and African American women to participate in survey research and other studies that use positivistic methodologies. This reluctance is especially strong among undocumented women, women who do not speak or are not fluent in English, and women who engage in nontraditional activities or activities involving the informal or the underground economy (Madriz, 1998). As a response, a few qualitative feminist researchers are advocating the use of focus groups for interviewing women (Fine, 1994; Jarrett, 1993; Madriz, 1997, 1998; Wilkinson, 1998). Jarrett (1993) has emphasized the importance of the use of focus groups in research with women of lower socioeconomic status, particularly women of color (see also Madriz, 1998).

Focus groups not only encourage researchers to listen to the voices of those who have been subjugated, they also represent a methodology that is consistent with the particularities and everyday experiences of women of color. Women have historically used conversation with other women as a way to deal with their oppression. For African American, Latina, and Asian American women, for example, sharing with other women has been an important way to confront and endure their marginality. Historically, women have gathered to talk about issues important to them and to get involved in political activism. Referring to African American women, for example, Cheryl Townsend Gilkes (1994, p. 235) documents how, after slavery ended, churchwomen and teachers gathered to organize throughout the South. Women's clubs were also important places where women learned from each other how to challenge male domination in the existing male-controlled organizations. Similarly, Mexican women have been instrumental in keeping traditional practices through getting together to cook, to organize birthday and *quinceaños* parties, and to talk and keep alive their rich oral traditions (Dill, 1994). Finally, Yen Le Espiritu (1997, p. 39) explains how, in 1937, Chinese women employed in San Francisco's Chinatown organized themselves and struck against the garment factory owned by the National Dollar Store. All these examples illustrate how women's gathering and sharing with other women has the potential to result in actions and movements for social change.

◆ Shattering Otherization as a Way to Promote Social Change

Focus groups are similar to other research methods in that they enable researchers to have access to the opinions, viewpoints, attitudes, and experiences of individuals. They also provide social scientists access to individual and collective life stories. However, as a qualitative methodology, focus groups have a lot to offer social researchers interested in building new paradigms of social research and promoting social change. Obviously, no research method per se can facilitate such change. My point, however, is that some methodologies are more suitable than others for shattering a colonizing discourse in which images of research subjects as the Other are constantly reproduced (Fine, 1994; Madriz, 1998).

Several feminist researchers who have worked with focus groups have reported how participants begin to discuss issues of interest to them without even waiting for questions from the moderator. Griffin (1986), for example, found in her research dealing with young women's experiences that some of her participants' focus group conversations did not even fall within the areas she had anticipated asking about. Thus group interviews heighten the opportunities for participants to decide the direction and content of the discussion.

As Michel Fine (1994) remarks, qualitative researchers collaborate in the construction of the self-other hyphen. In fact, it has been asserted that the relationship between researcher and participants reproduces colonial and postcolonial structures. I argue that group interviews minimize some of the self-other distance in various ways. First, the multivocality of the participants limits the control of the moderator, who has less power over a group than over a single individual (Holstein & Gubrium, 1995; Wilkinson, 1998). Second, the unstructured character of the focus group interview guide (the instrument favored by feminist ethnographers) decreases the control of the researcher over the interview process. Structured questionnaires, which consist of closed- or open-ended questions, maximize the influence of the researcher over the direction of the conversation and introduce the researcher's preconceived notions and opinions and even words and concepts. Indeed, it is possible to have a focus group without an interview guide, entirely eliminating the researcher's prejudices from the interaction (Morgan, 1988; Wilkinson, 1998). Finally, focus groups involve not only "vertical interaction," or interaction between the moderator and the interviewees, but also "horizontal interaction" among the group participants. Although it can be argued that there is a potential for power relations to surface among the participants, these relations, if they arise, are the participants' *own* power relations, in their *own* constructed hierarchies. Indeed, observing and documenting the development of these hierarchies may provide the researcher with some very important data.

Rather than giving voice to the other, or knowing the other, focus groups open possibilities of listening to the plural voices of Others "as constructors and agents of knowledge" (Fine, 1994, p. 75) and as agents of social change. Jenny Kitzinger (1994) explains how the group situation ensures that precedence is given to the participants' hierarchies of importance, their own words and language, and the frameworks they use to describe their own experiences. Language is of particular importance because a sensitive understanding of people's lives requires shared symbols, meanings, and vocabularies. Therefore, the power that research participants hold at the data collection stage of focus groups is not only a matter of ethics. Many researchers have also reported how the interaction among participants leads to the gathering of high-quality data (Wilkinson, 1998). By asking questions, participants contribute to challenge each other's contradictions and responses. In my own use of focus groups while doing research on fear of crime, participants confronted each other in this manner:

Maria: No, I tell you, *de verdad,* I am not afraid of crime.

Juana: Well, you are saying now that you are not afraid of crime. So, then why did you say before that you don't like to go out alone at night?

Rosa: Yes, that's true. You did say that before.

Maria: Okay, I am talking more in general. I try not to be afraid.

In this and many similar instances, participants challenged each other on responses that seemed to reflect contradictions between what they said and the ways they behaved when confronted with particular situations.

Group interviews are especially significant in that they allow the researcher to witness one of the most important processes for the social sciences—social interaction (Berg, 1998). Unlike more traditional research techniques, such as face-to-face interviews, in group interviews researchers observe participants engaging in dialogue, sharing ideas, opinions, and experiences, and even debating with each other. Indeed, it is this sharing that creates the socially constructed interactional experiences necessary for what Denzin (1989) calls "interpretive interactionism." The plurality of actors involved in the focus groups makes the process of interviewing more active and dynamic, facilitating the social construction of meaning (Holstein & Gubrium, 1995). Therefore, the group interaction becomes a very important aspect of the research, contributing to "the development of shared stocks of knowledge" (Holstein & Gubrium, 1995, p. 71). This shared stock of knowledge is essential to the process of writing history and culture together. For women of color, whose experiences—as researchers as well as subjects of research—have often been neglected in the social sciences, this writing is especially important because it contributes to tearing down the walls of silence that have hidden women of color's triple and overlapping marginality: being female, being of color, and, usually, being poor.

Obviously, focus groups are not a solution to the reproduction of the Other. However, at the data gathering stage, they facilitate researchers' hearing the *plural voices* of the participants (Fine, 1994, p. 75). The multi-vocality of the group situation validates the subjects' experiences with other subjects of similar socioeconomic, gender, and racial/ethnic backgrounds. This validation empowers participants, contributing to the construction of a research agenda embedded in the struggles for social justice (West, 1988). In a culture that highlights individualism and separation, shifting the research agenda in the direction of commonality and togetherness is, in itself, subversive.

When engaged in participant observation, the researcher is able to observe the unfolding of social processes in their actual social environment. It could be argued that this does not occur in the environment of the focus group, because the place where the group meets is decided by the researcher. As Frey and Fontana (1993) argue, qualitative research methods can be placed on a continuum; focus groups use more familiar settings than other research techniques and less familiar settings than field research or ethnographic studies. Evidently, there is a wide variation in how researchers use focus groups, with some even using special facilities, one-way mirrors, and videotaping in an attempt to create a more unfamiliar environment. Among feminist and postmodernist researchers, however, the tendency is to use the participants' own settings to carry out "in the field" group interviews. In my work, I have purposefully used participants' familiar settings, such as their living rooms and kitchens, a senior citizen's dining area, a church basement, a classroom, and even a teenager's bedroom. Using the participants' familiar spaces further diffuses the power of the researcher, decreasing the possibilities of "Otherization."

◆ The Use of Focus Groups as Collective Testimony

Feminist researchers have objected to the use of conventional, positivistic methodologies in the study of women and, more specifically, women of color and women of lower socioeconomic status (Etter-Lewis, 1991; Fonow & Cook, 1991; Reinharz, 1992). Some of the most compelling issues addressed by feminists deal with research into women's everyday lives and their particularities, and thus with gaining access into their lives. Hence feminists are attempting to use and develop research methods geared toward facilitating forms of communication with women and among women. Some the most common questions raised by feminist researchers include these: Doing research for whom and by whom? How is it conducted? Whose words are privileged (Benmayor, 1991)? One of the principles of feminist research has been expressed in the phrase "research by, about, and for women" (Acker, Barry, & Esseveld, 1983; Harding, 1987). This has resulted in a large amount of literature on women based on oral histories, in-depth interviews, and testimonies aimed at narrating the everyday reality of women's lives. Interestingly, very few books dealing with feminist research methods have included discussions on the use of focus groups (Wilkinson, 1998).

Since the 1960s, the entrance of African American, Latina, Asian American, and Native American women into the social sciences in small but unparalleled numbers has led to mounting criticism of the absence of women of color from many research projects and of the colonizing nature of many of those research projects. Third World feminists have joined these criticisms of the postcolonial nature of research practices.

As a Latina feminist researcher, I regard the use of focus groups as a form of collective testimony. "Multivocal conversations" have been used by women for generations in the form of exchanges with their mothers, sisters, and female neighbors and friends. In a male-centered culture, some of these conversations have been caricatured as "idle talk" or even "gossip." However, these dialogues have traditionally been a major way in which women have faced their social isolation and their oppression. Thus testimonies, individual or collective, become a vehicle for capturing the socioeconomic, political, and human challenges that women face (Randall, 1980).

The interaction occurring within the group accentuates empathy and commonality of experiences and fosters self-disclosure and self-validation. Communication among women can be an awakening experience and an important element in the consciousness-raising process. It asserts women's right to validate their own experience, and it allows them to build on each other's opinions and thoughts (Oakley, 1981). The awareness that other women experience similar problems or share analogous ideas is important in that it contributes to women's realization that their opinions are legitimate and valid. This awareness may contribute to raising consciousness among women that their problems are not just individual but structural and that these problems are shared by other women. This awareness is also consistent with a social research agenda inserted into movements for social change.

Latina women, for example, belong to a culture in which *mi familia y mi comunidad* (my family and my community) take precedence (Heyck, 1994; Marin & VanOss Marin, 1991; Moore, 1970). Because extended kinship groups are common, sharing is a customary practice, but sharing with other women is especially important for Latinas. In many Latina families, women sit around a kitchen table to plan the meals, drink coffee, and share stories and concerns. Hence communication exchange through the use of focus groups can be considered a practice with which many Latina women are accustomed. Similar claims can be made about African American women, who have faced centuries of oppression and the legacy of slavery. Sharing with other women has been an important way in which African American women have dealt with their oppression. Moreover, as Glenn (1986) notes, Asian American women "kept many customs alive by cooking ethnic foods, organizing traditional celebrations, practicing folk healing methods, and transmitting folklore" (p. 196). They performed most of these activities while engaging in dialogue and conversations with other women.

Rina Benmayor (1991), a Puerto Rican scholar, is one of the few to have pointed out the transformative experience of collective oral history. Benmayor asserts that group testimonies empower people, either individually or collectively: "Social empowerment enables people to speak and speaking empowers" (p. 159). Focus groups, as a form of collective testimony, can become an empowering experience for women in general, and for women of color in particular.

◆ Using Focus Groups to Study
Lower-Socioeconomic-Class Women of Color

Patricia Hill Collins (1998) argues that "breaking silence enables individual African-American women to reclaim humanity in a system that gains part of its strength by objectifying Black women" (p. 47). Similar words can be applied to Latina, Native American, and Asian American women, especially those of lower socioeconomic status. By speaking collectively, women of color not only reclaim their humanity but, at the same time, empower themselves by making sense of their experience of vulnerability and subjugation.

I decided to use focus groups based on several theoretical and methodological considerations. First, because fear of crime has been related to social vulnerability, I believed it was particularly important for me to gain access to women who, by virtue of their race and class, occupy socially devalued positions. More specifically, for my research goals it was crucial that I interview Latina and African American women of lower socioeconomic background. Second, I was concerned that women of color, who are usually more afraid of crime than members of other groups, would feel intimidated by face-to-face, one-on-one interviews. The fact that several women were present at the same time in a room definitely eased some of these concerns. Third, it was necessary to include undocumented women, who face unique situations of socioeconomic and political vulnerability. I believe that because the undocumented women involved in my project were interviewed in the company of other undocumented and documented women, rather than individually, they were more willing to participate in the study and were more open to entering into the discussion.

Collins (1990) has written about systems of inequality or matrices of domination. In the case of lower-socioeconomic-status women of color, the intersection of race, class, and gender puts them in an extremely vulnerable position, making it difficult in many cases for researchers to gain access into their lives. In the case of undocumented Latinas and Asian American women, who are considered "illegal" or "criminal" by virtue of their not having legal resident status in the United States, their situation places them in a particularly defenseless position. Indeed, the multiple and overlapping vulnerabilities of undocumented, lower-class Latinas and Asian American women make them one of the most extreme cases of "Otherization." Aura, a 16-year-old Puerto Rican who participated in one of the focus groups for my study and who lives in a Latino neighborhood in Brooklyn, New York, expressed her feelings of multiple subjugation in a vivid manner:

> Like my mother said, you are born with two strikes already: you are Puerto Rican and you are a woman. So, if something happens to you nobody is going to help. I think it is worse for us Latinas, because we are in the middle, between Black and white. . . . so, it's like, we get it from both ways, you know? (quoted in Madriz, 1997, p. 54)

In sum, I believed that traditional methodologies were not appropriate for my study. As a feminist, I wanted to minimize as much as possible the separation between myself and the participants, although my being a middle-class professor contributed to this separation. I believed that the focus group method would limit the imposition of my own ideas and beliefs onto the women and amplify the power of the participants while also diminishing my own influence on the conversations. It was also extremely important for me to observe the interaction among partici- pants and to witness how they were building on each other's words, ideas, and feelings. The following is an example of a conversation on the subject of carrying some form of protection. The participants are all Latina teenagers:

> *Carmen:* I usually carry something on me.
>
> *Isabel:* Like a weapon or something
>
> *Gloria:* I also carry a weapon with me . . . like keys or other sharp things to protect myself.
>
> *Carmen:* Come on! Tell her the truth.
>
> *Gloria:* Yes, I carry a knife.
>
> *Carmen:* And she carries a small gun. (quoted in Madriz, 1997, p. 141)

One important consideration for my study was how I might gain access to lower-socioeconomic-status women of color. As a Latina researcher, I believe that impersonal recruiting strategies—often preferred by positiv- istic researchers—do not work with lower-socioeconomic-status women of color, and especially with undocumented women. Other social scien- tists who have done research with women of color have reported similar experiences (Cannon, Higginbotham, & Leung, 1988; Jarrett, 1993). Jarrett (1993) considers impersonal recruiting strategies inappropriate for research with low-income minority populations. In her study of low-income African American women, she visited Head Start programs in poor neighborhoods throughout Chicago and talked to women directly about her study in order to gain their participation.

My sources of recruitment were personal networks such as friends, students, community leaders, and friends of friends who worked in non-profit, community organizations. The first contact with the recruiter was usually face-to-face; in a few instances, first contact took place over the telephone. In cases where I did not know the recruiter personally, I asked my friends and students to initiate the contact. They would mention my name to the recruiter, indicating that I was a professor doing a study on fear of crime and informing him or her that I would call at a later date. They usually informed the person that I was a professor involved in social justice and social change. As one of my students said, "I told the director of the organization that you are okay." This personalistic approach was extremely useful given the reluctance many people of color, and particularly undocumented women, feel about participating in research (Zinn, 1979).

Although this personal approach works better than other methods for reaching populations of color, it is still a challenge to gain the participation of members of some lower socioeconomic groups, such as lower-class Latinas. Some feel apprehensive about participating in group discussions, especially if they are recent immigrants or undocumented women, live on welfare or engage in any nonnormative behavior (such as alternative family living arrangements), or work in the underground economy. I found that economic incentives definitely increased the likelihood of participation in the project, and I believe participants should be offered such incentives as a reward for giving their time.

Some social scientists claim that Latinos are more willing to participate in research projects (Marin, Perez-Stable, & VanOss Marin, 1989). However, my experience in doing focus groups with low-income Latinas shows otherwise. Several factors influence the participation of Latinas in research projects. First, many Latinas, especially those of lower socioeconomic status, fulfill traditional roles within the family. Indeed, most of them carry full responsibility for the care of the children and the house. Second, traditional Latino families are hierarchical institutions in which men are considered the *cabeza de familia* (head of the family). Often, Latinas exercise their power in the family *por debajo* (behind the scenes; see Heyck, 1994). Frequently, in traditional Latino families—even in two-wage-earner families—women still perform more of the household work (Pesquera, 1993). Latinas fulfill many functions as mothers, caretakers, cooks, and keepers of the house. They often feel that they should be fully available to their spouses and to their children, making it difficult for some low-socioeconomic-status Latinas to attend activities outside of the house. Third, often these women have more unforeseen demands on their time and less control over their schedules than do other women (Krinitzky, 1990; Stack, 1974). Hence it is my experience that often Latinas fail to arrive at interviews or come late. In my experience, in spite of over-recruiting, only a few women will show up out of 12 to 15 who had confirmed their participation. Providing transportation for participants, either by picking them up or by sending drivers to bring them to the meeting place, or just offering to reimburse them for transportation costs improves attendance. But it is even better to meet them at their most convenient place, such as the soup kitchen where they have dinner or the church or English-as-a-second-language school they attend.

One reason for the high rate of nonattendance among lower-socioeconomic-status women is that they may feel uncomfortable saying no and turning down an invitation. In the case of Latinas, Latina *simpatía* emphasizes cordial and affable relationships. However, it may interfere with recruitment because it makes it more socially acceptable to say yes and accept an invitation. Thus a commitment to participate in a group may be made, but later the promise may not be fulfilled (Marin & VanOss Marin, 1991, p. 13).

In addition, I have found that it is not unusual for these women participants to encounter emergencies at the last minute that prevent them from participating in the group—a child gets sick or gets into trouble at school, a relative needs help with child care or needs to be accompanied to some appointment, or a basic service breaks down at home, such as water or electricity.

It was especially important for my study to have homogeneous groups in terms of age, class, and race because it was evident that participants felt freer to express their ideas about images and cultural representations of crime, criminals, and victims when discussing them with other women from their own backgrounds. Explaining this need to the recruiter, however, became a very sensitive issue. On several occasions, I was asked questions such as "Why do you want a group of all Latinas?" Or "Why only Black girls?" "Why can't we mix them up with White girls?" In most cases, after I carefully explained the nature of the topic, the recruiter understood the need for homogeneous focus groups.

I held 18 focus groups involving between 5 and 12 White, Black, and Latina women. I avoided using larger groups because of the difficulties they would pose for handling the discussion and keeping the conversation around the topic of research. Moreover, larger groups make it more difficult for all the participants to have their opinions heard. I acted as the facilitator in all the focus groups, except for one that was led by a student acting as a research assistant. The discussions typically lasted from 90 minutes to 2 hours. With the permission of the participants, the discussions were taped and later transcribed (Madriz, 1997).

One of the major dilemmas in data gathering concerns the question of the race/ethnicity of the facilitator versus that of the participants. My experience with focus groups has been similar to that found in other studies: A facilitator of the same race/ethnicity as participants usually enhances rapport and increases the willingness of participants to respond (Jarrett, 1993). A facilitator of the same racial or ethnic background contributes to participants' feelings that the facilitator shares with them common experiences. Although I believe this to be true with many other methodologies, it is especially important in the case of focus groups, where establishing rapport with the participants is key to eliciting high-quality information. Although research on Latinas and the race of the interviewer is scarce, studies with African Americans show that the race of the interviewer has an effect on responses (Jarrett, 1993). For example, a study on race-related attitudes of African Americans showed that when they were interviewed by Whites, they were more likely to express closeness toward Whites than when they were interviewed by African Americans (Anderson, Silver, & Abramson, 1988).

For my focus groups, I developed an unstructured interview guide with some introductory remarks. I first asked a very general question dealing with the participants' opinions about the incidence of crime in the place where they lived. Only after framing the topic did I begin to ask more specific questions about their fears and images of crime and the cultural representations associated with those fears. Because the topic of fear of crime was very relevant to the participants, they easily became willing participants in the discussion. On many occasions the participants moved away from the interview guide, tapping into areas of the topic that I had not previously considered. This process added a wealth of information to my research and gave me new insights into the topic of fear or crime.

One problem with the use of group interviews is that some lower-socioeconomic-status women have been socialized to reserve their opinions. Thus some may be less likely to participate in the discussion than others. Under these circumstances, it can be a challenge to elicit responses from particular women. They may feel uncomfortable in a group, especially when asked to express their opinions in front of strangers. Moreover, some women may feel uneasy disagreeing with others, and that may prevent them from expressing their opinions and feelings in the group. When there are a few timid or reticent participants in a group, the dynamic changes and interaction becomes less spontaneous and more directed by the facilitator. This problem may be minimized in groups that are homogeneous not only in terms of race, gender, and class, but in terms of ethnic cultures and languages. To include in the same group Latinas of different ethnic backgrounds—such as Caribbean and Mexican women—may be a mistake, because there are many differences among different Latina groups. For example, language differences may create problems of communication. Rules of interaction are also different among various Latina groups, with some being more comfortable when addressed with the formal pronoun *usted* and others being more comfortable with the use of the informal pronoun *tu.*

I found it very useful to let the groups know that the opinions of all the participants were important for the research project and were valued. Also, I emphasized that there could be no "right" or "wrong" answers to my questions. Because one of the dangers of the group discussion is that people may feel pressured to agree with others, it is important to let participants know that it is acceptable—and in fact desirable—for them to disagree on issues. Disagreements allow the researcher to understand the range of opinions on a topic. This is especially important in the case of focus groups with low-socioeconomic-status women, some of whom have been socialized to agree outwardly with others' opinions and to reserve their own.

Finally, it is important to note that conducting focus groups with people who speak Spanish, or Chinese, or any other language different from English, can result in additional expenses for such things as hiring bilingual facilitators, research assistants, and transcribers. In addition, given the time constraints and multiple demands experienced by lower socioeconomic women, researchers studying this group may find that cancellations are common. Group cancellations that lead to the need for replacement focus groups mean that the researcher incurs additional costs. In most social research, where funds are scarce, any unexpected expense can put a strain on the study budget. Researchers must take such likely expenses into consideration when applying for research grants. Because many social researchers are, like me, also professors with limited time for their research, cancellations impose additional hardships on their tight schedules.

◆ Focus Groups and the Ethics of Empowerment for Women of Color

Some scholars have pointed out the role of social theories in the reproduction of social inequality (Collins, 1998; van Dijk, 1993). According to Patricia Hill Collins (1998), elite discourses "represent the interest of those privileged by hierarchical power relations of race, economic class, gender, sexuality, and nationality" (pp. 44-45). For centuries, "scientific" theories justifying racial and gender inferiority have been commonplace. For example, in my area of research, criminology, biological theories have related physical characteristics of Blacks and other non-White groups to a predisposition to engage in criminal behavior. Similarly, theories of female criminality usually present women offenders as inferior beings who emulate male criminality because of "penis envy," or else as social misfits who do not follow mainstream gender expectations. Therefore, female offenders are often regarded as "bad girls" (Klein, 1995).

In the same way that elitist social theories have served to perpetuate inequalities, traditional methodologies have played an important role in the reproduction of race, class, and gender inequalities. Aside from perpetuating fallacious and insubstantial information about certain groups, the knowledge generated by positivistic research tends to reproduce discrimination and prejudice against those groups whose members do not "perform" according to social expectations or do not conform to the stereotypical ideas of researchers.

The predominant use of quantitative techniques and one-to-one interviewing among social scientists in the United States has resulted in an array of individualistic research methods. This individualism has even permeated ethnographic studies and feminist research. However, as Sue Wilkinson (1998) points out, "research methods that isolate individuals from their social context should clearly be viewed as inappropriate" for feminist researchers (p. 111). This observation is even more valid in the case of research with women of color and women of lower socioeconomic status. In the case of many women of color who belong to communitarian cultures, individualistic research methods place them in artificial, unfamiliar, and even "unsafe" environments.

As Rina Benmayor (1991) has stated, collective testimonies have the potential for "impacting directly on individual and collective empowerment" (p. 159). This, I believe, is the potential of focus groups for research into women's lives and particularly the lives of women of color. The shared dialogues, stories, and knowledge generated by the group interview have the potential to help such women to develop a sense of identity, self-validation, bonding, and commonality of experiences. Focus groups tend to create environments in which participants feel open to telling their stories and to giving their testimonies in front of other women like themselves.

Although the use of focus groups has plenty of challenges, this method is particularly well suited to research concerning low-socioeconomic-status women of color. Focus groups have great potential for uncovering the complexity of layers that shape women's collective, and individual, life experiences. Therefore, the properties inherent in focus groups allow them to be a culturally sensitive data gathering method. The experience of women of color in the United States is shaped by the intersection of multiple and overlapping hierarchies—gender, race, and class together with culture, language, and legal status. Some women of color, such as Asian and Latina immigrants in the United States, are trying to adapt to an alien culture and occupy socially, economically, and politically vulnerable positions. They are often part of cultures in which women's opinions and concerns are systematically devalued. In this context, I regard focus group interviewing as an appropriate methodology for women in general, and particularly for low-socioeconomic-status women of color. Focus groups offer a way of listening to multivocal conversations on topics relevant to the understanding of these women's lives, feelings, and thoughts. The collective experience of the focus group empowers participants to take control of the discussion process, moving the conversation toward areas of the topic relevant to *them,* sometimes encouraging and even compelling the researcher to reconsider her views on a certain subject. Focus group methods can contribute to correcting the individualistic bias existing in social research by offering a unique opportunity to study individuals in their social contexts, by generating high-quality interactive data, by contributing to the social construction of meaning, and by accessing women's shared, and often ignored, stocks of knowledge.

◆ The Future of Focus Groups

Although focus groups represent a sound method of inquiry with much potential for the study of women of color, their use in the future depends on researchers' abilities to understand when and where it becomes appropriate to use them. Some researchers may be lured into using the technique for many of the reasons developed in this chapter: the fact that participants enjoy the opportunity to take part in the discussion, the quality and quantity of information gathered, the possibility of interviewing several people at once and to witness their interaction, the empowerment of participants, and the enthusiasm generated toward the subject matter. However, it is important for researchers to recognize that in some instances other research techniques, such as individual interviews, may be more appropriate for the goals of the research. For instance, in a situation where a researcher needs participants to share very intimate details about their lives, a focus group would not be the most appropriate technique. Furthermore, researchers should avoid the use of focus groups in cases where participants may not feel comfortable with each other. For example, in some work situations, individuals may not feel comfortable opening up and presenting their views in front of their supervisors or other superiors (Morgan, 1998). Researchers should also avoid bringing together in a group individuals who have strong disagreements or who are hostile toward each other. Finally, focus groups are not appropriate when the researcher needs to be able to generalize from the research results. When generalizability is a requirement, the researcher must employ quantitative research techniques and adequate sampling methods.

Focus groups have become an important technique because they offer a way for researchers to listen to the plural voices of others. They are especially important for making audible the voices of oppressed people who are demanding to be heard. Many people want politicians, policy makers, academics, and others in position of power to listen to them (Krueger, 1994). Focus groups, although not a solution to the silencing of the oppressed, may help to facilitate this listening. For those social scientists interested in social change, the hope embedded in the use of focus groups is that they may contribute to some individuals' recognition and awareness of their own subjugation. Using their own words and their own framework, this awareness may lead to the participants' involvement as change agents in the affairs that affect their neighborhoods and their communities.

◆ References

Acker, J., Barry, K., & Esseveld, J. (1983). Objectivity and truth: Problems in doing feminist research. *Women's Studies International Forum, 6,* 423-435.

Anderson, B. A., Silver, B. D., & Abramson, P. R. (1988). The effects of the race of the interviewer on race-related attitudes of black respondents in SRC/CPS national election studies. *Public Opinion Quarterly, 52,* 289-324.

Benmayor, R. (1991). Testimony, action research, and empowerment: Puerto Rican women and popular education. In S. B. Gluck & D. Patai (Eds.), *Women's words: The feminist practice of oral history* (pp. 159-174). New York: Routledge.

Berg, B. L. (1998). *Qualitative research methods for the social sciences.* Boston: Allyn & Bacon.

Cannon, L. W., Higginbotham, E., & Leung, M. L. A. (1988). Race and class bias in qualitative research on women. *Gender & Society, 2,* 449-462.

Chow, E. N. (1987). The development of feminist consciousness among Asian American women. *Gender & Society, 1,* 284-299.

Collins, P. H. (1986). Learning from the outsider within: The sociological significance of black feminist thought. *Social Problems, 33,* 14-32.

Collins, P. H. (1990). *Black feminist thought: Knowledge, consciousness, and the politics of empowerment.* New York: Routledge, Chapman & Hall.

Collins, P. H. (1998). *Fighting words: Black women and the search for justice.* Minneapolis: University of Minnesota Press.

Denzin, N. K. (1986). A postmodern social theory. *Sociological Theory, 4,* 194-204.

Denzin, N. K. (1989). *Interpretive interactionism.* Newbury Park, CA: Sage.

Dill, B. T. (1994). Fictive kin, paper sons, and compadrazgo: Women of color and the struggle for family survival. In M. B. Zinn & B. T. Dill (Eds.), *Women of color in U.S. society* (pp. 149-169). Philadelphia: Temple University Press.

Espiritu, Y. L. (1997). *Asian American women and men: Labor, laws, and love.* Thousand Oaks, CA: Sage.

Etter-Lewis, G. (1991). Black women's life stories: Reclaiming self in narrative texts. In S. B. Gluck & D. Patai (Eds.), *Women's words: The feminist practice of oral history* (pp. 43-58). New York: Routledge.

Finch, J. (1984). "It's great to have someone to talk to": The ethics and politics of interviewing women. In C. Bell & H. Roberts (Eds.), *Social researching: Politics, problems, practice* (pp. 70-87). London: Routledge & Kegan Paul.

Fine, M. (1994). Working the hyphens: Reinventing self and other in qualitative research. In N. K. Denzin & Y. S. Lincoln (Eds.), *Handbook of qualitative research* (pp. 70-82). Thousands Oaks, CA: Sage.

Fonow, M. M., & Cook, J. A. (Eds.). (1991). *Beyond methodology: Feminist scholarship as lived research.* Bloomington: Indiana University Press.

Fontana, A., & Frey, J. H. (1994). Interviewing: The art of science. In N. K. Denzin & Y. S. Lincoln (Eds.), *Handbook of qualitative research* (pp. 361-376). Thousands Oaks, CA: Sage.

Frey, J. H., & Fontana, A. (1993). The group interview in social research. In D. L. Morgan (Ed.), *Successful focus groups: Advancing the state of the art* (pp. 20-34). Newbury Park, CA: Sage.

Garcia, A. M. (1989). The development of Chicana feminist discourse 1970-1980. *Gender & Society, 3,* 217-238.

Gilkes, C. T. (1994). "If it wasn't for the women . . . ": African American women, community work and social change. In M. B. Zinn & B. T. Dill (Eds.), *Women of color in U.S. society* (pp. 229-246). Philadelphia: Temple University Press.

Glenn, E. N. (1986). *Issei, nisei, war bride: Three generations of Japanese American women in domestic service.* Philadelphia: Temple University Press.

Griffin, C. (1986). Qualitative methods and female experience: Young women from school to the job market. In S. Wilkinson (Ed.), *Feminist social psychology: Developing theory and practice* (pp. 173-191). Milton Keynes, England: Open University Press.

Harding, S. (1987). Introduction: Is there a feminist method? In S. Harding (Ed.), *Feminism and methodology: Social science issues* (pp. 1-14). Bloomington: Indiana University Press.

Heyck, D. L. D. (1994). *Barrios and borderlands: Cultures of Latinos and Latinas in the United States.* New York: Routledge.

Holstein, J. A., & Gubrium, J. F. (1995). *The active interview.* Thousand Oaks, CA: Sage.

hooks, b. (1990). The politics of radical black subjectivity. In b. hooks, *Yearning: Race, gender, and cultural politics* (pp. 15-22). Boston: South End.

Jarrett, R. L. (1993). Focus group interviewing with low-income minority populations: A research experience. In D. L. Morgan (Ed.), *Successful focus groups: Advancing the state of the art* (pp. 184-201). Newbury Park, CA: Sage.

Kitzinger, J. (1994). The methodology of focus groups: The importance of interaction between research participants. *Sociology of Health and Illness, 16,* 103-121.

Klein, D. (1995). The etiology of female crime: A review of the literature. In B. R. Price & N. J. Sokoloff (Eds.), *The criminal justice system and women: Offenders, victims, and workers* (pp. 30-53). New York: McGraw-Hill.

Krinitzky, N. (1990). *Welfare dependence and psychological distress: A study of Puerto Rican women in New York City.* Unpublished doctoral dissertation, New York University.

Krueger, R. A. (1994). *Focus groups: A practical guide to applied research.* Thousand Oaks, CA: Sage.

Madriz, E. (1997). *Nothing bad happens to good girls: The impact of fear of crime on women's lives.* Berkeley: University of California Press.

Madriz, E. (1998). Using focus groups with lower socioeconomic status Latina women. *Qualitative Inquiry, 4,* 114-128.

Marin, G., Perez-Stable, E. J., & VanOss Marin, B. (1989). Cigarette smoking among San Francisco Hispanics: The role of acculturation and gender. *American Journal of Public Health, 79,* 196-198.

Marin, G., & VanOss Marin, B. (1991). *Research with Hispanic populations.* Newbury Park, CA: Sage.

Maynard, M., & Purvis, J. (1994). Doing feminist research. In M. Maynard & J. Purvis (Eds.), *Researching women's lives from a feminist perspective* (pp. 1-9). London: Taylor & Francis.

Merton, R. (1987). Focused interviews and focus groups: Continuities and discontinuities. *Public Opinion Quarterly, 51,* 550-566.

Moore, J. W. (1970). *Mexican-Americans.* Englewood Cliffs, NJ: Prentice Hall.

Morgan, D. L. (1988). *Focus groups as qualitative research.* Newbury Park, CA: Sage.

Morgan, D. L. (1998). *The focus group guidebook.* Thousand Oaks, CA: Sage.

Morgan, D. L., & Krueger, R. A. (1993). When to use focus groups and why. In D. L. Morgan (Ed.), *Successful focus groups: Advancing the state of the art* (pp. 3-19). Newbury Park, CA: Sage.

Oakley, A. (1981). Interviewing women: A contradictions in terms. In H. Roberts (Ed.), *Doing feminist research* (pp. 30-61). London: Routledge & Kegan Paul.

Olesen, V. (1994). Feminisms and models of qualitative research. In N. K. Denzin & Y. S. Lincoln (Eds.), *Handbook of qualitative research* (pp. 158-174). Thousand Oaks, CA: Sage.

Pesquera, B. M. (1993). In the beginning he wouldn't even lift a spoon: The division of household labor. In A. de la Torre & B. M. Pesquera (Eds.), *Building with our hands: New directions in Chicana studies* (pp. 181-195). Berkeley: University of California Press.

Randall, M. (1980). *Todas estamos despiertas.* Mexico City: Editorial Siglo XXI.

Reinharz, S. (1992). *Feminist methods in social research.* New York: Oxford University Press.

Stacey, J. (1991). Can there be a feminist ethnography? In S. B. Gluck & D. Patai (Eds.), *Women's words: The feminist practice of oral history* (pp. 111-119). New York: Routledge.

Stack, C. B. (1974). *All our kin: Strategies for survival in a black community.* New York: Harper & Row.

Stewart, D. W., & Shamdasani, P. N. (1990). *Focus groups: Theory and practice.* Newbury Park, CA: Sage.

van Dijk, T. A. (1993). *Elite discourse and racism.* Newbury Park, CA: Sage.

West, C. (1988). Marxist theory and the specificity of Afro-American oppression. In C. Nelson & L. Grossberg (Eds.), *Marxism and the interpretation of culture* (pp. 17-29). Urbana: University of Illinois Press.

Wilkinson, S. (1998). Focus groups in feminist research: Power, interaction, and the co-construction of meaning. *Women's Studies International Forum, 21,* 111-125.

Whyte, W. F. (1943). *Street corner society: The social structure of an Italian slum.* Chicago: University of Chicago Press.

Zinn, M. B. (1979). Field research in minority communities: Ethical, methodological and political observations by an insider. *Social Problems, 27,* 209-219.

11

Applied Ethnography

Erve Chambers

◆ There is no general agreement within the social sciences as to the definition or value of either of the words that make up the title of this chapter. Both words are imbued with assumptions of common meaning and yet subject to many conflicting and largely unexpressed distinctions. Accordingly, the subject of this chapter needs to be qualified in both of its terms. What is it that makes a piece of research or a kind of practice specifically *applied*, and what do we mean by the term *ethnography*?

The question of how social inquiry becomes applied is intriguing and can include considerations of intent as well as of research design and product. I opt here for a broad definition. Applied work helps people make decisions and is generally directed toward informing others of the possible consequences of policy options or of programs of directed change. These consequences may be anticipated (as in impact studies and forecasting), or they may be determined in retrospect (as in evaluation research). In this chapter I consider a variety of approaches to applied ethnography, focusing primarily on cognitive approaches, micro/macro analyses, and action or clinical models. A major difference between basic and applied research rests with the criteria used to judge their significance. For basic research, the ultimate measure of significance is a research product's contribution to theory and disciplinary knowledge. The most immediate measure of the significance of applied research is its contribution to decision making. This is not to say that a piece of research cannot be judged by both criteria, but only that it need not be. At any rate, the close association with decision making accounts for much of the variation in approaches to applied ethnography. It seems inevitable that the kinds of settings in which ethnographers work, ranging from federal bureaucracies to local activist organizations, should help determine the kinds of problems they are likely to address, as well as their methodological approaches to trying to understand those problems.

I reserve the term *applied research* for inquiry that is intentionally developed within a context of decision making and that is directed toward the interests of one or more clients. Basic research can certainly be usefully applied, but in order for the transition to occur between its potential for usefulness and its actual use, there must be a deliberate act of transfer from the one realm to the other. This can be accomplished through various kinds of *practice* in which individuals bring ethnographic knowledge to bear on particular human problems. Although this latter role might be realized in several ways (E. Chambers, 1985), I will discuss it here primarily in the context of what are sometimes referred to as clinical modes of practice.

In contrast to the above, my definition of *ethnography* will seem fairly narrow to some readers. This is because in many quarters the term has come to be regarded as virtually synonymous with qualitative research. Following Wolcott's (1995) clear but frequently unheeded counsel, I restrict my use of the term here to those varieties of inquiry that aim to describe or interpret the place of culture in human affairs. In other words, ethnography is principally defined by its subject matter, which is *ethnos,* or culture, and not by its methodology, which is often but not invariably qualitative.

The term *culture* is itself ambiguous and has been subject to a variety of interpretations, each implying somewhat different methodological approaches. In my view, culture is composed of those understandings and ways of understanding that are judged to be characteristic of a discernible group. As such, culture is an *abstraction* that has been applied, with various degrees of success, to small groups (i.e., the "culture" of the classroom) and to large groups (i.e., nation-states); an operational definition might be that culture is apparent when distinctly shared meanings are discovered to be present in any given group. Within most definitions of culture there is also an expectation that its features must have some lasting quality—durable enough, at least, to be acquired by newcomers to a group. It is important to recognize that cultural understanding can be acquired from a variety of data. It might, for example, be extracted out of observable patterns of human behavior, drawn from "native" accounts of explicit standards of value and behavior, discovered through the discernment of rules or patterns of interpretation that are particular to a group, or realized through the study of the more tacit dimensions of cognitive or symbolic processes. In practice, ethnographers often combine these data in ways that they feel will be productive given particular research aims.

The problem with the concept of culture as an abstraction that is attributed to particular societies or groups is that it has not been helpful for the anticipation of actual behaviors, which seem almost invariably to result from interaction between cultural groups. It has taken most anthropologists some time to realize that the concept is more useful and representational when applied to actual processes of cultural negotiation. Accordingly, the attribution of culture to shared meanings within groups does not necessarily imply that ethnographers are solely interested in describing such groups in isolation; in fact, they are becoming less so interested. Neither does the expectation of some degree of lastingness suggest that a group's culture is not subject to change. Early ethnographers generally did emphasize the uniqueness of neatly bounded cultures, and often assumed that cultural patterns were deeply rooted in human consciousness and resistant to change. They were more interested in describing durable and distinct cultural units than they were in discerning the processes by which culture becomes meaningful. More recently, however, many ethnographers have shifted their attention to these issues of process, trying to understand how culture is constructed and negotiated, particularly as a result of interactions between groups (or, if you will, between cultures). It is not yet entirely clear what this shift might mean to the special interests apparent in an *applied* ethnography, which has built most of its relationships with clients and with the general public on the basis of advocating for the significance of cultural understanding in its earlier incarnation.

◆ Early Applications of the Ethnographic Approach

Although ethnography is no longer the sole province of anthropologists, it clearly developed with a close relationship to the discipline, and its first applications follow closely on anthropology's early commitment to the study of presumably traditional and predominantly non-Western societies. By the time anthropology became established as a discipline in its own right, most such peoples were in one way or another politically or economically subject to Western nations. It is not surprising that many of the earliest opportunities to apply ethnography were closely related to problems that representatives of colonial or quasi-colonial systems encountered in administering these subject peoples. Two early defenses of an applied "anthropology" (i.e., ethnography) that is directed to the problems of administering subject peoples stand out, both for the reasonableness of their arguments and for their contrasting views of the kinds of data applied ethnographers might collect.

The first of these is Bronislaw Malinowski's essay "Practical Anthropology" (1929), which offers his views of how ethnographic understanding might assist British colonial administrators in Africa. Malinowski's argument for the usefulness of ethnographic data in colonial administration rests principally on the anthropologist's presumed grasp of what is sometimes called "the native point of view." Because the anthropologist has (more or less) lived within native communities and often participated in as well as observed their practices, he or she is in a better position to interpret the meanings and possible consequences of their behaviors in a cultural context. The promise of a distinctly applied ethnography rests, however, upon ethnographers' being willing to direct their research interests to matters of particular concern to administrators. Malinowski chided his colleagues for paying too little attention to understanding the subtleties of language use, and for ignoring such vital administrative issues as local practices related to land tenure, labor, and justice. He did not challenge the premises of colonial rule, but argued that a more practical ethnography would provide administrators with the kinds of information they needed to make more effective as well as more humane decisions regarding native peoples.

Malinowski's defense of applied ethnography rests primarily on the ethnographer's ability to observe behaviors and to explain their significance in relation to their functions in a larger institutional and cultural context. Another rationale for applied ethnography was offered by Clyde Kluckhohn in his article "Covert Culture and Administrative Problems" (1947). Writing on the basis of his experience with the U.S. Indian Service, Kluckhohn noted that the agency had made considerable strides in integrating cultural concepts and ethnographic data as part of their policy and program development. He argued that further progress might be made if ethnographers were to pay more attention to the covert dimensions of culture, or to those cultural configurations that lie somewhere beyond a people's conscious awareness of their own culture. This is a different justification for applied ethnography from one that relies solely on the discernment of the native point of view. Kluckhohn suggested that ethnography could uniquely serve to make explicit those cultural configurations that inform human behavior, even though they may not be explicitly recognized or easily verbalized by the "native." This kind of interpretation could be particularly useful in instances where there were striking differences between the configurations of particular Indian groups and those of the predominantly white administrators—two examples provided by Kluckhohn included Navajo configurations that relate sexual rights closely with property rights and the relative lack of "guilt" as a motivating or sanctioning factor in Navajo society. Kluckhohn was vague as to the kinds of ethnographic methods that might provide a better understanding of covert culture. He encouraged ethnographers not to limit themselves to those features of culture that could be "measured or quantitatively validated," and suggested that informed speculation based on long-term familiarity with another culture might well be appropriate.

A third distinct approach to applied ethnography was offered by Sol Tax (1958) as a result of his work with the Fox Indians in Iowa. Tax described his research team's efforts both as "action anthropology" and as "participant interference," playing on the familiarity of the term *participant observation* as a mainstay of ethnographic technique. Although action anthropology did not suggest any new methodological approaches, it did indicate a strikingly different way of applying ethnographic expertise. The Fox Project began in 1948, at a time when most of the ethnography devoted to American Indian communities was focused on documenting cultural traditions. Tax's team directed its interest instead to the problems that the Fox were then facing, most notably the effects of internal factionalism and difficulties in their relations with whites. The researchers committed themselves to a style of research and action that would permit them to "learn while helping." In terms of innovations in applying ethnography, the most notable characteristic of Tax's efforts was the extent to which the research team surrendered much of their control over the direction of their inquiries, which became increasingly dependent upon decisions made by the Fox in determining how they would respond to their own problems. The action anthropology proposed with the Fox Project (along with the work of sociologist Kurt Lewin) provided the impetus for much of the collaborative research to be discussed later in this chapter.

In the United States, much of the groundwork for an applied ethnography was established during and within the first decade after World War II. In addition to the contributions mentioned above, ethnographers of this era were involved in a wide variety of applications, including work in industrial relations and organizational behavior (e.g., Whyte, 1984); large-scale nutritional studies (Montgomery & Bennett, 1979); research with the War Relocation Authority related to the internment of the Japanese (Leighton, 1945; Spicer, 1979); ethnographic research in the Pacific Trust Territories, newly acquired by the United States (Barnett, 1956); and numerous projects in rural and international development (e.g., Foster, 1969; Holmberg, 1958; Spicer, 1952). At least some of the impetus for an increased interest in applied ethnography at this time can be attributed to the emergence of the United States as a global power and the recognition of a practical need for an improved understanding of cultural differences. The research clients of the time appear not to have been particularly interested in ethnography as a specific method; it just came along with the methodological preferences of most of the "cultural experts" of the time.

◆ From Stasis to Process

As noted above, the development of ethnographic methods and strategies has been closely associated with anthropology. Anthropologists continue to take the lead in insisting on linking their inquiries to the understanding of culturally based behaviors and values, thereby distinguishing ethnography from the broader category of qualitative research methods. By the same token, applied ethnography has never been defined solely as a property of anthropology. For example, the Society for Applied Anthropology was founded in 1941 as an organization devoted to encouraging interdisciplinary contributions to culturally based research and practice. Unlike the leaders of other professional organizations for anthropologists of the time, the founders of the Society for Applied Anthropology seemed less concerned with drawing disciplinary boundaries or maintaining methodological distinctions between disciplines than they were with establishing the status of culture as an important variable in matters of human change and adaptation.

Over the past few decades, a major shift in the way anthropologists, and some others, think about culture and its significance in human relations has led to a variety of innovations in ethnographic research. The kinds of inquiries discussed above were based on an assumption that the practical value of ethnography was to prepare cultural profiles of different human groups that could inform decision makers who were responsible for policies or programs that affected the lives of these people. Sol Tax's action anthropology was an exception to this trend, although it shared with the others a strong focus on viewing subjects in terms of the integrity of their "traditional," usually non-Western, cultural base.

Early applied ethnography was broadly influenced by anthropology's focus on peoples who had been marginalized, generally as a result of Western expansion, and by the discipline's prevailing interest in describing these peoples' traditional cultures before they disappeared altogether (another manifestation of early applied anthropology, sometimes called "salvage anthropology"). The consequence, if not the intent, of this research was to describe a people in terms of cultural ideals and behaviors that were presumed to be enduring and homogeneous. These "cultures" were often presumed to have changed little prior to Western contact, and their standards of behavior were generally described as being uniform within the prescribed statuses and roles of each culture. The usual ethnographic monograph of the time was written in what has been called the "ethnographic present," which was in reality an attempt to describe an idealized ethnographic past, largely out of time and with little or no reference to the present conditions of cultures that had been "adulterated" by Western influence (see, for example, Rosaldo, 1989). The impression was one of cultures that did not change in terms of any kind of internal dynamic, and that generally resisted change from the outside. Accordingly, much of the applied anthropology of the time was devoted to providing the kinds of cultural information that might help change agents respond to the resistance they almost invariably faced in the field.

So long as anthropologists focused their attention on small-scale societies and maintained the (generally erroneous) presumptions that the cultures they studied had been homogeneous, isolated from other major cultural influences, and had experienced little change prior to Western intrusion, their methods of research were based principally on their commitment to *being there* and on their ability to observe behaviors systematically in the cultural settings in which they naturally occurred. Anthropology emphasized, and undoubtedly romanticized, the position of the lone field-worker immersed in another culture and confident in her or his ability to discover the salient patterns of that culture through sustained participant observation. As a rule, anthropology students received little training in methods prior to entering the field, and fieldwork instructions were directed as much to practical matters of how to survive in another society as they were to methods of inquiry. The methods were much like, and frequently likened to, those of the naturalist, who assumed little significant variation in the patterns of species behavior that he or she observed in the wild.

Early ethnographic research was also influenced by a secondary mission within anthropology. A major goal of anthropology has been to serve as an antidote to ethnocentric values, especially when those values lead to misunderstandings about other cultures. This mission has led many anthropologists to emphasize the uniqueness of a culture and to focus on rationalizing and defending differences rather than similarities between cultures. The role of the anthropologist as an investigator came to play an interesting part in this quest. Ethnographies were frequently written as narratives in which the anthropologist validated his or her discovery of the rationale of human difference by recounting her or his own naïveté, misunderstandings, and eventual enlightenment during the process of doing fieldwork. Again, the methods that seemed best suited to such a perspective were those that were the most informal, experiential, and reflexive.

Although early anthropologists did on occasion apply ethnographic methods to a variety of situations outside the preferences described above, it seems fair to assert that this model did predominate until the late 1960s. At that time, several events served as stimuli to a fairly rapid transformation in the development of ethnographic methods and in the use of those methods in applied settings. One of these events was the advent of more systematic approaches to ethnographic inquiry, including ethnoscientific, or cognitive, research methods, and increased attention to the quantification of field data (Poggie, DeWalt, & Dressler 1992). During the same period of time, anthropology experienced a rather profound shift in orientation from its focus on small-scale societies in relative isolation to an increased interest in seemingly more complex and heterogeneous social groupings. This was not an entirely new situation for anthropologists, but its increased legitimation within in the field helped transform the discipline in at least three major ways. First, as anthropologists attempted to deal with larger, more stratified, and more diverse populations, the need for a systematic and somewhat more formal approach to field research and ethnographic methods became apparent. These new research interests also put anthropologists in closer association with practitioners of other social science disciplines—sometimes in cooperation, and occasionally in direct competition. Closer association with specific applied research strategies, such as evaluation research and social impact assessment, encouraged some applied ethnographers to adapt their inquiries to these models. Finally, and importantly, the experience of doing research with populations in which heterogeneity was obvious led some anthropologists to challenge many of their earlier assumptions concerning the relative "simplicity" and seeming passivity of the smallerscale societies in which they had been doing research.

These transformations were especially apparent in the development of applied ethnographic methods. Here, the greater and most apparent opportunity for anthropologists was still to try to assist change agents in interpreting the behaviors of marginal groups. It no longer seemed sufficient, however, to devote so much attention to traditional culture, at least not at the expense of understanding how these groups did indeed interact with, adapt to, and participate in the larger political and economic systems of which they were clearly a part. In ethnography devoted to agricultural development, for example, the original questions had focused on understanding what it was in a people's traditional culture that prevented them from participating fully in a newly introduced development scheme. The new research questions were framed in a context in which research subjects could be seen as rational actors in a development process (e.g., Bartlett, 1980; Warren, Slikkerveer, & Brokensha, 1995).

All these factors led to a rather rapid shift of focus. For many applied ethnographers, the object of research changed from the study of particular cultures or social groups in place to the study of the cultural processes that occur in efforts to respond to particular human problems. Applied ethnographers have become increasingly interested in such matters as how social groups collide and mix in situations of change and in the cultural meanings that result from the interactions of interested groups or stakeholders. They have become less convinced of the value of viewing culture as a quality that people possess (or, in turn, a quality that possesses them) and more interested in discovering how cultural meanings might be exchanged and negotiated as a result of intracultural attempts to find solutions to problems. In this sense, the culture described by many applied ethnographers has shifted from being a durable repository of a people's traditions to an unstable and mutable process by which people actively strive to derive meaning from their continually changing relationships and circumstances.

◆ Varieties of Applied Ethnography

Much of the value of ethnography lies in its narrative—in the telling of a story that is based in cultural representations. Whereas traditional ethnography has focused almost exclusively on telling stories about "other" and generally distant peoples, many contemporary ethnographic approaches tend to focus on the ways in which people fashion culturally meaningful expressions from fields of experience in which meaning is routinely contested, and where culture is perennially under construction. This has been particularly true of applied ethnography, which is by its very nature interventionist and culturally intrusive. As noted above, the problem of the applied ethnographer has largely shifted from telling stories about others to describing what happens when cultural systems overlap as a result of some sort of deliberate, recent, or anticipated intervention.

Cognitive Approaches

Cognitive, semiotic, and semantic approaches have played a significant role in the development of applied ethnography. These approaches follow a variety of language or discourse models and ethnographic methodologies in order to provide, much as Malinowski espoused, "the native point of view" in relation to particular kinds of interventions. Classic ethnographies in this vein include James Spradley's *You Owe Yourself a Drunk: An Ethnography of Urban Nomads* (1975), Michael Agar's *Ripping and Running: A Formal Ethnography of Urban Heroin Addicts* (1973), and Peter Manning's *Police Work: The Social Organization of Policing* (1977). These and similar contributions differ from standard (i.e., nonapplied) ethnographies in that they are focused on a research population that is at least in part defined by some larger social "problem." Spradley's study is grounded in public perception of the problem of street alcoholics and in police approaches to solving the problem, largely through incarceration. Agar's study was conducted in a treatment facility for heroin addicts. Other ethnographies, such as Manning's study of police work and Michael Agar's more recent *Independents Declared: The Dilemmas of Independent*

Trucking (1986a), focus on particular occupational groups that are subject to significant public interest or institutional intervention—Agar's study is concerned, for example, with the impacts of federal transportation regulation on independent truckers.

In an applied sense, the value of cognitive approaches to ethnography is that they often reveal patterns of cultural construction within a target group that vary considerably from the interpretations of that group that are made by outsiders, and most particularly by those who have some authority over the group under study. The ethnographies often reveal considerable disparities between policies, programs, or treatments directed to the group and the real-world exigencies that provide a cultural landscape and help determine behaviors within the group. To my mind, the most appealing of these ethnographies treat culture as a consequence of practical instances of intervention (including, interestingly enough, the interventions of research). As Agar (1994) notes in his discussion of the role of the intercultural practitioner (ICP), culture should not be thought of as an abstract set of principles that belong to a particular group, but rather as an orientation toward resolving differences:

> Culture is something the ICP creates, a story he or she tells that highlights and explains the differences that cause breakdowns. Culture is not something people *have*; it is something that fills the spaces *between* them. And culture is not an exhaustive description of anything; it focuses on differences, rich points, differences that can vary from task to task and group to group. (p. 236)

Cognitive approaches to applied ethnography derive much of their practical value from the fact that they tend to focus on failures of communication, or cultural "breakdowns" (see, e.g., Agar, 1986b; Briggs, 1986). Such failures are easily translated to applied situations, and cognitive ethnographic methods seem readily adaptable to the particular situations and communicative dilemmas that arise when one group attempts to intervene upon another. Although the approaches seem to hark back most closely to Malinowski's defense of applied ethnography in terms of eliciting a "native point of view," there are also parallels to Kluckhohn's attempt to describe a unique role for applied ethnographers in their ability to expose more tacit dimensions of culture. Cognitive and language-based ethnographies tend to be built on those communicative breakdowns that are directly experienced by the researcher and that are to be resolved by the researcher's attempts to understand what made the breakdowns occur. This is different from an applied approach that reports problems as expressed by change agents or by the groups they are attempting to change. There is also an assumption, seldom made entirely clear, that the ethnographer is better positioned to unravel communicative disorders between groups than are members of the groups themselves. This is not simply because researchers might have less at stake in anticipated actions, but also because they initially understand much less of the situation and are therefore more likely to experience firsthand the kinds of blunders and breakdowns that yield rich data and point toward communicative resolutions. Stakeholders, who are more closely associated with the problem at hand, are likely to have already developed cognitive defenses that insulate them from direct experience of the kinds of breakdowns that yield significant data or understanding. James Spradley (1979) has, for example, suggested that his own techniques of ethnosemantic elicitation seem to work best when the ethnographer comes to a cultural situation with little prior knowledge.

Approaches of Micro/Macro Analysis

Although ethnography has traditionally dwelled upon the local and relied heavily upon qualitative research techniques and methods, a variety of current approaches to applied ethnography have served to expand upon both the subjects and the methods of inquiry. Two factors have played major roles in this transition. One has been the recent tendency within the social sciences to resituate the local within the larger contexts of regional, national, and even global events. This focus seems particularly relevant to applied research and action, where deliberate efforts to intervene and bring about change invariably place the populations subject to such efforts in a relationship with a larger sphere of influence. Increasingly, applied ethnography is *about* these relationships, rather than about the experiences of particular groups or populations in isolation. The other factor has been the tendency for applied ethnography to expand its methodological reach, not only with the use of increasingly sophisticated qualitative methods, but also by adopting or at least responding to more quantitative research methods. Some of this shift can be attributed to changes in the ways in which social scientists and practitioners have become involved in applied work. (Again, I am speaking here primarily on the basis of my experience with applied anthropology, although I suspect these comments apply to the social sciences more generally.) In the past, anthropologists normally became involved in applied research when they were called upon to provide expertise based on their knowledge of a particular people. They were most likely to become involved in a project after something had already gone wrong, and their involvement in the overall project or research activity was minimal. In other words, their ethnography was largely independent of the larger intervention, and their role was primarily that of expert witness or troubleshooter.

There have always been exceptions to this practice, and now the exception is often the rule. Applied ethnographers are more likely, for example, to be involved in a project or research effort from its inception, and to play a role in research design. They are also more likely to be a part of the analysis or interpretation stage of applied research efforts. This greater degree of integration of applied ethnography within larger research projects and interventions has meant that a considerable amount of the qualitative, field-based applied ethnography being done today has been developed in studied relation to other research approaches. One way in which this has occurred is when the applied ethnographer becomes a participant in a larger, more quantitative research activity, generally as a qualitative researcher. The other approach has been when applied ethnographers themselves adopt quantitative methods as a part of their own ethnographic research plan—this has occurred to the extent that some applied ethnography now relies predominantly upon quantitative rather than qualitative methods. (Here it is again important to keep in mind that ethnography is being defined in this chapter in relation to its subject matter, rather than as a particular kind of methodology.)

In terms of methodological innovativeness, the most interesting examples of ethnographic inquiry that include qualitative and quantitative approaches, as well as varied levels of analysis, are those in which the ethnographer plays an active if not leading role in research design and is thereby able to maintain a primary interest in cultural analysis. Within anthropology, the qualitative/quantitative approaches to ethnography, with a focus on application, are perhaps most thoroughly described in Pertti Pelto and Gretel Pelto's *Anthropological Research: The Structure of Inquiry* (1978), H. Russell Bernard's *Research Methods in Anthropology: Qualitative and Quantitative Approaches* (1994), and Bernard's *Handbook of Research Methods in Cultural Anthropology* (1998). The shift within anthropology from local or community levels of analysis to approaches that include "macro" analyses in several dimensions (space, causal, and time) is evidenced by the contributions to be found in Billie DeWalt and Pertti Pelto's *Micro and Macro Levels of Analysis in Anthropology: Issues in Theory and Research* (1985) and in Poggie et al.'s *Anthropological Research: Process and Application* (1992).

These kinds of research experiences have provided opportunities for applied ethnographers to articulate ways in which the qualitative aspects of their work can be integrated with larger research activities. Qualitative approaches have, for example, proven particularly useful at the beginning of a research effort, often to help define the parameters of survey research (e.g., Kempton, Boster, & Hartley, 1995). In other work, qualitative field research has proven to be particularly useful at the analysis stage of research, in helping to explain anomalies in the data, especially in research that relies heavily upon reported data from a number of sites, where there might be unaccounted-for variation in how the sites interpret reporting requirements (Trend, 1978).

Where research requires accurate portrayals of stakeholder values or opinions, qualitative ethnographic data have often proven superior to survey data, particularly in cases that involve long-term field exposure and in situations where informants might feel at risk or have other reasons to provide incorrect responses, or where their "truer" responses might develop over time. In some cases, as I will discuss later in this chapter, qualitative ethnographic data have also proven to be more credible to particular research clients and stakeholders.

It is rare to find reports that explicitly compare qualitative and quantitative data obtained in the same applied research project. Susan Scrimshaw (1985) offers one such instance, related to a study of practices and attitudes concerning induced abortion in Ecuador. She notes that the ethnographic (i.e., field-based) data were in most cases validated through the comparison of these results with those obtained as a result of the larger and more rigorously defined sampling procedures developed for the surveys. On the other hand, Scrimshaw cautiously suggests that the ethnographic data might have been more accurate in those few instances in which significant anomalies between the two data sets did exist. This appears to have been the case, for example, where research subjects were asked to report practices or attitudes that were particularly sensitive or potentially embarrassing. In these instances, the longer-term familiarity gained as a result of ethnographic experience enabled the researchers to gain a deeper and more accurate grounding from which to discern the subjects' attitudes.

Action and Clinical Approaches

A number of current approaches to applied ethnography follow the early action or advocacy models offered by Sol Tax (1958) and, in another context, discussed by psychologist Kurt Lewin (1948), who emphasized participatory research based on client-oriented attempts to resolve particular social problems. Some of the models derive directly from these earlier examples, whereas others have been encouraged by recent interest on the part of research funding agencies, particularly some federal agencies, in sponsoring applied research that is participatory and that involves the "subjects" of research or intervention in one or several stages of inquiry. The actual extent of participation required for these activities varies considerably from one research effort to another, and in some cases mandated "participatory" research has earned a reputation for superficiality that is not dissimilar from earlier mandates that called for "citizen participation" in public decision making.

There is nothing necessarily ethnographic about action or advocacy research, although some researchers have suggested that ethnographic research strategies may be more accessible than other strategies, and, at the stage of interpretation, might provide kinds of data that are more convincing to those participants and community members who have not been trained as social scientists. As in the other approaches to applied research discussed here, much of what has been identified as applied "ethnography" would not conform to the definition offered above—it may be good and informative qualitative research, but it lacks the association with understanding cultural processes that would make it ethnographic.

Notwithstanding these provisos, there remain plenty of instances in which applied ethnographic methods have been incorporated into action and advocacy research strategies. Jean Schensul (1985) has described action-oriented research within the context of a collaborative model in which researchers and community activists form "policy research clusters" that are focused on important community problems. She notes that, in these settings, the ethnography is shaped in part by "the constraints of field situations including the social and political realities of the dissemination/utilization context," as well as by considerations that the research not violate "cultural principles" within the community (p. 193). William Foote Whyte (1984) has offered a similar model, which he calls "participatory action research." Dianne Argyris (1990) has provided perhaps the most detailed accounting of applied ethnography within the action context, and she suggests that a major goal of action research is to encourage participants to test their own "theories-in-use" as they relate to particular social problems.

The major innovation to applied ethnography resulting from action models has been the tendency to include individuals who are not professional social scientists in various stages of the research, including project selection and design, fieldwork, and research analysis. Conversely, and probably more than any other approach, advocacy research has also resulted in the professionalism of any number of traditional research subjects as social scientists in their own right—a practice extending back again to Sol Tax, who devoted considerable time during the later years of his career to facilitating the education of Native American students in the social sciences and in other fields. Davydd Greenwood and Morten Levin (1998) have offered a survey of action research that focuses on its criteria of scientific evidence and commitment to "democratizing" the research process.

Allied in many respects with action and advocacy research is the clinical approach to applied ethnography, which in the simplest of terms seeks to train people to use ethnographic strategies to gain a better understanding of their own cultural situations, or to understand more fully those cultural processes that influence others with whom they are involved. The clinical model has referred most often to those activities in which professionals of various kinds are encouraged to think about their practice in ethnographic terms. It has most often been applied to settings in which the professional is likely to encounter considerable cultural diversity, as in medicine and health (e.g., Shimkin & Golde, 1983), education (e.g., Heath, 1982), and social work (e.g., Green, 1982). Howard Stein (1982) describes the clinical model as one of "ethnographic teaching," in which the professionals (in this case, medical school students) are encouraged to use an ethnographic perspective and at least some methods of ethnographic inquiry to first conduct "self-ethnography," and later to apply principles of ethnography to understanding cultural diversity within the clinical setting.

Edgar Schein (1987) has argued the clinical perspective somewhat differently. His *clinicians* are organizational researchers and advisers who rely on fieldwork approaches that Schein claims are distinct in several respects from those of ethnographers. It is difficult, however, to determine how Schein derives his model of ethnography—what he describes as the opposing clinical model seems in actuality to be quite similar to the approaches of *applied* ethnography described in this chapter.

It seems likely that attention to ethnography as a way of thinking and problem solving will increase as social scientists learn that applied work is not simply a matter of affixing existing research paradigms to human problems. In the examples cited above, an ethnographic perspective is offered to aid practitioners in a variety of fields, presumably to increase their sensitivity toward issues related to cultural differences and cultural process. It is equally important to recognize that practitioners do have their own models of change and intervention, and that these models might conflict with an ethnographic perspective and militate against the effective use of ethnography in clinical or applied settings. Peter Rigby and Peter Sevareid (1992) have, for example, contrasted the ways in which lawyers and ethnographers deal with "facts" and "evidence," and Drake (1988) has contrasted ethnographic thinking with that of the government bureaucrat.

◆ Major Issues in Applied Ethnography

The increased use of ethnographic methods and perspectives in applied research has led to a variety of emergent issues, some of which are unique to the ethnographic approach and others of which are more general and relate primarily to differences between applied and basic research.

Criticisms of Ethnography in Applied Work

Issues of reliability and internal validity remain significant concerns related to the use of ethnographic approaches in applied research. These issues have become more prominent as ethnographers increase their involvement with research teams that include social scientists who approach their work from a more quantitative perspective. By the same token, such experiences have contributed to an increased sophistication on the part of many ethnographers, both in terms of expanding their methodological repertoires and in terms of their being better able to articulate measures of reliability and validity within the more qualitative aspects of their inquiries (e.g., Bernard, 1994; Kirk & Miller, 1986), although some ethnographers have argued that ethnographic research requires distinct criteria for judging the validity of its methods (e.g., Guba & Lincoln, 1989). As Hammersley (1992) notes, criteria of validity ultimately have their point of reference in concepts of "truth." This allows for the possibility that the "truths" derived from attempts to understand and interpret cultural processes are different from those of other phenomena (e.g., Geertz, 1983). It also allows for the certainty that the "truths" of applied research are generally more contingent and subject to varied criteria of utility (see below) than are those drawn from the framework of "pure" and discipline-bound research. If validity is not entirely in the eye of the beholder, it clearly does stand in relation to the needs and judgments of those who have in a stake in any particular applied research activity.

Another criticism of ethnography has related to the wealth and richness of the data that applied ethnographers typically retrieve, particularly when they are involved in large-scale research efforts that might involve collecting data over periods of several years, and that include a number of ethnographers or qualitative researchers producing data from several different research sites. Early efforts of this kind were often initiated without adequate attention to how the field data would later be analyzed or the extent to which data collected by different field-workers at different sites would be comparable. More recently, the adoption of computer-based ethnographic programs, such as NUD•IST and the Ethnograph, has proven useful, in terms of both managing ethnographic data and facilitating preliminary data analyses. The use of ethnography in applied research has also been criticized as taking too long to serve as an effective tool for decision making, and as being too broadly focused (ethnographers do not always stick to the "problem" specified by their clients). In regard to timeliness, ethnographers have made considerable progress in developing "rapid assessment" procedures, particularly in areas of development research and resource management. In defense of their usually broad or holistic focus, ethnographers have countered that their methods are often fundamental to exploring the extent to which the "problem" identified in applied research efforts might have been misconstrued or might fall off the mark—an argument that may have considerable merit but has not proved particularly comforting to some research clients.

The potential for perceptions of researcher bias in applied ethnographic research and practice extends beyond issues of reliability and validity. Whether their efforts are applied or not, ethnographers have often been regarded as advocates for the people they study, and at least some ethnographers would themselves not dispute such a claim. This seems particularly true of work in anthropology, where a claim to representing and protecting the "best" interests of those people typically studied by anthropologists has long been a part of the disciplinary standard. Although ethnographers certainly need to be attentive to the extent to which their traditions of advocacy contribute to biases, it is equally apparent that criticisms concerning possible bias can come about simply as a result of the kinds of conclusions for which ethnographers aim. In an applied setting, the strength of ethnography is its capacity to identify cultural patterns that provide reason and meaningfulness to human values and behaviors. Change agents and other potential clients for applied research are themselves usually close enough to the problem that they have their own interpretations of the values and behaviors that are being studied. Ethnography has the potential to provide alternative interpretations that might be greeted with enthusiasm by some research clients, or that might be so incompatible with client expectations as to be dismissed as biased and rejected outright.

Defenses of Ethnography in Applied Work

Many of the characteristics that have given rise to criticisms of the value of ethnography for applied research can also be offered as strengths particular to the method. The long-term and relatively intimate acquaintance with research subjects that is characteristic of much ethnography provides rich, contextual information that can increase the depth of our knowledge of particular subjects. Ethnographic and qualitative research approaches have been successfully applied to research situations in which subjects are not likely to be candid in response to such instruments as survey questionnaires, or where there are likely to be significant differences of interpretation regarding the appropriate responses to direct questions, cultural differences in the etiquette of inquiry, or even in the meaning of particular questions or responses. In terms of analysis and interpretation of research results, ethnography adds a cultural dimension that is likely to be absent in other approaches.

Recent approaches to applied ethnography have also served the useful purpose of simply helping people (clients, research subjects, and so on) think about the idea of culture, how culture "works," and culture's consequences. In some instances, this might require ethnographers to help others unlearn the popular, more static concepts of culture taught by earlier ethnographers, and most particularly by anthropologists (Chambers, 1986).

Research Clients and Applied Ethnographic Methods

Whereas basic research methods are generally developed within disciplinary boundaries and subject almost solely to peer review, applied research invariably entails convincing a client of the appropriateness and effectiveness of a research strategy. This may require the ethnographer to adapt his or her methods to the particular needs and constraints expressed by the client. Approaches to rapid ethnographic methods have, for example, derived specifically from the need of particular clients to receive data in a timely fashion (e.g., R. Chambers, 1985; Harris, Jerome, & Fawcett, 1997; van Willigan & Finan, 1991). Similarly, ethnographic methods have been adapted to the special needs of clients who feel the need to conduct assessments of the potential social or cultural impacts of their interventions (e.g., Cernea, 1985; Cochrane, 1979).

Rapid research might include a variety of techniques, but those that seem to be most commonly associated with ethnography are (a) the use of focus group interviews; (b) "stepwise" research, in which long-term field presence is replaced by brief ethnographic "visits" to solve particular research problems posed by an ongoing research project; and (c) participatory research strategies that involve those at the research site in data collection efforts. These approaches, as they relate to applied ethnographic research, are discussed in greater detail by the contributors to van Willigan and Finan's (1991) edited volume.

Applied ethnographers are not of a single mind as to the extent to which their research approaches should be adapted to the declared needs or expectations of research clients. For example, Wolcott (1994) has expressed concern about the influence of evaluation research models on ethnographic research in education. Wolcott argues for a more descriptive and nonevaluative approach. In contrast, others have built their approaches to applied ethnography directly upon evaluation research models (e.g., Fetterman 1984; Ryan, Greene, Lincoln, Mathison, & Mertens, 1998).

Criteria of Utility in Applied Ethnography

By and large, applied ethnographers have not been attentive to the task of proving the value of their inquiries. Although there has been considerable discussion of ways in which ethnographic research *might* be useful, there has been relatively little effort made to establish actual uses. Within anthropology, the usual genre for discussing the practical uses of ethnography has been the case study, which relies heavily upon establishing the reasonableness of an ethnographic interpretation, but seldom offers clues as to whether those interpretations were actually incorporated into client decision making, policy construction, or program intervention. A major exception is *Making Our Research Useful: Case Studies in the Utilization of Anthropological Knowledge* (van Willigan, Rylko-Bauer, & McElroy, 1989). Although the authors in this volume identify numerous factors that appear to contribute to effective utilization, many of them cluster around issues of collaboration and communication. The effective application of ethnography seems related to the extent to which the research client is actively involved in the research effort and the extent to which the ethnographers are willing to serve as advocates of their research and to communicate their findings in different ways to a variety of stakeholders.

In a similar vein, I have argued that criteria of utility are as vital for effective applied research as might be the more usual and variable criteria for establishing scientific reliability and validity (E. Chambers, 1985). I have identified five such criteria. The *accessibility* of research findings refers to the criterion that knowledge be available in an appropriate manner to those who have a stake in a program of change. Applied ethnography should also be *relevant* to the goals and prescribed activities of stakeholders and clients. It also needs to be responsive to different claims upon the *significance* of a course of action (understanding, for example, that the claims of the significance of maintaining historic structures might well be different among historic preservationists and among community members who more acutely feel the need for a modern shopping center). Fourth, applied ethnography should meet a criterion of *credibility* in terms of being responsive to those standards of evidence and proof that are favored by clients and stakeholders. Finally, applied research needs to address matters of *prospect* and judgment (or, in other words, to understand that stakeholders and clients are often more interested in what could be, or even in what should be, than they are in what currently is).

What Kind of Science?

As far as I can determine, there has never been agreement among applied ethnographers as to the kind of science they practice. I am certain this is true within anthropology. Early accounts range from the interpretive and even speculative sciences (e.g., Kluckhohn, 1947) to models that emulate the natural sciences in their attention to precision and predictability (e.g., Chapple, 1941). Most current applied ethnography follows one or the other of these models, with some researchers basing their work on a natural science paradigm that places emphasis on the search for testable and causal statements related to cultural processes (e.g., Bernard, 1994; Poggie et al., 1992) and others focusing on interpretive models that, to an extent at least, emphasize the uniqueness of particular cultural circumstances and events (e.g., Agar, 1996; Wolcott, 1994). In this regard, Wolcott has gone so far as to question whether a preoccupation with validity in applied ethnography might actually detract from an ethnographer's quest for understanding.

A major difference in the ways qualitative ethnography plays out in these two models is in the manner in which the method is integrated into a research project. For the natural science model, qualitative ethnography is often accompanied by, and sometimes dominated by, more quantitative methods. Interpretive researchers and practitioners tend to rely more fully on qualitative approaches as the basis for their inquiries.

In contrast to developments in general anthropology and elsewhere in the social sciences, postmodernism has played a relatively minor role in the further development of applied ethnography, and in some quarters there is open antagonism toward the approach (e.g., Young, 1998). Other have suggested that some aspects of the postmodern critique might contribute positively to a more critical understanding of applied ethnographers' own positions in the processes of inquiry, as well as to an exploration of alternative approaches to textual representation (e.g., Johannsen, 1992).

Issues of Ethics and Morality

Applied research often has immediate consequences for those who become subject to its gaze. In many cases, where applied ethnography is employed as a part of a knowledge base from which to make decisions about the fate of communities and their environments, the ethical and moral considerations can be daunting. Not infrequently, applied ethnography is conducted under conditions of planned or unplanned change, in which communities are experiencing the pressures of disruption and manipulation of their lives. Ethnographers vary considerably in the extent to which they feel their primary role in such situations is to try to understand what is going on or to try to help alleviate human suffering.

Beyond those issues that affect social science researchers in general, applied ethnographers have encountered a number of ethical and moral dilemmas that arise as a result of the researchers' unique relationships to research clients. One of the more intriguing of these is the question of whether or not ethnographers should be engaged in research with clients whose policies or actions might not conform to professional or personal standards of morality. In putting forth the idea that anthropologists could serve useful purposes related to British colonial administration in Africa, Malinowski (1929) walked a thin line between complicity and arguing that the presence of anthropology would help humanize the colonial mission. Similarly, social scientists involved as community analysts in the relocation camps established for Japanese Americans during World War II have sought to distance themselves from the policy and have described themselves primarily as "cultural brokers" between the Japanese internees and the War Relocation Authority (Spicer, 1979). This idea that involvement is better than boycott pervades much of current applied research, although others have argued that association is the equivalent of complicity and have recommended that applied researchers excuse themselves from work with a wide variety of clients (e.g., Berreman, 1991; Escobar, 1991).

Three issues of professional ethics have proven particularly difficult for applied ethnographers. One of these is the principle of informed consent. Within anthropology, Fluehr-Lobban (1994) has suggested that the tendency of field-workers to resist informed consent may result in part from their assumption that they are in a better position than their research subjects to determine and to mitigate any potentially harmful consequences of their research. She decries this attitude as being inappropriately paternalistic. On the other hand, Murray Wax (1995) has argued that there are instances in which strict adherence to principles of informed consent would make fieldwork difficult if not impossible—especially in cases where ethnographers are investigating illegal activity or are investigating elites (i.e., "studying up") who are likely to resist their inquiries.

Applied ethnographers also face ethical dilemmas related to the protection of the confidentiality of research subjects. This problem can relate to research subjects in general, as it does in cases in which research clients have or request access to records that identify research subjects. It can also relate to particular research subjects whose identities cannot be concealed by virtue of their unique positions in an institution. The professional codes of both the American Anthropological Association and the Society for Applied Anthropology, which at one time specified that the confidentiality of research subjects should be maintained in all cases, have recently been revised to indicate that subjects should at least be informed of those cases in which confidentiality cannot be assured.

In general, the social science professions have encouraged open and public dissemination of the results of research. During the 1960s, the American Anthropological Association went so far as to proscribe "secret" research altogether. This prohibition seemed unreasonable to some applied ethnographers, who found themselves engaged in research in which their clients appeared to have legitimate proprietary interests over the data. Such interests included, for example, research devoted to the test marketing of new products, evaluations of marketable techniques for counseling and consultation, and long-term social experiment research in which the early release of preliminary results might compromise the experiment. These claims have by and large been held to have merit, and most professional associations, including the American Anthropological Association in its 1998 revision of its principles of professional responsibility, have revised their codes to allow for the withholding of research results in cases in which there appear to be legitimate proprietary interests.

◆ Summary

Early attempts to apply ethnographic research to problem solving and social intervention introduced three major rationales that retain much of their influence. These point to the strengths of ethnography in eliciting the "native point of view," in uncovering the more tacit dimensions of culture, and in facilitating collaborative or "action" research strategies. On the other hand, a major change in the ethnographic perspective has been the gradual shift from viewing cultures as relatively closed and geographically bounded systems to focusing attention upon those cultural processes that emerge as a result of programs of intervention and change. In this respect, applied ethnographic research has kept pace with more general trends in tracing the interplay of local and global aspects of cultural expression.

The past two decades have seen changes and improvements in the development of applied ethnographic research methods and techniques. These changes have included the following:

♦ Increased sophistication in developing cultural (and cognitive) models in response to issues of intervention and problem solving;

♦ A greater diversification of research methodologies and techniques to include both qualitative and quantitative approaches, and the use of computer-assisted ethnographic research programs;

♦ More complete involvement of ethnographers in the various stages of applied research (project design, analysis, dissemination, and so on), resulting in greater understanding of specifically applied and policy-oriented research strategies;

♦ A greater tendency for ethnographers to work as members of research teams, either within their own disciplinary framework or as participants in interdisciplinary research;

♦ A tendency for ethnographers to pay greater attention to the importance of matching research strategies to specific client needs for information and insight, and to pay heed to "criteria of utility";

♦ Increased experience in applying ethnographic methods to participatory and "action" research strategies.

Within anthropology as a whole, this same period has seen increased acceptance of specifically applied research as a legitimate and important enterprise. Increased support and institutionalization of applied ethnography from within the discipline, as well as increased interest from outside the discipline, suggest that the progress made to date will continue well into the future.

Are there other areas in which applied ethnography has not progressed? I think there are. One of these is the failure of many ethnographers to follow up on the actual uses of their contributions. Except in occasional asides and anecdotes, no clear conceptualizations of utilization have emerged from the practice of applied ethnography. As in the past, ethnographers seem content to stress the supposed usefulness of their inquiries rather than to explore empirically what happens when their knowledge enters the fray of public recognition, intervention, and decision making. In this respect, much applied ethnography seems locked in the "positivist" assumption that good knowledge will find good uses without much effort or commitment on the part of the investigator. More critical analyses of the actual uses (and misuses) of ethnographic knowledge are badly needed.

Related to this is the ethical and moral stance of applied ethnography. Although guided in a general way by a preference for advocating for those who often have the least voice in public affairs, applied ethnographers have not resolved for themselves the vexing issue of the proper role for their inquiries. Are they specialists in the production of knowledge whose services should be available without discrimination, much as physicians and lawyers endeavor to respond equally to the needs of all potential clients? Or do they limit their participation to those clients they feel are most deserving? Although it might be that this issue will never be resolved beyond the level of individual choices, a higher level of discussion of the issues would be helpful.

Another area in which we have made few advances is in the translation of the ethnographic perspective to clinical modes of practice other than research. Although there is precedence for such an interest, which I have discussed above, our efforts to understand how ethnographic inquiry can better inform the practices of individuals who enter careers related to the human services, planning, and decision making fall short of the situation in which we find ourselves. In anthropology, for example, the dominant role of academic practice has begun to yield to a much broader sense of the kinds of careers that are appropriate to the discipline. We need to pay more attention to the ways in which such a major and distinct mode of inquiry as ethnography might prepare individuals for these new career modes—increasing our appreciation for the possibility that the "method" has salience beyond its more formal applications.

If I can speculate as to where the field will be 10 years from now, I would certainly hope for improvements in the areas just mentioned. Beyond this, I would place my bets on (a) increased sophistication in research methods and techniques, and advances in integrating ethnographic inquiries with other approaches to problem solving; and (b) in terms of research directions, greater emphasis upon convincing decision makers and research clients of the importance of paying heed to "indigenous knowledge systems," not only as means to understanding more fully the needs of people and their communities, but also as a vital source of potential solutions to communities' problems. Too often, "top-down" responses in attempts to solve social problems have served to erode if not destroy those very social and cultural resources and survival strategies that have helped keep troubled communities alive.

◆ References

Agar, M. H. (1973). *Ripping and running: A formal ethnography of urban heroin addicts.* New York: Seminar.

Agar, M. H. (1986a). *Independents declared: The dilemmas of independent trucking.* Washington, DC: Smithsonian Institution.

Agar, M. H. (1986b). *Speaking of ethnography.* Beverly Hills, CA: Sage.

Agar, M. H. (1994). The intercultural frame. *International Journal of Intercultural Relations, 18,* 221-237.

Agar, M. H. (1996). *The professional stranger: An informal introduction to ethnography.* San Diego, CA: Academic Press.

Argyris, D. (1990). The ethnographic approach to intervention and fundamental change. In C. Argyris, R. Putnam, & D. M. Smith (Eds.), *Action science* (pp. 158-189). San Francisco: Jossey-Bass.

Barnett, H. G. (1956). *Anthropology in administration.* Evanston, IL: Row, Peterson.

Bartlett, P. F. (Ed.). (1980). *Agricultural decision making: Anthropological contributions to rural development.* New York: Academic Press.

Bernard, H. R. (1994). *Research methods in anthropology: Qualitative and quantitative approaches* (2nd ed.). Walnut Creek, CA: AltaMira.

Bernard, H. R. (Ed.). (1998). *Handbook of research methods in cultural anthropology.* Walnut Creek, CA: AltaMira.

Berreman, G. D. (1991). Anthropological ethics in the 1980s: A positive approach. In C. Fluehr-Lobban (Ed.), *Ethics and the profession of anthropology: A dialogue for a new era* (pp. 36-71). Philadelphia: University of Pennsylvania Press.

Briggs, C. L. (1986). *Learning how to ask: A sociologuist appraisal of the role of the interview in social science research.* Cambridge: Cambridge University Press.

Cernea, M. M. (Ed.). (1985). *Putting people first: Sociological variables in rural development.* New York: Oxford University Press.

Chambers, E. (1985). *Applied anthropology: A practical guide.* Prospect Heights, IL: Waveland.

Chambers, E. (1986). The cultures of science and policy. In W. N. Dunn (Ed.), *Policy analysis: Perspectives, concepts, and methods* (pp. 93-110). Greenwich, CT: JAI.

Chambers, R. (1985). Shortcut and participatory methods for gaining social information for projects. In M. M. Cernea (Ed.), *Putting people first: Sociological variables in rural development* (pp. 515-537). New York: Oxford University Press.

Chapple, E. D. (1941). Anthropological engineering: Its use to administrators. *Applied Anthropology, 2*(2), 23-32.

Cochrane, G. (1979). *The cultural appraisal of development projects.* New York: Praeger.

DeWalt, B. R., & Pelto, P. J. (Eds.). (1985). *Micro and macro levels of analysis in anthropology: Issues in theory and research.* Boulder, CO: Westview.

Drake, H. M. (1988). *Mainstreaming anthropology: Experiences in government employment.* Washington, DC: American Anthropological Association.

Escobar, A. (1991). Anthropology and the development encounter: The making and marketing of development anthropology. *American Ethnologist, 18,* 658-682.

Fetterman, D. M. (Ed.). (1984). *Ethnography in educational evaluation.* Beverly Hills, CA: Sage.

Fluehr-Lobban, C. (1994). Informed consent in anthropological research: We are not exempt. *Human Organization, 53,* 1-10.

Foster, G. M. (1969). *Applied anthropology.* Boston: Little, Brown.

Geertz, C. (1983). *Local knowledge: Further essays in interpretive anthropology.* New York: Basic Books.

Green, J. W. (1982). *Cultural awareness in the human services.* Englewood Cliffs, NJ: Prentice Hall.

Greenwood, D. J., & Levin, M. (1998). *Introduction to action research: Social research for social change.* Thousand Oaks, CA: Sage.

Guba, E. G., & Lincoln, Y. S. (1989). *Fourth generation evaluation.* Newbury Park, CA: Sage.

Hammersley, M. (1992). *What's wrong with ethnography? Methodological explorations.* London: Routledge.

Harris, K. J., Jerome, N. W., & Fawcett, S. B. (1997). Rapid assessment procedures: A review and critique. *Human Organization, 56,* 375-378.

Heath, S. B. (1982). Questioning at home and at school: A comparative study. In G. Spindler (Ed.), *Doing the ethnography of schooling.* New York: Holt, Rinehart & Winston.

Holmberg, A. R. (1958). The research and development approach to the study of change. *Human Organization, 17,* 12-16.

Johannsen, A. M. (1992). Applied anthropology and post-modernist ethnography. *Human Organization, 51,* 71-81.

Kempton, W., Boster, J. S., & Hartley, J. A. (1995). *Environmental values in American culture.* Cambridge: MIT Press.

Kirk, J., & Miller, M. L. (1986). *Reliability and validity in qualitative research.* Beverly Hills, CA: Sage.

Kluckhohn, C. (1947). Covert culture and administrative problems. *American Anthropologist, 45,* 213-229.

Leighton, A. H. (1945). *The governing of men.* Princeton, NJ: Princeton University Press.

Lewin, K. (1948). *Resolving social conflicts.* New York: Harper & Row.

Malinowski, B. (1929). Practical anthropology. *Africa, 2,* 23-38.

Manning, P. K. (1977). *Police work: The social organization of policing.* Cambridge: MIT Press.

Montgomery, E., & Bennett, J. W. (1979). Anthropological studies of food and nutrition: The 1940s and the 1970s. In W. Goldschmidt (Ed.), *The uses of anthropology* (pp. 124-144). Washington, DC: American Anthropological Association.

Pelto, P. J., & Pelto, G. H. (1978). *Anthropological research: The structure of inquiry* (2nd ed.). New York: Cambridge University Press.

Poggie, J. J., Jr., DeWalt, B. R., & Dressler, W. W. (Eds.). (1992). *Anthropological research: Process and application.* Albany: State University of New York Press.

Rigby, P., & Sevareid, P. (1992). Lawyers, anthropologists, and the knowledge of facts. In R. F. Kandel (Ed.), *Double vision: Anthropologists at law* (pp. 5-21). Washington, DC: American Anthropological Association.

Rosaldo, R. (1989). *Culture and truth: The remaking of social analysis.* Boston: Beacon.

Ryan, K. E., Greene, J. C., Lincoln, Y. S., Mathison, S., & Mertens, D. (1998). Advantages and challenges of using inclusive evaluation approaches in evaluation practice. *American Journal of Evaluation, 19,* 101-122.

Schein, E. H. (1987). *The clinical perspective in fieldwork.* Newbury Park, CA: Sage.

Schensul, J. J. (1985). Systems consistency in field research, dissemination, and social change. *American Behavioral Scientist, 29,* 186-204.

Scrimshaw, S. C. M. (1985). Bringing the period down: Government and squatter settlement confront induced abortion in Ecuador. In B. R. DeWalt & P. J. Pelto (Eds.), *Micro and macro levels of analysis in anthropology: Issues in theory and research* (pp. 121-146). Boulder, CO: Westview.

Shimkin, D. B., & Golde, P. (Eds.). (1983). *Clinical anthropology: A new approach to American health.* Lanham, MD: University Press of America.

Spicer, E. H. (1952). *Human problems in technological change.* New York: John Wiley.

Spicer, E. H. (1979). Anthropologists and the War Relocation Authority. In W. Goldschmidt (Ed.), *The uses of anthropology* (pp. 217-237). Washington, DC: American Anthropological Association.

Spradley, J. P. (1975). *You owe yourself a drunk: An ethnography of urban nomads.* Boston: Little, Brown.

Spradley, J. P. (1979). *The ethnographic interview.* New York: Holt, Rinehart & Winston.

Stein, H. F. (1982). The ethnographic mode of teaching clinical behavioral science. In N. J. Chrisman & T. W. Maretzki (Eds.), *Clinically applied anthropology: Anthropologists in health science settings* (pp. 61-82). Boston: D. Reidel.

van Willigan, J., & Finan, T. L. (Eds.). (1991). *Soundings: Rapid and reliable research methods for practicing anthropologists.* Washington, DC: American Anthropological Association.

van Willigan, J., Rylko-Bauer, B., & McElroy, A. (Eds.). (1989). *Making our research useful: Case studies in the utilization of anthropological knowledge.* Boulder, CO: Westview.

Tax, S. (1958). The Fox Project. *Human Organization, 17,* 17-19.

Trend, M. G. (1978). On the reconciliation of qualitative and quantitative analysis: A case study. *Human Organization, 37,* 345-354.

Warren, D. M., Slikkerveer, L. J., & Brokensha, D. (Eds.). (1995). *The cultural dimension of development: Indigenous knowledge systems.* London: Intermediate Technology.

Wax, M. L. (1995). Informed consent in applied research: A comment. *Human Organization, 54,* 330-331.

Whyte, W. F. (with Whyte, K. K.). (1984). *Learning from the field: A guide from experience.* Beverly Hills, CA: Sage.

Wolcott, H. F. (1994). *Transforming qualitative data: Description, analysis, and interpretation.* Thousand Oaks, CA: Sage.

Wolcott, H. F. (1995). Making a study "more ethnographic." In J. Van Maanen (Ed.), *Representation in ethnography* (pp. 44-72). Thousand Oaks, CA: Sage.

Young, J. (1998). SfAA president's letter. *Society for Anthropology Newsletter, 9*(4), 1-2.

PART II

The Art
and Practices
of Interpretation,
Evaluation, and
Representation

In conventional terms, Part II of this volume signals the terminal phase of qualitative inquiry. The researcher or evaluator now assesses, analyzes, and interprets the empirical materials that have been collected. This process, conventionally conceived, involves a set of analytic procedures that produce interpretations, which are then integrated into a theory or put forward as a set of policy recommendations. The resulting interpretations are assessed in terms of a set of criteria, from the positivist or postpositivist tradition, that include validity, reliability, and objectivity. Those interpretations that stand up to scrutiny are put forward as the findings of the research.

The contributors to Part II explore the art, practices, and politics of interpretation, evaluation, and representation. In so doing, they return to the themes raised by the authors in Part I of Volume 1—asking, that is, *How can we use the discourses of qualitative research to help create and imagine a free democratic society?* It is understood that the processes of analysis, evaluation, and interpretation are neither terminal nor mechanical. They are like a dance, to invoke the metaphor used by Valerie Janesick in Chapter 12 of Volume 2. This dance is informed at every step of the way by a commitment to this civic agenda. The processes that define the practices of interpretation and representation are always ongoing, emergent, unpredictable, and unfinished.

We begin by assessing a number of criteria that have been used traditionally (as well as recently) to judge the adequacy of qualitative research. These criteria flow from the major paradigms now operating in this field (in Chapter 12, John Smith and Deborah Deemer explore these criteria in detail).

◆ Criteria for Evaluating Qualitative Research

Smith and Deemer remind us that we live in an age of relativism. They note that in the social sciences today there is no longer a God's-eye view that guarantees absolute methodological certainty; to assert such is to court embarrassment. Indeed, as Lincoln and Guba discuss in detail in Volume 1, Chapter 6, there is considerable debate over what constitutes good interpretation in qualitative research. Nonetheless, there seems to be an emerging consensus that all inquiry reflects the standpoint of the inquirer, that all observation is theory laden, and that there is no possibility of theory-free knowledge. We can no longer think of ourselves as neutral spectators of the social world.

Consequently, as Smith and Deemer observe, in the current discourses of qualitative inquiry it is no longer possible to speak in terms of a foundational epistemology and a direct ontological realism. No method is a neutral tool of inquiry, and hence the notion of procedural objectivity cannot be sustained. The days of naïve realism and naïve positivism are over. In their place stand critical and historical realism and various versions of relativism. The criteria for evaluating research are now relative.

Extending Smith and Deemer's argument, there are three basic positions on the issue of evaluative criteria: foundational, quasi-foundational, and nonfoundational. There are still those who think in terms of a foundational epistemology. They would apply the same criteria to qualitative research as are employed in quantitative inquiry, contending that is there is nothing special about qualitative research that demands a special set of evaluative criteria. As we indicate in our introduction to Part II of Volume 1, the positivist and postpositivist paradigms apply four standard criteria to disciplined inquiry: internal validity, external validity, reliability, and objectivity. The use of these criteria, or their variants, is consistent with the *foundational* position.

In contrast, *quasi-foundationalists* approach the criteria issue from the standpoint of a nonnaïve neorealism or subtle realism. They contend that the discussion of criteria must take place within the context of an ontological neorealism and a constructivist epistemology. They believe in a real world that is independent of our fallible knowledge of it. Their constructivism commits them to the position that there can be no theory-free knowledge.

Proponents of the quasi-foundational position argue for the development of a set of criteria unique to qualitative research. Hammersley (1992, p. 64; also 1995, p. 18; see also Wolcott, 1999, p. 194) is a leading proponent of this position. He wants to maintain the correspondence theory of truth while suggesting that researchers assess a work in terms of its ability (a) to generate generic/formal theory; (b) to be empirically grounded and scientifically credible; (c) to produce findings that can be generalized, or transferred to other settings; and (d) to be internally reflexive in terms of taking account of the effects of the researcher and the research strategy on the findings that have been produced.

Hammersley reduces his criteria to three essential terms: plausibility (Is a claim plausible?), credibility (Is the claim based on credible evidence?), and relevance (What is the claim's relevance for knowledge about the world?). Of course, these criteria require social judgments. They cannot be assessed in terms of any set of external or foundational criteria. Their meanings are arrived at through consensus and discussion in the scientific community. Smith and Deemer note that within Hammersley's model there is no satisfactory method for resolving this issue of how to evaluate an empirical claim.

For the *nonfoundationalists,* relativism is not an issue. They accept the argument that there is no theory-free knowledge. As Smith and Deemer note, relativism, or uncertainty, is the inevitable consequence of the fact that as human beings we have finite knowledge of ourselves and the world we live in. Nonfoundationalists contend that the injunction to pursue knowledge cannot be given epistemologically; rather, the injunction is moral and political.

Accordingly, the criteria for evaluating qualitative work are also moral and fitted to the pragmatic, ethical, and political contingencies of concrete situations. Good or bad inquiry in any given context is assessed in terms of such criteria as those outlined by Greenwood and Levin (Volume 1, Chapter 3), Fine, Weis, Weseen, and Wong (Volume 1, Chapter 4), Christians (Volume 1, Chapter 5), Lincoln and Guba (Volume 1, Chapter 6), Schwandt (Volume 1, Chapter 7), Kemmis and McTaggart (Volume 2, Chapter 11), Angrosino and Pérez (Chapter 3, this volume), and Madriz (Chapter 10, this volume). These are the criteria that flow from a feminist, communitarian moral ethic of empowerment, community, and moral solidarity. Returning to Christians, this moral ethic calls for research rooted in the concepts of care, shared governance, neighborliness, love, and kindness. Further, this work should provide the foundations for social criticism and social action.

◆ The Practices and Politics of Interpretation

In Chapter 13, Norman Denzin proposes to reengage the methods and promises of qualitative inquiry as forms of radical democratic practice. He explores new and older writing forms, working back and forth among the new, civic, and intimate journalism, calls for performance-based ethnographies, and variations on a Chicano/a and African American aesthetic. He explores the relationships between these practices and critical race theory. Like Ladson-Billings (Volume 1, Chapter 9), Denzin seeks to align critical theory with the poststructural turn in ethnography.

◆ Writing as Inquiry

Writers interpret as they write, so writing is a form of inquiry, a way of making sense of the world. In Chapter 14, Laurel Richardson explores new writing and interpretive styles that follow from the narrative, literary turn in the social sciences. She calls these different forms of writing CAP (creative analytic practices) ethnography. These new forms include auto-ethnography, fiction stories, poetry, drama, performance texts, polyvocal texts, readers' theater, responsive readings, aphorisms, comedy and satire, visual presentations, conversation, layered accounts, writing-stories, and mixed genres. Richardson discusses in detail one class of experimental genre that she calls evocative representations. Work in this genre includes narratives of the self, microprocess writing-stories, ethnographic fictional representations, poetic representations, ethnographic dramas, and mixed genres.

The crystal is a central image in Richardson's text; she contrasts the crystal with the triangle. Traditional postpositivist research has relied upon triangulation, including the use of multiple methods, as a method of validation. This model implies a fixed point of reference that can be triangulated. Mixed-genre texts, in contrast, do not triangulate. The central image is the crystal, which "combines symmetry and substance with an infinite variety of shapes, substances, transmutations, . . . and angles of approach." Crystals are prisms that reflect and refract, creating ever-changing images and pictures of reality. Crystallization deconstructs the traditional idea of validity, for now there can be no single, or triangulated, truth.

Richardson offers five criteria for evaluating CAP ethnography: substantive contribution, aesthetic merit, reflexivity, impactfulness, and ability to evoke lived experience. She concludes with a list of writing practices, ways of using writing as a method of knowing.

◆ Anthropological Poetics

Anthropologists have been writing experimental, literary, and poetic ethnographic texts for at least 40 years. In Chapter 15, Ivan Brady analyzes three subcategories of this writing: ethnopoetics, literary anthropology, and anthropological poetry. Ethnopoetics focuses on the poetic productions, proverbs, riddles, laments, prayers, and oral performances of indigenous verbal artists. Literary anthropology includes the fiction in realistic ethnographies, ethnographic novels, and the many different CAP ethnographies discussed by Richardson. Anthropological poetry is just that, poetry written by anthropologists.

In the literary, poetic form, anthropologists enact a moral aesthetic, an aesthetic that allows them to say things they could not otherwise say. In so doing, they push the boundaries of artful ethnographic discourse. Thus are the boundaries between the humanities and the human sciences blurred. In this blurring, our moral sensibilities are enlivened. We are able to imagine new ways of being ourselves in this bewilderingly complex world called the postmodern.

◆ The Practice and Promise of QualitativeProgram Evaluation

Program evaluation, of course, is a major site of qualitative research (the contributions to this *Handbook* by Greenwood & Levin, Stake, Kemmis & McTaggart, Miller & Crabtree, and Chambers help to establish this fact). Evaluators are interpreters. Their texts tell stories. These stories, Jennifer Greene argues in Chapter 16, are inherently moral and political. She examines four contemporary genres of evaluation work: postpositivism, utilitarian pragmatism, interpretivism/constructivism, and critical social science. She reviews the work of the major figures in this area, including Guba and Lincoln, Schwandt, Greenwood and Levin, and Stake. She presents evaluation as a narrative craft, asking, How good is this story? She calls for a morally engaged, constructivist, qualitative genre of evaluation practice.

◆ Influencing Policy With Qualitative Research

Qualitative researchers can influence social policy, and in Chapter 17, Ray Rist shows how they do this. He shows how qualitative research has pivotal relevance in each stage of the policy cycle, from the problem formulation to the implementation and accountability stages. Qualitative researchers can isolate target populations, show the immediate effects of certain programs on such groups, and isolate the constraints that operate against policy changes in such settings. Unlike other models that relegate qualitative research to a secondary position in this process, Rist's model gives this research a central part in the shaping of social policy.

Greene's and Rist's contributions here connect back to the applied research traditions identified by Greenwood and Levin, Stake, Chambers, and Kemmis and McTaggart. They show how the interpretive, qualitative text can morally empower citizens and shape government policies. At the same time, they chart new lines of action for evaluators who are themselves part of the ruling apparatuses of society (Ryan, 1995). Rist and Greene reclaim a new moral authority for the evaluator. This claim can also empower the qualitative researcher who does not engage in direct program evaluation.

◆ Conclusion

The readings in Part II affirm our position that qualitative research has come of age. Multiple discourses now surround topics that in earlier historical moments where contained within the broad grasp of the positivist and postpositivist epistemologies. There are now many ways to write, read, assess, evaluate, and apply qualitative research texts. This complex field invites reflexive appraisal, which is the topic of Part II of this volume.

◆ References

Hammersley, M. (1992). *What's wrong with ethnography? Methodological explorations*. London: Routledge.
Hammersley, M. (1995). *The politics of social research*. Thousand Oaks, CA: Sage.
Ryan, K. E. (1995). Evaluation ethics and issues of social justice: Contributions from female moral thinking. In N. K. Denzin (Ed.), *Studies in symbolic interaction: A research annual* (Vol. 19, pp. 143-151). Greenwich, CT: JAI.
Wolcott, H. F. (1999). *Ethnography: A way of seeing*. Walnut Creek, CA: AltaMira.

12

The Problem of Criteria in the Age of Relativism

John K. Smith and Deborah K. Deemer

◆ In the introduction to the third volume in his series on the nature of inquiry, Hazelrigg (1995) talks about "issues of relativism and its contrary" (p. ix). He then goes on to say about the latter, "which is what, now that we no longer speak the name of absolutism without embarrassment?" (p. ix). His point, which has been noted by many others, such as Bernstein (1983), is that there no longer is a "contrary" to place in opposition to relativism. If this is the case, then it is clear that in this age when the God's-eye view is no longer a realizable hope, relativism, in some form or another, is a consequence that is inescapable (Hesse, 1980, p. xiv). Thus any discussion of criteria for judging social and educational inquiry must confront the issue of relativism—but, of course, as we shall see, how relativism is understood or conceptualized matters greatly.

We begin this chapter with a brief historical review of how we have arrived at this point where we must accept relativism, not only as the crucial feature in any discussion of criteria, but also as the central condition of our very being in the world. At the core of this journey stands the realization, which has been expressed in innumerable ways, that all observation is theory laden or that there is no possibility of theory-free observation or

427

knowledge. Although this idea well predates the work of people such as Hanson (1958) and Kuhn (1962), one can argue it is their writings that have forced upon us the recognition that as knowing subjects we are intimately a part of any understanding we have of what counts as knowledge or of any claim we make to knowledge. With the end of the possibility that we could think of ourselves as neutral spectators at the game of knowledge, the central problem that has preoccupied the thoughts of numerous researchers for the past few decades is that of "Now what are we going to do with us?" This is a preoccupation that has been expressed with great frequency and in all manner of ways: Gallagher's (1995) revisiting of her role in her dissertation research, Sparkes's (1993) concerns over reciprocity, various aspects of Wolcott's (1995) discussion of the art of fieldwork, Punch's (1994) discussion of the politics and ethics of field inquiry, and on and on. The discussions that focus on the position or role of the inquirer seemingly have become endless.

Following this brief historical review, we examine some of the ways the issue of criteria has been addressed in this age of relativism. One of the most prominent of these is what we call the *quasi-foundationalist* response. At the center of the quasi-foundationalist project is the desire to deny the relativism that must accompany the realization that there can be no theory-free knowledge or observation. This group has drawn much of its intellectual sustenance from various neorealist philosophers (*neorealist* is a general term used to distinguish this group from what are often referred to, especially by the neorealists themselves, as naïve, direct, or unsophisticated realists). From at least the time of Popper's (1959) rejection of positivism in favor of a sophisticated or scientific realism, the neorealists have attempted to thread a line between their acceptance of a constructivist epistemology on the one side and, on the other, their adoption of a neorealist ontology. The latter commits them to the position that there is a reality out there that, because it can be known, at least in principle, as it really is, acts as a constraint on any claim to knowledge. The former announces their recognition that there can be no theory-free knowledge or theory-free observation.

In the second half of the chapter we address how our ideas about criteria must change when we realize that the epistemological project is over and relativism must be accepted. This examination begins with the very important point that relativism need not and must not be seen in terms of "anything goes." Rather, relativism is nothing more or less than our condition in the world—it announces that as human beings we are, and can be nothing but, finite. This understanding of relativism is then coupled with a concern that we must change our imageries and metaphors from those of discovery and finding to those of constructing and making. Based on this transition, the central issues become those of how do we as individuals make judgments, which we all must, and the extent to which we allow our judgments to move into a public space, which to a certain degree we also must, to engage the judgments of others.

As is always the case, before we begin at least two caveats are necessary. First, the issues we address are complex. Given the space available and, much more important, our limited capacities, there is no way we can do them full justice. Second, contrary to what is generally the case for others who have addressed this topic, we offer no particular criteria and instructions on how they might be applied. Our intent is to discuss the limits and possibilities of judgment—both individual and within social spaces—in this age of relativism.

◆ Historical Background

The long-standing problem empiricists constructed for themselves was how to reconnect that which they had separated—the knowing subject from the object of knowing. After having established a dualism of subject and object, empiricists of all varieties were compelled to spend considerable time and energy attempting to rework or get around this duality in a way that would allow them to claim the knowing subject could have access to reality in such a way that it could be depicted accurately. Put differently, empiricists had developed a situation in which the referent point for judging claims to knowledge was, and could only be, that which was outside, and independently so, of the knower. Knowledge was a matter of accurate representation, and thus was born the correspondence theory of truth. The solution of choice to make good on this correspondence theory was, as has long been announced in our research textbooks, a methodical one. The idea was quite straightforward: If the proper procedures or methods were properly applied, the subjectivities of the knowing subject would be contained and the knower would thereby gain an accurate, objective depiction of reality. This is what Kerlinger (1979) meant when he said that "the procedures of science are objective—not the scientists. Scientists, like all men and women are opinionated, dogmatic, ideological . . . that is the very reason for insisting on procedural objectivity; to get the whole business outside of ourselves" (p. 264).

Given this line of thought, a judgment about the quality of research, at least in the first instance, was a judgment about whether or not the proper procedures had been properly applied. The methods were seen as neutral and hence established that neutral arena within which judgments could be made about the goodness or badness of any individual research. Of course, there still remained a second level of interest—that of the significance of any particular study. It has long been recognized by the proceduralists that even the most appropriately conducted study could still be judged insignificant because it focused on a trivial problem. In any event, for empiricists the issue can be summarized as follows: Because method allowed for undistorted contact with reality, it was the basis for distinguishing good from bad inquiry but not important from unimportant research.

The attempts by empiricists over the past few hundred years to reconnect subject and object—from Locke's "blank slate" to the ostensive reference of the logical empiricists—need not be discussed. These moves are quite well-known and, more important, such a discussion would take us far afield from the main topic at hand (for a brief recounting of this history, see Smith, 1993). A few brief comments, however, must be made with regard to what has happened over the past 30 or 40 years as traditional empiricism has unraveled and we have witnessed the demise of the methodical solution to the problem of criteria. The problems associated with the dualism of subject and object were apparent to many philosophers prior to the middle of the 20th century. However, within Anglo-American philosophical circles, a good case can be made that it was Hanson (1958) and then, most definitely, Kuhn (1962) who brought the problematic associated with the dualism of subject and object to the forefront.

At the core of Hanson's (1958) arguments was the now seemingly obvious point that "the theory, hypothesis, framework, or background knowledge held by an investigator can strongly influence what is observed" (p. 7). A few short years later Kuhn (1962) followed up on this line of reasoning with his talk of incommensurable paradigms, paradigm shifts, that all knowledge is framework dependent, and so on. By the mid-to-late 1980s, the work of numerous people made it apparent that any claim of or hope for "theory-free knowledge" was untenable on all counts. To cite just a few examples, there were Putnam's (1981) arguments about "no God's-eye point of view," Nagel's (1986) claim that there was no possibility of a "view from nowhere," Bernstein's (1983) discussion of no "Archimedean point," Taylor's (1971) undermining of the hope for access to "brute data," Gadamer's (1995) discussion of "effective history," and Goodman's (1978) elaboration of the ways we make the world.

All of these arguments, and others, combined with another series of arguments that focused directly on, and cast grave doubt upon, the claim that method itself was neutral and could thereby be the repository of pro-cedural objectivity. This certainly was one of the main messages that could be taken from the work of Hesse (1980), Giddens (1976), MacKenzie (1981), Cherryholmes (1988), Smith (1985), and so on. In the end, the result of all of this intellectual ferment was the elaboration of a number of points of great consequence for any discussion of criteria: There is no pos-sibility of theory-free observation and knowledge, the duality of subject and object is untenable, no special epistemic privilege can be attached to any particular method or set of methods, and we cannot have the kind of objective access to an external, extralinguistic referent that would allow us to adjudicate from among different knowledge claims.

The legacy of all of this, of course, is that we no longer can talk in terms of a foundational epistemology and a direct ontological realism. To the contrary, if the discussions of the past few decades have made anything clear to us, it is that we cannot adopt a God's-eye point of view; all we can have are "the various points of view of actual persons reflecting various interests and purposes that their descriptions and theories subserve" (Putnam, 1981, p. 50). Under these conditions, with the demise of empiri-cism and the methodical stance, any discussion of criteria must come to terms, in one form or another or in one way or another, with the issue of relativism.

◆ The Quasi-Foundationalist Response

The quasi-foundationalists, who have attempted to address the criteria issue from the perspective of some form of nonnaïve realism, have had to contend with a very interesting problem. Any elaboration of criteria must take place within the context of their commitment to ontological realism on the one side and, on the other, their realization that they are obligated to accept a constructivist epistemology. The former announces a commitment to the proposition that there is a real world out there independent of our interest in, or knowledge of, it. The latter announces a commitment to the proposition that we can never know if we have depicted this real world as it really is. In short, nonnaïve realists or neorealists "assert a belief in a real world independent of our knowledge while also making it clear that our knowledge of this metacognitive world is quite fallible" (Leary, 1984, p. 918).

In light of these dual commitments, many neorealist philosophers have felt compelled to express their positions with the use of the term *relativism*. Bhaskar (1983), for example, says that his transcendental realism presupposes "ontological realism and epistemological relativism" (p. 259). Similarly, House (1991) notes that the world can be "known only under particular descriptions and is, in that limited sense, epistemologically relative" (p. 5). Even more directly, Manicas (1987) has written that "knowledge is a social product and the standards of inquiry are generated in the course of inquiry. This is a relativism. But it is not irrationalism, because it presupposes a realism" (p. 261).

There is no question, then, that neorealist acceptance of epistemological constructivism entails the realization that there can be no "God's-eye view" in that any claim to knowledge must take into account the perspective of the person making the claim. Maxwell (1992) notes quite clearly the key aspects of the neorealist response to the consequences of this realization. First, he recognizes that "as observers and interpreters . . . we cannot step outside of our own experience to obtain some observer-independent account of what we experience. Thus, it is always possible for there to be different, equally valid accounts from different perspectives" (p. 283). That said, however, it is also equally clear that he, like the other neorealists, does not accept a situation in which "all possible accounts . . . are equally useful, credible, or legitimate" (p. 283). Thus "understanding is relative," there is no account that can stand "independent of any particular perspective" (p. 284), but this does not mean that our only option is to descend into a relativism of all-accounts-are-equal or "anything goes." Finally, in that the neorealists acknowledge that the methodical stance of their empiricist predecessors is not possible, the way to avoid relativism is to call upon a "realist conception of validity that sees the validity of an account as inherent, not in the procedures used to produce and validate it, but in its relationship to those things that it is intended to be an account of " (p. 281).

To examine how well they have done with this quasi-foundationalist project, with its obvious truth-as-correspondence overtones, we turn to exemplars—beginning with a particular emphasis on the work of

Hammersley, in that he has presented one of the clearest and most sophisticated attempts to develop criteria from a neorealist perspective. In one very well attended piece of work, Hammersley (1990) begins with the assertion that "we do not need to abandon the concept of truth as correspondence to an independent reality. We can retain this concept of truth by adopting a more subtle realism" (p. 61). Following this assertion that we can retain the empiricist concept of truth but must reject naïve interpretations of it, he then attempts to elaborate criteria in order to prevent a slide into what is, for him, the void of relativism. These are criteria that must be worked out in light of a constructivist epistemology and a realist, however subtle, ontology. Hammersley frames this task in terms of how researchers can validate their accounts and argues that the only basis for validation is to engage in judgments of the "likelihood of error" (p. 61). This is a position that has distinct Popperian overtones and, accordingly, shares in the problems attendant to Popper's account of falsification. We return to this point shortly.

Hammersley (1990) proposes that the two key elements of validity are plausibility and credibility. The former issue is one of whether or not a claim seems plausible; "that is, whether we judge it as likely to be true given our existing knowledge" (p. 61). He adds that some claims are so plausible we can immediately accept them at face value, whereas others require the presentation of evidence. In the latter instance, a judgment about the credibility of a claim must be taken "given the nature of the phenomena concerned, the circumstances of the research" (p. 61), and so on. In both instances, then, Hammersley recognizes that when a claim has neither face plausibility nor face credibility, evidence is required. However, he further recognizes that the particular evidence presented by a researcher in support of the plausibility and credibility of a study must itself be assessed as to its own plausibility and credibility. And, as he continues, "we may require further evidence to support that evidence, which we shall judge in terms of plausibility and credibility" (p. 62).

It is clear Hammersley fully acknowledges that plausibility and credibility are social judgments, and, not surprisingly, his attempt to establish criteria has become entangled in an infinite regress—if not a hermeneutic circle. At this point, it would seem prudent to call upon ontological realism and make it do some serious work—in particular, the work of making contact with reality in such a way as to blunt the infinite regress of social judgments or, to put it differently, to blunt the relativism that would seem to lie at the end of it all.

This is not the case, however, and the notion of correspondence and realism, no matter how subtle or sophisticated, plays no role of consequence for the balance of his discussion. Hammersley's (1990) movement away from neorealism begins when he says that "plausibility and credibility form a relatively weak basis for judging claims, compared to the idea that we can assess claims directly according to their correspondence with reality or by relying on some body of knowledge whose validity is certain" (p. 62). He continues this movement when he reinvokes a constructivist epistemology and thereby acknowledges that judgments will not "necessarily be consensual, since there may be different views about what is plausible and credible" (p. 62).

Ultimately, Hammersley's line of argument ends in a discussion of the norms that should govern discourse among members of a scientific community. He lists what he considers to be three key features of this scientific community. First, all findings should be subject to "communal assessment," with an effort to "resolve disagreements by seeking common grounds . . . and trying to work back to a resolution of the dispute relying, only on what is accepted as valid by all disputants" (p. 63). Second, all involved should not only attempt to persuade, but be willing to be persuaded and to change their views. Finally, the community is open to those who are "willing to operate on the basis of the first two rules" (p. 63). In the end, then, judgments about plausibility and credibility are social judgments, and they should be made based upon as free and open a dialogue and discussion as possible. There is nothing in Hammersley's discussion that shows us how we can make contact with an external referent—a reality—that would give the criteria of plausibility and credibility a standing beyond the social process and the inevitable relativism that lurks behind this process.

A similar point can be made about the well-known work of Manicas and Secord (1983). They admit that "knowledge is a social and historical product" (p. 401), there is "no preinterpreted 'given' and the test of truth cannot be 'correspondence.' Epistemologically, there can be nothing known to which our ideas (sentences, theories) can correspond" (p. 401). But, if that is so, then, as Leary (1984) notes, "Exactly how Manicas and Secord propose to link experiences—which they admit to be culturally and historically mediated—with reality independent from experience is an issue I shall leave for them to clarify" (p. 918). They do not do well with this task, for as Leary further notes, their best response is the negative assertion that there is no theory-free observation, which "does not eliminate the possibility of objectivity, construed here as warranted assertibility" (p. 410). But, of course, the problem they face here is the same one Hammersley (1990) faces; the warrants one brings to judgments are themselves socially and historically conditioned—as are the warrants that warrant the warrants, and on and on. In both of these instances, and generally for neorealists, any attempt to elaborate on the issue of criteria in a way that gives criteria force beyond socially and historically conditioned judgments must involve an explanation of exactly how their ontological realism does some serious work and is not merely an assertion.

A further example of the same situation occurs in Maxwell's (1992) discussion of five aspects of validity: descriptive, interpretive, theoretical, generalizability, and evaluative. We focus only on his discussion of descriptive validity, as this is the one that seems to make the most use of the realist commitment. Maxwell argues that this is the first concern for qualitative inquirers in that it focuses on the factual accuracy of an account—that researchers are "not making up or distorting the things they saw and heard" (p. 285). On the face of it, this concern seems to be very unproblematic, especially if one confines description to the level of did the researcher actually speak with the person she said she did or did the researcher actually enter the classroom to observe the goings on. However, as soon as one moves that short distance to the level of "description" on the order of did or did not the student "throw an eraser on a specific occasion" (p. 286) or did she raise her arm or did she thrust her arm in the air, the prospects for a viable concept of descriptive validity disappear. Put differently, as soon as we move past the most minimal level of the depiction of the movement of physical bodies in time and space, the coercive or constraining quality that is desired from the real or from reality itself has been left behind long ago in the name of the need for context.

Maxwell (1992) recognizes this issue in that he further notes even descriptive validity is "by no means independent of theory . . . even if this theory is implicit or common sense" (p. 287). This understanding then leads to the comment that although there can be disagreement about the descriptive validity of an account, this can be resolved "in principle" by the data. Further, however, he brings this line of argument to its inevitable outcome when he notes, "Of course, the theory could be made problematic by one of the participants in the discussion—for example, by challenging the applicability of 'throwing' to what the student did with the eraser" (p. 287). One might counter at this point that to challenge the applicability of "throwing" is not only to make theory problematic, it is to make the

435

description problematic. For example, one might say that "throwing" cannot be applied here because the student "tossed" the eraser. If someone were to raise this point, then what would be at stake would not be just a matter of making the theory problematic; to the contrary, it would be a fundamental challenge to the very accuracy of depiction, with each accusing the other of an incorrect or inaccurate accounting of the facts.

Maxwell (1992) responds to this complication with a shift of validity categories and says that this then is no longer an issue of descriptive validity, but rather one of interpretive validity. But this will not do because the whole point of the idea that there can be no theory-free observation is that it is virtually impossible to disentangle the descriptive from the interpretive. How we describe the world is an interpretation—or, put differently, interpretation cuts very, very deep indeed. That much of the time we can agree on "throwing" versus "tossing" is not because reality stands over against us, but because we happen to share a theoretical or pretheoretical disposition and a language for depicting movement in time and space. In his next paragraph, Maxwell recognizes this point when he says, "Descriptive understanding pertains, by definition, to matters for which we have a framework for resolving such disagreement, a framework provided in large part by taken-for-granted ideas about time, space, physical objects, behavior, and our perception of these" (p. 286). In other words, if we start from the same perspective, sharing a language and so on, we will tend to describe/interpret things in basically the same ways. If we start from different theoretical or pretheoretical perspectives, our descriptions/interpretations of events and actions will differ. This is exactly the point made by Hanson (1958), Kuhn (1962), and many others, including the neorealists. Accordingly, just like Hammersley (1990) and Manicas and Secord (1983), Maxwell is unable to show us how to get reality to do some serious work—work that would give his discussion of validity, and by extension criteria, the kind of force that will allow it to stand over and against or beyond a process of socially and historically constrained judgments.

We close this section by noting that the problems faced by the neorealists are little different from the ones faced by one of their major intellectual precursors, Popper (1959, 1972), who, although he as much as anyone else contributed to the retreat from logical empiricism, still attempted to salvage something from the remains of that project. Popper freely accepted that there could be no theory-free observation. That point granted, he still wanted to preserve the capacity to test theories against observational statements. In order to do so, he appealed to a version of realism as the key element in our ability to falsify hypotheses. The problem with his appeal is that if falsification is a matter of a disjuncture between a theory, or a hypothesis derived from a theory, and the facts, the latter must be independent of the former. This is precisely what is not possible if all observation is theory laden. That is, it is impossible to think of the comparison of a hypothesis with theory-mediated facts as the same as testing a hypothesis against an independently existing reality. Hindess (1977) clearly notes the incoherence present in this line of thought: "If theory is inescapably implicated in observation then testing cannot be a rational procedure. If testing is a rational procedure then there must be an atheoretical mode of observation governed by a preestablished harmony between language and the real. To maintain . . . both the rationality of testing and the thesis that observation is an interpretation in light of theory is . . . [a] contradiction" (p. 186).

The problems with Popper's realism are further evident in his claims about inquiry and approximations to truth. This is a claim that Hammersley (1990) reiterates in slightly different terms when he mentions the possibility of research producing "cumulative knowledge" (p. 62). The basic idea sponsoring these claims is that over time our research gets us closer and closer to truth or reality. Unfortunately, this whole line of thought, as is well noted by Hazelrigg (1989), lacks cogency because the "notion of approximation requires an existent referent to which one can achieve proximity, yet how can we know that existent? According to Popper we cannot; but if we cannot, then how are we possibly to judge the question of proximity?" (p. 78). Again, the neorealist claim that it is reality itself that can serve as the bottom line for judgments cannot be made good.

In summary, then, it is clear the neorealists cannot grant us the kind of purchase on the criteria issue that they desire. This lack is evident in the work of Hammersley (1990), Maxwell (1992), and others. In the cases of the aforementioned, both begin with, in the first instance, the claim that we can retain the concept of "truth as correspondence to an independent reality" (p. 61) and, in the second, that a judgment about the validity of a study can be taken with regard to its "relationship to those things that it is intended to be an account of" (p. 281). However, in both cases this is as far as their neorealism goes, and both eventually turn to judgment as a social process. For Hammersley this move appears with full force when he fails to show us how to make contact with an external referent and, in response to this failure, he turns his full attention in the only direction possible—to the issue of the norms that should guide discourse among researchers. For Maxwell, the signal that he should abandon his neorealism comes when he notes that even a judgment about descriptive validity, which he says is about the "factual accuracy of [an] account" (p. 285), requires a shared framework for resolving disagreements (p. 287) and, accordingly, "validity is relative in this sense because understanding is relative" (p. 284).

◆ A Transition

With the failure of the neorealists to salvage the last remnants of the empiricist project, it is time to make a transition and begin to change the conversation. In other words, it is time to move beyond any lingering hopes for a foundational or quasi-foundational epistemology, to change our metaphors and imageries from those of discoverers/finders to those of constructors/makers, and to accept that relativism is our inescapable condition as finite beings. There is no question that we must, as both inquirers and laypersons, learn to live with uncertainty and contingency, and forgo the hope that something will come along that will enable us to transcend our human finitude. But, that said, the relativism that arrives with this perspective does not mean we must give ourselves over to the neorealist fear that all judgments are equally valid, or that "anything goes" in our assessments of the quality of inquiry. Schwandt (1996) summarizes the nonfoundationalist situation quite succinctly: "We must learn to live with uncertainty, with the absence of final vindications, without the hope of solutions in the form of epistemological guarantees. Contingency, fallibilism, dialogue, and deliberation mark our way of being in the world. But these ontological conditions are not the equivalent to eternal ambiguity, the lack of commitment, the inability to act in the face of uncertainty" (p. 59). In short, the problematic for nonfoundationalists, which is profoundly unsettling for us as individuals and as a community of inquirers (if such a sense of an overall community is even possible), is that of how to make and defend judgments when there can be no appeal to foundations or to something outside of the social processes of knowledge construction.

Discussion of this problematic, and of what it means for the judgments we make about inquiry, must begin by clearing some ground and establishing some points. Most immediately, a response is required to the oft-expressed charge that relativism is self-refuting. The refrain here is quite well-known: To say that all things are relative is to make a nonrelative statement. As such, relativism is self-refuting and an untenable position to adopt. We must address two issues in order to demonstrate why this charge is of no consequence.

First, is it the case that relativism is self-refuting? Given the form of logic we normally bring to such questions, the answer, of course, must be yes. But this then leads to the second point: Does it matter, again given this form of logic, that relativism is self-refuting? In this instance, the answer is no. This second point obviously requires elaboration.

One could attempt to argue that this point about being self-refuting should be a crippling blow to nonfoundationalists and their approach to criteria, if only because other schools of philosophical thought have met their demise in similar circumstances. For example, logical empiricism certainly unraveled over the verification issue. As is well-known, logical empiricists said that any statement that cannot be empirically verified is meaningless. But, of course, that statement itself cannot be empirically verified and so, logically, it is meaningless. As Putnam (1981) so clearly points out, it was this problem as much as anything else that led to the end of logical empiricism. So, why should not the same strictures be applied to relativism?

The initial answers to this self-refuting situation came from Gadamer and Rorty. Gadamer's (1995) response is to agree that relativism is self-refuting, but then to shrug it off by saying that to make this point is to make a point of no interest, or one that does "not express any superior insight of value" (p. 344). Rorty's (1985) tactic is to argue that it is a mistake to think of relativism as another theory of knowledge. Quite to the contrary, he dispenses with the self-refuting problem by saying that because his type of pragmatist is not interested in advancing any "epistemology, *a fortiori* he does not have a relativistic one" (p. 6).

Although we agree with much of how both Gadamer (1995) and Rorty (1985) have approached this issue, we feel a further comment remains necessary. One reason the self-refuting claim is and should be devastating to logical empiricism, and, for that matter, to other schools of thought, but not to relativism, depends on the aspirations expressed by these philosophical dispositions. We would argue that empiricism in any form, for example, was based on the claim and the hope that we could deny our human finitude and adopt a God's-eye point of view. That is, the claim was that we could "bracket" ourselves in some way or another, predominantly through submission to method, such that it would become possible for us to seize upon some external referent (i.e., reality known as it really is) to adjudicate different knowledge claims and resolve our differences. Given this claim, it is quite appropriate to apply the logic of self-refuting—the strength of the claim and the aspirations advanced must be directly related to the strength of the argument brought forth in support of those claims and aspirations.

Relativism as understood here, quite to the contrary, is not a theory of knowledge and advances no pretense that we can escape our finite condition of being in the world. As such, the issue of self-refuting, even though it is a logically correct position given a standard form of logic, is unimportant. Taking a page from Godel's idea of incompleteness (see Hofstadter, 1979), this situation is only what one would expect from any human, social and historical, construction. Relativism is not something to be transcended, it is merely something with which we, as finite beings, must learn to live.

Does this understanding of relativism leave nonfoundationalists enmeshed in a situation of "anything goes"—a situation where all judgments about inquiry, and, for that matter, everything else, are equal? There are two intimately related reasons why relativism should not and need not be understood in these terms. First, the charge of relativism as anything goes does not make sense because this charge requires for its vitality a viable concept of the absolute. As previously noted with reference to Hazelrigg (1995), if we no longer can speak of the absolute without embarrassment, then we must realize we cannot speak of "anything goes" without embarrassment.

Second, and more tangibly, it is very clear we all already do make judgments, and as far as anyone can see, we will continue to do so for a long time to come. To say these judgments cannot be grounded extralinguistically does not mean we are exempt from engaging in as open and unconstrained dialogue as possible in order to attempt to justify our assessments. But to attempt to persuade another further requires that one is open to being persuaded. All relativism brings to the table with regard to the issue of criteria is that to be a finite human being who must live with and make judgments in concert with other finite human beings can be, with some frequency, very tough work indeed. This is, in effect, what Schwandt (1996) means when he says, as noted above, that learning to live with uncertainty and the impossibility of final vindication does not mean that we must abandon commitment and our ability to make judgments.

What, then, does this understanding of relativism as a recognition and acceptance of our human finitude mean for social and educational inquiry—especially for the issue of criteria for judging the quality of our studies? One very important way to frame this question is to introduce the difference between depictions of inquiry with the use of the metaphors and imagery of discovery or finding versus the metaphors and imagery of making or constructing. If one accepts a constructivist stance, this means that, as Rorty (1979) so well notes, the metaphors and imageries of discovery and finding no longer can be made good. However, Rorty also goes on to add that we might as well stay with the language of a found world. Part of his justification for this injunction is that "nothing deep turns on the choice between these two phrases—between the imagery of making and of finding" (p. 344). However, Hazelrigg (1989) has been persuasive in helping us understand that a great deal of consequence turns on this distinction. This is so because, as he puts it, "the difference in consequence is not merely of imageries and stories but of practices—of who we are, of what we do, of what world we make" (p. 167). The problem is that to continue to employ the language of a "discovered world" is to continue a "passivity in regard to responsibility for the world" (p. 168). And, as Hazelrigg continues, to think in terms of finding is to place the world "outside the domain of human will. That is an enormously dangerous consequence of any retention of the 'found world' language of storytelling" (p. 168).

To illustrate this point, we note that in the histories, especially more recent, of both educational practice and research there has been a strong tendency to categorize children as this or that—as learning disabled (LD), for example. For those who operate with the image of researchers as "discoverers," LD is a natural category—there always were LD children, and the reason we have recently discovered them is that our inquiries have become increasingly sophisticated. For those who use the language of making or constructing, LD is a constructed category—a way we have chosen, for whatever social/historical reasons, to categorize children. The point is not that we dispense with categorization, which in any case is impossible for the finite human mind. To the contrary, the point is to examine and fully discuss why we construct the world as we do. This is a discussion that is practical and moral, framed by contingent social and historical circumstances, and certainly not epistemological in any theory-of-knowledge sense of the word. Put differently, for those possessed by the metaphors of discovery, issues of moral responsibility are at best contingent because "discovery" is only a matter of contact with reality and what reality is telling us. For those who accept the metaphors of constructing, moral responsibility is central because one must be morally responsible for what one constructs or makes (for a further example and discussion, see Smith, 1989, especially chap. 4).

It is in this sense that the relativism of the nonfoundationalists requires that inquiry be seen as an act of construction that is practical and moral and not epistemological. Likewise, as must follow from this requirement, any judgments about the goodness or badness of research must themselves be practical and moral judgments and not epistemological ones. For the nonfoundationalists, to move away from epistemology is to recognize inquiry as a social process in which we construct reality as we go along and as a social process in which we, at one and the same time, construct our criteria for judging inquiries as we go along.

◆ Changing the Conversation

Relativism is nothing more or less than the expression of our human finitude; we must see ourselves as practical and moral beings, and abandon hope for knowledge that is not embedded within our historical, cultural, and engendered ways of being. If this so, then to continue to talk in the vocabularies of theories of knowledge is to continue to talk in the shadows of the unrealizable desire that something will come along to allow us to get off of Montaigne's wheel or out of the hermeneutic circle. Chisholm's (1973) paraphrase of Montaigne clearly summarizes the unresolved and unresolvable epistemological problematic:

> To know whether things really are as they seem to be, we must have a *procedure* for distinguishing appearances that are true from appearances that are false. But to know whether our procedure is a good procedure, we have to know whether it really *succeeds* in distinguishing appearances that are true from appearances that are false. And we cannot know whether it does really succeed unless we already know which appearances are *true* and which ones are *false*. And so we are caught in a circle. (p. 3)

The neorealists have been unsuccessful in their attempt to cling to an organizing narrative of epistemology free of time and place. They have not been able to show us a way to get off of the wheel or out of the circle. We suspect it is time to move on; it is time to change the conversation by asking what making judgments is about when we can no longer be epistemological. Although we are certainly able to talk about knowledge, especially its social production, there is little point in talking about theories of knowledge and pursuing the ambition to solve the problematic.

That we can no longer play the game of philosophy as epistemology and find solace in a foundational narrative can be nothing but profoundly unsettling to us. This is a break, a rupture, that appears to leave social and educational inquiry "undone"—to use a word from the title of a recent book by Stronach and Maclure (1997). Put differently, all of this talk about judging can no longer take place within that seemingly abstracted, disembodied public space that was fostered by the desire to be epistemological and to thereby specify the context of judgment apart from the actual judgment process. In the age of relativism the issue of who is making judgments, about what inquiries, for what purposes, and with whom one shares these judgments is of critical importance. As individuals we must make judgments, and as members of social groups, however loosely organized, we must be witness to situations in which our individual judgments are played out with the judgments of other individuals.

But, we must immediately note, there is at least one very apparent and often practiced way to avoid the difficulty of judgment. Certainly one could turn to power, in one or another of its numerous guises, to render the social context and process of judgment very specifiable indeed. There is the use of power in a rather raw or open application—for example, the all-too-common situation where a reviewer rejects an article with little or no explanation. Or there is the power of the shrug of the shoulder that seems so popular today with various people when they are questioned. The questioner just does not get the point and the situation is so hopeless that there is no reason to attempt to engage any further. In these instances and many, many others of similar nature with which we are all familiar, an individual has made a judgment, criteria have been applied, but engagement with the judgment and criteria has been denied. To engage this defensive stance, based on the claim of theoretical, standpoint, or whatever differences, works to narrow the public space or social group with whom one shares judgments—all others are read out of the exchange. In any event, although the possibilities for the application of power to solve the problem of criteria seem almost endless, they also seem very unsatisfying and undesirable.

This should not be taken to mean that we are so naïve as to hold that power should and can be eliminated from judgments as they are played out socially. We have no intention to embrace some sort of romanticized "intellectualist flight from power" (Hazelrigg, 1995, p. 202). Rather, the issue for us centers on the responsible use of power while avoiding its excesses. But we also are well aware that it is impossible to specify in some permanent way exactly when one has crossed the line from responsible to excessive. Likewise, it would seem there are often good reasons to narrow the social group. When marginalized groups seek to have their voices heard, solidarity can be very important. In fact, we would argue that this was the case for many qualitative inquirers a few years ago. But, again, the question arises as to how to honor this need while avoiding its excesses—fully realizing that we are unable to specify exactly when the line has been crossed. In short, then, we recognize that power is ever and always present, but we also hold that the temptation (also ever and always present?) to use power as a way to avoid critique and the risk of one's prejudices denies the value of and need for public discourse. So the issue remains: What can be said about judgment when relativism demands attention to context and forgoes the possibility of appeal to an abstract, disembodied (epistemological) public space?

One response to this question from some people is the claim that any discussion of criteria is pointless. Although we will not engage Rosenau's (1992) rendering of affirmative versus skeptical postmodern and post-structural perspectives, we must acknowledge that some of her comments successfully surface issues that have been troubling many within the academy. Those whom Rosenau calls skeptic postmodernists argue that we can only be "nonjudgmental" (p. 55) because "good/bad criteria are unavailable" (p. 175) and all interpretations are equally interesting or uninteresting. In the absence of established criteria for sorting the good from the less so, there is no choice but to simply throw up our hands and leave the field of judgment behind. Certainly this sentiment is not unknown, at least to us. There are times as we review articles for publication, grade papers, accept the dissertation even though it disappointed, that the thought arises: Who are we to judge? The field should be left open to the play of differences, and so on. A similar arena of self-doubt, given the fallibility of human judgment, seems to be the driving force behind the often agonized and agonizing discussions of voice, writing the other, the crisis of representation, and so on.

But to begin from this point or to pretend (even hope?) that we can lead a life free of judgment is to immediately go astray, and obviously so. Judgments must be made and must be argued and justified, unless, in the latter instance, one simply resorts to raw power. As Schwandt (1996) has noted for us, that we all must live with uncertainty and contingency does not mean that we can dismiss commitment and abandon judgment (p. 59). There is no question that we all think some things are better than others and that we make judgments accordingly, often even when we say we do not. This process of judgment making has been going on for quite some time now, and will continue to do so for as far as can be seen.

It is impossible to imagine a person leading a life without making judgments or without making discriminations. To attempt to do so evokes the image of Ebenezer in Barth's novel *The Sot-Weed Factor* (1960), who, because he found all things equally interesting, "threw up his hands at choice" and "sat immobile in the window seat in his nightshirt and stared at the activity in the street below" (p. 11). The same immobility must be the fate of all those who would claim to find everything equally uninteresting. Taylor (1989) has expressed this situation and its consequences very clearly: "To know who you are is to be oriented in moral space, a space in which questions arise about what is good or bad, what is worth doing and what not, what has meaning and importance for you and what is trivial and secondary" (p. 28). To not make judgments is to lose sight of one's orientation in moral space, which is to lose one's grounding as a human being.

In our roles as inquirers, educators, evaluators, we are always making judgments about papers for publication, presentations, books, dissertations, student papers, and so on. As we approach judgment in any given case, we have in mind or bring to the task a list, for lack of a better term, of characteristics that we use to judge the quality of that production. The use of the term *list* should not be taken to mean that we are referring to something like an enclosed and precisely specified or specifiable shopping or laundry list. Put differently, to talk of a list in this sense is not at all to talk about, for example, an accumulation of 20 items, scaled 1 to 5, where everyone's presentation proposal is then numerically scored with a cutoff point for acceptance. Obviously, to think of a list in these terms is to miss the entire point, so much so that it makes a mockery of the idea of qualitative inquiry, of what relativism means, and of what it means to realize that we can no longer be epistemological.

To the contrary, for us a list of characteristics must be seen as always open-ended, in part unarticulated, and, even when a characteristic is more or less articulated, it is always and ever subject to constant reinterpretation. Moreover, the items on the list can never be the distillation of some

445

abstracted epistemology, they must inevitably be rooted in one's stand-point or, to use Gadamer's (1995) term, they must inevitably evolve out of and reflect one's "effective history" (pp. 301-302). These points require brief comment.

The lists we bring to judgment are and can only be open-ended in that we have the permanent capacity to add items to and subtract items from the lists—although, as we shall soon note, doing so involves risk. Should we accept the risk, then the limits for recasting our lists derive not from theoretical labor, but from the use to which the lists are put. The limits on modification are a practical matter; they are worked and reworked within the context of actual practices/applications and cannot be set down in abstracted formulas.

Second, any lists we bring to judgment are only partly articulated. Some items can be more or less specified, whereas others seem to resist such specification. Polanyi's (1962) idea of tacit knowledge applies here very well indeed. When we make judgments we more or less can specify some of the reasons, but other things seem to be out there—there is surplus that seems to stand just beyond our grasp, just beyond our language. This does not mean that we should not and do not attempt to bring this surplus to fuller conscious articulation; it only means that it can never be done completely. That this is so should not be surprising, because as finite beings we can never be fully transparent, not only to others, but even to ourselves. Similarly, even those items on our lists that are more or less well articulated can be reinterpreted, even if subtly and gradually over time. And, finally, the importance we assign to items on our lists may easily change over time. A characteristic of research that we thought important at one time and in one place may take on diminished importance at another time and place (D. Gallagher, personal communication, 1998).

But what is most important to reiterate here is that our lists are challenged, changed, and modified not through abstracted discussions of the lists and items in and of themselves, but in application to actual inquiries. That is, very often something "new" comes along, such as Sparkes's (1996) self-reflective narrative of the fragile body-self, the developing genre of ethnographic fiction, or readers' theater. The new does not fit well with one's existing list of characteristics. To read these "new" things that come along or to attend the challenge seriously immediately opens up the possibility that one must reformulate one's list and possibly replace the exemplars one calls upon in the never-ending process of making judgments. However, the key here is possibility, because inquirers may choose

446

to preserve their lists, as many often seem to do, and judge the production as not even qualifying to be considered research. The latter is a comment, by the way, that was often heard about qualitative inquiry in years past.

The lists we hold are part of us—they are expressions of our own particular standpoints or effective histories. In other words, to refer again to Gadamer (1995), a list is an expression of our prejudices and, as he notes, it is the prejudices of an individual that "constitute the historical reality of his being" (p. 277). In any encounter with a production, especially something "new," as noted above, one must be willing to risk one's prejudices. Just as in the process of judgment one asks questions of a text or a person, the person or a text must be allowed to ask questions in return. As per the example of Sparkes's (1996) work mentioned above, to approach this inquiry requires that one be open, that one be willing to allow the text to challenge one's prejudices and possibly change one's list and one's idea about what is and is not good inquiry. But two important points must be made here. First, to reiterate, the word *possibly* is crucial here because to be open does not mean automatically to accept. One may still offer reasons for not accepting something new. Second, there is no method for engaging in the risking of prejudices. If anything, to risk one's prejudices is a matter of disposition—or, better said, moral obligation—that requires one to accept that if one wishes to persuade others, one must be equally open to being persuaded.

It is time to turn to an exemplar to illustrate these points. The work of Lather (1986a, 1986b, 1993, 1998a, 1998b) over the past 10 or 12 years, in various articles and presentations and in her book with Smithies (1997), stands as an almost paradigmatic example of the fact that we all approach a piece of work with something in mind. Lather's discussions both participate in and trouble our discourse about criteria for judging inquiry. In the process, Lather struggles with lists of characteristics that are open, evolving over time, and always in flux, and that resist full articulation. The items Lather has brought forth under the banner of validity have clearly evolved over the years. In 1986, Lather was talking about validity with reference to triangulation, face validity, catalytic validity, and so on. By 1993 this list had evolved to a discussion of transgressive validity, with her interest focused on such concepts as simulacra/ironic validity, paralogy/neo-pragmatic validity, rhizomatic validity, and voluptuous/situated validity.

There are two important points to be noted here. First, Lather is well aware that her lists are not composed of highly specified items that are enclosed, complete, can be numerically scored, and so on. In fact, when she develops a "checklist" it is only to mimic and thereby disrupt the very idea or possibility of a checklist. Second, she also is well aware that her theorizing is and can only be grounded in practice or in the actual process of applying the lists and making judgments. This is a point she noted in her work in 1986 and that she has reiterated, to one degree or another, in her more recent efforts (1998a, 1998b).

Lather sees the task of judgment not only as a practical engagement, but also as a moral one. Although we must acknowledge her resistance to the appropriation of poststructuralist perspectives within unproblematized concerns of critical theorists, we also must acknowledge that she clearly is and has been concerned deeply with such things as oppression, exploitation, and domination. There is no question that she holds a normative frame of reference in which some definitive preferences are expressed. Not surprisingly, then, Lather holds, as we assume do most other inquirers, that social and educational inquiry can, should, and must have an ameliorative purpose—that what we do as inquirers has the purpose of contributing to making people's lives and futures better (again, with full recognition that whatever *better* might mean in any given context cannot be precisely specified).

However, at this point a version of the problem of Ebenezer's paralysis (as noted above) seems to be lurking in the shadows. Lather (1993, pp. 684-685) poses a number of worrisome questions that arose as she participated in a project involving women with HIV/AIDS. These are problems that are, as she puts it, "grounded in the crisis of representation" (p. 684). Her concerns range widely over issues about voice, the other, the methodological interest she advances, her goals as a researcher, and so on. These concerns seem to be echoed, even if expressed in a different sense and in different terminology, by Scheurich's (1997) fears about the "resourcefulness of the Same to reappear with new masks that only seem to be the Other" (p. 90) and about the "anonymous imperial violence that slips quietly and invisibly into our best intentions and practices" (p. 90). In both instances, we argue that at the core of the problem is these authors' concern that any judgment must close off other possibilities, that any writing discloses in its silences as much as it reveals in its articulations, that to write the other is to appropriate the other, that any judgment is quietly but immediately turned on itself, and so on.

We have no doubt that the questions are important and the concerns are genuine, and we agree that we must always question the judgments we make and guard against the reappearance of the Same. In this sense, both

Lather and Scheurich have raised important issues that have moved us at least partly away from the epistemological project. But still we must ask: Can this questioning be taken too far? Is the quest framed by a desire for answers that can never be had and guarantees that can never be given? In a text that presents the voices of the women who live with the reality of being HIV-positive, Lather and Smithies (1997) demonstrate that they understand what might be called the imperialist position of the author and own their particular judgments to do one thing as opposed to another in telling the stories of these women. However, in later discussions about her judgments, Lather (1998a, 1998b) seemingly works to undo the responsibility she has enacted, reinvoking a concern that she is still seeking a way to alleviate human vulnerability and contingency in judgment.

These points also can be noted in the responses of Lather (1993) and Scheurich (1997) to the questions she asks and the concerns he expresses. We argue that because the answers sought remain unavailable, as they must, and the concerns resist relief, as they must, they have turned too far to the other side with the call for a "loud clamor of a polyphonous, open, tumultuous, subversive conversation on validity as the wild, unknowable play of differences" (Scheurich, 1997, p. 90) and "a disjunctive affirmation of incommensurates" (Lather, 1993, p. 687). But if these injunctions that everything should be an unknowable play of differences and that all contributions are incommensurable are taken seriously or taken to conclusion, have they arrived at the point of "everything goes" such that nothing is left for judgment? Their lingering concern with the epistemological project has left them in an untenable situation where, intellectually or conceptually, they have rendered judgment pointless if not impossible, whereas practically and morally they do and must make judgments. A hypothetical example is necessary to make our point as clear as possible. We are confident that if Lather and Scheurich were to review for publication an article with racist overtones, as a practical and moral affair they would reject that paper for just that reason. However, at another level, on what basis could this be done? Given their comments above, why should not this paper be seen as simply another element in the play of differences or as another affirmation of incommensurates?

For us, it is time to accept our vulnerability and contingency, drop the last traces of the epistemological project, and thus change the conversation. There is no way off of the wheel or out of the circle and, in what may seem an odd twist, in a strange way there is no epistemological crisis of representation, but only a practical and moral problem of representation.

We are finite human beings who must learn to accept, for example, that anything we write must always and inevitably leave silences, that to speak at all must always and inevitably be to speak for the someone else, and that we cannot make judgments and at the same time have a "constantly moving speaking position that fixes neither subject or object" (Lather, 1993, p. 684). To lament this condition and to search for a solution to these "problems" is actually to lament and search for a solution to our human finitude. But that we are finite is something we can do nothing about. Hazelrigg (1995) puts it very well: These are our "deficiencies" as human beings, if you will. But they are deficiencies "proper to the fields of human knowing and doing" because "what the human creature is not, no matter what the strength of will, is omniscient and omnipotent" (p. 102).

But a caution must be reiterated lest we be misinterpreted. There is no doubt that there is a problem of representation. Silences must be questioned, we must be careful of what we speak in that we speak for others, and we must be cautious in our judgments and be willing to risk our prejudices as we share and justify our judgments in a public space. But these are not epistemological issues; to the contrary, they are practical and moral issues. We inquire, we make judgments about inquiries, we must give reasons for our judgments, offer up these reasons to others and simply attempt to do the best we can. Knowledge is a human social production. As finite beings, all we can do is construct social and educational worlds, social and educational constructed realities for which we are morally responsible. To realize that we are finite human beings is to realize that there may be little more to say than this about judgment, criteria, and validity.

Be that as it may, our remaining comments must turn more directly toward the fact that judgment obviously is not a solitary engagement. As teachers and researchers, we are members of social groups and, as briefly indicated at various times above, our individual judgments inevitably must be moved into a public space where they are placed in concert with the judgments of others. To a certain extent the public space for sharing judgments, certainly the initial and immediate public space, has been predetermined because of institutional and organizational arrangements. For example, grading papers must at least involve a public space with a student; dissertation approval/disapproval must involve the student, the committee, and whoever comes to the defense; reviewing a paper for journal publication must necessarily involve the author and the editor. In a broader sense, however, there is room for choice as to the public space within which or with whom one's judgments will be allowed play and the extent to which one allows one's prejudices to be tested and challenged.

This is possible because, although the ideal of community is important, in practice there is no overarching social and/or educational research community. Educational researchers, for example, are dispersed along numerous lines from what are referred to as subfields, to theoretical and methodological differences, to differences based on characteristics like gender, race, and sexual orientation, and so on. That we are dispersed in this way is what allows for some degree of individual choice in terms of with whom one will share judgments and risk one's prejudices.

There is no question that over the past few years the rejection of metanarratives and appeals to final vindications have promoted the concern to open new spaces of inquiry and increase the number of possible groups, however loosely formed, with which one can choose to share or not share judgments. This is a recognition that has appeared in the work of numerous people, including, for example, Denzin (1997) and Lincoln (1995). For the latter, one of the key points is that all texts "are always partial and incomplete; socially, culturally, historically, racially, and sexually located; and can therefore never represent any truth except those truths that exhibit the same characteristics" (p. 280). This is further coupled with the recognition "that research takes place in, and is addressed to, a community; it is also accurately labeled because of the desire of those who discuss such research to have it serve the purposes of the community in which it was carried out" (p. 280). And, very important, Lincoln says that these ideas must be understood within the context of ethics and social amelioration. About the latter she says we must have a "vision of research that enables and promotes social justice, community, diversity, civic discourse, and caring" (pp. 277-278).

For Denzin (1997), we have entered the era of the new ethnography, one that has left science behind, that finds no "break between empirical activity . . . theorizing and social criticism" (p. 86), and where we will encounter the continuing development of "standpoint epistemologies of race, class, nation, gender, and sexuality" (p. 87). Denzin continues by noting three shared commitments that stand behind the advent of standpoint epistemologies. First, our research must be undertaken from the "point of view of the historically and culturally situated individual" (p. 87). Second, "ethnographers will continue to work outward from their own biographies to the worlds of experience that surround them" (p. 87). Third, the desire is to produce inquiry that will "speak clearly and powerfully about these worlds [of experience]" (p. 87). Thus, in the end, "the stories ethnographers tell to one another will change, and the criteria for reading stories will also change" (p. 87).

To the extent that this new ethnography brings with it an increasing pluralism, multiplicity, and the play of differences to open new spaces and new possible futures, we think the move must be applauded. However, as alluded to above, the issue of honoring pluralism and multiplicity while avoiding its excesses is ever and always present. Schrag (1992) frames the possibilities quite well. On the one side, he says that it is possible that a multiplicity of stories can be "assembled in such a manner that lines of similitude remain operative and a binding of multiple discourses and practices remain possible" (p. 33). If this can be accomplished, then we could offer up our judgments to others in the name of the "possibilities for rational critique, articulation, and disclosure as these are geared to an understanding of shared experience, evaluation, and emancipation" (p. 49). However, on the other side, he also notes that if this multiplicity and plurality engage nothing beyond an endless play of local and localized stories, vocabularies, and judgments, then we may be ensnared in a never-ending process of "dissensus, incommensurability, irretrievable conflicts of interpretation, and hermeneutical nihilism" (p. 33).

As a practical and moral matter, Schrag (1992) centers a number of important questions: How does one preserve diversity and multiplicity while avoiding its excesses? With whom and under what conditions am I obligated to risk my prejudices by offering up my work and my judgments for comment and criticism? Or, put differently, What is there that will allow us to put faith in Denzin's (1997) claim that in the era of the new ethnography inquirers will work out from their own standpoints? But two points arise immediately to madden any discussion of these questions. First, what does it even mean to say that we have reached an excess of diversity; when and how does one know when the line of excess has been crossed? Second, it is naïve to hold that one should constantly offer work and judgments to a total diversity of localized communities or social spaces. At times there may be very good reasons, physical and mental exhaustion aside, for not reaching out and engaging in extended dialogue with others. For example, there are times when dialogue has been engaged, progress has not been made, and there seems no reason to continue. As has been so throughout this change of conversation, the issues are illusive indeed and resist easy solution.

That said, we begin by noting that we value Schrag's (1992) hope that lines of similitude can remain open and effective across a range of discourses and practices. The reason for this is framed by the fact that our inquiries do not discover reality, but rather construct reality—a constructed social and educational reality for which we are morally responsible, as individuals and collectively. And this point must be coupled with the injunction from Marx that our task is not merely to study the world, but to help change it. We thereby have a moral obligation to maximize our collective influence on actual policies and practices. To do this requires that we engage across lines, that we move out from our individual standpoints and risk our individual prejudices to keep lines of connection open to others.

If these lines cannot be kept open, then there may well be a Balkanization of, or a deep heterogeneity among, inquirer-based standpoints, theoretical differences, or whatever, and we could well end up with deep dissensus and a permanent conflict of interpretations. The play of differences to open spaces could easily tip over into little more than the announcement of differences, and the affirmation of incommensurates easily could become exactly that. This would seem to lead to inquirers' talking past one another, or not talking to each other at all, as they construct their localized communities, realities, and criteria. Under these conditions, it is difficult to imagine how our work can have moral purpose and social influence. The point is straightforward: If we cannot talk and listen to each other, it is difficult to imagine why anyone else would want to talk with us, listen to us, or attend to our judgments.

But the main problem is that there is no method or process to which we can appeal to energize Denzin's claim (hope?) that in this era of the new ethnography inquirers will work outward from their own biographies to engage the biographies of others. If inquirers are to do this, then it can only be a matter of disposition, not method. This is a disposition—or, as noted above, a moral obligation—that enjoins one to risk one's prejudices and defend one's judgments in a social space with others, even with those whose standpoints may seem seriously different from one's own. At the core of this moral obligation is the requirement that we accept that just as we attempt to persuade others to accept our judgments of good versus bad inquiries, we must in turn be equally willing to be persuaded by the judgments of others. And, to reiterate, it is only with this obligation in mind that we can maximize the possibility that our inquiries will assist in the construction of more just social and educational worlds.

◆ Summary

The quasi-foundationalists have attempted to establish criteria within the context of an epistemological constructivism on the one side and, on the other, an ontological realism. The latter announces their claim that there is a reality independent of us that can be known as it is—at least in principle; the former assumption directs their attention to the idea that knowledge is socially constructed and always fallible. This has led them to talk about criteria with the use of terms on the order of *plausibility, credibility,* and *descriptive validity.* Moreover, because the neorealists claim they are able to have contact with reality, however subtle this contact may be, they further claim that these criteria have force beyond particular time and place.

Unfortunately, the neorealists have not been able to present a convincing case, or an adequate justification, for their position. Neither Hammersley (1990) nor Maxwell (1992), for example, is able to demonstrate how his realist commitment does any real work in terms of moving us beyond a continual process of social judgments. In fact, were the neorealists to drop their realist ontology and their attempt to salvage something from the remains of empiricism, they would look very much like relativists of a Gadamerian variety.

Nonfoundationalists have fully accepted the relativist implications of the fact that there can be no theory-free observation or knowledge. However, for them relativism is not a problem, it is just the inevitable result of the fact that we, as human beings, are finite—a finitude we should learn to live with and not lament. For nonfoundationalists, the issue of criteria for judging inquiry is a practical and moral affair, not an epistemological one. They take very seriously Rorty's (1985) injunction that our pursuit of knowledge, as is the case for all human social activities, "has only an ethical base, not an epistemological or metaphysical one" (p. 6). Accordingly, criteria should not be thought of in abstraction, but as a list of features that we think, or more or less agree at any given time and place, characterize good versus bad inquiry. This is a list that can be challenged, added to, subtracted from, modified, and so on, as it is applied in actual practice—in actual application to actual inquiries. Relativists also recognize the need for and value of plurality, multiplicity, the acceptance and celebration of differences, and so on. The essential problem, however, is to honor this need without giving over to excesses—to inquiry that is so fragmented that lines of connection have been lost and the social amelioration possibilities of our work have been rendered moot.

So, we have come to the end with, as promised, no discussion of particular criteria and how to apply them. Rather, we have attempted to elaborate some of the conditions under which we must think about the possibility of criteria and the possibility of individual and collective judgment in this age of relativism.

◆ References

Barth, J. (1960). *The sot-weed factor.* Garden City, NY: Doubleday.

Bernstein, R. (1983). *Beyond objectivism and relativism.* Philadelphia: University of Pennsylvania Press.

Bhaskar, R. (1983). [Review of the book *Scientific revolutions*]. *Isis, 74,* 259.

Cherryholmes, C. (1988). *Power and criticism.* New York: Teachers College Press.

Chisholm, R. (1973). *The problem of the criterion.* Milwaukee, WI: Marquette University Press.

Denzin, N. K. (1997). *Interpretive ethnography: Ethnographic practices for the 21st century.* Thousand Oaks, CA: Sage.

Gadamer, H.-G. (1995). *Truth and method* (2nd rev. ed.; J. Weinsheimer & D. G. Marshall, Trans.). New York: Crossroad.

Gallagher, D. (1995). In search of the rightful role of method: Reflections on conducting a qualitative dissertation. In T. Tiller, A. Sparkes, S. Karhus, & F. Dowling-Naess (Eds.), *The qualitative challenge* (pp. 17-35). Oslo, Norway: Casper.

Giddens, A. (1976). *New rules of sociological method: A positive critique of interpretative sociologies.* New York: Basic Books.

Goodman, N. (1978). *Ways of worldmaking.* Indianapolis: Hackett.

Hammersley, M. (1990). *Reading ethnographic research: A critical guide.* London: Longman.

Hanson, N. (1958). *Patterns of discovery.* Cambridge: Cambridge University Press.

Hazelrigg, L. (1989). *Claims of knowledge.* Tallahassee: Florida State University Press.

Hazelrigg, L. (1995). *Cultures of nature.* Tallahassee: Florida State University Press.

Hesse, M. (1980). *Revolutions and reconstructions in the philosophy of science.* Brighton: Harvester.

Hindess, B. (1977). *Philosophy and methodology in the social sciences.* Atlantic Highlands, NJ: Humanities Press.

Hofstadter, D. (1979). *Godel, Escher, Bach: An eternal golden braid.* New York: Basic Books.

House, E. (1991). Realism in research. *Educational Researcher, 20*(6), 2-9.

Kerlinger, F. (1979). *Behavioral research.* New York: Holt, Rinehart & Winston.

Kuhn, T. S. (1962). *The structure of scientific revolutions.* Chicago: University of Chicago Press.

Lather, P. (1986a). Issues of validity in openly ideological research: Between a rock and a soft place. *Interchange, 17*(4), 63-84.

Lather, P. (1986b). Research as praxis. *Harvard Educational Review, 56,* 257-277.

Lather, P. (1993). Fertile obsession: Validity after poststructuralism. *Sociological Quarterly, 34,* 673-693.

Lather, P. (1998a, April). *Against empathy, voice, and authenticity.* Paper presented at the annual meeting of the American Educational Research Association, San Diego, CA.

Lather, P. (1998b, April). *Troubling praxis: The work of mourning.* Paper presented at the annual meeting of the American Educational Research Association, San Diego, CA.

Lather, P., & Smithies, C. (1997). *Troubling the angels: Women living with HIV/ AIDS.* Boulder, CO: Westview.

Leary, D. (1984). Philosophy, psychology, and reality. *American Psychologist, 39,* 917-919.

Lincoln, Y. S. (1995). Emerging criteria for quality in qualitative and interpretive inquiry. *Qualitative Inquiry, 1,* 275-289.

MacKenzie, D. (1981). *Statistics in Great Britain: 1885-1930.* Edinburgh: Edinburgh University Press.

Manicas, P. (1987). *A history and philosophy of the social sciences.* Oxford: Basil Blackwell.

Manicas, P., & Secord, P. (1983). Implications for psychology of the new philosophy of science. *American Psychologist, 38,* 399-413.

Maxwell, J. (1992). Understanding and validity in qualitative research. *Harvard Educational Review, 62,* 279-300.

Nagel, T. (1986). *The view from nowhere.* New York: Oxford University Press.

Polanyi, M. (1962). *Personal knowledge.* Chicago: University of Chicago Press.

Popper, K. (1959). *The logic of scientific discovery.* London: Hutchinson.

Popper, K. (1972). *Objective knowledge.* Oxford: Clarendon.

Punch, M. (1994). Politics and ethics in qualitative research. In N. K. Denzin & Y. S. Lincoln (Eds.), *Handbook of qualitative research* (pp. 83-97). Thousand Oaks, CA: Sage.

Putnam, H. (1981). *Reason, truth and history.* Cambridge: Cambridge University Press.

Rorty, R. (1979). *Philosophy and the mirror of nature.* Princeton, NJ: Princeton University Press.

Rorty, R. (1985). Solidarity or objectivity? In J. Rajchman & C. West (Eds.), *Post-analytic philosophy* (pp. 3-19). New York: Columbia University Press.

Rosenau, P. M. (1992). *Post-modernism and the social sciences: Insights, inroads, and intrusions.* Princeton, NJ: Princeton University Press.

Scheurich, J. J. (1997). *Research method in the postmodern.* London: Falmer.

Schrag, C. (1992). *The resources of rationality.* Bloomington: Indiana University Press.

Schwandt, T. A. (1996). Farewell to criteriology. *Qualitative Inquiry, 2,* 58-72.

Smith, J. (1985). Social reality as mind-dependent versus mind-independent and the interpretation of test validity. *Journal of Research and Development in Education, 1,* 1-9.

Smith, J. (1989). *The nature of social and educational inquiry: Empiricism versus interpretation.* Norwood, NJ: Ablex.

Smith, J. (1993). *After the demise of empiricism: The problem of judging social and educational inquiry.* Norwood, NJ: Ablex.

Sparkes, A. (1993). Reciprocity in critical research? Some unsettling thoughts. In G. Shacklock & J. Smyth (Eds.), *Being reflexive in critical educational and social research* (pp. 67-82). London: Falmer.

Sparkes, A. (1996). The fatal flaw: A narrative of the fragile body-self. *Qualitative Inquiry, 2,* 463-494.

Stronach, I., & Maclure, M. (1997). *Educational research undone.* Milton Keynes, England: Open University Press.

Taylor, C. (1971). Interpretation and the sciences of man. *Review of Metaphysics, 25,* 3-51.

Taylor, C. (1989). *Sources of the self.* Cambridge: Cambridge University Press.

Wolcott, H. F. (1995). *The art of fieldwork.* Walnut Creek, CA: AltaMira.

13

The Practices and
Politics of Interpretation

Norman K. Denzin

A marginalized group needs to be wary of the seductive
power of realism, of accepting all that a realistic
representation implies.

—Wahneema Lubiano, "But, Compared to What? Reading
Realism,Representation, and Essentialism in School Daze,
Do the Right Thing, and the Spike Lee Discourse," 1997

You've taken my blues and gone—
You sing 'em on Broadway
. . . And you fixed 'em
So they don't sound like me.
Yes, you done taken my blues and gone.

You also took my spiritual and gone.
. . . But someday somebody'll
Stand up and write about me,
And write about me—
Black and Beautiful—
And sing about me,
And put on plays about me!

AUTHOR'S NOTE: I would like to thank Meaghan Morris, Ivan Brady, Yvonna Lincoln, Jack
Bratich, Laurel Richardson, and Katherine Ryan for their comments on earlier versions of this
chapter. All asterisked material is used by permission.

I reckon it'll be
Me myself!
—Langston Hughes, "Yes, It'll Be Me," 1940/1994*

I
have seen it
and like it: The blood
the way like Sand Creek
even its name brings fear,
because I am an American
Indian and have learned
words are another kind of violence.
—Sherman Alexie, "Texas Chainsaw Massacre," 1993*

◆ At the beginning of the end of the sixth moment it is necessary to reengage the promise of qualitative research and interpretive ethnography as forms of radical democratic practice.[1] The narrative turn in the social sciences has been taken, we have told our tales from the field, and we understand today that we write culture (Brady, 1998; Richardson, 1998). Writing is not an innocent practice, although in the social sciences and the humanities there is only interpretation (Rinehart, 1998). Nonetheless, Marx (1888/1983, p. 158) continues to remind us that we are in the business of not just interpreting but changing the world.

In this chapter I explore new (and old) forms of writing, forms that are intended to forward the project of interpreting and changing the world—and this is the global world, not just the world as it is known in North America. Specifically, I work back and forth among three interpretive practices: the new civic, intimate, and literary journalisms (Charity, 1995; Dash, 1997; Harrington, 1992, 1997a, 1997b; Kramer, 1995; Sims, 1995); calls for critical, performance-based ethnographies (Ceglowski, 1997; Cohen-Cruz, 1998; Degh, 1995; Denison, 1996; Denzin, 1997, 1999a, 1999b, 1999c; Diversi, 1998; Dunbar, 1999; Jackson, 1998; Jones, 1999; Jordan, 1998; Lincoln, 1997; Rinehart, 1998; Ronai, 1998; Smith, 1993, 1994); and variations on a Chicano/a (Gonzalez, 1998; Pizarro, 1998) and African American aesthetic (Davis, 1998; hooks, 1990, 1996) and the relationship between these practices and critical race theory (Ladson-Billings, 1998; Parker, 1998).

459

Although there have been efforts to bring critical race theory into quali-tative research, few have merged this theory with the poststructural turn in ethnography (see hooks, 1990, pp. 123-134; also Ladson-Billings, Chapter 9, Volume 1). Nor have critical race theory and qualitative inquiry been connected to the radical performance texts stemming from the black arts movement of the 1960s and 1970s (Baker, 1997; Baraka, 1997; Harris, 1998). These interconnections are now being established in the various black cultural studies projects of the new black public in-tellectuals and cultural critics (Hall, Gilroy, hooks, Gates, West, Reed, Morrison, Wallace, Steele). A current generation of blues, rap, hip-hop, and popular singers, jazz performers, poets (Angelou, Dove, Jordan, Knight, Cortez), novelists (Walker, Morrison, Bambara), playwrights (Wilson, Shange, Smith), and filmmakers (Lee, Singleton, Burnett, Dash) are also making these links (see Christian, 1997, pp. 2019-2020; Harris, 1998, pp. 1344-1345).[2]

This chapter is a utopian project in which I attempt to bring these multi-ple discourses together into a unified framework. I present examples of writing from each these frameworks. In so doing, I assume that words and language have a material presence in the world—that words have effects on people. Amiri Baraka (1969/1998, p. 1502*) puts it this way:

> we want poems that wrestle cops into alleys
> and take their weapons . . .
> We want a black poem. And a Black World.
> Let the world be a Black Poem.
> And Let All Black People Speak This Poem
> Silently
> Or LOUD.

Words matter.

I imagine a world where race, ethnicity, class, gender, and sexual orien-tation intersect; a world where language empowers and humans are free to become who they can be, free of prejudice, repression, and discrimination (Jackson, 1998, p. 21; see also Parker, Deyhle, Villenas, & Nebeker, 1998, p. 5). Those who write culture must learn to use language in a way that brings people together. The goal is to create sacred, loving texts that "demonstrate a strong fondness . . . for freedom and an affectionate con-cern for the lives of people" (Joyce, 1987, p. 344). This writing addresses and demonstrates the benevolence and kindness that people should feel toward one another (Joyce, 1987, p. 344).

Thus I examine new ways of writing culture, new ways of making qualitative research central to the workings of a free democratic society. I begin with the civic, public affairs, and intimate journalists.

◆ An Intimate, Civic Journalism

As qualitative researchers engage experimental writing forms, a parallel movement is occurring in journalism, and there is much to be learned from these developments. Building on earlier calls for a new journalism (Wolfe, 1973), a current generation of journalists (Harrington, 1997a, 1997b; Kramer, 1995; Sims, 1995) is producing a new writing genre variously termed literary, intimate, or creative nonfiction journalism (Harrington, 1997a, p. xv). This intimate journalism extends the project of the new journalism of the 1970s. That project was based on seven understandings. The new writers of Wolfe's generation treated facts as social constructions. They blurred writing genres and combined literary and investigative journalism with the realist novel, the confession, the travel report, and the autobiography. They used the scenic method to show rather than tell. They wrote about real people and created composite characters. They used multiple points of view, including third-person narration to establish authorial presence, and deployed multiple narrative strategies (flashbacks, foreshadowing, interior monologues, parallel plots) to build dramatic tension. They positioned themselves as moral witnesses to the radical changes going on in U.S. society (Denzin, 1997, p. 131). These writers understood that social life and the reports about it are social constructions. Journalists do not map, or report on, an objective reality.

I have no desire to reproduce arguments that maintain some distinction between fictional (literary) and nonfictional (journalism, ethnography) texts. Nor do I distinguish literary, nonliterary, fictional, and nonfictional textual forms. These are socially and politically constructed categories. They are too often used to police certain transgressive writing forms, such as fictional ethnographies. There is only narrative—that is, only different genre-defined ways of representing and writing about experiences and their multiple realities. The discourses of the postmodern world constantly intermingle literary, poetic, journalistic, fictional, cinematic, documentary, factual, and ethnographic writing and representation. No form is privileged over others. Each simply performs a different function for a writer and an interpretive community.

461

These practices and understandings shape the work of the intimate journalists. Writers such as Harrington (1992) use the methods of descriptive realism to produce in-depth, narrative accounts of everyday life, lived up close. They use real-life dialogue, intimate first- and third-person voice, multiple points of view, interior monologues, scene-by-scene narration, and a plain, spare style (Harrington, 1997b, pp. xlii-xlv; Kramer, 1995, p. 24). The writer may be invisible in the text or present as narrator and participant. Here is Harrington (1992) talking about himself; the story is "Family Portrait in Black and White":

> My journey begins in the dentist's chair. The nurse . . . and the doctor are [telling] funny stories about their kids, when in walks another dentist. . . . "I've got a good one," he says cheerfully, and then he tells a racist joke. I can't recall the joke, only that it ends with a black man who is stupid. Dead silence. It's just us white folks here in the room, but my dentist and his nurse know my wife, who is black, and they know my son and daughter, who are, as they describe themselves, tan and bright tan. How many racist jokes have I heard in my life? . . . for the first time . . . I am struck with a deep sharp pain. I look at this man, with his pasty face, pale hair and weak lips, and I think: This idiot is talking about my children! (p. 1)

Compare this telling, with its first-person narration, to Leon Dash's (1997) description of Rosa Lee:

> Rosa Lee Cunningham is thankful that she doesn't have to get up early this morning. She is dozing, floating back and forth between sleep and drowsiness. Occasionally she hears the muted conversations of the nurses and doctors puttering around the nurse's station. . . . She's tired and worn down. . . . A full night's sleep and daylong quiet are rare luxuries in her life. This is the closest she ever comes to having a vacation. . . . Rosa Lee . . . is fifty-two years old, a longtime heroin addict . . . a member of the urban underclass. . . . [She] has no intention of ending her heroin use. (p. 3)

Harrington speaks only for himself. He is fully present in his text. Dash is invisible. He is the all-knowing observer. He is the fly on the wall narrating an unfolding scene. Dash describes a world, whereas Harrington talks about how it feels to be present in a world. Each writer creates a scene. Each penetrates the images that surround a situation. Harrington and Dash both use sparse, clean prose. Each creates a vivid image of his subject, Harrington of himself, Dash of Rosa Lee. On the other hand, Dash presumes to know what Rosa Lee is feeling and thinking. Hers is a story waiting to be told, and he will tell it. In contrast, Harrington's text suggests that stories are not waiting to be told; rather, they are constructed by the writer, who attempts to impose order on some set of experiences or perceived events.

Both writers ground their prose in facts and their meanings. Dash, however, works with so-called verifiable, factually accurate facts, whereas Harrington writes of impressions and truths that, although not necessarily factually accurate, are aesthetically and emotionally true. If something did not happen, it could have happened, and it will happen in Harrington's text.

Accounts like Harrington's and Dash's invoke the felt life. The goal of such writers is to understand "other people's worlds from the inside out, to understand and portray people as they understand themselves" (Harrington, 1997b, p. xxv). The intent is to build an emotional relationship joining the writer, the life told about, and the reader.

A year later, Harrington (1992) returns to his experience in the dentist's chair:

> What I discovered while waiting in the dentist's chair more than a year ago . . . still remains the greatest insight I have to share: *The idiot was talking about my kids!*
>
> I remember a time when my son was a baby. It was late at night . . . I sat in the dark of my son's room. . . . I watched his face grimace . . . in the shadows. And then, in time so short it passed only in the mind, my son was gone and I was the boy . . . and my father was me. . . . just as suddenly, I was gone again and the light was falling across the knees of my son, who was grown, who was a father, who was me. . . . this kind of understanding changes everything. Only when I *became* black by proxy—through my son, through my daughter—could I see the racism I had been willing to tolerate. Becoming black, even for a fraction of an instant, created an urgency for justice that I couldn't feel as only a white man, no matter how good-hearted. . . . no white man in his or her right mind would yet volunteer to trade places, become black, in America today. (p. 447)

Such writing connects readers to their newspapers by producing narratives about people in extreme and ordinary situations. These stories, or journalistic case studies, politicize the everyday world, illuminating the structures and processes that shape individuals' lives and their relations with others. In so doing, they "nurture civic transformation" (Harrington, 1997a, p. xiv; see also Harrington, 1997b, p. xviii).[3]

Civic Transformations

At the moment of civic transformation, intimate journalism joins with the call for public journalism, a critical ethnographic journalism that fuses persons and their troubles with public issues and the public arena. A pragmatic, civic journalism invites readers to become participants, not mere spectators, in the public dramas that define meaningful, engaged life in society today. Public journalism creates the space for local ethnographies of problematic community and personal experiences. This is a socially responsible civic journalism. It advocates participatory democracy. It gives a public voice to the biographically meaningful, epiphanic experiences that occur within the confines of the local moral community.[4] This form of journalistic ethnography speaks to the morally committed reader. This is a reader who is a coparticipant in a public project that demands democratic solutions to personal and public problems (Charity, 1995, p. 146).[5]

Taken to the next level, transformed into public-journalism-as-ethnography, this writing answers to the following goals. Critical, intimate, public ethnography does the following things:

◆ It presents the public with in-depth, intimate stories of problematic everyday life, lived up close. These stories create moral compassion and help citizens make intelligent decisions and take public action on private troubles that have become public issues, including helping to get these action proposals carried out (Charity, 1995, p. 2; Mills, 1959, p. 8).

◆ It promotes interpretive works that raise public and private consciousness. These works help persons collectively work through the decision-making process. They help isolate choices, core values, utilize expert and local systems of knowledge, and facilitate deliberative, civic discourse (Charity, 1995, pp. 4-8).

◆ It rejects the classic model of investigative journalism, where the reporter exposes corruption, goes on crusades, roots "out the inside story, tells the brave truth, faces down the Joseph McCarthy's and Richard Nixon's . . . comforts the afflicted and afflicts the comfortable" (Charity, 1995, p. 9).

◆ It seeks the ethnographer and journalist who is an expert in the history and public life of the local community, who knows how to listen to and talk to citizens, and how to hear and present consensus when it emerges, and who is also a full-time citizen and committed to the belief that public life can be made to work (Charity, 1995, p. 10).

♦ It sees the writer as a watchdog for the local community, a person who writes stories that contribute to deliberative, participatory discourse, thereby maintaining the public's awareness of its own voice (Charity, 1995, pp. 104-105, 127).

♦ It values writing that moves a public to meaningful judgment and meaningful action (Charity, 1995, p. 50). A central goal is civic transformation (Christians, Ferre, & Fackler, 1993, p. 14).

♦ It exposes complacency, bigotry, and wishful thinking (Charity, 1995, p. 146) while "attempting to strengthen the political community's capacity to understand itself, converse well, and make choices" (Rosen, 1994, p. 381).

♦ It seeks dramatic stories, narratives that separate facts from stories, telling moving accounts that join private troubles with public issues (Charity, 1995, p. 72; Mills, 1959, p. 8).

♦ It promotes a form of textuality that turns citizens into readers and readers into persons who take democratic action in the world (Charity, 1995, pp. 19, 83-84).

These are goals, ideals, ways of merging critical ethnography with applied action research, with the new public journalism, and with qualitative research in the seventh moment. (They presume the feminist, communitarian ethical model discussed by Christians in Chapter 5 of Volume 1.)

These goals assume an ethnographer who functions and writes like a literary and intimate public journalist. This means that ethnography as a performer-centered form of storytelling will be given greater emphasis (Degh, 1995, p. 8). A shared public consciousness is sought, a common awareness of troubles that have become issues in the public arena. This consciousness is shaped by a form of writing that merges the personal, the biographical, with the public. Janet Cooke's (1980) fictional story "Jimmy's World" is an instance of such writing. Such stories expose complacency and bigotry in the public sphere.

Writing Norms

A feminist, communitarian ethical model produces a series of norms for the public ethnographic writing project.[6] These norms build on and elaborate the four nonnegotiable journalistic norms of accuracy, nonmaleficence, the right to know, and making one's moral position public.[7] The ethnographer's moral tales are not written to produce harm for those who have been oppressed by the culture's systems of domination and repression (the principle of nonmaleficence). The identities of those written about should always be protected. These tales are factually and fictionally correct.[8] When fiction, or imaginative narrative, is written, or when composite cases are molded into a single story, the writer is under an obligation to report this to the reader (see Christians et al., 1993, p. 55).

The reader has the right to read what the ethnographer has learned, but the right to know should be balanced against the principle of nonmaleficence. Accounts should exhibit "interpretive sufficiency" (Christians et al., 1993, p. 120), that is, they should possess depth, detail, emotionality, nuance, and coherence. These qualities assist the reader in forming a critical interpretive consciousness. Such texts should also exhibit representational adequacy, including the absence of racial, class, and gender stereotyping.[9]

The writer must be honest with the reader.[10] The text must be realistic, concrete as to character, setting, atmosphere, and dialogue. The text should provide a forum for the search for moral truths about the self. This forum may explore the unpresentable in the culture; the discontents and violence of contemporary life are documented and placed in narrative form. This writer stirs up the world, and the writer's story ("mystory") becomes part of the tale that is told. The writer has a theory about how the world works, and this theory is never far from the surface of the text. Self-reflexive readers are presumed—readers who seek honest but reflexive works that draw them into the many experiences of daily life.

There remains the struggle to find a narrative voice that writes against a long tradition that favors autobiography and lived experience as the sites for reflexivity and self-hood (Clough, 1994, p. 157). This form of subjective reflexivity can be a trap. It too easily reproduces sad, celebratory, and melodramatic conceptions of self, agency, gender, desire, and sexuality. There is a pressing need to invent a reflexive form of writing that turns ethnography and experimental literary texts back "onto each other" (Clough, 1994, p. 162; 1998, p. 134).

Always a skeptic, this new writer is suspicious of conspiracies, alignments of power and desire that turn segments of the public into victims. So these works trouble traditional, realist notions of truth and verification, asking always who stands to benefit from a particular version of the truth. The intimate journalist as public ethnographer enacts an ethics of practice that privileges the client-public relationship. The ethnographer is a moral advocate for the public, although their own personal moral codes may lead individual researchers to work against the so-called best interests of their clients or particular segments of the public.

The ethnographer's tale is always allegorical, a symbolic tale, a parable that is not just a record of human experience. This tale is a means of experience, a method of empowerment for the reader. It is a vehicle through which readers may discover moral truths about themselves. More deeply, the tale is a utopian story of self and social redemption, a tale that brings a moral compass back into the reader's (and the writer's) life. The ethnographer discovers the multiple "truths" that operate in the social world, the stories people tell one another about the things that matter to them. The intimate journalist writes stories that stimulate critical public discourse. Thus these stories enable transformations in the public and private spheres of everyday life.

◆ Performing Ethnography

I turn next to the concept of the performance text (Conquergood, 1992; Turner, 1986), illustrating my arguments with materials drawn from an ongoing interpretive ethnography of a small Montana town (Denzin, 1999a, 1999b, 1999c).[11] I seek a set of writing practices that turn notes from the field into texts that are performed. A single, yet complex thesis organizes my argument.

We inhabit a performance-based, dramaturgical culture. The dividing line between performer and audience blurs, and culture itself becomes a dramatic performance. Performance ethnography enters a gendered culture with nearly invisible boundaries separating everyday theatrical performances from formal theater, dance, music, MTV, video, and film (Birringer, 1993, p. 182; Butler, 1990, p. 25; 1997, p. 159; 1999, p. 19). But the matter goes even deeper then blurred boundaries. The performance has become reality. Of this, speaking of gender and personal identity, Butler (1990) is certain. Gender is performative, gender is always doing, "though not a doing by a subject who might be said to preexist the deed. . . . there is no being behind doing. . . . the deed is everything. . . . there is no gender identity behind the expressions of gender. . . . identity is performatively constituted by the very 'expressions' that are said to be its results" (p. 25). Further, the linguistic act is performative, and words can hurt (Butler, 1997, p. 4).

Performance texts are situated in complex systems of discourse, where traditional, everyday, and avant-garde meanings of theater, film, video, ethnography, cinema, performance, text, and audience all circulate and inform one another. As Collins (1990, p. 210) has suggested, the meanings of lived experience are inscribed and sometimes made visible in these performances (see also Brady, 1999, p. 245).

Anna Deavere Smith's *Fires in the Mirror* (1993) is an example. In this play, Smith offers a series of performance pieces based on interviews with people involved in a racial conflict in Crown Heights, Brooklyn, on August 19, 1991. The conflict was set in motion when a young black Guyanese boy, Gavin Cato, was accidentally killed by an auto in a police-escorted entourage carrying Lubavitcher Grand Rebbe Menachem Schneerson. Later that day, a group of black men fatally stabbed Yankel Rosenbaum, a 29-year-old Hasidic scholar from Australia. This killing was followed by a racial conflict that lasted 3 days and involved many members of the community. A jury acquitted Yankel Rosenbaum's accused murderer, causing considerable pain for his family as well as feelings of victimization for the Lubavitchers (Smith, 1993, p. xiv).[12] Smith's play has speaking parts for gang members, police officers, anonymous young girls and boys, mothers, fathers, rabbis, the Reverend Al Sharpton, playwright Ntozake Shange, and African American cultural critic Angela Davis.

Cornel West (1993) observes that *Fires in the Mirror* is a "grand example of how art can constitute a public space that is perceived by people as empowering rather than disempowering" (p. xix). Thus blacks, gang members, the police, and the Jewish community all come together and talk in this play. The drama crosses racial boundaries. Smith's text shows that "American character lives not on one place or the other, but in the gaps between places, and in our struggle to be together in our differences" (p. xii).

An Anonymous Young Man #1 Wa Wa Wa, a Caribbean American with dreadlocks, describes the auto accident:

What I saw was
she was pushin'
her brother on the bike like
this,
right?
She was pushin'
him
and he keep dippin' around
like he didn't know how

to ride the bike . . .
So she was already runnin'
when the car was comin' . . .
we was watchin' the car
weavin',
and we was goin'
"Oh, yo
it's a Jew man.
He broke the stop light, they never get
arrested." (Smith, 1993, pp. 79-80)*

And so in performing this young man's words, Smith contextualizes this drama, showing how it looked from the standpoint of a person who watched the accident unfold.

Performance ethnography simultaneously creates and enacts moral texts, texts that move from the personal to the political, the local to the historical and the cultural. Following Conquergood (1985), these dialogical works create spaces for give and take, doing more than turning the other into the object of a voyeuristic, fetishistic, custodial, or paternalistic gaze.

Texts turned into radical street performances act to question and "re-envision ingrained social arrangements of power" (Cohen-Cruz, 1998, p. 1). Such works, in the forms of rallies, puppet shows, marches, vigils, choruses, clown shows, and ritual performances, transport spectators and performers out of everyday reality into idealized spaces where the taken for granted is contested (Cohen-Cruz, 1998, p. 3). Street, or public place, performances offer members of the culture alternative scripts or ways of acting in and hence of changing the world (Cohen-Cruz, 1998, p. 1).

Cohen-Cruz (1998, p. 5) suggests that these performances can take several overlapping forms, including *agit-prop,* or attempts to mobilize people around a partisan view; *witnessing,* or making a spectacle out of an act that perhaps cannot be changed; *confrontation,* or inserting a performance into people's everyday life, thereby asking them to confront a scenario that is otherwise distant; *utopia,* or enacting an idealized version of reality; and *tradition,* that is, honoring a set of culturally shared beliefs, as in Fourth of July parades in small-town America.

In my performance project I seek minimalist social science, one that uses few concepts. This is a dramaturgical (Branaman, 1997, p. xlix; Goffman, 1959; Lemert, 1997, p. xxiv) or performative anthropology (Jackson, 1998; Turner, 1986) that attempts to stay close to how people represent everyday life experiences. A performative ethnography simultaneously writes and studies performances, showing how people enact cultural meanings in their daily lives.

Shaped by the sociological imagination (Mills, 1959), this version of qualitative inquiry attempts to show how terms such as *biography, gender, race, ethnicity, family,* and *history* interact and shape one another in concrete social situations. These works are usually written in the first-person voice, from the point of view of the sociologist doing the observing and the writing. A minimalist, performative social science is also about stories, performances, and storytelling. When performed well, these stories create a ritual space "where people gather to listen, to experience, to better understand the world and their place in it" (Jenkins, 1999, p. 19).

The Performance Turn

The performance turn in the human disciplines (Bochner & Ellis, 1996; Conquergood, 1992) poses three closely interrelated problems for a critical, interdisciplinary interpretive project—namely, how to construct, perform, and critically analyze performance texts (see Stern & Henderson, 1993). Glossing the issues involved in construction and critical analysis, I will privilege performance and coperformance (audience-performer) texts in contrast to single performer, text-centered approaches to interpretation (see Denzin, 1997, p. 96). Through the act of coparticipation, these works bring audiences back into the text, creating a field of shared emotional experience. The phenomenon being described is created through the act of representation. A resistance model of textual performance and interpretation is foregrounded. A good performance text must be more than cathartic, it must be political, moving people to action and reflection.

The attention to performance is interdisciplinary; sociologists (Bochner & Ellis, 1996; Clough, 1994; Denzin, 1997; Ellis, 1997; Ellis & Bochner, 1992, 1996; Ellis & Flaherty, 1992; Kotarba, 1998; Richardson, 1997), anthropologists (Behar, 1996; Brady, 1999; Bruner, 1986, 1989, 1996; Cruikshank, 1997; Jackson, 1998; Turner, 1986), communication scholars (Conquergood, 1992; Hill, 1997), and education theorists (Lather, 1993; Lather & Smithies, 1997; Lincoln, 1995a, 1995b, 1997; Tierney, 1997) are calling for texts that move beyond the purely representational and toward the presentational. At the same time, action (Stringer, 1996), communitarian (Christians et al., 1993), feminist (Lather, 1993), constructivist (Lincoln, 1995a, 1995b, 1997), cooperative inquiry (Reason, 1993, 1994), and participant researchers (Carspecken, 1996) are exploring nontraditional presentational performance formats. Such works allow community researchers and community members to co-construct meaning through action-based performance projects (Stringer, 1996; see also Conquergood, 1998; Schwandt, 1997, p. 307). This call merges a feminist, communitarian ethic with a moral ethnography that presumes a researcher who builds collaborative, reciprocal, trusting, friendly relations with those studied (Lincoln, 1995a).

Performed texts "have narrators, drama, action, shifting points of view . . . [and] make experience concrete, anchoring it in the here and now" (Paget, 1993 p. 27; see also Donmoyer & Yennie-Donmoyer, 1995; Mienczakowski, 1995). Centered in the audience-researcher nexus, these texts are the site for "mystories" (Ulmer, 1989); that is, reflexive, critical stories that feel the sting of memory, stories that enact liminal experiences. These are storied retellings that seek the truth of life's fictions via evocation rather than explanation or analysis. In them ethnographers, audiences, and performers meet in a shared field of experience, emotion, and action.

Such performances return to memory, not lived experience, as the site of criticism, interpretation, and action. It is understood that experience exists only in its representation, it does not stand outside memory or perception. The meanings of facts are always reconstituted in the telling, as they are remembered and connected to other events. Hence the appeal of the performance text does not lie in its offer of the certainty of the factual. The appeal is more complicated than that. Working from the site of memory, the reflexive, performed text asks readers as viewers (or co-performers) to relive the experience through the writer's or performer's eyes. Readers thus move through the re-created experience with the performer. This allows them to relive the experience for themselves.

Thus we can share in Harrington's experiences when he tells us about remembering the night he held his young son in his arms. The writer acting in this manner re-creates in the mind's eye a series of emotional moments. Life is then retraced through that moment, interpreting the past from the point of view of the present. Here is Susan Krieger (1996):

> I have just come back from a trip to Florida to settle the affairs of my lover's aunt [Maxine], who died suddenly at the age of seventy. She was carrying

her groceries up the stairs to her apartment when she dropped dead of a heart attack. . .

. . . It was an otherworldly experience: going to Florida . . . to clean out the house of a woman I did not know—sorting through her clothes and jewelry, finding snapshots she recently took, using her bathroom, meeting her friends. (pp. 65, 68).

On her last day in Florida, Krieger finds Aunt Maxine's silver flatware inside an old accordion case in the back corner of a greasy kitchen cabinet. Maxine's silver is cheap. It had been a replacement set. It is tarnished, not the real thing like the family silver her mother had gotten from her mother. Krieger asks, "What determines the value of a person's life, is value different if you are a woman, how do you separate a woman from the things she owns, leaves behind, her clothes, the cheap family silver?" (p. 70). This cheap set of silver flatware is not an adequate measure of Aunt Maxine.

Laurel Richardson's mother died of breast cancer in Miami Beach on June 8, 1968. Nearly 30 years later, Richardson (1997) wrote about her mother's death:

On June 8, I awoke determined to drive to Key West for the day. I sponge-bathed Mother, greeted the nurse, kissed my parents good-bye, and drove off in Father's Dodge Dart. When I got to Long Key, I was overwhelmed with the need to phone my parents. Mother had just died—less than a minute ago—Father said. (p. 234)

Of this news she observes, "I was grateful to have not witnessed her passing-on. I was thirty years old" (p. 235).

Ten years after her mother's death, Richardson wrote a poem, "Last Conversation" (1997, p. 234):

I want to hold your
weightless body to my
breasts, cradle you,
rock you to sleep.

The truth of a person's and a culture's ways are given in texts like these. Such works, when performed or read, become symbolic representations of what the culture and the person values. In their performances, performers embody these values.

Now listen to Angela Davis. In her recent study of the female blues singers Ma Rainey, Bessie Smith, and Billie Holiday, Davis (1998) observes that within African American culture the "blues marked the advent of a popular culture of performance, with the borders of performer and audience becoming increasing differentiated. . . . this . . . mode of presenting popular music crystallized into a performance culture that has had an enduring influence on African-American music" (p. 5).

In their performances, Ma Rainey, Bessie Smith, and Billie Holiday presented a set of black feminist understandings concerning class, race, gender, violence, sexuality, marriage, men, and intimacy (Collins, 1990, p. 209). This blues legacy is deeply entrenched in an indigenous, class-conscious, black feminism. The female blues singers created performance spaces for black women, spaces to sing and live the blues, black female voices talking about and doing black culture on stage, a public, critical performance art (see Jones, 1999).

The blues are improvised songs sung from the heart about love and about women and men gone wrong (Collins, 1990, p. 210). Rainey, Smith, and Holiday sang in ways that went beyond the written text. They turned the blues into a living art form, a form that would with Holiday move into the spaces of jazz. And jazz, like the blues and culture, is an improvisational, not static, art form. Bill Evans, the great bebop pianist, put it this way, "Jazz is not a what . . . it is a how. If it were a what, it would be static, never growing. The how is that the music comes from the moment, it is spontaneous, it exists at the time it is created" (quoted in Lee, 1996, p. 426). The improvised coperformance text, the jazz solo, like Billie Holiday singing the blues, is a spontaneous production, it lives in the moment of creation. The how of culture as it connects people to one another in loving, conflictual, and disempowering ways is what performance ethnography seeks to capture (see Jackson, 1998, p. 21).

◆ Red Lodge, Montana: Experiences and Performances

William Kittredge (1996, p. 97) says that the West is an enormous empty and innocent stage waiting for a performance (see also Kittredge, 1987, 1994). He continues, "We see the history of our performances everywhere . . . inscribed on the landscape (fences, roads, canals, power lines, city plans, bomb ranges" (p. 97). Moreover, the West is contained in the stories people tell about it. Montana is both a performance and a place for performances. It is not possible to write an objective, authoritative, neutral account of performing Montana. Every account is personal and locally situated. Here are some of the ways Montana is performed.

In 1994, my wife and I bought a little piece of land outside Red Lodge, Montana, population 1,875.[13] We got an acre with a cabin on a river called Rock Creek and a big bluff of a rock outcropping behind the cabin. Our little valley is marked by lakes, snowcapped mountain ranges, alpine meadows, and sprawling ranches where people live in double-wide mobile homes. Early June brings fields of yellow sunflowers, Indian paintbrush, and lupine.

In the summer, horses and deer graze in the valley above the road to our cabin. Off the big boulder under the big cottonwood tree, I catch rainbow and brook trout for breakfast. I fish; my wife quilts, hikes, and collects wildflowers. Last Christmas my wife took up cross-country skiing. In the summer we go to auctions and yard sales, and drive into town for groceries.

Red Lodge is 4 miles from our cabin. It was primarily a mining town until the 1943 mine explosion that killed 74 miners. Hit hard by the Depression, even before the mines closed, looking for a way to stay alive, the town fathers pushed for a "high road" (the Hi-Road) that would connect Red Lodge to Cooke City and Silver Gate, the two little mining communities just outside the northeast entrance to Yellowstone National Park. It took a 1931 act of Congress and 5 years of hard work to build the road over the mountain; The Beartooth Highway officially opened in 1936. Ever since, Red Lodge has been marketed as the eastern gateway to Yellowstone. That's what got us there in 1990.[14]

After reading Kittredge and studying Turner (1986) and Bruner (1986, 1989, 1996), I have come to see our little part of Montana as a liminal place, a place for new performances, new stories. Caught up in the shadows of the new, mythologized culture of the West (Limerick, 1997, p. 151; Wilkinson, 1997, p. 114), we are learning how to perform Montana. We are learning to engage in the ritual performances that people do when they are in and around Red Lodge, performances such as going to parades; shopping in the little craft and antique stores; buying things for the cabin; driving over the mountain; eating out; having an espresso on the sidewalk in front of the Coffee Factory Roasters; having a fancy dinner at the Pollard (which is on the National Registry of Hotels); picking up pictures from Flash's Image Factory; buying quilting materials at Granny Hugs; volunteering in the local library, which is computerizing its entire collection; and chatting with the owner of the Village Shoppe, who at one time dated the niece of the former University of Illinois basketball coach.

We watch other people do what we are doing, separating the experience of being in Montana from its performances and representations, constructing culture and meaning as they go along (Bruner, 1989, p. 113). Three years ago, I overheard a man talking to the owner of the tackle shop in Big Timber. His BMW was still running out front, the driver's door open. He had on an Orvis fishing vest. He had driven with his family from Connecticut. "The kids saw that movie *A River Runs Through It*. Where do we have to go to catch fish like they did in that movie? Can somebody around here give me fly-fishing lessons?" The owner said no on the lessons, but told the man to "go about 20 miles upriver, past Four-Mile Bridge. You can't miss it" (see also Dawson, 1996, p. 11).

Of course, the meanings of these Montana performance experiences are constantly changing. It is not appropriate to judge them in terms of their authenticity or originality. There is absolutely no original against which any given performance can be measured. There are only performances that seem to work and those that don't.

Creating Local History

Every year, we try to observe part of Red Lodge's Festival of Nations celebration. This is a 9-day ritual performance that reenacts the town's white European ethnic history. It involves white rituals such as colorful Old World costumes; Finnish, Irish, and Scottish dances and songs; bagpipes and the New Caledonia Drum and Bugle Corps; and cowboy poets—"whiteness as race, as privilege, as social construction" (Fine, Powell, Weis, & Wong, 1997, p. vii). This is whiteness as moral community. The souls of white folk are on public display (Du Bois, 1920, p. 29; Hughes, 1962).

Each day of the festival is given a name—7 days are devoted to specific nationalities (Irish-English-Welsh, German, Scandinavian, Finnish, Italian, Slavic, and Scottish), and the other days are Montana Day and All Nations Day. At the beginning of the 20th century, men from the European countries saluted in the festival came to Montana and became miners. Later they married, and their wives taught school, cooked, had children, helped run little shops, and carried on native crafts from their home countries. Red Lodge tries to keep this history alive.

According to local history, the festival started shortly after World War II. Local community leaders decided to build a civic center. They wanted a place for community activities, for an annual summer music festival, for art and craft exhibits and the display of flags and cultural items from each of the nations represented in the town. Thus was born the Festival of Nations, and Red Lodge was soon transformed into a "tourist town, a place that offered good scenery, fine fishing, the Hi-Road, the rodeo, cool summers" (Red Lodge Chamber of Commerce, 1982, p. 4). But the town had more to offer: "The inhabitants themselves were a resource" (p. 4). For 9 days every summer, Red Lodge puts its version of local ethnic culture on display, turning everyday people into performers of their respective ethnic heritages.

In these performances, residents only had their own histories to go on, so they made it up as they went along, one day for each ethnic group, but each group would do pretty much the same thing: a parade down Broadway with national flags from the country of origin, people in native costume, an afternoon performance of some sort (singing, storytelling, rug making), ethnic food in the Labor Temple (every day from 3:00 to 5:00 p.m.), an evening of music and dance in the civic center. This is improvised ethnicity connected to the performance of made-up rituals handed down from one generation to the next, white privilege, white cultural memory, Montana style (see also Hill, 1997, p. 245).

Montana Jazz

I like Montana Day, especially that part that involves ranch women reading their stories about being Montana wives. This is improvised theater, cowgirl women singing their version of the blues—Montana jazz. A tent is set up over the dance pavilion in Lions Park, just next to the Depot Gallery, which is housed in a converted red train caboose, across the street from the Carnegie Library. White plastic chairs are lined up in rows on the lawn. Loudspeakers are on each side of the stage. An old-fashioned Montana rancher meal is served afterward: barbecued beef, baked beans, coleslaw, baked potatoes, Jell-o salad, brownies for dessert, coffee and ice tea for beverages.

Tall and short middle-aged suntanned women take the stage. These are hardworking women, mothers, daughters, and grandmothers who live in the ranches in the Beartooth Valley, along the East Rosebud, Rock Creek, Willow Creek, and Stillwater River south of Columbus and Absarokee.

Some have on cowboy boots, others wear Nike sneakers. They are dressed in blue jeans and decorated red, white, and blue cowboy shirts and skirts, and have red bandannas around their necks. They have short and long hair, ponytails and curls. They read cowboy poetry, tell short stories about hard winters and horses that freeze to death in snowbanks. Some sing songs. Country music plays quietly, and people come and go, some stopping and listening for a while. As these women perform, old ranchers in wide-brimmed cowboy hats close their eyes and tap their feet to the music. Young children run around through the crowd, and husbands proudly watch their wives read their poetry. Like Ma Rainey, Bessie Smith, and Billie Holiday, these women sing their version of the cowgirl blues. And there is a certain firm truth in the way they do this.

Dead Indians

Fiedler (1988) argues that Montana as a white territory became psychologically possible only after the Native Americans, the Nez Percé, Blackfeet, Sioux, Assinboine, Gros Ventre, Cheyenne, Chipewayan, Cree, and Crow were killed, driven away, or forced onto reservations. He asserts that the struggle to rid the West of the "noble savage" and the "redskin" was integral to the myth of the Montana frontier as a wild wilderness (p. 745). According to Fiedler, the Indian was Montana's Negro, an outcast living in an open-air ghetto (p. 752). With the passing of the redskin came trappers, mountain men, explorers, General Custer, Chief Joseph, and then ranchers and homesteaders. Indian sites were marked with names such as Dead Indian Pass.

Entering Red Lodge, you drive past a wooden statue of a Native American, a male Indian face sitting on a big stone. It was carved by a non-Native American. The history of Montana's relations with the Native American is folded into mountain man festivals and events like Montana Day in Red Lodge. It is a history that simultaneously honors the dead Indian while denying the violent past that is so central to white supremacy.

Two summers ago, we drove over Dead Indian Pass, taking the Chief Joseph Highway back from Yellowstone Park. Chief Joseph led the Nez Percé over this pass just months before Custer's last stand. At the top of the mountain there is a turnoff where you can stop and look back across the valley, 10,000 feet below. Although this place is called Dead Indian Pass, there is no mention of Chief Joseph on the little plaque at this viewing spot. Instead, there is a story about the ranch families who settled the valley while fighting off the Indians—hence the name Dead Indian Pass. The whites, and not the Indians, are honored in popular memory.

Performing Montana

There are many ways to perform Montana. Montana is a place where locals and tourists constantly commingle, where Orvis-outfitted fly fishermen from Connecticut connect with Huck Finn look-alike local kids who fish with worms and old bamboo poles. These Montana performances mix up many different things at the same time—different identities, different selves: cowboys, rodeos, classical music, antique hunters, skiers, mountain men, Finnish women who make rugs, ranchers' wives who write poetry, fishing for trout.

Being in nature is a major part of the Montana self. My wife and I enact nature; we bring it to ourselves through the very act of bending down and smelling a wildflower, of walking along the river. This contact with the "natural world is an experience that comes to us like a gift" (Kittredge, 1996, p. 108). And so our corner of Montana is a sacred place, a hole, or house of sky, to use phrases from Kittredge (1994) and Doig (1978), a place where wonderful things happen, and they happen when we perform them.

These are the kinds of things a minimalist, storytelling, performative form of qualitative inquiry makes visible. In these tellings the world comes alive. The qualitative researcher attempts to make these meanings available to the reader, hoping to show how this version of the sociological imagination engages some of the things that matter in everyday life. But sometimes words fail, for in its naturalness Montana is a place that is stunning in its beauty, a world of images beyond words.

I turn now to an aesthetic of color[15] and critical race theory. I explore how critical race theory can use experimental forms of narrative to criticize and resist racist cultural practices.

◆ An Aesthetic of Color and Critical Race Theory

A feminist, Chicano/a, and black performance-based aesthetic uses art, photography, music, dance, poetry, painting, theater, cinema, performance texts, autobiography, narrative, storytelling, and poetic, dramatic language to create a critical race consciousness, thereby extending the post-civil rights Chicano/a and black arts cultural movements into the next century (see Harrington, 1992, p. 208). These practices serve to implement critical race theory (Anzaldúa, 1987; Collins, 1990; Davis, 1998, p. 155; Gonzalez, 1998; hooks, 1990, p. 105; Joyce, 1987; Ladson-Billings, 1998; Parker, 1998; Parker et al., 1998; Scheurich, 1997, pp. 144-158; Smith, 1993, p. xxvi; Smith, 1994, p. xxii; Trinh, 1992). Critical race theory "seeks to decloak the seemingly race-neutral, and color-blind ways . . . of constructing and administering race-based appraisals . . . of the law, administrative policy, electoral politics . . . political discourse [and education] in the USA" (Parker et al., 1998, p. 5).

Thus Collins's (1990, 1998) Afrocentric feminist agenda for the 1990s is moved into the next century; that is, theorists and practitioners enact a standpoint epistemology that sees the world from the point of view of oppressed persons of color. Representative sociopoetic and interpretive works in this tradition include those of Baraka (1969/1998), Jones (1966), Shange (1977), Joyce (1987), Neal (1988), and Jordan (1998), as well as the more recent arguments of hooks (1990, 1996), Smith (1993, 1994), Davis (1998), Anzaldúa (1987), Noriega (1996), and others. This aesthetic is also informed by the successive waves of activism among Asian Americans and Native Americans, women, and gays, lesbians, and bisexuals who "use their art as a weapon for political activism" (Harris, 1998, p. 1384; also Nero, 1998, p. 1973).

Theorists critically engage and interrogate the anti-civil rights agendas of the New Right (see Jordan, 1998), but this is not a protest or integrationist initiative aimed solely at informing a white audience of racial injustice. It dismisses these narrow agendas. In so doing it rejects classical Eurocentric and postpositivist standards for evaluating literary, artistic, and research work.

The following understandings shape this complex project:

♦ Ethics, aesthetics, political praxis and epistemology are joined; every act of representation, artistic or research, is a political and ethical statement (see Neal, 1988/1998, p. 1451). There is not a separate aesthetic or epistemological realm regulated by transcendent ideals, although an ethics of care should always be paramount.

♦ Claims to truth and knowledge are assessed in terms of multiple criteria, including asking if a text (a) interrogates existing cultural, sexist, and racial stereotypes, especially those connected to family, femininity, masculinity, marriage, and intimacy (Neal, 1988/1998, p. 1457); (b) gives primacy to concrete lived experience; (c) uses dialogue and an ethics of personal responsibility, values beauty, spirituality, and love of others; (d) implements an emancipatory agenda committed to equality, freedom, social justice, and participatory democratic practices; and (e) emphasizes community, collective action, solidarity, and group empowerment (Denzin, 1997, p. 65; hooks, 1990, p. 111; Pizarro, 1998, pp. 63-65).

♦ No topic is taboo, including sexuality, sexual abuse, death, and violence.

♦ This project presumes an artist and social researcher who is part of, and a spokesperson for, a local moral community, a community with its own symbolism, mythology, and heroic figures.

♦ This project asks that the writer-artist draw upon vernacular, folk, and popular culture forms of representation, including proverbs, work songs, spirituals, sermons, prayers, poems, choreopoems (Shange, 1977), folktales, blues (Davis, 1998), jazz, rap, film, paintings, theater, movies, photographs, performance art, murals, and *corridos* (see Fregoso, 1993; Gates & McKay, 1997, p. xxvii; Hill, 1998; Noriega, 1996; Pizarro, 1998, p. 65).

♦ This project includes a search for texts that speak to women and children of color and to persons who suffer from violence, rape, and racist and sexist injustice.

♦ This project seeks artists-researchers-writers who produce works that speak to and represent the needs of the community (e.g., concerning drug addiction, teenage pregnancy, murder, gang warfare, AIDS, school dropout).

♦ It is understood, of course, that no single representation or work can speak to the collective needs of the community. Rather, local communities are often divided along racial, ethnic, gender, residential, age, and class lines.

Thus this project seeks emancipatory, utopian texts grounded in the distinctive styles, rhythms, idioms, and personal identities of local folk and vernacular culture. As historical documents, these texts record the histories of injustices experienced by the members of oppressed groups. They show how members of local groups have struggled to find places of dignity and respect in a violent, racist, and sexist civil society (see Gates & McKay, 1997, p. xxvii).

These texts are sites of resistance. They are places where meanings, politics, and identities are negotiated. They transform and challenge all forms of cultural representation: white, black, Chicano/a, Asian American, Native American, gay or straight.

In her poem "Power," black lesbian poet Audre Lorde (1978/1998b, p. 1627)* talks about taking action in the world:

The difference between poetry and rhetoric
is being
ready to kill
yourself
instead of your children.

In lines such as these, critical race theory is connected to a heightened reflexive and moral sense of race consciousness. Lorde (1973/1998a, pp. 1626-1627)* again, this time from "Coal":

I
is the total black, being spoken
from the earth's inside.
There are many kinds of open
how a diamond comes into a knot of flame
how a sound comes into a word coloured
by who pays what for speaking . . .

Love is a word, another kind of open.
As the diamond comes into a knot of flame
I am black because I come from the earth's inside
Now take my word for jewel in the open light.

Lorde (1986/1998c, pp. 1630-1631)* once more, from her poem "Stations":

Some women love
to wait
for life for a ring
for a touch . . . for another
woman's voice to make them whole . . .
Some women wait for something
to change and nothing
does change
so they change
themselves.

In "Taking in Wash," Rita Dove (1993/1998, pp. 1966-1967)* speaks to drinking, drunkenness, and violence in the house:

Papa called her Pearl when he came home
drunk, swaying as if the wind touched
only him . . . Mama never changed:

when the dog crawled under the stove
and the back gate slammed, Mama hid
the laundry . . . Papa is making the hankies
sail. Her foot upon a silk
stitched rose, she waits
he turns, his smile sliding over.
Mama a tight dark fist.
Touch that child
And I'll cut you down
Just like the Cedar of Lebanon.

Ntozake Shange's (1977)* powerful, Obie Award-winning choreo-poem *For Colored Girls Who Have Considered Suicide When the Rainbow Is Enuf* ends this way. Six of the seven women in the company, the ladies in red, purple, orange, blue, green, and yellow, have spoken. The lady in red summarizes (pp. 60, 63-64):

lady in red
i waz missin somethin . . .
i sat up one nite walkin a boardin house
screamin/cryin/the ghost of another woman
who was missin what I waz missin
i wanted to jump up outta my bones
& be done wit myself
leave me alone . . .
i fell into a numbness
til the only tree I cd see . . .
held me in the breeze
made me dawn dew
that chill at daybreak
the sun wrapped me up swingin rose light everywhere
the sky laid over me like a million men
i waz cold/I waz burnin up/a child
& endlessly weaving garments for the moon
wit me tears

i found god in myself
& i loved her/i loved her fiercely

All of the ladies repeat to themselves softly the lines 'i found god in myself & I loved her.' It soon becomes a song of joy, started by the lady in blue. The ladies sing first to each other, then gradually to the audience. After the song peaks the ladies enter a closed tight circle.

lady in brown
& this is for colored girls who have considered
suicide/but are movin to the ends of their own
rainbows

And so the world is taken back, and we dream of another day of lightness and being free, of making our own rainbow.

Aesthetics and Cinematic Practices

Within the contemporary black and Chicano/a film communities, there are specific sets of film practices associated with this aesthetic project.[16] These practices inform and shape the narrative and visual content of these experimental texts. They include the following:

- ♦ Experiments with narrative forms, folk ballads, and *corridos* that honor long-standing Chicano/a discourse traditions (Fregoso, 1993, pp. 70-76; Noriega, 1992, pp. 152-153);
- ♦ The use of improvisation, mise-en-scène, and montage to fill the screen with multiracial images and to manipulate bicultural visual and linguistic codes;
- ♦ The use of personal testimonials, life stories, voice-overs, and offscreen narration to provide overall narrative unity to texts (Noriega, 1992, pp. 156-159);
- ♦ Celebration of key elements in Chicano/a culture, especially the themes of resistance, maintenance, affirmation, and neoindigenism, or *mestizaje* (Noriega, 1992, p. 150), thereby challenging assimilation and melting-pot narratives;
- ♦ Production of texts that deconstruct machismo, the masculine identity, and the celebration of works that give the Chicana subject an active part in the text while criticizing such timeworn stereotypes as the virgin, whore, supportive wife, and homegirl (Fregoso, 1993, pp. 29, 93-94);
- ♦ Rejection of essentializing approaches to identity and emphasis on a processual, gendered, performance view of self and the location of identity within, not outside of, systems of cultural and media representation;
- ♦ Refusal to accept the official race-relations narrative of the culture, which privileges the ideology of assimilation while contending that black and Hispanic youth pose grave threats to white society (Fregoso, 1993, p. 29).

Return to Anna Deavere Smith's *Fires in the Mirror* (1993)*, and listen now to An Anonymous Young Man #2 Bad Boy. The time is evening; the season, spring. The setting is the same recreation room where the interview with Anonymous Young Man #1 took place. Young Man #2 has dreadlocks. On his head is a "very odd-shaped multicolored hat" (p. 100). He is wearing a black jacket over his clothes. He has a gold tooth. He is soft-spoken.

> That youth,
> that sixteen-year-old
> didn't murder that Jew . . .
> mostly the Black youth in Crown Heights have two things to do—
> You either
> DJ, be a MC, a rapper
> or Jamaican rapper,
> ragamuffin,
> or you be a bad boy
> you sell drugs or you rob people.
> What do you do?
> I sell drugs
> What do you do?
> I rap.
> That's how it is in Crown Heights. (pp. 100, 102)

In this speech Smith catches the language of youth, its rhythm, syntax, and semantics. She uses the personal testimonial as a way of bringing another voice into the text, as well as providing narrative unity to the play. Her young man rejects essentializing views of identity, but notes that in Crown Heights young people have few choices or options in life. Young Man #2 resists these interpretations.

Artistic representations such as those presented here from Lorde, Dove, and Smith (and Jordan—see below) are based on the notion of a radical and constantly changing set of aesthetic practices. As hooks (1990) observes: "There can never be one critical paradigm for the evaluation of artistic work. . . . a radical aesthetic acknowledges that we are constantly changing positions, locations, that our needs and concerns vary, that these diverse directions must correspond with shifts in critical thinking" (p. 111).

At this level, there is no preferred aesthetic. For example, realistic art is not necessarily better than abstract, expressionist, or impressionist art. In the worlds of jazz, ragtime, New Orleans, classic, and swing are not necessarily more or less politically correct or aesthetically better than bebop, cool, hard bop, Latin, avant-garde, and fusion. Nor is Charlie Parker less politically correct then Lester Young, or Ben Webster, Ella Fitzgerald, Nina

Simone, Nancy Wilson, Billie Holiday, Bessie Smith, John Coltrane, or Miles Davis.

But then, June Jordan (1998)* might put it differently. In her jazz prose poem "A Good News Blues," she pays homage to Billie and Louis, Nina, and Bessie, to anyone who sings the blues. In the following lines she praises Billie Holiday (pp. 199-200):

> Since the blues left my sky
> I'm runnin out on Monday
> To chase down all my Sundays
> Now a man must be pushing and shoving
> But a woman's born to strut and stretch
> To go outside (for /catch some) lovin
> Get over past regrets
> I'm liftin' weights and wearin sweats . . .
> And thrillin through the night . . .
> And if I want to rewrite
> all the sorry-ass/
> victim/passive/feminine/
> traditional
> propaganda
> spinnin out here
>   ain' nobody's business
>   if I do
> I been lost
> but
> I been found
>   I am bound
>   for Billie's land
> that place of longing
> where the angels learn
> to sing and play
>   the syncopated music
>   of my soul

And brilliant rainbows cut through the blue-and-white clouds, connecting distant hills and mountains to the places where I live.

Each text, each performance should be valued in terms of the collective and individual reflection and critical action it produces, including conversations that cross the boundaries of race, class, gender, and nation. We ask how each work of art and each instance of qualitative inquiry promotes the development of human agency, "resistance . . . and critical consciousness" (hooks, 1990, p. 111).

This aesthetic also seeks and values beauty, and looks to find beauty in the everyday, especially in "the lives of poor people" (hooks, 1990, p. 111). Here is an illustration from bell hooks, who recalls the houses of her childhood, especially the house of Baba, her grandmother. Looking back into her childhood, hooks observes that she now sees how this black woman was struggling to create, in spite of poverty and hardship, an oppositional world of beauty. Baba had a clean house crowded with many precious objects. Baba was also a quilt maker. She turned worn-out everyday clothing into beautiful works of art, and her quilts were present in every room of her small house.

Baba's house was like an art gallery. Late at night, hooks would sit alone in an upstairs room in the house, and light from the moon would send crisscrossing patterns and shadows across the floor and the wall. In the stillness of the night, in the reflections from the moon's light, hooks came to see darkness and beauty in different ways.

Now, in a different time, late at night, she and her sisters "think about our skin as a dark room, a place of shadows. We talk often about color politics, and the ways racism has created an aesthetic that wounds us, we talk about the need to see darkness differently. . . . in that space of shadows we long for an aesthetic of blackness—strange and oppositional" (hooks, 1990, p. 113). Baba, the quilt maker, shows her how to do this.

Aesthetics, art, performance, history, culture, and politics are thus intertwined, for in the artful, interpretive production, cultural heroes, heroines, mythic pasts, and senses of moral community are created. It remains to chart the future—to return to the beginning, to reimagine the ways in which qualitative inquiry and interpretive ethnography can advance the agendas of radical democratic practice, to ask where these practices will take us next.

◆ Into the Future

Of course, persons who do interpretations feel uncomfortable making predictions. But where the fields of interpretation, qualitative inquiry, and the practices and politics of telling stories will be in 10 years must be addressed. If the past predicts the future, and if the decade of the 1990s is to be taken seriously, then interpretation is moving more and more deeply into the regions of the postmodern, multicultural sensibility. A new postinterpretive, postfoundational paradigm is emerging. This framework is attaching itself to new and less foundational interpretive criteria. A more expansive framework shaped by an aesthetics of color and critical race theory principles informs these criteria.

Epistemologies and aesthetics of color will proliferate, building on Afrocentric, Chicano/a, Native American, Asian, and Third World perspectives. More elaborated epistemologies of gender (and class) will appear, including queer theory (see Gamson, Chapter 12, Volume 1) and feminisms of color (see Ladson-Billings, Chapter 9, Volume 1). These interpretive communities and their scholars will draw on their group experiences as the basis of the texts they write, and they will seek texts that speak to the logic and cultures of these communities. They will be committed to advancing the political, economic, cultural, and educational practices of critical race theory.

These race-, ethnic-, and gender-specific interpretive communities will fashion interpretive criteria out of their interactions with postpositivist, constructivist, critical theory, and poststructural sensibilities. These criteria will be local, aesthetic, emic, existential, political, and emotional. They will push the personal to the forefront of the political, where the social text becomes the vehicle for the expression of politics.

This projected proliferation of interpretive communities does not mean that the field of qualitative research will splinter into warring factions, or into groups that cannot speak to one another. Underneath the complexities and contradictions that define this field rest four common commitments. The first reflects the belief that the world of human experience must be studied from the point of view of the historically and culturally situated individual. Second, qualitative researchers will persist in working outward from their own biographies to the worlds of experience that surround them. Third, scholars will continue to value and seek to produce works that speak clearly and powerfully about these worlds. As Raymond Carver (1989, p. 24) observes, the real experimenters will always be those who make it new, who find things out for themselves, and who want to carry this news from their world to ours. Thus will qualitative researchers find new and different ways of joining their interpretive work with constantly changing forms of radical democratic practice.

Fourth, these texts will be committed not just to describing the world, but to changing it. These texts will be performance based and informed by the practices of civic, intimate, and public journalism. They will be committed to creating civic transformations and to using minimalist social theory. They will inscribe and perform utopian dreams, dreams shaped by critical race theory, dreams of a world where all are free to be who they choose to be, free of gender, class, race, religious, or ethnic prejudice or discrimination. The seventh moment will be one in which the practices of qualitative inquiry finally move, without hesitation or encumbrance, from the personal to the political. This move is a spiraling process. It builds on previous levels of expression. It does not abandon the personal, for example, in the name of the political.[17]

So the stories we tell one another will change, and the criteria for reading stories will also change. And this is how it should be. The good stories are always told by those who have learned well the stories of the past but are unable to tell them any longer. This is so because the stories from the past no longer speak to them or to us.

In the end, then, to summarize, I seek an existential, interpretive ethnography, an ethnography that offers a blueprint for cultural criticism. This criticism is grounded in the specific worlds made visible in the ethnography. It understands that all ethnography is theory and value laden. There can be no objective account of a culture and its ways (see Smith & Deemer, Chapter 12, this volume). Taking a lead from midcentury African American cultural critics (Du Bois, Hurston, Ellison, Wright, Baldwin, Hines), we now know that the ethnographic, the aesthetic, and the political can never be neatly separated. Ethnography, like art, is always political.

Accordingly, after Ford (1950/1998), a critical, civic, literary ethnography is one that must meet four criteria. It must evidence a mastery of literary craftsmanship, the art of good writing. It should present a well-plotted, compelling, but minimalist narrative. This narrative should be based on realistic, natural conversation, with a focus on memorable, recognizable characters. These characters should be located in well-described, "unforgettable scenes" (Ford, 1950/1998, p. 1112). Second, the work should present clearly identifiable cultural and political issues, including injustices based on the structures and meanings of race, class, gender, and sexual orientation. Third, the work should articulate a politics of hope. It should criticize how things are and imagine how they could be different. Finally, it should do these things through direct and indirect symbolic and rhetorical means. Writers who do these things are fully immersed in the oppressions and injustices of their time. They direct their ethnographic energies to higher, utopian, morally sacred goals.

Finally, this performative ethnography searches for new ways to locate and represent the gendered, sacred self in its ethical relationships to nature. An exploration of other forms of writing is sought, including personal diaries, nature writing, and performance texts anchored in the natural world (see Denzin, 1999a; see also Lincoln & Denzin, Chapter 14, Volume 1).

◆ Notes

* I am indebted to Sage Publications and the Institute of Communications Research for supplying the funds to pay the permissions fees for quoted material used in this chapter.

1. To repeat, as Yvonna Lincoln and I assert in Chapter 1 of this series, the seven moments of qualitative inquiry are traditional (1900-1950); modernist (1950-1970); blurred genres (1970-1986); crisis of representation (1986-1990); postmodern, a period of experimental and new ethnographies (1990-1995); postexperimental inquiry (1995-2000); and the future, which is now (2000-).

2. A parallel movement (see below) is occurring in the worlds of cinema, where Chicano/a and black filmmakers are using voice-overs, first-person and offscreen narration, mise-en-scène, and montage as ways of disturbing traditional gendered images of the racial subject (Fregoso, 1993, pp. 70-76; Noriega, 1992, pp. 152-153; see also Hall, 1989). This movement is a consequence, in part, of a 1968 U.S. Office of Economic Opportunity-funded program called the New Communicators, "designed to train minorities for employment in the film industry" (Noriega, 1996, p. 7).

3. The following section draws from Denzin (1997, pp. 280-281).

4. At the same time, it is understood that "participating in a citizen's initiative to clean up a polluted harbor is no less political than debating in cultural journals the pejorative presentation of certain groups in terms of stereotypical images" (Benhabib, 1992, p. 104).

5. Public journalism is not without its critics, including those who say it is news by focus group, that it is a marketing device to sell newspapers, that it is a conservative reform movement aimed at increasing the power of professional journalists, and that its advocates do not understand the real meanings of community, public life, and civic discourse. See the essays in Graber, McQuail, and Norris (1998) and Glasser (1999), but see also Carey (1995).

6. This ethic values community, solidarity, care, love, empowerment, morally involved observers, and caring relations with the community (see Denzin, 1997, p. 275).

7. These are extensions of the norms that Christians et al. (1993, pp. 55-57) see as operating for journalists.

8. Things are known only through their representations. Each representational form is regulated by a set of conventions. Factual tales should be objective and should conform to certain rules of verification. Fictional tales are regulated by understandings connected to emotional verisimilitude, emotional realism, and so on.

9. I thank Clifford Christians for this principle.

10. The rules in this paragraph plagiarize Raymond Chandler's "Twelve Notes on the Mystery Story" (1995).

11. This section draws from and reworks portions of Denzin (1999b).

12. As Meaghan Morris has indicated to me in conversation, the Australians involved in this case felt that justice was not served, that they had to deal with the loss of a loved one strictly within American political terms. Rosenbaum became a cipher in these accounts.

13. There are various stories about how the town got its name. "The generally accepted theory is that the Crow Indians who inhabited the area colored their lodges with red clay" (Graetz, 1997, p. 23).

14. The town has a Web site. Using a search engine such as Yahoo, you can simply type "Red Lodge, Montana" and within seconds you can be looking at a map of downtown Red Lodge.

15. I borrow this phrase from bell hooks's (1990) essay "An Aesthetic of Blackness."

16. The implementation of the 1968 New Communicators program (see note 2, above) at the University of Southern California and the University of California at Los Angeles produced first- and second-generation minority filmmakers called by some the black and brown Los Angeles schools (see Diawara, 1993; Fregoso, 1993, pp. 31, 129; Masilela, 1993; Noriega, 1992, p. 142; Noriega, 1996, pp. 7-8). Among this group of filmmakers are such names as Burnett, Dash, Van Peebles, Rich, Duke, Trevino, Vasquez, Martinez, Valdez, Nair, Wang, hooks, and Nava. More recent names include Lee, Singleton, and Hughes. These post-civil rights filmmakers are implementing a cinematic version of critical race theory, and their works should be read alongside those of hooks, West, and others. Funding for this project was cut back under the Reagan administration in the 1980s.

17. Ivan Brady clarified this point for me.

◆ References

Alexie, S. (1993). *Old shirts and new skins.* Los Angeles: University of California, American Indian Studies Center. (Used by permission.)

Anzaldúa, G. (1987). *Borderlands/la frontera: The new mestiza.* San Francisco: Aunt Lute.

Baker, H., Jr. (1997). The black arts movement. In H. L. Gates, Jr., & N. Y. McKay (Eds.), *The Norton anthology of African American literature* (pp. 1791-1806). New York: W. W. Norton.

Baraka, A. (1997). *The autobiography of Leroi Jones.* Chicago: Lawrence Hill.

Baraka, A. (1998). Black art. In P. L. Hill (Ed.), *Call and response: The Riverside anthology of the African American literary tradition* (pp. 1501-1502). Boston: Houghton Mifflin. (Original work published 1969. Reprinted by permission of Sterling Lord Literistic, Inc. Copyright by Amiri Baraka.)

Behar, R. (1996). *The vulnerable observer: Anthropology that breaks your heart.* Boston: Beacon.

Benhabib, S. (1992). *Situating the self: Gender, community and postmodernism in contemporary ethics.* New York: Routledge.

Birringer, J. (1993). *Theatre, history, postmodernism.* Bloomington: Indiana University Press.

Bochner, A. P., & Ellis, C. (1996). Taking ethnography into the twenty-first century. *Journal of Contemporary Ethnography, 25,* 3-5.

Brady, I. (1998). A gift of the journey. *Qualitative Inquiry, 4,* 463.

Brady, I. (1999). Review essay: Ritual as cognitive process, performance as history. *Current Anthropology, 40,* 243-248.

Branaman, A. (1997). Goffman's social theory. In C. Lemert & A. Branaman (Eds.), *The Goffman reader* (pp. xvi-lxxxii). Malden, MA: Blackwell.

Bruner, E. M. (1986). Experience and its expressions. In V. Turner & E. M. Bruner (Eds.), *The anthropology of experience* (pp. 3-30). Urbana: University of Illinois Press.

Bruner, E. M. (1989). Tourism, creativity, and authenticity. In N. K. Denzin (Ed.), *Studies in symbolic interaction: A research annual* (Vol. 10, pp. 109-114). Greenwich, CT: JAI.

Bruner, E. M. (1996). Abraham Lincoln as authentic reproduction: A critique of postmodernism. *American Anthropologist, 96,* 397-415.

Butler, J. (1990). *Gender trouble: Feminism and the subversion of identity.* New York: Routledge.

Butler, J. (1997). *Excitable speech: A politics of the performative.* New York: Routledge.

Butler, J. (1999). Revisiting bodies and pleasures. *Theory, Culture & Society, 16,* 11-20.

Carey, J. W. (1995). The press, public opinion, and public discourse. In T. L. Glasser & C. T. Salmon (Eds.), *Public opinion and the communication of consent* (pp. 380-402). New York: Guilford.

Carspecken, P. F. (1996). *Critical ethnography in educational research: A theoretical and practical guide.* New York: Routledge.

Carver, R. (1989). *Fires.* New York: Vantage.

Ceglowski, D. (1997). That's a good story, but is it really research? *Qualitative Inquiry, 3,* 188-201.

Chandler, R. (1995). Twelve notes on the mystery story. In R. Chandler, *Later novels and other writings* (pp. 1004-1011). New York: Penguin.

Charity, A. (1995). *Doing public journalism.* New York: Guilford.

Christian, B. T. (1997). Literature since 1970. In H. L. Gates, Jr., & N. Y. McKay (Eds.), *The Norton anthology of African American literature* (pp. 2011-2020). New York: W. W. Norton.

Christians, C. G., Ferre, J. P., & Fackler, P. M. (1993). *Good news: Social ethics and the press.* New York: Oxford University Press.

Clough, P. T. (1994). *Feminist thought: Desire, power and academic discourse.* Cambridge, MA: Blackwell.

Clough, P. T. (1998). *The end(s) of ethnography: From realism to social criticism* (2nd ed.). New York: Peter Lang.

Cohen-Cruz, J. (1998). General introduction. In J. Cohen-Cruz (Ed.), *Radical street performance: An international anthology* (pp. 1-6). New York: Routledge.

Collins, P. H. (1990). *Black feminist thought: Knowledge, consciousness, and the politics of empowerment.* New York: Routledge, Chapman & Hall.

Collins, P. H. (1998). *Fighting words: Black women and the search for justice.* Minneapolis: University of Minnesota Press.

Conquergood, D. (1985). Performing as a moral act: Ethical dimensions of the ethnography of performance. *Literature in Performance, 5,* 1-13.

Conquergood, D. (1992). Ethnography, rhetoric and performance. *Quarterly Journal of Speech, 78,* 80-97.

Conquergood, D. (1998). Health theatre in a Hmong refugee camp: Performance, communication and culture. In J. Cohen-Cruz (Ed.), *Radical street performance: An international anthology* (pp. 220-229). New York: Routledge.

Cooke, J. (1980, September 28). Jimmy's world. *Washington Post,* p. A1.

Cruikshank, J. (1997). Negotiating with narrative: Establishing cultural identity at the Yukon International Storytelling Festival. *American Anthropologist, 99,* 56-69.

Dash, L. (1997). *Rosa Lee: A mother and her family in urban America.* New York: Penguin.

Davis, A. Y. (1998). *Blues legacies and black feminism: Gertrude Ma Rainey, Bessie Smith,* and Billie Holiday. New York: Pantheon.

Dawson, P. (1996). Not another fish story from occupied Montana. In R. Newby & S. Hunger (Eds.), *Writing Montana: Literature under the big sky* (pp. 10-23). Helena: Montana Center for the Book.

Degh, L. (1995). *Narratives in society: A performer-centered study of narration.* Bloomington: Indiana University Press.

Denison, J. (1996). Sports narratives. *Qualitative Inquiry, 2,* 351-362.

Denzin, N. K. (1997). *Interpretive ethnography: Ethnographic practices for the 21st century.* Thousand Oaks, CA: Sage.

Denzin, N. K. (1999a). An interpretive ethnography for the next century. *Journal of Contemporary Ethnography, 28,* 510-519.

Denzin, N. K. (1999b). Performing Montana. In B. Glassner & R. Hertz (Eds.), *Qualitative sociology as everyday life* (pp. 147-158). Thousand Oaks, CA: Sage.

Denzin, N. K. (1999c). Performing Montana, part II. *Symbolic Interaction, 23,* 76-89.

Diawara, M. (1993). Black American cinema: The new realism. In M. Diawara (Ed.), *Black American cinema* (pp. 3-25). New York: Routledge.

Diversi, M. (1998). Glimpses of street life: Representing lived experience through short stories. *Qualitative Inquiry, 4,* 131-137.

Doig, I. (1978). *This house of sky.* New York: Harcourt Brace.

Donmoyer, R., & Yennie-Donmoyer, J. (1995). Data as drama: Reflections on the use of readers theater as a mode of qualitative data display. *Qualitative Inquiry, 1,* 402-428.

Dove, R. (1998). Taking in wash. In P. L. Hill (Ed.), *Call and response: The Riverside anthology of the African American literary tradition* (pp. 1966-1967). Boston: Houghton Mifflin. (Reprinted from R. Dove, *Selected poems,* 1993, New York: Vantage)

Du Bois, W. E. B. (1920). *Darkwater: Voices from within the veil.* New York: Schocken.

Dunbar, C., Jr. (1999). Three short stories. *Qualitative Inquiry, 5,* 130-140.

Ellis, C. (1997). Evocative autoethnography: Writing emotionally about our lives. In W. G. Tierney & Y. S. Lincoln (Eds.), *Representation and the text: Re-framing the narrative voice* (pp. 115-139). Albany: State University of New York Press.

Ellis, C., & Bochner, A. P. (1992). Telling and performing personal stories: The constraints of choice in abortion. In C. Ellis & M. G. Flaherty (Eds.), *Investigating subjectivity: Research on lived experience* (pp. 79-101). Newbury Park, CA: Sage.

Ellis, C., & Bochner, A. P. (Eds.). (1996). *Composing ethnography: Alternative forms of qualitative writing.* Walnut Creek, CA: AltaMira.

Ellis, C., & Flaherty, M. G. (Eds.). (1992). *Investigating subjectivity: Research on lived experience.* Newbury Park, CA: Sage.

Fiedler, L. (1988). The Montana face. In W. Kittredge & A. Smith (Eds.), *The last best place: A Montana anthology* (pp. 744-752). Seattle: University of Washington Press.

Fine, M., Powell, L. C., Weis, L., & Wong, L. M. (1997). Preface. In M. Fine, L. C. Powell, L. Weis, & L. M. Wong (Eds.), *Off white: Readings on race, power and society* (pp. vii-xii). New York: Routledge.

Ford, N. A. (1998). A blueprint for Negro authors. In P. L. Hill (Ed.), *Call and response: The Riverside anthology of the African American literary tradition* (pp. 1112-1114). Boston: Houghton Mifflin. (Original work published 1950)

Fregoso, R. L. (1993). *The bronze screen: Chicana and Chicano film culture.* Minneapolis: University of Minnesota Press.

Gates, H. L., Jr., & McKay, N. Y. (1997). Preface: Talking books. In H. L. Gates, Jr., & N. Y. McKay (Eds.), *The Norton anthology of African American literature* (pp. xxvii-xli). New York: W. W. Norton.

Glasser, T. L. (Ed.). (1999). *The idea of public journalism.* New York: Guilford.

Goffman, E. (1959). *The presentation of self in everyday life.* Garden City, NY: Doubleday.

Gonzalez, F. E. (1998). Formations of Mexicananess: Trenzas de identidades multiples/Growing up Mexicana: Braids of multiple identities. *International Journal of Qualitative Studies in Education, 11,* 81-102.

Graber, D., McQuail, D., & Norris, P. (Eds.). (1998). *The politics of news: The news of politics.* Washington, DC: Congressional Quarterly Press.

Graetz, R. (1997, July-August). Sojourn to the sky: The Beartooth Highway. *Montana Magazine,* pp. 18-26.

Hall, S. (1989). Cultural identity and cinematic representation. *Framework, 36,* 68-81.

Harrington, W. (1992). *Crossings: A white man's journey into black America.* New York: HarperCollins.

Harrington, W. (1997a). Prologue: The job of remembering for the tribe. In W. Harrington (Ed.), *Intimate journalism: The art and craft of reporting everyday life* (pp. vii-xvi). Thousand Oaks, CA: Sage.

Harrington, W. (1997b). A writer's essay: Seeking the extraordinary in the ordinary. In W. Harrington (Ed.), *Intimate journalism: The art and craft of reporting everyday life* (pp. xvii-xlvi). Thousand Oaks, CA: Sage.

Harris, W. J. (1998). Cross roads blues: African American history and culture, 1960 to the present. In P. L. Hill (Ed.), *Call and response: The Riverside anthology of the African American literary tradition* (pp. 1343-1385). Boston: Houghton Mifflin.

Hill, P. L. (Ed.). (1998). *Call and response: The Riverside anthology of the African American literary tradition.* Boston: Houghton Mifflin.

Hill, R. T. G. (1997). Performance and the "political anatomy" of pioneer Colorado. *Text and Performance Quarterly, 17,* 236-255.

hooks, b. (1990). *Yearning: Race, gender, and cultural politics.* Boston: South End.

hooks, b. (1996). *Reel to real: Race, sex, and class at the movies.* New York: Routledge.

Hughes, L. (1962). *The ways of white folks.* New York: Vintage.

Hughes, L. (1994). *Collected poems by Langston Hughes.* New York: Alfred A. Knopf. (Permission granted by the Estate of Langston Hughes. Reprinted by permission of Alfred A. Knopf, a Division of Random House, Inc.)

Jackson, M. (1998). *Minima ethnographica: Intersubjectivity and the anthropological project.* Chicago: University of Chicago Press.

Jenkins, J. E. (1999, May 2). Narrating the action while taking part in it. *New York Times,* Arts and Leisure sec., pp. 9, 19.

Jones, L. (1966). *Home: Social essays.* Hopewell, NJ: Ecco.

Jones, S. H. (1999). Torch. *Qualitative Inquiry, 5,* 235-250.

Jordan, J. (1998). *Affirmative acts.* Garden City NY: Anchor. (Copyright © 1998 by June Jordan. Used by permission of Doubleday, a division of Random House, Inc.)

Joyce, J. A. (1987). The black canon: Reconstructing black American literary criticism. *New Literary History, 18,* 335-344.

Kittredge, W. (1987). *Owning it all.* San Francisco: Murray House.

Kittredge, W. (1994). *Hole in the sky: A memoir.* San Francisco: Murray House.

Kittredge, W. (1996). *Who owns the West?* San Francisco: Murray House.

Kotarba, J. A. (1998). Black men, black voices: The role of the producer in synthetic performance ethnography. *Qualitative Inquiry, 4,* 389-404.

Kramer, M. (1995). Breakable rules for literary journalists. In N. Sims & M. Kramer (Eds.), *Literary journalism: A new collection of the best American nonfiction* (pp. 21-34). New York: Ballantine.

Krieger, S. (1996). *The family silver: Essays on relationships among women.* Berkeley: University of California Press.

Ladson-Billings, G. (1998). Just what is critical race theory and what is it doing in a "nice" field like education? *International Journal of Qualitative Studies in Education, 11,* 7-24.

Lather, P. (1993). Fertile obsession: Validity after poststructuralism. *Sociological Quarterly, 34,* 673-693.

Lather, P., & Smithies, C. (1997). *Troubling the angels: Women living with HIV/ AIDS.* Boulder, CO: Westview.

Lee, G. (1996). The poet: Bill Evans. In R. Gottlieb (Ed.), *Reading jazz: A gathering of autobiography, reportage, and criticism from 1919 to now* (pp. 419-444). New York: Pantheon.

Lemert, C. (1997). Goffman. In C. Lemert & A. Branaman (Eds.), *The Goffman reader* (pp. ix-xliii). Malden, MA: Blackwell.

Limerick, P. N. (1997). The shadows of heaven itself. In W. E. Reibsame (Ed.), *Atlas of the new West* (pp. 151-178). New York: W. W. Norton.

Lincoln, Y. S. (1995a). Emerging criteria for quality in qualitative and interpretive inquiry. *Qualitative Inquiry, 1,* 275-289.

Lincoln, Y. S. (1995b). The sixth moment: Emerging problems in qualitative research. In N. K. Denzin (Ed.), *Studies in symbolic interaction: A research annual* (Vol. 19, pp. 37-55). Greenwich, CT: JAI.

Lincoln, Y. S. (1997). Self, subject, audience, text: Living at the edge, writing in the margins. In W. G. Tierney & Y. S. Lincoln (Eds.), *Representation and the text: Re-framing the narrative voice* (pp. 37-56). Albany: State University of New York Press.

Lincoln, Y. S. (1998, November). *When research is not enough: Community, care, and love.* Presidential Address delivered at the annual meeting of the Association for the Study of Higher Education, Miami, FL.

Lorde, A. (1998a). Coal. In P. L. Hill (Ed.), *Call and response: The Riverside anthology of the African American literary tradition* (pp. 1626-1627). Boston: Houghton Mifflin. (Copyright © 1986 by Audre Lorde, from *Collected Poems* by Audre Lorde. Used by permission of W. W. Norton & Company, Inc.)

Lorde, A. (1998b). Power. In P. L. Hill (Ed.), *Call and response: The Riverside anthology of the African American literary tradition* (p. 1627). Boston: Houghton Mifflin. (Reprinted from A. Lorde, *The black unicorn: Poems,* 1978, New York: W. W. Norton)

Lorde, A. (1998c). Stations. In P. L. Hill (Ed.), *Call and response: The Riverside anthology of the African American literary tradition* (pp. 1630-1631). Boston: Houghton Mifflin. (Copyright © 1988 by Audre Lorde, from *Collected Poems* by Audre Lorde. Used by permission of W. W. Norton & Company, Inc.)

Lubiano, W. (1997). But, compared to what? Reading realism, representation, and essentialism in *School Daze, Do the Right Thing,* and the Spike Lee discourse. In V. Smith (Ed.), *Representing blackness: Issues in film and video* (pp. 1-12). New Brunswick, NJ: Rutgers University Press.

Marx, K. (1983). Theses on Feuerbach. In E. Kamenka (Ed.), *The portable Karl Marx* (pp. 155-158). New York: Penguin. (Original work published 1888)

Masilela, N. (1993). The Los Angeles school of black filmmakers. In M. Diawara (Ed.), *Black American cinema* (pp. 107-117). New York: Routledge.

Mills, C. W. (1959). *The sociological imagination.* New York: Oxford University Press.

Mienczakowski, J. (1995). The reconstruction of ethnography into theater with emancipatory potential. *Qualitative Inquiry, 1,* 360-375.

Neal, L. (1988). *Visions of a liberated future.* New York: Thunder's Mouth.

Neal, L. (1998). The black arts movement. In P. L. Hill (Ed.), *Call and response: The Riverside anthology of the African American literary tradition* (pp. 1450-1458). Boston: Houghton Mifflin. (Reprinted from L. Neal, *Visions of a liberated future,* 1988, New York: Thunder's Mouth)

Nero, C. L. (1998). Toward a gay black aesthetic: Signifying in contemporary black gay literature. In P. L. Hill (Ed.), *Call and response: The Riverside anthology of the African American literary tradition* (pp. 1973-1987). Boston: Houghton Mifflin.

Noriega, C. A. (1992). Between a weapon and a formula: Chicano cinema and its contexts. In C. A. Noriega (Ed.), *Chicanos and film: Representation and resistance* (pp. 141-167). Minneapolis: University of Minnesota Press.

Noriega, C. A. (1996). Imagined borders: Locating Chicano cinema in America/ America. In C. A. Noriega & A. M. López (Eds.), *The ethnic eye: Latino media arts* (pp. 3-21). Minneapolis: University of Minnesota Press.

Paget, M. A. (1993). *A complex sorrow* (M. L. DeVault, Ed.). Philadelphia: Temple University Press.

Parker, L. (1998). Race is . . . race ain't: An exploration of the utility of critical race theory in qualitative research in education. *International Journal of Qualitative Studies in Education, 11,* 43-55.

Parker, L., Deyhle, D., Villenas, S., & Nebeker, K. C. (1998). Guest editors' introduction: Critical race theory and qualitative studies in education. *International Journal of Qualitative Studies in Education, 11*, 5-6.

Pizarro, M. (1998). "Chicana/o power": Epistemology and methodology for social justice and empowerment in Chicana/o communities. *International Journal of Qualitative Studies in Education, 11*, 57-79.

Red Lodge Chamber of Commerce. (1982). *Festival of Nations, Red Lodge, Montana* [brochure]. Red Lodge, MT: Author.

Reason, P. (1993). Sacred experience and sacred science. *Journal of Management Inquiry, 2*, 10-27.

Reason, P. (Ed.). (1994). *Participation in human inquiry*. London: Sage.

Richardson, L. (1997). *Fields of play: Constructing an academic life*. New Brunswick, NJ: Rutgers University Press.

Richardson, M. (1998). Poetics in the field and on the page. *Qualitative Inquiry, 4*, 451-462.

Rinehart, R. (1998). Fictional methods in ethnography: Believability, specks of glass, and Chekhov. *Qualitative Inquiry, 4*, 200-224.

Ronai, C. R. (1998). Sketching with Derrida: An ethnography of a researcher/erotic dancer. *Qualitative Inquiry, 4*, 405-420.

Rorty, R. (1979). *Philosophy and the mirror of nature*. Princeton, NJ: Princeton University Press.

Rosen, J. (1994). Making things more public: On the political responsibility of the media intellectual. *Critical Studies in Mass Communication, 11*, 362-388.

Scheurich, J. J. (1997). *Research method in the postmodern*. London: Falmer.

Schwandt, T. A. (1997). Textual gymnastics, ethics and angst. In W. G. Tierney & Y. S. Lincoln (Eds.), *Representation and the text: Re-framing the narrative voice* (pp. 305-311). Albany: State University of New York Press.

Shange, N. (1977). *For colored girls who have considered suicide when the rainbow is enuf*. New York: Simon & Schuster. (Reprinted with the permission of Scribner, a Division of Simon & Schuster. Copyright © 1975, 1976, 1977 by Ntozake Shange.)

Sims, N. (1995). The art of literary journalism. In N. Sims & M. Kramer (Eds.), *Literary journalism: A new collection of the best American nonfiction* (pp. 3-19). New York: Ballantine.

Smith, A. D. (1993). *Fires in the mirror: Crown Heights, Brooklyn, and other identities*. Garden City, NY: Anchor. (Copyright © 1993 by Anna Deavere Smith. Used by permission of Doubleday, a division of Random House, Inc.)

Smith, A. D. (1994). *Twilight: Los Angeles, 1992*. Garden City, NY: Anchor.

Stern, C. S., & Henderson, B. (1993). *Performance texts and contexts*. New York: Longman.

Stringer, E. T. (1996). *Action research*. Thousand Oaks, CA: Sage.

Tierney, W. G. (1997). Lost in translation: Time and voice in qualitative research. In W. G. Tierney & Y. S. Lincoln (Eds.), *Representation and the text: Re-framing the narrative voice* (pp. 23-36). Albany: State University of New York Press.

Trinh T. M. (1992). *Framer framed.* New York: Routledge.

Turner, V. (1986). *The anthropology of performance.* New York: Performing Arts Journal Publications.

Ulmer, G. (1989). *Teletheory.* New York: Routledge.

West, C. (1993). Foreword. In A. D. Smith, *Fires in the mirror: Crown Heights, Brooklyn, and other identities* (pp. xvii-xxii). Garden City, NY: Anchor.

West, C. (1994). *Race matters.* New York: Vantage.

Wilkinson, C. (1997). Paradise revisited. In W. E. Reibsame (Ed.), *Atlas of the new West* (pp. 15-65). New York: W. W. Norton.

Wolfe, T. (1973). The new journalism. In T. Wolfe & E. W. Johnson (Eds.), *The new journalism: An anthology* (pp. 1-52). New York: Harper & Row.

14

Writing

A Method of Inquiry

Laurel Richardson

> The writer's object is—or should be—to hold the reader's attention. . . . I want the reader to turn the page and keep on turning to the end.
> —Barbara Tuchman, New York Times, February 2, 1989

◆ In the spirit of affectionate irreverence toward qualitative research, I consider writing as a *method of inquiry,* a way of finding out about yourself and your topic. Although we usually think about writing as a mode of "telling" about the social world, writing is not just a mopping-up activity at the end of a research project. Writing is also a way of "knowing"—a method of discovery and analysis. By writing in different ways, we discover new aspects of our topic and our relationship to it. Form and content are inseparable.

AUTHOR'S NOTE: I thank Ernest Lockridge for many discussions about this chapter, and his reading of it multiple times. I also thank Arthur Bochner, Norman Denzin, Carolyn Ellis, Michelle Fine, Patti Lather, Yvonna Lincoln, Meaghan Morris, and John Van Maanen for their generous and valuable critiques. And, finally, I am grateful to the many students who have told me they found the earlier version of this chapter useful; they have given me the energy and the will to revise it.

Writing as a method of inquiry departs from standard social science practices. It offers an additional—or alternative—research practice. In standard social scientific discourse, methods for acquiring data are distinct from the writing of the research report, the latter presumed to be an unproblematic activity, a transparent report about the world studied. When we view writing as a *method,* however, we experience "language-in-use," how we "word the world" into existence (Rose, 1992). And then we "reword" the world, erase the computer screen, check the thesaurus, move a paragraph, again and again. This "worded world" never accurately, precisely, completely captures the studied world, yet we persist in trying. Writing as a method of inquiry honors and encourages the trying, recognizing it as embryonic to the full-fledged attention to the significance of language.

Writing as a method of inquiry, then, provides a research practice through which we can investigate how we construct the world, ourselves, and others, and how standard objectifying practices of social science unnecessarily limit us and social science. Writing as method does not take writing for granted, but offers multiple ways to learn to do it, and to nurture the writer.

I have composed this chapter into two *equally* important, but differently formatted, sections. I emphasize the *equally* because the first section, an essay, has rhetorical advantages over its later-born sib. In the first section, "Writing in Contexts," I position myself as a reader/writer of qualitative research. Then, I discuss (a) the historical roots of social scientific writing, including its dependence upon metaphor and prescribed writing formats; (b) the postmodernist possibilities for qualitative writing, including creative analytic practices and their ethnographic products; and (c) the future of ethnography. In the second section, "Writing Practices," I offer a compendium of writing suggestions and exercises.

Necessarily, the chapter reflects my own process and preferences. I encourage researchers to explore their own processes and preferences through writing. Writing from our Selves should strengthen the community of qualitative researchers and the individual voices within it, because we will be more fully present in our work, more honest, more engaged.

◆ Writing in Contexts

I have a confession to make. For 30 years, I had yawned my way through numerous supposedly exemplary qualitative studies. Countless numbers of texts I abandoned half read, half scanned. I would order a new book with great anticipation—the topic was one I was interested in, the author was someone I wanted to read—only to find the text boring. It was not that the writing was complex and difficult, but that it suffered from acute and chronic passivity: passive-voiced author, passive "subjects." "Coming out" to colleagues and students about my secret displeasure with much of qualitative writing, I found a community of like-minded discontents. Undergraduates, graduates, and colleagues alike say they have found much of qualitative writing—yes—boring.

We have a serious problem: Research topics are riveting and research valuable, but qualitative books are underread. Unlike quantitative work, which can be interpreted through its tables and summaries, qualitative work carries its meaning in its entire text. Just as a piece of literature is not equivalent to its "plot summary," qualitative research is not contained in its abstracts. Qualitative research has to be read, not scanned; its meaning is in the reading.

Qualitative work could be reaching wide and diverse audiences, not just devotees of individual topics or authors. It seems foolish at best, and narcissistic and wholly self-absorbed at worst, to spend months or years doing research that ends up not being read and not making a difference to anything but the author's career. Can something be done? That is the question that drives this chapter: How do we create texts that are vital? That are attended to? That make a difference? One way to create those texts is to turn our attention to writing as a method of inquiry.

I write because I want to find something out. I write in order to learn something that I did not know before I wrote it. I was taught, however, as perhaps you were, too, not to write until I knew what I wanted to say, until my points were organized and outlined. No surprise, this static writing model coheres with mechanistic scientism and quantitative research. But, I will argue, this static writing model is itself a sociohistorical invention that reifies the static social world imagined by our 19th-century foreparents. The model has serious problems: It ignores the role of writing as a dynamic, creative process; it undermines the confidence of beginning qualitative researchers because their experience of research is inconsistent with the writing model; and it contributes to the flotilla of qualitative writing that is simply not interesting to read because adherence to the model requires writers to silence their own voices and to view themselves as contaminants.

Qualitative researchers commonly speak of the importance of the individual researcher's skills and aptitudes. The researcher—rather than the survey, the questionnaire, or the census tape—is the "instrument." The more honed the researcher, the better the possibility of excellent research. Students are taught to be open, to observe, listen, question, and participate. Yet they are taught to conceptualize writing as "writing-up" the research, rather than as an open place, a method of discovery. Promulgating "writing-up" validates a mechanistic model of writing, shutting down the creativity and sensibilities of the individual writer/researcher.

One reason, then, that some of our texts may be boring is that our sense of Self is diminished as we are homogenized through professional socialization, rewards, and punishments. Homogenization occurs through the suppression of individual voices and the acceptance of the omniscient voice of science as if it were our own. How do we put ourselves in our own texts, and with what consequences? How do we nurture our own individuality and at the same time lay claim to "knowing" something? These are both philosophically and practically difficult problems.

Historical Contexts: Writing Conventions

Language is a constitutive force, creating a particular view of reality and of the Self. Producing "things" always involves value—what to produce, what to name the productions, and what the relationship between the producers and the named things will be. Writing "things" is no exception. No textual staging is ever innocent (including this one). Styles of writing are neither fixed nor neutral but reflect the historically shifting domination of particular schools or paradigms. Social scientific writing, like all other forms of writing, is a sociohistorical construction, and, therefore, mutable.

Since the 17th century, the world of writing has been divided into two separate kinds: literary and scientific. Literature, from the 17th century onward, was associated with fiction, rhetoric, and subjectivity, whereas science was associated with fact, "plain language," and objectivity (Clifford, 1986, p. 5). Fiction was "false" because it invented reality, unlike science, which was "true" because it purportedly "reported" "objective" reality in an unambiguous voice.

During the 18th century, assaults upon literature intensified. John Locke cautioned adults to forgo figurative language lest the "conduit" between "things" and "thought" be obstructed. David Hume depicted poets as professional liars. Jeremy Bentham proposed that the ideal language would be one without words, only unambiguous symbols. Samuel Johnson's dictionary sought to fix "univocal meanings in perpetuity, much like the univocal meanings of standard arithmetic terms" (Levine, 1985, p. 4).

Into this linguistic world the Marquis de Condorcet introduced the term *social science*. He contended that "knowledge of the truth" would be "easy and error almost impossible" if one adopted precise language about moral and social issues (quoted in Levine, 1985, p. 6). By the 19th century, literature and science stood as two separate domains. Literature was aligned with "art" and "culture"; it contained the values of "taste, aesthetics, ethics, humanity, and morality" (Clifford, 1986, p. 6) and the rights to metaphoric and ambiguous language. Given to science was the belief that its words were objective, precise, unambiguous, noncontextual, and nonmetaphoric.

But because literary writing was taking a second seat to science in importance, status, impact, and truth value, some literary writers attempted to make literature a part of science. By the late 19th century, "realism" dominated both science and fiction writing (Clough, 1992). Honoré de Balzac spearheaded the realism movement in literature. He viewed society as an "historical organism" with "social species" akin to "zoological species." Writers deserving of praise, he contended, must investigate "the reasons or causes" of "social effects"—the "first principles" upon which society is based (Balzac, 1842/1965, pp. 247-249). For Balzac, the novel was an "instrument of scientific inquiry" (Crawford, 1951, p. 7). Following Balzac's lead, Emile Zola argued for "naturalism" in literature. In his famous essay "The Novel as Social Science," he argued that the "return to nature, the naturalistic evolution which marks the century, drives little by little all the manifestation of human intelligence into the same scientific path." Literature is to be "governed by science" (Zola, 1880/1965, p. 271).

As the 20th century unfolded, the relationships between social scientific writing and literary writing grew in complexity. The presumed solid demarcations between "fact" and "fiction" and between "true" and "imagined" were blurred. The blurring was most hotly debated around writing for the public—or journalism. In what Tom Wolfe dubbed the "new journalism," writers consciously blurred the boundaries between "fact" and "fiction" and consciously made themselves the center of the story. (For an excellent extended discussion of the new journalism, see Denzin, 1997, chap. 5.)

New journalists also encroached upon ethnography's province, borrowing its methods and reporting social and cultural life not as "reporters," but as social analysts. Joining those trespassers were fiction writers such as Truman Capote, Joan Didion, and Norman Mailer. Professors of literature awakened and reawakened interest in novels by minority and postcolonial writers by positioning them as "ethnographic novels"—narratives that tell about cultures through characters (see Ba, 1987; Hurston, 1942/1991).

By the 1970s, "crossovers" between writing forms spawned the naming of oxymoronic genres: "creative nonfiction," "faction," "ethnographic fiction," the "nonfiction novel," and "true fiction." By 1980, the novelist E. L. Doctorow would assert, "There is no longer any such things as fiction or nonfiction, there is only narrative" (quoted in Fishkin, 1985, p. 7).

Despite the actual blurring of genres, and despite our contemporary understanding that all writing is narrative writing, I would contend that there is still one major difference separating fiction from science writing. The difference is not whether the text *really* is fiction or nonfiction, but the claim the author makes for the text. Claiming to write "fiction" is different from claiming to write "science" in terms of the audience one seeks, the impact one might have on different publics, and how one expects "truth claims" to be evaluated. These differences should not be overlooked or minimized.

Whenever there are changes in writing styles and formats, we can expect intellectual interest in documenting and tracing those changes. Today, scholars in a host of disciplines are tracing the relationships between scientific and literary writing and are deconstructing the differences between them (see Agger, 1989; Brodkey, 1987; Brown, 1977; Clough, 1992; Edmondson, 1984; Mishler, 1989; Nelson, Megill, & McCloskey, 1987; Simons, 1990). Their deconstructive analyses concretely show how all disciplines have their own sets of literary devices—not necessarily *fiction writing* devices—and rhetorical appeals such as probability tables, archival records, and first-person accounts.

Each social science writing convention could be discussed at length, but I will address here only (a) metaphor and (b) writing format. I choose these conventions because they are omnipresent, and because I believe they are good sites for experimenting with writing as a method of inquiry (see the section headed "Writing Practices").

504

Metaphor

Metaphor, a literary device, is the backbone of social science writing. Like the spine, it bears weight, permits movement, is buried beneath the surface, and links parts together into a functional, coherent whole. As this metaphor about metaphor suggests, the essence of metaphor is experiencing and understanding one thing in terms of another. This is accomplished through comparison (e.g., "My love is like a green, green toad") or analogy (e.g. "the evening of life").

Social scientific writing uses metaphors at every "level." Social science depends upon a deep epistemic code regarding the way "that knowledge and understanding in general are figured" (Shapiro, 1985-1986, p. 198). Metaphors external to a particular piece of research prefigure the analysis with a "truth-value" code belonging to another domain (Jameson, 1981). For example, the use of *enlighten* for knowledge is a light-based metaphor, what Derrida (1982) refers to as the heliocentric view of knowledge, the passive receipt of rays. Immanent in such metaphors are philosophical and value commitments so entrenched and familiar that they can do their partisan work in the guise of neutrality, passing as literal.

Theoretical schemata are always situated in complex, systematic metaphors. Consider the following statements about theory (examples inspired by Lakoff & Johnson, 1980, p. 46):

- What is the *foundation* of your theory?
- Your theory needs *support.*
- Your position is *shaky.*
- Your argument is *falling apart.*
- Let's *construct* an argument.
- The *form* of your argument needs *buttressing.*
- Given your *framework,* no wonder your argument *fell apart.*

The italicized words express our customary, unconscious use of the metaphor "Theory is architecture." The metaphor, moreover, structures the actions we take in theorizing and what we believe constitutes theory. We try to *build* a theoretical *structure,* which we then experience as a *structure,* which has a *form* and a *foundation,* which we then experience as an *edifice,* sometimes quite *grand,* sometimes in need of *shoring up,* and sometimes in need of *dismantling,* or, more recently, *deconstructing.*

Historically, theory constructors have *deployed* combative metaphors. *Sport, game,* and *war* are common ones. These metaphoric schemes do not resonate with many women's interests, and, in addition, they have contributed to an academic intellectual culture of hostility, argumentativeness, and confrontation. In the 1970s, feminist researchers introduced and acted upon a different metaphor: "Theory is story." Not only is the personal the political, the personal is the grounding for theory. With the new metaphor for their work, many feminists altered their research and writing practices; women talking about their experience, narrativizing their lives, telling individual and collective stories became understood as women *theorizing* their lives. The boundary between "narrative" and "analysis" dissolved.

Metaphors are everywhere. Consider *functionalism, role* theory, *game* theory, *dramaturgical* analogy, *organicism,* social *evolutionism,* the social *system, ecology, labeling* theory, *equilibrium, human capital, resource mobilization,* ethnic *insurgency, developing* countries, *stratification* and *significance* tests. Metaphors organize social scientific work and affect the interpretations of the "facts"; indeed, facts are interpretable ("make sense") only in terms of their place within a metaphoric structure. The "sense making" is always value constituting—making sense in a particular way, privileging one ordering of the "facts" over others.

Writing Format

In addition to the metaphoric basis of social scientific writing, there are prescribed writing formats: How we are expected to write affects what we can write about. The referencing system in social science, for example, discourages the use of footnotes, a place for secondary arguments, novel conjectures, and related ideas. Knowledge is constituted as "focused," "problem" (hypothesis) centered, "linear," straightforward. Other thoughts are extraneous. Inductively accomplished research is to be reported deductively; the argument is to be abstracted in 150 words or less; and researchers are to identify explicitly with a theoretical label. Each of these conventions favors—creates and sustains—a particular vision of what constitutes knowledge. The conventions hold tremendous material and symbolic power over social scientists. Using them increases the probability of one's work being accepted into "core" social science journals, but they are not prima facie evidence of greater—or lesser—truth value or significance than social science writing using other conventions.

Additional social science writing conventions have governed ethnographies. Needful of distinguishing their work from travelers' and missionaries' reports as well as from imaginative writing, ethnographers adopted an impersonal, third-person voice to explain "observed phenomena" and to trumpet the authenticity of their representations (see Tedlock, Chapter 6, Volume 2). John Van Maanen (1988) identifies four conventions used in traditional ethnographies, or "realist tales": (a) *experiential author(ity)*, where the author exists only in the preface to establish "I was there" and "I am a researcher" credentials; (b) *documentary style*, or a plethora of concrete, particular details that presume to represent the typical activity, pattern, culture member; (c) *the culture member's point of view*, putatively presented through quotations, explanations, syntax, cultural clichés, and so on; and (d) *interpretive omnipotence* of the ethnographer. Many of the classic books in the social sciences are realist tales. These include Kai Erikson's *Everything in Its Path* (1976), William Foote Whyte's *Street Corner Society* (1943), Elliot Liebow's *Tally's Corner* (1967), and Carol Stack's *All Our Kin* (1974).

Other genres of qualitative writing—such as texts based on life histories or in-depth interviews—have their own sets of traditional conventions (see Mishler, 1989; Richardson, 1990). In these qualitative texts, researchers establish their credentials in the introductory or methods section; they write the body of the text as though the document and quotation snippets are naturally present, valid, reliable, and fully representative, rather than selected, pruned, and spruced up by the author for their textual appearance. As in cultural ethnographies, the assumption of *scientific authority* is rhetorically displayed in these other qualitative texts. Examples of conventional "life story" texts include Lillian Rubin's *Worlds of Pain* (1976), Sharon Kaufman's *The Ageless Self* (1986), and my own *The New Other Woman* (Richardson, 1985).

Postmodernist Context

We are fortunate, now, to be working in a postmodernist climate (see Agger, 1990; Clifford & Marcus, 1986; Denzin, 1986, 1991, 1995; Hutcheon, 1988; Lehman, 1991; Lyotard, 1984; Nicholson, 1990; Turner & Bruner, 1986), a time when a multitude of approaches to knowing and telling exist side by side. The core of postmodernism is the *doubt* that any method or theory, discourse or genre, tradition or novelty, has a universal and general claim as the "right" or the privileged form of authoritative knowledge. Postmodernism *suspects* all truth claims of masking and serving particular interests in local, cultural, and political struggles. But it does not automatically reject conventional methods of knowing and telling as false or archaic. Rather, it opens those standard methods to inquiry and introduces new methods, which are also, then, subject to critique.

The postmodernist context of *doubt,* then, distrusts all methods equally. No method has a privileged status. The superiority of "science" over "literature"—or, from another vantage point, "literature" over "science"—is challenged. But a postmodernist position does allow us to know "something" without claiming to know everything. Having a partial, local, historical knowledge is still knowing. In some ways, "knowing" is easier, however, because postmodernism recognizes the situational limitations of the knower. Qualitative writers are off the hook, so to speak. They don't have to try to play God, writing as disembodied omniscient narrators claiming universal, atemporal general knowledge; they can eschew the questionable metanarrative of scientific objectivity and still have plenty to say as situated speakers, subjectivities engaged in knowing/ telling about the world as they perceive it.

A particular kind of postmodernist thinking that I have found especially helpful is *poststructuralism* (for an overview, see Weedon, 1987; for application of the perspective in a research setting, see Davies, 1994). Poststructuralism links language, subjectivity, social organization, and power. The centerpiece is language. Language does not "reflect" social reality, but produces meaning, creates social reality. Different languages and different discourses within a given language divide up the world and give it meaning in ways that are not reducible to one another. Language is how social organization and power are defined and contested and the place where our sense of selves, our *subjectivity,* is constructed. Understanding language as competing discourses, competing ways of giving meaning and of organizing the world, makes language a site of exploration and struggle.

Language is not the result of one's individuality; rather, language constructs the individual's subjectivity in ways that are historically and locally specific. What something means to individuals is dependent on the discourses available to them. For example, being hit by one's spouse is differently experienced if it is thought of within the discourse of "normal marriage," "husbands' rights," or "wife battering." If a woman sees male violence as "normal" or a "husband's right," then she is unlikely to see it as "wife battering," an illegitimate use of power that should not be tolerated.

Similarly, when a man is exposed to the discourse of "childhood sexual abuse," he may recategorize and remember his own traumatic childhood experiences. Experience and memory are thus open to contradictory interpretations governed by social interests and prevailing discourses. The individual is both site and subject of these discursive struggles for identity and for remaking memory. Because individuals are subject to multiple and competing discourses in many realms, their subjectivity is shifting and contradictory, not stable, fixed, rigid.

Poststructuralism thus points to the *continual cocreation of Self and social science:* Each is known through the other. Knowing the self and knowing about the subject are intertwined, partial, historical, local knowledges. Poststructuralism, then, permits—nay, invites—no, incites—us to reflect upon our method and explore new ways of knowing.

Specifically, poststructuralism suggests two important things to qualitative writers: First, it directs us to understand ourselves reflexively as persons writing from particular positions at specific times; and second, it frees us from trying to write a single text in which we say everything at once to everyone. Nurturing our own voices releases the censorious hold of "science writing" on our consciousness, as well as the arrogance it fosters in our psyche: Writing is validated as a method of knowing.

Creative Analytic Practices: CAP Ethnography

In the wake of postmodernist—including poststructuralist, feminist, queer, and critical race theory—critiques of traditional qualitative writing practices, qualitative work now appears in multiple venues in different forms. Science-writing prose is not held sacrosanct. The ethnographic genre has been blurred, enlarged, altered to include poetry, drama, conversations, readers' theater, and so on. These ethnographies are like each other in that they are produced through *creative analytic practices.* I have settled upon calling this class of ethnographies *creative analytic practice ethnography,* or *CAP ethnography.* This label can include new work, future work, and older work, wherever the author has moved outside conventional social scientific writing.

I know that any concept or acronym is problematic, subject to critique. Yet the more I thought about what to name these genre-breaking ethnographies, the more I liked the complex metaphoric resonances of the acronym CAP. The English word *cap* comes from the Latin for head, *caput.*

Using "head" to signal ethnographic breaching work can help break down the mind/body duality. The "head" is both mind and body and more, too. Producers of CAP ethnography are using their "heads." The products, although mediated throughout the body, cannot manifest without "headwork."

Cap—both noun (product) and verb (process)—has multiple common and idiomatic meanings and associations, some of which refract the playfulness of the genre: a rounded head covering; a special head covering indicating occupation or membership in a particular group; the top of a building, or fungus; a small explosive charge; any of several sizes of writing paper; putting the final touches on; lying on top of; surpassing, outdoing. And then there are the other associated words from the Latin root, such as *capillary* and *capital(ism)*, which humble and contextualize the labor.

The practices that produce CAP ethnography are *both* creative *and* analytic. Those holding the dinosaurian belief that "creative" and "analytic" are contradictory and incompatible modes are standing in the path of a meteor. They are doomed for extinction. Witness the evolution, proliferation, and diversity of new ethnographic "species" during the past two decades.

Here is but a sampling of the many "species" of CAP ethnography: *autoethnography* (Behar, 1993, 1996; Bruner, 1996; Church, 1995; Ellis, 1993, 1995a, 1995b, 1998; Frank, 1995; Geertz, 1988; Gerla, 1995; Goetting & Fenstermaker, 1995; Karp, 1996; Kondo, 1990; Krieger, 1991, 1996; Lawrence-Lightfoot, 1994; McMahon, 1996; Shostak, 1996; Slobin, 1995; Steedman, 1986; Yu, 1997; Zola, 1982), *fiction-stories* (Cherry, 1995; Diversi, 1998a, 1998b; Frohock, 1992; Richardson & Lockridge, 1998; Rinehart, 1998; Shelton, 1995; Sparkes, 1997; Stewart, 1989; Williams, 1991; Wilson, 1965; Wolf, 1992), *poetry* (Baff, 1997; Brady, 1991; Diamond, 1982; Glesne, 1997; Norum, in press; Patai, 1988; Prattis, 1985; Richardson, 1992a), *drama* (Ellis & Bochner, 1992; Paget, 1990; Richardson, 1993, 1996a; Richardson & Lockridge, 1991), *performance texts* (Denzin, 1997; McCall & Becker, 1990; Mienczakowski, 1996; Richardson, 1998, 1999a, 1999b), *polyvocal texts* (see Butler & Rosenblum, 1991; Daly & Dienhart, 1998; Krieger, 1983; Pandolfo, 1997; Schneider, 1991), *readers' theater* (see Donmoyer & Yennie-Donmoyer, 1995), *responsive readings* (see Richardson, 1992b), *aphorisms* (Rose, 1992, 1993), *comedy and satire* (see Barley, 1986, 1988), *visual presentations* (see Harper, 1987; Jacobs, 1984; McCall,

Gammel, & Taylor, 1994), *allegory* (Lawton, 1997, pp. 193-214), *conversation* (see Ellis & Bochner, 1996b; Richardson & Lockridge, 1998), *layered accounts* (Jago, 1996; Ronai, 1992, 1995), *writing-stories* (see Lawton, 1997; Richardson, 1995, 1997; St. Pierre, 1997a, 1997b), and *mixed* genres (see Angrosino, 1998; Brown, 1991; Church, 1999: Davies, 1989; Dorst, 1989; Fine, 1992; hooks, 1990; Jipson & Paley, 1997; Jones, 1998; Lather, 1991; Lather & Smithies, 1997; Lee, 1996; Linden, 1992; Pfohl, 1992; Richardson, 1997; Rose, 1989; Stoller, 1989; Trinh, 1989; Ulmer, 1989; Visweswaran, 1994; Walkerdine, 1990; Williams, 1991; Wolf, 1992).

For more than a decade, what I am calling CAP ethnography has been labeled *experimental* or *alternative* (see Van Maanen, 1995). Unintentionally, however, those labels have reinscribed traditional ethnographic practices as the standard, the known, accepted, preferred, tried-and-true mode of doing and representing qualitative research. I believe that reinscription is now unnecessary, false, and deleterious. CAP ethnographies are not alternative or experimental; they are in and of themselves valid and desirable representations of the social. Into the foreseeable future, these ethnographies may indeed be the most valid and desirable representations, for they invite people in; they open spaces for thinking about the social that elude us now.

CAP ethnography displays the *writing process* and the *writing product* as deeply intertwined; both are privileged. The product cannot be separated from the producer or the mode of production or the method of knowing. Because all research—traditional and CAP ethnography—is now produced within the broader postmodernist climate of "doubt," readers (and reviewers) want and deserve to know how the researcher claims to know. How does the author position the Self as a knower and teller? These questions engage intertwined problems of subjectivity, authority, authorship, reflexivity, and process on the one hand and representational form on the other.

Postmodernism claims that writing is always partial, local, and situational, and that our Self is always present, no matter how much we try to suppress it—but only partially present, for in our writing we repress parts of ourselves, too. Working from that premise frees us to write material in a variety of ways: to tell and retell. There is no such thing as "getting it right"—only "getting it" differently contoured and nuanced. When using creative analytic practices, ethnographers learn about their topics and about themselves that which was unknowable and unimaginable using conventional analytic procedures, metaphors, and writing formats. Even if one chooses to write an article in a conventional form, trying on different modes of writing is a practical and powerful way to expand one's interpretive skills, raise one's consciousness, and bring a fresh perspective to one's research.

It is beyond this chapter's scope for me to outline or comment here on the scores of new ethnographic practices and forms. And it is far beyond that scope for me to discuss practices that exceed the written page—performance pieces, readers' theater, museum displays, choreographed research findings, fine-art representations, hypertexts, and so on—although I welcome these additions to the qualitative repertoire. Instead, I will address a class of genres that deploy literary devices to re-create lived experience and evoke emotional responses. I call these *evocative representations*. I resist providing the reader with snippets from these forms, because snippets will not do them justice. I will describe some texts, but I have no desire to valorize a new canon. Again, *process* rather than product is the purpose of this chapter.

Evocative forms display interpretive frameworks that demand analysis of themselves as cultural products and as methods for rendering the social. Evocative representations are a striking way of seeing through and beyond social scientific naturalisms. Casting social science into evocative forms reveals the rhetoric and the underlying labor of the production, as well as social science's potential as a human endeavor, because evocative writing touches us where we live, in our bodies. Through it we can experience the self-reflexive and transformational process of self-creation. Trying out evocative forms, we relate differently to our material; we know it differently. We find ourselves attending to feelings, ambiguities, temporal sequences, blurred experiences, and so on; we struggle to find a textual place for ourselves and our doubts and uncertainties.

One form of evocative writing is *autoethnography*. (This topic is fully covered by Ellis & Bochner in Chapter 6 of this volume; see also Fine et al., Volume 1, Chapter 4.) Autoethnographies are highly personalized, revealing texts in which authors tell stories about their own lived experiences, relating the personal to the cultural. The power of these narratives depends upon their rhetorical staging as "true stories," stories about events that really happened to the writers. In telling these stories, the writers call upon such fiction-writing techniques as dramatic recall, strong imagery, fleshed-out characters, unusual phrasings, puns, subtexts, allusions, flashbacks and flashforwards, tone shifts, synecdoche, dialogue, and interior monologue. Through these techniques, the writers construct sequences of events, or "plots," holding back on interpretation, asking readers to "relive" the events emotionally, with the writers. These narratives seek to meet literary criteria of coherence, verisimilitude, and interest. Some narratives of the Self are staged as imaginative renderings; others are staged as personal essays, striving for honesty, revelation, the "larger picture." In either case, autoethnographers are somewhat relieved of the problem of speaking for the "Other," because they are the "Other" in their texts.

Related to autoethnography without necessarily invoking the writing strategies mentioned above are narratives about the writing process itself. I call these *writing-stories* (Richardson, 1997). These are narratives about contexts in which the writing is produced. They situate the author's writing in other parts of the author's life, such as disciplinary constraints, academic debates, departmental politics, social movements, community structures, research interests, familial ties, and personal history. They offer critical reflexivity about the writing-self in different contexts as a valuable creative analytic practice. They evoke new questions about the self and the subject; they remind us that our work is grounded, contextual, and rhizomatic. They can evoke deeper parts of the Self, heal wounds, enhance the sense of self—or even alter one's sense of identity.

In *Fields of Play: Constructing an Academic Life* (1997), I make extensive use of writing-stories to contextualize 10 years of my sociological work, creating a text more congruent with poststructural understandings of the situated nature of knowledge. Putting my papers and essays in the chronological order in which they were conceptualized, I sorted them into two piles—"keeper" and "reject." When I reread my first keeper—a presidential address to the North Central Sociological Association—memories of being patronized, marginalized, and punished by my department chair and dean reemerged. I stayed with those memories and wrote a writing-story about the disjunction between my departmental life and my disciplinary reputation. Writing the story was not emotionally easy; in the writing I was reliving horrific experiences, but writing it released the anger and pain. Many academics who read that story recognize it as congruent with their experiences, their untold stories.

I worked chronologically through the keeper pile, rereading and then writing the writing-story evoked by the rereading. Different facets, different contexts. Some stories required checking my journals and files, but most did not. Some stories were painful and took an interminable length of time to write, but writing them loosened their shadow hold on me. Other stories are joyful and remind me of the good fortunes I have in friends, colleagues, family.

Writing-stories sensitize us to the potential consequences of all of our writing by bringing home—inside our homes and workplaces—the ethics of representation. Writing-stories are not about people and cultures "out there"—ethnographic subjects (or objects)—they are about ourselves, our work spaces, disciplines, friends, and families. What can we say? With what consequences? Writing-stories bring the danger and poignancy of ethnographic representation up close and personal.

Each writing-story offers its writer an opportunity to make a situated and pragmatic ethical decision about whether and where to publish the story. For the most part, I have found no ethical problem in publishing stories that reflect the abuse of power by administrators; I consider the damage done by them far greater than any discomfort my stories might cause them. In contrast, I feel constraint when writing about my family members. Anything I have published about them, I have checked out with them; in the case of more distant family members, I have changed their names and identifying characteristics. Some of my recent writing I will not publish for a while because it would be too costly to me and my familial relations to do so.

Graduate students have found the idea of the writing-story useful for thinking through and writing about their research experiences. Some use the writing-story as an alternative or supplement to the traditional methods chapter and, as Judith Lawton (1997) has done, to link the narratives of those they have researched.

Yet to be developed as a subgenre of writing-stories are what we might call *microprocess writing-stories* (see also Meloy, 1993). Who has not looked at the computer screen, read a paragraph he or she has written, and then chosen to alter it? Who has not had their subsequent writing affected by what they have already written? How does the process of writing passages and reading them back to yourself "open new questions and issues that feed back and emanate from the earlier passages?" (A. P. Bochner, personal communication, May 10, 1998). How is a changed Self evoked through the hands-on/eyes-on feedback process?

Related to this subgenre is computer technology and the textual page layout: typefaces, font sizes, split pages, boxed inserts, running bottom text, images, frames. How are choices made? With what impact on the producer and the reader? How does the ease of manipulating page formats and typographical style contribute to—or distract from—the evocativeness of the text? Authors' discoveries about their topics and themselves? These are questions looking for writing-stories.

Unlike the two forms discussed above, an evocative form about which there is an extensive literature is *ethnographic fiction* (see Banks & Banks, 1998). (For a more extended discussion of this and other narrative forms, see Tedlock, Volume 2, Chapter 6.) "Fiction writing," according to novelist Ernest Lockridge (personal communication, 1998), "is using the imagination to discover and embody truth." Social science writers who claim that their work is fiction privilege their imaginations, seeking to express their visions of social scientific "truth." Usually they encase their stories—whether about themselves or a group or culture—in settings they have studied ethnographically; they display cultural norms through their characters. In addition to the techniques used by self-narrators (see above), ethnographic fiction writers might draw upon devices such as alternative points of view, deep characterization, third-person voice, and the omniscient narrator. (I do not think any ethnographic fiction writers, yet, write from the point of view of the unreliable narrator; see Lockridge, 1987.)

There are some advantages and some disadvantages to claiming one's ethnographic writing is fiction. Staging qualitative research as fiction frees the author from some constraints, protects the author from criminal or other charges, and may protect the identities of those studied. But competing in the publishing world of "literary fiction" is very difficult. Few succeed. Moreover, if one's desire is to effect social change through one's research, fiction is a rhetorically poor writing strategy. Policy makers prefer materials that claim to be not "nonfiction" even, but "true research."

Another evocative form is *poetic representation*. A poem, as Robert Frost articulates it, is "the shortest emotional distance between two points"—the speaker and the reader. Writing sociological interviews as poetry, for example, displays the role of the *prose trope* in constituting knowledge. When we read or hear poetry, we are continually nudged into recognizing that the text has been constructed. But all texts are constructed—prose ones, too; therefore, poetry helps problematize reliability, validity, transparency, and "truth."

Writing "data" as poetic representations reveals the constraining belief that the purpose of a social science text is to convey information as facts or themes or notions existing independent of the contexts in which they were found or produced—as if the story we have recorded, transcribed, edited, and written up in prose snippets is the one and only true one: a "science" story. Standard prose writing conceals the handprint of the sociologist who produced the final written text.

When people talk, moreover, whether as conversants, storytellers, informants, or interviewees, their speech is closer to poetry than it is to sociological prose (Tedlock, 1983). Writing up interviews as poems, honoring the speaker's pauses, repetitions, alliterations, narrative strategies, rhythms, and so on, may actually better represent the speaker than the practice of quoting in prose snippets. Further, poetic devices—rhythms, silences, spaces, breath points, alliterations, meter, cadence, assonance, rhyme, and off-rhyme—engage the listener's body, even if the mind resists and denies. "Poetry is above all a concentration of the power of language which is the power of our ultimate relationship to everything in the universe. It is as if forces we can lay claim to in no other way become present to us in sensuous form" (DeShazer, 1986, p. 138). Settling words together in new configurations lets us hear, see, and *feel* the world in new dimensions. Poetry is thus a *practical* and *powerful* method for analyzing social worlds.

"Louisa May's Story of Her Life" is an example of poetic construction that challenges epistemological assumptions (Richardson, 1997). It is a 5-page narrative poem I created from a 36-page transcript of my in-depth interview with "Louisa May," an unwed mother. In writing Louisa May's story, I drew upon both scientific and literary criteria. This was a greater literary challenge than a sociological one because Louisa May used no images or sensory words and very few idioms. The poem, therefore, had to build upon other poetic devices, such as repetition, pauses, meter, rhyme, and off-rhyme. Without putting words in her mouth, which would violate my sociological sensibilities, I used her voice, diction, hill-southern rhythms, and tone. I wrote her life—as she told it to me—as a historically situated exemplar of sense making. Her life, as she speaks it, is a "normal one." The political subtext, as I wrote it, is "Mother Courage in America."

Ethnographic drama is another evocative way of shaping an experience without losing the experience. It can blend realist, fictional, and poetic techniques; it can reconstruct the "sense" of an event from multiple "as-lived" perspectives; it can allow all the conflicting "voices" to be heard, relieving the researcher of having to be judge and arbiter (Davies et al., 1997; Johnston, 1997); and it can give voice to what is unspoken but present, for example, "cancer" as portrayed in Paget's (1990) ethnographic drama or abortion as in Ellis and Bochner's (1992) drama. When the material to be displayed is intractable, unruly, multisited, and emotionally laden, drama is more likely to recapture the experience than is standard writing.

Constructing drama raises the postmodern debates about "oral" and "written" texts. Which comes first? Which one should be (is) privileged, and with what consequences? Why the bifurcation between "oral" and "written"? Originating in the lived experience, encoded as field notes, transformed into an ethnographic play, performed, taped-recorded, and then reedited for publication, the printed script might well be fancied the definitive or "valid" version, particularly to those who privilege the published over the "original," the performance, or even the lived experience. What happens if we accept this validity claim? Dramatic construction provides multiple sites of invention and potential contestation for validity, the blurring of oral and written texts, rhetorical moves, ethical dilemmas, and authority/authorship. It doesn't just "talk about" these issues, *it is* these issues (see Davies et al., 1997; Johnston, 1997; Richardson, 1997).

A last evocative form to consider is *mixed genres*. The scholar draws freely in his or her productions from literary, artistic, and scientific genres, often breaking the boundaries of each of those as well. In these productions, the scholar might have different "takes" on the same topic, what I think of as a postmodernist deconstruction of triangulation.

In traditionally staged research, we valorize "triangulation." (For discussion of triangulation as method, see Denzin, 1978; Flick, 1998. For an application, see Statham, Richardson, & Cook, 1991). In triangulation, a researcher deploys "different methods"—such as interviews, census data, and documents—to "validate" findings. These methods, however, carry the *same domain* assumptions, including the assumption that there is a "fixed point" or "object" that can be triangulated. But in postmodernist mixed-genre texts, we do not triangulate; we *crystallize*. We recognize that there are far more than "three sides" from which to approach the world.

I propose that the central imaginary for "validity" for postmodernist texts is not the triangle—a rigid, fixed, two-dimensional object. Rather, the central imaginary is the crystal, which combines symmetry and substance with an infinite variety of shapes, substances, transmutations, multidimensionalities, and angles of approach. Crystals grow, change, alter, but are not amorphous. Crystals are prisms that reflect externalities *and* refract within themselves, creating different colors, patterns, and arrays, casting off in different directions. What we see depends upon our angle of repose. Not triangulation, crystallization. In postmodernist mixed-genre texts, we have moved from plane geometry to light theory, where light can be *both* waves *and* particles.

Crystallization, without losing structure, deconstructs the traditional idea of "validity" (we feel how there is no single truth, we see how texts validate themselves), and crystallization provides us with a deepened, complex, thoroughly partial, understanding of the topic. Paradoxically, we know more and doubt what we know. Ingeniously, we know there is always more to know.

The construction and reception of the narrative poem mentioned above, "Louisa May's Story of Her Life" (Richardson, 1997), is emblematic of crystallization. That work generated alternate theories and perspectives for writing and for living, deconstructed traditional notions of validity, glancingly touching some projects, lighting others. My life has been deeply altered through the research and writing of the poem, and "Louisa May" has touched wide and diverse audiences, even inspiring some to change their research and writing practices.

In one section of *Fields of Play* (1997), I tell two interwoven stories of "writing illegitimacy": Louisa May's story and the research story—its production, dissemination, reception, and consequences for me. There are multiple illegitimacies in the stories: a child out of wedlock; poetic representation of research findings; a feminine voice in social sciences; ethnographic research on ethnographers and dramatic representation of that research; emotional presence of the writer; and work *jouissance*.

I had thought the research story was complete, not necessarily the only story that could be told, but one that reflected fairly, honestly, and sincerely what my research experiences have been. I still believe that. But missing from the research story, I came to realize, were the personal, biographical experiences that led me to author such a story.

The idea of "illegitimacy," I have come to acknowledge, has had a compelling hold on me. In my research journal I wrote, "My career in the social sciences might be viewed as one long adventure into illegitimacies." I asked myself, Why am I drawn to constructing "texts of illegitimacy," including the text of my academic life? What is this struggle I have with the academy—being in it and against it at the same time? How is my story like and unlike the stories of others struggling to make sense of themselves, to retrieve suppressed selves, to act ethically?

Refracting "illegitimacy" through allusions, glimpses, extended views, I came to write a personal essay, "Vespers," the final essay in *Fields of Play*.

"Vespers" located my academic life in childhood experiences and memories; it deepened my knowledge of myself and has resonated with others' experiences in academia. In turn, the writing of "Vespers" has refracted, again, giving me desire, strength, and enough self-knowledge to narrativize other memories and experiences—to give myself agency, to construct myself anew, for better or for worse.

We also see this crystallization process in several recent mixed-genre books. Margery Wolf, in *A Thrice-Told Tale* (1992), takes the same event and tells it as fictional story, field notes, and a social scientific paper. John Stewart, in *Drinkers, Drummers and Decent Folk* (1989), writes poetry, fiction, ethnographic accounts, and field notes about Village Trinidad. In *Schoolgirl Fictions* (1990), Valerie Walkerdine develops/displays the theme that "masculinity and femininity are fictions which take on the status of fact" (p. xiii) by incorporating into the book journal entries, poems, essays, photographs of herself, drawings, cartoons, and annotated transcripts. Ruth Linden's *Making Stories, Making Selves: Feminist Reflections on the Holocaust* (1992) intertwines autobiography, academic writing, and survivors' stories in a Helen Hooven Santmyer Prize in Women's Studies book, which was her dissertation. John Van Maanen's *Tales from the Field* (1988) presents his research on police as realist, confessional, and impressionist narratives. Patti Lather and Chris Smithies's *Troubling the Angels: Women Living With HIV/AIDS* (1997) displays high theory, researchers' stories, women's support group transcripts, and historical and medical information, using innovative text layouts. John Dorst's *The Written Suburb* (1989) presents a geographic site as site, image, idea, discourse, and an assemblage of texts. Stephen Pfohl's *Death at the Parasite Cafe* (1992) employs collage strategies and synchronic juxtapositions, blurring critical theory and militant art forms.

In some mixed-genre productions, the writer/artist roams freely around topics, breaking our sense of the externality of topics, developing our sense of how topic and self are twin constructed. Susan Krieger's *Social Science and the Self: Personal Essays on an Art Form* (1991) is a superb example. The book is "design oriented," reflecting Krieger's attachment to Pueblo potters and Georgia O'Keeffe, and, as she says, it "looks more like a pot or a painting than a hypothesis" (p. 120). Trinh T. Minh-ha's *Woman Native Other* (1989) breaks down writing conventions within each of the essays that constitute the book, mixing poetry, self-reflection, feminist criticism, photographs, and quotations to help readers experience postcoloniality. In *I've Known Rivers: Lives of Loss and Liberation* (1994), Sara Lawrence-Lightfoot uses fiction-writing techniques and self-reflexivity to tell stories of being Afro-American and professional. Anthologies also reflect these mixed genres. My own book *Fields of Play: Constructing an Academic Life* (1997) in its entirety tells the story of my intellectual and political struggles in academia through personal essays, dramas, poems, writing-stories, e-mail messages, and sociology articles. Anthologies also present mixed genres. Some examples are Carolyn Ellis and Arthur Bochner's *Composing Ethnography: Alternative Forms of Qualitative Writing* (1996a), Ellis and Michael Flaherty's *Investigating Subjectivity: Research on Lived Experience* (1992), Ruth Behar and Deborah Gordon's *Women Writing Culture* (1995). The book series *Studies in Symbolic Interaction,* and the journal *Qualitative Inquiry* mix genres in their pages.

Whither and Whence?

The contemporary postmodernist context in which we work as qualitative researchers is a propitious one. It provides an opportunity for us to review, critique, and re-vision writing. Although we are freer to present our texts in a variety of forms to diverse audiences, we have different constraints arising from self-consciousness about claims to authorship, authority, truth, validity, reliability. Self-reflexivity brings to consciousness some of the complex political/ideological agendas hidden in our writing. Truth claims are less easily validated now; desires to speak "for" others are suspect. The greater freedom to experiment with textual form, however, does not guarantee a better product. The opportunities for writing worthy texts—books and articles that are "good reads"—are multiple, exciting, and demanding. But the work is harder. The guarantees are fewer. There is a lot more for us to think about.

One thing for us to think about is whether writing CAP ethnography for publication is a luxury open only to those who have academic sinecure. Are the tenured doing a disservice to students by introducing them to these different forms of writing? Will teaching students hereticisms "deskill" them? Alienate them from their discipline? (Would we ask these questions about students' learning a second language?) A related issue is, if students are taught writing as inquiry, what criteria should be brought to bear upon their work? These are heady ethical, pedagogical, aesthetic, and practical questions. I struggle with them in my teaching, writing, and collegial discussions. I have no definitive answers, but I do have some thoughts on the issues.

Writing is a process of discovery. My purpose is not to turn us into poets, novelists, or dramatists—few of us will write well enough to succeed in those competitive fields. Most of us, like Poe, will be at best only almost poets. Rather, my intention is to encourage individuals to accept and nurture their own voices. The researcher's self-knowledge and knowledge of the topic develop through experimentation with point of view, tone, texture, sequencing, metaphor, and so on. Another skill, another language—the student's own—is added to the student's repertoire. The science-writing enterprise is demystified. The deepened understanding of a Self deepens the text. Even the analysis paralysis that afflicts some readers of postmodernism is attenuated when writers view their work as process rather than as definitive representation.

Students will not lose the language of science when they learn to write in other ways, any more than students who learn a second language lose their first (Y. S. Lincoln, personal communication, 1998). Rather, acquiring a second language enriches students in two ways: It gains them entry into a new culture and literature, and it leads them to a deepened understanding of their first language, not just grammatically, but as a language that constructs how they view the world.

Writing in traditional ways does not prevent us from writing in other ways for other audiences at other times (Denzin, 1994; Richardson, 1990). There is no single way—much less one "right" way—of staging a text. Like wet clay, the material can be shaped. Learning alternative ways of writing increases our repertoires, increases the numbers and kinds of audiences we might reach.

As I write this chapter, I imagine four friendly audiences: graduate students, curious quantitative researchers, traditionally inclined qualitative researchers, and creative analytic practitioners. I want to clarify and teach—and, yes, proselytize.

Who is your audience? What are your purposes? Understanding how to stage your writing *rhetorically* increases your chances of getting published and reaching your intended audiences. Deconstructing traditional writing practices makes writers more conscious of writing conventions and, therefore, more competently able to make choices.

The new ways of writing do, however, invoke conversation about criteria for judging an ethnographic work—new or traditional. Traditional ethnographers of goodwill have legitimate concerns about how their students' work will be evaluated if they choose to write CAP ethnography. I have no definitive answers to ease their concerns, but I do have some ideas and preferences.

I see the ethnographic project as humanly situated, always filtered through human eyes and human perceptions, bearing both the limitations and the strengths of human feelings. Scientific superstructure is always resting on the foundation of human activity, belief, understandings. I emphasize ethnography as constructed through *research practices*. Research practices are concerned with enlarged understanding. Science offers some research practices; literature, creative arts, memory work (Davies, 1994; Davies et al., 1997), and introspection (Ellis, 1991) offer still others. Researchers have many practices from which to choose, and ought not be constrained by habits of other people's minds.

I believe in holding CAP ethnography to high and difficult standards; mere novelty does not suffice. Here are five of the criteria I use when reviewing papers or monographs submitted for social scientific publication.

1. *Substantive contribution:* Does this piece contribute to our *understanding* of social life? Does the writer demonstrate a deeply grounded (if embedded) social scientific perspective? How has this perspective informed the construction of the text? (See "Writing Practices," below, for some suggestions on how to accomplish this.)

2. *Aesthetic merit:* Rather than reducing standards, CAP ethnography adds another standard. Does this piece succeed aesthetically? Does the use of creative analytic practices open up the text, invite interpretive responses? Is the text artistically shaped, satisfying, complex, and not boring? (Creative writing is a skill that can be developed through reading, courses, workshops, and practice; see the suggestions listed in the "Writing Practices" section.)

3. *Reflexivity:* Is the author cognizant of the epistemology of postmodernism? How did the author come to write this text? How was the information gathered? Are there ethical issues? How has the author's subjectivity been both a producer and a product of this text? Is there adequate self-awareness and self-exposure for the reader to make judgments about the point of view? Does the author hold him- or herself accountable to the standards of knowing and telling of the people he or she has studied?

4. *Impact:* Does this affect me? Emotionally? Intellectually? Does it generate new questions? Move me to write? Move me to try new research practices? Move me to action?

5. *Expression of a reality:* Does this text embody a fleshed out, embodied sense of lived experience? Does it seem "true"—a credible account of a cultural, social, individual, or communal sense of the "real"?

These are five of my criteria. Science is one lens; creative arts another. We see more deeply using two lenses. I want to look through both lenses, to see a "social science art form."

I strongly disagree, then, with those who claim ethnography should be a "science guild," a "craft" with "tacit rules," apprentices, trade "secrets," and "disciplined," "responsible" journeymen (i.e., professors) who enact rules that check "artistic pretensions and excesses" (see Schwalbe, 1995; see also Richardson, 1996b). This medieval vision limits ethnographic exploration, patrols the boundaries of intellectual thought, and aligns qualitative research ideologically with those who would discipline and punish postmodern ideas within social science. Policing, however, is always about bodies. It is always about real live people. Should the medieval vision triumph, what real live people are likely to be excluded?

What I have learned from my teaching and conversations with colleagues is this: Minorities within academia, including ethnic and racial, postcolonial, gay and lesbian, physically challenged, and returning students, find the turn to creative analytic practices as beckoning. These researchers desire the opportunity to be "responsible" to the "guild" while honoring their responsibilities to their traditions, their cultures, and their sense of the meaningful life.

Welcoming these researchers creates an enriched, diversified, socially engaged, nonhegemonic community of qualitative researchers. Everyone profits—the communities of origin and identification and the qualitative research community. The implications of race and gender would be stressed not because it would be "politically correct," but because race and gender *are axes* through which symbolic and actual worlds have been constructed. Members of nondominant worlds know that, and would insist that this knowledge be honored (see Margolis & Romero, 1998). The blurring of humanities and social sciences would be welcomed not because it is "trendy," but because the blurring coheres more truly with the life senses and learning styles of so many. This new qualitative community could, through its theory, analytic practices, and diverse membership, reach beyond academia, teaching all of us about social injustice and methods for alleviating it. What qualitative researcher interested in social life would not feel enriched by membership in such a culturally diverse and inviting community?

Furthermore, CAP ethnography is now firmly established within the social sciences. There are prestigious places for students and others to publish. *Sociological Quarterly, Symbolic Interaction, American Anthropologist, Journal of Contemporary Ethnography, Journal of Aging Studies, Qualitative Inquiry, International Journal of Qualitative Research in Education, Qualitative Studies in Psychology, Qualitative Sociology, Waikato Journal of Education,* and *Text and Performance Quarterly* routinely publish CAP ethnography. The annuals *Studies in Symbolic Interaction* and *Cultural Studies* showcase evocative writing. Publishers such as Routledge, University of Chicago Press, University of Michigan Press, Indiana University Press, University of Pennsylvania Press, Rutgers University Press, Temple University Press, and Sage Publications regularly publish new ethnography by both well-known and lesser-known authors. Alta-Mira Press (formerly a division of Sage) boasts the excellent Ethnographic Alternatives book series, which is dedicated to qualitative research that blurs the boundaries between the social sciences and humanities. New York University Press has launched the Qualitative Studies in Psychology series, which is receptive to creative-analytic texts. Trade and university presses are increasingly resistant to publishing old-style monographs, and traditional ethnographers are writing more reflexively and self-consciously (see Thorne, 1993). Even those opposed to postmodernism legitimate it through dialogue (Whyte, 1992). Throughout the social sciences, convention papers include transgressive presentations. Entire conferences are devoted to experimentation, such as the "Redesigning Ethnography" conference at the University of Colorado and the Year 2000 Couch-Stone Symbolic Interaction Symposium.

At least three well-respected interpretive programs—at the University of Illinois (under Norman Denzin), the University of South Florida (under Arthur Bochner and Carolyn Ellis), and the University of Nevada at Las Vegas (with Andrea Fontana and Kate Hausbreck)—teach creative analytic practices. The Ohio State University's Folklore Studies (under Amy Shuman) and its Cultural Studies in Education Ph.D. program (under Patti Lather) privilege postpositivism. Dissertations violating the traditional five-chapter, social science writing style format are accepted in the United States, Canada, England, New Zealand, and Australia. Elliot Eisner

(1996), art educator and past president of the American Educational Research Association, has gone further. He proposes that novels should be accepted as Ph.D. dissertations in education. All of these changes in academic practices are signs of *paradigm changes.*

In the 1950s, the sociology of science was a new, reflexively critical area. Today, the sociology of science undergirds theory, methods, and interdisciplinary science studies. In the 1960s, "gender" emerged as a theoretical perspective. Today, gender studies is one of the largest (if not the largest) subfield in the social sciences. In part, science studies and gender studies thrived because they identified normative assumptions of social science that falsely limited knowledge. They spoke "truly" to the everyday experiences of social scientists. The new areas hit us where we lived—in our work and in our bodies. They offered alternative perspectives for understanding the experienced world.

Today, the postmodernist critique is having the same impact on the social sciences that science studies and gender have had, and for similar reasons. Postmodernism identifies unspecified assumptions that hinder us in our search for understanding "truly," and it offers different practices that work. We feel its "truth"—its moral, intellectual, aesthetic, emotional, intuitive, embodied pull. Each researcher is likely to respond to that pull differently, which should lead to writing that is more diverse, more author centered, less boring, and humbler. These are propitious times. Some even speak of their work as spiritual.

And Thence

The ethnographic life is not separable from the Self. Who we are and what we can be—what we can study, how we can write about that which we study—is tied to how a knowledge system disciplines itself and its members, its methods for claiming authority over both the subject matter and its members.

We have inherited some ethnographic rules that are arbitrary, narrow, exclusionary, distorting, and alienating. Our task is to find concrete practices through which we can construct ourselves as ethical subjects engaged in ethical ethnography—inspiring to read and to write. Some of these practices involve working within theoretical schemata (sociology of knowledge, feminism, critical race theory, constructionism, poststructuralism) that challenge grounds of authority; writing on topics that matter, personally and collectively; *jouissance*; experimenting with different writing formats and audiences simultaneously; locating ourselves in multiple discourses and communities; developing critical literacy; finding ways to write/present/teach that are less hierarchal and univocal; revealing institutional secrets; using positions of authority to increase diversity, both in academic appointments and in journal publications; self-reflexivity; giving in to synchronicity; asking for what we want, like cats; not flinching from where the writing takes us, emotionally or spiritually; and honoring the embodiedness and spatiality of our labors.

What creative analytic practices in ethnography will eventually produce, I do not know. But I do know that the ground has been staked, the foundation laid, the scaffolding erected, and diverse and adventurous settlers have moved on in.

. . . and Forever After

The *Handbook* editors really do want all the contributors to predict the future of qualitative research. I thought I had. Oh, how I resist! But here goes.

Forty years ago, I was an undergraduate who detested the yearlong course "History of Western Civilization"—2,500 years, five continents, 700 countries, six trillion names, dates, wars, and places. I thought the final would decimate me. But fortune smiled. In addition to the zillions of "objective" questions, we were given a take-home essay: "What is the future of history?" I said—in 10 pages or less—that the future of history was *both* toward unity *and* toward diversity. I got an A+ on that essay. I think I'll stick with it. That's the way I see the future of qualitative research, too. We will be clearer about its domain and more welcoming of diverse representations.

The domain's metaphor will be the "text"—or some other equally outrageously encompassing image—but the meaning and construction of text will far exceed the written page, the computer screen, and even the hypertext: two-dimensional, three-dimensions, refractive, layered texts. Discussions of the boundaries between literature and science will seem quaint, as "writing"—in the future understood as any textual construction—will be routinely understood as a "method of inquiry." And, therefore, it will have to be challenged!

Oh, dear!

◆ Writing Practices

> Writing, the creative effort, should come first—at least for some
> part of every day of your life. It is a wonderful blessing if you
> will use it. You will become happier, more enlightened, alive,
> impassioned, light hearted and generous to everybody else. Even
> your health will improve. Colds will disappear and all the other
> ailments of discouragement and boredom.
>
> —Brenda Ueland, *If You*
> *Want to Write*, 1938/1987

In what follows, I suggest some ways of using writing as a method of knowing. I have chosen exercises that have been productive for students because they demystify writing, nurture the researcher's voice, and serve the process of discovery. I wish I could guarantee them to bring good health as well. The practices are organized around topics discussed in the text.

Metaphor

Using old, worn-out metaphors, although easy and comfortable, after a while invites stodginess and stiffness. The stiffer you get, the less flexible you are. Your ideas get ignored. If your writing is clichéd, you'll not "stretch your own imagination" (Ouch! Hear the cliché of pointing out the cliché!) and you'll bore people.

1. In traditional social scientific writing, the metaphor for theory is that it is a "building" (structure, foundation, construction, deconstruction, framework, grand, and so on). Consider a different metaphor, such as "theory as a tapestry" or "theory as an illness." Write a paragraph about "theory" using your metaphor. Do you "see" differently and "feel" differently about theorizing using an unusual metaphor?

2. Consider alternative sensory metaphors for "knowledge" other than the heliocentric one mentioned in the text. What happens when you rethink/resense "knowledge" as situated in voice? In touch?

3. Look at one of your papers and highlight your metaphors and images. What are you saying through metaphors that you did not realize you were saying? What are you reinscribing? Do you want to? Can you find different metaphors that change how you "see" ("feel") the material? your

relationship to it? Are your mixed metaphors pointing to confusion in yourself or to social science's glossing over of ideas?

4. Take a look at George Lakoff and Mark Johnson's *Metaphors We Live By* (1980). It is a wonderful book, a compendium of examples of metaphors in everyday life and how they affect our ways of perceiving, thinking, and acting. What everyday metaphors are shaping your knowing/writing?

Writing Formats

1. Choose a journal article that exemplifies the mainstream writing conventions of your discipline. How is the argument staged? Who is the presumed audience? How does the paper inscribe ideology? How does the author claim authority over the material? Where is the author? Where are you in this paper? Who are the subjects and who are the objects of research?

2. Choose a journal article that exemplifies excellence in qualitative research. How has the article built upon normative social science writing? How is authority claimed? Where is the author? Where are you in the article? Who are the subjects and who are the objects of research?

3. Choose a paper you have written for a class or that you have published that you think is pretty good. How did you follow the norms of your discipline? Were you conscious of doing so? How did you stage your paper? What parts did the professor/reviewer laud? How did you depend upon those norms to carry your argument? Did you elide some difficult areas through vagueness, jargon, calls to authorities, or other rhetorical devices? What voices did you exclude in your writing? Who is the audience? Where are the subjects in the paper? Where are you? How do you feel about the paper now? About your process of constructing it?

Creative Analytic Writing Practices

1. Join or start a writing group. This could be a writing support group, a creative writing group, a poetry group, a dissertation group, or another kind of group. (On dissertation and article writing, see Becker, 1986; Fox, 1985; Richardson, 1990; Wolcott, 1990.)

2. Work through a creative writing guidebook. Natalie Goldberg (1986, 1990), Rust Hills (1987), Brenda Ueland (1938/1987), and Deena Weinstein (1993) all provide excellent guides.

3. Enroll in a creative writing workshop or class. These experiences are valuable for both beginning and experienced researchers.

4. Use "writing up" your field notes as an opportunity to expand your writing vocabulary, habits of thought, and attentiveness to your senses, and as a bulwark against the censorious voice of science. Where better to develop your sense of self, your voice, than in the process of doing your research? Apply creative writing skills to your field notes. You may need to rethink what you've have been taught about objectivity, science, and the ethnographic project. What works for me is to give different labels to different content. Building on the work of Glaser and Strauss (1967), I use four categories, which you may find of value:

- *Observation notes* (ON): These are as concrete and detailed as I am able to make them. I want to think of them as fairly accurate renditions of what I see, hear, feel, taste, and so on. I stay close to the scene as I experience it through my senses.
- *Methodological notes* (MN): These are messages to myself regarding how to collect "data"—who to talk to, what to wear, when to phone, and so on. I write a lot of these because I like methods, and I like to keep a process diary of my work.
- *Theoretical notes* (TN): These are hunches, hypotheses, poststructuralist connections, critiques of what I am doing/thinking/seeing. I like writing these because they open my field note texts to alternative interpretations and a critical epistemological stance. They provide a way of keeping me from being hooked on one view of reality.
- *Personal notes* (PN): These are uncensored feeling statements about the research, the people I am talking to, my doubts, my anxieties, my pleasures. I want all my feelings out on paper because I know they are affecting what/how I lay claim to know. I also know they are a great source for hypotheses; if I am feeling a certain way in a setting, it is likely that others might feel that way too. Finally, writing personal notes is a way for me to know myself better, a way of using writing as method of inquiry into the self.

5. Keep a journal. In it, write about your feelings about your work. This not only frees up your writing, it becomes the "historical record" for the writing of a narrative of the Self or a writing-story about the writing process.

6. Write a writing autobiography. This would be the story of how you learned to write: the dicta of English classes (topic sentences? outlines? the five-paragraph essay?), the dicta of social science professors, your experi-

ences with teachers' comments on your papers, how and where you write now, your idiosyncratic "writing needs," your feelings about writing and about the writing process. (This is an exercise that Arthur Bochner uses.)

7. If you wish to experiment with evocative writing, a good place to begin is by transforming your field notes into drama. See what ethnographic rules you are using (such as fidelity to the speech of the participants, fidelity in the order of the speakers and events) and what literary ones you are invoking (such as limits on how long a speaker speaks, keeping the "plot" moving along, developing character through actions). Writing dramatic presentations accentuates ethical considerations. If you doubt that, contrast writing up an ethnographic event as a "typical" event with writing it as a play, with you and your hosts cast in roles that will be performed before others. Who has ownership of spoken words? How is authorship attributed? What if people do not like how they are characterized? Are courtesy norms being violated? Experiment here with both oral and written versions of your drama.

8. Experiment with transforming an in-depth interview into a poetic representation. Try using only the words, rhythms, figures of speech, breath points, pauses, syntax, and diction of the speaker. Where are you in the poem? What do you know about the interviewee and about yourself that you did not know before you wrote the poem? What poetic devices have you sacrificed in the name of science?

9. Experiment with writing narratives of the self. Keep in mind Barbara Tuchman's warning: "The writer's object is—or should be—to hold the reader's attention. . . . I want the reader to turn the page and keep on turning to the end. This is accomplished only when the narrative moves steadily ahead, not when it comes to a weary standstill, overlaced with every item uncovered in the research" (in *New York Times,* February 2, 1989).

10. Try writing a text using different typefaces, font sizes, and textual placement. How have the traditional ways of using print affected what you know and how you know it?

11. Write a "layered text" (see Lather & Smithies, 1997; Ronai, 1992). The layered text is a strategy for putting yourself into your text and putting your text into the literatures and traditions of social science. Here is one possibility. First, write a short narrative of the Self about some event that is especially meaningful to you. Then step back and look at the narrative from your disciplinary perspective and insert into the narrative—beginning, midsections, end, wherever—relevant analytic statements or

references, using a different typescript, alternative page placement, split pages, or other ways to mark the text. The layering can be multiple, with different ways of marking different theoretical levels, theories, speakers, and so on. (This is an exercise that Carolyn Ellis uses.)

12. Try some other strategy for writing new ethnography for social scientific publications. Try the "seamless" text, in which previous literature, theory, and methods are placed in textually meaningful ways, rather than in disjunctive sections (for a excellent example, see Bochner, 1997); try the "sandwich" text, in which traditional social science themes are the "white bread" around the "filling" (C. Ellis, personal communication, April 27, 1998); or try an "epilogue" explicating the theoretical analytic work of the creative text (see Eisner, 1996).

13. Consider a fieldwork setting. Consider the various subject positions you have or have had within it. For example, in a store you might be a salesclerk, customer, manager, feminist, capitalist, parent, child, and so on. Write about the setting (or an event in the setting) from several different subject positions. What do you "know" from the different positions? Next, let the different points of view dialogue with each other. What do you discover through these dialogues?

14. Consider a paper you have written (or your field notes). What have you left out? Who is not present in this text? Who has been repressed or marginalized? Rewrite the text from that point of view.

15. Write your "data" in three different ways—for example, as a narrative account, as a poetic representation, and as readers' theater. What do you know in each rendition that you did not know in the other renditions? How do the different renditions enrich each other?

16. Write a narrative of the Self from your point of view (such as something that happened in your family or in a seminar). Then interview another participant (such as family or seminar member) and have that person tell you his or her story of the event. See yourself as part of the other person's story in the same way he or she is part of your story. How do you rewrite your story from the other person's point of view? (This is an exercise Carolyn Ellis uses.)

17. Collaborative writing is a way to see beyond one's own naturalisms of style and attitude. This is an exercise that I have used in my teaching, but it would be appropriate for a writing group as well. Each member writes a story of his or her life. It could be a feminist story, a success story, quest story, cultural story, professional socialization story, realist tale, confessional tale, or another kind of story. All persons' stories are photocopied

for the group. The group is then broken into subgroups (I prefer groups of three), and each subgroup collaborates on writing a new story, the collective story of its members. The collaboration can take any form: drama, poetry, fiction, narrative of the selves, realism, whatever the subgroup chooses. The collaboration is shared with the entire group. All members then write about their feelings about the collaboration and what happened to their stories, their lives, in the process.

18. Memory work (see Davies, 1994; Davies et al., 1997) is another collaborative research and writing strategy. Stories shared in the group are discussed and then rewritten, with attention paid to the discourses that are shaping the stories in each of their tellings. As more people tell their stories, individuals remember more details of their own stories, or develop new stories. Participants discover what their stories have in common, perhaps even writing what Bronwyn Davies (1994) calls a "collective biography."

19. Consider a part of your life outside of or before academia with which you have deeply resonated. Use that resonance as a "working metaphor" for understanding and reporting your research. Students have created excellent reports by using unexpected lenses, such as choreography, principles of flower arrangement, art composition, and sportscasting, to view their lives and the lives of others. Writing from that which resonates with your life nurtures a more integrated life.

20. Different forms of writing are appropriate for different audiences and different occasions. Try writing the same piece of research for an academic audience, a trade audience, the popular press, policy makers, research hosts, and so on (see Richardson, 1990). This is an especially powerful exercise for dissertation students who may want to share their results in a "user-friendly" way with those they studied.

21. Write writing-stories (see Richardson, 1997), or reflexive accounts of how you happened to write pieces you have written. Your writing-stories can be about disciplinary politics, departmental events, friendship networks, collegial ties, family, and personal biographical experiences. Writing-stories situate your work in contexts, tying what can be a lonely and seemingly separative task to the ebbs and flows of your life, your self. Writing these stories reminds us of the continual cocreation of the self and social science.

> Willing is doing something you know already—there is no new imaginative understanding in it. And presently your soul gets

frightfully sterile and dry because you are so quick, snappy, and efficient about doing one thing after another that you have no time for your own ideas to come in and develop and gently shine.

—Brenda Ueland, If You
Want to Write, 1938/1987

◆ References

Agger, B. (1989). *Reading science: A literary, political and sociological analysis.* Dix Hills, NY: General Hall.

Agger, B. (1990). *The decline of discourse: Reading, writing and resistance in post-modern capitalism.* Bristol, PA: Falmer.

Angrosino, M. V. (1998). *Opportunity House: Ethnographic stories of mental retardation.* Walnut Creek, CA: AltaMira.

Ba, M. (1987). *So long a letter* (M. Bode-Thomas, Trans.). Portsmouth, NH: Heinemann.

Baff, S. J. (1997). Realism and naturalism and dead dudes: Talking about literature in 11th grade English. *Qualitative Inquiry, 3,* 468-490.

Balzac, H. de (1965). Preface to *The human comedy,* from *At the Sign of the cat and racket* (C. Bell, Trans., 1897). In R. Ellman & C. Feidelson, Jr. (Eds.), *The modern tradition: Backgrounds of modern literature* (pp. 246-254). New York: Oxford University Press. (Original work published 1842)

Banks, A., & Banks, S. P. (Eds.). (1998). *Fiction and social research: By ice or fire.* Walnut Creek, CA: AltaMira.

Barley, N. (1986). *Ceremony: An anthropologist's misadventures in the African bush.* New York: Henry Holt.

Barley, N. (1988). *Not a pleasant sport.* New York: Henry Holt.

Becker, H. S. (1986). *Writing for social scientists: How to finish your thesis, book, or article.* Chicago: University of Chicago Press.

Behar, R. (1993). *Translated woman: Crossing the border with Esperanza's story.* Boston: Beacon.

Behar, R. (1996). *The vulnerable observer: Anthropology that breaks your heart.* Boston: Beacon.

Behar, R., & Gordon, D. A. (Eds.). (1995). *Women writing culture.* Berkeley: University of California Press.

Bochner, A. (1997). It's about time: Narrative and the divided self. *Qualitative Inquiry, 3,* 418-438.

Brady, I. (Ed.). (1991). *Anthropological poetics.* Savage, MD: Rowman & Littlefield.

Brodkey, L. (1987). *Academic writing as social practice.* Philadelphia: Temple University Press.

Brown, K. M. (1991). *Mama Lola: A Vodou priestess in Brooklyn.* Berkeley: University of California Press.

Brown, R. H. (1977). *A poetic for sociology.* Cambridge: Cambridge University Press.

Bruner, E. M. (1996). My life in an ashram. *Qualitative Inquiry, 2,* 300-319.

Butler, S., & Rosenblum, B. (1991). *Cancer in two voices.* San Francisco: Spinster.

Cherry, K. (1995). The best years of their lives: A portrait of a residential home for people with AIDS. *Symbolic Interaction, 18,* 463-486.

Church, K. (1995). *Forbidden narratives: Critical autobiography as social science.* Newark, NJ: Gordon & Breach.

Church, K. (1999). *Fabrications: Stitching ourselves together* [Online]. Ottawa: Canadian Museum of Civilization. Available Internet: http://www/grannyg.bc.ca/Fabrications/index.html

Clifford, J. (1986). Introduction: Partial truths. In J. Clifford & G. E. Marcus (Eds.), *Writing culture: The poetics and politics of ethnography* (pp. 1-26). Berkeley: University of California Press.

Clifford, J., & Marcus, G. E. (Eds.). (1986). *Writing culture: The poetics and politics of ethnography.* Berkeley: University of California Press.

Clough, P. T. (1992). *The end(s) of ethnography: From realism to social criticism.* Newbury Park, CA: Sage.

Crawford, M. A. (1951). *Introduction to* Old Goriot. New York: Penguin.

Daly, K., & Dienhart, A. (1998). Navigating the family domain: Qualitative field dilemmas. In S. Grills (Ed.), *Doing ethnographic research: Fieldwork settings* (pp. 97-120). Thousand Oaks, CA: Sage.

Davies, B. (1989). *Frogs and snails and feminist tales: Preschool children.* St. Leonards, Australia: Allen & Unwin.

Davies, B. (1994). *Poststructuralist theory and classroom practice.* Geelong, Victoria, Australia: Deakin University Press.

Davies, B., Dormer, S., Honan, E., McAllister, N., O'Reilly, R., Rocco, S., & Walker, A. (1997). Ruptures in the skin of silence: A collective biography. *Hecate: A Woman's Interdisciplinary Journal, 23*(1), 62-79.

Denzin, N. K. (1978). *The research act: A theoretical introduction to sociological methods* (2nd ed.). New York: McGraw-Hill.

Denzin, N. K. (1986). A postmodern social theory. *Sociological Theory, 4,* 194-204.

Denzin, N. K. (1991). *Images of postmodern society.* Newbury Park, CA: Sage.

Denzin, N. K. (1994). Evaluating qualitative research in the poststructural moment: The lessons James Joyce teaches us. *International Journal of Qualitative Studies in Education, 7,* 295-308.

Denzin, N. K. (1995). *The cinematic society: The voyeur's gaze.* Thousand Oaks, CA: Sage.

Denzin, N. K. (1997). *Interpretive ethnography: Ethnographic practices for the 21st century.* Thousand Oaks, CA: Sage.

Derrida, J. (1982). *Margins of philosophy* (A. Bass, Trans.). Chicago: University of Chicago Press.

DeShazer, M. K. (1986). *Inspiring women: Reimagining the muse.* New York: Pergamon.

Diamond, S. (1982). *Totems.* Barrytown, NY: Open Book/Station Hill.

Diversi, M. (1998a). Glimpses of street life: Representing lived experience through short stories. *Qualitative Inquiry, 4,* 131-147.

Diversi, M. (1998b). Late for school. *Waikato Journal of Education, 4,* 78-86.

Donmoyer, R., & Yennie-Donmoyer, J. (1995). Data as drama: Reflections on the use of readers theater as a mode of qualitative data display. *Qualitative Inquiry, 1,* 402-428.

Dorst, J. D. (1989). *The written suburb: An American site, an ethnographic dilemma.* Philadelphia: University of Pennsylvania Press.

Edmondson, R. (1984). *Rhetoric in sociology.* London: Macmillan.

Eisner, E. (1996). Should a novel count as a dissertation in education? *Research in the Teaching of English, 30,* 403-427.

Ellis, C. (1991). Sociological introspection and emotional experience. *Symbolic Interaction, 14,* 23-50.

Ellis, C. (1993). Telling the story of sudden death. *Sociological Quarterly, 34,* 711-730.

Ellis, C. (1995a). *Final negotiations: A story of love, loss, and chronic illness.* Philadelphia: Temple University Press.

Ellis, C. (1995b). The other side of the fence: Seeing black and white in a small southern town. *Qualitative Inquiry, 1,* 147-168.

Ellis, C. (1998). "I hate my voice": Coming to terms with minor bodily stigmas. *Sociological Quarterly, 39,* 517-537.

Ellis, C., & Bochner, A. P. (1992). Telling and performing personal stories: The constraints of choice in abortion. In C. Ellis & M. G. Flaherty (Eds.), *Investigating subjectivity: Research on lived experience* (pp. 79-101). Newbury Park, CA: Sage.

Ellis, C., & Bochner, A. P. (Eds.). (1996a). *Composing ethnography: Alternative forms of qualitative writing.* Walnut Creek, CA: AltaMira.

Ellis, C., & Bochner, A. P. (1996b). Introduction: Talking over ethnography. In C. Ellis & A. P. Bochner (Eds.), *Composing ethnography: Alternative forms of qualitative writing* (pp. 13-48). Walnut Creek, CA: AltaMira.

Ellis, C., & Flaherty, M. G. (Eds.). (1992). *Investigating subjectivity: Research on lived experience.* Newbury Park, CA: Sage.

Erikson, K. T. (1976). *Everything in its path: Destruction of the community in the Buffalo Creek flood.* New York: Simon & Schuster.

Fine, M. (1992). *Disruptive voices: The possibility of feminist research.* Ann Arbor: University of Michigan Press.

Fishkin, S. F. (1985). *From fact to fiction: Journalism and imaginative writing in America.* Baltimore: Johns Hopkins University Press.

Flick, U. (1998). *An introduction to qualitative research: Theory, method and applications.* London: Sage.

Fox, M. F. (Ed.). (1985). *Scholarly writing and publishing: Issues, problems, and solutions.* Boulder, CO: Westview.

Frank, A. (1995). *The wounded storyteller: Body, illness, and ethics.* Chicago: University of Chicago Press.

Frohock, F. (1992). *Healing powers.* Chicago: University of Chicago Press.

Geertz, C. (1988). *Works and lives: The anthropologist as author.* Stanford, CA: Stanford University Press.

Gerla, J. P. (1995). An uncommon friendship: Ethnographic fiction around finance equity in Texas. *Qualitative Inquiry, 1,* 168-188.

Glaser, B. G., & Strauss, A. L. (1967). *The discovery of grounded theory: Strategies for qualitative research.* Chicago: Aldine.

Glesne, C. E. (1997). That rare feeling: Re-presenting research through poetic transcription. *Qualitative Inquiry, 3,* 202-221.

Goetting, A., & Fenstermaker, S. (1995). *Individual voices, collective visions: Fifty years of women in sociology.* Philadelphia: Temple University Press.

Goldberg, N. (1986). *Writing down the bones: Freeing the writer within.* Boston: Shambala.

Goldberg, N. (1990). *Wild mind: Living the writer's life.* New York: Bantam.

Harper, D. (1987). *Working knowledge: Skill and community in a small shop.* Chicago: University of Chicago Press.

Hills, R. (1987). *Writing in general and the short story in particular.* Boston: Houghton Mifflin.

hooks, b. (1990). *Yearning: Race, gender, and cultural politics.* Boston: South End.

Hurston, Z. N. (1991). *Dust tracks on a road.* New York: HarperCollins. (Original work published 1942)

Hutcheon, L. (1988). *A poetics for postmodernism: History, theory, fiction.* New York: Routledge.

Jacobs, J. (1984). *The mall: An attempted escape from everyday life.* Prospect Heights, IL: Waveland.

Jago, B. J. (1996). Postcards, ghosts, and fathers: Revising family stories. *Qualitative Inquiry, 2,* 495-516.

Jameson, F. (1981). *The political unconscious: Narrative as a socially symbolic act.* Ithaca, NY: Cornell University Press.

Jipson, J., & Paley, N. (Eds.). (1997). *Daredevil research: Re-creating analytic practice.* New York: Peter Lang.

Johnston, M. (with Educators for Collaborative Change). (1997). *Contradictions in collaboration: New thinking on school/university partnerships.* New York: Teachers College Press.

Jones, S. H. (1998). *Kaleidoscope notes: Writing women's music and organizational culture.* Walnut Creek, CA: AltaMira.

Karp, D. (1996). *Speaking of sadness.* New York: Oxford University Press.

Kaufman, S. (1986). *The ageless self: Sources of meaning in later life.* Madison: University of Wisconsin Press.

Kondo, D. K. (1990). *Crafting selves: Power, gender, and discourses of identity in a Japanese workplace.* Chicago: University of Chicago Press.

Krieger, S. (1983). *The mirror dance: Identity in a women's community.* Philadelphia: Temple University Press.

Krieger, S. (1991). *Social science and the self: Personal essays on an art form.* New Brunswick, NJ: Rutgers University Press.

Krieger, S. (1996). *The family silver: Essays on relationships among women.* Berkeley: University of California Press.

Lakoff, G., & Johnson, M. (1980). *Metaphors we live by.* Chicago: University of Chicago Press.

Lather, P. (1991). *Getting smart: Feminist research and pedagogy with/in the postmodern.* New York: Routledge.

Lather, P., & Smithies, C. (1997). *Troubling the angels: Women living with HIV/AIDS.* Boulder, CO: Westview.

Lawrence-Lightfoot, S. (1994). *I've known rivers: Lives of loss and liberation.* Boston: Addison-Wesley.

Lawton, J. E. (1997). *Reconceptualizing a horizontal career line: A study of seven experienced urban English teachers approaching career end.* Unpublished doctoral dissertation, Ohio State University.

Lee, V. (1996). *Granny midwives and black women writers.* New York: Routledge.

Lehman, D. (1991). *Signs of the times: Deconstruction and the fall of Paul de Man.* New York: Poseidon.

Levine, D. N. (1985). *The flight from ambiguity: Essays in social and cultural theory.* Chicago: University of Chicago Press.

Liebow, E. (1967). *Tally's corner: A study of Negro street corner men.* Boston: Little, Brown.

Linden, R. R. (1992). *Making stories, making selves: Feminist reflections on the Holocaust.* Columbus: Ohio State University Press.

Lockridge, E. (1987). F. Scott Fitzgerald's *Trompe l'oeil* and *The great Gatsby's* buried plot. *Journal of Narrative Technique, 17,* 163-183.

Lyotard, J.-F. (1984). *The postmodern condition: A report on knowledge* (G. Bennington & B. Massumi, Trans.). Minneapolis: University of Minnesota Press.

Margolis, E., & Romero, M. (1998). The department is very male, very white, very old, and very conservative: The functioning of the hidden curriculum in graduate sociology departments. *Harvard Educational Review, 68,* 1-32.

McCall, M. M., & Becker, H. S. (1990). Performance science. *Social Problems, 37,* 116-132.

McCall, M. M., Gammel, L., & Taylor, S. (1994). *The one about the farmer's daughter: Stereotypes and self portraits.* Minneapolis: Country Characters.

McMahon, M. (1996). Significant absences. *Qualitative Inquiry, 2,* 320-336.

Meloy, J. M. (1993). Problems of writing and representation in qualitative inquiry. *International Journal of Qualitative Studies in Education, 6,* 315-330.

Mienczakowski, J. (1996). An ethnographic act: The construction of consensual theater. In C. Ellis & A. P. Bochner (Eds.), *Composing ethnography: Alternative forms of qualitative writing* (pp. 244-266). Walnut Creek, CA: AltaMira.

Mishler, E. G. (1989). *Research interviewing: Context and narrative.* Cambridge, MA: Harvard University Press.

Nelson, J. S., Megill, A., & McCloskey, D. N. (Eds.). (1987). *The rhetoric of the human sciences: Language and argument in scholarship and human affairs.* Madison: University of Wisconsin Press.

Nicholson, L. J. (Ed.). (1990). *Feminism/postmodernism.* New York: Routledge.

Norum, K. E. (in press). School patterns: A sextet. *International Journal of Qualitative Studies in Education.*

Paget, M. (1990). Performing the text. *Journal of Contemporary Ethnography, 19,* 136-155.

Pandolfo, S. (1997). *Impasse of the angels: Scenes from a Moroccan space of memory.* Chicago: University of Chicago Press.

Patai, D. (1988). Constructing a self: A Brazilian life story. *Feminist Studies, 14,* 142-163.

Pfohl, S. J. (1992). *Death at the Parasite Cafe: Social science (fictions) and the postmodern.* New York: St. Martin's.

Prattis, I. (Ed.). (1985). *Reflections: The anthropological muse.* Washington, DC: American Anthropological Association.

Richardson, L. (1985). *The new other woman: Contemporary single women in affairs with married men.* New York: Free Press.

Richardson, L. (1990). *Writing strategies: Reaching diverse audiences.* Thousand Oaks, CA: Sage.

Richardson, L. (1992a). The consequences of poetic representation: Writing the other, rewriting the self. In C. Ellis & M. G. Flaherty (Eds.), *Investigating subjectivity: Research on lived experience.* Newbury Park, CA: Sage.

Richardson, L. (1992b). Resisting resistance narratives: A representation for communication. In N. K. Denzin (Ed.), *Studies in symbolic interaction: A research annual* (Vol. 13, pp. 77-83). Greenwich, CT: JAI.

Richardson, L. (1993). The case of the skipped line: Poetics, dramatics and transgressive validity. *Sociological Quarterly, 34,* 695-710.

Richardson, L. (1995). Writing-stories: Co-authoring "The sea monster," a writing-story. *Qualitative Inquiry, 1,* 189-203.

Richardson, L. (1996a). Educational birds. *Journal of Contemporary Ethnography, 25,* 6-15.

Richardson, L. (1996b). A sociology of responsibility. *Qualitative Research, 19,* 519-524.

Richardson, L. (1997). *Fields of play: Constructing an academic life.* New Brunswick, NJ: Rutgers University Press.

Richardson, L. (1998). The politics of location: Where am I now? *Qualitative Inquiry, 4,* 41-48.

Richardson, L. (1999a). Dead again in Berkeley. *Qualitative Inquiry, 5,* 141-144.

Richardson, L. (1999b). Paradigms lost [Distinguished Lecture]. *Symbolic Interaction, 22,* 79-91.

Richardson, L., & Lockridge, E. (1991). *The sea monster:* An ethnographic drama. *Symbolic Interaction, 14,* 335-340.

Richardson, L., & Lockridge, E. (1998). Fiction and ethnography: A conversation. *Qualitative Inquiry, 4,* 328-336.

Rinehart, R. (1998). Sk8ing. *Waikato Journal of Education, 4,* 87-100.

Ronai, C. R. (1992). The reflexive self through narrative: A night in the life of an erotic dancer/researcher. In C. Ellis & M. G. Flaherty (Eds.), *Investigating subjectivity: Research on lived experience* (pp. 102-124). Newbury Park, CA: Sage.

Ronai, C. R. (1995). Multiple reflections of child sexual abuse: An argument for a layered account. *Journal of Contemporary Ethnography, 23,* 395-426.

Rose, D. (1989). *Patterns of American culture: Ethnography and estrangement.* Philadelphia: University of Pennsylvania Press.

Rose, E. (1992). *The werald.* Boulder, CO: Waiting Room.

Rose, E. (1993). *The worulde.* Boulder, CO: Waiting Room.

Rubin, L. B. (1976). *Worlds of pain: Life in the working-class family.* New York: Basic Books.

Schneider, J. (1991). Troubles with textual authority in sociology. *Symbolic Interaction, 14,* 295-320.

Schwalbe, M. (1995). The responsibilities of sociological poets. *Qualitative Sociology, 18,* 393-412.

Shapiro, M. (1985-1986). Metaphor in the philosophy of the social sciences. *Cultural Critique, 2,* 191-214.

Shelton, A. (1995). The man at the end of the machine. *Symbolic Interaction, 18,* 505-518.

Shostak, A. (Ed.). (1996). *Private sociology: Unsparing reflections, uncommon gains.* Dix Hills, NY: General Hall.

Simons, H. W. (1990). *Rhetoric in the human sciences.* London: Sage.

Slobin, K. (1995). Fieldwork and subjectivity: On the ritualization of seeing a burned child. *Symbolic Interaction, 18,* 487-504.

Sparkes, A. C. (1997). Ethnographic fiction and representing the absent other. *Sport, Education, and Society, 2,* 25-40.

Stack, C. B. (1974). *All our kin: Strategies for survival in a black community.* New York: Harper & Row.

Statham, A., Richardson, L., & Cook, J. A. (1991). *Gender and university teaching: A negotiated difference.* Albany: State University of New York Press.

Steedman, K. (1986). *Landscape for a good woman: A story of two lives.* New Brunswick, NJ: Rutgers University Press.

Stewart, J. (1989). *Drinkers, drummers and decent folk: Ethnographic narratives of Village Trinidad.* Albany: State University of New York Press.

Stoller, P. (1989). *The taste of ethnographic things: The senses in anthropology.* Philadelphia: University of Pennsylvania Press.

St. Pierre, E. A. (1997a). Circling the text: Nomadic writing practices. *Qualitative Inquiry, 3,* 403-417.

St. Pierre, E. A. (1997b). Nomadic inquiry in the smooth spaces of the field: A preface. *International Journal of Qualitative Studies in Education, 10,* 175-189.

Tedlock, D. (1983). *The spoken word and the work of interpretation.* Philadelphia: University of Pennsylvania Press.

Thorne, B. (1993). *Gender play.* New Brunswick, NJ: Rutgers University Press.

Trinh T. M. (1989). *Woman, native, other: Writing postcoloniality and feminism.* Bloomington: Indiana University Press.

Turner, V., & Bruner, E. M. (Eds.). (1986). *The anthropology of experience.* Urbana: University of Illinois Press.

Ueland, B. (1987). *If you want to write: A book about art, independence and spirit.* Saint Paul, MN: Graywolf. (Original work published 1938)

Ulmer, G. (1989). *Teletheory: Grammatology in the age of video.* New York: Routledge.

Van Maanen, J. (1988). *Tales of the field: On writing ethnography.* Chicago: University of Chicago Press.

Van Maanen, J. (Ed.). (1995). *Representation in ethnography.* Thousand Oaks, CA: Sage.

Visweswaran, K. (1994). *Fictions of feminist ethnography.* Minneapolis: University of Minnesota Press.

Walkerdine, V. (1990). *Schoolgirl fictions.* London: Verso.

Weedon, C. (1987). *Feminist practice and poststructuralist theory.* New York: Basil Blackwell.

Weinstein, D. (1993). *Writing for your life: A guide and companion to the inner worlds.* New York: HarperCollins.

Whyte, W. F. (1943). *Street corner society: The social structure of an Italian slum.* Chicago: University of Chicago Press.

Whyte, W. F. (1992). In defense of *Street corner society. Journal of Contemporary Ethnography, 21,* 52-68.

Williams, P. J. (1991). *The alchemy of race and rights: Diary of a law professor.* Cambridge, MA: Harvard University Press.

Wilson, C. (1965). *Crazy February: Death and life in the Mayan highlands of Mexico.* Berkeley: University of California Press.

Wolcott, H. F. (1990). *Writing up qualitative research.* Newbury Park, CA: Sage.

Wolf, M. A. (1992). *A thrice-told tale: Feminism, postmodernism, and ethnographic responsibility.* Stanford, CA: Stanford University Press.

Yu, P.-L. (1997). *Hungry lightning: Notes of a woman anthropologist in Venezuela.* Albuquerque: University of New Mexico Press.

Zola, E. (1965). The novel as social science. In R. Ellman & C. Feidelson, Jr. (Eds.), *The modern tradition: Backgrounds of modern literature* (pp. 270-289). New York: Oxford University Press. (Original work published 1880)

Zola, I. K. (1982). *Missing pieces: A chronicle of living with a disability.* Philadelphia: Temple University Press.

15

Anthropological Poetics

Ivan Brady

◆ Poetics is a topic usually associated with the systematic study of literature, but, especially in its modern concern with texts as "cultural
artifacts," it extends to anthropology in several ways.[1] One obvious connection is that, like other academic disciplines, anthropology is "literary"
in that it conveys its information primarily through writing. This textual
base lets anthropology share with more conventional studies of poetics an
interest in text construction, the authority of the text, semiotic behavior
and the production of meaning in discourse, and, in general, all the philosophical and critical problems associated with mimesis—the representation and successful communication of experience in any form, especially
as problematized in texts. It also brings to the fore something that anthropology is predisposed to engage because of its own diverse history: debate
over the place of art and science in the social sciences and the humanities.
Anthropology has intellectual camps at both extremes, that is, strong
science orientations that conscientiously attempt to exclude more artistic

AUTHOR'S NOTE: This chapter is a substantially revised and expanded version of Brady
(1996). It has benefitted from generous readings by James A. Boon, Norman K. Denzin,
Robert Borofsky, Dan Rose, Miles Richardson, Yvonna S. Lincoln, James W. Fernandez, and
Barbara Tedlock, and I wish to thank them. Any remaining wrongheadedness is entirely my
own. "Shaman's Song" is reprinted with permission of Station Hill Press (Barrytown, New
York), from Stanley Diamond's *Totems* (1982, p. 94).

or humanistic methods and interpretations, and vice versa (see Fujimara, 1998). Overall there is a compromise of identity: Anthropology sees itself as an "artful science" (Brady, 1990a, 1993). That leaves room for engaging a variety of postmodern challenges from other disciplines, including much that has arisen under the labels *literary* and *poetic* (Brady, 1991b).

Cultural anthropology in particular encompasses both individualized studies and systematic comparisons of cross-cultural experience, so its potential poetic sources are broadly based. That has allowed anthropologists to feed into and draw reciprocally on several disciplines while developing their own specialized studies of the forms and content of poetic production in their own societies, in other cultures, as well as in their communications *about* other cultures.[2] Playing in such fields begs a variety of critical issues, from cultural relativism to competing philosophies of representation that have long histories of contemplation in other disciplines and less attention in anthropology. Theorists from other disciplines have reached into anthropology on similar issues (see Clifford, 1988; Clifford & Marcus, 1986; Krupat, 1992). But the cross-poaching that underwrites anthropology's "literarization" and the "anthropologizing" of literary studies is hard to measure and subject to various interpretations.[3] It has also resulted in some confusion over the degree to which anthropology ought to rely on other disciplines instead of creating its own adaptive solutions to the challenges posed, for example, regarding "the effort to situate discourses sociologically, to show how discourses function, compete, and clash within sociopolitical arenas, and to trace how discourses are transformed historically" (Fischer, 1988, p. 8; compare Krupat, 1992, pp. 51-52; Taylor, 1996).

One famous connection between anthropology and other disciplines that study poetics is structuralism. Although now less popular (having been relegated mistakenly by some to the graveyard of things buried by "postmodern" growth—see Brady, 1993), the structuralism developed in this century by linguists Ferdinand de Saussure and Noam Chomsky, psychologist Jean Piaget, and especially anthropologist Claude Lévi-Strauss had a profound impact on literary studies in the 1960s and 1970s.[4] The concept of poetics and what might constitute a legitimate study of it has been permanently changed as a result, and the possibilities for demarcating something clearly as *anthropological* poetics have been complicated in the process.[5] That doesn't disappoint most of the modern critics who operate happily between the cracks of conventional divisions. Poetics is now more than ever an interdisciplinary topic that rightfully resists such reductions. Nevertheless, anthropology's footprints tend to be distinctive, so marking its path through this terrain is not impossible. Even though anthropological inquiry into poetics lacks coherence as a specialized field, we can locate it pragmatically by inspecting what anthropologists have done with it and by marking the intersections of their work with like-minded activities from elsewhere.

Without departing entirely from the common literary grounds of writing as a form of expression and what constitutes *author*-ity in the first place, anthropological studies of poetics differ from those of most other disciplines by reaching into performance issues in discourse, including studies of ritual and worldview, from tribal societies to modern theater, and their relationships to language and culture.[6] Ethnopoets in particular—cultural anthropologists, linguists, and poets who study other cultures from a poetic perspective—never lose sight of the language that structures and facilitates discourse, in oral or written form.[7] These are some of the reasons the subject of anthropological poetics gravitates naturally to sociolinguistics and linguistics in general (which has its own gradations of science-minded versus more artful practitioners), residually to the empirically rigorous studies of semantics and culture popularized in anthropology in the 1960s and 1970s as "cognitive anthropology" (see Tyler, 1969), and directly to discourse-centered production in any form, including writing. They are tied together by the instrumental role language plays in each instance.

The emphasis on the centrality of language in culture was also one of the original attractions of structuralism and poetics to linguistics and at the same time a brace for some of the earliest discontents with logical positivism in ethnography, which historically has tried to keep its rhetorical bases and authorship "invisible" as a pretext of clinical distance. An increased understanding of the collaborative nature of fieldwork and the need for more "reflexive" perspectives on it relative to constructivist (e.g., the reader reception theories of scholars such as semiologist Umberto Eco and literary critic Roland Barthes) and multivocal interpretations of literature (following especially the seminal work of Russian critic Mikhail Bakhtin) have also spurred the development of a critical dialogics for linguistics and anthropology as a whole.[8] The challenge for a dialogic poetics is that it "must first of all be able to identify and arrange relations between points of view: It must be adequate to the complex architectonics that shape the viewpoint of the author toward his characters, the characters toward the author, and all of these toward each other" (Holquist, 1990,

p. 162). Ethnographers have been attracted to this kind of argument precisely because it defines both the relationships and the constraints on self-conscious cross-cultural research and writing. But the subsequent turn to linguistics as science and model for cultural and textual studies and to language in some strict sense as the key to ethnographic investigation has proved to be inadequate—or at least incomplete—and is the source of many of the indeterminacies in philosophy and method that characterize current debate on ethnographic representation and interpretation.[9]

The interdisciplinary stretch of what can be marked as the anthropological version of poetics thus covers a lot of ground. It ranges from a self-conscious interest in *poetry,* conceived brightly by poet Rita Dove (1994) as "the art of making the interior life of one individual available to others" (p. 25; see also Prattis, 1986, 1997), on the one hand, to much more inclusive analytic interests that are perhaps best contained by French critic Paul Valéry's (1964) concept of poetics as "everything that bears on the creation or composition of works having language at once as their substance and their instrument" (p. 86; see also Brady, 1991a), on the other. Splicing into that fuzzy framework from many directions, anthropological poetics nevertheless settles mainly into three subcategories of inquiry, which are not mutually exclusive: (a) ethnopoetics, (b) literary anthropology, and (c) anthropological poetry.

◆ Ethnopoetics

Ethnopoetics may be the most conspicuously anthropological activity in a poetic domain. Dennis Tedlock (1992), a pioneer in the field, defines it as the "study of the verbal arts in a worldwide range of languages and cultures" (p. 81). It focuses primarily on "the vocal-auditory channel of communication in which speaking, chanting, or singing voices give shape to proverbs, riddles, curses, laments, praises, prayers, prophecies, public announcements, and narratives" (p. 81). The goal in such studies is "not only to analyze and interpret oral performances but also to make them directly accessible through transcriptions and translations that display their qualities as works of art" (p. 81). Much has been done to reach this goal since ethnopoetics was invented as a special genre of inquiry in the United States in the late 1960s.

Poet-ethnographer Jerome Rothenberg coined the term *ethnopoetics* in 1968 and is properly considered to be "the father of American ethnopoetics" (Tarn, 1991, p. 75). His most instructive thoughts on this topic are collected in edited volumes that also illustrate the diverse intellectual inspiration this movement owes to various social scientists, ethnographers, and poets (including especially Henry David Thoreau, Gertrude Stein, Ezra Pound, Arthur Rimbaud, and William Blake), and to other influential social thinkers (such as Giambattista Vico and surrealist Tristan Tzara—see Rothenberg & Rothenberg, 1983). Some of Rothenberg's other work (e.g., 1981, 1985) digs deeper into the roots of "oral poetry" (see Finnegan, 1992a, 1992b) and related traditions as old as the late Pleistocene (see Brady, 1990b; Tarn, 1991, p. 15) and as momentous as the birth of theater and poetry in shamanism (Rothenberg, 1981). A common theme throughout is an attempt to close the distance modern thinking tends to put between "us" and "them," both historically and as these artificial boundaries are used to separate us from the performative traditions of "ex-primitives" around the globe today (see Bauman, 1977, 1992; MacCannell, 1992; Schechner, 1995). The author of numerous books of poetry, Rothenberg was also a cofounder (with Dennis Tedlock) and co-editor of the radical magazine *Alcheringa/Ethnopoetics,* which featured "transcripts, translations, and tear-out disc recordings of performances by indigenous verbal artists from Africa, Asia, Oceania, and the Americas" (D. Tedlock, 1992, pp. 81-82). It was keenly focused on developing ethnopoetics, on freeing poetries of all kinds from the "monolithic great tradition" of Western literature, and on exploring new techniques of translating the poetry of tribal societies. Although *Alcheringa* is no longer in print, its experimentalism continues to characterize the field of ethnopoetics today (see especially Tedlock, 1983, 1990, 1992).

The innovative work of linguist-anthropologists Dell Hymes, Robert Duncan, and George Quasha, anthropologist-poet Stanley Diamond, and other poets who, like Rothenberg, have had some training in anthropology or linguistics, including David Antin and Gary Snyder, must also be considered in calculating the intellectual history of ethnopoetics. Their collective scholarship has influenced all the others who have contributed to the development and preservation of this genre since the early 1970s. One such person was anthropologist Victor Turner. Writing more than a decade and half ago about the connection of ethnopoetics to his own work on ritual, Turner (1983) suggested that ethnopoetics offers a way of renewing recognition of "the deep bonds between body and mentality, unconscious and conscious thinking, species and self" that "have been treated without respect, as though they were irrelevant for analytical purposes" in much of the intellectual discourse from anthropology's colonial period (p. 338). He also noted poignantly that the resurgence of ethnopoetics "comes at a time when knowledge is being increased of other cultures, other worldviews, other life styles, when Westerners, endeavoring to trap non-Western philosophies and poetries in the corrals of their own cognitive constructions, find that they have caught sublime monsters, eastern dragons, lords of fructile chaos, whose wisdom makes our knowledge look somehow shrunken and inadequate" (p. 338). Appropriate to bridging ethnopoetics and anthropology's struggle for a postcolonial identity, such concerns also lead directly into the realm of humanistic anthropology.[10]

Anthropologist-linguist Keith Basso (1988) points to another major problem still on the ethnopoetic horizon that is centered in the larger issue of hegemonic discourse—a cultural bias or override in the linguistic and intellectual forms we use to appropriate and represent cross-cultural experience. There is, Basso says, "a growing conviction among linguistic anthropologists that the oral literatures of Native American people have been inaccurately characterized, wrongly represented, and improperly translated." For the better part of a century, "the spoken productions of Native American storytellers have been presented as pieces of prose whose formal divisions are marked by paragraphs and sentences." Recent research indicates that this is a fundamental distortion of the record. It appears that "Native American storytellers often spoke—and in some Indian communities continue to speak today—in forms of measured verse" (p. 809).[11] The ethnopoetic task is to decide on the kinds of evidence that "attest to the existence of these poetic forms" and to answer a variety of related questions: "Given a properly recorded text, together with a knowledge of the language in which it was made, how should analysis proceed? What kinds of theoretical constructs are called for along the way, and how should these constructs be modified and refined?" (Basso, 1988, p. 809).[12] Answering these questions sweeps through many of the postmodern challenges that have surfaced in ethnopoetics and anthropology in general in the past 20 years. The concerns cluster around cultural and historical "situatedness"—our inability to devise a culture-free or purely objective view of anything. It is hard to avoid the argument that scholarly work is culturally constructed, rhetorically conditioned, tropological, empowered with a point of view, and addled with imperfections, distortion, and incompleteness. Everything a scholar produces is, in effect, "textual" in every sense of the term (see also Rorty, 1979, 1981; White,

1973, p. xii). Just how "literary" anthropology wants to be in the face of these challenges has emerged as a serious question and a point of much debate.

◆ Literary Anthropology

While the study of relations between anthropology and literary theory is still unfolding,[13] the major points of entry into them were pioneered in anthropology by Clifford Geertz (1973, 1983, 1988). In much the same way that Hayden White's celebrated "contention of the inherent 'literariness' of history significantly prefigured the way a number of theorists and historians are now reading anthropology, that is, as text, as writing that is necessarily bound within the parameters of discourse," so it is that "Clifford Geertz's anthropological writings over the past two decades have similarly affirmed the ultimately discursive nature of anthropology by holding that cultural interplay is itself semiotic, a system of signs that can be interpreted by the culture-reader" (Manganaro, 1990b, p. 15). Pursuing this has had a dramatic effect on ideas about the craft and purpose of ethnography, but the linking up with literary interests has not been too much of a stretch for anthropology in some respects: "We know many reasons to emphasize what literature shares with other kinds of human expression. We know how readily we transform literary to non-literary knowledge, and vice versa. We also know how fuzzy matters may be at their intellectual margins" (Miner, 1990, p. 12)—and therein lies much of the problem: It is "fuzzy" on the boundaries. That notwithstanding for the moment, with both the same and a different subject by metaphoric extension—"texts" and "cultures as texts"—some anthropologists have pushed Geertz's premises to argue that their discipline can function as a form of cultural critique not unlike that promoted in more obviously literary circles.[14] Transcending the naïve conception of ethnography as easily apprehended cross-cultural description, influential anthropologist-critic George Marcus (1988) gives its poetic a simultaneous shot of aesthetic value and authority: "When done artfully," he says, "description takes the form of authoritative narration of cultural processes" (p. 68). It has the character of allegory (Clifford, 1988) in any case and produces a kind of layered artifact loaded with variable cultural dispositions and competing political concerns that are situated in "terms of the social construction of literary realism" (Feld,

1987, p. 190). The much-discussed perspectives of "interpretive anthropology" were born of such concerns.[15]

By keeping questions of authorship at center focus and by exploring the evocative equation of cultures *as* texts that participant observers must learn how to "read" in culturally authentic ways,[16] Marcus and several other anthropologists have since the early 1980s devoted considerable effort to evaluating the utility of such metaphors and to understanding how the methods and theories of interpreting literature might transfer to the interpretation of their own writings, to the study of other cultures so conceived, as well as to the specific study of indigenous oral narratives.[17] The "rich contemporary production of fiction and literature from most parts of the third world" is another "object of analysis that combines ethnography and literary criticism" (Marcus & Fischer, 1986, p. 74).[18] It is "important not only as a guide for . . . inquiries in the field . . . [but also] for suggesting ways in which the form of the ethnography might be altered to reflect the kind of cultural experiences that find expression both in indigenous writing and in the ethnographer's fieldwork" (Marcus & Fischer, 1986, p. 74) and ultimately function "as a form of cultural critique of ourselves" (Marcus & Fischer, 1986, p. 1; see also Williams, 1998).

This work has been expanded critically[19] and extended creatively[20] in various ethnographic and historical contexts. But the growing literariness of the process has become increasingly problematic, including the issue of *how* to write as an anthropologist and questions about the place of fiction in "realistic" ethnographies (see Banks & Banks, 1998; Ellis & Bochner, 1996; Rapport, 1997). Geertz (1988) first raised the issue of anthropological writing's being inescapably fictional in the sense of being "something made, something constructed"—a strategic fabrication that is not necessarily untrue, but cannot escape its fictional character simply by adopting realism as a mode of exposition or by claiming clear authority on another form of life only on the basis of having "been there" (pp. 4-5). Ethnographic authority derives necessarily from a much more creative, self-interested, historically and culturally situated circumstance in which the author is inevitably a confabulator between his or her own experiences and those of Others in some mutually constructed communication. It is established most directly as a "writerly act" (Geertz, 1988); ethnographic knowledge is "*really* created by conventions of writing" (Fabian, 1990, p. 762). By being dedicated generally to representing peoples without writing, ethnography differentiates itself from the writing of literature and history per se (Manganaro, 1990b). But, despite its needs for objectivity and the defiance of ethnocentrism, ethnographic writing can "no longer be seen as a natural or organic extension of content"; the anthropological writer "either plugs into preexisting plot structures or creates a new structure out of the amalgam of old forms" (Manganaro, 1990b, p. 15). By allowing no culturally or linguistically unconstructed access to reality—no story structures unconditioned by history—and by virtue of its roots in the "fuzzy" cross-cultural margins of anthropological fieldwork, ethnographic representation is thus conducive to developing the kinds of competing interpretations that go with the declaration of "fuzzy" boundaries on any topic. In that capacity it easily lends itself to further analogizing of the situation as ambiguous "text." [21]

The attempt to reconcile the role of the author, the place of fiction, and related literary enmeshments in ethnography's realist writing tradition leads to two underexamined developments in the field, one old and one new, and it begs a third. First, it shows the need for a critical reexamination of writing constructions and realist assumptions in anthropology's only established poetic genre, the ethnographic novel.[22] Second, there is an active search on in many quarters of anthropology to adopt more obviously literary forms that can be used to enhance communication of the ethnographic experience in the realist tradition, including those with greater "writer consciousness" (e.g., where the author appears in first person as narrator and actor in the ethnographic account, contrary to the positivist tradition).[23] Although there are now many variations on this theme,[24] Lévi-Strauss's *Tristes Tropiques* (1961) is by far the best known of all such works and was foundational in "its resistance to the duty of directly rendering the anthropological subject."[25] It "represents the anthropological text that perhaps most influenced current speculation on the nature of anthropological representation" (Manganaro, 1990b, p. 17). One enduring consequence is that anthropologists are much more alert to their roles as writers and critics today in ethnographic and historical research,[26] and to the role of writing and criticism more generally in anthropological method and theory.[27]

Third, the new emphasis on creative construction and prolonged attention to anthropology's inevitable textual involvement has created a kind of epistemological havoc. It not only pits positivism against all of the great deconstructive "undoings" of late, it also means the loss of invisibility in writing as part of the realist tradition. That is a direct challenge to science's mythical perpetuation of the unobtrusive sign (compare Barthes, 1972). By accentuating the form of the message rather than the contents of its speech acts, the literary or poetic takes for its primary object what science does not. In the formalist sense, we can cull out a measure of literariness in any text and call it *poeticity:* the degree to which a work flags the linguistic nature of its own being; the degree to which it emphasizes materiality versus transparency through self-referencing linguistic forms (see Jakobson, 1987). A text high in poeticity, whether prose or verse, in this sense signals itself in place instead of disappearing; it celebrates the signifier over the signified without abandoning the basic communication function it shares as discourse with more scientific or historically authentic calculations, albeit through very different channels (compare Levine, 1987, 1994). Writing in a way that does not call attention to itself in order to allow the objective observer to focus directly on the "reality" of the subject is a delusion—a special kind of fiction and desire that helps to turn "culture" into "nature" in the common view. It hides precepts and politics alike behind the power of the sign and makes them look invisible (Brady, 1991a, p. 216). The narrative discourse of science, as in art, is created out of the interaction of such cultural conventions and situations, the way the author deploys them through particular language codes, and the reader's process of reception (creative construction) that releases meaning from the text. Clarity of meaning itself takes on new meaning in this context. It lacks absolutes. It becomes a manipulable cultural code, reckoned with familiarity and history—still "fuzzy" around the edges. It cannot be a culture-free peek at the universe enabled by a mythical objectivity (Brady, 1991b, p. 19; see also Bruner, 1986, 1990; compare Barthes, 1968).

Science, of course, needs language to function, but unlike literature, it neither asserts nor sees itself as situated *within* language. The conspicuously poetic author willingly appears in his or her text as an artisan whose constant display is the craft of language (the language and form of the poem is claimed by the poet and must be read through that claim—a proprietary function) or as a person who visibly leads the prose narrative from within. The scientific author tries to avoid both, aspiring to invisibility in every place except the opening credits of his or her cover page (compare Geertz, 1988, pp. 7-8; Manganaro, 1990b, pp. 15-16). The resulting gap between author and text is a pit for various detached composition strategies, including anthropology's great timeless fiction of writing in the ethnographic present. Authorial invisibility enhances the prospect for smuggling distancing time frames (we are "present" and full of time; Others are "past" and "timeless")[28] into the argument, not to mention excessively clinical assumptions of philosophy, including the possibility of "mirror of nature minds" in observation and communication and related forms of objectivity (Rorty, 1979). Calling "into question the very language by which modern science knows its language," thereby bringing its invisible signs back into conscious orbit, Barthes (1986, p. 5) concludes, can thus only be done by writing, itself a condition of language.

Philosophical justification in the criticism of interpretive anthropology and its textual turn have waned since Dreyfus and Rabinow's (1983) challenging evaluation of Michel Foucault's thinking and its relevance to cultural anthropology.[29] Any serious reengagement of interpretive anthropology with modern science (and, to some degree, with archaeology and physical anthropology—compare Hodder, 1986; Tilley, 1990) will have to resurrect the historical points at which epistemological concerns began to recede in anthropology and then build from there. Literary anthropology, as part of the emerging critical tradition in textual studies, rests on a similar fate if it is ever to close the loop of its critical departure from modern science concerns with *explanation* per se and much that has been rejected arbitrarily in the zeal to construct powerful arguments about representation, historical situatedness, and *author*-ity in general. As Fabian (1990) suggests, "Dialogical and poetic conceptions of ethnographic knowledge touch the heart of questions about othering. But they have a chance to change the shape of ethnography only if they lead to literary processes that are hermeneutic-dialectical, or 'practical,' rather than representational" (p. 766). On the other hand, many of the participants in anthropology's literary turn have no interest whatsoever in closing that larger loop with any method, theory, or language that resembles the status quo ante in their field (Brady, 1991b, pp. 12-13). Theirs is a more creative turn to be considered critically before any larger inclusions are attempted.[30] Following ideas that have "already been claimed by various forms of radical anthropology," which see "the discipline as a handmaiden to an era of European and American imperialism," Nathaniel Tarn (1991) suggests that intellectual studies—perhaps properly conceived as Wittgensteinian language games—should keep their identities as such and not be promoted to some Archimedian level of essential Truth or "used for oppressive purposes or any pretence at superior knowledge" (p. 57).[31] Anthropological poetry has surfaced in a similar humanistically grounded context as a distinctly literary activity crossed over to social science.

◆ Anthropological Poetry

If ethnopoetics is the most conspicuous anthropological activity in a poetics domain, anthropological poetry is easily qualified in the converse as the most conspicuously poetic activity in an anthropological domain.[32] Such work tends to focus on cross-cultural themes, esoteric cultural information, the experiences of doing fieldwork in other cultures, and so on. Its distinctive characteristic is the presentation of that information in marked poetic form. Set in an anthropological mode, poetry is a conspicuously linguistic message loaded with critical commentary on the nature of the world and our place in it (Brady, 1991a, p. 216). Through poetic portrayal, although perhaps fictional at the level of precise time and sequence of events, anthropological poets often attempt to convey the cross-cultural circumstances and events of their fieldwork in an authentic and penetrating way (see Flores, 1982, 1999; Prattis, 1986). The aim in this poetry is not to exist only for its own sake or self, or merely to entertain, but to flag its language without losing its historical or ethnographic referentiality and authenticity—thereby constituting a paradox of the first order.[33] But it is the conspicuously linguistic forms (such as the self-halting process of poetic line phrasing) that give it poeticity, not its commentary—that is its anthropological part. This raises the issue of writer consciousness once again, the degree to which authors should or must appear as such in their discourse, and therefore crosses the boundary that traditionally has divided scientific writing (and observation) from other forms.

Poetics leads to the aesthetic, which, as part of a general concern for the making of meaning in what we do and study (see Brady, 1991b; Flores, 1985), can be engaged in radical forms, including but not limited to poetry, without completely abandoning seemingly contrary interests such as scientific observation. Although poetry is not science and does not aspire to be science (Diamond, 1986c, p. 132), some of the work of at least the kind of science produced by ethnographers is intruded upon by the anthropological poet. By varying their forms of expression to include poetry, anthropologists attempt to say things that might not be said as effectively or at all any other way. This is consistent with the need to discover and examine critically all of the ways a subject (including social and cultural relationships) can be represented. In that diversity the anthropological poet finds a measure of truth. But the Cartesian critic sees another version: By reporting fieldwork experiences through poetry, the author invokes a form of subjectivity to do the work of a form of objectivity, the conventional ethnography (see Tarn, 1991, p. 246). In the process, information may be conveyed more as what "might" or "could be" than "what is" or "what was" as concrete historical fact, and that is problematic (counterintuitive) to modern science and to ethnography that emulates its methods.

The pecking order of arguments in this instance has not always been the same. Poetry has occupied more respectable positions in some of the Truth camps of the past. It has not always been so marginalized as intellectual activity.[34] Aristotle recognized 2,400 years ago that because poetry exacts universal judgments from action, from history, it can be considered (with more than a little irony for the present argument) at one level *more* scientific (or philosophical) than history. It is a medium in which "the lessons of history do not become any more intelligible and they remain undemonstrated and therefore merely probable, but they become more compendious and therefore more useful" (Collingwood, 1956, p. 25). Nevertheless, rejected as method by the received wisdom of science since the Enlightenment, in part for its declaration of "ringing true" rather than "being true" in some particular empirical and historical accountability of "what actually happened," in part for working in a kind of "fifth dimension," independent of time and therefore "of a sort that scientists cannot recognize" (Graves, 1971, p. 35; see also Bruner, 1986, p. 52), poetry is reintroduced only with difficulty to any context of specific empirical accountability, such as concerns anthropology and the social sciences.[35]

The challenge of poetry for anthropology thus has several aspects. In addition to studying the uses to which poetry can be put, the contexts in which it appears as discourse, and the variability of its forms in specific cultures (its ethnopoetic dimensions), the challenge includes the development of a genre of writing and reporting that systematically tries to incorporate satisfying and edifying poetic quality (foregrounding for clarity as well as aesthetic functions and the practical use of metaphor as a tool of discovery) without sacrificing the essence of ethnographic accountability. In writing anthropological poetry, an author attempts to evoke a comparable experience or set of experiences through the reader's experience with the text on the twin assumptions that all humans are tied together through certain substantive universals of being and that the beings we encounter are sufficiently like ourselves to be open to empathic construction, discovery, and reporting (Quine's principal of charity—see Shweder, 1996).

Perhaps one can also "extend to all discourse what has been said of poetic discourse alone, because it manifests to the highest degree, when it is successful, the effect which consists in awakening experiences which vary from one individual to another. . . . The paradox of communication is that it presupposes a common medium, but one which works—as is clearly seen in the limiting case in which, as often in poetry, the aim is to transmit emotions—only by eliciting and reviving singular, and therefore socially marked, experiences" (Bourdieu, 1991, p. 39). In this way, whether through poetry, a great novel, or a play, the anthropological writer invites us to "live through" other experiences vicariously and, "through the power of metaphor, to come away with a deeper understanding of . . . the human condition" (Coward & Royce, 1981, p. 132). Anthropological humanists (some of whom are poets) look at this as the challenge of writing "from within" rather than "without" and that of "good writing" in general, which, as mentioned earlier, is an important part of anthropology's emerging poetics.[36]

Clifford Geertz is well-known for the quality of his writing, as are a few other anthropologists.[37] But theirs is not typical writing in the discipline. In fact, as noted previously, and contrary to the kind of disciplinary protection history claims generally for the public accessibility of its writings against the obtuse jargonizing of the social sciences, not all anthropologists strive for more interesting and edifying ways of communicating anthropological experience. Appearing "too literary" (and certainly writing poetry begs the issue) is generally believed to undermine scientific authority.[38] It can put the writer in the "wrong" intellectual camp, and that can have severe career consequences for research funding, promotions, and other political concerns. Some of the resistance is simply against passion in discourse (see Fabian, 1994, p. 100; Taussig, 1987). For holistic anthropology (with its interest in preserving the four-field character of the discipline: cultural anthropology, archaeology, physical anthropology, and linguistics), the real danger in exaggerating the focus on "author-centrism" is slipping into a purely rhetorical or aesthetic legitimation of ethnography "by ontologizing representation, writing, and literary form" (Fabian, 1994, p. 91). That may elide or preempt altogether the question of objectivity, which—as one of the few gates of conversation open to reconciling conventional scientific concerns with advancing poetics and the need for epistemological study in ethnography—nevertheless is a neglected issue in postmodern anthropology (Fabian, 1994, p. 91; see also Megill, 1994; Tiles, 1984). In the middle of it all is an ongoing confusion between powerful explanation and good vocabulary (Rorty, 1981, p. 158; see also Abrahams, 1986; Brady, 1991b).

Lamenting the generally sad state of anthropological discourse today—that it is often "painful to read," enormously self-serving, corrupted with esoteric and bland jargon, incestuous in its preoccupations when it might be better served with a more outward vision of its purposes and communication strategies—Tarn (1991) suggests that "if the latest generation writes well it may be due to mass alienation from the academic side of the discipline (with all its dangers) and to such phenomena as 'ethnopoetics' " (p. 56)—with its emphasis on comparative expression. A properly modern anthropology would find a way to reintegrate its writing of science and its humanisms. "It would pay the greatest attention to the way in which . . . ethnography was written, striving to go beyond *belles lettres* toward a language with scientific and literary properties both, but governed primarily by literature, so that its results could be available to all culturally literate readers" (Tarn, 1991, p. 57). Addressing in particular what authors have attempted in what he calls "auto-anthropologies" ("personal ethnography," "reflexive ethnography," and so on; see Crapanzano, 1980; Dumont, 1978; Rabinow, 1977), Tarn (1991) says that such efforts run parallel to his "argument that the genre so long looked for which would assure a complete union of the poetic and anthropological enterprises [without reducing either completely to the other, without sacrificing the option of lopsided emphasis, of an anti-union, or of for all practical purposes complete independence in the conscious formulation of anthropological discourse] (should such be desirable) lies not in the keeping of the anthropologist who cannot, for all his/her efforts, get beyond *belles lettres,* but with the poet who, in theory, still can. This is the question of a language which, without turning away from scientific veracity, abdicates not one jot of its literary potential. Undoubtedly utopian, the search is at home in poetry, incurably utopian, and probably nowhere else" (p. 256; see also Richardson, 1994; Rose, 1991b).

As poets, anthropologists still have to get some purchase on their audiences. Will it be poetry addressed to the existing elite, to anthropologists as such, perhaps as a form of extending the ethnographic tradition, or addressed to "the people at large, or that section of it which has not been consumerized out of existence as a reading and listening public?" (Tarn, 1991, p. 64). Market matters, and some poetry published in the social sciences is of dubious quality by literary standards and therefore less marketable.[39] But what makes the distinction? What is defensibly good or agreeably bad poetry? There is a whole industry of writing about this in general, of course, and there has been since the first critics forayed as experts into a world not of their own making. I will not attempt to sort that pile out here, especially at the level of craft (although such discussion is relevant), except to echo some early-in-the-century thinking by I. A. Richards (1929): "It is less important to like 'good' poetry and dislike 'bad,' than to be able to use them both as a means of ordering our minds"; and that what matters is the quality of the reading we give to poems, "not the correctness with which we classify them" as good or bad, right or wrong (p. 327). The ease with which a poem might slip into the mind to good effect is as much a function of the reader's susceptibility by topic and variable inclination to appropriate such things as it is a function of form. There may be wide agreement on the value of a particular poem or body of work, but there are no absolutes of poetic stimulation and effectiveness. Much depends on the situation at hand. As with any text, the same poem can travel with very different effects across personal and cultural boundaries.

Nonetheless, after all is said and done, perhaps we can agree that the most effective poetry stirs something up in you—an emotion or passion that reaches beyond the shallow, that gravitates to deeper experiences and the sublime. The best of it is powerfully orienting, inspirational, if not more directly mantic or prophetic.[40] In ethnographic or cross-cultural poetry, the effect is likely to be a significant realization of identity with what otherwise could not possibly be claimed as Own. Through words and their specialized forms, a kinship is evoked that is grounded in empathy and interpretation. It huddles with the universality of being human and sends a large message: Perhaps we are all Cheyenne, Arapaho, Tuvaluan, and Ik. Perhaps we are also all ethnographers now, as Rose (1991b, 1993) says. The best poets can make these things work as ideas and as platforms for social action (compare Rothenberg, 1994).

The late anthropologist-poet-social-activist Stanley Diamond (1987), reflecting on the ugly, the beautiful, and the sublime in poetry (and quarreling with Keats's famous line that "a thing of beauty is a joy for ever"), wrote:

The mere deepening of gratification from the "joyful" experience of beauty as truth does not achieve the sublime. The experience of the sublime is both transcendental and quintessentially cultural at the same time. Language itself is the transcendence of the biological, it is the medium of culture, and culture is a rope-bridge thrown across a biological chasm. As the objective realizations of the human essence, that is, as the existentializing of our human possibilities, culture(s) is the arena for the construction of meanings: it

557

represents a struggle that is constant and renewed in each generation, and evident in the lives of individuals as they strive to become cultured human beings.... There are no certainties here, only struggle and contingency, pain and realization. Gratification, satisfaction, or happiness are not at issue. But, we encounter *joy*. This is the joy that one finds in Lear, as he hurls his words into the terrible gulf that engulfs him. The joy is in the words, in his matured sensibility, in his challenge to nature and human defeat. The joy is in the challenge, and in the formulation of his meanings. Or observe the final shuffling off of guilt by Oedipus at Colonnus, as Sophocles etherealizes him in a beam of light. Or the conclusion of the Winnebago medicine rite, when the initiate finally achieves his emancipation from society, after bearing all the abuse that society may heap upon him. Or, for that matter, the ordinary rituals of maturing and variegated experience known in every primitive society, whereby growth is attended by pain, where a new name may be earned, and where the past is arduously incorporated into the present, preparing the individual for the next ritual round as he moves higher in the spiritual hierarchy of his society. That is where the joy is. And finally, it is this joy, not Keats's beauty or truth, which defines the sublime, beyond the confines of the merely aesthetic, breaking all the formal rules of aesthetics, beyond the range of the romantic imagination. For we are not talking of imagination here, but of experience and its meanings, whether in the culture of dreams, the culture of the hunt, or in the ceremonies of rebirth. And finally, I am talking of the sacred space, the sacred silence that lies beyond language, but remains grounded in language. (pp. 270-271; compare Burke, 1958)

All but the most serious and sensitive writers would be hard-pressed to capture these existential dimensions in generally accessible language. Ethnopoets strive for such experience and communication, even as they eschew as unrealistic any expectations of ever reducing the sacred or the sublime to strictly clinical or analytic forms. A battle is fit on this very quest: If the artist sees it, she believes she has some prospect of saying it poetically, of conveying with less prospect of empirical distortion the nature of the experience as panhuman emotion; if the scientist sees it or grips its "felt meaning," she can only hasten its transformation into something else (or some things else) by attempting to appropriate and express it through clinical forms. Either way, there is a problem. Coleridge's "The Rime of the Ancient Mariner" refuses reduction to the subject of sailors and seawater or to critical summaries of its formal properties and inspirations, just as the statistical expression of cross-cultural trait distributions in the ancient Middle East cannot yield its exactness and rhetorical integrity to interpretive statements high in poeticity or uncommon metaphor.[41] Poetizing such things may reveal new dimensions of the problem, to be sure, and that can be a profound contribution to humanistic concerns, but it is not necessarily a proper substitute for the original statement or form. While the upshot of such things can be shared widely in language, culture, and experience, the confining exactitudes of competing poetic and scientific linguistic forms restrict movements and thus hook again into that entangled truth of disciplinary and intellectual discourse: Not all subjects travel equally well.[42] The movement is not hopeless. Translation is possible. But it is by definition a changing frame.

Beyond that we need to ask who does the poet speak *for?* There is debate over this in anthropology, not only for its poets but for all of its writers, as there is in every discipline that has entered the crisis of representation. Sticking to anthropological poets for the moment, for they may have stretched the forms of representation in the social sciences the most, consider Diamond's (1982, p. 94) poem "Shaman's Song":

I talk to flowers
My fingertips withstand
The glance of roses
What do you know of the Bear
His body, my spirit
Rises everywhere
Seeing what the leaf sees
And the cloud
Ambiguous as a woman
Drifting through stones

I have lain with the otter
Under white water
On beds softer than birds

What do you know of the Fox
Bearing the message of death?

Diamond was not a shaman. He was not a Native American, although the spirit of indigenous cultures of the Americas resonates through this work and through the multiple (Native American, Anglo, and anthropomorphized animal) voices that structure his epic poem *Going West* (1986a).[43] In these works, as in all others he produced, especially in the waning years of his life, Diamond aimed for the sublime by drawing on the Everyman he met time and again through cross-cultural experience and by taking on that persona. Here was Aristotle's universal—and Diamond's mine. Penetrating and conspicuous experiences were laid out before him like so much crackable glass and Diamond felt it under his feet with every cross-cultural step. Tread lightly, he said, and his poetry was the gateway sign: "Things can break here." In that he spoke for everyone, as brother, as kin, as alienated Jew, as Everyman who has ever suffered the great smotherings of life and identity that flow from cross-cultural oppression. Translation and multivoice reporting of human commonalities in purpose, interests, pasts, and futures were not only possible, they were, to Diamond's eternal credit, imperative (see Rose, 1983/1991a). Everyman was for him simultaneously author, subject, and audience, a social unit whose variable parts were collapsed into reciprocal self-awareness through the rituals of poetry.

Two related themes found throughout Diamond's work, including his provocative "How to Die in America" (1986b), are that individuals and cultures transcend that which consumes them, no matter how painful the circumstances, or perhaps because of the pain, and that vast unintended consequences come from colonial cannibalizing, with its miles and miles of cross-cultural casualties on the beachheads of the world, in Biafra, India, New Mexico, the Dakotas, New York, and California—not to mention the great erasures of tribal peoples in Russia, Spain, Iraq, Australia, China, and the other Americas. Diamond's poetry seems to come from everywhere because his quest for internalizing and expressing the sublime had no firm cultural boundaries. Transcultural mysteries and truths were in his view everywhere subject to appropriation through the carefully opened eye and ear, once saturated with experience. Diamond believed that no culture could hide its fundamental life from the prying eyes of the mystic or the excavations of the traveling poet, especially when a mature social scientist carried them both on his shoulders. His discourse was full of crossovers and changing centers. He knew that anthropology struggled for such knowledge and he believed that none of it would come without intellectual passion in discovery and representation. By shucking preconceptions to the best of his ability and immersing himself in the lives of others, he devoted the last years of his life to saying these things through poetry, having been, as he said, "first a poet, then an anthropologist, then a poet again" (personal communication, March 1983; see also Diamond, 1982; Rose, 1991b). His writings make it obvious that he never really changed professions, only from time to time his manner of professing.

Is the truth of Diamond's poetic work mixed up with beauty and yet anchored empirically in valid ethnography (compare McAllister, 1998)? Is it best judged as poetry, as skill in form, plussed by the enJOYment or illuminating and edifying introspection it produces? Or is it best judged like all fiction, not exclusively or necessarily in terms of its historical accuracy, but on a sliding scale of erotics and believability in the realm of being human? Does it stir something valuable up in us, perhaps rare or otherwise unobtainable, even as it rings true on life as we know it, or argue it, or both? These are but a few problematic slices of Geertz's (1973) claim that all ethnography is in important ways fictional—something constructed, something fashioned, and never from whole cloth. The crisis of representation in anthropology followed most directly from that pioneering work. The poets have never held center stage in the ensuing melee, but we can assert here that the fundamental issues of ethnographic representation do not change for conspicuously poetic versus more clinical texts. They are textual through and through, no matter what the purported form of representation.[44]

By the same token, as convention would have it in society generally, and specifically in the curious mix of subtle inferences, methodological mandates, and editorial imperialism in the Western world concerning appropriate language for scientific reporting, the form of address often depends heavily on the nature of the problem to be addressed. As it happens, Miles Richardson (1998a) says, "social scientists have long turned to poetry" as a reportorial mode, but the content generally has diverged from the academic centers of their fieldwork and therefore from a collision course with more conventional forms of ethnographic reporting: "Their poems . . . rarely addressed the rich ethnographic record they compiled nor the anguish they felt about the free individual encountering coercive culture" (p. 461). Some of the most notable poetry written by anthropologists in previous generations—by Edward Sapir, Loren Eiseley, and Ruth Benedict, who make up most of a short list—was similarly decentered as ethnography per se but competitive enough to be published in nonanthropological media oriented toward such concerns. But no anthropology journals catered to such interests, and the mainstream sentiment was generally then what it is now: Poetry is an aside, an amusement, that belongs elsewhere. Other than what might be called a "poetic mentality" in the humanism of the times, and for some an affinity with the enticingly poetic work of Sir James Frazer, there was no ideology afoot that might sponsor or enfranchise a more specifically poetic genre of anthropological writing, including poetry.

That climate has changed perceptibly with the growth of more explicitly interpretive works in the field, that is, with the advent of postmodernism, the growth of "textualism" because of its focus on text construction and consumption, and the linguistic emphases of influential structuralists such as Jakobson (1987) and Lévi-Strauss (1962). Iain Prattis's *Reflections: The Anthropological Muse* (1986), a collection of poetry and artwork specifically addressed to fieldwork experiences by cultural anthropologists and linguists, established a precedent. So did reviews of Stanley Diamond's and Paul Friedrich's poetry in anthropology's flagship journal, the *American Anthropologist,* in the early 1980s.[45] At a time when much of this was at least a source of heated debate in the field, then editor George Marcus published Diamond's "How to Die in America" (1986b) poem in the first volume of *Cultural Anthropology.* As the editor of *Anthropology and Humanism Quarterly,* Miles Richardson initiated a poetry and fiction competition that featured the winners in the journal. The competition has been continued by the present editor, Edith Turner, and by her poetry editor, Dell Hymes, and the topics continue to widen. Friedrich's *Bastard Moons* (1979a), Diamond's *Going West* (1986a), and Dennis Tedlock's Turner Prize-winning *Days From a Dream Almanac* (1990) "explore issues of language, ethnographic truth, and shamanic dreams" (Richardson, 1998a, p. 461). Recent poetry in the *American Anthropologist,* under the editorship of Barbara and Dennis Tedlock, includes contributions by Friedrich (1995), Hymes (1995), and Richardson (1998b) on a variety of themes central to ethnographic experience. A new journal devoted to poetry, poetics, ethnography, and cultural and ethnic studies, called appropriately *Cross-Cultural Poetics [Xcp]* and edited by Mark Nowak, published its first issue in 1997. Now the journal *Qualitative Inquiry,* under the editorship of Yvonna Lincoln and Norman Denzin, is following suit (see Brady, 1998a; Richardson, 1998a). It will carry poetry and fiction as regular features, not because it is trendy to do so, say the editors, but because "social scientists have for too long ignored these important forms of ethnographic representation and interpretation" (N. K. Denzin, personal communication, November 8, 1998).

Looking in another direction, if the anthropologist-poets have been few in number to date (albeit increasing in the postmodern afterglow), anthropology as a whole has inspired numerous poets from other disciplines. "Poets precisely because of their 'otherness' in their home societies are attuned to otherness wherever it may be found. Hence they find an affinity, and to their own delight a *social* affinity, with the fruits of other cultures, particularly those of the 'despised and rejected' " (Turner, 1983, p. 339). To which Tarn (1991) adds: "The inspiration that anthropology has afforded poets—to go no further back than Pound or Eliot, or St. John Perse and Segalen, or Neruda, Vallejo, and Paz, in the age of Frazer, Harrison, or the author of *From Ritual to Romance*—to say nothing of Marx and Engles, Freud or Jung, Mauss, Durkheim or Lévi-Strauss—can scarcely be said to have abated when we now have a virtual school of 'ethnopoetics' devoted both to the accessing of 'primitive and archaic poetries' into our culture through the best available techniques of *twentieth century* translation *and* to the mutual effect upon each other of such poetries and our own—granted that Native poets very much continue to produce poetry all over this world" (p. 63).

Anticipating mutual effects, it is reasonable to ask where one goes with a penchant to write poetry in anthropology. Just adopting poetry as a form of writing guarantees nothing. But poetry can be informative and useful, even exhilarating when it reaches the sublime. Properly cast, it can be both fire bellows for and bubbling lid on the pot of intellectual life, a source of transformation that is admirably unquiet in any position: It "turns everything into life. It is that form of life that turns everything into language" (Meschonnic, 1988, p. 90). It is in fact an art "far larger than any description of its powers" (Vendler, 1988, p. 6). For these reasons and others already detailed, some competition between poetry and science as genres may in fact be "healthy and entertaining" (Fabian, 1990, p. 766), even functional (Brady, 1993). It follows that having a hall full of poets (as nightmarish as that may seem to some scientists) can give academies of arts and sciences a better overall pulse, if not a better future of discourse and discovery. Writing poetry has also "helped individual anthropologists to overcome alienation from experience" (Fabian, 1990, p. 766) and that, as much as anything, has serious implications for engaging postmodern concerns about authority in ethnography. The penchant of the anthropologist to wax poetic, if honed and pointed in these ways, can push into the heart of ethnographic contemplation, epistemology, and theory. Hanging out in that zone for a while (as nightmarish as that may seem to some poets) might give way to progress in the conversation over what divides us so readily in the academy today.

There are many other paths to that end, of course. Poetry is not necessarily the right tool for every job. As the old adage goes, if one has only a hammer to work with, after a while everything starts to look like a nail. In this instance, "To seek the solution for a problem regarding the production of knowledge in different or better representations of knowledge is to reaffirm, not to overcome, the representationist stance," with all of its compulsions to order in conceptions of language and culture and related problems (Fabian, 1990, p. 766; see also Friedrich, 1979b). Remaining attentive to "the transformative, creative aspects of ethnographic knowledge" (Fabian, 1990, p. 766) is not entailed automatically by writing poetry (or reproducing dialogues) as an alternative to strict representational ethnography. "To preserve the dialogue with our interlocutors, to assure the Other's presence against the distancing devices of anthropological discourse, is to continue conversing with the Other on all levels of writing, not just to reproduce dialogues" (Fabian, 1990, p. 766) or to slip unwittingly from being "natural historians into itinerant bards, clowns, or preachers" in a humanistic or poetic commitment to "being with others" (Fabian, 1990, pp. 766-767; see also Tarn, 1991, p. 75). We can do better—and more.

One more thing to do in this writer's arena is to counter sole reliance on the centrifugal or "distancing" devices of anthropological discourse—the "Others are never Us" ideas, substituting third-person writing for first-person experiences, writing in the ethnographic present, and so on. Developing alternatives depends on paying special attention to the processes through which ethnographic knowledge is produced in the first place (Fabian, 1994).[46] That does not require a lapse into the old static models of structuralism, although much of what a poetics yields as the sublime might be seen as the recognition of common deep structures (*langue*) in a variable field of surface particulars (*parole*). Certainly there is room for some edifying resuscitation here. But the movement to more centripetal or "closing" discourse in anthropology should at minimum include an ontological and ethnopoetic emphasis on the performative aspects of culture, those that can be "acted out," as opposed to focusing exclusively on the more limited category of "what members of a culture know [that] is 'informative' in the sense that it can be elicited and produced as discursive information" (Fabian, 1994, p. 97).[47]

Such concerns necessarily draw ethnographers and poets into the larger philosophical fields of process, structure, and agency—including the dynamics of knowledge and ritual, theater and history (see Brady, 1999;

Richardson, 1994)—and thereby increase the prospects of producing larger-level understandings of the experiential fields we draw from as observers and contribute to as actors and writers. But it should also be remembered that the original point of creative mystery in every study is also where the Muses call on the writer, and that is precisely "where humanistic anthropology must both stall the process of knowing and open it up intellectually—where we must catch ourselves in the act of rushing headlong into conventional formats, of jumping to conclusions about where the experience must take us and how to communicate it to others, and begin to build a successful poetics into the framework" (Brady, 1991b, p. 20). By attempting to reconcile the spread in this connection between analytic problems and the substance of fieldwork, anthropological poetics can do more than capture (or create) and convey the poetries and literatures of various cultures. It can require greater philosophical justification for its ethnographic endeavors and at the same time help to erase some unnecessary distortions of detachment from its objects of inquiry.

◆ Coda

Here, then, is the poetic turf more anthropologists than ever are traversing nowadays. It is neither defined nor covered exclusively by anthropologists or traditional anthropological interests. As observers of common problems (in and out of their own societies), anthropologists differ in research methods and strategies and sometimes produce incomparable results. Adding other disciplines from the wings only seems to complicate matters. But common ground for all is not beyond the pale. One source of that for anthropologists and other social scientists is that they all seek ways of "speaking in the name of the real" about the people and behaviors they study—of representing fairly and accurately what cannot easily be known or demonstrated in the foggy partialities of cross-cultural experience, the imperfections of culturally situated observations, and the many voices insinuated in mutually constructed truths (compare Brady, 1983, 1991c). Another, as poet Tarn (1991) says, lies in the knowledge that "nothing can hide from us for long the fact that we all face the same problems in the end; that the poetic fate, like the human, is universal" (p. 14).

Discovering and assessing the common denominators of human existence has always had some priority in anthropology,[48] and the need to bridge the inherently hermeneutic studies of ethnography and larger-level statements about the whole organism (universals of language, culture, cognition, and behavior) is getting renewed attention—in full view of past limitations, such as incommensurate theory construction, language biases, political and pragmatic relations between ethnographers and the groups they study, the impossibility of absolute objectivity, and the need for successful measures of validity in ethnographic assertions.[49] But the poets have traditionally approached human commonalities differently, hanging more on meaning than behavior—more on humanistic interpretations than clinically validatable truths. From the perspective of anthropological poetics, resurrecting a systematic scientific examination of what is universal in life and culture—"thinking big" again (see Simpson, 1994)—is more than a big task. It requires jumping the gap of irony and paradox from a great (Geertzian) descent into details of local knowledge, "thick descriptions," and related critical intellectual developments over the past 20 years, back into the whole package of logical positivist methods and assumptions that have been criticized so extensively by the great descenders. Besides, as Aristotle discovered, the poets' generality is exposed in the rich particulars of their work. The poets believe that the commonalities of life can be plucked from there by large-minded observers of whatever persuasion. Whether or not these apparent sharings can be defended as unassailable or universal truths by other standards is another matter. The paths for collecting them are different, so are the logbooks, and therefore the form of the arguments down the line. Scientists normally create conglomerates from heavily laundered particulars, drawn from wide fields of clinically cut cloth, to reach their generalities.

So which to choose? No matter which extreme is harnessed—soft art, hard science—let me reiterate what can be called by now (via my pressing redundancies) the maxim that some things can't be said exactly or as effectively any other way. Extremes are validated and perpetuated by that defensible fact, even as the proponents themselves exaggerate it in their bookend fights over turf and exclusivity. But what about the stretch in between? Rifts are made to be mended; the challenge in gulfs is to bridge them. The boldest of anthropology's new interpreters and poets have gone halfway around the horns of this problem by trying to raise the illumination of our human commonalities to an art form without losing the ability to inform more traditional social science concerns at the same time, in part on the premise that the collective work of scientists and poets is in the broadest view complementary. In the pool of common knowledge, the pattern is ancient and very human: many in the one, one in the many. How you travel depends on where you start. The destination is in the longest of long runs the same: the audiovisual room, the bookshelf, the electronic library, and, perhaps above all else, the mirror in the center of the house of Who-Are-We?[50] Inquiring minds want to know. We have always wanted to know. Who has the key? Never mind. There seems to be more than one door and some of them aren't locked. See you inside.

[Refrain: *Is this just more anthropological borrowing from the multiple-reality world of physics? No. An argument for uncompromising relativism, or just for tolerance of diversity of argument and approach in the absence of an overarching paradigm for cultural anthropology? Neither. Do ethnographic methods have to be reduced to "deep hanging out" (Geertz, 1998)? No. Do we have to abandon the search for commensurate theories and universals of language, culture, and behavior? No. Should we force nostalgia-driven models of the past on present ethnographic research for the next millennium? No need to ask. Won't work.*]

◆ Notes

1. But compare Bachelard (1964) on the "poetics of space," Bachelard (1971) on the "poetics of reverie," Brown (1977) on a "poetic for sociology," and Hallyn (1990) on the "poetic structure of the world."

2. For ethnographers, the poetic focus on communications about other cultures is as much a concern about how the story of fieldwork is told as anything else. See Bruner (1984), Prattis (1986), Van Maanen (1988), Manganaro (1990a), Brady (1991a), and O'Nell (1994).

3. See Beaujour (1987, p. 470) and Fischer (1988, p. 8); compare Burke (1989, p. 188), Krupat (1992, pp. 51-52), Robbins (1987), Tarn (1991, p. 63), Tsing (1994), and James, Hockey, and Dawson (1997).

4. See Lévi-Strauss (1962, 1967, 1969), Riffaterre (1970), Scholes (1974), Culler (1975, 1977), Todorov (1977, 1981), and Harland (1987).

5. See Boon (1972), Todorov (1981), Eagleton (1983), Brady (1991a), and Brooks (1994). The burgeoning domain of "cultural studies" also begs the question of disciplinary division and proprietary interests in these subjects (compare Marcus, 1998). Although there is much more in book form and articles elsewhere using this label, a comparison of the range of interests covered in the literary journals *Cultural Critique* and *Poetics Today* relative to those of the *American Anthropologist, Cultural Anthropology,* and *Anthropology and Humanism* is instructive.

6. See Turner (1974, 1982a, 1982b), Bauman (1977, 1992), Schechner (1985, 1995), Graham (1995), Dening (1996), and Brady (1999).

7. Drawing on the oral behavior of the speech community, for example, ethnopoet David Antin (1983), paraphrasing Dell Hymes, writes: "All over the world in a great variety of languages people announce, greet, take leave, invoke, introduce, inquire, request, demand, command, coax, entreat, encourage, beg, answer, name, report, describe, narrate, interpret, analyze, instruct, advise, defer, refuse, apologize, reproach, joke, taunt, insult, praise, discuss, gossip. Among this grab-bag of human language activities are a number of more or less well-defined universal discourse genres, whose expectation structures are the source of all poetic activity. If there is any place that we should look for an ETHNO-POETICS it is here, among these universal genres, where all linguistic invention begins. . . . I take the 'poetics' part of ETHNOPOETICS to be . . . the structure of those linguistic acts of invention and discovery through which the mind explores the transformational power of language and discovers and invents the world itself" (p. 451). Albeit less dynamic in orientation and less concerned with cultural process than product, there is also connective tissue in that perception for structural studies of the ways what has been discovered and invented is put into place in particular societies, that is, the logical and symbolic arrangements that characterize the cognitive content and social relations of whole cultures (including anthropology itself—see Boon, 1982, 1984, 1989; Brady, 1993).

8. For more on dialogics, see Tedlock (1983, 1987b), Hill (1986), Feld (1987), Holquist (1990), Weiss (1990), Brady (1991b), Bruner and Gorfain (1991), Duranti (1993), and Emerson (1997).

9. See Harland (1987), Clifford and Marcus (1986), Clifford (1988), Fabian (1994), Marcus (1998), and Geertz (1998).

10. See, for example, Tarn (1991), Wilk (1991), Scott (1992), and Brady and Turner (1994).

11. See also Rothenberg (1981, 1985), Swann (1983), Tedlock (1983), Tedlock and Tedlock (1985), Kroskrity (1985), and Sherzer and Woodbury (1987). On the anthropology of folk narratives, see Jackson (1982), Wilbert and Simoneau (1982), Swann (1983), Sherzer and Woodbury (1987), Narayan (1989), Abu-Lughod (1993), Basso (1995), Graham (1995), Candre and Echeverri (1996), and Reichel-Dolmatoff (1996).

12. Compare D. Tedlock (1972, 1985, 1987a, 1991, 1993), Culler (1977, p. 8), Riffaterre (1984), Sherzer (1987), and Graham (1995).

13. If not literature per se—see, for example, Spradley and McDonough (1973), Langness and Frank (1978), Dennis and Aycock (1989), Handler (1983, 1985, 1990), Handler and Segal (1987), Richardson (1990), and Benson (1993).

14. See also Marcus and Fischer (1986), Handler (1983, 1985, 1990), Handler and Segal (1987), Fischer (1991), and Marcus (1998).

15. Of course, the whole enterprise is "interpretive." Furthermore, interpretive anthropology—as part of the poststructuralist, deconstructionist movement in contemporary philosophy and social science—is not necessarily (a) antiempirical (How can any discipline operate without an empirical ground?), (b) antiobjective (see Brady, 1991b; Rorty, 1979, pp. 361-363; Spiegelberg, 1975, pp. 72-73), or (c) antiscience (compare Barrett, 1996; Holton, 1993; Jennings, 1983; Knauft, 1996; Lett, 1997; Maxwell, 1984; O'Meara, 1989; Sangren, 1991; Shankman, 1984). But responsible social science of this kind does reject (as necessarily incomplete, among other problems) dogmatic empiric-*ism* that forecloses on the study of meaning in favor of an exclusive focus on behavior (see Brady, 1993, p. 277, n. 28; Fernandez, 1974; Polanyi & Prosch, 1975; Rabinow & Sullivan, 1987).

16. Following especially Geertz's (1973) classic observations on a Balinese cockfight.

17. See Marcus and Fischer (1986, p. 72), Marcus (1980, 1998), Marcus and Cushman (1982), Boon (1972, 1982, 1989), Clifford and Marcus (1986), Fernandez (1974, 1985, 1986, 1988, 1989), and much that has been published in the journal *Cultural Anthropology*, the discussion of anthropology and Irish discourse in Taylor (1996), and note 11, above, on folk narratives. See also Fischer (1988, 1989, 1991), Fabian (1990, p. 767: "If writing is part of a system of intellectual and political oppression of the Other, how can we avoid contributing to that oppression if we go on writing?"), Manganaro (1990a), Tarn (1991), Karp and Levine (1991), Said (1991), Krupat (1992), Marcus's (1993) review of Krupat, and Mascia-Lees, Sharpe, and Cohen (1993) on some important aspects of the politicizing that follows from ethnographic encapsulations of other people's texts and customs.

18. See, for example, the best-selling novels by Silko (1977) and Momaday (1989), and Slater's (1982) ethnographic exegesis of Brazilian *literatura de cordel*.

19. See, for example, Dennis and Aycock (1989), Rosaldo (1989), Manganaro (1990a), B. Tedlock (1991), Brady (1991b), Benson (1993), James et al. (1997), and Marcus (1998).

20. See, for example, Feld (1982), Jackson (1986), Turner (1987), Dennis (1989), Fox (1989), Stewart (1989), Richardson (1990), B. Tedlock (1992), Gottlieb and Graham (1993), Limón (1994), Behar (1993, 1996), Stewart (1996), and Dening (1998a, 1998b).

21. For related readings on textual authority and ethnographic representation, see Geertz (1973, 1983, 1988, 1995, 1998), Lanser (1981), Bruner (1984), Fernandez (1985, 1986), Webster (1986), Fabian (1990), Weinstein (1990a, 1990b), Simms (1991), Tsing (1994), Dening (1996, 1998a, 1998b), Rapport (1997), and Banks and Banks (1998); compare Taussig (1993) and Motzafi-Haller (1998). For a recent debate on who speaks for whom in historical ethnography, see Obeyesekere (1992), Sahlins (1996), and Borofsky (1997); compare Brady (1985).

22. On that account, see the diverse works of LaFarge (1929), Bohannan (writing as Elenore Smith Bowen, 1954), Turnbull (1962), Stewart (1962), Matthiessen (1963, 1975), Kurten (1980), Thomas (1987), Handy (1973), Thompson (1983), Jackson (1986), and Knab (1995); compare the narrative form in Turner's (1987) empathic memoir.

23. See Turnbull (1962, 1972), Rabinow (1977), Dumont (1978), Crapanzano (1980), Turner (1987), Dennis (1989), Dennis and Aycock (1989), and B. Tedlock (1992).

24. See especially the innovative combination of Gottlieb and Graham (1993), Fischer (1988) on Michel Leiris's effort "to combine sympathetic observation of the Other, the unavoidability of literary self-inscription, and the imperative of cultural critique" (p. 8); compare Beaujoir (1987), Tarn (1991), and Wolf (1992).

25. Tarn (1991) echoes a sentiment shared by many about Lévi-Strauss: He might have been a creative writer with equal success, "had he chosen that path of expression" (p. 56). Manganaro (1990b) adds, "The writerly sense of *Tristes Tropiques*, importantly, arises not only out of a literary style adopted by the anthropologist-author, but from the very perspective that the writer takes to his subject" (p. 16). It is also noteworthy that Lévi-Strauss has been roundly criticized for the formalism of his other works (see, e.g., Eagleton, 1983; Geertz, 1973, pp. 345-359; Harland, 1987; Prattis, 1986; compare Boon, 1972, 1982; Brady, 1993). The large-minded Lévi-Strauss seems to have touched all the bases at one time or another.

26. A theme plainly visible in Dening (1980, 1998a), Geertz (1998), and Borofsky (2000).

27. See Fox (1991), Poggie, DeWalt, and Dressler (1992), Borofsky (1994), Barrett (1996), Jessor, Colby, and Shweder (1996), Knauft (1996), Denzin (1997), Lett (1997), James et al. (1997), Layton (1997), Rapport (1997), and Marcus (1998); compare O'Meara (1997).

28. For important statements on this problem, see Wolf (1982), Fabian (1983), Borofsky (1987, 2000), Thomas (1989, 1991), and Dening (1995, 1996).

29. See Rabinow (1983, 1984, 1986), Jarvie (1983), Wuthnow, Hunter, Bergesen, and Kurzweil (1984), Ulin (1984), Rabinow and Sullivan (1987), Boon (1982), Swearingen (1986), Loriggio (1990), Brady (1991a, 1993), Duranti (1993), and Rapport (1997); compare Scholte (1966) for some earlier thinking, and, more recently, continuing the epistemological effort in anthropology with smart and practical arguments, Davies (1999).

30. See, for example, Reck's (1978) Mexican ethnography, Rose (1993) on the death of "Malinowski-style" ethnography and the birth of a more poetic and multigenre manifesto as its replacement, Boon (1982, pp. 9-12) on some of the confusions of this style and its supposed differentiation as "ethnography" from the "armchair" speculations of Sir James George Frazer, Burke (1989, pp. 188ff.) on the need for anthropologists to "recognize the factor of rhetoric in their own field" (Marcus, 1980), and Boon (1982) on "standards of 'convincingness' in various cross-cultural styles and genres, just as there are canons of verisimilitude in realist ethnography" (p. 21).

31. For more on the relativity and eligibility of such material as language games or similar focus frames, see Guetti (1984), de Zengotita (1989), Denzin (1997), and Gellner (1998).

32. This is less true on both counts in linguistics—see, for example, Napoli and Rando (1979) and Bright (1983, 1985).

33. Dilemma is the other side of paradox. As Paul de Man once observed: "It is in the essence of language to be capable of origination, but of never achieving the absolute identity with itself that exists in the natural object. Poetic language can do nothing but originate anew over and over again; it is always constitutive, able to posit regardless of presence but, by the same token, unable to give a foundation to what it posits except as an intent of consciousness" (quoted in Donoghue, 1989, p. 37).

34. See Vendler (1985, 1988) on the variable marginality of poetry. Not all cultures share America's questionable valuation of poetry. It has conspicuously more status as an activity elsewhere (Brazil, Spain, England—to name a few). See Bishop and Brasil (1972), Lorde (1984, p. 87) on poetry being something other than a luxury, Tarn (1991, p. 15) on poetry's "survival value" for humankind, Lavie (1990) and Behar's (1993) sensitive and rich texts on the tribulations of letting their poetry and poetic mentalities out in oppressive contexts, and Richardson (1994) on poetry being a "*practical* and *powerful* method for analyzing social worlds" (p. 522).

35. Tarn (1991, p. 254) sees this as a kind of competition of "vocations" that can be most discouraging in its personal, political, and philosophical entanglements. But it should be remembered that these seemingly insurmountable problems do not prevent great artists from also being great scientists (and vice versa—e.g., Goethe; see Gould, 1991), that "contempt for one is no qualification for citizenship in the other" (Brann, 1991, p. 775), and that the opposition that pits imagination against reason, when overdrawn on the battlegrounds of art and science, may be a kind "synecdochic fallacy" anyway—a category mistake in its opposition (see Brady, 1991a; Burke, 1989, p. 87).

36. For more on anthropological humanism and writing, see Wilk (1991) and Brady and Turner (1994); compare Harris (1997, p. 293) and Lett (1997).

37. See, for example, Lévi-Strauss (1961), Turnbull (1962, 1972), Van Lawick-Goodall (1971), Harris (1977, 1987), Dening (1980), Sahlins (1981, 1985, 1996), Jackson (1986), Thomas (1987), Rosaldo (1989), Narayan (1989), D. Tedlock (1990), Laderman (1991), B. Tedlock (1992), Rose (1993), and Behar (1993, 1996). Fabian (1990) notes wryly that "Geertz probably deserves credit for initiating the new literary awareness in anthropology not so much because he fraternized with literary critics but because he dared to write well and got away with it" (p. 761). Fernandez (personal communication, February 27, 1998), playing on some of his own influential work (e.g., 1974, 1986), says that Geertz is above all else a "master metaphorist."

38. However, separating these genres and doing both can generate a laudable effect. Scientists who also write novels, poetry, or very "literary" memoirs only seem to enhance their reputations (see, e.g., Levi, 1984; Lightman, 1993; Sagan, 1980, 1985). On a related matter, when asked if his exercises in poetry improved his science, Nobel Prize-winning chemist and estimable poet Roald Hoffmann said no, at least not directly. Writing poetry for Hoffmann makes him feel better about himself as a person, as a human being, and *that* helps his science considerably (personal communication, February 26, 1997; see also Chandrasekhar, 1987; Hoffmann, 1987, 1990a, 1990b, 1995). Even with separation in practice or redefinition in humanistic terms, the functional linkage of art-*in*-science cannot be denied. It may be less direct, less obvious, less explored, and less reported than it could be. But it is always present.

39. There are important exceptions. See, for example, Friedrich (1979a), Diamond (1982, 1986a, 1986b), some of Prattis (1986), various contributions over the years to *Anthropology and Humanism (Quarterly)*, Fox (1989), Stewart (1989), Tedlock (1990), Richardson (1998a, 1998b), and Flores (1999); compare Hall (1988) on phases in becoming a poet.

40. Leavitt (1997) is pioneering work on poetry and prophecy, words and power, mantic prose and ecstatic experiences—"stirrings" that range from the aesthetic and emotional to fundamentally physical responses and their diverse cultural expressions in ritual, politics, healing, and messianic movements, to name a few. See also Abu-Lughod (1986), Trawick (1988, 1997), Dobin (1990), and Csordas (1997).

41. See Fernandez (1974) for an important argument (with discussion) on sensitivity to and the mastery of metaphors (tropes) in ethnographic narration and related highly organized expressive activities, Lakoff and Johnson (1980) and Lakoff and Turner (1989) for a clear enunciation of common versus uncommon metaphors in everyday life, Van Den Abbeele (1992) on travel as a common metaphor and much that is smuggled into its use, and Fernandez (1986) and Fernandez and Herzfeld (1998) on the place of social and cultural poetics in the study of meaning in performance.

42. Playing out these constraints is in part how logical positivism got to be known less as the backbone of universally applicable methods and more as a list of things that could not (or were not allowed to) be studied in depth, or at all (e.g., meaning versus behavior, aesthetics and emotions, and so on).

43. It is not the same thing as letting multiple authentic voices surface in a single text or performance (see Trawick, 1997), of course, but Diamond believed in—and displayed (by assuming the roles of other speakers) in some of his poetry—the prospect that some people

could speak for others to advantage for all on some occasions; that certain knowledge boundaries could be crossed with insight and power, without imperialism or blind cultural exploitation, without a franchise of superiority or oppressive ethnocentrism. Early in his *Going West* (1986a), for example, the anthropomorphized Otter speaks for the Mohicans and Algonquins (as representatives of still other Native Americans) through esoteric knowledge of their impending collision with history: "Because we knew the future / And we understood their [Mohican, Algonquin] legends / Better than they did" (p. 11). A larger point of this boundary crossing that is not always obvious, especially where ethnic pride is at stake, is that indigenous identity doesn't necessarily translate to expert on all that contextualizes it. Much depends on the form and cultural origins of the questions asked and the cultural and intellectual range of answers sought (see Brady, 1985).

44. There are no separate languages for science and poetry, only specialized vocabularies and variable contexts—cultural "pre-texts" and "subtexts" that reassure, inform, and might even misinform through manipulations designed to present the truth we *want* to find, as opposed to something that might be calculated through other measures as more accurate, analytically satisfying, or less prejudicial. Moreover, there is plenty of slippage in the division of labor between scientific and poetic texts. Asserting bias control, for example, including unmasking ethnocentrism, is seen as obligatory in scientific observation. Disclosing observational bias directly by emulating ("flagging") it in performance and text is a poetic option that may accomplish much the same thing, albeit through a radically different channel and probably for different ends. Here, as elsewhere, context is practically everything for determining meaning, and on occasion it can itself be all but slave to authorial intentions and sociolinguistic form.

45. As book review editor of the *American Anthropologist* at the time, I commissioned these reviews (see Rose, 1983/1991a; Tyler, 1984). One earlier and interesting example of poetry in the *AA* was published by then editor Sol Tax. Referred to as "Puzzled Ph.D. Candidate," and published anonymously (Anonymous, 1954), the poem was sent to Tax by Melville Herskovits, who took it off the bulletin board at the Department of Anthropology, Northwestern University. It was actually "Wasn't It a Thought Titanic" by then graduate student (and now anthropologist and poetics scholar at the University of Chicago) James W. Fernandez.

46. For special takes on the production of ethnographic knowledge, see Borofsky (1987, 2000), Geertz (1973, 1983, 1988, 1995, 1998), Dening (1980, 1996, 1998a, 1998b), Brady (1991b), and Behar (1993, 1996).

47. See also Tedlock (1983, 1990), Schechner (1985, 1995), Fernandez (1988), Graham (1995), Dening (1996), and Taylor (1996). Poetry, of course, fits into the performative traditions of its makers directly, and it can be an important source for understanding indigenous histories. As Charlot (1985) says of Hawaiian poetry, "The fact that poetry has been used frequently for important occasions and purposes suggests that it has a utility thus far overlooked by historians" (p. 29). See also Vendler (1995, p. 6) on the historical meaning of rhythms, stanza forms, personae, and genre; and Fernandez and Herzfeld (1998) for a strong argument that "poetic principles guide all *effective* and *affective* social interaction" (p. 94) and a discussion of how that articulates with the problem of performativity in human action generally.

48. See Brown (1991) and Lévi-Strauss's whole corpus of writings; see also Whitten (1988) and Kilbride (1993),

49. See, for example, Jessor et al. (1996), Shore (1996), Bloch (1998), and Brady (1998b); compare Wierzbicka (1996).

50. Some poets live there, along with a group of narcissists, clever historians, and a tinhorn totalitarian or two. They are visited regularly by social and natural scientists. The project is to see what makes the residents tick. The problem is that everyone in the room is ticking. Everyone is looking back at everyone who's looking at. Nobody knows for sure who's studying whom, or, for that matter, whose conversation should dominate. Somebody said there was order in the chaos. Two poets and the ghost of Aristotle said, "We told you so." Two scientists wanted to bottle it but couldn't get a grip on either its substance or its meaning. New schools of methods grew up in the exact spot of this discovery. A plaque marks it to this very day: THE FOUNTAIN OF MUSES STARTED HERE. LANGUAGE OF TRUTH SOLD NEAR HERE. PLEASE DO NOT LOITER.

◆ References

Abrahams, R. D. (1986). Ordinary and extraordinary experience. In V. Turner & E. M. Bruner (Eds.), *The anthropology of experience* (pp. 45-72). Urbana: University of Illinois Press.

Abu-Lughod, L. (1986). *Veiled sentiments: Honor and poetry in a Bedouin society.* Berkeley: University of California Press.

Abu-Lughod, L. (1993). *Writing women's worlds: Bedouin stories.* Berkeley: University of California Press.

Anonymous (J. W. Fernandez). (1954). Puzzled Ph.D. candidate. In S. Tax, This issue and others. *American Anthropologist, 56,* 742.

Antin, D. (1983). Talking to discover. In J. Rothenberg & D. Rothenberg (Eds.), *Symposium of the whole: A range of discourse toward an ethnopoetics* (pp. 450-461). Berkeley: University of California Press.

Bachelard, G. (1964). *The poetics of space.* Boston: Beacon.

Bachelard, G. (1971). *On poetic imagination and reverie* (C. Gandin, Trans.). Indianapolis: Bobbs-Merrill.

Banks, A., & Banks, S. P. (Eds.). (1998). *Fiction and social research: By ice or fire.* Walnut Creek, CA: AltaMira.

Barrett, S. R. (1996). *Anthropology: A student's guide to theory and method.* Toronto: University of Toronto Press.

Barthes, R. (1968). *Writing degree zero* (A. Lavers & C. Smith, Trans.). New York: Noonday.

Barthes, R. (1972). *Mythologies* (A. Lavers, Trans.). New York: Hill & Wang.

Barthes, R. (1986). From science to literature. In R. Barthes, *The rustle of language* (R. Howard, Trans.; pp. 3-10). Berkeley: University of California Press.

Basso, K. (1988). A review of *Native American discourse: Poetics and rhetoric* (J. Sherzer & A. C. Woodbury, Eds.). *American Ethnologist, 15,* 805-810.

Basso, E. (1995). *The last cannibals: A South American oral history.* Austin: University of Texas Press.

Bauman, R. (1977). *Verbal art as performance.* Prospect Heights, IL: Waveland.

Bauman, R. (Ed.). (1992). *Folklore, cultural performances, and popular entertainments.* New York: Oxford University Press.

Beaujoir, M. (1987). Michel Leiris: Ethnography or self-portrayal? Review essay of Sulfur 15, featuring new translations of Michel Leiris's work. *Cultural Anthropology, 2,* 470-480.

Behar, R. (1993). *Translated woman: Crossing the border with Esperanza's story.* Boston: Beacon.

Behar, R. (1996). *The vulnerable observer: Anthropology that breaks your heart.* Boston: Beacon.

Benson, P. (Ed.). (1993). *Anthropology and literature.* Urbana: University of Illinois Press.

Bishop, E., & Brasil, E. (Eds.). (1972). *An anthology of twentieth-century Brazilian poetry.* Middletown, CT: Wesleyan University Press.

Bloch, M. E. F. (1998). *How we think they think: Anthropological approaches to cognition, memory, and literacy.* Boulder, CO: Westview.

Boon, J. A. (1972). *From symbolism to structuralism: Lévi-Strauss in a literary tradition.* New York: Harper & Row.

Boon, J. A. (1982). *Other tribes, other scribes: Symbolic anthropology in the comparative study of cultures, histories, religions, and texts.* Cambridge: Cambridge University Press.

Boon, J. A. (1984). Folly, Bali, and anthropology, or satire across cultures. In E. M. Bruner (Ed.), *Text, play, and story: The construction and reconstruction of self and society* (pp. 156-177). Washington, DC: American Ethnological Society.

Boon, J. A. (1989). *Affinities and extremes: Criss-crossing the bittersweet ethnology of East Indies history, Hindu-Balinese culture, and Indo-European allure.* Chicago: University of Chicago Press.

Borofsky, R. (1987). *Making history: Pukapukan and anthropological constructions of knowledge.* New York: Cambridge University Press.

Borofsky, R. (1994). *Assessing cultural anthropology.* New York: McGraw-Hill.

Borofsky, R. (1997). Cook, Lono, Obeyesekere, and Sahlins [with commentary]. *Current Anthropology, 38,* 255-282.

Borofsky, R. (Ed.). (2000). *Remembrance of Pacific pasts: An invitation to remake history.* Honolulu: University of Hawaii Press.

Bourdieu, P. (1991). *Language and symbolic power.* Cambridge, MA: Harvard University Press.

Bowen, E. S. (pseudonym of L. Bohannan). (1954). *Return to laughter: An anthropological novel.* New York: Harper & Row.

Brady, I. (Ed.). (1983). Speaking in the name of the real: Freeman and Mead on Samoa [Special section]. *American Anthropologist, 85,* 908-947.

Brady, I. (1985). Review of *Tuvalu: A history,* by S. Faniu, V. Ielemia, T. Isako, et al. In *Pacific History Bibliography and Comment, 1985* (pp. 52-54). Canberra: Journal of Pacific History.

Brady, I. (1990a). Comment on "Is anthropology art or science?" by M. Carrithers. *Current Anthropology, 31,* 273-274.

Brady, I. (1990b). Review of *The violent imagination,* by R. Fox. *American Anthropologist, 92,* 1078-1079.

Brady, I. (Ed.). (1991a). *Anthropological poetics.* Savage, MD: Rowman & Littlefield.

Brady, I. (1991b). Harmony and argument: Bringing forth the artful science. In I. Brady (Ed.), *Anthropological poetics* (pp. 3-30). Savage, MD: Rowman & Littlefield.

Brady, I. (1991c). The Samoa reader: Last word or lost horizon? *Current Anthropology, 32,* 497-500.

Brady, I. (1993). Tribal fire and scribal ice. In P. Benson (Ed.), *Anthropology and literature* (pp. 248-278). Urbana: University of Illinois Press.

Brady, I. (1996). Poetics. In D. Levinson & M. Ember (Eds.), *The encyclopedia of cultural anthropology* (Vol. 3, pp. 951-959). New York: Holt.

Brady, I. (1998a). A gift of the journey. *Qualitative Inquiry, 4,* 463.

Brady, I. (1998b). Two thousand and what? Anthropological moments and methods for the next century. *American Anthropologist, 100,* 510-516.

Brady, I. (1999). Ritual as cognitive process, performance as history. *Current Anthropology, 40,* 243-248.

Brady, I., & Turner, E. (1994, June). Introduction. In I. Brady & E. Turner (Eds.), Humanism in anthropology, 1994 [Special issue]. *Anthropology and Humanism, 19,* 3-11.

Brann, E. T. H. (1991). *The world of the imagination: Sum and substance.* Savage, MD: Rowman & Littlefield.

Bright, W. (Ed.). (1983). *Discovered tongues: Poems by linguists.* San Francisco: Corvine.

Bright, W. (1985). *Word formations: Poems by linguists.* San Francisco: Corvine.

Brooks, P. (1994). Aesthetics and ideology: What happened to poetics? *Critical Inquiry, 20,* 509-523.

Brown, D. E. (1991). *Human universals.* New York: McGraw-Hill.

Brown, R. H. (1977). *A poetic for sociology: Toward a logic of discovery for the human sciences.* Cambridge: Cambridge University Press.

Bruner, E. M. (Ed.). (1984). *Text, play, and story: The construction and reconstruction of self and society.* Washington, DC: American Ethnological Society.

Bruner, E. M., & Gorfain, P. (1991). Dialogic narration and the paradoxes of Masada. In I. Brady (Ed.), *Anthropological poetics* (pp. 177-203). Savage, MD: Rowman & Littlefield.

Bruner, J. (1986). *Actual minds, possible worlds.* Cambridge, MA: Harvard University Press.

Bruner, J. (1990). *Acts of meaning.* Cambridge, MA: Harvard University Press.

Burke, E. (1958). *A philosophical enquiry into the origin of ideas of the sublime and beautiful.* Notre Dame, IN: University of Notre Dame Press.

Burke, K. (1989). *On symbols and society* (J. R. Gusfield, Ed.). Chicago: University of Chicago Press.

Candre, H., & Echeverri, J. A. (1996). *Cool tobacco, sweet coca: Teachings of an Indian sage from the Colombian Amazon.* Devon: Themis.

Chandrasekhar, S. (1987). *Truth and beauty: Aesthetics and motivations In science.* Chicago: University of Chicago Press.

Charlot, J. (1985). *The Hawaiian poetry of religion and politics.* Honolulu: Institute for Polynesian Studies.

Clifford, J. (1988). *The predicament of culture: Twentieth-century ethnography, literature, and art.* Cambridge, MA: Harvard University Press.

Clifford, J., & Marcus, G. E. (Eds.). (1986). *Writing culture: The poetics and politics of ethnography.* Berkeley: University of California Press.

Collingwood, R. G. (1956). *The idea of history.* New York: Oxford University Press.

Coward, H. G., & Royce, J. R. (1981). Toward an epistemological basis for humanistic psychology. In J. R. Royce & L. P. Mos (Eds.), *Humanistic psychology: Concepts and criticisms* (pp. 109-134). New York: Plenum.

Crapanzano, V. (1980). *Tuhami: Portrait of a Moroccan.* Chicago: University of Chicago Press.

Csordas, T. J. (1997). Prophecy and the performance of metaphor. *American Anthropologist, 99,* 321-332.

Culler, J. (1975). *Structuralist poetics: Structuralism, linguistics, and the study of literature.* Ithaca, NY: Cornell University Press.

Culler, J. (1977). Foreword. In T. Torodov, *The poetics of prose* (pp. 7-13). Ithaca, NY: Cornell University Press.

Davies, C. A. (1999). *Reflexive ethnography: A guide to researching selves and others.* New York: Routledge.

Dening, G. (1980). *Islands and beaches: Discourse on a silent land: Marquesas 1774-1880.* Honolulu: University of Hawaii Press.

Dening, G. (1995). *The death of William Gooch: A history's anthropology.* Honolulu: University of Hawaii Press.

Dening, G. (1996). *Performances.* Chicago: University of Chicago Press.

Dening, G. (1998a). *Readings/writings.* Victoria: Melbourne University Press.

Dening, G. (1998b). Writing, rewriting the beach: An essay. *Rethinking History,* 2(2), 143-172.

Dennis, P. A. (1989). Oliver LaFarge, writer and anthropologist. In P. A. Dennis & W. Aycock (Eds.), *Literature and anthropology* (pp. 209-219). Lubbock: Texas Tech University Press.

Dennis, P. A., & Aycock, W. (Eds.). (1989). *Literature and anthropology.* Lubbock: Texas Tech University Press.

Denzin, N. K. (1997). *Interpretive ethnography: Ethnographic practices for the 21st century.* Thousand Oaks, CA: Sage.

de Zengotita, T. (1989). On Wittgenstein's remarks on Frazer's *Golden bough. Cultural Anthropology, 4,* 390-398.

Diamond, S. (1982). *Totems.* Barrytown, NY: Open Book/Station Hill.

Diamond, S. (1986a). *Going west.* Northhampton, MA: Hermes House.

Diamond, S. (1986b). How to die in America. *Cultural Anthropology, 1,* 447-448.

Diamond, S. (1986c). Preface. *Dialectical Anthropology, 11,* 131-132.

Diamond, S. (1987). The beautiful and the ugly are one thing, the sublime another: A reflection on culture. *Cultural Anthropology, 2,* 268-271.

Dobin, H. (1990). *Merlin's disciples: Prophecy, poetry, and power in Renaissance England.* Stanford, CA: Stanford University Press.

Donoghue, D. (1989, June 29). The strange case of Paul de Man. *New York Review of Books,* pp. 32, 37.

Dove, R. (1994, January-February). What does poetry do for us? *Virginia* (University of Virginia alumni newsletter), pp. 22-27.

Dreyfus, H. L., & Rabinow, P. (1983). *Michel Foucault: Beyond structuralism and hermeneutics* (2nd ed.). Chicago: University of Chicago Press.

Dumont, J.-P. (1978). *The headman and I: Ambiguity and ambivalence in the fieldworking experience.* Austin: University of Texas Press.

Duranti, A. (1993). Truth and intentionality: An ethnographic critique. *Cultural Anthropology, 8,* 214-245.

Eagleton, T. (1983). *Literary theory: An introduction.* Minneapolis: University of Minnesota Press.

Eco, U. (1979). *The role of the reader: Explorations in the semiotics of texts.* Bloomington: Indiana University Press.

Ellis, C., & Bochner, A. P. (Eds.). (1996). *Composing ethnography: Alternative forms of qualitative writing.* Walnut Creek, CA: AltaMira.

Emerson, C. (1997). *The first hundred years of Mikhail Bakhtin.* Princeton, NJ: Princeton University Press.

Fabian, J. (1983). *Time and the other: How anthropology makes its object.* New York: Columbia University Press.

Fabian, J. (1990). Presence and representation: The other and anthropological writing. *Critical Inquiry, 16,* 753-772.

Fabian, J. (1994). Ethnographic objectivity revisited: From rigor to vigor. In A. Megill (Ed.), *Rethinking objectivity* (pp. 81-108). Durham, NC: Duke University Press.

Feld, S. (1982). *Sound and sentiment: Birds, weeping, poetics, and song in Kaluli expression*. Philadelphia: University of Pennsylvania Press.

Feld, S. (1987). Dialogic editing: Interpreting how Kaluli read sound and sentiment. *Cultural Anthropology, 2,* 190-210.

Fernandez, J. W. (1974). The mission of metaphor in expressive culture [with commentary]. *Current Anthropology, 15,* 119-145.

Fernandez, J. W. (1985). Exploded worlds: Texts as a metaphor for ethnography (and vice-versa). In S. Diamond (Ed.), Anthropology after '84: State of the art, state of society, part II [Special issue]. *Dialectical Anthropology, 10*(1-2), 15-26.

Fernandez, J. W. (1986). *Persuasions and performances: The play of tropes in culture*. Bloomington: Indiana University Press.

Fernandez, J. W. (1988). Andalusia on our minds: Two contrasting places in Spain as seen in a vernacular poetic duel of the late 19th century. *Cultural Anthropology, 3,* 21-35.

Fernandez, J. W. (1989). Comment on Keesing's exotic readings of cultural texts. *Current Anthropology, 30,* 470-471.

Fernandez, J. W., & Herzfeld, M. (1998). In search of meaningful methods. In H. R. Bernard (Ed.), *A handbook of method in cultural anthropology* (pp. 89-129). Thousand Oaks, CA: Sage.

Finnegan, R. (1992a). Oral poetry. In R. Bauman (Ed.), *Folklore, cultural performances, and popular entertainments* (pp. 119-127). New York: Oxford University Press.

Finnegan, R. (1992b). *Oral poetry: Its nature, significance, and social context*. Bloomington: Indiana University Press.

Fischer, M. M. J. (1988). Scientific dialogue and critical hermeneutics. *Cultural Anthropology, 3,* 3-15.

Fischer, M. M. J. (1989). Museums and festivals: Poetics and politics of Representations Conference, the Smithsonian Institution, September 26-28, 1988, I. Karp and S. Levine, organizers. *Cultural Anthropology, 4,* 204-221.

Fischer, M. M.J. (1991). Anthropology as cultural critique: Inserts for the 1990s: Cultural studies of science, visual virtual-realities, and post-trauma politics. *Cultural Anthropology, 6,* 525-537.

Flores, T. (1982). Field poetry. *Anthropology and Humanism Quarterly, 7*(1), 16-22.

Flores, T. (1985). The anthropology of aesthetics. In S. Diamond (Ed.), Anthropology after '84: State of the art, state of society, part II [Special issue]. *Dialectical Anthropology, 10*(1-2), 27-41.

Flores, T. (1999). *In place: Poems by Toni Flores*. Geneva, NY: Hobart & William Smith Colleges Press.

Fox, R. (1989). *The violent imagination*. New Brunswick, NJ: Rutgers University Press.

Fox, R. G. (Ed.). (1991). *Recapturing anthropology: Working in the present*. Santa Fe, NM: School of American Research Press.

Friedrich, P. (1979a). *Bastard moons*. Chicago: Benjamin & Martha Waite.

Friedrich, P. (1979b). Linguistic relativity and the order-to-chaos continuum. In J. Maquet (Ed.), *On linguistic anthropology: Essays in honor of Harry Hoijer* (pp. 89-139). Malibu, CA: Undena.

Friedrich, P. (1995). The world-listener & Cities (two poems). *American Anthropologist, 97,* 658-659.

Fujimara, J. H. (1998). Authorizing knowledge in science and anthropology. *American Anthropologist, 100,* 347-360.

Geertz, C. (1973). *The interpretation of cultures: Selected essays*. New York: Basic Books.

Geertz, C. (1983). *Local knowledge: Further essays in interpretive anthropology*. New York: Basic Books.

Geertz, C. (1988). *Works and lives: The anthropologist as author*. Stanford, CA: Stanford University Press.

Geertz, C. (1995). Disciplines. *Raritan, 14*(3), 65-102.

Geertz, C. (1998, October 22). Deep hanging out. *New York Review of Books,* pp. 69-70.

Gellner, E. (1998). *Language and solitude: Wittgenstein, Malinowski, and the Habsburg dilemma*. New York: Cambridge University Press.

Gottlieb, A., & Graham, P. (1993). *Parallel worlds: An anthropologist and a writer encounter Africa*. New York: Crown.

Gould, S. J. (1991). More light on leaves: Can a great artist also be a great scientist? *Natural History, 2,* 16-23.

Graham, L. (1995). *Performing dreams: Discourse of immortality among the Xavante of central Brazil*. Austin: University of Texas Press.

Graves, R. (1971, December 2). Science, technology, and poetry. *New Scientist,* pp. 34-35.

Guetti, J. (1984). Wittgenstein and literary theory. *Raritan, 4*(2), 67-84.

Hall, D. (1988). *Poetry and ambition: Essays 1982-88*. Ann Arbor: University of Michigan Press.

Hallyn, F. (1990). *The poetic structure of the world: Copernicus and Kepler*. New York: Urzone.

Handler, R. (1983). The dainty and the hungry man: Literature and anthropology in the work of Edward Sapir. In G. W. Stocking, Jr. (Ed.), *Observers observed: Essays on ethnographic research* (pp. 208-231). Madison: University of Wisconsin Press.

Handler, R. (1985). On dialogue and destructive analysis: Problems in narrating nationalism and ethnicity. *Journal of Anthropological Research, 41,* 171-181.

Handler, R. (1990). Ruth Benedict and the modernist sensibility. In M. Manganaro (Ed.), *Modernist anthropology: From fieldwork to text* (pp. 163-180). Princeton, NJ: Princeton University Press.

Handler, R., & Segal, D. (1987). Narrating multiple realities: Some lessons from Jane Austen for ethnographers. *Anthropology and Humanism Quarterly, 12*(4), 15-21.

Handy, W. C. (1973). *Thunder from the sea.* Honolulu: University of Hawaii Press.

Harland, R. (1987). *Superstructuralism: The philosophy of structuralism and post-structuralism.* New York: Methuen.

Harris, J. (1997). Giotto's invisible sheep: Lacanian mirroring and modeling in Walcott's "Another life." *South Atlantic Quarterly, 96,* 293-309.

Harris, M. (1977). *Cannibals and kings.* New York: Random House.

Harris, M. (1987). *The sacred cow and the abominable pig: Riddles of food and culture.* New York: Simon & Schuster.

Hill, J. H. (1986). The refiguration of the anthropology of language. *Cultural Anthropology, 1,* 89-102.

Hodder, I. (1986). *Reading the past: Current approaches to interpretation in archaeology.* New York: Cambridge University Press.

Hoffmann, R. (1987). *The metamict state: Poems by Roald Hoffmann.* Gainesville: University Presses of Florida.

Hoffmann, R. (1990a). *Gaps and verges: Poems by Roald Hoffmann.* Gainesville: University Presses of Florida.

Hoffmann, R. (1990b). Molecular beauty. *Journal of Aesthetics and Art Criticism, 48,* 191-204.

Hoffmann, R. (1995). *The same and not the same.* New York: Columbia University Press.

Holquist, M. (1990). *Dialogism: Bakhtin and his world.* New York: Routledge.

Holton, G. (1993). *Science and anti-science.* Cambridge, MA: Harvard University Press.

Jackson, M. (1982). *Allegories of the wilderness: Ethics and ambiguity in Kuranko narratives.* Bloomington: Indiana University Press.

Jackson, M. (1986). *Barawa and the ways birds fly in the sky.* Washington, DC: Smithsonian Institution Press.

Jakobson, R. (1987). *Language in literature* (K. Pomorska & S. Rudy, Eds.). Cambridge, MA: Harvard University Press.

James, A., Hockey, J., & Dawson, A. (Eds.). (1997). *After writing culture: Epistemology and praxis in contemporary anthropology.* New York: Routledge.

Jarvie, I. C. (1983). The problem of the ethnographic real. *Current Anthropology, 24,* 313-325.

Jennings, B. (1983). Interpretive social science and policy analysis. In D. Callahan & B. Jennings (Eds.), *Ethics, the social sciences, and policy analysis* (pp. 3-35). New York: Plenum.

Jessor, R., Colby, A., & Shweder, R. A. (Eds.). (1996). *Ethnography and human development: Context and meaning in social inquiry.* Chicago: University of Chicago Press.

Karp, I., & Levine, S. D. (Eds.). (1991). *Exhibiting cultures: The poetics and politics of museum display.* Washington, DC: Smithsonian Institution Press.

Kilbride, P. L. (1993). Anti-anti-universalism: Rethinking cultural psychology and anti-anti-relativism. *Reviews in Anthropology, 22*(1), 1-11.

Knab, T. J. (1995). *A war of witches: A journey into the underworld of the contemporary Aztecs.* New York: HarperCollins.

Knauft, B. M. (1996). *Genealogies for the present in cultural anthropology.* New York: Routledge.

Kroskrity, P. V. (1985). Growing with stories: Line, verse, and genre in an Arizona Tewa text. *Journal of Anthropological Research, 41,* 183-199.

Krupat, A. (1992). *Ethno-criticism: Ethnography, history, literature.* Berkeley: University of California Press.

Kurten, B. (1980). *Dance of the tiger.* New York: Berkeley.

Laderman, C. (1991). *Taming the wind of desire: Psychology, medicine, and aesthetics in Malay shamanistic performance.* Berkeley: University of California Press.

LaFarge, O. (1929). *Laughing boy.* Boston: Houghton Mifflin.

Lakoff, G., & Johnson, M. (1980). *Metaphors we live by.* Chicago: University of Chicago Press.

Lakoff, G., & Turner, M. (1989). *More than cool reason: A field guide to poetic metaphor.* Chicago: University of Chicago Press.

Langness, L. L., & Frank, G. (1978). Fact, fiction, and the ethnographic novel. *Anthropology and Humanism Quarterly, 3*(1-2), 18-22.

Lanser, S. S. (1981). *The narrative act.* Princeton, NJ: Princeton University Press.

Lavie, S. (1990). *The poetics of military occupation: Mzeina allegories of Bedouin identity under Israeli and Egyptian rule.* Berkeley: University of California Press.

Layton, R. (1997). *An introduction to theory in anthropology.* Cambridge: Cambridge University Press.

Leavitt, J. (Ed.). (1997). *Poetry and prophecy: The anthropology of inspiration.* Ann Arbor: University of Michigan Press.

Lett, J. (1997). *Science, reason, and anthropology: The principles of rational inquiry.* Lanham, MD: Roman & Littlefield.

Levi, P. (1984). *The periodic table.* New York: Schocken.

Levine, G. (1987). Literary science—scientific literature. *Raritan, 6*(3), 24-41.

Levine, G. (1994). Why science isn't literature: The importance of differences. In A. Megill (Ed.), *Rethinking objectivity* (pp. 65-79). Durham, NC: Duke University Press.

Lévi-Strauss, C. (1961). *Tristes tropiques: An anthropological study of primitive societies in Brazil* (J. Russell, Trans.). New York: Atheneum.

Lévi-Strauss, C. (1962). "Les chats" de Charles Baudelaire. *L'Homme, 2*(1), 5-21.

Lévi-Strauss, C. (1967). *Structural anthropology* (C. Jacobson & B. G. Schoepf, Trans.). Garden City, NY: Doubleday.

Lévi-Strauss, C. (1969). *The raw and the cooked* (J. Weightman & D. Weightman, Trans.). New York: Harper & Row.

Lightman, A. (1993). *Einstein's dreams.* New York: Time Warner.

Limón, J. (1994). *Dancing with the devil: Society and cultural poetics in Mexican-American South Texas.* Madison: University of Wisconsin Press.

Lorde, A. (1984). *Sister outsider.* Trumansburg, NY: Crossing.

Loriggio, F. (1990). Anthropology, literary theory, and the traditions of modernism. In M. Manganaro (Ed.), *Modernist anthropology: From fieldwork to text* (pp. 215-242). Princeton, NJ: Princeton University Press.

MacCannell, D. (1992). *Empty meeting grounds: The tourist papers.* New York: Routledge.

Manganaro, M. (Ed.). (1990a). *Modernist anthropology: From fieldwork to text.* Princeton, NJ: Princeton University Press.

Manganaro, M. (1990b). Textual play, power, and cultural critique: An orientation to modernist anthropology. In M. Manganaro (Ed.), *Modernist anthropology: From fieldwork to text* (pp. 3-47). Princeton, NJ: Princeton University Press.

Marcus, G. E. (1980). Rhetoric and the ethnographic genre in anthropological research. *Current Anthropology, 21,* 507-510.

Marcus, G. (1988). Parody and the parodic in Polynesian cultural history. *Cultural Anthropology, 3,* 68-76.

Marcus, G. E. (1993). A review of *Ethno-criticism: Ethnography, history, literature,* by A. Krupat. *American Anthropologist, 395,* 766.

Marcus, G. E. (1998). *Ethnography through thick and thin: A new research imaginary for anthropology's changing professional culture.* Princeton, NJ: Princeton University Press.

Marcus, G. E., & Cushman, D. (1982). Ethnographies as texts. *Annual Review of Anthropology, 11,* 25-69.

Marcus, G. E., & Fischer, M. M. J. (1986). *Anthropology as cultural critique: An experimental moment in the human sciences.* Chicago: University of Chicago Press.

Mascia-Lees, F. E., Sharpe, P., & Cohen, C. B. (1993). The postmodernist turn in anthropology: Cautions from a feminist perspective. In P. Benson (Ed.),

Anthropology and literature (pp. 225-248). Urbana: University of Illinois Press.

Matthiessen, P. (1963). *At play in the fields of the Lord.* New York: Vintage.

Matthiessen, P. (1975). *Far Tortuga.* New York: Vintage.

Maxwell, N. (1984). *From knowledge to wisdom: A revolution in the aims and methods of science.* New York: Blackwell.

McAllister, J. W. (1998). Is beauty a sign of truth in scientific theories? *American Scientist, 86,* 178-183.

Megill, A. (Ed.). (1994). *Rethinking objectivity.* Durham, NC: Duke University Press.

Meschonnic, H. (1988). Rhyme and life. *Critical Inquiry, 15,* 90-107.

Miner, E. (1990). *Comparative poetics: An intercultural essay on theories of literature.* Princeton, NJ: Princeton University Press.

Momaday, N. S. (1989). *The ancient child.* New York: HarperCollins.

Motzafi-Haller, P. (1998). Beyond textual analysis: Practice, interacting discourses, and the experience of distinction in Botswana. *Cultural Anthropology, 13,* 522-547.

Napoli, D. J., & Rando, E. N. (Eds.). (1979). *Linguistic muse.* Edmonton: Linguistic Research.

Narayan, K. (1989). *Storytellers, saints, and scoundrels: Folk narrative in Hindu religious teaching.* Philadelphia: University of Pennsylvania Press.

Obeyesekere, G. (1992). *The apotheosis of Captain Cook: European mythmaking in the Pacific.* Princeton, NJ: Princeton University Press.

O'Meara, J. T. (1989). Anthropology as empirical science. *American Anthropologist, 91,* 354-369.

O'Meara, J. T. (1997). Causation and the struggle for a science of culture [with commentary]. *Current Anthropology, 38,* 399-418.

O'Nell, T. D. (1994). Telling about whites, talking about Indians: Oppression, resistance, and contemporary Indian identity. *Cultural Anthropology, 9,* 94-126.

Poggie, J. J., Jr., DeWalt, B. R., & Dressler, W. W. (Eds.). (1992). *Anthropological research: Process and application.* Albany: State University of New York Press.

Polanyi, M., & Prosch, H. (1975). *Meaning.* Chicago: University of Chicago Press.

Prattis, J. I. (Ed.). (1986). *Reflections: The anthropological muse.* Washington, DC: American Anthropological Association.

Prattis, J. I. (1997). *Anthropology at the edge: Essays on culture, symbol, and consciousness.* Lanham, MD: University Press of America.

Rabinow, P. (1977). *Reflections on fieldwork in Morocco.* Berkeley: University of California Press.

Rabinow, P. (1983). Humanism as nihilism. In N. Haan, R. N. Bellah, P. Rabinow, & W. M. Sullivan (Eds.), *Social science as moral inquiry* (pp. 52-75). New York: Columbia University Press.

Rabinow, P. (Ed.). (1984). *The Foucault reader.* New York: Pantheon.

Rabinow, P. (1986). Representations are social facts: Modernity and post-modernity in anthropology. In J. Clifford & G. E. Marcus (Eds.), *Writing culture: The poetics and politics of ethnography* (pp. 234-261). Berkeley: University of California Press.

Rabinow, P., & Sullivan, W. M. (Eds.). (1987). *Interpretive social science: A second look.* Berkeley: University of California Press.

Rapport, N. (1997). *Transcendent individual: Towards a literary and liberal anthropology.* New York: Routledge.

Reck, G. G. (1978). *In the shadow of Tlaloc: Life in a Mexican village.* Prospect Heights, IL: Waveland.

Reichel-Dolmatoff, G. (1996). *Yuruparí: Studies of an Amazonian foundation myth.* Cambridge, MA: Harvard University Press.

Richards, I. A. (1929). *Practical criticism.* New York: Harcourt Brace Jovanovich.

Richardson, L. (1994). Writing: A method of inquiry. In N. K. Denzin & Y. S. Lincoln (Eds.), *Handbook of qualitative research* (pp. 516-529). Thousand Oaks, CA: Sage.

Richardson, M. (1990). *Cry lonesome and other accounts of the anthropologist's project.* Albany: State University of New York Press.

Richardson, M. (1998a). Poetics in the field and on the page. *Qualitative Inquiry, 4,* 451-462.

Richardson, M. (1998b). The poetics of a resurrection: Re-seeing 30 years of change in a Colombian community and in the anthropological enterprise. *American Anthropologist, 100,* 11-21.

Riffaterre, M. (1970). Describing poetic structures: Two approaches to Baudelaire's "Les chats." In J. Ehrmann (Ed.), *Structuralism* (pp. 189-230). Garden City, NY: Doubleday.

Riffaterre, M. (1984). *Semiotics of poetry.* Bloomington: Indiana University Press.

Robbins, B. (1987). Poaching off the disciplines. *Raritan, 6*(4), 81-96.

Rorty, R. (1979). *Philosophy and the mirror of nature.* Princeton, NJ: Princeton University Press.

Rorty, R. (1981). Nineteenth-century idealism and twentieth-century textualism. *Monist, 64,* 155-174.

Rosaldo, R. (1989). *Culture and truth: The remaking of social analysis.* Boston: Beacon.

Rose, D. (1991a). In search of experience: The anthropological poetics of Stanley Diamond. In I. Brady (Ed.), *Anthropological poetics* (pp. 219-233). Savage, MD: Rowman & Littlefield. (Reprinted from *American Anthropologist,* 1983, *85*)

Rose, D. (1991b). Reversal. In I. Brady (Ed.), *Anthropological poetics* (pp. 283-301). Savage, MD: Rowman & Littlefield.

Rose, D. (1993). Ethnography as a form of life. In P. Benson (Ed.), *Anthropology and literature* (pp. 192-224). Urbana: University of Illinois Press.

Rothenberg, J. (1981). *Pre-faces and other writings.* New York: New Directions.

Rothenberg, J. (Ed.). (1985). *Technicians of the sacred: A range of poetries from Africa, America, Asia, Europe, and Oceania.* Berkeley: University of California Press.

Rothenberg, J. (1994). "Je est un autre": Ethnopoetics and the poet as other. *American Anthropologist, 96,* 523-524.

Rothenberg, J., & Rothenberg, D. (Eds.). (1983). *Symposium of the whole: A range of discourse toward an ethnopoetics.* Berkeley: University of California Press.

Sagan, C. (1980). *Cosmos.* New York: Ballantine.

Sagan, C. (1985). *Contact.* New York: Pocket Books.

Sahlins, M. (1981). *Historical metaphors and mythical realities: Structure in the early history of the Sandwich Islands kingdom.* Ann Arbor: University of Michigan Press.

Sahlins, M. (1985). *Islands of history.* Chicago: University of Chicago Press.

Sahlins, M. (1996). *How "natives" think: About Captain Cook, for example.* Chicago: University of Chicago Press.

Said, E. (1991). The politics of knowledge. *Raritan, 11*(1), 17-31.

Sangren, P. S. (1991). Rhetoric and the authority of ethnography. In S. Silverman (Ed.), *Inquiry and debate in the human sciences* (pp. 277-307). Chicago: University of Chicago Press.

Schechner, R. (1985). *Between theater and anthropology.* Philadelphia: University of Pennsylvania Press.

Schechner, R. (1995). *The future of ritual: Writings on culture and performance.* New York: Routledge.

Scholes, R. (1974). *Structuralism in literature: An introduction.* New Haven, CT: Yale University Press.

Scholte, B. (1966). Epistemic paradigms: Some problems in cross-cultural research on social anthropological history and theory. *American Anthropologist, 68,* 1192-1201.

Scott, D. (1992). Anthropology and colonial discourse: Aspects of the demonological construction of Sinhala cultural practice. *Cultural Anthropology, 7,* 301-326.

Shankman, P. (1984). On semiotics and science: Reply to Renner and Scholte. *Current Anthropology, 25,* 691-692.

Sherzer, J. (1987). A discourse-centered approach to language and culture. *American Anthropologist, 89,* 295-309.

Sherzer, J., & Woodbury, A. C. (Eds.). (1987). *Native American discourse: Poetics and rhetoric.* New York: Cambridge University Press.

Shore, B. (1996). *Cognition, culture, and the problem of meaning.* New York: Oxford University Press.

Shweder, R. A. (1996). True ethnography: The lore, the law, and the lure. In R. Jessor, A. Colby, & R. A. Shweder (Eds.), *Ethnography and human devel-*

opment: Context and meaning in social inquiry (pp. 4-52). Chicago: University of Chicago Press.

Silko, L. M. (1977). *Ceremony.* New York: Penguin.

Simms, N. T. (1991). *Points of contact: A study of the interplay and intersection of traditional and non-traditional literatures, cultures, and mentalities.* New York: Pace University Press.

Simpson, D. (1994). Literary criticism, localism, and local knowledge. *Raritan, 14*(1), 70-88.

Slater, C. (1982). *Stories on a string: The Brazilian literatura de cordel.* Berkeley: University of California Press.

Spiegelberg, H. (1975). *Doing phenomenology: Essays on and in phenomenology.* The Hague: Martinus Nijhoff.

Spradley, J. E., & McDonough, G. P. (Eds.). (1973). *Anthropology through literature.* Boston: Little, Brown.

Stewart, J. (1962). *Curving road: Stories by John Stewart.* Urbana: University of Illinois Press.

Stewart, J. (1989). *Drinkers, drummers, and decent folk.* Albany: State University of New York Press.

Stewart, K. (1996). *A space on the side of the road: Cultural poetics in an "other" America.* Princeton, NJ: Princeton University Press.

Swann, B. (Ed.). (1983). *Smoothing the ground: Essays in Native American oral literature.* Berkeley: University of California Press.

Swearingen, J. (1986). Oral hermeneutics during the transition to literacy: The contemporary debate. *Cultural Anthropology, 1,* 138-156.

Tarn, N. (1991). *Views from the weaving mountain: Selected essays in poetics and anthropology.* Albuquerque: University of New Mexico.

Taussig, M. (1987). *Shamanism, colonialism, and the wild man.* Chicago: University of Chicago Press.

Taussig, M. (1993). *Mimesis and alterity: A particular history of the senses.* New York: Routledge.

Taylor, L. J. (1996). "There are two things that people don't like to hear about themselves": The anthropology of Ireland and the Irish view of anthropology. *South Atlantic Quarterly, 95,* 213-226.

Tedlock, B. (1991). From participant observation to the observation of participation: The emergence of narrative ethnography. *Journal of Anthropological Research, 47,* 69-94.

Tedlock, B. (1992). *The beautiful and the dangerous: Dialogues with the Zuni Indians.* New York: Penguin.

Tedlock, B., & Tedlock, D. (1985). Text and textile: Language and technology in the arts of the Quich Maya. *Journal of Anthropological Research, 41,* 121-146.

Tedlock, D. (Trans.). (1972). *Finding the center: Narrative poetry of the Zuni Indians.* New York: Dial.

Tedlock, D. (1983). *The spoken word and the work of interpretation.* Philadelphia: University of Pennsylvania Press.

Tedlock, D. (Trans. & Commentator). (1985). *Popol Vuh: The Mayan book of the dawn of life.* New York: Simon & Schuster.

Tedlock, D. (1987a). Hearing a voice in an ancient text: Quich Maya poetics in performance. In J. Sherzer & A. C. Woodbury (Eds.), *Native American discourse: Poetics and rhetoric* (pp. 140-175). Cambridge: Cambridge University Press.

Tedlock, D. (1987b). Questions concerning dialogical anthropology (with a response from Stephen Tyler). *Journal of Anthropological Research, 43,* 325-344.

Tedlock, D. (1990). *Days from a dream almanac.* Urbana: University of Illinois Press.

Tedlock, D. (1991). The speaker of tales has more than one string to play on. In I. Brady (Ed.), *Anthropological poetics* (pp. 309-340). Savage, MD: Rowman & Littlefield.

Tedlock, D. (1992). Ethnopoetics. In R. Bauman (Ed.), *Folklore, cultural performances, and popular entertainments* (pp. 81-85). New York: Oxford University Press.

Tedlock, D. (1993). *Breath on the mirror: Mythic voices and visions of the living Maya.* Albuquerque: University of New Mexico Press.

Thomas, E. M. (1987). *Reindeer moon.* New York: Pocket Books.

Thomas, N. (1989). *Out of time: History and evolution in anthropological discourse.* New York: Cambridge University Press.

Thomas, N. (1991). Against ethnography. *Cultural Anthropology, 6,* 306-322.

Thompson, W. I. (1983). *Blue jade from the morning star: An essay and a cycle of poems on Quetzalcoatl.* West Stockbridge, MA: Lindisfarne.

Tiles, M. (1984). *Bachelard: Science and objectivity.* New York: Cambridge University Press.

Tilley, C. (Ed.). (1990). *Reading material culture.* Cambridge, MA: Blackwell.

Todorov, T. (1977). *The poetics of prose* (R. Howard, Trans.). Ithaca, NY: Cornell University Press.

Todorov, T. (1981). *Introduction to poetics* (R. Howard, Trans.). Minneapolis: University of Minnesota Press.

Trawick, M. (1988). Spirits and voices in Tamil song. *American Ethnologist, 15,* 193-215.

Trawick, M. (1997). Time and mother: Conversations with a possessing spirit. In J. Leavitt (Ed.), *Poetry and prophecy: The anthropology of inspiration* (pp. 61-75). Ann Arbor: University of Michigan Press.

Tsing, A. L. (1994). From the margins. *Cultural Anthropology, 9,* 279-297.

Turnbull, C. (1962). *The forest people*. Garden City, NY: Doubleday.

Turnbull, C. (1972). *The mountain people*. New York: Simon & Schuster.

Turner, E. (1987). *The spirit and the drum: A memoir of Africa*. Tucson: University of Arizona Press.

Turner, V. (1974). *Dramas, fields, and metaphors: Symbolic action in human society*. Ithaca, NY: Cornell University Press.

Turner, V. (Ed.). (1982a). *Celebration: Studies in festivity and ritual*. Washington, DC: Smithsonian Institution Press.

Turner, V. (1982b). *From ritual to theatre: The human seriousness of play*. New York: Performing Arts Journal Publications.

Turner, V. (1983). A review of "Ethnopoetics." In J. Rothenberg & D. Rothenberg (Eds.), *Symposium of the whole: A range of discourse toward an ethnopoetics* (pp. 337-342). Berkeley: University of California Press.

Tyler, S. A. (Ed.). (1969). *Cognitive anthropology*. New York: Holt, Rinehart & Winston.

Tyler, S. A. (1984). The poetic turn in postmodern anthropology: The poetry of Paul Friedrich. *American Anthropologist, 86*, 328-336.

Ulin, R. C. (1984). *Understanding cultures: Perspectives in anthropology and social theory*. Austin: University of Texas Press.

Valéry, P. (1964). *Aesthetics* (R. Mennheim, Trans.). New York: Bollingen Foundation.

Van Den Abbeele, G. (1992). *Travel as metaphor: From Montaigne to Rousseau*. Minneapolis: University of Minnesota Press.

Van Lawick-Goodall, J. (1971). *In the shadow of man*. New York: Delta.

Van Maanen, J. (1988). *Tales of the field: On writing ethnography*. Chicago: University of Chicago Press.

Vendler, H. (1985, November 7). Looking for poetry in America. *New York Review of Books,* pp. 53-60.

Vendler, H. (1988). *The music of what happens: Poems, poets, critics*. Cambridge, MA: Harvard University Press.

Vendler, H. (1995). *Soul says: On recent poetry*. Cambridge, MA: Harvard University Press.

Webster, S. (1986). Realism and reification in the ethnographic genre. *Critique of Anthropology, 6*, 39-62.

Weinstein, F. (1990a). *History and theory after the fall: An essay on interpretation*. Chicago: University of Chicago Press.

Weinstein, F. (1990b). Who should write history? *SUNY Research, 10*(3), 20-21.

Weiss, W. A. (1990). Challenge to authority: Bakhtin and ethnographic description. *Cultural Anthropology, 5*, 414-430.

White, H. (1973). *Metahistory: The historical imagination in nineteenth-century Europe*. Baltimore: Johns Hopkins University Press.

Whitten, N. E., Jr. (1988). Toward a critical anthropology. *American Ethnologist,* *15,* 732-742.

Wierzbicka, A. (1996). *Semantics: Primes and universals.* Oxford: Oxford University Press.

Wilbert, J., & Simoneau, K. (Eds.). (1982). *Folk literature of the Mataco Indians.* Los Angeles: UCLA Latin America Center Publications.

Wilk, S. (1991). *Humanistic anthropology.* Knoxville: University of Tennessee Press.

Williams, B. (1998, November 19). The end of explanation? *New York Review of Books,* pp. 40-44.

Wolf, E. (1982). *Europe and the people without history.* Berkeley: University of California Press.

Wolf, M. A. (1992). *A thrice-told tale: Feminism, postmodernism, and ethnographic responsibility.* Stanford, CA: Stanford University Press.

Wuthnow, R., Hunter, J. D., Bergesen, A., & Kurzweil, E. (Eds.). (1984). *Cultural analysis: The work of Peter L. Berger, Mary Douglas, Michel Foucault, and Jürgen Habermas.* Boston: Routledge & Kegan Paul.

16

Understanding
Social Programs
Through Evaluation

Jennifer C. Greene

◆ Social program evaluation is a field of applied social inquiry uniquely distinguished by the explicit value dimensions of its knowledge claims, by the overt political character of its contexts, and by the inevitable pluralism and polyvocality of its actors.[1] Social program evaluators use the methods and tools of the social sciences to address not abstract theoretical questions of interest to some scholarly colleagues, but rather the priority policy and practice questions of diverse social actors—decision makers, program administrators, direct service staff, program participants, and others. Social program evaluators aim to inform and improve the services, programs, policies, and public conversations at hand, in contexts like these:

Annette Barlow directs a county United Way in rural Georgia. Like the boards of directors of United Ways elsewhere, Annette's board has increasingly asked for information about the *outcomes* of the programs they fund. Are babies in the county being born any healthier as a result of the prenatal program? Are children who participate in the peer tutoring program reading any better? Are seniors in the volunteer grandparent program less isolated, and, if so, does this meaningfully affect their physical health, their quality of life, and their economic self-sufficiency?

Martin Seguro is a newly elected U.S. senator from Arizona who finds himself the junior minority member on the Senate Foreign Relations Committee. As he learns more about American relationships around the world, he wonders about the influence on these relationships of international monetary policies, such as structural adjustment, tariffs, and trade agreements.

Evelyn Reynolds has 20 years of service as a social worker in her county social service department, working primarily with public assistance programs and clients. As the programs have changed over the years—from a proliferation of categorical benefits to more-integrated benefit and service packages to a phasing out of welfare altogether—so has Evelyn's job. She finds herself with increasingly less authority yet more responsibility and with more and more desperate demands for fewer and fewer resources. "There must be some way to make this system work better!" she asserted at a recent staff meeting.

Thomas Greenbaum is the director of social services in Evelyn Reynolds's state. He is also experiencing tensions and contradictions in his job. However, the pressures Thomas experiences—and thus his priority information needs—revolve around minimizing program costs, meeting federal regulations, and responding to the conflicting demands of political action lobbyists.

Michael Grey Wolf has been active in the Native American sovereignty movement for more than a decade. His recent work has focused on comparing Native and non-Native public elementary and secondary schools, toward the goal of developing charter school legislation for Native schools in his home state.[2]

In this chapter, I endeavor to use these and other specific contexts to redirect attention to the sociopolitical role of evaluation. I do so by highlighting the sociopolitical dimensions of evaluation approaches that incorporate qualitative methods and the changing face of this genre as it responds to challenges from within and without. These highlights are embedded within the following organization for the chapter. The next two sections locate evaluation within the social policy arena and qualitative approaches within the overall landscape of social program evaluation, respectively. The subsequent two sections portray the philosophy and practice of evaluation approaches that rely on qualitative methods.

591

Philosophy refers to the general epistemological logic of justification for these approaches, and *practice* describes key facets of application. The final section then locates approaches in this genre historically, connects them to significant theoretical developments in evaluation, and guides them through contemporary challenges toward a promising future identity and role.

◆ The Contexts of Program Evaluation

The scenarios just above, presented as characteristic contexts of social program evaluation, clearly evince its political inherence (Cronbach & Associates, 1980; Patton, 1987; Weiss, 1987). They directly engage the pluralistic values of contemporary American democracy. These are contexts about contested social policies and programs, about how and by whom resources are allocated, and about competing civic values, both in the global arena and in the local community. The core content of social program evaluation is thus intertwined with political power and decision making about societal priorities and directions. Evaluators working in these politicized contexts must negotiate identities for themselves that maximize their credibility and potential effectiveness. Different evaluators choose different grounds for negotiation, grounds that lead to different evaluation purposes and roles, yet all are concerned with power and all are value based (Greene, 1997).

Moreover, the work of social program evaluators is steered by the interests of selected members of the setting being evaluated. (Interests here are value-based claims on resources.) In all evaluation contexts there are multiple, often competing, potential audiences for evaluation—groups and individuals who have vested interests in the programs being evaluated, called *stakeholders* in evaluation jargon. These range from the powerful to the powerless, from policy makers and funders like Annette Barlow's United Way board and the U.S. Senate to program administrators like Thomas Greenbaum and program staff members like Evelyn Reynolds, to advocates like Michael Grey Wolf, and to the citizenry at large. Thus evaluators must also negotiate whose questions will be addressed and whose interests will be served by their work, negotiations that again are inherently value based.

Evaluation results then enter the political arena of social program and policy decision making not as decontextualized, abstract, or theoretical knowledge claims, but rather as interested knowledge claims, as empirically justified value judgments about the merit or worth of the programs evaluated. Evaluators do not just claim to know about something, they claim to know how good it is from selected vantage points. At root, evaluation is about valuing (Scriven, 1967) and judging (Stake, 1967). Values permeate the evaluation landscape, from values that are constitutive of the programs being evaluated to values as professional ethics, to values as the ethical aim of the practice of evaluation (Schwandt, 1997b). Hence, in addition to negotiating evaluation purpose and audience, evaluators must negotiate the criteria and standards upon which judgments of quality will be made. These criteria and the resulting judgments are inescapably power and value based and thereby matters of debate and conflict in all contemporary democracies.

◆ Locating QualitativeProgram Evaluation

Because social program evaluation is inextricably intertwined with politics and values, and because evaluators must navigate carefully amid competing political and value agendas, it is essential that evaluators have a diverse set of approaches to help guide practice. Currently, the diverse approaches available to evaluators offer not only choices of methods, but also alternative epistemological assumptions (about knowledge, the social world, human nature) and distinct ideological stances (about the desired ends of social programs and of social inquiry). These alternative philosophies and methods (concerned with what and how we know) and alternative ideological stances (concerning the meaning of social and community life) are constitutive of their respective approaches.

Table 16.1 offers a *descriptive* categorization of four contemporary genres of evaluation approaches. Like all such categorizations, the boundaries of these genres are clear only in the presentation of them. In historical evolution, conceptual argument, and actual practice, genre boundaries are considerably more fluid. The first genre, which represents the historically dominant tradition in program evaluation, is oriented around the interests of policy makers and funders—characteristically, it involves causal questions about the degree to which a program has attained desired outcomes while retaining cost-efficiency compared to its critical competitors. Recurrent demands for accountability in social expenditures are well addressed by this genre. These include Annette Barlow's United Way board's desire for information on program outcomes and state

TABLE 16.1 Major Contemporary Approaches to Formal Program Evaluation

Epistemology	Primary Values Promoted	Key Audiences	Preferred Methods	Typical Evaluation Questions
Postpositivism (Cook, 1985)	Efficiency, accountability, cost-effectiveness, policy enlightenment	High-level policy and decision makers, funders, the social science community	Quantitative: experiments and quasi-experiments, surveys, causal modeling, cost-benefit analysis	Are intended outcomes attained and attributable to the program? Is this program the most efficient alternative?
Utilitarian pragmatism (Patton, 1997)	Utility, practicality, managerial effectiveness	Midlevel program managers and on-site administrators	Eclectic, mixed: structured and unstructured surveys, interviews, observations, docuent analyses, panel reviews	Which program components work well and which need improvement? How effective is the program with respect to the organization's goals and mission? Who likes the program?
Interpretivism, constructivism (Stake, 1995)	Pluralism, understanding, contextualism, personal experience	Program directors, staff, and beneficiaries	Qualitative: case studies, open-ended interviews and observations, document reviews, dialectics	How is the program experienced by various stakeholders? In what ways is the program meaningful?
Critical social sciences (Fay, 1987)	Emancipation, empowerment, social change, egalitarianism, critical enlightenment	Program beneficiaries and their communities, activists	Participatory, action oriented: stakeholder participation in evaluation agenda setting, data collection, interpretation, and action	In what ways are the premises, goals, or activities of the program serving to maintain power and resource inequities in this context?

administrator Thomas Greenbaum's need for information on his social welfare program's costs versus benefits. Also in this genre, science, in the guise of program evaluation, is especially valued for its presumed objectivity and truth claims, still held as regulative ideals.

The second genre of evaluation approaches arose largely in response to the failure of classic experimental science to provide trustworthy, timely, and useful information for program decision making. As early trials clearly demonstrated (one classic is the Head Start evaluation; Cicirelli & Associates, 1969), the logic of experimentalism simply does not transfer well to real-world social contexts. This second genre then refocused attention on the needs of decision makers, especially the practical needs of on-site decision makers for program information useful for management decisions. Evelyn Reynolds's plea for information useful for program improvement is well answered by this genre. With its utilitarian value base, this genre of evaluation embraces eclectic methods choices in the service of practical problem solving. Michael Patton's (1997) utilization-oriented evaluation is a quintessential example of this genre. His approach to qualitative evaluation also falls within this genre, given its utilitarian value base (Patton, 1990).

But it is in the third cluster that qualitative approaches to evaluation that are rooted in long-standing philosophical and disciplinary traditions, such as interpretivism and ethnography, respectively, have found their home. In both theory and practice, qualitative approaches to evaluation span multiple "moments" in qualitative inquiry (see Lincoln & Denzin, Chapter 14, Volume 1), from the blurred genres and representation/legitimation crises of the 1970s and 1980s to the experimental postmodernism of today. Yet most of these approaches *in evaluation* share a hermeneutic view of social scientific knowledge claims, a value orientation that promotes pluralism, and a preference for qualitative methods. Also influenced by the responsive tradition within program evaluation (Abma, 1997a; Stake, 1975), these approaches characteristically seek to address the interests and honor the experiences of stakeholders closest to the programs evaluated—namely, program staff and beneficiaries—by giving voice to their contextualized program understanding. In-depth, contextualized understanding may also be of interest to other stakeholders, for example, Arizona Senator Martin Seguro's interest in the connections between international monetary policies and U.S. relations abroad. The early work of Robert Stake (1975) and of Egon Guba and Yvonna Lincoln (1981) significantly shaped the contours of this genre. As discussed later in this chapter (and as illustrated throughout this volume), contemporary work in this genre is reshaping it in significant ways.

Finally, the fourth genre represents evaluation approaches that are "openly ideological," that explicitly advance a particular value agenda, for example, of Rawlsian social justice (House, 1990), empowerment (Fetterman, 1994), critical race consciousness (Ladson-Billings, 1998), or social change (Ryan, Greene, Lincoln, Mathison, & Mertens, 1998; Whitmore, 1994). Michael Grey Wolf's explicit desire to advocate for Native American sovereignty in his evaluative work well illustrates this genre. As noted, all evaluation approaches advance certain ideals and values. "They privilege the stakeholder audiences who share those ideals and they summon the methodologies that enable their realization" (Greene, 1997, p. 27). Distinctively in the fourth genre, the essential rationales for evaluation are, first, the advocacy of ideals and values and, second, the answering of certain program questions. For most other evaluators, answering program questions is the stated first priority. Within this fourth genre of contemporary evaluation approaches are a diverse array of philosophical arguments, including critical social science, feminisms, and neo-Marxism. Within evaluation, British and Australian democratic evaluation (MacDonald, 1976) and action-oriented evaluation (Carr & Kemmis, 1986) are early exemplars. Guba and Lincoln's (1989) fourth-generation evaluation also warrants examination as it advances an activist ideology with grounding in a constructivist philosophy.

Even as I endeavor in Table 38.1 to present the four genres of evaluation approaches as significantly differentiated by ideology, in addition to epistemology and technique, the methodological domination of evaluative thinking still reigns (Greene, 1992; Schwandt, 1998). This is nowhere more evident than in the naming of different approaches to evaluation by their primary methods, as in *qualitative evaluation.* This naming obscures important differences among evaluative approaches that rely on qualitative methods, such as those promoted by Stake, Guba and Lincoln, Patton, Eisner, Schwandt, and MacDonald (which I discuss in my contribution to the first edition of this *Handbook*; Greene, 1994). It also misdirects attention toward *how* an evaluation is done (qualitatively) instead of *why* (to be contextually responsive, to help improve the program, to promote democratizing conversations, to advocate for pluralism). Further, the methodological domination of evaluative theory and practice falsely simplifies the political complexities of the contexts in which evaluators work.

◆ The Logic of Justification for Evaluations Conducted Qualitatively

Although variations exist in the philosophical underpinnings of different qualitative approaches to evaluation, most share a core set of assumptions and stances that are aptly labeled *constructivist* or *interpretivist*. As Schwandt (1994) notes:

> Proponents of these persuasions share the goal of understanding the complex world of lived experience from the point of view of those who live it. This goal is variously spoken of as an abiding concern for the life world, for the emic point of view, for understanding meaning, for grasping the actor's definition of a situation, for *Verstehen*. The world of lived reality and situation-specific meanings that constitute the general object of investigation is thought to be constructed by social actors. That is, particular actors, in particular places, at particular times, fashion meaning out of events and phenomena through prolonged, complex processes of social interaction involving history, language, and action. (p. 118)

He goes on:

> Constructivists are deeply committed to the . . . view that what we take to be objective knowledge and truth is the result of perspective. Knowledge and truth are created, not discovered by mind. They emphasize the pluralistic and plastic character of reality—pluralistic in the sense that reality is expressible in a variety of symbol and language systems; plastic in the sense that reality is stretched and shaped to fit purposeful acts of intentional human agents. (p. 125)

Constructivism

Constructivist inquirers seek to *understand contextualized meaning,* to understand the meaningfulness of human actions and interactions—as experienced and construed by the actors—in a given context. This aim is based on the assumption that the social world, as distinct from the physical world, does not exist independently, "out there," waiting to be discovered by smart and technically expert social inquirers. Rather, the emotional, linguistic, symbolic, interactive, political dimensions of the social world—and their meaningfulness, or lack thereof—are all constructed by agentic human actors. These constructions are influenced by specific historical, geopolitical, and cultural practices and discourses, and by the intentions—noble and otherwise—of those doing the constructing. So these constructions are multiple and plural, contingent and contextual.

And so the basic task of social inquiry is not to discover lawful properties of the external world, to answer population representation questions, or to extract and connect observed effects with causes. Rather, the first task is to understand people's constructions of meanings in the context being studied, because it is these constructions that constitute social realities and underlie all human action. This task itself is an interpretive one, requiring the inquirer to "elucidate the process of meaning construction... to construct a reading of these meanings; it is to offer the inquirer's construction of the constructions of the actors one studies" (Schwandt, 1994, p. 118). That is, the interpretive inquirer cannot know the meanings of another's life experience, but only the inquirer's own inscriptions or representations of said meanings (Lather, 1991). In these ways, interpretivist, constructivist inquiry is unapologetically subjectivist—the inquirer's worldview becomes part of the construction and representation of meaning in any particular context. Inquirer bias, experience, expertise, and insight are all part of the meanings constructed and inscribed.

Values are therefore also intertwined with knowing, as knowing is intertwined with being and acting. In constructivist, interpretive work, there are "no facts without values, and different values can actually lead to different facts" (Smith, 1989, p. 111). That is, different knowers holding different ideals and values can construct different meanings, even in the same situation. So constructivist, interpretive inquiry honors the value dimensions of lived experience and human meaning, but does not prescribe or advance any particular set of values. Rather, the values of a particular constructivist inquiry become those held dear by the constructors of meaning in that inquiry—the members of the setting studied, the inquirer, and the larger society. Constructivism is thereby value pluralistic.

Methodologically, constructivism is most consonant with natural settings, with the human inquirer as the primary gatherer and interpreter of meaning, with qualitative methods, with emergent inquiry designs, and with contextual, holistic understanding, in contrast to interventionist prediction and control, as the overall goal of inquiry (Guba & Lincoln, 1989; Lincoln, 1990; Patton, 1990).

Perhaps more significant, constructivism supports the decentering of inquiry/evaluation discourse from questions of method to questions of purpose and role. The quality of technique becomes secondary to the quality and meaningfulness of understanding. Yet, unlike some of their more radical peers who disclaim the existence of any privileged procedures that will enhance the acceptability of an inquirer's interpretations (e.g., Barone, 1992; Smith, 1989, p. 160), most constructivist evaluators favor some procedural structure for their work. This is partly because the contexts of social program evaluation continue to demand assurances of methodological quality and data integrity. Evaluations conducted qualitatively can make little contribution to social policies and programs if they are not perceived as credible—defensible, enlightening, and useful—by at least some evaluation users.

In this respect, evaluators are particularly concerned about criteria and methods for warranting their evaluative knowledge claims as empirically based representations of program experiences and not as biased inquirer opinions. Philosophically, this poses a contradiction, that being "the attempt to provide a methodological foundation for knowledge based on nonfoundational assumptions" (Smith, 1989, p. 159). The practice section that follows outlines some of the ways evaluators do this, for example, using time-honored procedures of triangulation. These responses to the criteria problem generally follow Smith's (1989, 1990) lead in recasting the concerns from ones of foundational methods to ones of heuristic procedures, appealing, for example, to procedural criteria as grounds for judging the goodness of interpretations (Schwandt, 1994, p. 130). For many qualitative evaluators, nonetheless, the contradictory demands of philosophy and practice, especially around criteria and procedures for warranting quality, remain strong.

Beyond Constructivism

Constructivism characterizes the philosophical logic justifying many of the evaluations conducted qualitatively today. But constructivism itself is not unchallenged, and some evaluators have engaged these challenges. Two brief examples here will illustrate these developments at the level of philosophy.[3] I will return to the topic of contemporary challenges and future directions in the concluding section of the chapter.

First, for more than a decade, Thomas Schwandt (1989, 1996, 1997a, 1997c, 1998) has offered *practical philosophy* as an alternative way of conceptualizing the practice and discourse of social science, including evaluation. "Practical philosophy is concerned with the mode of activity called the practical (praxis). Its subject matter is how an individual conducts her or his life and affairs as a member of society" (Schwandt, 1998, p. 9). To practice evaluation practically means to shift radically from a methodological to a political-ethical frame, and to be less concerned about perfecting and warranting our knowledge claims (Schwandt, 1996) and more concerned about helping practitioners to deliberate well and to develop their own wise practice.

Second, postmodern challenges exist to all contemporary forms of evaluation practice (Mabry, 1997). In much postmodern thought, for example, claims to know are not just partial and contingent, but also fundamentally indeterminate. Further, not only is the author of a postmodern representation of knowing also a major constructor of what is claimed to be known, but so is the reader. One response to these challenges is to abandon modernist principles and preoccupations in favor of actually practicing evaluation postmodernly. Tineke Abma (1997a, 1997b, 1998) offers inspirational examples of postmodern evaluation practice that accept postmodern incredulity and doubt without giving way to nihilism and disengagement. For example, Abma (1997a) promotes in her work the idea and experience of *playfulness:* "A playful person is not too attached to his or her personal persuasions and appreciates the power of redescribing, the power of language to make new and different things possible and important" (p. 44). Abma also invokes the "self-reflexive, polyvocal, and multiinterpretable" (1998, p. 434) texts of postmodern writers in endeavoring to craft her evaluation reports as "open, ambiguous, and unpredictable . . . without summary, conclusions and recommendations" (1997b, p. 106) and thereby as invitations to dialogue (1998).

◆ The Practice of Evaluations Conducted Qualitatively

So far, I have described the unique contexts and character of social program evaluation, presented a typology of contemporary genres of evaluation theory and practice, and explicated the constructivist philosophy underlying most "qualitative" evaluation approaches. In turning now to practice, I need to acknowledge that in the field, evaluators rarely practice a "pure" form of their craft, either philosophically or methodologically. The complex, pluralistic demands of evaluation field contexts evoke instead multiple, diverse frames for guiding practice and invite dialogue among them. In fact, evaluation expertise today is marked by its *dialectical, dialogical temperament,* its openness to multiple forms and layers of understanding, and its responsiveness to contextual needs for understanding, rather than its adherence to any singular philosophy or approach.

I offer here an example of evaluation practiced qualitatively that illustrates common features of this genre. After highlighting these features, I will discuss the continuing challenges of this approach to evaluation.

An Example

Envision an evaluation of a state-level welfare reform initiative, a reform that aims to shift three-quarters of the people currently on the state's welfare rolls to sustainable jobs over the next 5 years. This reform is based on the premise that long-term economic self-sufficiency for many of the people currently dependent on welfare requires an approach that first concentrates on "developing human capital" and then shifts to work placements. The development phase of this program includes intensive, individualized education, personal development, job training, and job search activities.

To address evaluative questions about the quality and effectiveness of this welfare reform for both policy and local program audiences, the qualitatively minded evaluator would seek primarily to *understand* how the program is experienced by individual participants—welfare clients, program staff, educational and economic development leaders—in particular contexts, for it is in these contextualized experiences that the meanings of program quality and effectiveness are shaped and molded. The qualitative evaluator of this welfare reform would likely purposefully sample for intensive data gathering a small number of program communities and participants to obtain heterogeneous samples on relevant characteristics (for example, demographics, economic and employment histories, cultural norms) in order to capture a broad range of diversity of experiences and meanings expected. For this sample, then, the evaluator would likely conduct extended on-site observations in order to develop a descriptive portrayal of what happens in the new welfare program and how this portrayal varies across contexts. How is the concept of "human capital" envisioned and implemented in these varied program sites? What is a typical program experience like for different types of welfare clients? How do community characteristics shape the definitions of *long-term employment* variously adopted by the program sites?

The evaluator would likely sample 10-15 welfare clients in each site for individual interviews and reviews of their program records in order to understand what program participants find meaningful, or not, in the program and how this meaning is reflected in their program journeys. The evaluator would also likely sample some program staff and managers, some economic development leaders, and some key community members in each site for individual or group interviews regarding their perceptions of and experiences with the new welfare program. What is the range of views regarding the human and the economic development emphases of the new program? What agreements and disagreements exist within the community about the kinds of economic self-sufficiency being fostered in the new program? Alternatively, these program staff and community perceptions might be more effectively and representatively gathered with structured, quantitative mail surveys.

The evaluator would then integrate these multiple individual stories about program engagement and experience into community narratives. These community narratives would convey the evaluator's representations of the contextualized, experiential meaning of the welfare reform initiative in each locality studied. One community narrative, for example, might highlight the disjuncture between the "professional advancement" rhetoric of the welfare reform program and the program's limited, mostly low-skilled set of educational offerings. Another might highlight the complementarity of the program's activity schedule with the daily rhythms and practices of a significant proportion, although not all, of the program participants in that setting. Yet another might centrally feature program participants' experiences of *their* program as oppressive and dehumanizing, and core program staff who are bitterly resentful about their recent transfer to this, "the worst of the neighborhood welfare offices." Community narratives, that is, would holistically describe and analyze or explain the meaningful connections and disjunctures of this welfare reform initiative within each of its multiple contexts. Beyond description and analysis, political policy and action interpretations of these narratives (Wolcott, 1994) would invoke the values and beliefs of individual evaluators and stakeholders.

Furthermore, these community narratives are shaped not just by micro-level events and interactions, but also by macro-level economic, political, and especially job market factors, forces, and trends. The narratives would gain more meaning if placed within their larger state and regional economic and political context. Further, a cost-benefit analysis of this reform initiative is, in all probability, an expected part of the evaluation. So, in addition to the intensive study of selected community cases, this evaluation would access and analyze macro-level information—most probably in quantitative form—on relevant welfare dependence, economic, and job market indicators and would assess program costs against outcomes.

These evaluative data would then be woven into an overall portrayal of program quality and effectiveness as grounded in insider experiences and meanings and as bounded by the opportunities and constraints of the broader marketplace. This portrayal would be offered as a holistic representation of those studied, with possible but not assured extensions and relevance to those not studied. This portrayal would be filled with snapshots of program activities and vignettes about accomplishment and disappointment, fulfillment and disengagement. This portrayal would thus offer a contextualized, complex, dynamic, value-laden, but necessarily partial statement about welfare reform. Although holistic, hermeneutic understanding is the goal of evaluation practice qualitatively, human phenomena in their sociopolitical contexts remain extraordinarily complex. All representations of interpretive understanding are thus necessarily partial.

Evaluation as the Telling of Stories

As highlighted by this example, evaluation practiced qualitatively is a narrative craft that involves the telling of *stories*—stories about individuals and groups of people in their own complex and dynamic communities, stories that enable understanding of what these communities share with others and what is unique to them, stories with an explicit authorial signature (Barone, 1992), and stories with the aim of understanding, and often action, as the improvement of practice or the reframing of the policy conversation, toward the appreciation of pluralism and complexity.

As a narrative craft, this approach to evaluation heavily favors *qualitative methods,* methods that require direct engagement with members of the settings being studied and that gather information about their experiences in their own words. Such methods uniquely enable understanding of insider experiences and perspectives. On-site observations and personal interviews are thus the mainstays of evaluation practiced qualitatively, supported by reviews of relevant documents and records. However, most evaluations also require information about a large, representative sample of program participants or information about macro social-political-economic factors and trends or cost-benefit information, as illustrated by the welfare reform example above. For these kinds of purposes, *quantita-*

tive methods are clearly acceptable within qualitative evaluation. In fact, in all genres of evaluation practice, evaluators are likely to attain more comprehensive and in-depth program understanding by explicitly inviting dialogue around data from different methods and approaches (Greene & Caracelli, 1997).

Good storytellers carefully select and richly portray their settings and make the actions of their protagonists explicable within these settings. In like fashion, qualitative evaluations are framed by the careful selection of one or more *cases* to study and by the rich, multilayered descriptions of the *contexts* of those cases. The welfare reform example is framed by the selection of several communities as *instrumental cases* (Stake, 1995)—cases selected not for their intrinsic interest but for their potential to provide insight into the overall reform initiative. Understanding the interpersonal, civic, socioeconomic, cultural rhythms of these communities is essential, as constructivist meaning is greatly embedded in context. What community characteristics, for example, might influence a program participant's sense of hopefulness or despair, connectedness or isolation, and then how are these feelings related to her or his program experience? Locating these instrumental cases within the larger state economic context—through more quantitative methods and indicators—is also a critical part of meaning making and understanding the overall reform endeavor.

As a narrative craft, evaluation practiced qualitatively is highly dependent on the narrator-evaluator. Different evaluators will tell different stories, and more experienced, knowledgeable, sensitive, and insightful evaluators can usually tell more meaningful stories. An *evaluator's own position* in his or her work reflects both personal biography and political partisanship, both who the evaluator is, as an individual and an evaluator, and whose interests he or she chooses to advance in the study (Greene, 1996, p. 285). With a constructivist worldview, most evaluators in this genre are partial to the interests of those closest to the program being studied, namely, program staff and participants. These are the voices and perspectives most prominently featured in the welfare reform example above. But, with a constructivist worldview, most evaluators in this genre are also committed to pluralism and thus to representing the full array of perspectives and meanings in their stories—for a comprehensive story, all are also needed.

Finally, evaluators must define and position not just themselves in their work, but their work in the world (Greene, 1996, 1998b). Evaluators must be accountable for the differences their stories make. With their constructivist worldview, evaluators in this genre most comfortably *position their stories* as guides for the improvement of specific contextual practices (Patton, 1997), as opportunities for program learning and insight by diverse interested stakeholders (Stake, 1997), or as vehicles for reframing the larger policy conversation (Weiss, 1998). Perhaps less comfortably, constructivist and interpretivist evaluators can position their stories as insistent demands to attend to the vital complexities, the legitimate pluralism, and the politics of power that constitute the fabric of contemporary social life in the United States. To have a voice in the future direction of the social practices and policies they study, evaluators in this genre must offer not only convincing stories, but challenging ones, and they need not only to tell their stories but also actively and assertively to claim space on the social agenda for them.

The Challenges of Evaluation as Storytelling

But how do those who read and listen to the evaluator's story about the meaningfulness of this state-level welfare reform decide if it is a good story? How do they know the evaluator is not just advocating for her own viewpoint about welfare reform in the telling of this story? How does the evaluator know where the boundaries of her own advocacy lie? And how does she as a "qualitative" evaluator fairly and justly fulfill her responsibilities—to those who have commissioned the evaluation, to the members of the settings studied, and to the larger citizenry, the collective good? Whose interests are advanced, for example, when the evaluator judges this state's approach to welfare reform to be an effective one, but welfare reform itself to be a misguided policy direction?

These questions reveal the essential value dimensions of all social program evaluation, across all genres. They contest the criteria to be used in judging the quality of the inquiry (How good is this story?) and the quality of the program evaluated (How good is this program?). They challenge the presence of the evaluator in the story (Are you just advocating for your own viewpoint?) and they query the very purpose of evaluation (Whose interests are being advanced?). As noted, these questions are germane to all forms of evaluation. They are more visible in evaluations practiced qualitatively because this evaluation genre explicitly acknowledges the value strands of knowledge claims. And they are more problematic because this evaluation genre is philosophically nonfoundational and

605

practically value pluralistic. The constructivist justification for this genre provides no ready answers to these challenges, which instead must be addressed by each evaluator in each context.

In the welfare reform evaluation example above, the evaluator may rely on recognizable inquiry criteria, for example, some of the trustworthiness criteria of Lincoln and Guba (1985). These criteria (credibility, applicability, dependability, and confirmability) are constructed to parallel conventional inquiry criteria (internal validity, external validity, reliability, and neutrality, respectively) and thus can be recognized as familiar and understood as legitimate by critical evaluation audiences, site-level program staff, and state-level program decision makers alike.[4] Procedural guides for fulfilling these criteria are also familiar, as they rely heavily on methodological arguments and techniques—sampling for diversity, triangulating for agreement, and monitoring bias. Many important evaluation clients need familiar or recognizable evaluation constructs like these in order to accept unfamiliar ways of knowing and thinking. Although not as respectful of the nature of constructivist thought as some other proposed lists of inquiry criteria—for example, Harry Wolcott's (1990) *understanding,* Guba and Lincoln's (1989) *authenticity,* and action researchers' *warranted action* (Greenwood & Levin, 1998)—these trustworthiness constructs are pragmatic choices for evaluators concerned about the acceptability and usefulness of their stories, especially for "modernist clients" (Robert Stake, personal communication, May 6, 1999).

But still, usefulness for what purposes, for whose aims? Whereas qualitative inquirers in other domains can uninhibitedly experiment with various political and action agendas for their work, social program evaluators are more constrained, both by tradition and by context. Advocacy is a daunting specter in many evaluation circles, challenging as it does the traditional stance of the disinterested, distanced, neutral evaluator whose only job is to find out the "truth" about the effectiveness of the social program at hand (Greene, 1997). But advocacy as the promotion of some interests over others is unavoidable in contemporary social program evaluation. There are simply too many stakeholders with too many varied interests for any single evaluation to address all of their concerns fairly and justly. In this regard, evaluation practiced qualitatively—characteristically more than other genres—strives to reach pluralistic ideals while clearly acknowledging its partialities. Pluralistic ideals imply inclusiveness of perspective and voice. That is, the views of both the usually vocal and the usually silent stakeholders are sought, the latter often with an extra stretch of an outreached hand. But even such concerted efforts will fall short, and pluralistic inclusiveness is rarely fully attained.

Moreover, evaluators in this genre know that their claims to understand are constitutive of the perspectives that do get privileged and thereby unavoidably interested and partial. The welfare reform evaluator, with her constructivist worldview, is likely to emphasize contextual meaningfulness over cost-efficiency in her judgments of program quality. In like manner, Patton's (1990, 1997) utilization ideals privilege the interests of on-site decision makers, Guba and Lincoln's (1989) fourth-generation evaluation integrates a constructivist philosophy with an empowerment ideology to champion the interests of the least powerful, and Stake's (1997) constructivist beliefs and reformist principles engender sympathies for those who are also struggling mightily and meaningfully with reform. In short, while soundly disclaiming advocacy as bias, evaluators of this genre recognize the undeniable leanings of all evaluation and embrace those most comfortable with their own philosophy and biography. My own leanings underscore the importance of complexity and pluralism as critical markers of social meaning and action.

◆ The Journey of Evaluations Conducted Qualitatively

Beginnings

Constructivist, qualitative approaches to program evaluation emerged within the U.S. evaluation community in the 1970s (Stake, 1967, 1975), in tandem with two significant evolutions in intellectual thought and societal beliefs (Cook, 1985; Greene & McClintock, 1991).[5] The first (r)evolution was the dethroning of experimental science as the paradigm for social program evaluation (and other applied social sciences), a dethroning resulting from major fractures in the positivist philosophy of science that had guided most scientific practice since the Enlightenment era of the 18th century.[6] It was amid the debates and discussions that ensued regarding alternatives to experimentalism that interpretivist philosophies and qualitative approaches entered evaluative discourse. Initially contested on both methodological and practical grounds (as expressed in evaluation's *qualitative-quantitative debate,* e.g., Cook & Reichardt, 1979; Reichardt & Rallis, 1994), qualitative approaches to evaluation took strong root in the thinking of many evaluation theorists and methodologists. Largely through their sensible and appealing practice, such approaches have now become an accepted alternative throughout the evaluation community.

The second major set of changes that encouraged and enabled the emergence and growth of qualitative approaches to evaluation involved changes in the belief systems of the larger U.S. society during the 1960s and 1970s. Thomas Cook (1985) describes these changes as follows:

1. The decline in authority accorded standard social science theory following the perceived failures of the Great Society (see also House, 1993);

2. The decline in authority accorded political figures following the Vietnam War, the Watergate scandal, and other government debacles; and,

3. An increase in the cultural, value, and political pluralism of society, as manifest, for example, in the civil rights and women's movements.

There was considerable consonance between these shifts in societal thinking and the emergence of alternative paradigms, including interpretivism and constructivism, for understanding and doing social science.

Present-Day Connections to Important Evaluation Theories

In its contemporary form, social program evaluation is a young field, just beginning to develop and refine its own theories (Shadish, Cook, & Leviton, 1991). Among the important theoretical developments likely to continue to shape evaluative thinking and practice over the coming decade are two sets of ideas: (a) the reclamation of *theories of program action and change* as significant conceptual frameworks for evaluation, and (b) the redefinition of evaluation's primary role as an opportunity for *active, generative, and inclusive learning,* a redefinition that emphasizes the process of evaluation over its products. What these developments in evaluation theory share is a recentering of evaluation around its sociopolitical role, instead of its methods and techniques, and a valuing of the educative and action potential of evaluation. They also derive strength from evaluation practiced qualitatively, through significant but not exclusive reliance on interpretive methods, and through support for, if not complete allegiance to, a constructivist worldview. I describe each development briefly below.

Evaluating Program Theories

Early program evaluations in the Great Society era of the United States were styled after experimental tests of program theories, of the hypothesized causal links between program inputs and expected program outcomes. Evaluations of that era aspired to measure outcomes for program participants and to compare these to measured outcomes for similar people who did not participate in the programs. Little attention was given to gathering data on the actual programs, as implemented or experienced. So the processes by which observed program effects happened or did not happen were unknown—thus the label of "black box" evaluations for these early studies, signaling the disfavor into which they generally fell as stand-alone studies. As Lee Cronbach and Associates (1980) observed, "A good evaluative question invites a differentiated answer instead of leaving the program plan, the delivery of the program, and the response of clients as unexamined elements within a closed black box" (p. 5).

Starting in the early 1980s, a number of evaluation theorists (notably Len Bickman, 1987; Huey Chen & Peter Rossi, 1983; and Carol Weiss, 1972) began to reargue for the importance of "theory-driven evaluation" and evaluation directed at understanding and assessing a program's "theory of change." From Carol Weiss (1998):

The [program] theory gives guidance to the evaluator about where to look and what to find out. (p. 65)

The mere construction of a [program] theory can expose naïve and simplistic expectations. . . . The . . . theory can be a learning tool long before the evaluation begins. (p. 66)

Once the data are in hand, [the analysis assesses] how well the theory describes what actually happened. . . . This is important information for the directors and staff of the program under study, so that they can rethink the understandings and replan the activities that did not work out as anticipated. (p. 66)

Theory-based evaluation [also] provides explanations, stories of means and ends, that communicate readily to policymakers and the public. (p. 68)

Another key argument for theory-based evaluation is its potential to contribute to generalizable knowledge about how social interventions work and the conditions and factors that enable and obstruct their success (Cronbach, 1982; Weiss, 1998). Evaluation practiced qualitatively has much to offer this goal of social problem solving. Holistic program portrayals can translate program constructs into contextualized lived experiences within diverse community values. Evaluators' program portrayals can complement regression coefficients, say, for net earnings increases of job training program participants, with stories of human pride and shame, accomplishment and failure. Program portrayals can also challenge the generation of effect sizes, which homogenize and centralize program participation, with the dissonance and complexity of human diversity. Indeed, this increasingly urgent dialogue about social problems and how best to solve them requires the dialectical participation of all evaluation perspectives, and a critical if not leadership role for the insistence on complexity, contextuality, and human agency offered by qualitative approaches to evaluation.

Evaluating With Stakeholder Engagement

Offering some counterpoint to the reclamation of program theory as an important evaluation agenda is the expanding development and application of participatory and collaborative approaches to evaluation (Ryan et al., 1998; Whitmore, 1998). These approaches emphasize the active engagement of stakeholders in the evaluation process for purposes of enhancing ownership and thus usefulness of the evaluation results (Cousins & Earl, 1995; Patton, 1997) *or* for purposes of promoting some form of democratizing social change, such as social justice (House, 1990) or empowerment (Fetterman, 1994).[7] In these (admittedly diverse) ways, participatory evaluators frame evaluation primarily as an opportunity for engagement, learning, and action in that context. And the *process* of conducting the evaluation—the ways in which stakeholders are involved, which particular stakeholders participate, how less-powerful voices can be fairly heard, who speaks for and with whom—becomes of central importance, not the issue of what methods are used or even what substantive results are obtained.

In ongoing developments, utilization-oriented participatory evaluators are advancing the significant role evaluation can play in *organizational learning,* forging connections to contemporary emphases on strategic planning and quality management within organizational development circles (Cousins & Earl, 1995; Patton, 1994; Preskill & Torres, 1998). And social action-oriented participatory evaluators are advancing the significance of evaluation's potential for broadening and deepening our deliberations and dialogues about important social issues (Greene, 1997; House & Howe, 1998; Ryan et al., 1998). In all dimensions of these ongoing advances in participatory evaluation, qualitative evaluation is playing and will continue to play a central, although again not exclusive, role. Inclusion, not exclusivity, is the defining character of contemporary dialectical, dialogical evaluation.

◆ Future Directions

As vividly illustrated throughout this volume, ways of thinking about and doing "qualitative research" continue to evolve and change. Social program evaluators, like other applied social scientists, are challenged by the ongoing evolutions in the philosophy and ideology of science. Here is a sampling.[8]

Challenges to the Very Nature of Our Qualitative Data

> The [qualitative] interview is fundamentally indeterminate. The complex play of conscious and unconscious thoughts, feelings, fears, powers, desires, and needs on the part of both the interviewer and interviewee cannot be captured and categorized. . . . When we think we "interpret" what the meaning or meanings of an interview are, through various data reduction techniques, we are overlaying indeterminacy with the determinacies of our meaning-making, replacing ambiguities with [our] findings or constructions. When we proceed as if we have "found" or "constructed" the best, or the key, or the most important interpretation, we are misportraying what has occurred. . . . [Instead in the analysis] the researcher fills . . . [the interview's] indeterminate openness with her or his interpretive baggage; imposes names, categories, constructions, conceptual schemes, theories upon the unknowable; and believes that the indeterminate is now located, constructed, known. Order has been created. The restless, appropriative spirit of the researcher is (temporarily) at peace. (Scheurich, 1995, p. 249)

Challenges to Our Representations as Meanings

> Postmodernism opens space for new forms of representing social science inquiry by challenging the assumptions of what are seen as accepted forms of

611

presenting the findings of inquiry. Paget . . . points out, "there is something odd about privileging an analysis of discourse in its least robust form, a written text, exploring it in great detail while ignoring the speakers' miens and intentions.". . .

. . . In the creation of new representations of inquiry, we need to struggle to represent the complexities and indeterminacies of participants' experiences . . . [and] to acknowledge our role in the construction of the representation, our voice in the presentation. [Further] as, in postmodern terms, knowledge is partial, conditional and contextual, so are representations. (Goodyear, 1997, pp. 64-65, 69)

Challenges Regarding the Political Ethics of Our Work

How do we handle "hot" information, especially in times when poor and working-class women and men are being demonized by the Right and by Congress? . . . For instance, what do we do with information about the ways in which women on welfare virtually have to become welfare cheats to survive? *("Sure he comes once a month and gives me some money. I may have to take a beating, but the kids need the money.")* A few [of those we study] use more drugs than we wish to know . . . some underattend to their children well beyond neglect. . . . To ignore these data is to deny the effects [of hard economic times]. To report the data is to risk their likely misinterpretation.

In a moment in history when there are few audiences willing to reflect on the complex social roots of community and domestic violence and the impossibility of sole reliance on welfare, or even to appreciate the complexity, love, hope, and pain that fills the poor and working class, how do we display the voyeuristic dirty laundry that litters our database? At the same time, how can we risk romanticizing or denying the devastating impact of the current assault on poor and working-class families launched by the State, the economy, neighbors, and sometimes kin? (Fine & Weis, 1996, pp. 258-259)

These challenges to the very core of what it is we do when we practice the craft of social program evaluation with a constructivist, qualitative worldview are daunting but not defeating. They continue the erosion, partially initiated by constructivism, of evaluation's preoccupation with methodological rigor and technical expertise. They affirm the constructivist evaluator's emphasis on the meaningfulness of lived experience, even as they unravel our confidence in our ability to know, understand, and interpret such experience. They also substantiate constructivist evaluators' self-consciousness about values, about our own position in our work, and about the location of our work in the world.

612

As social program evaluators, we have responsibilities to multiple audiences, including the powerful policy makers, the all-but-powerless poor people who are often the intended beneficiaries of the programs we evaluate, and the citizenry at large. Our work, therefore, must respectfully balance social scientific theories of knowledge construction, interpretation, and representation with the political realities of social policy making. Such balance is attained not through partisanship, but through explicit commitment to inclusiveness, to pluralism, to ensuring that all stakeholder voices are part of the conversation (Datta, 1999; House & Howe, 1998). Inclusiveness respects both constructivist holism *and* democratic dialogue. We must acknowledge that making such a commitment explicit is often viewed as advocacy or partisanship, and so our challenge becomes one of creating impartial, nonconfrontational expressions of this commitment (Datta, 1999).

The need is not to find the *one correct way* to do program evaluation, but rather to conduct our craft so that it responds to multiple audiences, includes multiple perspectives, constructs multiple and diverse understandings and equally diverse representations of those understandings, and encourages dialogue and conversations. I believe that the constructivist, qualitative genre of evaluation—with its valuing of responsiveness and pluralism—is extremely well positioned to be an active player in this dialogical evaluation evolution. It is now up to us, each of us as constructivist evaluators, to claim a seat at the table.

◆ Notes

1. Social program evaluators work at all levels of government and thus social programming, from positions both inside and external to government agencies. Their work is frequently mandated by program funders—namely, government and foundations—traditionally for knowledge, development, or accountability purposes (Chelimsky, 1997). Practicing evaluators have been trained in applied social science graduate programs or in policy analysis and evaluation graduate programs. In addition to social programs, evaluations are conducted on objects (product evaluation), on people (personnel evaluation), and on programs in the private sector such as executive development and human resource training. Although Scriven (1995) and others argue that the logic of evaluation is the same across these different objects of evaluation, I believe they constitute essentially different tasks, and so require qualitatively and politically different responses. In this chapter, I focus on qualitative evaluation of social programs and the policies they embody, predominantly in the U.S. public domain. My arguments here may not transfer well to other evaluation contexts; this is a judgment for the reader.

2. I am indebted to Alyce Spotted Bear for the idea of this evaluation context.

3. These two examples are drawn from Greene (1998a).

4. From Lincoln and Guba (1985): Evaluation findings will be (a) *credible* when consonant with contextualized lived experience, (b) *applicable* to other similar contexts when so
judged by those doing the applying, (c) *dependable* when the methods decisions made are
defensible and reasonable for that context, and (d) *confirmable* when inferences can be
traced back through analyses to data actually collected.

5. See my chapter in the first edition of this *Handbook* for an elaborated discussion of
the history of qualitative program evaluation (Greene, 1994).

6. Among the numerous accounts of this revolution in the philosophy of science, the
works of philosopher Richard Bernstein (1983, 1992) are among the most accessible.

7. These two clusters of purposes for participatory evaluation reflect its dual origins in
(a) utilization (Patton, 1997) and stakeholder-based (Gold, 1983) evaluation, and (b) from
outside the evaluation field, liberatory traditions of participatory and participatory action
research (Freire, 1972; Greenwood & Levin, 1998). See Whitmore (1998) for elaborated
discussions of participatory evaluation's histories, theories, and practices.

8. These examples are drawn from Greene (1998a).

◆ References

Abma, T. A. (1997a). Playing with/in plurality. *Evaluation, 3,* 25-48.

Abma, T. A. (1997b). Sharing power, facing ambiguity. In L. Mabry (Ed.), *Evaluation and the postmodern dilemma* (pp. 105-119). Greenwich, CT: JAI.

Abma, T. A. (1998). Text in an evaluative context: Writing for dialogue. *Evaluation,
4,* 434-454.

Barone, T. E. (1992). On the demise of subjectivity in educational inquiry. *Curriculum Inquiry, 22,* 25-38.

Bernstein, R. J. (1983). *Beyond objectivism and relativism.* Philadelphia: University
of Pennsylvania Press.

Bernstein, R. J. (1992). *The new constellation: The ethical-political horizons of
modernity/postmodernity.* Cambridge: MIT Press.

Bickman, L. (Ed.). (1987). *Using program theory in evaluation.* San Francisco:
Jossey-Bass.

Carr, W. L., & Kemmis, S. (1986). *Becoming critical: Education, knowledge, and
action research.* London: Falmer.

Chelimsky, E. (1997). The coming transformations in evaluation. In E. Chelimsky
& W. R. Shadish (Eds.), *Evaluation for the 21st century* (pp. 1-26). Thousand
Oaks, CA: Sage.

Chen, H.-T., & Rossi, P. H. (1983). Evaluating with sense: The theory-driven
approach. *Evaluation Review, 7,* 283-302.

Cicirelli, V. G., & Associates. (1969). *The impact of Head Start: An evaluation of
the effects of Head Start on children's cognitive and affective development*

(Report to the Office of Economic Opportunity). Athens: Ohio University/ Westinghouse Learning Corporation.

Cook, T. D. (1985). Postpositivist critical multiplism. In L. Shotland & M. M. Mark (Eds.), *Social science and social policy* (pp. 21-62). Beverly Hills, CA: Sage.

Cook, T. D., & Reichardt, C. S. (Eds.). (1979). *Qualitative and quantitative methods in evaluation research.* Beverly Hills, CA: Sage.

Cousins, J. B., & Earl, L. (1995). *Participatory evaluation in education: Studies in evaluation use and organizational learning.* New York: Falmer.

Cronbach, L. J. (1982). *Designing evaluations of educational and social programs.* San Francisco: Jossey-Bass.

Cronbach, L. J., & Associates. (1980). *Toward reform of program evaluation.* San Francisco: Jossey-Bass.

Datta, L.-E. (1999). The ethics of evaluation neutrality and advocacy. In J. L. Fitzpatrick & M. Morris (Eds.), *Current and emerging ethical challenges in evaluation* (pp. 77-88). San Francisco: Jossey-Bass.

Fay, B. (1987). *Critical social science.* Ithaca, NY: Cornell University Press.

Fetterman, D. M. (1994). Empowerment evaluation. *Evaluation Practice, 15,* 1-16.

Fine, M., & Weis, L. (1996). Writing the "wrongs" of fieldwork: Confronting our own research/writing dilemmas in urban ethnographies. *Qualitative Inquiry, 2,* 251-274.

Freire, P. (1972). *Pedagogy of the oppressed.* New York: Herder & Herder.

Gold, N. (1983). Stakeholders and program evaluation: Characterizations and reflections. In A. S. Bryk (Ed.), *Stakeholder-based evaluation* (pp. 63-72). San Francisco: Jossey-Bass.

Goodyear, L. K. (1997). *"A circle that it's time to open": Using performance as a representation of a participatory evaluation.* Unpublished master's thesis, Cornell University.

Greene, J. C. (1992). The practitioner's perspective. *Curriculum Inquiry, 22,* 39-45.

Greene, J. C. (1994). Qualitative program evaluation: Practice and promise. In N. K. Denzin & Y. S. Lincoln (Eds.), *Handbook of qualitative research* (pp. 530-544). Thousand Oaks, CA: Sage.

Greene, J. C. (1996). Qualitative evaluation and scientific citizenship: Reflections and refractions. *Evaluation, 2,* 277-289.

Greene, J. C. (1997). Evaluation as advocacy. *Evaluation Practice, 18,* 25-35.

Greene, J. C. (1998a). Balancing philosophy and practicality in qualitative evaluation. In R. Davis (Ed.), *Proceedings of the Stake Symposium on Educational Evaluation* (pp. 35-49). Champaign-Urbana: University of Illinois Press.

Greene, J. C. (1998b). Qualitative, interpretive evaluation. In A. J. Reynolds & H. J. Walberg (Eds.), *Evaluation research for educational productivity* (pp. 135-154). Greenwich, CT: JAI.

Greene, J. C., & Caracelli, V. J. (Eds.). (1997). *Advances in mixed-method evaluation: The challenges and benefits of integrating diverse paradigms.* San Francisco: Jossey-Bass.

Greene, J. C., & McClintock, C. (1991). The evolution of evaluation methodology. *Theory Into Practice, 30,* 13-21.

Greenwood, D. J., & Levin, M. (1998). *Introduction to action research.* Thousand Oaks, CA: Sage.

Guba, E. G., & Lincoln, Y. S. (1981). *Effective evaluation: Improving the usefulness of evaluation results through responsive and naturalistic approaches.* San Francisco: Jossey-Bass.

Guba, E. G., & Lincoln, Y. S. (1989). *Fourth generation evaluation.* Newbury Park, CA: Sage.

House, E. R. (1990). Methodology and justice. In K. A. Sirotnik (Ed.), *Evaluation and social justice* (pp. 23-36). San Francisco: Jossey-Bass.

House, E. R. (1993). *Professional evaluation: Social impact and political consequences.* Newbury Park, CA: Sage.

House, E. R., & Howe, K. (1998). *Deliberative evaluation.* Paper presented at the annual meeting of the American Evaluation Association, Chicago.

Ladson-Billings, G. (1998). Just what is critical race theory and what is it doing in a "nice" field like education? *International Journal of Qualitative Studies in Education, 11,* 7-24.

Lather, P. (1991). *Getting smart: Feminist research and pedagogy with/in the postmodern.* New York: Routledge.

Lincoln, Y. S. (1990). The making of a constructivist: A remembrance of transformations past. In E. G. Guba (Ed.), *The paradigm dialog* (pp. 67-87). Newbury Park, CA: Sage.

Lincoln, Y. S., & Guba, E. G. (1985). *Naturalistic inquiry.* Beverly Hills, CA: Sage.

Mabry, L. (1997). A postmodern test on postmodernism? In L. Mabry (Ed.), *Evaluation and the postmodern dilemma* (pp. 1-19). Greenwich, CT: JAI.

MacDonald, B. (1976). Evaluation and the control of education. In D. A. Tawney (Ed.), *Curriculum evaluation today: Trends and implications.* London: Falmer.

Patton, M. Q. (1987). Evaluation's political inherency: Practical implications for design and use. In D. J. Palumbo (Ed.), *The politics of program evaluation* (pp. 100-145). Newbury Park, CA: Sage.

Patton, M. Q. (1990). *Qualitative evaluation and research methods* (2nd ed.). Newbury Park, CA: Sage.

Patton, M. Q. (1994). Development evaluation. *Evaluation Practice, 15,* 311-320.

Patton, M. Q. (1997). *Utilization-focused evaluation: New century edition.* Thousand Oaks, CA: Sage.

Preskill, H. S., & Torres, R. (1998). *Evaluative learning in organizations.* Thousand Oaks, CA: Sage.

Reichardt, C. S., & Rallis, S. F. (Eds.). (1994). *The qualitative-quantitative debate: New perspectives.* San Francisco: Jossey-Bass.

Ryan, K. E., Greene, J. C., Lincoln, Y. S., Mathison, S., & Mertens, D. (1998). Advantages and challenges of using inclusive evaluation approaches in evaluation practice. *American Journal of Evaluation, 19,* 101-122.

Scheurich, J. J. (1995). A postmodern review of research interviewing. *International Journal of Qualitative Studies in Education, 8,* 239-252.

Schwandt, T. A. (1989). Recapturing moral discourse in evaluation. *Educational Researcher, 18*(8), 11-16, 34.

Schwandt, T. A. (1994). Constructivist, interpretivist approaches to human inquiry. In N. K. Denzin & Y. S. Lincoln (Eds.), *Handbook of qualitative research* (pp. 118-137). Thousand Oaks, CA: Sage.

Schwandt, T. A. (1996). Farewell to criteriology. *Qualitative Inquiry, 2,* 58-72.

Schwandt, T. A. (1997a). Evaluation as practical hermeneutics. *Evaluation, 3,* 69-83.

Schwandt, T. A. (1997b). Reading the "problem of evaluation" in social inquiry. *Qualitative Inquiry, 3,* 4-25.

Schwandt, T. A. (1997c). Whose interests are being served? Program evaluation as a conceptual practice of power. In L. Mabry (Ed.), *Evaluation and the postmodern dilemma* (pp. 89-104). Greenwich, CT: JAI.

Schwandt, T. A. (1998, April). *Recapturing moral discourse in evaluation—revisited.* Keynote address delivered at the annual Kelly Conference, Ottawa, ON.

Scriven, M. (1967). The methodology of evaluation. *AERA Monograph Series in Curriculum Evaluation, 1,* 39-83.

Scriven, M. (1995). The logic of evaluation and evaluation practice. In D. Fournier (ed.), *Reasoning in evaluation: Inferential links and leaps* (pp. 49-70). San Francisco: Jossey-Bass.

Shadish, W. R., Cook, T. D., & Leviton, L. C. (1991). *Foundations of program evaluation.* Newbury Park, CA: Sage.

Smith, J. K. (1989). *The nature of social and educational inquiry: Empiricism versus interpretation.* Norwood, NJ: Ablex.

Smith, J. K. (1990). Alternative research paradigms and the problem of criteria. In E. G. Guba (Ed.), *The paradigm dialog* (pp. 167-187). Newbury Park, CA: Sage.

Stake, R. E. (1967). The countenance of educational evaluation. *Teachers College Record, 68,* 523-540.

Stake, R. E. (1975). *Evaluating the arts in education: A responsive approach.* Columbus, OH: Merrill.

Stake, R. E. (1995). *The art of case study research.* Thousand Oaks, CA: Sage.

Stake, R. E. (1997). The fleeting discernment of quality. In L. Mabry (Ed.), *Evaluation and the postmodern dilemma* (pp. 41-59). Greenwich, CT: JAI.

Weiss, C. H. (1972). *Evaluation.* Englewood Cliffs, NJ: Prentice Hall.

Weiss, C. H. (1987). Where politics and evaluation research meet. In D. J. Palumbo (Ed.), *The politics of program evaluation* (pp. 47-70). Thousand Oaks, CA: Sage.

Weiss, C. H. (1998). *Evaluation* (2nd ed.). Upper Saddle River, NJ: Prentice Hall.

Whitmore, E. (1994). To tell the truth: Working with oppressed groups in participatory approaches to inquiry. In P. Reason (Ed.), *Participation in human inquiry* (pp. 82-98). Thousand Oaks, CA: Sage.

Whitmore, E. (Ed.). (1998). *Understanding and practicing participatory evaluation.* San Francisco: Jossey-Bass.

Wolcott, H. F. (1990). On seeking—and rejecting—validity in qualitative research. In E. W. Eisner & A. Peshkin (Eds.), *Qualitative inquiry in education: The continuing debate* (pp. 121-152). New York: Teachers College Press.

Wolcott, H. F. (1994). *Transforming qualitative data: Description, analysis, and interpretation.* Thousand Oaks, CA: Sage.

17

Influencing the
Policy Process With
Qualitative Research

Ray C. Rist

◆ More than 20 years ago, James Coleman wrote, "There is no body of methods; no comprehensive methodology for the study of the impact of public policy as an aid to future policy." This now-famous quote still rings true. Indeed, one can argue that in the intervening decades, the tendency in policy research and analysis has become ever more centrifugal, spinning off more methodologies and variations on methodologies, more conceptual frameworks, and more disarray among those who call themselves policy analysts or see themselves working in the area of policy studies. A number of critics of the current scene of policy studies and the attendant applications of so many different methodologies have argued that any improvements in the techniques of policy research have not led to greater clarity about what to think or what to do. More charitably, it could be said that the multiplicity of approaches to policy research should be

AUTHOR'S NOTE: The views expressed here are those of the author, and no endorsement by the World Bank is intended or should be inferred.

welcomed, as they bring different skills and strengths to what are admittedly difficult and complex issues.

Regardless of whether one supports or challenges the contention that policy research has had a centrifugal impact on the knowledge base relevant to policy making, the bottom line remains much the same: What policy researchers tend to consider as improvements in their craft have not significantly enhanced the role of research in policy making. Instead, the proliferation of persons, institutes, and centers conducting policy-related work has led to more variation in the manner by which problems are defined, more divergence in the ways in which studies are designed and conducted, and more disagreement and controversy over the ways in which data are analyzed and findings reported. The policy maker now confronts a veritable glut of differing (if not conflicting) research information.

A sobering but provocative counterintuitive logic is at work here: Increased personnel, greater allocation of resources, and growing sophistication of methods have not had the anticipated or demonstrated effect of greater clarity and understanding of the policy issues before the country. Rather, current efforts have led to a more complex, complicated, and partial view of the issues and their solutions. Further, as Smith (1991) would argue, this tendency to greater complexity has left both the policy makers and the citizens less able to understand the issues and to see how their actions might affect the present condition.

Whereas one may grant that early analyses, for example, in the areas of education or social welfare, were frequently simplistic and not especially sophisticated in either the design or application of policy methods, the inverse does not, in and of itself, work to the advantage of the policy maker. Stated differently, to receive a report resplendent with "state-of-the-art" methodologies and complex analyses that tease out every nuance and shade of meaning on an issue may provide just as little guidance for effective decision making as did the former circumstances. The present fixation on the technical adequacy of policy research without a commensurate concern for its utilization is to relegate that work to quick obscurity (Chelimsky, 1982).

If this admittedly brief description of the current state of policy research approximates the reality, then a fundamental question arises: Is the presumption correct that research cannot be conducted that is relevant to the policy process? It is my view that the presumption is not correct. Research can contribute to informed decision making, but the manner in which this is done needs to be reformulated. We are well past the time when it is possible to argue that good research will, because it is good, influence the policy process. That kind of linear relation of research to action simply is not a viable way in which to think about how knowledge can inform decision making. The relation is both more subtle and more tenuous. Still, there is a relation. It is my intent in this chapter to address how some of the linkages of knowledge and action are formed, particularly for the kinds of knowledge generated through qualitative research.[1]

◆ The Nature of Policy Decision Making

Policy making is multidimensional and multifaceted. Research is but one (and often minor at that) among the number of frequently contradictory and competing sources that seek to influence what is an ongoing and constantly evolving process. The emphasis here on policy making being a *process* is deliberate. It is a process that evolves through cycles, with each cycle more or less bounded, more or less constrained by time, funds, political support, and other events. It is also a process that circles back on itself, iterates the same decision issue time and again, and often does not come to closure. Choosing not to decide is a frequent outcome.

Such a description of the policy process suggests the need for a modification, if not a fundamental reframing, of the traditional understanding of policy making. In this latter, more traditional approach, decision making in the policy arena is understood as a discrete event, undertaken by a defined set of actors working in "real time" and moving to their decision on the basis of an analysis of their alternatives. Weiss (1982) has nicely summarized this notion of "decision making as an event":

> Both the popular and the academic literature picture decision making as an event; a group of authorized decision makers assemble at particular times and places, review a problem (or opportunity), consider a number of alternative courses of action with more or less explicit calculation of the advantages and disadvantages of each option, weigh the alternatives against their goals or preferences, and then select an alternative that seems well suited for achieving their purposes. The result is a decision. (p. 23)

She also nicely demolishes this view when she writes:

Given the fragmentation of authority across multiple bureaus, departments, and legislative committees, and the disjointed stages by which actions coalesce into decisions, the traditional model of decision making is a highly stylized rendition of reality. Identification of any clear-cut group of decision makers can be difficult. (Sometimes a middle-level bureaucrat has taken the key action, although he or she may be unaware that his or her action was going to be—or was—decisive.) The goals of policy are often equally diffuse, except in terms of "taking care of" some undesirable situation. Which opinions are considered, and what set of advantages or disadvantages are assessed, may be impossible to tell in the interactive, multiparticipant, diffuse process of formulating policy. The complexity of governmental decision making often defies neat compartmentalization. (p. 26)

Of particular relevance here is that the focus on decision making as an ongoing set of adjustments, or midcourse corrections, eliminates the bind of having to pinpoint the event—that is, the exact time, place, and manner—in which research has been influential on policy. Parenthetically, because the specifics can seldom be supplied, the notion that research *should* have an impact on decision making seems to have become more and more an article of faith. That researchers have so persistently misunderstood decision making, and yet have constantly sought to be of influence, is a situation deserving of considerably more analysis than it receives. So long as researchers presume that research findings must be brought to bear upon a single event, a discrete act of decision making, they will be missing those circumstances and processes where, in fact, research can be useful. However, the reorientation away from "event decision making" and to "process decision making" necessitates looking at research as serving an "enlightenment function" in contrast to an "engineering function" (see Janowitz, 1971; Patton, 1988; Weiss, 1988).

Viewing policy research as serving an enlightenment function suggests that policy researchers work with policy makers and their staffs over time to create a contextual understanding about an issue, build linkages that will exist over time, and strive constantly to educate about new developments and research findings in the area. This is in contrast to the engineering perspective, where it is presumed that sufficient data can be brought to bear to determine the direction and intensity of the intended policy initiative, much as one can develop the specifications for the building of a bridge. If the policy direction is sufficiently explicit, then the necessary information relevant to the development of the policy can be collected, so this view would contend, and the policy actions can be deliberate, directed, and successful.

These comments should not be taken as a diatribe against research or an argument that knowledge counts for naught. Quite the contrary. Systematic knowledge generated by research is an important and necessary component in the decision-making process. Further, it is fair to note that there is seldom enough research-based information available in the policy arena. William Ruckelshaus once noted that although he was the administrator of the Environmental Protection Agency, he made many decisions when there was less than 10% of the necessary research information available to him and his staff. The relevance and usefulness of policy research will not become apparent, however, unless there is a reconsideration of what is understood by decision making in the policy process. A redefinition is needed of the context in which to look for a linkage between knowledge and action. Unpacking the nature of the policy cycle is the strategy employed here to address this redefinition of policy decision making.

◆ The Policy Cycle and Qualitative Research

There are two levels of decision making in the policy arena. The first involves the establishment of the broad parameters of government action, such as providing national health insurance, establishing a national energy policy, restructuring the national immigration laws, or reexamining the criteria for determining the safety and soundness of the country's financial institutions. At this level and in these instances, policy research input is likely to be quite small, if not nil. The setting of these national priorities is a political event, a coming together of a critical mass of politicians, special interest groups, and persons in the media who are able among them to generate the attention and focus necessary for the items to reach the national agenda.

"Iron triangles" built by the informal linking of supporters in each of these three arenas are not created by the presence or absence of policy research. One or another research study might be quoted in support of the contention that the issue deserves national attention, but it is incidental to the more basic task of first working to place the issue on the national agenda. If one wishes to influence any of the players during this phase of the policy process, it is much more likely to be done through personal contact, by organizations taking positions, or through the creation of sufficient static in the policy system (for example, lining up special interest groups in opposition to a proposal, even as there are groups in favor). This works to the benefit of the opposition in that media coverage will have to be seen to be "balanced" and coverage of the opposition can create the impression that there is not the strong unified support for a position that otherwise would seem to be the case.

Once the issue is on the agenda of key actors or organizations within the policy establishment, there are possibilities for the introduction and utilization of policy research. It is here at this second level of policy making—the level where there are concerns about translating policy intentions into policy and programmatic realities—that I will focus in this chapter.

The framework in which the contributions of policy research in general and qualitative research in particular can best be understood is that of the policy cycle, a concept that has been addressed for more than a decade (see, e.g., Chelimsky, 1985; Guba, 1984; Nakamura & Smallwood, 1980; Rist, 1989, 1990, 1993). I will develop my discussion of the policy cycle here according to its three phases—policy formulation, policy implementation, and policy accountability. Each of these three phases has its own order and logic, its own information requirements, and its own policy actors. Further, there is only some degree of overlap among the three phases, suggesting that they do merit individual analysis and understanding.

The opportunities for qualitative research within the policy cycle are thus defined and differentiated by the information requirements at each phase. The questions asked at each phase are distinct, and the information generated in response to these same questions is used to different ends. It is to a detailed examination of these three phases of the policy cycle and the manner in which qualitative research can inform each phase that I now turn.

◆ Policy Formulation

Nakamura and Smallwood (1980) define a policy as follows: "A policy can be thought of as a set of instructions from policy makers to policy implementers that spell out both goals and the means for achieving those goals" (p. 31). How is it that these instructions are crafted, by whom, and with what relevant policy information and analysis? The answers can provide important insights into the process of policy formulation. Nakamura and

Smallwood offer a relevant departure point with their description of the actors involved in policy formulation:

> In general, the principal actors in policy formulation are the "legitimate" or formal policy makers: people who occupy positions in the governmental arena that entitle them to authoritatively assign priorities and commit resources. These people include elected officials, legislators, and high-level administrative appointees, each of whom must follow prescribed paths to make policy. . . . Since these formal policy makers represent diverse constituencies—electoral, administrative, and bureaucratic—the policy making process offers many points of access through which interest groups and others from arenas outside government can exercise influence. Thus policy making usually involves a diverse set of authoritative, or formal, policy makers, who operate within the governmental arena, plus a diverse set of special interest and other constituency groups from outside arenas, who press their demands on these formal leaders. (pp. 31-32)

As the formulation process begins, there are a number of pressing questions. Answering each question necessitates the compiling of whatever information is currently available plus the development of additional information when the gaps are too great in what is currently known. The information needs can generally be clustered around three broad sets of questions. Each of these clusters is highly relevant to policy formulation; in each there are important opportunities for the presentation and utilization of qualitative research.

The first set of information needs revolves around an understanding of the policy issue at hand. What are the contours of this issue? Is the problem or condition one that is larger now than before, about the same, or smaller? Is anything known about whether the nature of the condition has changed? Do the same target populations, areas, or institutions experience this condition now as earlier? How well can the condition be defined? How well can the condition be measured? What are the different interpretations and understandings about the condition, its causes and its effects? The issue here, stated differently, is one of the ability of policy makers to define clearly and understand the problem or condition that they are facing and for which they are expected to develop a response.

Charles Lindblom (1968) has nicely captured some of the conceptual complexity facing policy makers as they try to cope with the definition of a policy problem or condition:

Policy makers are not faced with a given problem. Instead they have to identify and formulate their problem. Rioting breaks out in dozens of American
cities. What is the problem? Maintaining law and order? Racial discrimination? Incipient revolution? Black power? Low income? Lawlessness at the
fringe of an otherwise relatively peaceful reform movement? Urban dis-
organization? Alienation? (p. 13)

The second cluster of questions focuses on what has taken place previously in response to this condition or problem. What programs or projects
have previously been initiated? How long did they last? How successful
were they? What level of funding was required? How many staff members
were required? How receptive were the populations or institutions to
these initiatives? Did they request help or did they resist the interventions?
Did the previous efforts address the same condition or problem as currently exists, or was it different? If it was different, how so? If it was the
same, why are yet additional efforts necessary? Are the same interest
groups involved? What may explain any changes in the present interest
group coalition?

The third cluster of questions relevant to the policy formulation stage
of the cycle focuses on what is known of the previous efforts and their
impacts that would help one choose among present-day options. Considering trade-offs among various levels of effort in comparison to different levels of cost is but one among several kinds of data relevant to
considering the policy options. There may also be data on the time
frames necessary before one could hope to see impacts. Trade-offs between the length of the developmental stage of the program and the eventual impacts are relevant, particularly if there are considerable pressures
for short-term solutions. The tendency to go to "weak thrust, weak effect"
strategies is well understood in these circumstances. Alternatively, if previous efforts did necessitate a considerable period of time for measurable
outcomes to appear, how did the policy makers in those circumstances
hold on to the public support and keep the coalitions intact long enough
for the results to emerge?

Qualitative research is highly relevant to the information needs at this
stage in the policy cycle. Studies on the social construction of problems, on
the differing interpretations of social conditions, on the building and sus-
taining of coalitions for change, on previous program initiatives and their
impacts, on community and organizational receptivity to programs, on
organizational stability and cohesion during the formulation stage, and on

the changing nature of social conditions are all germane to the questions posed here.

There is an additional contribution that qualitative work can make at this stage of the policy process, and it is that of studying the intended and unintended consequences of the various policy instruments or tools that might be selected as the means to implement the policy (Salamon, 1989). There is a present need within the policy community to ascertain what tools work best in which circumstances and for which target populations. Very little systematic work has been done in this area—which frequently leaves policy makers essentially to guess as to the trade-offs between the choice of one tool and another.

Information of the kind provided by qualitative research can be of significant help in making decisions, for example, about whether to provide direct services in health, housing, and education or provide vouchers to recipients, whether to provide direct cash subsidies or tax credits to employers who will hire unemployed youth, and whether to increase funding for information campaigns or to increase taxes as strategies to discourage smoking. These are but three examples where different policy tools are available and where choices will have to be made among them.

Key among the activities in the policy formulation stage is the selection of the most appropriate policy strategy to achieve the desired objective. Central to the design of this strategy is the selection of one or more tools available to the government as the means to carry out its intentions. Qualitative studies of how different tools are understood and responded to by target populations is of immense importance at this stage of the policy process.

Unfortunately, although the demand for analysis of this type is great, the supply is extremely limited. The qualitative study of policy tools is an area that is yet to be even modestly explored within the research community.

Although qualitative research can be relevant at this stage, it is also the case that its applications are problematic. The basic reason is that seldom is there enough time to both commission and complete new qualitative research within the existing window of opportunity during policy formulation. Thus the applications have to rely on existing qualitative research—and that may or may not exist. Here is one key means by which good, well-crafted qualitative work on topical social issues can find its way into the policy arena. As policy makers start on the formulation effort, their need to draw quickly on existing work puts a premium on those research studies that have worked through matters of problem definition, the social construction of problems, community studies, retrospective assessments of prior initiatives, and so on.

The problematic nature of the applications of qualitative research at this stage is further reinforced by the fact that seldom are research funds available for studies that address the kinds of questions noted above in the three clusters. If the problem or condition is not seen to be above the horizon and thus on the policy screen, there is little incentive for a policy maker or program manager to use scarce funds for what would appear to be nonpragmatic, "theoretical" studies. And by the time the condition has sufficiently changed or become highly visible as a social issue for the policy community, qualitative work is hard-pressed to be sufficiently time sensitive and responsive. The window for policy formulation is frequently very small and open only a short time. The information that can be passed through has to be ready and in a form that enhances quick understanding.

The above constraints on the use of qualitative research at this stage of the policy cycle should not be taken as negative judgments on either the utility or the relevance of such information. Rather, it is only realistic to acknowledge that having the relevant qualitative research available when it is needed for policy formulation is not always possible. As noted earlier, this is an area where there are potentially significant uses for qualitative studies. But the uses are likely to come because of scholars and researchers who have taken on an area of study for their own interest and to inform basic understandings in the research community, rather than presuming before they begin that they would influence the formulation process. It is only the infrequent instance where there is sufficient time during the formulation stage for new qualitative work to be conducted.

It should be stressed here that the restrictions on the use of qualitative **work during the formulation phase of the policy cycle come much more** from the nature of the policy process than from the nature of qualitative work. The realities of the legislative calendar, the short lives of most senior political appointees in any one position, the mad scramble among competing special interest groups for their proposals to be addressed and acted upon, and the lack of concentration by the media on any issue for very long all inhibit the development of research agendas that address the underlying issues. This is ironic because it is clear that the country will face well into the foreseeable future the issues of health care allocation and quality, immigration controls and border security, educational retraining of dislocated workers, and youth unemployment, to name but four areas that have heretofore persistently stayed near or at the top of the national policy agenda. Basic, in-depth qualitative work in these and other key areas could inform the policy formulation process for years to come. But the pressures and structural incentives in the policy system all go in the other direction. To wit: Develop short-term proposals with quick impacts to show responsiveness and accommodate all the vested interests in the iron triangle.

In sum, with respect to this first phase of the policy cycle, qualitative research can be highly influential. This is particularly so with respect to problem definition, understanding of prior initiatives, community and organizational receptivity to particular programmatic approaches, and the kinds of impacts (both anticipated and unanticipated) that might emerge from different intervention strategies. This information would be invaluable to policy makers. But, as noted, the use of the material can be hindered by such factors as whether or not the information exists, is known to the policy community, and is available in a form that makes it quickly accessible. Overcoming these obstacles does not guarantee the use of qualitative research in the formulation process, but one can be strongly assured that if these obstacles are present, the likelihood of the use of qualitative material drastically diminishes.

◆ Policy Implementation

The second phase of the policy cycle is that of policy implementation. It is in this stage that the policy initiatives and goals established during policy formulation are to be transformed into programs, procedures, and regulations. The knowledge base that policy makers need to be effective in this phase necessitates the collection and analysis of different information from that found in policy formulation. With the transformation of policies into programs, the concern moves to the operational activities of the policy tool and the allocation of resources. The concern becomes one of how to use the available resources in the most efficient and effective manner in order to have the most robust impact on the program or condition at hand. As Pressman and Wildavsky (1984) have written in this regard:

> Policies imply theories. Whether stated explicitly or not, policies point to a chain of causation between initial conditions and future consequences. If X, then Y. Policies become programs when, by authoritative action, the initial

conditions are created. X now exists. Programs make the theories operational by forging the first link in the causal chain connecting actions to objectives. Given X, we act to obtain Y. Implementation, then, is the ability to forge subsequent links in the causal chain so as to obtain the desired results. (p. xxii)

The research literature on policy and program implementation indicates that that is a particularly difficult task to accomplish (see, e.g., Hargrove, 1985; Pressman & Wildavsky, 1984; Yin, 1985). Again, quoting Pressman and Wildavsky:

Our normal expectations should be that new programs will fail to get off the ground and that, at best, they will take considerable time to get started. The cards in this world are stacked against things happening, as so much effort is required to make them work. The remarkable thing is that new programs work at all. (p. 109)

It is in this context of struggling to find ways of making programs work that the data and analyses from qualitative research can come into play. The information needs from qualitative research at this stage of the policy cycle cluster into several areas. First, there is a pressing need for information on the implementation process per se. Qualitative researchers, through case studies, program monitoring, and process evaluations, can inform program managers responsible for the implementation of the policy initiative.

Qualitative work can focus on such questions as the degree to which the program is reaching the intended target audience, the similarities and contrasts in implementation strategies across sites, the aspects of the program that are or are not operational, whether the services slated to be delivered are in fact the ones delivered, and the operational burdens placed on the institution or organization responsible for implementation (i.e., Is there the institutional capacity to respond effectively to the new policy initiative?). The focus is on the day-to-day realities of bringing a new program or policy into existence. This "ground-level" view of implementation is best done through qualitative research. The study of the rollout of an implementation effort is an area where qualitative work is at a clear advantage over other data collection strategies.

A second cluster of research questions amenable to qualitative work in the implementation arena focuses on the problem or condition that prompted the policy or program response in the first place. No problem or condition stands still simply because the policy community has decided to take action on what was known at the time the decision was made. Problems and conditions change—both before and after a policy response is decided upon. Thus the challenge for qualitative researchers is to continue to track the condition, even as the implementation effort swings into action. Qualitative work can provide ongoing monitoring of the situation—whether the condition has improved, worsened, remained static; whether the same target population is involved as earlier; whether the condition has spread or contracted; and whether the aims of the program still match the assumptions and previous understandings of the condition. Qualitative work can provide an important reality check for program managers as to whether the program is or is not appropriate to the current condition. Qualitative work that monitors the condition in real time can play a key role in the continuous efforts of program managers to match their services or interventions to the present circumstances.

The third cluster of necessary policy questions during this implementation phase of the policy cycle focuses on the efforts made by the organization or institution to respond to the initiative. Here, for example, qualitative data would be relevant for learning how the organizational response to the condition or problem has been conceptualized. Are the social constructions of the problem that were accepted at the policy formulation stage by federal policy makers accepted during implementation by the program managers and staff months later and perhaps thousands of miles away? What has been the transformation of the understandings that have taken place when the policy or program is actually being implemented? Do the policy makers and the program implementation folks accept the same understandings as to the intent of the policy—let alone the same understandings of the problem that the policy is suppose to address?

Another aspect of this need for qualitative data concerns the organizational response. Here questions would be asked that address the expertise and qualifications of those responsible for the implementation effort, the interest shown by management and staff, the controls in place regarding the allocation of resources, the organizational structure and whether it adequately reflects the demands on the organization to respond to this initiative, what means exist in the organization for deciding among competing demands, the strategies the organization uses to clarify misunderstandings or ambiguities in how it defines its role in implementation, and, finally, what kinds of interactive information or feedback loops are in place to assist managers in their ongoing efforts to move the program toward the stated objectives of the policy. It is information of precisely this type on the implementation process that Robert Behn (1988) notes is so critical to managers as they struggle to "grope along" and move toward organizational goals.

◆ Policy Accountability

The third stage in the policy cycle comes when the policy or program is sufficiently mature that one can address questions of accountability, impacts, or outcomes. Here again, the information needs are different from those in the two previous stages of the policy cycle. The contributions of qualitative research can be pivotal in assessing the consequences of the policy and program initiative. Just as the questions change from one part of the policy cycle to another, so too does the focus of the qualitative research necessary to answer these same questions.

First there is the matter of what the program or policy did or did not accomplish: Were the objectives for the program met? Qualitative research can specifically help in this regard by addressing, for example, whether the community and police were actively working together in a neighborhood "crime watch" program, whether the appropriate target audience of homeless persons in another program received the health services they were promised, and whether in a third program youth were given the type and quantity of on-the-job training that resulted in successful placements in permanent positions.

When a program reaches the stage that it is appropriate to discuss and assess impacts, qualitative research provides a window on the program that is simply not available in any other way. Qualitative research allows for the study of both anticipated and unanticipated outcomes, changes in understandings and perceptions as a result of the efforts of the program or policy, the direction and intensity of any social change that results from the program, and the strengths and weaknesses of the administrative/ organizational structure that was used to operationalize the program. Policy makers have no equally grounded means of learning about program impacts and outcomes as they do with qualitative research findings.

These grounded means of knowing also carry over into what one might traditionally think of as quantitative assessments of policy. Qualitative work can provide to program managers and policy makers information on how confident they can or should be in the measures being used to determine program influence. Although the intent may be that of a highly reliable and replicable instrument that allows for sophisticated quantification, it is the qualitative work that can address the issue of validity.

The issues of reliability and validity are well known in the research literature and need not be reviewed here. Suffice it to say that policy makers and program managers have been misled more than once by investing a great deal of time and effort on their instrumentation without equal emphasis on answering the question of whether their measures were the appropriate ones to the problem or condition at hand. Studies of school desegregation and busing or health care in nursing homes are but two areas where a heavy emphasis on quantifying outcomes and processes have left key aspects of the condition undocumented and thus unattended to by those who should have been paying attention.

There is an additional aspect of this first cluster of information needs that merits special attention vis-à-vis qualitative research. This has to do with whether the original objectives and goals of the policy stayed in place through implementation. One message has come back to policy makers time and again: Do not take for granted that what was intended to be established or put in place through a policy initiative will be what one finds after the implementation process is complete. Programs and policies make countless midcourse corrections, tacking constantly, making changes in funding levels, staff stability, target population movements, political support, community acceptance, and the like.

It is through the longitudinal perspective of qualitative work that such issues can be directly addressed. Blitzkrieg assessments of programs are simply unable to pick up the backstage issues and conflicts that will inevitably be present and that may directly influence the direction and success of the program (Rist, 1980). To ignore staff turnover in a program that is highly staff-intensive in the provision of services, for instance, is to miss what may be the key ingredient in any study of implementation. But recognizing that it may be an issue in the first place is one of the ways in which qualitative work distinguishes itself from other research strategies.

The second cluster of information needs that emerge when a program is being assessed for impacts and outcomes is that of addressing whether and what changes may have occurred in the problem or condition. Central to any study of outcomes is the determination of whether in fact the condition itself has changed or not and what relevance the program or policy did or did not have to the present circumstances.

Although it is rudimentary to say so, it is worth stating explicitly that problems can change or not, totally independently of any policy or program initiative. Conceptually what we have is a situation in which impacts could or could not have occurred, and the consequence would be change or no change in a program or condition.

For example, a positive outcome of a policy could be no worsening of a condition, that is, no change in the original status that first prompted the policy response. Developing local intervention programs that stalled any growth in the number of child abuse cases could be considered a positive outcome. The key question is, of course, whether the evidence of no growth can be attributed to the intervention program or some other factor that was affecting the community independent of the intervention program itself, such as broad media coverage of a particularly savage beating of a child and, in the aftermath, considerable additional media coverage of how parents can cope with their urges to injure their children.

Qualitative work in this instance could focus on such impacts as the outreach efforts of the program to attract parents who had previously abused their children; efforts to reach parents who are seeking help to build better skills in working with their children; patterns and trends in child abuse as discussed by school teachers, day care providers, and others who have ongoing and consistent contact with children; and whether and how parents are now coping with the stresses that might cause them to abuse their children.

The above discussion also generates an additional area in which qualitative work can assist at this stage of the policy cycle. It is the close-in and intensive familiarity with the problem or condition that comes from conducting qualitative work that would allow the researcher to make judgments on whether the situation is of a magnitude and nature that further action is necessary. If the study indicates that the problem or condition is diminishing in severity and prevalence, then further funding of a programmatic response may not be necessary. As a contrary example, the data from qualitative work may suggest that the condition has changed directions—that is, moved to a new target population—and a refocusing of the program is necessary if it is to be responsive.

Social conditions do not remain static, and the realization that the characteristics of a condition can change necessitates periodic reexamination of the original policy intent (policy formulation). Qualitative researchers can position themselves so that they can closely monitor the ongoing characteristics of a condition. With this firsthand and close-in information, they are well suited to suggest any necessary changes to both the policy formulation and implementation strategies for subsequent intervention efforts.

The third information need at this stage of the policy cycle where qualitative work can be of direct use comes with the focus on accountability. Here qualitative work can address concerns of management supervision, leadership of the organization with clear goals in mind, the attention to processes and procedures that would strengthen the capacity of the organization to implement the policy initiative effectively, the use of data-based decision making, and the degree of alignment or congruence between the leadership and the staff. All of these issues speak directly to the capacity of an organization to mobilize itself to provide effective service to its customers. If the organization is not positioned to do so, then there are clear issues of accountability that rest with the leadership.

Qualitative researchers who come to know an organization thoroughly and from the inside will be in a unique position from which to address the treatment and training of staff, reasons for attrition and low morale, the service-oriented philosophy (or lack of it) among the staff and leadership, the beliefs of the staff in the viability and worthiness of the program to address the problem, the quality and quantity of information used within the program for decision making, and the like. These are true qualitative dimensions of organizational life. It is essential that these be studied if judgments are to be made on the efficiency and effectiveness of any particular programmatic strategy. These judgments become central to subsequent decisions on the potential selection of a policy tool that would require a similar program intervention.

There are clear concerns of management accountability that must be discussed and assessed whenever programs are to be funded anew or redirected. Some of these concerns deal directly with impacts on the problem or condition, whereas others focus on the internal order and logic of the organization itself. Stated differently, it is important during the accountability phase to determine the degree to which any changes in the condition or problem can be directly attributed to the program and whether the program optimized or suboptimized the impact it had. Likewise, it is important to ascertain whether the presence (or absence) of any documented impacts is the result of the coherence of the policy formulation or the nature of program implementation. Finding that instance where coherent and robust policy initiatives are operationalized within a well-managed organization necessitates the complex assessment of what impacts can be attributed to the policy and what to its successful implementation. Qualitative research has a perspective on how to undertake this kind of assessment that other research approaches do not and for which the other approaches would have to rely heavily on proxy measures.

◆ Policy Tools

The analysis thus far has focused on the nature of the policy cycle and how each phase of the cycle has different information requirements for policy makers and program managers. The effort has been to document how qualitative research can play an active and positive role in answering the information needs at each of these phases and for both the policy makers and the program managers. In this section, the attention shifts to a focus on what are termed *policy tools.*

Such an emphasis is important because a deeper understanding of the tools available to government and how each can be more or less effectively used to achieve policy objectives can clearly inform all three stages of the policy cycle. Key to the efforts in policy formulation is the selection of an appropriate tool—be it a grant, a subsidy, a tax credit, a loan, a new regulation, the creation of a government-sponsored enterprise, or the provision of direct services, to name but 7 of the more than 30 tools currently used by government.

The selection of one tool rather than another is a policy choice for which few guiding data are available. Further, research to help policy makers in this regard is extremely sparse. Policy makers decide either based on past experience with a tool ("We used tax credits before, let's use tax credits again") or because they have a clear proclivity for or against a particular tool (conservatives would resist direct government services and seek instead a tool that locates the activity in the private sector, e.g., grants for the construction of public housing or the privatization of all concessions in national parks). It is safe to assert that neither qualitative nor quantitative researchers have shown much interest in this area. Beyond the works of Linder (1988), Linder and Peters (1984, 1989), May (1981), and Salamon (1981, 1989), there is not much research, either theoretical or empirical, to be cited.

What follows is an effort to identify four areas where qualitative work could be highly valuable to discussions regarding policy tools. For each of these areas, there is at present a nearly complete research void. It should be stressed that the short discussion to follow is not meant to be a definitive statement on how qualitative work can address the information needs of policy makers as they choose among tools, nor is it the definitive research agenda on the strengths and weaknesses of different tools.

It needs to be restated that few researchers of any persuasion have moved into this difficult but highly policy-relevant area. The reasons for this hesitancy are outside the bounds of this discussion, but it is clear that the policy analysis and research communities have, with few exceptions, steered wide of this port of inquiry. Building primarily on the works of Linder, Peters, and Salamon, what follows is offered as a modest agenda for those qualitative researchers who are interested in exploring new and untested ways of involving qualitative work within the policy arena. A more elaborate and detailed research agenda in this area is still well over the horizon.

As noted, four areas amenable to qualitative study will be briefly discussed. These are resource intensiveness, targeting, institutional constraints, and political risks. The tentativeness of this proposal has to be stressed yet again. There may well be multiple other ways in which to frame the qualitative study of policy tools. What follows here is predicated on the previous discussion regarding the policy cycle. The framework for the qualitative study of policy tools is essentially a matrix analysis, whereby each of these four areas can be studied in each of the three phases of the policy cycle. All 12 combinations will not be individually addressed here; rather, the focus will be on the four broad areas that can help to clarify the trade-offs among tools.

Resource intensiveness refers to the constellation of concerns involving the complexity of the operations, the relative costliness of different options, and the degree of administrative burden that different tools place on organizations. Tools vary widely in their complexity, their demands on organizations for technical expertise to administer and manage, their direct and indirect costs by sector, and the degree to which they are direct or indirect in their intent. And just to complicate matters more, the mix of these concerns for any given tool will shift as one moves from one phase of the policy cycle to another. Keeping the financial costs low and federal involvement to a minimum, for example, may be high priorities in Washington during the policy formulation stage, but these will also have the consequences during the policy implementation stage of serving few of the eligible target population, adding complexity through mandated state administration, and reducing direct impacts. Managing toxic waste clean-ups is but one example that is somewhat parallel to this brief scenario.

For qualitative researchers, the challenges here are multiple, not the least because they would necessitate more direct attention to organizational analysis. But there is also the clear opportunity to ask questions within organizations and to assess organizational capacity in ways that have not traditionally been done. Administrative burden has not been a topic of much (if any) qualitative research, but it is a very real consideration in the policy arena. Learning more of how to conceptualize this concern, how it is understood at various levels of government and within the private sector, and how different tools vary in this regard would be of considerable interest to policy makers in departments as well as those responsible for regulator and administrative oversight in organizations such as the Office of Management and Budget in the White House.

At present, a concept such as administrative burden is ill defined and subject to widely varying interpretations. In the absence of any systematic research, one person's definition and experience with "administrative burden" is as good as any other person's—and maybe better if he or she has more institutional or organizational influence. Additional examples concerning such concepts as "operational complexity" and "institutional capacity" are readily apparent.

Targeting refers to the capacity of the policy tool to be aimed at particular populations, problems, or institutions for whom the tool is primarily intended. A tool that, for example, seeks to help homeless persons who are mentally ill and also veterans would be highly targeted. Such a tool would be differentiated from a tool that is either diffuse or low in target specificity, for example, a tax credit for the interest earned in individual retirement accounts.

There are several key aspects of the targeting issue for a policy tool that qualitative researchers could address. First, there is the matter of the precision of the targeting. Qualitative researchers, in reference to the example just given, could help policy makers work through the strategies and definitional problems inherent in determining who is or is not homeless, who has or has not been diagnosed as mentally ill, and how to screen homeless veterans for service when documentation, service records, and so on are all likely to be lost or when persons simply cannot remember their own names.

A second aspect of targeting in selecting a policy tool is that of the amenability of the tool to adjustment and fine tuning. If the characteristics of the target population start to change, can the tool be adjusted to respond to this change? Flexibility in some instances would be highly desirable, whereas in others it may be irrelevant. For example, it would be beneficial to choose a policy instrument that responds to fluctuations and variations in the refugee populations coming into the United States, whereas it would be unnecessary in the instance of an entitlement program for which age is the only criterion for access to services.

Qualitative studies of different populations targeted by tools and the need (or lack thereof) of specificity in the targeting would be highly useful in policy formulation. There is also the opportunity in this area to explore whether those who have been targeted by a program believe this to be the case. Establishing community mental health centers could have some in the target population coming because of the "community health" emphasis, others coming for the "mental health" emphasis, and still others not showing up at all because they are not certain whose community is being referred or because they would never want anyone in their own neighborhood to know they have mental health problems. Linking services to target populations in the absence of such qualitative information suggests immediately the vulnerability and precariousness of presuming to establish service centers without the detailed knowledge of the populations for whom the effort is intended.

The example of community mental health centers leads to a third consideration in the targeting area—that of adaptability across uses. Can community mental health centers also serve other needs of the designated population, for example, nutrition and education, as well as serve as centers for entirely other target populations who are in the same residential vicinity? Can they serve as centers for the elderly, for latchkey children, for infant nutrition programs, and so on? The issue is one of flexibility and acceptance as well as neutrality in the perceptions of the other target groups. There may be groups who would not want to come to a mental health center, but who would be quite pleased to meet in a church or at a school. Gaining insight on these matters is clearly important as decisions are made on the location and mix of community services to be offered at any one location. Qualitative studies on these issues can inform policy makers and program managers in ways that will clearly affect the success or failure of different strategies.

Institutional capacity refers to the ability of the institution to deliver on the tasks that have been delegated to it. When a policy option clearly relies on a single institution to achieve certain objectives—for example, using the public schools as the vehicle to teach English to non-English-speaking children—there has to be some degree of certainty that the institution has the capacity to do so. Countless experiences with different policy initiatives have shown time and again that some institutions simply did not have, at the time, the capacity to do what was expected of them.

Further, there can be constraints placed on the institution that make it difficult if not impossible for the objective to be achieved. In addition to the more readily anticipated constraints of funding, staff availability, quality of facilities, and low political support, there are also constraints associated with the degree of intrusiveness the institution can exercise as well as the level of coerciveness allowed. The hesitancy of policy makers to allow intrusive efforts by the Internal Revenue Service to collect unpaid taxes has a clear impact on the ability of the organization to do so. The same can be said with respect to the IRS on the matter of coerciveness. Policy makers have simply decided to keep some organizations more constrained than others in carrying out their functions, for fear of abuse. Policy tools that have to rely on voluntary compliance or are framed to have an indirect effect face constraints different from those where these do not apply.

Qualitative research into the domain of institutional constraints and how it is that these constraints play out in the relation of the organization to the fulfillment of its mission is not, to my knowledge, now being done. It may be argued that it is not necessary, as the constraint dimension for any policy tool is too removed from research influence. That is, any constraints on an organization are more philosophical and ideological than operational. Yet the issue of institutional capacity and what does or does not hinder the ability of the organization to achieve its stated objectives is important to understand explicitly. If policy makers establish the parameters around an organization to the degree that it can never clearly achieve its goal (e.g., the IRS and unpaid back taxes), then there is a built-in level of failure that ought not be ignored and for which the institution should not be held accountable.

Political risk is the fourth dimension of the study of policy tools where qualitative research can directly contribute. Here the issues cluster around concerns of unanticipated risk, chances of failure, and timing. The selection of a policy tool is made with some outcome in mind—either direct or indirect. Yet there is always the possibility of unanticipated outcomes— again either direct or indirect. The selection of a tool necessarily has to take into account the risk of unknown outcomes and how these might affect the success of the policy.

Qualitative research, by the nature of its being longitudinal, done in naturalistic settings, and focused on the constructions of meaning developed by participants, is in a unique position from which to assess the possibility of tools having the impacts intended by policy makers. Low risk of unknown outcomes—for example, in increasing the security at U.S. federal courthouses—eliminates some level of uncertainty from the decision that does not happen when the risk of unknown outcomes is quite high, such as moving to year-round school schedules or as was learned when the movement to deinstitutionalize the mentally ill resulted in tens of thousands of mentally ill persons being left on their own with no means of support or treatment.

One other aspect of the political risk factor that qualitative research can address is the sustainability of the policy initiative. Close-in studies of the operational life of a policy initiative can gain a perspective on the commitment of those involved, their belief in the worthiness of the effort, the amount of political support they are or are not engendering, and the receptivity of the target population to the effort. If all these indicators are decidedly negative, then the sustainability of the initiative is surely low.

It is difficult to achieve success in policy efforts in the best of circumstances; it is that much harder when all the indicators point in the opposite direction. Qualitative research should have a distinct window from which to judge matters of political risk. Understanding of the participants, willingness to assume the causal linkage posited in the policy itself, and the degree of risk of unknown outcomes all influence the likelihood that any policy tool will achieve its intended results.

◆ Concluding Observations

In reviewing this assessment of the contributions of qualitative work to the policy process, it is apparent that the contributions are more in the realm of the potential than the actual. There is no broad-based and sustained tradition within contemporary social science of focusing qualitative work specifically on policy issues, especially given the real time constraints that the policy process necessitates. Yet it is also clear that the opportunities are multiple for such contributions to be made. The issue is chiefly one of how to link those in the research and academic communities who are knowledgeable in conducting qualitative research studies to those in the policy arena who can commission such work and who will make use of the findings. The analysis of different strategies for building these linkages would require a separate chapter; suffice it to say here that much hard thinking and numerous exploratory efforts will be required for the potential to become the actual. The issues of institutional cultures, academic reward systems, publication requirements, funding sources, and methodological limitations are but five among many that will have to be addressed if the linkages are to be built. And even beyond the resolution of (or at least the careful thinking about) these issues is the fundamental question of whether there is the will to bring qualitative work directly into the policy arena. Much of what has been written here will remain speculative unless and until there is some consensus among the practitioners of qualitative research that making this transition is worthwhile. The policy community is, I believe, ready for and would be receptive to anything those in the qualitative research community could offer, should they choose to make the effort to do so.

◆ Note

1. I want to stress early on that in this chapter I will not seek to develop distinctions among various conventionally used terms for qualitative research. Thus, in the pages that follow, terms such as *qualitative work, qualitative research,* and *qualitative methods* will all be used to denote the same frame of reference. I most frequently use the term that appears in the title of this handbook, *qualitative research.* I leave it to other authors in this volume to develop those distinctions as appropriate. I would also note, in defense of not trying to specify in much detail just exactly what the meaning is behind the use of any one of these terms, that early reviewers of this chapter suggested at least four other terms I might use in lieu of those I have. These terms included *naturalistic, constructionist, interpretive,* and *ethnographies.* I am sure that the delineation of distinctions has an important place in this book; it is just not my intent to do so here.

I also want to note early on that I am not going to try to differentiate among various qualitative data collection strategies, or means of analysis, as to their particular spheres of potential influence. Thus in this chapter I will not try to indicate what policy relevance or influence one might expect from case studies (and there are multiple variations in this single area alone) in contrast, for example, to multimethod studies. My intent is to place qualitative work broadly within the policy arena, not to develop a prescriptive set of categories about which methods or modes of analysis are likely to lead to what types of influence.

◆ References

Behn, R. D. (1988). Managing by groping along. *Journal of Policy Analysis and Management, 7*(4).

Chelimsky, E. (1982). Making evaluations relevant to congressional needs. *GAO Review, 17*(1).

Chelimsky, E. (1985). Old patterns and new directions in program evaluation. In E. Chelimsky (Ed.), *Program evaluation: Patterns and directions*. Washington, DC: American Society for Public Administration.

Guba, E. G. (1984). The effect of definitions of policy on the nature and outcomes of policy analysis. *Educational Leadership, 42*(2).

Hargrove, E. (1985). *The missing link: The study of the implementation of social policy*. Washington, DC: Urban Institute Press.

Janowitz, M. (1971). *Sociological methods and social policy*. New York: General Learning Press.

Lindblom, C. E. (1968). *The policy making process*. Englewood Cliffs, NJ: Prentice Hall.

Linder, S. H. (1988). Managing support for social research and development: Research goals, risk, and policy instruments. *Journal of Policy Analysis and Management, 7*(4).

Linder, S. H., & Peters, B. G. (1984). From social theory to policy design. *Journal of Public Policy, 4*(3).

Linder, S. H., & Peters, B. G. (1989). Instruments of government: Perceptions and contexts. *Journal of Public Policy, 9*(1).

May, P. J. (1981). Hints for crafting alternative policies. *Policy Analysis, 7*(2).

Nakamura, R. T., & Smallwood, F. (1980). *The politics of policy implementation*. New York: St. Martin's.

Patton, M. Q. (1988). *Qualitative evaluation and research methods* (2nd ed.). Newbury Park, CA: Sage.

Pressman, J. L., & Wildavsky, A. (1984). *Implementation* (3rd ed.). Berkeley: University of California Press.

Rist, R. C. (1980). Blitzkrieg ethnography: On the transformation of a method into a movement. *Educational Researcher, 9*(2).

Rist, R. C. (1989). Management accountability: The signals sent by auditing and evaluation. *Journal of Public Policy, 9*(3).

Rist, R. C. (Ed.). (1990). *Program evaluation and the management of government: Patterns and prospects across eight nations*. New Brunswick, NJ: Transaction Books.

Rist, R. C. (1993). Program evaluation in the United States General Accounting Office: Reflections on question formulation and utilization. In R. Conner et al. (Eds.), *Advancing public policy evaluation: Learning from international experiences*. Amsterdam: Elsevier.

Salamon, L. M. (1981). Rethinking public management: Third-party government and the changing forms of government action. *Public Policy, 29*(3).

Salamon, L. M. (1989). *Beyond privatization: The tools of government action*. Washington, DC: Urban Institute Press.

Smith, J. A. (1991). *The idea brokers: Think tanks and the rise of the new policy elite*. New York: Free Press.

Weiss, C. H. (1982). Policy research in the context of diffuse decision making. In R. C. Rist (Ed.), *Policy studies review annual.* Beverly Hills, CA: Sage.

Weiss, C. H. (1988). Evaluations for decisions: Is anybody there? Does anybody care? *Evaluation Practice, 9*(1).

Yin, R. K. (1985). Studying the implementation of public programs. In W. Williams (Ed.), *Studying implementation.* Chatham, NJ: Chatham House.

◆ Suggested Further Readings

Bemelmans-Videc, M. L., Rist, R. C., & Vedung, E. (Eds.). (1998). *Carrots, sticks, and sermons: Policy instruments and their evaluation.* New Brunswick, NJ: Transaction Books.

Elmore, R. (1987). Instruments and strategy in public policy. *Policy Studies Review, 7*(1), 63-78.

Gray, A., Jenkins, B., & Segsworth, B. (Eds.). (1992). *Budgeting, auditing and evaluation: Functions and integration in seven governments.* New Brunswick, NJ: Transaction.

Hood, C. C. (1986). *The tools of government.* Chatham, NJ: Chatham House.

Leeuw, F. L., Rist, R. C., & Sonnichsen, R. (Eds.). (1994). *Can governments learn? Comparative perspectives on evaluation and organizational learning.* New Brunswick, NJ: Transaction.

Mayne, J., & Zapico-Goni, E. (Eds.). (1997). *Monitoring performance in the public sector: Future directions from international experience.* New Brunswick, NJ: Transaction Books.

Rist, R. C. (1990). Management accountability: The signals sent by auditing and evaluation. *Journal of Public Policy, 9,* 355-369.

Toulemonde, J., & Rieper, O. (Eds.). (1997). *Politics and practices of intergovernmental evaluation.* New Brunswick, NJ: Transaction Books.

Vedung, E. (1997). *Public policy and program evaluation.* New Brunswick, NJ: Transaction Books.

Suggested Readings

◆ Chapter 2

Gubrium, J. F., & Holstein, J. A. (Eds.) (2002). *Handbook of interview research: Context and methods*. Thousand Oaks: Sage.

◆ Chapter 3

Babbie, E. (1998). *Observing ourselves: Essays in social research*. Prospect Heights, IL: Waveland.

Evans, J., & Hall, S. (Eds.) (1999). *The visual culture reader*. London: Sage.

Gold, R. L. (1997). The ethnographic method in sociology. *Qualitative Inquiry, 3,* 388-402.

Schensul, S. L., Schensul, J. R., & LeCompte, M. D. (1999). Essential ethnographic methods: Observations, interviews, and questionnaires. In J. Scheusel & M. D. LeCompte (Eds.), *Ethnographer's Toolkit,* Vol. 2. Walnut Creek, CA: AltaMira.

Wolcott, H. F. (1995). *The art of fieldwork*. Walnut Creek, CA: AltaMira.

◆ Chapter 5

Emmison, M., & Smith, P. (2000). *Researching the visual*. London: Sage.

◆ Chapter 6

Bochner, A. P. (2001). Narrative's virtues. *Qualitative Inquiry, 7,* 131-157.

Bochner, A., & Ellis, C. (2002). *Ethnographically speaking: Autoethnography, literature, and aesthetics*. Walnut Creek, CA: AltaMira.

Goodall, H. L. (2000). *Writing the new ethnography.* Walnut Creek, CA: AltaMira.

Rosenwall, G., & Ochberg, R. (1992). *Storied lives: The cultural politics of self-understanding.* New Haven: Yale University Press.

Tillmann-Healy, L. (2001). *Between gay and straight: Understanding friendship across sexual orientation.* Walnut Creek, CA: AltaMira.

◆ Chapter 7

Bernard, H. R. (2002). *Research methods in anthropology, 3rd edition.* Thousand Oaks, CA: Sage.

Dey, I. (1993). *Qualitative data analysis: A user friendly guide for social scientists.* London: Routledge.

Krippendorf, K. (1980). *Content analysis: An introduction to its methodology.* Beverly Hills, CA: Sage.

Miles, M. B., & Huberman, A. M. (1994). *Qualitative data analysis: An expanded sourcebook, 2nd edition.* Thousand Oaks, CA: Sage.

Strauss, A., & Corbin, J. (1990). *Basics of qualitative research: Grounded theory procedures and techniques.* Newbury Park, CA: Sage.

Weller, S. W., & Romney, A. K. (1988). *Systematic data collection.* Thousand Oaks, CA: Sage.

◆ Chapter 8

Flick, U. (2002). *An introduction to qualitative research,* 2nd edition. (See especially Part 6.) London: Sage.

◆ Chapter 9

Sacks, H. (1992). *Lectures on conversation* (G. Jefferson, Ed.). Oxford, UK: Blackwell.

Silverman, D. (Ed.). (1997). *Qualitative research: Theory, method, and practice.* London: Sage.

Silverman, D. (1998). *Harvey Sacks: Social science and conversation analysis.* New York: Oxford University Press.

Silverman, D. (2000). *Doing qualitative research: A practical handbook.* London: Sage.

Silverman, D. (2001). *Interpreting qualitative data: Methods for analysing talk, text and interaction,* 2nd edition. London: Sage.

ten Have, P. (1998). *Doing conversation analysis: A practical guide.* London: Sage.

◆ Chapter 10

Greenbaum, T. L. (1998). *The handbook for focus group research, 2nd edition.* Thousand Oaks: Sage.

◆ Chapter 11

Agar, M. H.(1996). *The professional stranger: An informal introduction to ethnography.* Orlando, FL: Academic Press.

Bernard, H. R. (2001). *Research methods in anthropology: Qualitative and quantitative approaches.* Walnut Creek, CA: AltaMira.

Fetterman, D. M. (1998). *Ethnography: Step by step.* Thousand Oaks, CA: Sage.

LeCompte, M. D., & Schensul, J. J. (1999). *Designing and conducting ethnographic research.* Walnut Creek, CA: AltaMira.

Wolcott, H. F. (1999). *Ethnography: A way of seeing.* Walnut Creek, CA: AltaMira.

◆ Chapter 12

Gadamer, H-G (1995). *Truth and method* (2nd rev. ed.; J. Weinsheimer & D. G. Marshall, Trans.). New York: Crossroad.

Hazelrigg, L. (1989). *Claims of knowledge.* Tallahassee, FL: Florida State University Press.

Jones, R. (1992). *Physics for the rest of us.* Lincolnwood, IL: Contemporary Books.

Rorty, R. (1985). Solidarity or objectivity? In J. Rajchman & C. West (Eds.), *Postanalytic philosophy* (pp. 3-19). New York: Columbia University Press.

Sheman, N. (1993). *Engenderings: Constructions of knowledge, authority and privilege.* New York: Routledge.

Smith, J. (1993). *After the demise of empiricism: The problem of judging social and educational inquiry.* Norwood, NJ: Ablex.

◆ Chapter 13

Bochner, A. P., & Ellis, C. (Eds.) (2002). *Ethnographically speaking: Auto-ethnography, literature, and aesthetics.* Walnut Creek, CA: AltaMira.

◆ Chapter 14

Behar, R. (1993). *Translated woman: Crossing the border with Esperanzo's story.* Boston: Beacon.

Bochner, A., & Ellis, C. (Eds.). (2002). *Ethnographically speaking.* Thousand Oaks, CA: Sage.

Denzin, N. (1997). *Interpretive ethnography: Ethnographic practices for the 21st century.* Thousand Oaks, CA: Sage.

Ellis, C., & Bochner, A. (Eds). (1996). *Composing ethnography: Alternative forms of qualitative writing.* Walnut Creek, CA: AltaMira.

Jones, S. H. (1998). *Kaleidoscope notes: Writing women's music and organizational culture.* Walnut Creek, CA: AltaMira.

Lather, P., & Smithies, C. (1997). *Troubling the angels: Women living with HIV/AIDS.* Boulder, CO: Westview.

Richardson, L. (1990). *Writing strategies: Reaching diverse audiences.* Thousand Oaks, CA: Sage.

Richardson, L. (1997). *Fields of play: Constructing an academic life.* New Brunswick, NJ: Rutgers University Press.

Trinh T. M. (1989). *Woman, native, other: Writing postcoloniality and feminism.* Bloomington, IN: Indiana University Press.

Van Maanen, J. (1988). *Tales of the field: On writing ethnography.* Chicago, IL: University of Chicago Press.

◆ Chapter 15

Brady, I. (2002). *The time at Darwin's reef: Poetic explorations in anthropology and history.* Walnut Creek, CA: AltaMira.

Denzin, N. K., & Lincoln, Y. S. (Eds.). (2002). *The qualitative inquiry reader.* Thousand Oaks, CA: Sage.

Hirsch, E. (1999). *How to read a poem and fall in love with poetry.* New York: Harcourt Brace.

Koch, K. (1998). *Making your own days: The pleasures of reading and writing poetry.* New York: Simon and Schuster.

Nowak, M. (2000). *Revenants.* Minneapolis: Coffee House Press.

◆ Chapter 16

House, E. R., & Howe, K. R. (1999). *Values in evaluation and social research.* Thousand Oaks, CA: Sage.

Kushner, S. (2000). *Personalizing evaluation.* London: Sage.

Mertens, D. M. (1999). Inclusive evaluation: Implications of transformative theory for evaluation. *American Journal of Evaluation, 20,* 1-14.

Patton, M. Q. (2002). *Qualitative research and evaluation methods,* third edition. Thousand Oaks, CA: Sage.

Ryan, K. R., & DeStefano, L. (Eds.). (2000). *Evaluation as a democratic process: Promoting inclusion, dialogue, and deliberation.* New Directions for Evaluation no. 85. San Francisco: Jossey-Bass.

Schwandt, T. A. (forthcoming). *Evaluation practice reconsidered*. Baltimore, MD: Peter Lang.

◆ Chapter 17

Narayan, D. (Ed.). (2000). *Voices of the poor: Can anyone hear us?* Oxford, UK: Oxford University Press.

Rist, R. (1999). Linking evaluation utilization and governance: Fundamental challenges for countries building evaluation capacity. In R. Boyle & D. Lemaire (Eds.) *Building effective evaluation capacity: Lessons from practice*. New Brunswick, NJ: Transaction Books.

Roche, C. (1999). *Impact assessments for development agencies: Learning to value change*. Oxford, UK: Oxfam Publishers.

Author Index

Subject Index

About the Authors

Michael V. Angrosino is Professor of Anthropology at the University of South Florida, where he specializes in mental health policy analysis, the influence of organized religion on contemporary social policy, and the methodology of oral history. He has served as editor of *Human Organization*, the journal of the Society for Applied Anthropology, and is currently general editor of the *Southern Anthropological Society Proceedings Series* for the University of Georgia Press. His most recent book, *Opportunity House: Ethnographic Stories of Mental Retardation* (1998), is an experiment in alternative ethnographic writing.

H. Russell Bernard (Ph.D., Illinois, 1968) is Professor of Anthropology at the University of Florida. He has taught at Washington State University, West Virginia University, and the University of Florida. He has also taught or done research at the University of Athens, the University of Cologne, the National Museum of Ethnology (Osaka), and Scripps Institution of Oceanography. He works with indigenous people to develop publishing outlets for works in previously nonwritten languages. He also does research in social network analysis, particularly on the problem of estimating the size of uncountable populations. His publications include *Native Ethnography: An Otomí Indian Describes His Culture* (with Jesús Salinas Pedraza; 1989), *Technology and Social Change* (edited with Pertti Pelto; second edition, 1983), *and Research Methods in Anthropology* (second edition, 1994). He has served as editor of *Human Organization* (1976-1981), the *American Anthropologist* (1981-1989), and *Cultural*

Anthropology Methods Journal (1989-1998), and is currently editor of *Field Methods*.

Arthur P. Bochner is Professor of Communication and Codirector of the Institute for Interpretive Human Studies at the University of South Florida. He is the coauthor of *Understanding Family Communication* and coeditor of *Composing Ethnography: Alternative Forms of Qualitative Writing* (1996) as well as the AltaMira Press book series *Ethnographic Alternatives*. He has published more than 50 articles and monographs on close relationships, communication theory, and narrative inquiry. His current research focuses on geriatric care managers as ethnographers of aging.

Ivan Brady is Distinguished Teaching Professor of Anthropology at the State University of New York at Oswego and a SUNY Faculty Exchange Scholar. He is a former President of the Society for Humanistic Anthropology and book review editor for the *American Anthropologist*. His primary research has been in the Pacific Islands. His poetry has appeared in various books and journals, including *Reflections: The Anthropological Muse* (edited by I. Prattis; 1985), the *Neuroanthropology Network Newsletter*, and *Anthropology and Humanism* (Quarterly).

Erve Chambers is Professor of Anthropology at the University of Maryland, College Park. He is founding editor of the publication *Practicing Anthropology* and a past President of the Society for Applied Anthropology. His current research interests include ethnographic approaches to decision making in the areas of tourism development, natural resources management, and urban and regional planning. He is the author of *Applied Anthropology: A Practical Guide* (1985) and *Native Tours: The Anthropology of Travel and Tourism* (1999). His edited volumes include *Housing, Culture, and Design: A Comparative Perspective* (1989) and *Tourism and Culture: An Applied Perspective* (1997).

Deborah K. Deemer is Assistant Professor of Education at the University of Northern Iowa. Her interest in criteria for qualitative inquiry began when she was working in program evaluation as a Research Associate at Alverno College's Office of Research and Evaluation. For more than a decade she has struggled to disentangle her subjectivity from realist pretensions. Her coauthored contribution to this volume reflects her movement into working fully within the qualitative paradigm. In her current writing she continues to grapple with the meaning of quality while striving to utilize qualitative inquiry in writing the self, in depicting the lives of women, and in reflecting on educational practice.

Norman K. Denzin is Distinguished Professor of Communications, College of Communications Scholar, and Research Professor of Communications, Sociology and Humanities at the University of Illinois, Urbana-Champaign. He is the author of numerous books, including *Interpretive Ethnography: Ethnographic Practices for the 21st Century, The Cinematic Society: The Voyeur's Gaze, Images of Postmodern Society, The Research Act: A Theoretical Introduction to Sociological Methods, Interpretive Interactionism, Hollywood Shot by Shot, The Recovering Alcoholic*, and *The Alcoholic Self*, which won the Charles Cooley Award from the Society for the Study of Symbolic Interaction in 1988. In 1997 he was awarded the George Herbert Award from the Study of Symbolic Interaction. He is the editor of the Sociological Quarterly, coeditor of Qualitative Inquiry, and editor of the book series Cultural Studies: A Research Annual and Studies in Symbolic Interaction.

Carolyn Ellis is Professor of Communication and Sociology and Codirector of the Institute for Interpretive Human Studies at the University of South Florida. She is the author of *Final Negotiations: A Story of Love, Loss, and Chronic Illness* (1995) and *Fisher Folk: Two Communities on Chesapeake Bay* (1986). She is coeditor of *Composing Ethnography: Alternative Forms of Qualitative Writing* (1996), *Investigating Subjectivity: Research on Lived Experience* (1992), *Social Perspectives on Emotion* (volume 3), and the AltaMira book series *Ethnographic Alternatives*. Her current research focuses on illness narratives, autoethnography, and emotional sociology.

Andrea Fontana is Professor of Sociology at the University of Nevada, Las Vegas. He received his Ph.D. from the University of California, San Diego, in 1976. He has published articles on aging, leisure, theory, and postmodernism. He is the author of *The Last Frontier: The Social Meaning of Getting Old*, coauthor of *Social Problems and Sociologies of Everyday Life*, and coeditor of *The Existential Self in Society and Postmodernism and Social Inquiry*. He is former President of the Society for the Study of Symbolic Interaction and a former editor of the journal *Symbolic Inter-*

action. His two most recently published essays are, respectively, a deconstruction of the work of Hieronymus Bosch and a performance/play about Farinelli, the castrato.

James H. Frey is Dean of the College of Liberal Arts, Professor of Sociology and founder and former Director of the Center for Survey Research at the University of Nevada, Las Vegas. He is author of *Survey Research by Telephone* and *Government and Sport: Public Policy Issues*. He has published papers on survey research, group interviewing, sport sociology, deviance, and work in the leisure industry. He recently edited an issue of the *Annals of the American Academy of Political and Social Science* on the social and economic impacts of gambling.

Jennifer C. Greene received her Ph.D. in educational psychology from Stanford University in 1976. Since then, she has been engaged in the field of social and educational program evaluation. Working first at the University of Rhode Island, then at Cornell University, and currently at the University of Illinois, she has concentrated on making her work useful and socially responsible, both in theory and in practice. Her work has emphasized the development and refinement of various approaches to evaluation, primarily using qualitative methodologies, participatory approaches, and "mixed-method" perspectives and value stances. She has evaluated a wide range of programs, including public policy education, natural resource leadership training, remedial education, and youth employment. Her work generally focuses on educational programs and programs for families and children. In her publications she endeavors to share the lessons she has learned about evaluation practice across multiple contexts.

Douglas Harper is Professor and Chair of the Department of Sociology and Codirector of the Graduate Center for Social and Public Policy at Duquesne University. He has held faculty appointments at the University of Amsterdam, the University of Bologna, the State University of New York at Potsdam, and the University of South Florida. He is the founding editor of *Visual Sociology*, the journal of the International Visual Sociology Association. His books include *Good Company* (the sociology of the tramp), *Working Knowledge: Skill and Community in a Small Shop* (the microsociology of the shop), and *Changing Works* (on cows and their keepers). He has coedited books on visual sociology published by academic presses in Italy and Holland. His first book, *Good Company*, has been translated into Italian and French; his papers have appeared in translation in French, German, and Italian. He is also codirector of the film *Ernie's Sawmill*. His current sociological interests center on the sociology of jazz. His 1998 ASA panel on that topic featured the first musical sociology in ASA history, as performed by H. S. Becker and Robert Faulkner.

Ian Hodder obtained his B.A. degree in archaeology from the University of London in 1971 and his Ph.D. from Cambridge University in 1975. From 1974 to 1977 he taught in the Department of Archaeology at Leeds University, and since then he has taught at Cambridge, ending up as Professor of Archaeology. Since September 1999 he has been Professor in the Cultural and Social Anthropology Department at Stanford University. He is also a Fellow of the British Academy and has taught as a Visiting Professor at the University of Amsterdam, Paris 1/Sorbonne, the State University of New York at Binghamton, the University of California at Berkeley, and the University of Vienna. His books include *Spatial Analysis in Archaeology* (with Clive Orton, 1976), *Reading the Past* (1986), *The Domestication of Europe* (1990), and *The Archaeological Process* (1999).

Yvonna S. Lincoln is Professor of Higher Education, Texas A&M University, and coeditor of this volume and the first edition of the *Handbook of Qualitative Research* (1994). She is also coeditor of the journal *Qualitative Inquiry*, with Norman K. Denzin. She is, with her husband Egon G. Guba, coauthor of *Effective Evaluation* (1981), *Naturalistic Inquiry* (1985), and *Fourth Generation Evaluation* (1989); she is also the editor of *Organizational Theory and Inquiry* (1985) and coeditor of *Representation and the Text* (1997). She has been the recipient of numerous awards for research, including the AERA-Division J Research Achievement Award, the AIR Sidney Suslow Award for Research Contributions to Institutional Research, and the American Evaluation Association's Paul Lazarsfeld Award for Contributions to Evaluation Theory. She is the author of numerous journal articles, chapters, and conference presentations on constructivist and interpretive inquiry, and also on higher education.

Esther Madriz is Associate Professor of Sociology and Associate Director of the Center for Latino Studies in the Americas at the University of San Francisco. She has a master's degree in criminal justice administration from California State University in Sacramento and a Ph.D. in sociology from Vanderbilt University. She previously taught at Hunter College in New York City. She teaches classes in criminology, violence against women, and juvenile delinquency. Her field of expertise is fear or crime. She is the author of many articles on the topic and has also published papers on the use of focus groups as a feminist methodology. Her recent book *Nothing Bad Happens to Good Girls: Fear of Crime in Women's Lives* (1997) was nominated for the C. Wright Mills Award in 1998. She is a member of the board of directors of the Instituto Familiar La Raza in San Francisco and sits on the editorial boards of *Social Justice* and *Peace Review*.

Kimberly A. Mays de Pérez is a nontraditional student holding a B.A. in anthropology from the University of South Florida. She is especially interested in the role of culture in the practice of medicine. She currently works as a medical translator at a Tampa, Florida, clinic that serves a variety of Hispanic populations. She plans to use her background in anthropology in her chosen career as a medical doctor.

Laurel Richardson is Professor Emerita of Sociology, Professor of Cultural Studies in the College of Education, and Graduate Professor of Women's Studies at the Ohio State University. She has written extensively on qualitative research methods, ethics, and issues of representation. She is the author of seven books, including *Fields of Play: Constructing an Academic Life* (1997), which was honored with the C. H. Cooley Award for the 1998 Best Book in Symbolic Interaction. Currently, she is interested in the relationships between conceptual and personal constructions of "timeplaces," narratives of the self, and knowledge practices.

Ray C. Rist is the Evaluation Adviser for the World Bank Institute (WBI). He is also the Head of the Evaluation and Scholarship Unit within the WBI. Prior to his coming to the World Bank in 1996, his career had included 15 years in the U.S. government, with appointments in both the executive and legislative branches. He also served for 12 years as a university professor, with positions at the Johns Hopkins University, Cornell University, and George Washington University. He was the Senior Fulbright Fellow at the Max Planck Institute in Berlin, Germany, in 1976 and 1977. He has authored or edited 23 books, written more than 125 articles, and lectured in more than 40 countries. For the past 15 years, he has chaired an international working group with representative from 17 countries who are collaborating on research related to evaluation and governance. He also has a 4-year-old granddaughter named Molly.

Gery W. Ryan is Assistant Professor of Anthropology at the University of Missouri–Columbia. He has served as coeditor of *Cultural Anthropology Methods Journal* (1993-1998) and has written and lectured on qualitative data collection and analysis techniques, ethnographic decision modeling, and response biases in the field. For 2 years, he was Associate Director of the Fieldwork and Qualitative Data Laboratory at the UCLA Medical School, where he consulted with and trained researchers in text analysis. His substantive interests in medical anthropology focus on how laypersons select among treatment alternatives across illnesses and cultures. He has conducted fieldwork in Mexico and Cameroon and has published in *Social Science and Medicine, Human Organization*, and *Archives of Medical Research*.

David Silverman's interests are in nonromantic qualitative methodologies, professional-client communication, and conversation analysis. He is the author of 14 books, the most recent of which are *Interpreting Qualitative Data* (1993), *Discourses of Counselling* (1997), *Harvey Sacks: Social Science and Conversation Analysis* (1998), and *Doing Qualitative Research: A Practical Handbook* (1999). Since 1999, he has been Professor Emeritus at Goldsmiths College, London University. He continues to argue for a rigorous, theoretically based social science that maintains a dialogue with the wider community.

John K. Smith is Professor of Education at the University of Northern Iowa. For the past 20 years, his interests have centered on the philosophy of social and educational inquiry, with a special emphasis on the issue of criteria. His work has appeared in such journals as the *Educational Researcher, Journal of Educational Administration*, and *Educational Evaluation and Policy Analysis*. He also has published two books: *The Nature of Social and Educational Inquiry* and *After the Demise of Empiricism*.

Eben A. Weitzman received his Ph.D. in social and organizational psychology from Columbia University. He is currently Assistant Professor, Graduate Programs in Dispute Resolution, University of Massachusetts, Boston, and Research Associate at the International Center for Cooperation and Conflict Resolution. He is also the book and software reviews editor for the journal *Field Methods*. During 1993-1995, he was a Visiting Professor of Psychology in the New York University Psychology Department's program in industrial/organizational psychology. His interests are in organizational development, cross-cultural conflict, conflict resolution, and intergroup relations. His current research focuses on intragroup conflict in mediation, cultural differences in attitudes toward conflict, organizational conflict, and the effects of cooperation and competition on small group processes. He is the recipient of recent grants to study "intragroup conflict in mediation" and "cross-cultural conflict on campus." His recent publications on the use of software in qualitative research include articles such as "Analyzing Qualitative Data With Computer Software" and, with the late Matthew B. Miles, "The State of Qualitative Analysis Software: What Do We Need?" and "Choosing Software for Qualitative Data Analysis: An Overview," and the book *Computer Programs for Qualitative Data Analysis* (1995), which he is currently revising in collaboration with Nigel Fielding and Ray Lee.